Lincoln's Autocrat

Civil War America

PETER S. CARMICHAEL,
CAROLINE E. JANNEY, and
AARON SHEEHAN-DEAN,
editors

This landmark series interprets broadly the history and culture of the Civil War era through the long nineteenth century and beyond. Drawing on diverse approaches and methods, the series publishes historical works that explore all aspects of the war, biographies of leading commanders, and tactical and campaign studies, along with select editions of primary sources. Together, these books shed new light on an era that remains central to our understanding of American and world history.

Lincoln's Autocrat

THE LIFE OF EDWIN STANTON

William Marvel

THE
UNIVERSITY
OF NORTH
CAROLINA
PRESS
Chapel Hill

© 2015 The University of North Carolina Press
All rights reserved
Set in Miller and Clarendon by codeMantra
Manufactured in the United States of America

The paper in this book meets the guidelines for permanence
and durability of the Committee on Production Guidelines for Book Longevity
of the Council on Library Resources.

The University of North Carolina Press has been a member of
the Green Press Initiative since 2003.

Jacket illustration: Edwin M. Stanton in the summer of 1865
(courtesy of the New Hampshire Historical Society).

Title page photograph of Edwin M. Stanton: Dover Publications
(Courtesy of the New-York Historical Society).

Library of Congress Cataloging-in-Publication Data
Marvel, William.
Lincoln's autocrat : the life of Edwin Stanton / William Marvel.
pages cm. — (Civil War America)
Includes bibliographical references and index.
ISBN 978-1-4696-2249-1 (cloth : alk. paper) —
ISBN 978-1-4696-2250-7 (ebook)
1. Stanton, Edwin M. (Edwin McMasters), 1814–1869.
2. Cabinet officers—United States—Biography. 3. United States.
War Department—Biography. 4. Statesmen—United States—Biography.
5. United States—History—Civil War, 1861–1865—Biography. 6. Reconstruction
(U.S. history, 1865–1877)—Biography. 7. United States—Politics and government—
1861–1865. 8. United States—Politics and government—1865–1869.
9. Lincoln, Abraham, 1809–1865—Friends and associates.
I. Title. II. Title: Life of Edwin M. Stanton.
E467.1.S8M37 2015
973.7092—dc23
[B]
2014032690

For Nell

CONTENTS

MAPS & ILLUSTRATIONS

His heart was full of tenderness for every form of suffering and sorrow, and he always had a word of sympathy for the smitten and afflicted.
—Senator Henry Wilson, "Edwin M. Stanton,"
Atlantic Monthly, *February, 1870*

He cared nothing for the feelings of others. In fact it seemed pleasanter to him to disappoint than to gratify.
—*Ulysses S. Grant on Stanton,* Personal Memoirs

It will be regretted by the impartial historian of the future that Stanton was capable of impressing his intense hatred so conspicuously upon the annals of the country, and that Lincoln, in several memorable instances, failed to reverse his War Minister when he had grave doubts about the wisdom or justice of his methods.
—*Alexander K. McClure,* Abraham Lincoln and Men of War-Times

Edwin Stanton was never false—to a principle of truth, honesty, justice, or honor!
—*Pamphila Stanton Wolcott on her brother, unpublished memoir*

Stanton is, by nature, an intriguer, courts favor, is not faithful in his friendships, is given to secret, underhand combinations.
—*Navy Secretary Gideon Welles, diary entry of December 20, 1862*

Mr. Stanton . . . believes in mere force,
so long as he wields it, but cowers before it,
when wielded by any other hand.
—Ex-Attorney General Edward Bates,
diary entry of May 25, 1865

He was always on my side & flattered me ad nauseam.
—James Buchanan to Harriet Lane, January 16, 1862

Stanton . . . has no sincerity of character,
but is hypocritical and malicious.
—Orville Hickman Browning,
diary entry of February 15, 1867

PREFACE

In the century after his death, Edwin Stanton became the subject of five published biographies. The best known of these is Harold M. Hyman's *Stanton: The Life and Times of Lincoln's Secretary of War*, which was begun by Benjamin H. Thomas. Thomas died in 1956 with the project unfinished, and Hyman took it up by 1958, graciously giving primary title-page credit to Thomas when the book was published in 1962. For more than half a century Hyman has stood as the principal authority on Stanton, whom he characterized as a devoted patriot—brusque and quirky, but compulsively truthful and dedicated to his vision of justice and the common good. That view has guided much of the subsequent historical literature, and colored most of it.

Hyman was the most objective of the biographers, but even he favored Stanton visibly, often giving him the benefit of the doubt when the sources appeared to dictate otherwise. Hyman leaned toward generous interpretations of episodes that raised serious questions about Stanton's integrity, and occasionally he presented negative sources in a positive light, often by missing obvious sarcasm. His tendency to overlook or discount Stanton's administrative mistakes and his failure to assess the impact of Stanton's divisive departmental and interdepartmental scheming undermines Hyman's complimentary estimate of Stanton's service in three administrations. Hyman apparently did not consider that Stanton might have misrepresented James Buchanan in order to ingratiate his new Republican friends, or that his battle with Andrew Johnson served his own interests.

Frequent misreading of the evidence may have reflected the posthumous handoff of Thomas's notes, which predated the era of photocopiers. That offered abundant opportunity for accumulated misunderstanding, which seems rife in Hyman's biography, where errors and omissions run from the amusing to the disturbing. In one instance, because of a correspondent's colloquial reference to dropping in on "the Macy tribe" on Nantucket, Hyman supposed that Stanton visited an Indian village instead of the Quaker Macy family from which he was descended. Elsewhere, Hyman asserted that Stanton feared Johnson wanted to use the U.S. Army to suppress Congress, but he documented that claim with two letters from Oliver Morton and John Pope that have no relation to so alarming a prospect. In 2009 David Stewart repeated Hyman's unsupported claim more stridently in his book on Johnson's impeachment, demonstrating the general danger of relying on secondary sources for factual information and illustrating how

Hyman's book has distorted the interpretation of that era over the past half-century. Scores of documentary discussions of such errors, amounting to a small book by themselves, have been removed from the notes in the editing process because of their sheer volume.

The lenience of Hyman's treatment inevitably exaggerates any contrast with a critical portrait, and many who have been influenced by his biography will think me too harsh on Stanton. The preponderance of testimony suggests that, at least in his public life, Stanton tended to be insincere, devious, and dedicated to self-preservation: some of the evidence comes from acquaintances who were not hostile to him, or who were even friendly, and some is in his own hand. When studied with the skepticism that is as important in history as it is in journalism, Edwin Stanton's legacy shines less brightly, suggesting a need to reexamine his relations with those near him. Stanton's close collaborator, Joseph Holt, seems undeserving of the gleaming armor he wore in Elizabeth Leonard's recent biography, while Stanton's assistant secretary, Charles Dana, comes away tainted with unbecoming portions of self-interest, hypocrisy, and vindictiveness. President Lincoln's association with Stanton endures a measure of reappraisal, as well.

The dearth of reliable information on Stanton's early development poses an irksome impediment to a definitive examination of his life. As might be expected of someone born during the presidency of James Madison, no contemporary observations of the young Stanton survive. All glimpses of his youth suffer from conscious or subliminal recognition of his ultimate achievements and his established public image. Like most reminiscences (and particularly those involving Lincoln and his immediate associates), many of those vignettes convey a distinct air of invention or exaggeration designed to inflate the role of the raconteurs. The private Stanton remains largely hidden, except to those willing to accept memoir accounts, some of which border on the ludicrous. It is mainly circumstantial evidence that suggests what might have spawned chronic insecurity in a man of such obvious intelligence, who rose to such prominence and gained so much acclaim: that he was afflicted with deep insecurity seems clear unless one denies all the evidence of Stanton's sycophancy, double-dealing, and self-congratulatory storytelling. In the absence of a dependable and disinterested picture of his youth and his family, one can only extrapolate from the basic facts about the oldest son of an apparently imprudent father, who was raised in genteel but worsening poverty and who never completed his formal education, yet increasingly competed against and associated with men of more advantageous backgrounds. Why those circumstances wrought such unpleasant consequences in Stanton, when Abraham Lincoln surmounted worse difficulties with no apparent degradation in character, necessarily remains a matter of speculation.

Equally frustrating is the paucity of reliable information on Stanton's family life, and particularly the women who probably exerted softening influences on him. Trustworthy evidence about his first wife is virtually nonexistent, and little enough can be found about his second, whose voice is confined to a handful of transcribed letters. A few other family-owned letters from Ellen Stanton seen by Hyman, at least in excerpt, could not be tracked down for this study. Drawn shades like that inevitably hide humanizing details that might yield a more balanced biography. Stanton's most complimentary assessments came from his immediate family, for which he appears to have harbored unrelenting devotion, and the unpleasant aspects of his public deportment may not have emerged at home. Even the bias of blood could not entirely account for the intense loyalty of his sister and his oldest son, while his younger son left a legacy of generosity and personal integrity that suggests an exemplary upbringing in a healthy, happy home. Direct testimony and indirect evidence from family members indicate that Stanton showed his best qualities to them, and reserved his more objectionable talents for the confrontational arenas of his professional and public life. Caleb Cushing deemed Stanton a "duplex character," meaning that he played a double role, but as a father, son, and husband he appears to have acted a third part, and evidently with much more credit to himself.

A close examination of Stanton's conduct in the legal profession raises occasional questions of ethical propriety, including at least one instance where he pursued a case as government counsel in a manner that significantly benefited a private client. With no bar association to set standards, conflicts like that were not uncommon or technically illegal at the time, yet they do not appear to have been regarded as innocent even then. His furtive habits raised suspicion among many of his associates, causing some to believe that he profited from bribes and kickbacks from War Department contracts, but that was almost certainly not true. If he ever misappropriated a dollar for his own enrichment, no evidence of it has ever surfaced, and in that regard Stanton appears to have exceeded the ethical deportment of most of his contemporaries. Had he succumbed to graft, his financial circumstances during government service would have improved rather than deteriorated, and the pecuniary distress in which Stanton died testifies against his accumulation of much wealth by that means. He did, however, occasionally put public resources to his own use, or accept private considerations for his own convenience, and he rarely hesitated to dip into public funds to finance political vendettas. Such behavior may have been fairly common in his generation, but it was not openly condoned. More to the point, Stanton's willingness to engage in it conflicted with the path of absolute propriety that he and his admiring biographers consistently claimed he trod.

There is no question that Stanton possessed remarkable professional talents. He could organize and control volumes of information in preparation for a complicated legal case. By dint of obfuscation, sarcasm, theatrics, and the browbeating of witnesses, he could sway judges and juries in the face of overwhelming contradictory evidence. Within the adversarial legal system those are all qualities that are admired and envied. The problem came when Stanton carried those same manipulative tactics into public service—where, for the first time, he tasted the attraction of power over others, and found that he had a weakness for it. The amalgamation of those professional virtues with that personal failing moved him to authoritarian excess, and allowed him to rationalize it. His new dictatorial manner and his old partisan intolerance fueled roundups of dissidents so extensive that they skewed the public perception of what constituted repression, and blighted what Lincoln called "the jewel of liberty" with corrosive constitutional precedents. Tragically, Stanton's propensity for panic drove many of those infringements unnecessarily. Through the use of military commissions and the subversion of civil law, he eventually gained a measure of control over the civilian population as well as the army, and with that control he set in motion some of the more shameful injustices in American history. In so doing, he tarnished the legacy of a president who should more often have overruled him. The most important result of subjecting Stanton to a more critical examination than he has thus far endured may be its effect on the prevailing image of Lincoln's personal strengths. It has been suggested that Lincoln used Stanton to do his political dirty work, and that seems substantially true—sometimes to the point of leaving the gentle-spirited president uncomfortable with the results. At the same time, however, Stanton appeared to exploit some of Lincoln's weaknesses, such as his trusting nature and his discomfort with disagreeable personalities.

Stanton went to his grave mourned by many in his last phalanx of political allies as a model of humanitarianism and a monument to selfless sacrifice in the public interest. Warmed by their camaraderie with him, and lacking the sting of political or personal betrayal that others had felt, those late-life associates portrayed his battle with Andrew Johnson from their own perspective: not as a struggle for personal political survival but as a stoic defense of altruistic principles, some of which Stanton had purportedly imbibed in childhood. Former political associates whom Stanton had turned against found that fray less creditable to him. Senator Henry Wilson's description of Stanton as reflexively sensitive and empathetic typified the admiring Radical view of Stanton, but Ulysses Grant found him without a shred of sympathy for anyone. Stanton's sister stridently emphasized her brother's honorable, truthful nature, while most of his cabinet colleagues who remarked on him thought Stanton malicious, hypocritical, and untrustworthy. Their darker perception had its own political coloring, but the surviving evidence often seems to bear them out, despite the accident of Stanton's alliance with the Radical faction that enjoys greater historical sympathy today.

Too much testimony survives to deny any longer that Stanton habitually presented a false face under the pressure of personal or political conflict. He played insincere roles with mounting enthusiasm and intricacy as the influence of his audience increased, until finally he reached a pinnacle of influence himself, whereupon those various faces blended into one surly, overbearing persona. He flattered his superiors in business and politics so persistently that two presidents and several associates remarked upon it distastefully, but he often showed no mercy to those over whom he exerted complete control. In his memoirs General Grant used backhanded phrasing to convey that he considered Stanton a coward and a bully. Many others, including some with no ax to grind, expressed that same estimate more bluntly.

Stanton also betrayed a vindictive streak, and he played a central role in renowned instances of injustice. The worst example of that trait appears to have been meant to disguise his own share of responsibility for the tragedy he ostensibly avenged. Conspiracy theorists need not pursue the nonsense of Stanton's involvement in the Lincoln assassination to paint him with a brutal side: that seems well enough illustrated by the orchestrated conviction and execution of the hapless Andersonville commandant Henry Wirz—whose death appears to have been meant, at least in part, to address a chorus of criticism over Stanton's own resistance to prisoner exchanges.

Stanton was said to possess legendary energy, and it may once have been prodigious, despite evident exaggeration, but he might have served his country better had he devoted less of that energy to political intrigue. His organizational skill and attention to detail did make the largest army on the planet more manageable, leading William Seward to bestow on him the borrowed title "organizer of victory" that was originally applied to Lazare Carnot during the French Revolution. Yet his frequent intrigues worsened mistrust of (and suspicion within) the Lincoln and Johnson administrations. His cronyism, meanwhile, often discouraged independence and bred parasitism in his department and in the army. He exercised brazen personal and political favoritism that inevitably seeped through the system, dampening morale and impeding the war effort in subtle ways. The point here, again, is not so much that he engaged in it, because most politicians and bureaucrats of his day did, but that he and his assorted eulogists and biographers have consistently denied it.

Early in his tenure, Stanton's factional scheming may also have helped indirectly to prolong the conflict, while his first major executive blunder contributed more directly to that result. He was universally credited, even by some of his worst enemies, with cleaning up the graft and waste of Simon Cameron's War Department. There was some truth in that, but corruption remained rife in the supply bureaus to the end of the war, and for political purposes Stanton would partake in it himself: to help fund partisan electoral victory, he readily conspired with department quartermasters who knew the safest methods of skimming money from army contractors, although he frequently court-martialed officers who committed the same crime for personal profit.

Lincoln's old friend Joshua Speed remarked in 1861 that the president was too honest to believe that others were not, and someone who could switch faces as easily as Stanton presented him with a particular challenge. Rigorous scrutiny of Stanton's tenure as a cabinet officer hints that Lincoln's ability to judge men was not so exceptional as some have presumed, and suggests deficiencies in the existing analyses of the presidents who preceded and followed Lincoln—all of which may provide the most salient historical insights in reconsidering Stanton's role. His mendacious portrayal of the last ten weeks of the Buchanan administration is still widely credited, to the detriment of a president whose historical reputation cannot afford unwarranted aspersions, and Stanton's disloyalty to Andrew Johnson may have worsened the obstinacy of that beleaguered president, who was already too reluctant to compromise. Stanton's talent for administrative constriction and entrapment, meanwhile, appears to have guided the Radical campaign against Johnson during Reconstruction, and that helps explain the fluctuating favor Stanton has endured. For nearly three generations, while racial issues remained subordinate in the public eye, Johnson's battle against Congress elicited great sympathy from historians who deplored the unconstitutional methods of the men they called Jacobins, and Stanton suffered for his collusion with them. Conversely, when the modern civil rights struggle spawned a revision of the Radicals' image by historians who admired their presumed altruistic motives, Stanton's stock rose—although his own devotion to racial justice may have been theatrical and motivated by personal political expediency. Stanton might have contributed nearly as much to factional polarization during Reconstruction as Johnson's stubbornness did, by reinforcing the president's inflexibility at crucial junctures and misrepresenting his positions to Radical congressmen. Reactionary initial interpretations of Reconstruction emphasized Stanton's mischief but largely ignored Johnson's failings, while most treatments over the past five decades have reversed that imbalance. Both interpretations are equally obsolete, leaving that era in sore need of a dispassionate new examination that applies neither the antiquated assumptions of the nineteenth century nor the anachronistic expectations of the twenty-first.

Let me say a preliminary word about sources. I normally mistrust memoirs, and usually avoid them altogether. My preference is to depend on the most contemporary primary sources—diaries, letters, official documents, and newspaper observations from the period in question. All those sources suffer from personal and political prejudices, but those are usually easier biases to detect than those absorbed unconsciously, over the passage of decades. However, in piecing together a life that began two centuries ago, the absence of other sources has forced me to frequently consider observations recorded long after the event. That is particularly true early in Stanton's life. For instance, an intriguing reminiscence in the introductory scene documented the notorious rumor, very likely false, that Stanton had been conceived out of wedlock. Memoirs, indirectly supported by a suspiciously ambiguous obituary, also revealed the secret of his brother's suicide. Reminiscences alone relate—and probably invent—the famous tale of Stanton snubbing Abraham Lincoln in Cincinnati in 1855. Some of the best-known anecdotes about Stanton originate in recollections, many of which seem to have been deliberately crafted to buff his image, or to mar it, and if I did not address them the lapse would be glaring. The confidentiality of cabinet meetings and the absence of witnesses to conversations in the office, hall, or parlor often demanded some consideration of memoirs when documents or diaries failed to record the discussions. It also seemed necessary to compare some dueling posthumous recollections of Stanton, especially regarding his association with Abraham Lincoln. Whenever retrospective evidence of that type appears, the reader should remain alert—as I have tried to be—to the added potential for distortion through hindsight, calculation, or faulty memory.

Lincoln's Autocrat

1

BANKS OF THE OHIO

At midwinter of 1862 most of Virginia remained undisturbed by Union armies. In the six months since the battle of Manassas the counties of Fauquier and Culpeper had seen little of war beyond the passage of Confederate troops to and from their encampments and hospitals. A gentleman the caliber of John Murray Forbes could still travel unmolested wherever business interests and legal proceedings took him, just as he had before the war. In pursuit of such matters he frequently rode from his farm near Warrenton to Culpeper Court House, from which he sometimes continued on to Fredericksburg, and when he did he liked to rest his horse at Zimmerman's Tavern, in Stevensburg, run by a widow named Martha Wale. She seemed to know everyone in the vicinity, and everything about them.

If Squire Forbes related the story faithfully, it was probably late in January when he dropped in at the tavern to find the old woman in a dither over news that had filtered down from above the Potomac. President Lincoln had recently installed Edwin M. Stanton as his secretary of war, and Mrs. Wale interpreted the appointment as evidence that the war would now escalate into a long, bitter struggle, from which the Lincoln government might never relent. Stanton was the grandson of Thomas Norman, from right there in Stevensburg: Norman's home, "Fairfield," lay just a short distance from the tavern, and the widow remembered him as the most stubborn man ever to inhabit Culpeper County. She suspected that Norman's grandson shared his ancestor's obstinacy, and thought it boded ill for the Confederacy's bid for independence.[1]

Thomas Norman had lived his entire life in the watershed of the upper Rappahannock. In the American Revolution he served in the Western Battalion of the Virginia Line, with which he descended the Ohio River in bateaux to the falls of the Ohio, between Kentucky and the Illinois country. There the battalion built a fort and garrisoned it until December of 1781, never encountering the British but losing a fair number of officers and men in skirmishes with the Shawnee.[2] Afterward, Norman returned to his home below the Rappahannock, where he accumulated substantial property in different parts of the county. His first wife bore him a host of children before she died; when he remarried, his daughter Lucy moved into the household of David McMasters, a Methodist minister who had married a friend of hers. Folks in Culpeper remembered that Lucy "ran away" from her father's home, but she appears to have left with his blessing. McMasters and his wife then migrated to Ohio, settling in the town of Mount Pleasant, and Lucy moved there with them.[3]

Mount Pleasant lay a league or two from the Ohio River, in Jefferson County. It consisted of a few hundred residents, many of them Quakers from eastern Pennsylvania, Virginia, North Carolina, and even England, some of whom were drawn there by the ban on slavery in the Northwest Territory. One such family was the Stanton clan, the matriarch of which had led most of her children and sons-in-law there from North Carolina: after the death of her husband Benjamin, in 1798, Abigail Macy Stanton had sold off his shipyard and much of his land in Carteret County to finance the family's passage. The Stantons retained their membership in the Society of Friends, carrying certificates of their worthiness from the Core Sound Monthly Meeting to the Westland Meeting, in western Pennsylvania, which admitted the entire family on May 14, 1800; four years later the Westland Meeting transferred authority over Jefferson County Quakers to the newly formed Short Creek Monthly Meeting. Abigail and her sons established themselves in that community with the proceeds of her husband's estate, and over the years more cash came from North Carolina as cousins there sold their remaining lands for them.[4]

Abigail had named her eighth child David. He was only ten when his father died, and barely twelve when his mother brought him to Ohio, but he was not the last of Abigail's children by far: the youngest of her brood was still a toddler during the hegira to the free country of the Old Northwest. David was old enough, however, to imbibe an early hatred of slavery from his parents, who had evidently adopted the predominant Quaker scruples against it. The expensive and arduous journey to free territory from their well-established community illustrates the Stantons' collective aversion to slavery, which drove many Southerners into the free states above the Ohio. Eventually David Stanton imitated antislavery Friends by shunning coffee and other fruits of slave labor, and as a young man he would inevitably have encountered Benjamin Lundy, a zealous antislavery newspaperman who sojourned for a time among the Quakers of Mount Pleasant.[5] More than half a century later, after David Stanton's son Edwin had allied himself with the political descendants of such militant abolitionists, he told at least one of them that Lundy frequently visited the Stanton home, and that the perennially straitened David Stanton contributed money for his cause.[6]

No one bothered to record how David Stanton passed his bachelor years at Mount Pleasant. In his mid-twenties he met Lucy Norman, who was still in her teens, and early in 1814 he married her, with David McMasters conducting the ceremony.[7] According to John Murray Forbes, Mrs. Wale maintained that David Stanton was working as a tailor when he met Lucy, and that the two married hastily to disguise a pregnancy. Clearly they did wed without pausing for David to seek his Quaker meeting's sanction to marry an outsider, and for that he was expelled from the Society of Friends, to which his ancestors had belonged for a century. The omission may simply have reflected Lucy's refusal to accept Quaker doctrine, and the date of his expulsion, on March 22, 1814, is consistent with the official record of their February 25 wedding. Family tradition maintained that their first child, Edwin McMasters Stanton, was born nearly ten months later, on December 19. Fragments of garbled truth cling to the Culpeper profile of the couple as told by Mrs. Wale through Forbes, but Edwin could not have been conceived out of wedlock unless his parents postdated his birth, for which there is no contemporary documentation.[8]

Edwin M. Stanton arrived in the midst of turbulent times. The country was at war with England for the second time, and during Lucy's confinement Andrew Jackson was preparing to defend New Orleans against a British army sailing up the Mississippi River. Far away in Belgium, representatives of the United States and Britain sought the restoration of peace and were nearing a settlement. At the same juncture, Federalist delegates from New England were meeting in Hartford, Connecticut, to discuss their future relations with the rest of the states: New England lacked enthusiasm for the war, the consequences of which had fallen heavily on that coastal region, and the debate included talk of seceding from the federal union. The final resolutions from the convention omitted that provocative notion, focusing instead on complaints about the political power exercised by the Southern states.[9]

The Stantons were then renting a small, plain, two-story brick house at the corner of Market Street and Fifth in the growing shire town of Steubenville, on the banks of the Ohio River twenty miles from Mount Pleasant. Slaveholding Virginia lay not half a mile from their front door. A traveler visiting Steubenville less than two years later found the place thriving, with an iron foundry, cotton and woolen factories, a steam mill, a brewery, and its own newspaper, the *Steubenville Western Herald*.[10]

The critical Mrs. Wale (or Mr. Forbes) insinuated that Thomas Norman frowned on his new son-in-law's humble vocation. In fact, Stanton family lore remains curiously silent about David Stanton's early occupation, and whatever work he did follow at the time of his marriage must have proven inadequate to support a family. About the time he turned twenty-seven, while Edwin was an infant, David began "reading" medicine with an established physician whose name, along with most of David Stanton's early life, remains unknown. A year into his studies Lucy bore a second boy, whom they called Erasmus Darwin Stanton, and the year after that David made a roundabout 400-mile trek with his wife and sons to visit Thomas Norman and his third wife at "Fairfield," in the section of Culpeper County then called St. Mark's. They made the trip in their own carriage, covering much of the distance on the new Cumberland Road that was then approaching Wheeling, and on the return they brought Lucy's oldest sister Elizabeth, who stayed with them for several years. Subsisting perhaps on contributions from David's mother or from Lucy's father, or both, they remained in the rented Market Street house until May 13, 1818, when David passed an examination by a panel of doctors representing the State of Ohio Medical District.[11] At the age of thirty he opened his own practice in a furnished house he had bought on Third Street, six doors from the Jefferson County courthouse. The $1,600 purchase price of the home appears to have come from no cash reserves of David Stanton's, and may have followed from his recent introduction of two healthy grandsons to Thomas Norman.[12]

The family remembered Edwin being able to read by the age of three, and credited his aunt, Elizabeth Norman, with helping him achieve that feat. He then went to a "dame school," taught by a local woman—the informal environment where most children of that era learned their letters. A neighbor whose son attended with him came in one day and found the two of them leaning fast asleep against their teacher; she concluded that Edwin and her boy were both too young for school. Private schools like that, all within a few hundred yards of his home, grounded him in grammar and ciphering. The curriculum broadened a bit when he gravitated to a frontier academy on the next street, where male teachers claimed a measure of education themselves and followed teaching as a vocation. An older classmate later described attending an evening grammar school where an itinerant teacher instructed a group of boys and young men, of whom he remembered Edwin as the youngest of them and the puniest—but a serious student. Recollections solicited from childhood acquaintances by Stanton's first two biographers and by his adoring younger sister, Pamphila, portray him almost entirely in a positive light: he was courteous and devout, studied hard, shunned games, avoided fisticuffs even in self-defense, and was never abusive, although one playmate admitted that Edwin could be "imperious."[13]

Forty years later, after President Lincoln had chosen Edwin Stanton to head the War Department, the antagonistic editor of the *New York Herald*, James Gordon Bennett, inquired into the new secretary's early history. Perhaps through acquaintances in the newspaper business, Bennett learned of a terse criticism that he thought illustrated the fundamental aspect of Stanton's personality, although it may have been no more reliable than the retrospective accolades of Stanton's friends and kin. Bennett shared the story with James Steedman, a former newspaperman and Union general, and in 1873 Steedman revealed Bennett's unpleasant observation to a professional in gravestone biography, who enthusiastically wrote it down: when Stanton was young, Bennett's informant claimed, "he kissed the [asses] of the big boys and kicked those of the little ones!" Hatred or hindsight may have spawned the recollection, but that uncomplimentary schoolyard characterization is not inconsistent with the experiences of many whom Stanton encountered during his years in public office. Two of the three presidents Stanton served under remarked on his excessively flattering, obsequious manner with them, while numerous subordinates, supplicants, and peers viewed him as a bully—dictatorial, mean, and vindictive.[14]

The shadow of genteel poverty stalked Edwin's youth. Evidence of local economic difficulties surfaced almost as soon as his father began treating his first patients. Businesses in Steubenville began advertising for customers to settle their accounts, and tradesmen who had produced or repaired goods for delinquent customers warned them that those items would be sold if the bills were not settled within a short, specified period; merchants began offering discounts to patrons who paid cash on their orders. At least one of the major factories changed hands, apparently to rectify a financial embarrassment, while nearly every week's issue of the Steubenville newspaper during 1819 included the sheriff's announcement that he would be forced to sell someone's land or belongings. Those broad hints of economic constriction reflected Steubenville's share in the Panic of 1819—which started with an epidemic of speculation and worsened after the Bank of the United States attempted to repair the consequences of its own inflationary policies by contracting its currency. Hard cash all but disappeared in Ohio, launching an epidemic of business failures and personal penury. The first hope of relief came in the summer of 1820, when newly appointed commissioners began laying out the next segment of the Cumberland Road, westward from opposite Wheeling.[15]

Such a downturn would have weighed heavily on a doctor anxious to nurture a new practice. Turning away patients would have been unthinkable, but indigents who had already accumulated debts with the established physicians in the neighborhood would naturally flock to the newest one, and David Stanton seems to have been an easy mark for the poor and underprivileged. In what may have been an effort to improve his profession and the economic vitality of his community, Dr. Stanton joined a new medical society and accepted a position on a committee to promote Jefferson County industry.[16]

For the office of a fledgling physician, the Stanton home on Third Street bore the unfortunate distinction of having originally belonged to Steubenville's coroner. Perhaps no potential patients were superstitious enough to shun Dr. Stanton on that account, but some may have lost confidence when he failed to save three of his own children. In 1820 he and Lucy lost Lucretia, a two-year-old girl. On April 13, 1821, they greeted another "sweet little daughter" who could not be made to breathe regularly for an hour or two, and when she finally did she betrayed severe brain damage from the prolonged anoxia, lapsing into convulsions. She died the following morning, yet they named her Lucy, after her mother, who did not recover as quickly as she had after the births of her boys. Elizabeth Norman, who still lived with the Stantons, could not tend her sister, either, for she was recuperating from something Dr. Stanton was only able to identify as "an inflammatory fever."[17]

The newborn Lucy may have inherited the respiratory ailment that killed her so quickly. Thomas Norman struggled with severe asthma for most of his life, according to one of his younger daughters. Lucy suffered increasingly from it herself, and Edwin showed early symptoms, but if his father prescribed any remedies or palliatives, no one made note of it. Traditional treatments involved a range of vile concoctions containing pulverized vegetable matter and animal ingredients as revolting as skunk's scent glands and powdered fox intestines, usually dissolved in generous drafts of rum or brandy, none of which would have offered much relief beyond intoxication. The realization that asthma was related to dietary and environmental allergies lay many decades in the future. Those born with the condition therefore usually died with it—or of it.[18] Barely a year after the death of this little girl, Lucy bore David another daughter, whom they called Oella. A third boy, Theophilus, died in 1824, and their last child, a girl named Pamphila, arrived in the summer of 1827.[19]

Three nights after Christmas that year, guests had left the Stantons' modest home and the family had retired when Dr. Stanton collapsed with a violent stroke. Soon the seizure subsided, but he lay unconscious through the next day, Saturday. At 10:00 A.M. on Sunday, December 30, at the age of thirty-nine, he breathed his last. Forty-eight hours later, on New Year's Day, the bell rang in Steubenville's Presbyterian meetinghouse, calling the teachers and students of the various Sunday schools to form in procession for a last visit to Dr. Stanton's home. When pallbearers brought out his coffin, all these mourners followed the hearse to the cemetery, on the northwest corner of South Street and Fourth, to bid him farewell.[20]

The turnout reflected high regard for the doctor, but his obituary hinted how little he had profited from his practice by emphasizing his "kind and benevolent" behavior toward the needy, which helped account for his own poverty. The court-appointed administrators for David Stanton's estate strove to squeeze the doctor's patients and other debtors for their delinquent accounts, and with the proceeds of these actions they alternately paid the debts of the deceased and provided some support for his widow and children. They sold his surplus property, the most valuable of which was probably a quarter-section of undeveloped land in Marietta that may have come from his mother. Other than the house on Third Street, the assets amounted to so little that in desperation, or determination, Lucy collected some produce and dry goods to offer for sale in the front room of her home, alongside some of her late husband's medicines. This pitiful inventory drew far fewer customers than the tavern across the street, and the independent girl who had left her father's home became the impoverished widow dependent on more of her father's charity.[21]

Lucy Stanton also had to remove her oldest son from school, for she could not afford tuition and needed any money he might be able to earn. Rather than ask thirteen-year-old Edwin to go to work in one of the mills or on the river, though, she apprenticed him to James Turnbull, a Steubenville bookbinder. Turnbull also sold books and stationery from his Market Street location, and the apprenticeship resembled little more than a lengthy indenture as a clerk. Only a few months into young Stanton's contract his employer began to see competition cropping up, with schoolbooks, blank books, and writing paper for sale from the local paper mill "at the lowest Pittsburgh Cash Prices," and then newspaper editor James Wilson set his son up as a bookbinder, just down the street from Turnbull's store.[22]

Apprenticeship at that time required a boy to serve his master exclusively during the life of the contract. Runaway-apprentice advertisements appeared in Ohio newspapers, even in Steubenville, with rewards offered for the return of young men in their late teens. Falling back on a statutory authority similar to the one that would mark the worst of the sectional dispute over slavery, the master sometimes threatened to prosecute anyone who harbored the fugitive.[23]

Apprentices saw little leisure, as the paucity of specific anecdotes about Edwin Stanton's teenage years in Steubenville implies. Most of the late-life recollections offered by those who knew him at that time revolve around the bookstore. John Lloyd, who was about the same age as Stanton, worked as a clerk in the store next to Turnbull's, and one morning he and Stanton opened their opposing windows at the same moment: Stanton greeted Lloyd with the remark that he was ahead of him for once, but that opportunity to speak to each other must have been rare. The hours would have been long, as they were in most occupations, and the parsimonious James Turnbull seemed inclined to wring as much work as he could from a lad. Stanton's principal benefit may have been access to a variety of books available to few boys of his economic stratum, and a passion for reading was a trait that his family and most of his young friends remembered about him. James Turnbull evidently frowned on his apprentice's fascination with books because it distracted him from his duties and customers, whom he was said to have frequently ignored because he was so absorbed in reading.[24]

The unusually serious, studious attitude attributed to the adolescent Stanton bespoke abundant natural curiosity, but his deliberate cultivation of that quality would also have been understandable in a boy who suddenly found himself the oldest male member of a family in reduced circumstances. Childhood ended early in Jacksonian America, where most boys were expected to do a man's work at least by the time they reached sixteen, and even that rapid maturity was often accelerated by the common disaster of a family breadwinner's death. That had been the case with Andrew Jackson himself. One of the few consistent observations made by those who knew Stanton, either in youth or maturity, commended him on a virtually inexhaustible capacity and appetite for reading and paperwork. Childhood poverty that then included the specter of possible starvation may have led him to pursue such occupation with exaggerated industry, especially in light of a chronic respiratory condition that left him unfit for physical labor. No one would ever accuse him of being lazy. Nature and necessity apparently combined to light his professional path: he revealed an unusual ability to grasp the essence of a complicated issue even as he immersed himself in the details, and that rare talent became more obvious and advantageous when he entered the law.

The apprenticeship at Turnbull's bookstore lasted three years. Considering the schedule of graduated compensation that Turnbull purportedly offered him, that would have been the limit of their contract, and by April of 1831 Edwin had appealed for his freedom with the intention of continuing his formal education. The years of voracious reading had probably anticipated this very step. With money borrowed from the court-appointed legal guardian of his father's estate, Steubenville lawyer Daniel L. Collier, sixteen-year-old Edwin enrolled at Kenyon College.[25]

Kenyon sat on the fringe of the village of Gambier, Ohio, on a plateau above the Walhonding River. Stanton would have made the journey by stagecoach, probably traveling from Steubenville through New Philadelphia and Millersburg to Mount Vernon, from which a local omnibus shuttled passengers the four miles to Gambier. The college, founded seven years before by Ohio's Episcopal bishop, Philander Chase, consisted primarily of a single stone building sitting on the edge of the hardwood forest that still covered most of the state. A few straggling frame and log buildings housed the faculty and the artisans who were working on a chapel, and sheltered the cultivating equipment for the extensive gardens on which the school subsisted. The spring semester began on April 21, by which time the new freshman from Jefferson County had presumably arrived on campus. He paid a prorated portion of the $70 annual fee, covering tuition, room and board, and enough firewood and candles for two twenty-week semesters. During his first two weeks he visited William K. Lamson, the chief clerk of the college store, who recorded $4.25 in charges for a chair, an inkstand, a toothbrush, a $2.25 copy of Day's *Algebra*, and a Latin grammar.[26]

His first classes would have been with Latin and Greek professor Chauncey Fitch, and with the instructor of mathematics and natural philosophy, George Denison, both of whom—like most of the faculty—were Episcopal priests. Edwin followed a rigid schedule of course work, mandatory religious services, and chores in the garden and elsewhere, but he had matriculated just as the faculty glided into a quiet but determined rebellion against the autocratic rule of Bishop Chase. That rebellion came to a head three months into Stanton's sojourn at Kenyon, and Chase resigned as president of the college just as Stanton's first semester was drawing to a close.[27]

College commencements in the early nineteenth century usually came late in the summer. Kenyon held its ceremony on the first Wednesday of September, and by that date in 1831 Stanton's account at the college store had reached $14 for quills, ink powder, paper, and an assortment of personal items including extra candles, cream of tartar, frequent purchases of sugar, two combs, two brooms, a pair of suspenders, socks, alterations to a pair of pants, and the mending of a shirt. With eight weeks of vacation following, during which the college library was closed, there was nothing for Stanton to do but return home by stagecoach at a cost of about $10.[28]

The first semester of the next academic year began early in November, just as the state of Georgia started forcing the Choctaws from their ancestral lands. The following February the United States Supreme Court confirmed that only the federal government held jurisdiction over Indian land, but President Andrew Jackson refused to enforce the decision. His inaction outraged the political opposition and pained those who sympathized with the plight of the once-powerful Creeks, Cherokees, and Choctaws. In Steubenville alone, scores of women petitioned Congress to sustain federal promises to those tribes in the name of humanity, Christianity, and national honor. The wives of Edwin Stanton's guardian and the guardian's brother (and law partner) both endorsed the document. At least one of Stanton's early teachers signed it, as did many of his family's close friends and some of his own early companions. Lucy Stanton's name did not appear on the petition—despite David Stanton's activism on behalf of the oppressed, and his reputed opposition to Jackson. With so many of her friends and neighbors signing the plea, Edwin's mother would probably have been asked to do so—unless it was already understood that she did not share her late husband's sympathies.[29]

In February Stanton joined Kenyon's literary club, the Philomathesian Society. The members met weekly, usually on Friday evenings, engaging in formal debates on subjects designed to hone their logic and rhetorical skills. One night in mid-July the society heard Stanton debate his friend Andrew McClintock over whether "the life of the agriculturalist" was more gratifying than that of a lawyer. Stanton took the affirmative side and McClintock the negative, although both would soon choose the law for a career. The next week Stanton defended the execution of Louis XVI while David Davis, who would manage Abraham Lincoln's presidential campaign in 1860, denounced the regicide. In that debate the two seventeen-year-olds took the respectively radical and conservative positions they would occupy in more momentous disputes, three decades later, but early in August they combined to defend the premise that "the extraordinary ecclesiastical power of the middle ages [was] of more benefit than injury to Literature."[30]

The same month that Stanton joined the Philomathesians, South Carolinians met in convention to consider nullifying a federal tariff that fell heavily on the South's slave-based agricultural economy, and when their nullification initiative escalated into a discussion about secession the rancor reached even the Kenyon campus. Eventually the Philomathesian Society split along sectional lines, with the Southern students resigning to form a new club, where they might debate in perfect harmony. Stanton remained with the Northern faction, which would have been logical enough for a lifelong resident of Ohio, but his decision implied a measure of enhanced nationalism as well as regional loyalty. One of those who clung to the old group with him exaggerated that aspect half a lifetime later, boasting "we fought the South together at Kenyon, and whipped."[31]

Although President Jackson had backed Georgia when it defied federal law by stealing Indian lands, he stood firm for federal power in the showdown with South Carolina. His rejection of the nullifiers won him praise from many citizens and politicians who did not otherwise support him or his party, with Daniel Webster foremost among them. Stanton's decision to side with the society members from his region therefore provides no evidence that he had yet spurned his father's politics and "gone over to Jackson," as one Whig phrased Stanton's ultimate connection to the Democrats.[32]

The pomp and glory of military service bore little charm for the youthful Stanton. Perhaps because his constitution and nervous temperament did not incline him toward physical rigor and personal danger, he echoed his Quaker ancestors' pacifism with barbs of bitter sarcasm. It was probably for a Philomathesian Society debate that Stanton prepared an indictment of militarism that challenged the very foundation of Old Hickory's political popularity, not to mention the martial threat behind some of Jackson's more confrontational positions. Admiration of military character, Stanton wrote, was one of mankind's worst inconsistencies: a great battle might leave thousands dead, but rather than pitying the beaten and grieving over the slain it was the human tendency to heap honors on the victorious general, impure though his own character might be. Admiration for such men came naturally enough "in a rude and ignorant state of society," he continued, but not in the forenoon of the nineteenth century. On rare occasions wars were necessary, he vaguely conceded, and at such times so were military leaders, but even then he questioned canonizing the victor.[33]

An argument in debate need not reflect sincere opinion, but Stanton reinforced his stance against generals and war by lampooning the military spirit mercilessly in private correspondence from the same period. His earliest surviving letter describes the 1832 Fourth of July celebration in Gambier for his Steubenville friend, Alexander Beatty: Stanton informed him that the day passed quite happily without any "valiant guard" to march back and forth on the plateau, "choking themselves with dust, for our amusement." Having learned that the Steubenville militia had decided to travel downriver to parade at Wheeling, he speculated that the "admirable corps" had probably "made themselves 'very sufficiently' ridiculous by traveling so far for an exhibition not of their strength but of their weakness." The observances in nearby Mount Vernon, he added, had entailed three patriotic addresses, all plagiarized, with a feast and fandango where "every man, woman and child were drunk as a fidler's bitch."[34] If he did embrace the national union with particular ardor, that did not translate into any regard for the military pomp or raucous patriotism that so often commemorated it.

Young Stanton took an active interest in the opposite sex while he studied at Kenyon, and—probably with the usual leavening of embellishment—he regaled friends with his adventures in that arena. The same letter in which Stanton mocked the Independence Day festivities contained a bit of boast about going diligently "in chase of a petticoat," describing an evening at a young lady's home, three miles from Kenyon, where he remained until one o'clock in the morning. The night was cold, he said, and evidently so dark that he lost his way coming back to campus, while enough precipitation fell that he reached his room wet and chilled, near dawn. He claimed the exploit cost him several days in bed with a fever. "So much for love," he lamented, but he held out hope that his attentions might yet avail him something to compensate for his misery.[35]

Colds and respiratory infections like the one Stanton described caused special concern in an era when tuberculosis carried away so many, for they often seemed to presage that dreaded disease, but in the summer of 1832 cholera posed the most acute threat. It had appeared in New York by July and spread west from there, following the wagon routes and steamboat corridors. Those with the means to escape the seemingly infectious filth of the cities fled into the countryside, but they merely took the panic with them, and sometimes the cholera as well. Authorities tried to curtail the spread of the disease and protect their communities by imposing quarantines. The governor of Ohio issued a frantic proclamation to that effect late in June, which Stanton must have been scoffing at when he told his Steubenville correspondent that to prevent cholera the Kenyon faculty had "prohibited bathing, and almost everything else but studying—would to God they may prohibit that shortly."[36]

The epidemic passed by the end of summer, by which time Stanton had more pressing worries of his own. As his third semester at college drew to a close, he addressed a letter to his guardian, Daniel Collier, requesting funds to settle accounts and travel home, but he added a final sentence hinting at previous discussions about the dwindling resources available for his education. He asked to be forewarned if there was any probability that he might not be able to afford another semester, and Collier replied that in fact a shortage of money did weigh against him continuing. Stanton lingered in Kenyon a few weeks after commencement before boarding the coach for home, leaving behind a trunk that his friend McClintock promised to forward if Stanton could not persuade his guardian to let him return. The two boys rode together as far as Millersburg, forty miles from Gambier, after which McClintock turned for his home in eastern Pennsylvania and the disconsolate Stanton traveled the rest of the way in miserably wet weather. He arrived in Steubenville still hoping to alter Collier's plans.[37]

Daniel Collier had come to Steubenville from Connecticut with his older brother James, and the two of them had opened a law office. James, at least, dove into Ohio politics, identifying himself with the rising Whig Party, to which his brother also seemed sympathetic. Daniel Collier appears to have undertaken the guardianship of the Stanton children conscientiously, attending to the family's needs and advancing money to the oldest son so long as enough remained in the estate to cover the loan. By the late summer of 1832 the administrators had begun to advise Squire Collier that the assets of David Stanton's estate had shrunk to little more than the house Mrs. Stanton and her daughters occupied, and it was this reality that prompted him to insist that Edwin interrupt his education until he had earned something to defray his expenses.[38]

The solution Collier found was to bind his ward once again to James Turnbull, who had opened a new bookstore in Columbus early that year with his brother, Benjamin. It was there the erstwhile scholar was to go, not as an apprentice but as manager of the entire business, while his friend Alexander Beatty had taken over the Steubenville store. Almost from the moment Stanton stepped down from the stage he objected to the bookstore position, resisting so vociferously that he even won "churlish assent" from Turnbull to annul the agreement Collier had already made. His guardian insisted on the contract, though—apparently disapproving of the youth taking a loan he had been offered by a third party to finance another year at Kenyon. Without spelling out exactly what he was paying Beatty, Turnbull implied that he would compensate his Columbus manager more generously than he did Beatty, and Stanton reluctantly signed the articles for another year's employment. In conveying his disappointment to McClintock, he alluded melodramatically to the instantaneous evaporation of all his cherished "dreams of future greatness."

"This I consider an absolute sacrifice of myself soul and body," he mourned, "an utter destruction, of all hopes and expectation. . . . I shall henceforth be regardless of life, fortune, character, everything, and shall continue to live on, from day, to day, objectless, hopeless, without end to be reached, or design to be accomplished, being literally 'nipt in the bud' I shall go on cursing and being cursed." His accompanying claim to have begun indulging in self-destructive behavior bears a hint of embroidery, but he seemed genuinely devastated by the setback. Recognizing that Collier would exercise legal authority over him until he turned twenty-one, he affected a cordially subordinate demeanor, but it was a disconsolate and perhaps resentful young man who boarded the stage in Steubenville on October 15.[39]

The coach eventually stopped in Mount Vernon, where the town square lay on a slanting hillside. Here—at least as his sister told the story—Reverend William Preston climbed aboard, having perhaps just concluded some duty as a trustee of Kenyon College. Stanton had recently begun to smoke, under the common misconception that it actually relieved the symptoms of asthma, but before he lighted a cigar he offered one to his fellow passenger. At first Preston declined, rather than risk public revelation of his fondness for that vice, but eventually he succumbed and they bounded on toward Columbus in a nicotine haze. The cigars may have been responsible for Stanton coming down with "the belly-ache" when he arrived in Columbus: when he wrote to McClintock for his trunk he described himself as "devilishly sick."[40]

Turnbull and Collier must have struck their bargain before the last term at Kenyon had even ended. Anticipating a full-time clerk at the Columbus store, Turnbull began to run a new series of long, top-corner newspaper advertisements for his stock. He listed textbooks on law, medicine, music, and theology, besides a wide assortment of history, biography, and classical literature, with a heavy concentration in British poetry.[41] The new store manager found trade slow enough that he spent much of his time reading, as he had in the Steubenville shop, but his three semesters at Kenyon had inevitably trained him to direct his study more profitably. He recoiled at the notion of remaining a store clerk, or pursuing business on his own hook: it may have been James Turnbull's tightfisted ways that led Stanton to summarize standard business training as "learning how to cheat, and avoid being cheated," while he feared his new job would transform him into an "accomplished villain." Before many months had elapsed he identified the legal profession as his best chance for a remunerative and interesting career—with the mercenary incentive probably posing the greater of the two attractions, after a life in the shadow of want. In the state capital he may also have observed that attorneys, unlike tradesmen and businessmen, tended not to subordinate themselves to their clientele.[42]

When McClintock returned to Kenyon in late October he forwarded Stanton's trunk to Columbus. Stanton moved it, and himself, into the home of Horton Howard and his wife, Hannah, who had four adult daughters, at least one of whom was married. The new boarder, not yet eighteen, immediately observed that none of the daughters was particularly attractive, although they were all kind, intelligent, and pleasant. For that matter, two weeks into his sojourn at Columbus, Stanton judged the town's women disappointing in general, as much as he preferred them to the "impudent, ignorant" men of the place. At first he made only one exception, for one girl whom a Kenyon lad had warmly recommended: Stanton clearly deemed her quite appealing. Through the kindness of another Kenyon classmate he was invited to a party, but he complained about the "affectation" of the girls there, and of the "dullness" of the young men; the next morning, to his mortification, he discovered that his threadbare trousers had worn completely through, and that he had been "showing my arse in more ways than one," although he presumed he had been subject to "the admiring gaze of the ladies." He nevertheless claimed to like Columbus "pretty well," if for no other reason than that so many of Ohio's prominent figures circulated there.[43]

His satisfaction with the place blossomed all the more when he began to see Mary Lamson. She was the sister-in-law of Reverend Preston, of the smoke-filled stagecoach ride, and she had recently been orphaned, so her sister and the reverend had taken her into their home. Mary had lived at Gambier previously, where her father was chief clerk of the college store Stanton had so often patronized, but somehow he missed meeting her in that tiny community, although she was only a year younger. He later admitted that she caught his eye because she was so pretty, describing her as a lovely brunette, with dark eyes and an appealing smile that showed bright, even teeth in an age before orthodontics, when decay and tooth loss were common. Her skin was fair, her figure slim, her manner gentle, and her voice soothingly sweet. So attractive a girl must have seemed an odd match and a tremendous prize for Stanton, who was once described as "not handsome, but on the contrary, rather pig-faced," but she seemed intellectually ambitious and admired the same quality in him. Her presence may have lured him to Reverend Preston's Trinity Episcopal Church in Columbus—try as

Kenyon loyalists might to credit obligatory attendance at the college chapel with winning Stanton for the denomination.[44]

While his relationship with Mary evolved from calling to courting, his mother and siblings left the home where they had lived for fifteen years. The estate had finally evaporated, except for the house, and it had to be sold to provide for the children's support and education: this was the calamity Daniel Collier had foreseen when he insisted on Edwin working for Turnbull. In May, Lucy Stanton relinquished her dower right in the house to free it for faster sale, and on August 17 it went on the block. Lucy moved her three children and what remained of her furnishings into a tiny, three-room house a furlong up Third Street, on what was then the edge of town. Her eldest child only learned of this latest reversal in family fortunes weeks later, through a letter from his eleven-year-old sister, Oella.[45]

Worse trouble followed even as Collier advertised the house for sale. Cholera had returned with the hot weather, and by May it was spreading down the Ohio River. By the end of that month it appeared in Wheeling, not thirty miles from Steubenville, and mortality ran high. It also spread west, reaching Columbus on Sunday, July 14, and by July 27 it had claimed ten victims in the city. A week later the *Ohio State Journal* added seven more citizens and nine state-prison convicts to the toll, which the editor still considered fairly light in a town of nearly three thousand residents. On August 9, the disease fell with a vengeance at the home where Stanton boarded, first killing twenty-two-year-old Ann Howard. Her father died five days later, and her mother on August 20; two nights after that one of Ann's older sisters lost her husband. In two weeks, half the family had been buried.[46]

More than seventy years after the epidemic, a grisly story surfaced about Stanton's reaction to Ann's death. She was said to have served him his noon meal on August 9, with the symptoms overcoming her after he went back to the bookstore, and she died so quickly that when he returned home she had already been buried. According to the earliest published version of this legend, Stanton doubted she was really dead, and enlisted other men to help him reopen the grave and open the coffin to be certain she had not been buried alive. All who later heard or read of the episode interpreted it as evidence of great courage on the part of Stanton, whose generation believed the disease could be communicated by mere contact with the bodies of those it had killed.[47]

Cholera was deadly enough for Ann to have felt well at noon and be buried by late evening, but that would have allowed little time for finding a casket, digging a grave, and filling it in. Stanton's sister remembered hearing her mother relate the incident when she was a child, but a Columbus resident who was born two decades after the epidemic offers the only corroboration for the story, which is discredited by two very newsy letters that

Stanton wrote immediately afterward.[48] Had the dark-of-night disinterment actually happened, Stanton would have felt the wrath of the surviving Howard family and all their neighbors. The very element that would have given the undertaking heroic flavor—the misconception that the corpses of cholera victims were dangerously contagious—would have made the amateur undertakers seem directly responsible for bringing the fatal disease back to kill the other members of that family. Yet Stanton was welcome in the Howard home well into the epidemic, if not afterward, for he told his guardian that he "sat up" with the family on the night Mr. Howard died.[49]

The epidemic did not stop Stanton from attending Kenyon's commencement exercises. The campus reminded him how badly he wanted to resume his studies there, and as soon as he returned to Columbus he wrote to his guardian about his wish to pass another year at Kenyon and then begin the study of law. He complained that James Turnbull had taken unfair advantage of him—had cheated him, really—with the implied promise to pay him more than Alexander Beatty was earning in Steubenville. He knew, probably from Beatty himself, that Beatty was getting $250 a year, with another $3 a month for "extra services," while his own salary was at least no higher, and Turnbull allowed him no bonus at all, even with the entire business of the Columbus store falling on his responsibility. His income so little exceeded his expenses, which were far greater in Columbus than Beatty's were, that he had nothing with which to either continue in college or arrange for reading law. He told Collier he would therefore renew his engagement if Turnbull would "make any thing like an equitable bargain," but he had written to Turnbull on that subject already and had not received a reply. [50]

Meanwhile, cholera lingered in Columbus. John Miner, a recent Kenyon graduate of his acquaintance, had fallen ill, as did Miner's brother-in-law, and Stanton tended both of them, once staying up all night again. The city's last victim died September 21, and no further cases developed, but a new threat that doctors diagnosed as bilious fever had already infected certain wards, killing an occasional sufferer. Like cholera, malignant fever, and numerous other obscure ailments of that century, bilious fever produced diarrhea, vomiting, and high temperatures. Stanton may have had a touch of that, as well, for at the tail end of the epidemic he admitted coming down with another brief bout of something that resembled cholera for a few anxious hours.[51]

With nothing but the sale price of the house to support the Stanton children until the last of them had reached adulthood, Daniel Collier balked at the idea of the oldest boy doing anything but keep his job, and he told him to renew his contract with Turnbull. While remaining outwardly obedient, having promised to abide by Collier's judgment, Stanton tried to make private arrangements that amounted to rebellion. His attachment to Mary

Lamson had evidently fostered impatience for the independence that a profession would bring, and he schemed to pursue a career while remaining within reach of a young woman he now admitted being "desperately in love with." He had evidently cultivated a relationship with John W. Campbell, the federal district judge for Ohio, and the two may have forged an agreement about Stanton coming into Campbell's office in some capacity that would have allowed him enough salary to subsist on while still training for the law. Collier's reply, directing him to stay on at the bookstore, reached Columbus as the cholera scare waned, and Stanton was probably waiting to present Collier with his new legal tutelage as a fait accompli, but two or three days later Judge Campbell inconveniently died.[52]

That brought Stanton's world crashing down again, but still he did not renew the contract with Turnbull. To McClintock he hinted that he had tried next to secure a position in the office of a circuit court judge in Columbus, but then President Jackson filled Campbell's place with one of his loyal electors from the election of 1832—Benjamin Tappan Sr. of Steubenville. Tappan's social position had always been a few steps above that of the Stanton family, and as a fervent Jacksonian his politics would have been repugnant to David Stanton (and probably to Daniel Collier, for that matter). Yet the hometown connection must have given Stanton great hope, for he had developed a cordial friendship with Judge Tappan's son and namesake, Benjamin Jr. The judge expected to move his office to Columbus, and any decision about staffing would probably have been deferred even if Stanton inquired about a position, so when October came to an end so did the job at Turnbull's store. It was doubtless another bittersweet homecoming for him early in November, with the pleasure of seeing his family clouded by the distance he had suddenly put between himself and Mary Lamson.[53]

For a month or more Stanton loitered in Steubenville, living in the three-room house with his mother, two sisters, and Darwin, who had begun to show an interest in medicine. Daniel Collier had been retained for a case in the national capital and was not in town. Sometime in December, around his nineteenth birthday and on the day that Collier was scheduled to come back to Steubenville, Stanton concluded in evident desperation to return to Columbus. As much as Mary may have figured in his decision, he likely justified the journey with a plan for committing himself to study under Judge Tappan or some other prominent jurist, but his mother and five-year-old Pamphila intercepted him on the porch of the tiny house as he started to meet the stage, begging him not to leave them alone again. Their supplications at last dissuaded him, and he agreed to wait for Collier's return. That evening (as little Pamphila remembered it, fifty or sixty years afterward) he called at his guardian's home, revealing his intention to defy instructions and undertake legal studies in Columbus.[54]

Perhaps frustrated with his obstinate ward, or impressed with his determination, Collier relented in his insistence on the bookstore position, but he tried to persuade Stanton of the advantages his native town offered, over Columbus, for studying the law. Admitting that the sixty-year-old Tappan might be more eminent as an attorney than most Steubenville lawyers, Collier contended that as a federal district judge and a prominent Democrat Tappan would not have much time for actually teaching a novice. The younger local men in the profession had more incentive to prepare competent new colleagues and potential partners for the Steubenville bar, Collier reasoned. So many youths had been reading law recently that something akin to a regular curriculum had developed, and at that moment four others were already studying. One lawyer in this informal consortium reputedly owned the best law library west of the Alleghenies. There was a weekly lyceum in the sciences and humanities, and an "athenaeum" offered not only a reading room and library but Monday night debates. Collier may also have mentioned a mock court the lawyers were planning to establish, where students could hone their rhetoric and learn the finer points of procedure. Above all, Collier noted, the cost of living was cheaper in Steubenville. In the end he offered to take Stanton into his own office as a student, with a $150 fee for his legal education to be paid after he had been licensed to practice. The prospect of long absence from Mary clearly posed the biggest hurdle, and Stanton argued earnestly for finding a place in Columbus. The longings of his heart may have flavored his opinion of the professional advantages to be had in that city, and he confessed to McClintock with typical hyperbole that "I thought my whole future success, nay my very existence depended on my going there," but in the end he accepted Collier's offer. With his career under way he was able to cast off the dismal uncertainty that had dogged him since summer, and within weeks he conceded that his guardian had been wiser than he.[55]

2

THE WIFE OF HIS YOUTH

Living with his family and settling into a routine of study toward his career goal quickly restored Stanton's humor, as much as he missed Mary Lamson. Letters written during his first months in Collier's office reveal a youth who seemed contented and playful again, although the playfulness took a vulgar turn. Of one Kenyon student who was preparing to enter private medical practice, Stanton remembered that he "used to have a singular itching to put his fingers into other mens eyes," and remarked that as a physician he would soon "have a chance to put them into other mens arses!" He commented even more crudely on the wife of a Kenyon professor, perhaps indicating a prurient preoccupation not inconsistent with separation from the object of his affection. Stanton planned months in advance to make the long trek to Gambier for Kenyon's 1834 commencement, undoubtedly arranging to meet Mary, and the prospect of seeing her must have softened his disappointment over learning that the closest of his former classmates, Andrew McClintock, would not be there.[1]

McClintock's absence from commencement would only mean that Stanton could spend more time with Mary, with whom he corresponded as often as his office schedule and study permitted. His portion of their exchanges bore no resemblance to his boastful and bawdy letters to college friends, instead focusing on ambitions for himself and them. Based on such declarations, and probably on his industrious application to his books, she sensed that he lusted for fame, and confessed that she admired him for it. She described her own studies and lamented that her schooling was over, asking if he would prescribe a reading regimen. Mary had read a collection of Byron's works, and while Stanton replied that he enjoyed Byron's poetry he echoed her disapproval of its licentious character, albeit with an evident lack of candor. Mary might have suffered a shock had she seen one of his letters to McClintock from that period.[2]

Stanton had been with Collier six months when a young man in Virginia's Shenandoah Valley by the name of Cyrus McCormick patented a horse-drawn mechanical device for harvesting wheat: the machine would not only enhance the production of food and accelerate settlement of the

American prairies and plains but, two decades later, would provide a mature Edwin Stanton with one of his more profitable and conspicuous legal cases. Around the same time, President Jackson enlisted Roger B. Taney in his battle against the Bank of the United States, and for his loyal services in that struggle Jackson felt a considerable debt, so when Chief Justice John Marshall died in 1835 Jackson named Taney to that position. The Senate approved the appointment, and Taney—the future author of the divisive decision in the Dred Scott case—lived long enough that Stanton himself entertained some hope of filling his place.

The struggle over banks would also ensnare Stanton. It all began when the Bank of the United States attempted to renew a charter that granted it extensive privileges and considerable power. An agreement made by the Madison administration in financial desperation after the War of 1812 stipulated that federal funds would supply much of the capital for that private corporation, while the bank handled the government's deposits and fund transfers. During the postwar land boom the bank encouraged expansionary practices that spread to state banks, but in 1819 panic ensued when the Bank of the United States curtailed credit to curb inflation during an economic downturn. Federalist influence on the Supreme Court, meanwhile, had guaranteed the Philadelphia-based bank and its branches exemption from taxation by the states. Jackson and his supporters believed the bank was guilty of manipulating the currency to benefit investors and influence trade, and denounced it as a dangerous monster. Advocates of the bank deemed it vital to territorial expansion and internal improvements, and saw Jackson's opposition as rabble-rousing recklessness. The charter was due to expire in 1836, but congressional friends passed a renewal bill just before the election of 1832, hoping to force Jackson's hand. That plan backfired when Jackson vetoed the legislation, creating an issue that seemed to secure his reelection, and throughout his second term he carried on a campaign to kill the bank. Jackson won a significant round when he began withdrawing the public deposits. The bank retaliated, trying to create a panic by shutting off credit again, but for all that political pressure Jackson refused to return the government's deposits. By the summer of 1835 the bank relented and reversed course, issuing a new flood of loans. That only precipitated another round of speculation and inflation.[3]

The conflict with the Bank of the United States occupied center stage in Jackson's war against the privileged class just as Stanton finished his legal education. Eventually he would cast his fortunes with the Jacksonians, the party that advocated less government, but he took no part in the contest yet. Instead, he concentrated on the bar examination, which he passed before reaching his majority. He argued at least one case alongside Collier before he turned twenty-one, prosecuting a trover against a warehouseman who had misappropriated three hundred barrels of flour, but Ohio law delayed his license to practice until his birthday, on December 19. One of his Kenyon friends had moved to Cincinnati and tried to persuade him to settle in that "great city," but so distant a place held no charm for Stanton. He could already claim a fairly intimate association with Judge Tappan, whose clout in Ohio and with the president could be helpful to a young man just setting out, and that connection would be lost in Cincinnati. Nor did any young women interest him save Mary, whom he visited in Columbus in the waning days of 1835. With the close of the year he found himself a legal adult, free from commitments to any master, and he promptly moved out of the family home. As a novice with no reputation, no library, and little experience, Stanton was obliged to find an established attorney willing to share his profits and his caseload. That brought him to Chauncey Dewey, a forty-one-year-old lawyer who had an office in Cadiz, the seat of neighboring Harrison County.[4]

Cadiz lay as much as thirty miles from Steubenville by the indirect roads of 1836, but it was close enough that Stanton could enjoy occasional contact with his family, friends, and associates while he dove into the legal affairs of a community where he was still a stranger. He bought no property at first, so presumably he boarded with another family. He must have hinted to someone that he sympathized with the nascent abolition movement, for he had not been in town six months before the Cadiz Antislavery Society asked him to speak, but there is no evidence that he ever did. Like most lawyers new to the bar, he began by handling property transactions, estate matters, and lawsuits over minor indebtedness. His name first appears in court documents on April 4, 1836, when he represented three orphans for whom he recommended a guardian and the administrators of two different estates. The next day Stanton defended five individuals in separate cases pressed by the Farmers and Mechanics Bank of Steubenville: Daniel Collier prosecuted for the bank, and won judgments against all of Stanton's clients. An increasing number of debtors found themselves in the same predicament, as the latest inflationary bubble expanded toward the bursting point. Three months into Stanton's partnership with Dewey, a New York newspaper was already looking for the economic collapse that "the banks have been preparing for us."[5]

The rented three-room house where Lucy Stanton and her daughters had been living was sold out from under them, and they moved into another house on Market Street, right alongside the Farmers and Mechanics Bank that was suing Stanton's delinquent clients. His younger brother Darwin had gone to Philadelphia to study medicine at the University of Pennsylvania. Their mother's bad health and shrinking resources created a domestic crisis that Stanton could not resolve from Cadiz, and the solution seemed to be for Lucy to visit her aging father for the first time in nearly two decades. She took Oella and Pamphila with her, for Thomas Norman had never seen those two granddaughters.[6]

With his income rising, his family scattered, and Mary patiently waiting, Stanton concluded it was time to unite everyone under one roof. Mary consented to his proposal, although she anticipated marital responsibilities with "fear and trembling." On December 14 Stanton boarded the stage for Columbus, where he fell ill for a week, but he had recovered by Christmas and on the last morning of 1836 he and Mary stood before Reverend Preston to be married. Judge Tappan's son Benjamin, who had gone to Paris for his own medical education, learned of the nuptials and congratulated Stanton on winning the lovely, gentle Mary. "You have taken a ticket in that lottery in which the blanks are at least as numerous as the prizes," he wrote. "I am inclined to believe that you have drawn a prize." So did Stanton: he later acknowledged that happiness required him to have someone to love, and someone to love him, and Mary supplied both. He credited her with bringing out the good in him and suppressing his darker tendencies (including his temper, perhaps), and said she made him so happy that he strove to see her content in return. Through three years of separation they had remained single-mindedly constant, and for Stanton the devotion may have lasted long after death had sundered their bond.[7]

It was his plan to proceed to Virginia immediately after the wedding, to fetch his mother and sisters. Judge Tappan's wife offered to let Mary stay with them while he was gone, but the newlyweds spent the rest of the winter at the Tappan home. Not until well into spring, after the April term of court had ended, did Stanton start over the mountains for his mother and the girls. The journey still entailed travel by stagecoach all the way to Frederick, Maryland, but from there the railroad had been completed to Baltimore and thence to Washington, where steamboats carried passengers down the Potomac to within easy coach distance of Fredericksburg and Stevensburg. It was the second and last opportunity for Stanton to see his grandfather, and the only instance he probably remembered. The old man died a year and a half later, leaving a sprawling estate that included thirty-five slaves, but his three marriages had also produced a huge brood, of whom thirteen children survived: his only bequest to Lucy Stanton and her line consisted of $800 as a trust for her support, with the principal to be distributed among her children after she died.[8]

The financial collapse that hard-money proponents had been anticipating began as Stanton started for Virginia, and it peaked as he escorted his mother and sisters home. To curb the spiraling inflation of land speculation between the Alleghenies and the Mississippi, President Jackson had issued his "Specie Circular," directing the Treasury to accept only gold or silver coin for the sale of government land: that brought the pyramid of artificial land values crashing down, and caught speculators owing high-interest notes on land they could not sell. The interruption of land sales stifled the payment of other debts, and—in the face of a simultaneous contraction of British currency—banks and businesses began failing with dizzying speed. Late in March New Orleans, New York, and Philadelphia all saw one or two of their bigger merchant houses abruptly close their doors, and through April one or another retail institution failed in each city almost daily. New York City alone counted 250 major mercantile failures by May 3, and another score on May 4. Then came a run on the banks, as crowds demanded coin for the paper currency each bank had issued, or tried to withdraw their funds in gold and silver, and by May 10 even the big Eastern banks started suspending specie payments. On the streets of Philadelphia, where Darwin Stanton pursued his course in medicine, a pedestrian overheard the vocabulary of the panic whenever he passed two or more people standing together.[9]

This crash only further inflamed the anti-bank sentiments of radical Democrats, who by then had embraced the pejorative nickname of Locofocos that conservative bank Democrats had given them. In a few years Judge Tappan would proudly count himself among the Locofocos, steadfastly opposing all banks, and that stance won political allies in the state capital. Tappan came from a family of Massachusetts reformers, and while his younger brothers leaned toward the abolition movement he took up the cause of economic egalitarianism. Stanton's straitened youth had probably produced similar sympathies, and he adopted the politics of his new mentor, yet there may have been an element of professional calculation in the choice as well.[10]

Stanton inadvertently annoyed Tappan that spring with a letter he wrote to young Benjamin. At the age of twenty-five Benjamin Jr. remained dependent on his father for his education and living expenses, and the judge had grown impatient for him to finish school in Paris and begin medical practice. Stanton interfered, trying to explain the judge's wishes, but he exaggerated a case of erysipelas that afflicted the judge, and the son seemed to use that as his excuse for coming home before he finished his course of study. After what may have been a fortnight of dissipation that he disguised as a debilitating fever, the younger Tappan returned from France in the face of his father's disapproval, but he satisfied the old man by beginning at least a nominal practice. He also started courting fifteen-year-old Oella Stanton.[11]

As young as Oella was, a marital connection with the prominent Tappan family would almost certainly have pleased Stanton. Since their winter with the elder Tappans, he and Mary socialized with them enough that Mary developed a reputation for beating the old man at checkers, and when the judge advertised his return to private practice late in May he announced that Stanton would be working with him. They were soon involved in a number of legal cases, and in their correspondence Stanton referred to the judge and himself in the first person plural, but their publicly acknowledged collaboration initially fell short of a full partnership. Stanton stuck with Dewey, and for the present lived just outside of Cadiz with Mary, his mother, and the two girls. At the same time, he collected evidence, interviewed witnesses, and suggested strategies in the cases he took with Tappan. He looked out for the judge's political interests and ambitions, too, and as Tappan's protégé he adopted identical political views. For the first time, he revealed a definite preference for the party of Jackson, alluding to the Democrats as "our side" when reporting to the judge on political affairs in Harrison County, and the more hostile the judge grew to the banks, the more stridently Stanton opposed them. Only after Tappan had taken him under his wing did Stanton align himself with the party publicly as well as privately, taking the field as a Democratic candidate.[12]

Hard times often bring good times to lawyers, and clients multiplied as the boom of 1836 deteriorated into the Panic of 1837. Stanton engaged in numerous courtroom contests with the Farmers and Mechanics Bank, but creditors usually prevailed in their actions against debtors, and he lost every case that spring, as well as a significant slander suit. Each case improved Stanton's financial standing, win or lose, but losing did little to attract clients, and that may have led him to seek the job that often falls to lawyers who need to enhance their prestige, or bolster a dwindling clientele. In the autumn elections of 1837 he filed as a Democrat for prosecuting attorney of Harrison County, and won. Criminal cases proliferated with the financial crash, and Stanton was soon busy with burglaries, larcenies, varying degrees of assault, at least one riot, and a string of bastardy and seduction cases that he pursued with a particular zeal. So much criminal business did he drum up in his first year as prosecutor that the court awarded him twice as much compensation for the November term as it had in the spring term.[13]

Stanton relished the additional workload. A decade later he confessed that something in his nature made it unbearable to be idle—a compulsion that may have been driven by the memory of the poverty his family had endured, especially after the death of his imprudently generous father. As prosecutor he accumulated more victories than defeats, but his private practice still produced more losses. Juries seemed susceptible to his rhetoric and relentless cross-examinations when he prosecuted defendants in criminal trials, where he enjoyed the latitude to bring forward only those cases for which he could present abundant evidence. Civil actions necessarily constituted the bulk of his private practice while he served as county prosecutor, and in that arena he—like most young lawyers—accepted any client who could afford to pay, regardless of the merits of the case. That naturally increased his odds of failure.[14]

The ties to the Tappans grew tighter on June 7, 1838, when the Paris-educated, freshly licensed Dr. Benjamin Tappan married Oella Stanton, who had turned sixteen a few days before. In the lottery of blanks and prizes the doctor had mentioned, he would eventually conclude that he had drawn a blank, and it would ultimately become clear that Oella had won no prize, either, but for the nonce romance prevailed. A few weeks later the Democratic Central Committee, which now included Stanton, called voters in the counties of Jefferson, Harrison, and Tuscarawas who were "friendly to the Administration" of Martin Van Buren to meet in convention for the nomination of candidates for state and local offices. Enough of their candidates filled the legislature to select a Democrat for the U.S. Senate seat, and by Christmas they had chosen sixty-five-year-old Judge Tappan by seven votes. That left Stanton in charge of their legal business during Tappan's long absences in Washington, during which he also acted as Tappan's eyes and ears at Democratic functions, reporting on the party conventions in Columbus and the political leanings of various candidates.[15]

In the spring of 1838 Darwin returned from Philadelphia with a medical degree, having satisfied the university trustees with an essay on the phenomenon of irritable uterus. He chose to settle in Holliday's Cove, Virginia, right across the Ohio River from his native town, where the local doctor had recently died. His mother and Pamphila moved in with him as housekeepers, bringing them that much closer to Oella and giving Stanton and Mary the privacy they had never had as newlyweds: living in close quarters with his mother and prepubescent sister may have helped them to pass more than two years of married life without conceiving a child. That privacy lasted only until the following summer, for on July 4, 1839, Darwin married Nancy Hooker, a girl of fifteen, whereupon Lucy and her youngest daughter moved back in with Stanton and Mary—who may not yet have known that Mary was pregnant. Stanton went to court to assume legal guardianship over Pamphila, then only twelve, but early marriage seemed fashionable for girls along that stretch of the Ohio River, and it was barely two more years before an aspiring colleague of Stanton's asked for Pamphila's hand, too.[16]

The court record asserts that Pamphila asked to have her oldest brother as her guardian, and in old age she remembered him acting as her caretaker "since my earliest recollection." In taking legal responsibility, Stanton relieved Daniel Collier of his last charge in the care of David Stanton's children and paved the way for final settlement of that pitiful estate. It also allowed Stanton to distance himself from the Whiggish Colliers: in his professional, political, and personal association with Senator Tappan he would inevitably come into conflict with the family that included his former guardian and mentor.[17]

As a member of the Democratic Central Committee for the 19th Congressional District, Stanton attended the party conventions in Columbus each winter, where the logrolling for state nominations served as a prognosticator for larger issues. Although Stanton was not a member of the nominating committee, he cultivated acquaintances with prominent members, consulted with them about candidates, and became his district delegation's spokesman on resolutions for the convention of 1840. He and Senator Tappan vehemently opposed the reelection of Reuben Wood as an Ohio Supreme Court judge, and Stanton composed a letter for the *Ohio Statesman* exposing Wood's obligations to the bank lobby, which he had courted with favorable judicial decisions; the letter noted that the obnoxious interpretation of a bank charter as an inviolable contract dated from Wood's first appearance on the high court. Stanton dropped the letter off at the newspaper as soon as he reached Columbus, but it never ran.[18]

Stanton may also have had a hand in composing the interrogatories presented to the leading candidates for the state Supreme Court that year, so dominated were they by questions on the bank issue. Delegates asked the aspirants' opinions on the constitutionality of the Bank of the United States, their attitudes toward banks in general, and their position on President Van Buren's efforts to establish an independent U.S. Treasury for the deposit of federal funds. It was a reflection of Locofoco power that both candidates expressed antagonism toward banks and enthusiasm for an independent treasury. Stanton thought he caught Reuben Wood in a contradictory reply to the committee, and collected information that would expose the falsehood. Wood submitted a revised interrogatory, however, and marshaled enough powerful supporters to prevail before Stanton could spring his trap. Noting defections from radical Democratic ranks, and the weakness of the party's candidates, including the man they had run for the state court, Stanton predicted that with a little brains and integrity Ohio's Whigs would probably carry the state election and perhaps even beat Van Buren.[19]

Returning from the convention on January 15, Stanton mailed Senator Tappan the only surviving copy of Wood's initial interrogatory, containing the inconsistent response. He included the evidence demonstrating the lie he said it contained, and—reflecting a practice he would follow with later enemies—he urged saving those papers in a dossier for potential future use against Wood. He also counseled Tappan to ingratiate himself with George Flood, an influential assemblyman whom Stanton had earlier endorsed as a person who commanded the greatest confidence. Now Stanton warned that Flood was not reliable and had powerful friends, suggesting that Tappan should appease him and get him out of the state with a federal appointment. In the same letter Stanton described a rising star in the party, David Tod, whom he recommended as a loyal ally in their campaign against banks and paper money. "Tod is true as steel," Stanton assured the senator, but Tappan would not finish his term before he learned to discount that over-zealous encomium, too.[20]

Eight weeks after Stanton returned from the 1840 convention, Mary bore her first child, whom they named Lucy Lamson Stanton. By the end of Stanton's term as county prosecutor he had shifted his focus from the partnership with Chauncey Dewey to the practice with Tappan, and had brought his wife, mother, and sister back to Steubenville, selling the Cadiz homestead to Dewey for $250. A couple of months after his daughter's birth he installed all three generations in a small house on a half-lot, only a few doors up Third Street from the house where he had grown up.[21]

The presidential campaign of 1840 began early, and radical hostility to the banks still smoldered within the Democratic Party. Stanton took immediate action against a Steubenville bank in which director Samuel Stokely held a leading interest, attacking it for usury and suggesting its charter be repealed. He proposed that his district Democratic committee highlight the generous fees banks had paid for title searches by officials who had subsequently become Whig stump speakers, insinuating that those transactions amounted to veiled bribes, and he suspected that Harrison County's most effective speaker had made so much from them that publishing the amount would silence him. Generally Stanton referred to the Whigs merely as "the opposition," or more pejoratively as "Federalists," and he advised a no-holds-barred struggle, cautioning that "delicacy and forbearance is not to be expected from our adversaries."[22]

The Democrats nominated Martin Van Buren again, just as Congress considered a bill for his independent treasury that so many of the common folk believed would liberate them from bondage to the banks. To counteract nearly a decade of Democratic rhetoric against the privileged classes, the Whigs usurped the Jacksonian mantle and cast their own candidate, William Henry Harrison, as a man of the people. Harrison was born in a magnificent manor house on a James River plantation and lived in a sprawling home at North Bend, Ohio, but his managers portrayed him as a cider-sipping rustic living in a log cabin. Whigs could offer so little in the way of populist policies that they abstained from proclaiming any platform at all, harping on the myth of the log cabin and the cider barrel. Except for a few ambiguous speeches, their candidate lay low, and he was reputedly not even trusted to answer his own mail, lest he inadvertently reveal an actual opinion.[23]

While the Democrats focused on slander and scandal, the Whig campaign quickly degenerated into the brandishing of tokens, the chanting of slogans, and the invention of gimmicks. Log cabins appeared in every imaginable form, from lapel pins, flags, bottles, and illuminations, to scale models transported by wagon. Newspapers sprang into existence called the *Log Cabin*—most notably in New York, under the eye of Horace Greeley. Harrison became "Tippecanoe," to commemorate his first victory over the Indians, and his champions shouted "Tyler, too," in honor of his running mate, John Tyler. Harrison supporters rolled big, slogan-covered tin balls from one town to another, to the sound of brass bands or their own cheering. Cider—and not usually sweet cider—flowed at every Harrison meeting. Occasionally a local orator might allude to some complicated, substantive matter: state legislator Abraham Lincoln, for instance, enlightened a crowd at Tremont, Illinois, about the legitimacy of the Bank of the United States and the evils of the independent treasury. Like the Democrats, however, the Harrison team stuck mainly to visceral issues that resonated with the masses. Lincoln himself appealed to the baser instincts of Illinois voters by alluding disapprovingly to Van Buren's support for giving free Negroes the franchise in New York. The ease with which so many were drawn into this cultivated hysteria disgusted even some of the more staid observers who were, themselves, hoping for a Whig victory.[24]

The *Log Cabin Farmer* flourished in Steubenville that election year, with much of its space devoted to lists of local Democrats who vowed they would not vote again for Van Buren. Their grievances included the passage of the independent-treasury "scheme," the "warfare carried on against the Banks and the currency," and continuing hostility to protective tariffs. The apostates included Stanton's former master, James Turnbull, who had suffered as much as any business owner from the bursting of the speculative bubble.[25]

Stanton spent many weekends that summer speaking for Van Buren and hard money at Democratic gatherings in the eastern part of the state. He appeared at one grand rally in his home town, where the secretaries of Democratic committees from other counties liked the barbs he cast and solicited him for other meetings, especially to counter the glib Whig newcomer John Bingham. Stanton leaped into the campaign with all the determined concentration that he applied to his legal cases, haranguing voters in the newspapers as well as from the rostrum. He composed an anonymous brief for a bill he claimed would rob chartered banks of their "irresponsible monopoly" and reduce them to economic equality with the farmer, mechanic, and manufacturer by forcing them to rely on the reputations of their owners instead of surviving on special privileges granted by the legislatures. After requiring stockholders to identify themselves by their names, addresses, and their other business interests, the proposed legislation would prohibit the banks from issuing notes of lower denomination than twenty dollars, in order to assure that all but the largest transactions were carried on with sound money. The bill preached the classic Jacksonian doctrine of the commoner.[26]

It was all to no avail. The Panic of 1837 and an aftershock in 1839 still reverberated through the economy in 1840, and Whigs found it easy to blame the Democrats' aversion to banks and paper money. Through the *Log Cabin Farmer* James Collier accused Senator Tappan of favoring policies that would cut day laborers' wages to the equivalent of barely a penny an hour, and prospective voters tended to credit even obviously false rumors that constituted a threat to their livelihoods. By the end of August, sixty-two Steubenville Democrats had announced their support for Harrison. Early in September the paper posted what it called the "Democratic Whig Ticket," and before the middle of that month it seemed to Harrison's followers that his election was "beyond doubt." The prediction proved accurate, and in November Harrison carried nineteen of the twenty-six states, including Ohio.[27]

Disappointed by the national contest, Stanton tried manipulating a local one. The spoils system that Jackson himself had inaugurated made it certain that the new president would dismiss all Democratic postmasters, including the one in Steubenville, and it had come to Stanton's attention that the Colliers were plotting to win the job for one of their family. Stanton supposed it would go to Daniel Collier, the guardian for whom he had once expressed such respect and gratitude. With more cunning than conscience, Stanton devised a convoluted plan to either rob the Colliers of the postal position or embarrass President Harrison among the Steubenville Whigs. Reasoning that the Democrat who held the job was going to be replaced anyway, Stanton suggested that Senator Tappan persuade President Van Buren to fill the post, just before he left office, with a prominent Whig who was antagonistic to the "Collier influence." If Harrison followed through with his reported promise to appoint a Collier, that would cause a rift within the local Whig ranks and perhaps alienate them against Harrison. Stanton started the wheels rolling on that scheme, enlisting some Democrats to offer endorsements for their pet Whig and perhaps even approaching that man directly. Tappan reacted so indignantly that Stanton wrote an abrupt apology, signed also by his chief conspirator: they pleaded that they were acting only under instructions from "a respectable meeting of their fellow citizens," and self-righteously assured the senator that they only meant to circumvent the regrettable consequences of a president who was guided by "the hands of unprincipled men." To regain Tappan's favor, Stanton offered more glowing compliments on one of Tappan's speeches, with which he said the senator had bested Senate legend Henry Clay, whom Stanton characterized as the "Autocrat of Kentucky."[28]

With his party out of power, Stanton could only take political satisfaction in whatever troubles afflicted the opposition, including the seemingly imminent collapse of half a dozen local state-chartered banks. In the final month of Van Buren's administration the Farmers and Mechanics Bank, the biggest in Steubenville, began refusing the paper currency issued by Whig congressman Samuel Stokely's bank, and Stanton contentedly observed the hard feelings engendered among the Whigs who served as directors of both banks. When state commissioners seized the assets of Stokely's bank, Stanton reveled in his access to its financial records as counsel for Stokely's opponents in a civil suit. He hastened as well to embarrass Steubenville's Whig business cliques, trying through the newspaper to paint a town council initiative to narrow High Street as a ploy to enlarge a crony's lot.[29]

The political defeat of 1840 left more time for Stanton's legal practice, and without the conflict of serving as a county prosecutor he never had to turn down a criminal case unless the client could not afford his services. One of his more notorious early defendants faced that difficulty, but Stanton solved it for him by accepting the man's home as security. John Gaddis, an aging Richmond tavern keeper who had been indicted on charges of beating his wife to death, put his farm up as collateral on February 3, 1841, and at the March term of the Jefferson County court Stanton entered a plea of not guilty on his behalf. That seemed a bold move: Gaddis's wife had lingered for four days after he repeatedly struck her with a brick, and before dying she had identified him as her assailant. In criminal as well as civil law, the adversarial system observed in American courtrooms can subordinate evidence to the personal persuasiveness of the advocate, and that clearly helped the widower Gaddis. Despite the victim's deathbed testimony, Stanton somehow won an acquittal, sending Gaddis back into society free, if homeless. By now the partnership with Tappan had become official, for when Gaddis failed to come up with the fee Stanton promptly foreclosed, taking joint ownership of the farm with the senator.[30]

Even in the relatively routine estate and property cases he took with Tappan, Stanton leaned toward the procedural equivalent of going for the jugular, which put him in demand among the desperate. Publicity from the Gaddis case may have led Joseph Thomas to select Stanton to defend him against an accusation that he murdered his wife. In an indictment dated August 16, 1841, a Harrison County grand jury alleged that Thomas had poisoned Mary Thomas with "corrosive sublimate," or mercuric chloride, on May 24, causing her death on June 2. His trial came late in the fall, and before presenting his case Stanton had the sheriff stand witness while he swallowed a small amount of the same poison Thomas was supposed to have mixed in his wife's food and drink. Evidently Stanton had consulted with a doctor beforehand, for a physician sat by with the antidote. Whether he wished to learn the effect of the chemical, or simply to demonstrate that it was not necessarily lethal, his experiment met with only limited success. The best he could do for Thomas was avoid a conviction for murder in the first degree. The jury spared the defendant from the gallows but sentenced him to life in the state penitentiary.[31]

That summer of 1841 Stanton met with the first great family loss since the death of his father. His little girl Lucy, not quite a year and a half old, died on August 24, while district Democrats were meeting in Bloomfield. The blow fell hard enough that Christopher Wolcott, a young law student in the firm (and Pamphila Stanton's suitor), assumed Stanton's correspondence with Senator Tappan for a couple of weeks. William Buchanan, another of the students in the office, remembered Stanton's sorrow persisting so doggedly that after a year he had Lucy's remains exhumed and sealed by coppersmith Samuel Wilson in a brazed metal box that Stanton "kept in his own room." Buchanan may have attributed too much of the macabre to a decision that Stanton probably had forced upon him by the impending relocation of one of Steubenville's two badly overcrowded cemeteries: if the little girl's body had to be disinterred, it was not so unusual to keep the remains hermetically sealed at home until another lot was found, although the necessity may well have reawakened parental grief.[32] Intense sentimentality over his family may have been Stanton's most endearing trait, and it showed particularly with Mary and her children, but he had seemed to recover within a reasonable period after Lucy died. Three months later he performed memorably in Joseph Thomas's murder trial, and ten weeks or so after Lucy's death his spirits had revived enough to father another child. His first son, Edwin Lamson Stanton, was born nine months later.[33]

By the end of 1841 those who followed courthouse theater in eastern Ohio might reasonably have assumed that Stanton would pursue a specialty in criminal defense. He soon discovered, however, that civil actions provided much higher fees, and that perhaps helped persuade him to move steadily away from the seamy, less profitable side of life and law. His involvement in criminal cases dwindled precipitously after he parted from Tappan, although he occasionally assisted in the prosecution of criminal defendants for well-heeled complainants—or, more rarely, represented a wealthy defendant.[34]

Stanton had taken the case of Mordecai Moore in 1840. Moore, a very prosperous Quaker farmer from Ross Township, in northwestern Jefferson County, had borrowed $23,000 from the United States Bank of Pittsburgh a couple of years previously, offering much of his extensive property as collateral. The bank failed, and during its death throes the directors called in all outstanding loans. Moore resisted the foreclosure and the case dragged on for years, but in 1845 Stanton finally persuaded the court to cancel the debt by declaring the mortgage void. Although Moore had entered into the contract willingly, Stanton successfully argued that the bank had been a creation of the state of Pennsylvania and therefore had no authority to exact a lien on property outside the state.[35]

In the same court term that saw him save John Gaddis from the hang-man, Stanton immersed himself in the infamous "pork case," involving three Ohioans trying to make a killing in the growing Cincinnati meatpack-ing business. William Talbott, a Jefferson County speculator, contracted with Cincinnati investors Aaron Gano and William Thoms to buy hogs and drive them to the city for butchering and shipment in brine-filled barrels. Bad timing foiled their plans, for the Panic of 1837 caused pork prices to plummet. Their chief creditor and Talbott's partner in another enterprise, John Moore of Cincinnati (no relation to Mordecai), sued Talbott, Gano, and Thoms: the latter pair avoided the summons, but Moore won a $16,000 judgment that Talbott could never have paid. Stanton initiated another suit to bring the wealthier partners in as defendants, and secured a decision in Moore's favor in the spring term of 1841, but the Supreme Court of Ohio reversed the decision. That seemed to end the case to Moore's disadvan-tage until Stanton and Henry Stanbery, a Lancaster attorney, moved for a new trial based on judicial misdirection in the reversal, and when they surmounted that hurdle the case was virtually won. The second trial was not held until the spring of 1845, but Stanton triumphed on the principle that the contract between the speculator and his investors should be held sacred—precisely the opposite position he took, about the same time, to rescue Mordecai Moore from the defunct bank.[36]

Stanton had more than one encounter with a litigious Irish physician named Benjamin Mairs, who lived just north of Steubenville. The most complicated involved a boardinghouse owner named Rectina McKinley, who sued Mairs over $8.25 for boarding the doctor's hired man, and in re-taliation Mairs countersued for $10.50, claiming that Miss McKinley owed him that much for an abortion. Stanton used Dr. Mair's affidavit as the basis of a suit for slander and libel, asking $5,000. Mairs produced a witness—"an Irishman he had picked up from the gutter in Pittsburgh," sneered Stanton—who testified to McKinley's promiscuous character. It may have been the defendant herself who recognized that the witness was wearing the doctor's own clothes, and under cross-examination Stanton wormed it out of him that he had been living with Mairs and taking wages from him. That seemed to convince the court that the witness had been suborned. The doctor's petition was denied; fearing the defeat would fatally prejudice the libel suit against him, he settled it for $900.[37]

With growing confidence in his courtroom prowess, in the spring of 1842 Stanton went fishing for business in an action against the very founder of Steubenville, as well as against his own former guardian. Bezaleel Wells, who had laid out the town nearly half a century before, had fallen on hard times during the depression of 1819, and B. Wells & Co. had failed alto-gether the next year. As administrator, Daniel Collier had been assigned to pay the firm's debts at the same time that he was looking out for the Stanton children's interests. Stanton offered to sue both Wells and Collier on behalf of Baltimore creditors who still remained unpaid, but the action appears not to have gone far: Senator Tappan had been an associate of the company at one time, and his inquiries must have revealed that too little remained to make the suit profitable.[38]

Tension may already have existed between the Collier family and Stanton because of a letter Tappan had written to the newspaper lambasting the Collier brothers for their political and professional practices. Stanton, who praised Tappan for something nearly every time he wrote, complimented him particularly for the carefully accusative "Collier letter." Joking that Tappan had been so acerbic that he must have wished to invite a libel action, Stanton ironically observed that the senator had discouraged the Colliers from filing suit by crafting it too adroitly. Stanton added that he had goaded the Colliers with an offer to sue Tappan himself, but he caustically lamented that they could "neither be driven nor coaxed into harness."[39]

The approach of the biennial elections of 1842 rejuvenated Stanton's political hopes. Steubenville Democrats chose him as one of their two delegates to the January state convention, and in the middle of February he traveled to Washington to see Judge Tappan and meet the other senator from Ohio, William Allen. While there, he grew sanguine about seeing the Whigs thoroughly trounced in the fall elections. Stanton's brother Darwin was drawn to the flame, as well, running for the Virginia House of Delegates in Brooke County as a Whig. Darwin and his child bride already had one son and a girl on the way (respectively named after his parents, David and Lucy), but Darwin showed signs of his father's impractical spirit. He had evidently never settled in at Holliday's Cove, and over the winter of 1841 he had been planning to pull up stakes for a move to Missouri, only to abandon the plan at the last moment. His decision to seek a time-consuming state office suggested, further, that his medical practice was not exactly thriving. Although he was running on the opposition ticket, his protective older brother joined him during part of Virginia's spring campaign, offering moral support and at least enough strategic advice to win the race; afterward, Stanton reported extensively to Tappan on Democratic weakness in that county.[40]

The economy had not improved under the Whigs, in Steubenville or anywhere else in Ohio. A new state bankruptcy law allowed debtors to evade their responsibilities, and it gave creditors no protection against fraud. Besides foreclosures, town clerks had begun listing an unusual number of houses, land tracts, and commercial properties (including a few mills) to be sold for unpaid taxes. The bank failures Stanton and others had been predicting on the eve of President Harrison's inauguration had come to pass by the end of that year: directors of the Bank of Zanesville had reportedly closed their doors and begun burning their paper currency in mid-January of 1842, and angry crowds had mobbed four Cincinnati banks that had stopped making payments. Banks and private moneylenders had begun filing a flood of lawsuits again, "putting the screws to their debtors very tightly," as Stanton phrased it. Factories had closed for want of demand, and the shops were empty. Democrats smelled opportunity in the air.[41]

Their opportunity had been enhanced by Harrison's death, only one month into his term. That had ushered John Tyler of Virginia into the White House, and he had quickly antagonized many in his own party, provoking all but one member of his cabinet to resign barely five months into his presidency. Political affiliations turned nebulous and ephemeral again without Andrew Jackson as the focal point of loyalty or hostility. When Tyler next sought office he would run with the Democrats—as would Darwin Stanton. On May 17, Steubenville Democrats met at the courthouse in the biggest rally Stanton had ever seen in Jefferson County, and he blamed the lackluster resolutions on his own absence from the preparatory meeting a few days earlier. Former governor and current gubernatorial candidate Wilson Shannon joined them there. A few renegade Democrats softened their opposition to the banks, holding a rump session at James Dillon's hotel, but the faithful at the courthouse "fairly read them out of meeting"—as Stanton told Senator Tappan. The next night the Whigs met at the courthouse to praise the still-solvent Farmers and Merchants Bank, and to hear the Colliers denounce President Tyler with "gall and bitterness" that Stanton judged "could only be distilled and concentrated from such hearts." It appeared that Stanton had drawn a dark veil over the memory of his "beloved guardian."[42]

Perhaps with the help of Tappan's influence, Stanton had been chosen by the state legislature that spring for a three-year term as reporter for the Ohio Supreme Court. Between chasing down case records, compiling court decisions, and pursuing their own firm's business, he was absent from home much of the summer, and he seemed never to cease moving even during sporadic stops in Steubenville. On one visit he attended the auction of a foreclosed farm where he deliberately bid against James Means, whom he claimed to despise as the leader of Steubenville's apostate Democrats. The doctor who had first taken Darwin Stanton into his office as a student was present and had his heart set on that farm, so Stanton bid against Means up to $14,000. Means said that was enough for him and withdrew, whereupon Stanton let the doctor make the next bid and take the place.[43]

At this point Stanton may have been weighing the possibilities of a career in politics. He had been considered for "president judge" of one of the state's judicial districts, but Senator Tappan had advised him to decline the position if it were offered, warning that his law business might suffer too much to compensate for the salary and honors. "If you are ambitious," Tappan urged, "(and who is not?), *look this way.*" He may have been hinting that Stanton should seek cases that would bring him to the Supreme Court, in Washington, but more likely he meant that the young lawyer should consider the political course Tappan had followed. Stanton came to Columbus early in December to be sworn in as reporter of the Ohio Supreme Court, and his presence in the capital again threw him into frequent (and perhaps infectious) contact with the mandarins of state and national politics.[44]

Governor Shannon won reelection that fall, and Stanton attended the inaugural ball. In a Christmas Day letter to his little sister he described the costumed and coiffed ladies and gentlemen leaping to the tunes of the fiddlers, and while he took no evident part in the dancing he obviously enjoyed mingling with Ohio notables. He toured the various asylums for the deaf, the blind, and the insane, and sat in on the legislature's debate over a bill to extend the charters of the state's surviving banks. With pro-bank legislators in the majority, the bill seemed certain to pass, but Stanton rejoiced at the long-odds fight waged by a few hard-money men while bankers packed the lobby to coax and coerce the reluctant. Caleb McNulty, of Mount Vernon, stalled the assembly all afternoon when Whigs and recusant Democrats finally forced it to the floor. A colleague spelled McNulty when he tired, talking into the evening, until Dr. Edson B. Olds stood to answer them. Olds rebutted the day's attacks until 9:00 P.M., and then called for an immediate vote. McNulty jumped to his feet to ask a point of order, which took precedence over any other motion, and when the speaker answered him McNulty challenged his ruling. McNulty "then sprung motion after motion," Stanton told Tappan, "question after question, appeal after appeal," until he had so thoroughly confused the speaker and the "paper money men" that when the body finally voted on the issue enough of them voted the wrong way that the bill failed. The next day was devoted to a motion for reconsideration.[45]

Shannon represented the Democrats who could brook equivocation on the matter of banks and currency, and they had begun promoting the idea of Lewis Cass as a contender for the presidency, on the presumption that he favored paper money and easy credit. Cass had just returned from a six-year mission to France, and in February of 1843 he visited Columbus in the hope of impressing potential supporters. Stanton professed to share Tappan's support of Martin Van Buren for the next presidential election, but he may have been exploring the advantages of other options. When he returned to the capital to enter the last few cases in his latest volume of the *Ohio Reports*, he sidled up to Governor Shannon as though he were interested in Cass, presenting himself as a prospective convert so Shannon would introduce him to that ponderous personage. In a conspiratorial tone Stanton explained to Tappan that he was merely associating with the Cass men so he could discover their plans, the better to serve Van Buren, and he offered the preliminary intelligence that the Cass clique expected Van Buren and John C. Calhoun to wound and smear each other so badly by the 1844 convention that Cass could step in as an unsullied compromise candidate. At the same time, Stanton reported that Cass appeared not to favor soft money much at all, notwithstanding a published letter to that effect. Instead, Stanton informed the senator, "he has here given strong intimations of being a hard money man," and had specifically said so to their friend Samuel Medary, the editor and publisher of the radically Democratic *Ohio Statesman*. Stanton mentioned that Shannon had told him that "Sam Medary has it in his power to make Cass President," but he assured Tappan that "a truer man never breathed" than Medary. Tappan, who would not live to learn of Stanton intriguing against two of the presidents he later served, appeared not to suspect his young partner of cultivating contingent alliances.[46]

In the end, Stanton did adhere to Van Buren. As chairman of Democrats in Carroll and Jefferson counties he marshaled his troops from late spring—first to local meetings, where townspeople selected delegates to a district convention, and then, on July 14, to choose Democratic candidates for senator and representative. That summer the eleventh volume of the *Ohio Reports* came out in the edition known as "Stanton's Reports," which made his name familiar to every lawyer in the state. In the fall, he was again designated as one of the district delegates to the state convention.[47]

By autumn, Mary Stanton had fallen into a pattern of deteriorating health that suggested she had contracted the plague of that century. No one ever called it tuberculosis, but she grew progressively more fragile while her husband's strained expressions of optimism betrayed underlying doubt. He continued to work as relentlessly as ever, to provide for their financial comfort and security to be sure, but also perhaps to escape the leisure that fostered discouraging reflection. Late in September they risked a trip to Pittsburgh by carriage, combining rare pleasure with the ancillary motive of medical consultation. They had been invited to spend a few days at the nearby estate of William Wilkins, on whom Stanton had bestowed a rather fawning letter the previous year, right after Wilkins was elected to Congress. The smoky city wilted Mary before they could start for the Wilkins home, and they decided to return by steamboat, rather than subject her to another forty-mile ride over rough roads in the elements. She was moving so slowly that they missed the boat, and in their anxiety to reach home they resorted to the carriage once again. Her strength gave out, forcing them to put up at a spa, where Mary remained a few days to recover while a distracted Stanton drove back to Steubenville. He sent his regrets to Wilkins for failing to make his visit, remarking that "Mrs. Stanton's state of health prevented the enjoyment of that, and every other pleasure."[48]

A few weeks later Stanton moved his family out of the house he had bought in 1840 and into a spacious, two-and-a-half-story brick house on the corner of Third Street and Logan, three blocks farther north. It was a fairly new house in a more quiet and exclusive neighborhood of Steubenville, and it had never been occupied. He may have made the exchange in unanticipated haste, to lift Mary's spirits and make her more comfortable: for a few months he retained ownership of the smaller house and leased the new one, but he bought three adjoining lots for gardens and buffer. He had little time to enjoy their expansive new quarters, for December dragged him back to Columbus again, to collect information for the next annual volume on cases in the state's high court. Mary wrote him on the thirteenth that everyone in the Steubenville house was well, implying that her own health remained stable. Stanton stayed in the capital through Christmas, and for their New Year's Eve wedding anniversary he wrote a letter containing what sounded like a despairing wish that they could enjoy many more new years together.[49]

The state Democratic convention followed, as usual, on January 8—the anniversary of Jackson's victory at New Orleans. Muddy roads diminished attendance from communities in the hinterlands, where hatred for the banks ran deepest, but the anti-bank men gained strategic advantages nevertheless. The hard-money contingent seated a sympathetic chairman in former congressman William Medill, and it won a coup in nomination strategy over the Cass machine of Governor Shannon, who tried to amend the rules to the disadvantage of Van Buren supporters. A string of Cass men endorsed the amendment, but Stanton and another delegate spoke against it and it failed: Medill described the two of them as "a tower of strength" for party unity, and an observer of Shannon's attempted divisiveness reported that Stanton had "killed him [i.e., Shannon] dead on the spot." After naming the delegates for Baltimore's national convention in May, the convention voted to instruct them to nominate Van Buren, and Medill remembered that the crowd's reaction "shook the very building itself." Almost without dissent, David Tod emerged as the candidate for governor, giving radical, hard-money Democrats something else to applaud.[50]

With the party's prospects fairly glowing and all going his way, Stanton probably spent the next month at home with Mary, returning reluctantly to the capital early in February as he had the previous year, to work on the court reports. Mary's brother, Nathan Lamson, traveled to Steubenville to visit his ailing sister, but hurried back to Columbus to warn Stanton that she had taken a turn for the worse. Stanton raced home to find her failing fast. She died on March 13, and for a time her husband seemed to lose his reason. At first he gave way to unmitigated grief, weeping uncontrollably and wailing for Mary to come back to him. Then he retreated into denial:

Pamphila later wrote that she found her brother wandering through the house at night, in a daze, carrying a lamp and asking where Mary was.[51]

A week later he managed to compose a letter, but it only served to illustrate the force of the blow he had suffered. He wrote to Senator Tappan's brother Lewis, in New York, to ask for the name of a stonecutter so he could order a marble monument to erect over the grave of his wife and daughter. Even in the businesslike request for an artisan's address he could not hold back a wrenching admission of the "utter desolation" he felt.

"It has pleased God," he wrote, in manifest despair, "within a few days past, to take from me my beloved wife, upon whom all my affections & happiness rested. . . . This calamity has overwhelmed me. I know not where to look or whither to turn. . . . We were both young & happy in each other, looking forward to a long life of joy & happiness. By incessant toil & industry we were gathering around us all that we thought would promote our comfort & enjoyment and this Spring had in our thoughts attained these. A few days ago I laid her in her grave, and to me they are now ashes, ashes."[52]

3

THE GOLDEN TRIANGLE

The Democratic juggernaut that had seemed so formidable when Stanton hurried home from Columbus began to disintegrate even as he knelt by Mary's deathbed. Gubernatorial candidate David Tod published a letter in which he retreated from the radicals' position on banks, leading one irate newspaper editor to brand him a "Bank Coon" and another to dismiss him as "the temporizing, time-serving candidate of the Loco Focos." Then, just before the national convention, Van Buren came out against the annexation of Texas, which outraged the slaveholding South. In a spiritless letter written six weeks after Mary's funeral, Stanton told Senator Tappan that Tod's equivocation had "dampened and subdued the ardor of our friends throughout the whole state." He feared that the "moral force of the campaign has been lost," at least in Ohio. He had not yet learned of Van Buren's courageously impolitic stand on Texas, but he knew that there were already movements afoot to sabotage the nomination.[1]

The presidential campaign of 1844 proved as tumultuous as any since the rise of Jackson. Texas loomed so large that it virtually decided the race, dooming both the presumptive Democratic nominee Van Buren and his Whig rival Henry Clay, who also opposed annexation. Van Buren's opposition pleased Northerners like Tappan, who worried that Texas could be divided into several new slave states, but it angered Southern Democrats who would have to support his nomination if Van Buren was to receive the two-thirds majority required by the Baltimore convention. He fell a score or so delegates short, and for a time the contest wavered between him and Cass until the convention finally settled on a relative unknown by the name of James K. Polk—former governor of Tennessee, onetime Speaker of the House of Representatives, and a disciple of Old Hickory.[2]

Stanton claimed that business commitments kept him from the convention, but he probably lacked the heart for it. Reminiscences from the late nineteenth century described him as so grief-stricken that his court cases for the March term all had to be postponed, while he became obsessively protective of Mary's grave. Those tales may have been exaggerated, and inevitably the pain of her death subsided, but he mourned over Mary for years, and perhaps forever: nearly four years later he told a friend that she was responsible for any good in him, while "whatever evil tendencies there may be, are less restrained since God took her from me." With a child, a sister, and his mother to support he ultimately forced himself to work, and that may be all that dragged him back from the brink of despair. He remarked more than once on his need for perpetual occupation, and that need would have been acute through the spring of 1844. He retained the chairmanship of his party's district committee, organizing rallies and caucuses the next summer, and six months after Mary died he managed to keep an audience of Steubenville Democrats applauding and cheering for an hour.[3]

It was about this time that Darwin grew restless again. He had served one term in the Virginia House of Delegates as a Whig, and had finished a second term as a Democrat, but rather than resuming his medical practice he sought government employment, again with the likely assistance of his brother. Caleb McNulty, who had stalled the bank bill on the floor of the Ohio House in 1842, had been rewarded a year later with the post of Clerk of the U.S. House of Representatives by appreciative hard-money Democrats like Senator Tappan. Stanton, who had contributed to McNulty's rise, probably interceded with him about a place for Darwin, or asked Tappan to do so for him. McNulty, who had dismissed a host of Whig underlings to make way for Democrats, hired Darwin as an assistant recording clerk, so he moved to Washington, leaving Nancy and their two children in Holliday's Cove under Edwin's eye until he found lodging for them in the capital.[4]

Senator Tappan came home in the final weeks of the national campaign. He chaired a mass meeting of Democrats on September 4, where Stanton called the crowd to order and David Tod explained his wavering on the banks. Ten days later an "enthusiastic" crowd of Democrats reconvened at Steubenville to hear Senator Tappan talk about Texas—which candidate Polk wanted to annex as U.S. territory. Tappan had reason to regard Texas as the center of a slaveholding conspiracy, and had already spoken against annexation in Senate debate, but how he reconciled his opinion with Polk's without damaging the Democratic nominee was not revealed in friendly newspaper coverage.[5]

The October elections in Ohio proved disastrous to Democrats, in large part because of uncertainty over Tod's attitude toward banks. Jefferson County went for Tod by twenty-five votes out of nearly five thousand, but equivocation cost him the election. Clay won Ohio, too, but his strongest support came from New England and the upper fringe of slave states. Polk went to Washington, where he would quickly steer the nation in the very direction dreaded most by Tappan and many others who helped elect him.[6]

The impending expiration of Tappan's term in the U.S. Senate had partly motivated his campaign efforts in Ohio. The Whigs had taken complete control of the legislature—they arranged all legislation in secret caucuses, Stanton observed, and used the state assembly as a mere "court of registration"—so Tappan had little chance to return to Washington. When Stanton traveled to Columbus to cover the December court session he reported that the Democrats were turning to Cass for favors. "It seems as if every man in the state wanted & must have something," he wrote when he arrived in the capital. Three weeks later he professed to Tappan that it disgusted him to see so many of their firm former allies "truckling and yielding to the Cass influence." Cass had reportedly said he was to be Polk's secretary of state, which he was not, but it was also rumored that he might be elected to the Senate, which he was. Another scramble for the post of U.S. District Attorney for Ohio included mention of Stanton's own name, but he said he would not accept it. The federal judge there was Humphrey H. Leavitt, who had sat on that bench since 1834, after the Senate had rejected Judge Tappan's nomination. In an apparent display of personal loyalty, Stanton told Tappan he would not practice in Leavitt's court "while I can make my bread elsewhere."[7]

When Tappan came home to Steubenville in the spring of 1845, he was approaching his seventy-second birthday. Stanton had essentially carried their partnership for the previous six years, but a man born before the American Revolution would have been thinking of retirement by then. Stanton had already taken a young lawyer under his own wing—twenty-two-year-old George W. McCook, who had been raised thirty miles from Steubenville and who had a younger brother named Edwin Stanton McCook. George had helped Stanton with estate cases the previous summer, and soon the *American Union* carried front-page "cards" for Stanton & McCook. After the connection with Tappan had been severed, Stanton's letters to his former partner contained no more expressions of contempt for the Collier brothers, who had been such bitter political enemies of the senator, and within a few weeks Stanton joined forces with one of the Colliers for the first time in years, to defend an indigent client charged with murder.[8]

The closing of his patron's political career seemed to bring Stanton's to an abrupt end, too, at least for the moment. District Democrats quickly chose another chairman for their central committee, and the appointment as reporter for the Ohio Supreme Court expired, depriving Stanton of his best opportunity to brush sleeves with the state's power brokers. Having lost his most influential friend in the nation's capital, he cultivated acquaintances with Ohio's remaining Democrat in the Senate and with one of the state's congressmen, and he began by complimenting each of them on speeches that contradicted each other.[9]

Dissolving the partnership with Tappan also relieved Stanton of growing discomfort over domestic strife between the senator's son and Stanton's sister, Oella. Dr. Tappan had seemed immature and irresponsible a decade before, as a medical student on the paternal dole, and his behavior only worsened with age. A couple of years into his marriage he stopped working, and not until early 1842, according to Stanton, did "the doctor" resume his practice, attracting a few patients. The next year Dr. Tappan disappeared for a time, evidently on a trip to South America that may have constituted one of his frequent excursions on the excuse of health, and while he was gone he ignored at least one piece of Steubenville real estate long enough that the town seized it for taxes. After he returned, Oella took the children and moved out of Senator Tappan's house, where they had all been living since 1840, and she did not return until after the election, when the senator went back to Washington. Stanton appears to have housed her and the children in the interim, and afterward he complained that the couple had reconciled "at my expense." The doctor turned "sour," snubbed him, and refused to allow the children to visit their grandmother—clearly blaming the Stantons for Oella's sudden independence. Dr. Tappan informed his father that he and his wife were finally dwelling together in harmony, that her housekeeping had improved, and that she was trying to make herself agreeable, but he did not want "her mother and brothers about the house." When his father was about to return from Washington, Dr. Tappan sent him a whining letter about the expense it had caused him to maintain the family home, in which he had been living rent-free for five years. Senator Tappan showed occasional impatience with his namesake's behavior, and must have sensed his shortcomings, because he tried to hide them from others, but eventually he took his son's side in the dispute with Oella. The doctor's troubled marriage must have created enough tension between Stanton and the senator to grace their professional separation with a measure of relief.[10]

An errant son may have been the least of the judge's problems as he pondered the conclusion of his public career. As one of those who had recommended Caleb McNulty for Clerk of the House of Representatives, Senator Tappan had stood with Ohio congressman John Weller as surety for McNulty's faithful disposition of the public funds that passed through the hands of that officer. When the House charged McNulty with defalcation to the tune of nearly $50,000, Tappan and Weller faced either having to pay it all to save their honor, or forfeiting their $20,000 bond to satisfy the law.[11]

When McNulty filed his report for the year ending December 1, 1844, $47,000 remained unaccounted for. The Committee on Accounts had twice called for him to appear and explain the discrepancy, without response from McNulty, so committee members investigated. They found that he had advanced $30,000 to E. G. Woodward, a produce dealer in McNulty's home town of Mount Vernon, besides paying thousands out elsewhere. The committee recommended immediate dismissal, civil action to recover the missing money, and criminal prosecution by the executive branch. The topic consumed most of the day in the House on January 17, 1845, after which the sergeant at arms was dispatched to bring McNulty in. McNulty walked into the House that afternoon and denied using "one dollar of the public funds." He offered some excuses, and said he could account for every penny by ten o'clock the next morning, so the House agreed to postpone the matter until two o'clock the following afternoon, by which time McNulty was expected to have resolved everything with the committee.[12]

His promises notwithstanding, McNulty never appeared the next day. In the afternoon the Committee on Accounts received letters confirming that McNulty had deposited most of the money in the Bank of America, and then forwarded much of it to Woodward. It all looked very bad for McNulty. Besides having technically defaulted by his failure to produce the unspent funds at the appointed hour, he gave every sign of trying to mislead and deceive the House, as though stalling for time to cover the missing funds. Even his loyal friend Weller, who still doubted any embezzlement, could not find McNulty that morning, and joined in what became a unanimous decision to summarily dismiss the elusive clerk.[13]

That left McNulty unemployed and disgraced, and then a District of Columbia grand jury indicted him for embezzlement. He likely fell back on his sureties for bail, because his trial was not scheduled until December, probably so all the pertinent witnesses could be conveniently subpoenaed when they returned for the opening of the Twenty-ninth Congress.[14]

Stanton appears to have been in Washington for a week already when, on the bitterly cold morning of December 16, he, McNulty, and McNulty's Washington lawyer, James M. Carlisle, appeared at the city court and heard the five separate charges of the indictment read. When the acting district attorney, P. R. Fendall, brought forward the fifth count first, Stanton asked for a day's postponement, saying he had prepared on the assumption that the charges would be tried in order, and Judge Thomas H. Crawford consented to the postponement.[15]

The trial lasted more than a week. In his first case widely reported by major newspapers, Stanton leaped immediately from the defense to the offense, combating damaging testimony by badgering the witnesses. Fendall called Chauncey Bestor, cashier of the Patriotic Bank, who recounted handling a suspicious check. On cross-examination Stanton wore down the witness with rapid-fire volleys all afternoon, nullifying his testimony finally and hopelessly confusing him. The reporter for the *Baltimore Sun* remarked that the "cross-examination of Mr. Bestor, by Mr. Stanton, was the severest I ever listened to." A Washington newspaperman would recall Stanton's aggressiveness nearly fifteen years later, at the outset of another trial, observing that with Stanton "his weapon in attack is rather the sledge hammer than the rapier."[16]

Prosecution witnesses offered damning testimony, but with satire and sarcasm Stanton neutralized it all. On the fourth day, while members of Congress were scheduled to testify, one of the House messages to McNulty came into discussion, but after a diligent search of the House and the Treasury Department no one was able to find it. The chief clerk of the Treasury Department testified that it had passed through his hands but had since been mislaid. After this exchange Representative William Taylor was supposed to appear on behalf of the Committee on Accounts, but he was lying in his room, less than a month away from death: when Fendall said that Taylor would not be able to appear, Stanton quipped that he hoped the moribund congressman had "not been lost with the other valuable evidence."[17]

The defense did not put McNulty on the stand, and it called only character witnesses, including numerous sitting members of both chambers of Congress, a justice of the Ohio Supreme Court, and David Tod. Stanton and Carlisle spent the entire fifth day of the trial pumping these dignitaries for all the praise they would provide. In his summation, on December 22, Fendall reminded the jury that testimony of character appertained only to cases of doubt, while no doubt intruded in McNulty's.[18]

Addressing the jury for the defense, Stanton began with an anecdote about a prominent, unnamed American who, when asked what he considered the nation's most precious asset, replied that it was "trial by jury." Then, after complimenting the jurors for their acuity, he engaged in some sophistry over the indictment—which accused McNulty of converting thousands of dollars to his own use, lending it to Woodward, or buying merchandise with it. The second count contradicted the other two, Stanton contended, and the prosecution had never specified which of the three counts the defendant should be convicted for. He ridiculed the secretary of the treasury, the district attorney, "and all concerned" in McNulty's prosecution, specifically rebuking the Committee on Accounts as "hasty, ill-tempered, and uncharitable." Finally, he resorted to sheer pity. He told the jury that McNulty, as a "posthumous" child, "had never known a father's smile" and had crossed the Ohio River at the age of nineteen, "poor[,] friendless, and unprotected," to make his own way in the world. By admirable talents he had become Clerk of the Ohio House of Representatives, and then Clerk of the Ohio Senate, and had twice been elected to the legislature himself. Along the way, however, he had accumulated political enemies "as unprincipled and reckless as any to be found in the Union," and on those enemies Stanton blamed the defendant's tribulations.[19]

He saved the best for last. Lamenting the prosecutor's efforts to malign the unfortunate former clerk, Stanton recalled that the last time he had seen McNulty, the defendant had been wrapped in the loving arms of "his young and blooming wife," and he invited the jurors to cast their eyes on the awful change the prosecution had wrought on him. On cue, apparently, McNulty burst into tears, and the reporter noted that Stanton had wrought the same effect from plenty of others in the courtroom. In the middle of the afternoon on Christmas Eve the jury returned a verdict of "not guilty," to resounding applause. With an acquittal issuing from such solid grounds for conviction, the district attorney decided to dismiss the other four indictments. McNulty and Stanton both returned to Ohio—the first burdened by heavy debts and a tainted reputation, but free, while the second came home to an editorial chorus of applause for having essentially done the impossible for McNulty, for Judge Tappan, and for Ohio.[20]

Fresh from that remarkable triumph in Washington, Stanton headed to Columbus for the 1846 state Democratic convention, where David Tod again won the nomination for governor. The linked issues of slavery and Texas had divided the party, which had pushed for annexation and statehood against the objections and warnings of adherents like Senator Tappan and Congressman Jacob Brinkerhoff of Mansfield. Early in 1845 Brinkerhoff had delivered a scathing speech on Texas, asking why President Polk so passively met British occupation of the Oregon territory at the same time he championed the acquisition of Texas to save it from the imagined designs of Great Britain. Brinkerhoff, a Van Buren man to the last, accused the president of catering to the slave power and of having been mesmerized by "the beauties of bondage, and the sweet harmonious music of fetters." Implying that they shared an abhorrence of slavery and opposition to Texas statehood, Stanton congratulated Brinkerhoff on his rebuke to slaveholders, but the January convention named someone else to fill Brinkerhoff's seat and Stanton promptly aligned himself with the Southern-born Senator William Allen. Allen was one of the Senate's loudest cheerleaders for the taking and keeping of Texas, but he still had three years left on his term, and Stanton praised him as warmly as he had the deposed Brinkerhoff—Allen's political opposite.[21]

Texas brought trouble, the worst of which would not be realized for years, but the first became obvious by the middle of spring. The new state had come with a disputed southern border, and in direct contrast with the diplomatic patience he showed in the Pacific Northwest the president directed U.S. troops under Zachary Taylor to occupy the southernmost fringe of the disputed portion. As might have been expected, hostilities erupted, and by the middle of May Congress obliged Polk with an official declaration of war. Ridiculously exaggerated accounts of Taylor's victories were soon racing up the Mississippi or around the tip of Florida from the Gulf of Mexico, with rumors that seven hundred Mexicans—or twelve hundred—had been killed in battle and only a single American.[22]

Stanton lost his new partner to the patriotic frenzy. George McCook raised a company of volunteers that he called the Steubenville Greys, filling it in a little over a week. Captain McCook and his command steamed down the river for Cincinnati early in June, to join their regiment and head for Mexico. At Cincinnati the regiment picked up a company from Mount Vernon that included Private Caleb McNulty, age twenty-nine, who died a few weeks later as they descended the Mississippi. Stanton used his new acquaintance with Senator Allen to seek a surgeon's appointment for Dr. Tappan, but that effort to mollify his brother-in-law failed, despite a second letter to Allen six months later and a separate appeal to their congressman.[23]

Darwin Stanton sought no surgeon's commission, although it would not have been out of character for him to take leave of his family and go off with the army. In the previous decade he had often acted impulsively— abandoning the profession that had cost his brother and himself so much to prepare for, and making plans to leave his home community for the uncertainty of Missouri, only to give up that dream for politics. Then he left that career for a minor federal sinecure, holding the job through a couple of sessions before returning to Holliday's Cove after the August adjournment in 1846 with Nancy and their three children, who included a baby girl just born in Washington. Six weeks later the Steubenville newspaper reported that he "was seized with a violent disease, accompanied with inflammation of the brain, and after a severe illness, he was sent off." The obituary seemed to use a good measure of diagnostic euphemism to disguise what sounded more like severe emotional disturbance. Darwin ended the drama himself on the evening of September 23, apparently by taking up a knife or scalpel and severing an artery, from which he bled to death.[24]

Darwin's death is clouded by a mist of memoirs numerous enough to confirm the suicide, but conflicting enough to doubt the details. Alfred Taylor, Edwin Stanton's onetime gardener, said decades later that his employer wandered out of the bloodstained house and disappeared into the woods, apparently in shock. Taylor was responsible for a number of maudlin and obviously embroidered anecdotes, yet it seems perfectly plausible that Stanton should have been stunned by the second death of an intimate family member in only thirty months, especially considering the unexpected, needless cause, as well as the gory means. William Brown, a neighbor of Darwin's, evidently corroborated the story: he said he went chasing after Stanton that night, found him stumbling blindly through the darkness, and led him back to the house.[25]

A few days later they buried Darwin, who had just turned thirty, and Stanton filed a motion to name Nancy administrator of the estate—standing as surety with his new brother-in-law, Christopher P. Wolcott, who had just married Pamphila. Stanton's old employer, James Trumbull, assessed the property, but it yielded little after the assets had been liquidated and the debts paid. Darwin had left a life insurance policy, rare enough in that day, but there is no indication whether his widow was able to collect on it because of the suicide. With his customary generosity to close family, Stanton opened his big home at Logan and Third to Nancy and her children after the house at Holliday's Cove had been sold. The child bride of seven years before would live to mourn her husband for nearly seven decades.[26]

A couple of months before Darwin's death, Stanton had developed a friendship with Salmon P. Chase, whose career would later intersect closely with his. The two shared certain life experiences: like Stanton, Chase had lost his father to a stroke while still a boy, and he had known the sorrow of watching a young wife die—twice already, in fact, and he had buried the second only the year before. Chase was seven years older than Stanton, and taller by half a foot, but they had the connection of Chase's uncle, Bishop Philander Chase, who still held sway at Kenyon College when Stanton first matriculated, and of Stanton's Kenyon classmate John L. Miner, who had studied law in Chase's office. Chase lived on the far side of the state in Cincinnati, and he had never been a Democrat, but they had encountered each other more than once in Columbus, usually around the holiday season, when Stanton was reporting for the Ohio Supreme Court. They fell in together long enough in July of 1846 to become intimate, talking politics and religion in Chase's hotel room. Chase was soliciting Democrats who shared the sentiments of the Liberty Party, hoping to graft that antislavery faction to the national organization. Stanton's propensity for exaggerated expressions of concurrence must have convinced Chase that the younger man was ripe for conversion, but his actions would never match the enthusiasm of his words. In August Stanton offered encouragement for Chase's success in the venture, but he gave no hint of wanting to join him in it.[27]

Nine weeks after Darwin's death, Chase wrote to announce that he had married for the third time; he also proposed a presidential candidate for the Liberty Party, and asked whether Stanton would help defend an Ohioan named John Van Zandt, who had been convicted of harboring a fugitive slave. Stanton congratulated Chase enthusiastically on his third wedding, discounted the proposed candidate as too much of a "sham," and thanked him for the compliment of asking his assistance in the Van Zandt matter, but he declined to participate. Although he complained of Ohio Democrats trying to galvanize support by promising to preserve the state's repressive racial laws, he seemed reluctant to openly declare the antislavery views he had expressed in private to Chase, and earlier to Brinkerhoff: as Martin Van Buren had illustrated, antislavery sentiments could pose a severe liability for a Democrat. Stanton professed great interest in the Van Zandt case, but backhandedly maintained that he was not competent for the job, at least at present. Without mentioning Darwin's suicide, he described a malaise sounding very much like the depressive side of a manic personality. "Events of the past summer have broken my spirits," he explained, "crushed my hopes, and without energy or purpose in life, I feel indifferent to the present, careless of the future, in a state of bewilderment the end of which is hidden."[28]

The risk of losing a conspicuous case like the Van Zandt appeal may have contributed to his hesitation, for he later let it slip that he had no confidence in the Supreme Court on that issue, but he did sink into a long, deep despondency that autumn. While Chase wrote every few weeks, Stanton's replies came slowly, with excuses for his tardiness; even after he finished a letter it often lay on his escritoire for weeks. With little court business to handle he seldom left home that bleak winter, blaming his sudden and uncharacteristic reclusiveness on an overwhelming physical and psychological lassitude. He spent time reading material that reinforced his early attachment to Andrew Jackson's popular revolution, leading him to scorn conservatism as a selfish, cruel, and cowardly readiness to "uphold every form of injustice." To Chase he denounced the "wicked frauds," "bloody crimes," and "unjust privilege" of aristocracies, for which he deemed most historical accounts to be nothing but "lying apologies." The slave South replicated all the evils of aristocracies in the classical age, he fumed. Still, whenever Chase waved him into the antislavery melee he shrank from the struggle. As late as May Day he waited passively for the opening of the common pleas court to pry him out of his lethargy.[29]

Chase was a man who embraced ideas wholeheartedly. His persistent proselytizing for Liberty Party doctrine and other reform movements reflected his evangelical nature, manifested by a pious devotion that might have seemed extreme even in the shadow of the Second Great Awakening. He sublimated those impulses through political activism, but he found it difficult to understand why others would disagree with him, and the subject of religion usually found its way into his conversations. At the commencement of their friendship in July, in evident response to Stanton's continued mourning over Mary, Chase had read the fifteenth chapter of First Corinthians to him while they lounged in Chase's room. After what Stanton called the "calamity" of the previous September, which had surely compounded the impact of Mary's death, psychological depression left Stanton even more vulnerable to that comforting message of life after death, and he gratified Chase with the news that he had been consulting that chapter. He wrote that he had been reading the Bible generally, too, and had started attending church regularly again. Playmates depicted Stanton briefly effervescing with religious zeal in childhood, and he had alternated his bawdy correspondence to classmates with occasional professions of faith to Mary Lamson, but the most direct and convincing evidence of any particular spirituality began with his letters to Chase as he emerged from his torpor. That religiosity may have lighted his path out of depression, and the flame flickered long enough for him to sustain a pietistic correspondence of a few years' duration with Marie Bates, the devout wife of a colleague, who had known Mary as a girl. Their correspondence bore heavily on the idea that he and Mary would meet again in heaven, which appeared to give him great comfort for a time, but then the world seemed to reclaim him.[30]

The advent of court helped to revive him, too, for by June he was back at the helm of the local Democratic Central Committee. Then on July 4, 1847, the Steubenville Greys returned from their year of war in northern Mexico, with George McCook commanding the regiment. McCook had given up his lodging in Steubenville, so Stanton boarded him at his house before taking leave to visit Chase, in Columbus, but Stanton rushed back when McCook collapsed with chills and fever. The sign over their Third Street office now read "Stanton & McCook," and once the conquering hero had recovered they resumed the joint practice, in an office across the street from the Stanton home. They became friends as well as partners, and when McCook began courting a local girl Stanton extended her his warm congratulations.[31]

Having McCook back in the office freed Stanton to accept more remunerative work beyond his native town. The most promising opportunities for a Steubenville resident in that era of the steamboat lay at Cincinnati and Pittsburgh, but Cincinnati was four hundred miles away—a long enough journey downriver, with an even longer return against the current. Pittsburgh could be reached in a few hours, and it was there that he cast his net, perhaps soliciting potential partners through his acquaintance, the former senator and secretary of war William Wilkins, who had also been a federal judge for the western district of Pennsylvania. It might have required a recommendation of that caliber to secure an association with Charles Shaler, a well-established jurist who had just dissolved a partnership.[32]

Stanton traveled to Pittsburgh in the late summer and early autumn to meet Shaler and discuss a potentially significant case, but as the leaves fell Stanton prepared a trunk or two to take upriver for an extended stay. As though to confirm for his family that he had every intention of remaining in Steubenville, just before he left he paid two brothers $2,600 for four connected lots on the opposite side of Third Street from his house, one block closer to town. The previous owners' glass factory stood on the corner of the nearest parcel, and under his direction workmen converted it to a home, where he installed a caretaker to transform those city lots into a farmstead, complete with livestock, orchard, and truck gardens. Forty years after Stanton's death, when this little estate had been re-subdivided and covered in houses, it was still called "Stanton's Patch."[33] He had owned that oasis three weeks when he boarded the boat for Pittsburgh. Local newspapers heralded his arrival there late in October, covering his admission to the bar and the official start of his partnership with Shaler.[34]

When people spoke of Pittsburgh in 1847, they usually referred collectively to Pittsburgh and Allegheny City, which faced each other across the Allegheny River, just above its confluence with the Monongahela. Those communities and the adjacent towns boasted a population approaching 100,000. Fire had ravaged most of downtown Pittsburgh two years before, consuming a thousand houses and destroying the business district, but the reconstruction gave the city the semblance of a boomtown. Vast deposits of bituminous coal in the region had made it an inviting spot for smelting and forging iron, and the smokestacks of rolling mills and foundries towered over the waterfront, spewing billows of smoke: residents on the surrounding hills might enjoy bright sunshine while gazing down on a dense cloud shrouding both cities, with nothing to indicate they were there, save the roar of the factories. Many found employment beneath that gritty cloud, and a few parlayed their industry into prosperity. The Ohio River, which began its long journey to the Gulf of Mexico at the westernmost tip of triangular Pittsburgh, served as the commercial highway.[35]

Stanton was less than a stranger upon his arrival. He still maintained a friendship with Judge Wilkins, who left him a standing invitation to visit his estate. As a boy in Steubenville, Stanton had also been friendly with John Harper, who had since become a banker and the secretary of Pittsburgh's Board of Trade. Those two and men like them held a deep interest in Pittsburgh's future, and they may have influenced Stanton's decision to practice there. Such moguls may even have recruited him to confront a looming threat to their smoky city, for he began almost immediately to take testimony in a protracted legal dispute that reflected a simple matter of regional economic rivalry. He and everyone associated with it would come to call it the "Bridge case."[36]

The previous March, the Virginia General Assembly had issued a charter for a suspension bridge over the Ohio River at Wheeling. Below Pittsburgh only ferries crossed the river, and the very existence of a bridge raised the specter of serious competition—not especially from the National Road that passed through Wheeling, but from the railroad that would almost certainly follow it. In 1847 the predominance of river travel made Pittsburgh the gateway to the Old Northwest and the Mississippi Valley, but a railroad passing far below Pittsburgh could change all that. The builder had no sooner begun work on the bridge than Stanton started looking for an excuse to seek an injunction against it. The tort on which he would ultimately base his suit did not surface until two years after he began collecting evidence, when the bridge had been completed and opened to traffic. Until then, Stanton prepared a tentative brief in secret, leaving a blank space where he could fill in a cause of action, while others with a stake in Pittsburgh's dominance pursued funding for the contest.[37]

The potentially remunerative connection with bankers and industrialists of predominately Whig sympathies may have persuaded Stanton to curb his Jacksonian rhetoric, and perhaps to suppress whatever convictions may have lain behind that rhetoric. That also precluded him from resuming political activity with his former zeal, lest he show too glaring a divergence from his old rant against privilege. At that very moment, Chase was trying to push him toward politics, so they could combat slavery together, but Stanton would reveal no sympathy with the antislavery movement, either. Doing so might have actually gratified Pittsburghers like John Harper, who considered slavery "a dark stain on our national escutcheon," but abolition remained unpopular, and Stanton never showed much courage for expressing political opinions without the strength of at least a healthy plurality behind him. He had been elected as a delegate to Ohio's Democratic convention again, and he led Chase to believe he intended to go, implicitly to work with him for the nomination of antislavery, hard-money candidates. When January 8 came, however, Stanton could not be found in Columbus: instead, he sent the fervently abolitionist Christopher Wolcott as a nonvoting proxy. Chase, whom he had teased with the prospect of meeting him there, came up from Cincinnati "almost solely" to see him, only to be disappointed at his unexplained absence. Chase's regret deepened when the convention endorsed Cass as the Democratic candidate and equivocated over allowing slavery in any territory the United States might wrest from Mexico. Stanton felt Chase's implied censure for not being present, but maintained that his presence would have made no difference.[38]

As the year progressed, Chase pressed friends and associates to organize a new coalition, the Free Soil Party, to run a presidential candidate. He asked for the support of Judge Tappan, who had shown such loyalty to Martin Van Buren, and he wrote Stanton twice that spring, probably on the same subject. Van Buren ended up winning the Free Soil nomination, but Stanton—who had once touted Van Buren as vigorously as anyone, and who wrote Chase that he deplored the lack of a strong candidate to oppose the spread of slavery—kept perfectly still during the entire campaign. Meanwhile, he corresponded with conservative Democrats who implored him to take their side of the contest, but he shied away from them, as well.[39]

Stanton's silence in the seminal year of 1848 casts a different light on a man who, at the brink of slavery's demise years later, portrayed himself as having been mesmerized by his father's antislavery discussions with Benjamin Lundy in the Stanton home. He was busy establishing himself in a new partnership and a new city, but his renowned energy ought to have been able to accommodate such a distraction had he been inclined—just as he later took up the cause while he was finding his way at the War Department. Irreconcilable accounts of Stanton's political positions recorded during and after his life implied, by their number and discordance, that he often ingratiated himself to opposing factions by privately voicing support for each, at least until he could determine which side might prevail. His failure to utter a public word against slavery before 1862 appears to reflect that habit, and if Stanton evinced little overt sensitivity to slavery he showed even less concern for the exploited working class. A couple of months after the 1848 campaign had been decided, he and Shaler prosecuted striking laborers on behalf of Pittsburgh mill owners.[40]

Factories along the Allegheny River had known unrest before, when violence had seemed the only answer to long hours and low pay, but Pennsylvania addressed the workers' complaints by legislating a ten-hour day, with the contractual assent of the employee required for anything beyond that; the legislature also banned any further employment of children under the age of twelve. The Ten Hour Law went into effect on the first of July, 1848, and to pressure their employees into twelve-hour contracts the owners of textile mills in Allegheny City closed their doors. The lockout lasted until the end of the month, when about a hundred operatives finally agreed to waive their new statutory right and go to work for the Penn Cotton Mill. They filed into the factory on July 31 to the hisses and jeers of their mostly female former colleagues, who surrounded the grounds all morning and occasionally threw stones, eggs, and potatoes over the fence. Some witnesses testified that R. T. Kennedy, one of the owners, carried a gun, and then someone inside the fence turned a steam hose on those outside, badly scalding at least one little girl. That infuriated the protesters, and a sheriff's posse arrived to find as many as a thousand people tearing at the fence and breaking through, including one girl in a huge sunbonnet who hacked at the front gate with an ax. A few police and Kennedy suffered cuts and bruises before the mob dispersed, and much glass was broken, but the riot produced no significant damage or serious injuries, except to the little girl.[41]

The next few days saw several editorials condemning the rioters and supporting the beleaguered owners. The *Daily Commercial Journal* carried a pseudonymous guest piece that chastised the textile workers for resorting to violence. While recognizing their nominal right to bargain for a ten-hour day, the author "Mechanic" insisted that they had no right to impede the operation of the factories "in an unlawful manner." The language of this one-sided argument bore the distinct flavor of Stanton's prose, and in fact he would use that very rhetoric to help send some of those operatives to jail. "Mechanic" added that the conflict between the hands and their employers was hurting everyone, but he implicitly blamed the workers, while the *Daily Gazette* incited anger against the strikers with rumors that the owners were considering removing their factories to Virginia. By the middle of September the owners finally agreed to limit their operations to ten-hour days, but only if workers who had been earning between fifty cents and two dollars a day agreed to take less. After ten idle weeks the employees submitted, and the next year industrial pressure led the legislature to repeal the Ten Hour Law altogether.[42]

Seventeen mill operatives were arraigned the following December for participation in the riot, with four girls as young as sixteen among them. Stanton and Shaler conducted the prosecution on behalf of the factory owners, with two other lawyers assisting them. A battery of attorneys appeared with the defendants, who commanded the sympathy of the greater part of Pittsburgh's laboring population. When the judge asked who stood for the accused, lead attorney Samuel Black replied "the whole bar and one or two others from Mercer." The case was heard, however, in the Court of Quarter Sessions before Judge Benjamin Patton, an acquaintance of Stanton's whose sympathies seemed to lie with the owners.[43]

The trial ran for four days in mid-January, beginning with the testimony of John Scott, an Allegheny City policeman who blamed the worst of the riot on the scalding of the protesters. When witnesses for the defense testified, they revealed that the decision to break into the factory arose from the belief that Kennedy, the gun-toting owner, had seized a boy and was holding him inside the company office. When Kennedy took the stand a defense lawyer asked him if he had held a boy imprisoned in the office that day, but Judge Patton refused to allow the question; the jury had heard it nonetheless, and to counter any bias it might have incurred the prosecution allowed Kennedy a chance to claim that he had caught the boy climbing the fence and took him inside for his own safety. Black argued that the owners were still trying to exact more than ten hours' work from unwilling operatives, and accentuated the scalding of the women and girls outside the fence, but Stanton and Shaler (like "Mechanic") objected that one illegal act by the owners did not justify another by the protesters. In cross-examination Stanton got Scott to admit that the weapon Kennedy had carried might not have been a gun, although a woman insisted that it was. A cavalcade of young girls testified for the defendants, including one not yet fourteen, who had already been working at the Blackstone factory for more than four years.

The owner-friendly *Daily Dispatch* predicted that the witnesses were so pretty that they might make it too difficult for the "gallant" all-male jury to find the defendants guilty.[44]

The *Dispatch* had no cause for worry. After a day of closing remarks by attorneys for the prosecution and the defense, Stanton concluded with a lengthy disquisition on the importance of maintaining the supremacy of law, regardless of grievances. Judge Patton issued a charge to the jury so damning to the defendants and so favorable to the complainants that some believed Stanton had written it himself, and the owners of six of Allegheny City's seven textile factories had it circulated in a pamphlet. Thirteen of the defendants were found guilty and sentenced to jail, including all four girls. Stanton's appeal to the sanctity of the law notwithstanding, no action ensued against the owners of the Penn mill for conduct that their own attorneys seemed to concede was illegal.[45]

The trial of the rioters hinted that, in moving to Pittsburgh, Stanton—the son of an improvident champion of the poor and oppressed, and himself formerly the professed enemy of privilege—was drifting toward the privileged class. His emergence as the champion of Pittsburgh's industrial gentry suggested at least the beginning of an ideological metamorphosis for a man who, less than a year before, had venomously damned aristocracies in private. Material success, however, had been the goal of all Stanton's hard work; he might have agreed with another Ohio attorney who, years later, warned an aspiring law student that "as a lawyer, a man sacrifices independence to ambition."[46]

Charles Shaler kept his office in Pittsburgh's recently reconstructed downtown, in the middle of the banking district at 81 Fourth Street, closer to Wood Street than to Market. There Stanton joined him. For at least his first few months in the city he lived a block away, on the corner of Wood and Third Streets, at the new St. Charles Hotel. Almost everything was new in Pittsburgh so soon after the great fire, and when a five-story Monongahela House rose from the ashes of its wooden predecessor, on the corner of Smithfield and Water streets, Stanton moved there. That added four blocks to his morning and evening walks, but it took him a little farther out of the city's smoky center, which was probably more important for an asthmatic than his generation realized: tradition, for instance, then held that smoking actually helped to allay the symptoms of asthma, and Stanton apparently believed it. It may have been more important to him that the Monongahela House overlooked the steamboat docks along the Monongahela River, thereby reducing the distance he had to carry his baggage when he traveled.[47]

Every few weeks Stanton boarded one of those boats to spend a few days with his mother and son in Steubenville, and the journey itself often proved productive. Returning from his first sojourn at home after joining Shaler, he met both the U.S. senator from Florida, David Yulee, and the reformer Robert Dale Owen, who had just been defeated for reelection to Congress from Indiana. Both men impressed him, although Yulee held fervent proslavery views—and Stanton implied they discussed that issue, among other salient topics of the day. Yulee would become a client a few years hence, and when Stanton rose to national office he would find Owen helpful. During the May and September terms of the Jefferson County Court of Common Pleas, Stanton's visits to Steubenville sometimes lasted for weeks while he tried local cases with McCook. State Supreme Court appeals sometimes took him to Columbus—where he won one of his last cases against a bank—and on a stop there in July of 1848 he met Marie Bates, who undertook the role of his spiritual overseer. For nearly three years they exchanged letters of a largely theological nature, but she was already married and he met no women who appealed to him in more than a platonic way. On occasion he admitted that he still carried a torch for Mary, to whom he appeared to remain more steadfastly loyal than to almost any living person. The allure of his fleeting religious devotion seemed tied to the posthumous connection it promised with his lost wife, whose unrelenting affection and admiration may have given him the only sense of complete personal security he ever knew.[48]

Like any waterfront, the Monongahela docks near Stanton's hotel could be a dangerous place, and in the spring of 1849 Stanton represented a white bartender from the steamer *Atlantic* who had shot a black porter to death there the previous November. His defense consisted of turning the victim into the villain by showing that the deceased had bought a knife the very morning he was killed, and although the knife was still in his pocket after he died Stanton painted the dead man as a violent, pugnacious character who had threatened the defendant. In a three-hour summation of "burning eloquence," Stanton persuaded the jury that the bartender had acted in self-defense. Such captivating exhortations became his trump card whenever facts or sentiment weighed against him, but he seldom wasted his elocutionary talents when his clients seemed safely in the right. No reporter commended him for either prolixity or passion that same week when, at the behest of offended parents, he prosecuted a doctor for digging up and dissecting the body of their freshly buried daughter.[49]

The bridge case consumed most of his time during 1849. The Wheeling and Belmont Bridge Company had nearly completed its span across the Ohio by summer, and Stanton was able to pencil in his cause of action by arguing that the bridge would not be high enough to allow the smokestacks of the tallest steamboats to pass under it. Thanks to the efforts of influential backers in Pittsburgh, a paying plaintiff had appeared in the form of the aggrieved state of Pennsylvania, for Stanton had concluded to argue that the bridge would pose a hazard to navigation for Pennsylvania craft venturing down the Ohio River. Interstate disputes required a federal hearing, so he filed a petition for injunction with the U.S. Circuit Court in Philadelphia, where the first step in the case would be decided by Associate Supreme Court Justice Robert C. Grier, a Pennsylvanian.[50]

Stanton feared he would be turned down on the matter of jurisdiction, but he surmounted that hurdle without having to present any physical or anecdotal evidence to support his complaint. He appeared in Philadelphia that August, nominally acting for the attorney general of Pennsylvania, and after two days of argument Grier took the matter under advisement. He issued his decision barely two weeks later, hinting that the bridge violated its own charter provision to pose no navigation hazard. He stopped short of granting the injunction, but he realized that the technological revolution in transportation had complicated the law by permitting an entity like the bridge company to injure citizens of another state without intruding on their borders, so he allowed for a timely appeal to the Supreme Court. That was evidently what Stanton had wanted most, and it boded so well for the state's case that newspapers welcomed him back to Pittsburgh with lavish praise. In a letter to a friend, Stanton betrayed his fear that the decision would persuade the bridge company to accept defeat and raise the bridge without waiting for a court order. That would have been the cheapest outcome for the industrialists whom he really represented, but it would not have prevented rail-borne competition, and so quick a victory would have robbed him of the chance to argue his first case before the highest court in the land.[51]

Undaunted by Grier's decision, the Wheeling builders finished their bridge for vehicular traffic in October. They dedicated it the following month, inviting Henry Clay to ridicule the Pennsylvania lawsuit and commend the engineering marvel as an example of the internal improvements so central to his American System. The ceremony seemed to discourage Pittsburgh opponents, who understood that one of their hometown engineers had proposed a similar bridge far downriver at Cincinnati.[52]

None of that fazed Stanton. He spent the summer and fall collecting more evidence of fluctuation in the river's level, the height of steamboat chimneys, and the reasons for that height. After the bridge was finished, he documented instances of obstructed navigation. He learned that boats had begun carrying chimneys as tall as eighty feet in order to prevent hot cinders from dropping directly on the deck, and to create enough draft for maximum heat and steam power, especially on the upstream route. The bridge at its highest point hovered less than ninety-four feet over the low-water mark, while the flood of 1832 had raised the river nearly forty-five feet above low water. Lowering the chimneys burdened river vessels with additional costs, delays, and danger even when that solution proved mechanically feasible, and Stanton contended that the bridge would close the river to larger vessels above Wheeling, which would harm the economy of Pittsburgh and western Pennsylvania. Pittsburgh industry depended on those tall, first-class boats, many of which were built right there—along with seagoing vessels that needed tall stacks but could not pass the Wheeling bridge on their way to the open sea. He immersed himself in the details, having perhaps discovered that excessive preparation counterbalanced any sense of inadequacy that may have lingered from his abbreviated education—not to mention that mastering the minutiae enabled him to control his opponent in the courtroom.[53]

A legend insists that Stanton instructed Captain Charles Batchelor, of the riverboat *Hibernia*, to run his vessel into the Wheeling bridge at full steam, to bring down his smokestacks. Even if it were credible that a captain and owner would have risked the possible destruction of his craft to document someone else's uncertain lawsuit, Stanton used no such evidence in his legal brief, and Batchelor never mentioned any such incident in his memoirs. Completion of the bridge did, however, allow Stanton to collect three examples in which the structure actually did obstruct river traffic. On November 10 the steamboat *Messenger* came upon the bridge at the average stage of twenty-one feet of water and found that it could not pass until workmen had cut seven feet off the top of her chimneys. The next day the *Telegraph* had to lower its adjustable chimneys to pass under, and it could not have negotiated the span at all had the river been three feet higher. In an experience that apparently gave birth to the *Hibernia* myth, that boat encountered the same problem on its way upstream: after the crew had taken on all the coal the boat could carry, and drilled a hole in the hull to let water into its shallow hold, one of her chimneys still caught on the bridge as it passed under.[54]

The bridge case did involve one serious accident, and the victim was Stanton himself. The only account of what actually happened came from his sister, who had moved to Akron with her husband and learned of the mishap by mail: she described her brother falling into the open hatch of one of the riverboats and breaking—as she said—his kneecap. Stanton always referred to his injured "limb," and Chase inquired about his broken "leg," while no contemporary source specifically alluded to his knee. The injury, which happened in November, immediately after the *Hibernia*'s tribulations at the bridge, probably required opiates at first, because owners of the bridge company heard stories of Stanton lapsing into a delirium and raving at his servant to deliver his argument to the jury. By the third week of November he lay flat on his back at home in Steubenville, evidently free enough of drugs to keep up with his correspondence. Weeks passed before he could walk, and his doctor told him he would not be able to travel before the middle of January. With the bridge case due for a hearing at the January term of the Supreme Court, he perfected his brief while wondering whether he would be able to deliver the argument himself. As a contingency he sought the services of Robert Walker, a former Mississippi senator and cabinet officer who had once practiced in Pittsburgh, but the case could not be heard before late February, when Stanton appeared in Washington with a distinct limp.[55]

He began his first argument before the Supreme Court on February 25, along with several other attorneys, including Vice President Millard Fillmore and his friend Salmon Chase, who had come to Washington as Ohio's junior senator. Stanton immediately reopened the issue of jurisdiction, contending that the federal government alone had the right to regulate trade between the states, and owned a "constitutional obligation to preserve the Ohio River as a free and common highway." He cited case law that confirmed the right of Congress to extend its regulation of interstate trade to navigation and held federal authority on that matter superior to any contradictory state legislation. If states could override that federal authority, he declared, then "the Constitution would be a rope of sand." His staccato delivery of case after case convinced all but one of the justices that no inferior court held jurisdiction over the dispute, and that Stanton had appealed to the proper body.[56]

Next he addressed the question of whether the bridge posed a hazard to navigation, reciting the historic rising and falling of the river against the maximum height of the bridge and the much greater heights necessary for first- and even second-class boats to pass safely beneath the structure. Noting each of the potential mechanical remedies the bridge company had suggested for boats, from shorter stacks to hinged chimneys that could be tilted back, he explained the impracticality of them all. To establish the extent of the damage he documented the investment Pennsylvania had made to accommodate and improve its river traffic, the amount of tonnage that was constructed in Pittsburgh shipyards, and the volume of traffic it sent or received on the river. The following May, with a lone dissent on the jurisdiction question, the court remanded the case to a commissioner, Reuben H. Walworth of New York, who was charged with determining whether the bridge posed a hazard and what modifications might remove the obstruction.[57]

The case dragged on for years. Commissioner Walworth ruled against the bridge company, declaring their masterpiece an obstruction, and debate turned to whether a draw might not be cut into the bridge rather than raising the entire structure twenty feet higher. No satisfactory engineering solution appeared, and Stanton again appealed successfully for demolition:

in May of 1852 the court decreed that the bridge would have to come down by the first day of February, 1853. One Pittsburgh newspaper let slip the underlying purpose of the suit by sounding the alarm about the Baltimore & Ohio Railroad, which was expanding westward across Virginia, on its way to Parkersburg and Wheeling: when it reached the Ohio, the editor warned, Pittsburgh would became a backwater to Wheeling if the bridge remained in place.[58]

Congress intervened on behalf of Virginia, declaring the bridge part of the National Road and therefore a legitimate route for the U.S. Mail. In the spring of 1854, before Stanton could challenge the constitutionality of that act, high winds took the bridge down and he finally obtained an injunction from Grier to prevent its reconstruction unless it met the Supreme Court's height requirements. The company rebuilt the bridge at the same height within six months, in open violation of the order. Stanton filed a petition for contempt, but the court declined to hear it and removed the injunction. At that failure some in Pittsburgh began to raise editorial questions about the quality of Stanton's performance, but the newspapers that had backed the suit defended him and blamed the court instead—playing the slavery card by charging that the decision had gone Virginia's way because it was a slave state. In the end the bridge remained where it was, but the economic damage proved much less devastating than expected. It all mattered little to Stanton, for he could ascribe the ultimate defeat to a partisan Congress, while the victories that preceded it had all been his. A Pittsburgh proponent of the bridge case had informed a Philadelphia friend that Stanton stood "at the head of the western bar." A measure of fame and fortune were finally his.[59]

4

THE PRINCESS OF PENN STREET

In Stanton's time the Supreme Court met in the U.S. Capitol, in a room beneath the Senate chamber. On the day Stanton first appeared to argue the bridge case, Henry Clay took the floor overhead to ask the Senate's indulgence on his compromise measure for California's admission to the Union, which would dominate congressional debate through the spring and summer of 1850.[1] In the treaty that ended the Mexican War, the United States had realized a vast amount of new territory—half barren desert, half lush paradise, and all trouble, because it could be carved into several new slave states. Citizens of California had applied for admission to the Union as a free state: that would have upset the balance between free and slave states in the U.S. Senate, which the increasingly paranoid slaveholding faction deemed crucial to its protection. Southern representatives wanted another slave state admitted from the Mexican Cession, or at least the creation of a territory that might become a slave state, but that in turn provoked Northerners who had been insisting all along that slavery should be banned in any territory realized from that war. Clay's solution consisted of admitting free California and abolishing the slave trade in the national capital to satisfy the antislavery element in the North, while giving Southerners an enhanced law for the recapture of fugitive slaves; the final version of the compromise included the two new territories of Utah and New Mexico, which could decide whether they wanted to come in as slave or free when they applied for statehood.

In his first year as a senator, Salmon P. Chase gravitated to the more obstinate antislavery position. Stanton had given him to believe that he shared that view, so Chase again tried to bring him into the fray. Clay had hardly introduced his mutual concessions before Chase wrote Stanton, urging him to organize a public meeting in Pittsburgh to demand that Congress prohibit slavery in any of the territories, and refuse to enact any laws for catching runaway slaves. "For Heaven's sake and for the sake of the good cause go to work and get up a rousing meeting forthwith," Chase pleaded. Stanton did nothing of the kind, and many weeks later Chase wrote again, complaining of the stolid conservatism in Pittsburgh that allowed for such silence against the slave power. "What are you doing?" he asked. "Gathering gold dust I suppose, not in wet diggings, but in dry—aye, as dry as Parchments & Law Books can be."[2]

Stanton replied a month later, reassuring Chase that he agreed with him about Clay's compromise: let California into the Union if the South would stand it, he advised, but accept none of the conditions imposed by the slave power. Let slavery be confined to those states where it already existed, where it "might fester and rot in God's own appointed time." In answer to Chase's inquiry about his leg, he admitted that he would always have a limp, and he seemed to use that lameness as an excuse for devoting all his energy to his law practice instead of to the cause Chase held sacred. Chase retorted that Stanton's physical disability had been divinely intended to divert him to "higher duties than those of a lawyer."[3]

On the same day that he conveyed his concurrence with Chase's views, Stanton implied in a letter to another friend that Clay's plan could—and would—be made acceptable to him. Major John Sanders, an army engineer with whom he occasionally corresponded on professional and political topics, had expressed pessimism about sectional differences, but in consolation Stanton predicted that the difficulty was about to be "adjusted." At that particular moment the only adjustment likely would have been Clay's compromise, and satisfaction with that probability contradicted the intense animosity Stanton indicated to Chase within a few hours of writing to Sanders. Meanwhile, he responded to none of Chase's appeals for action at home. He still lamented the hidebound conservatism—the "Hunkerism"—that Chase thought he detected in Pittsburgh, but he continued to represent and socialize with his affluent and decidedly conservative clients from the industrial upper crust.[4]

The president and vice president took unexpectedly differing positions on the Compromise of 1850. President Zachary Taylor, a native and resident of slave states who owned slaves himself, hoped to admit California and Utah as one gigantic free state, and when that idea fizzled he still backed concessions that favored the free states. Then, on July 9, Taylor died and Millard Fillmore ascended to the presidency. Fillmore hailed from New York, but Senator Chase worried that he would dilute Taylor's appealing formula for sectional balance, at least as far as the territories were concerned, and his fears were soon borne out. Congress passed the numerous parts of the compromise over the course of that long summer, and Fillmore signed them all. California theoretically added two senators to the Northern bloc (although one was a slave-state native and sympathizer), and the slave market disappeared from Washington. The slave power gained the potential to expand into the territories of New Mexico and Utah, while a stringent Fugitive Slave Act transformed the federal government into an enforcement agency for Southern slave catchers.[5]

The last ingredient offered the most valuable concession to slave owners, for it not only revived hope for recapturing runaways who had already slipped into free states but further discouraged those still in bondage from attempting to escape. The law sparked immediate indignation in the North, where every citizen had become a statutory accomplice to the return of fugitives. Supreme Court Justice Robert C. Grier, who had accommodated Stanton in the first hearing on the bridge case, won initial praise from antislavery observers when he signaled his disapproval of the Fugitive Slave Act, but before long he began enforcing it through his U.S. Circuit Court rulings with enough vigor to attract compliments from the opposite quarter. Abolitionists across the North promoted the idea of repudiating and resisting the statute, either on constitutional grounds or in obedience to a "higher law." Chase responded to this free-state nullification of slave legislation by striving to magnify Ohio's Free Soil representation in the Senate. Still believing Stanton hated slavery, Chase suggested him as a candidate for a seat that had just opened.[6]

Then and for the rest of his life, Stanton declined to run for political office, or for the Ohio Supreme Court, with its limited terms. Besides the insecurity of elective office, it would have forced him to declare himself on controversial issues, depriving him of the luxury of private equivocation that so clearly appealed to him. He went only so far as to allow his name to be mentioned for the judicial nomination, to undermine an antagonist and, perhaps, to reassert his Ohio residency. That first case under the Fugitive Slave Act excited Pittsburgh early in 1851, but—unlike his friend Chase—Stanton made no overture to help defend the prisoner, whom the judge remanded to his captors with the remark that the law gave him no alternative.[7]

Except for the attenuated saga of the Wheeling bridge, Stanton could hardly plead an onerous workload as a reason to avoid involvement in the fugitive case, which would almost certainly have been a pro bono representation. He defended the Monongahela Navigation Company against an irate shareholder, winning by luck or judicial partiality after the jury awarded the plaintiff $20,000: the judge took the unusual step of declaring that the jurors had misunderstood his instructions, and over the understandably strident protests of the plaintiff's attorney he ordered them to retire again and come up with a different decision. A week later Stanton rescued a Pittsburgh doctor from a malpractice claim when the jury ruled in the plaintiffs' favor but allowed them only six cents in damages. Those were the most demanding of Stanton's cases that spring, and his work in the bridge case had abated after a preliminary ruling against the bridge company. The heaviest continuing task from that suit involved pressing the governor and legislature of Pennsylvania for funds to pay the Supreme Court's commissioner and his engineer.[8]

Stanton nevertheless cited continual occupation as his reason for not visiting Chase, and for refusing the case of an individual whom Chase had proposed as a client. Chase made no attempt to challenge those apparent excuses, but he might well have raised one of his bushy eyebrows at Stanton's sharp criticism of those who, by the late summer of 1851, seemed to have abandoned earlier principles in favor of new and more convenient ones. Stanton hinted that he regretted the rise of James Buchanan's political star, and he frowned even on Pennsylvania congressman David Wilmot, who had introduced the resolution to prohibit slavery in the Mexican Cession but had reportedly pledged himself to a proponent of the Fugitive Slave Act for governor. As for himself, Stanton assured Chase that he intended to "practice law in a small way" and "stick to sound democratic sentiments."[9]

The "small way" in which Stanton practiced law increasingly involved corporations. These cases could usually be depended on to produce larger judgments, and therefore larger fees. The Democratic press could still be found lamenting the power and privilege of these statutory corporations, with their alliances of wealthy stockholders and guaranteed monopolies that Democrats had opposed since Jackson's heyday. Pittsburgh's *Commercial Journal* criticized the Pennsylvania legislature for the favoritism and freehandedness with which it chartered new corporations, even as Stanton digested the latest decision in his case against the Wheeling and Belmont Bridge Company.[10]

The Harmony Society represented a more casual variety of private association, akin to an unofficial corporation. A decade before Stanton's birth, George Rapp, the charismatic leader of a German millennial sect, had settled several hundred followers in western Pennsylvania, where they lived a communal, agricultural life in relative seclusion from society. At Rapp's insistence the entire membership adopted lifelong celibacy, which may have contributed to the disharmony Joshua Nachtrieb found in the society, although he bore it for twenty-seven years before asking to be released in 1846. In 1827 Rapp had changed an article in the membership contract: instead of allowing departing followers the equivalent of what they had brought into the society, the trustees were authorized (but not required) to grant apostates a "donation" to start life anew. The society then owned property valued at about $1 million, and had barely three hundred members. At the age of forty-eight, feeling worn out by the labor of more than half a lifetime, Nachtrieb took $200 into the world with him, signing a receipt for it and acknowledging his separation from the separatists.[11]

After reflecting for a few years, and probably spending his $200, Nachtrieb and another former Harmonist hired Stanton, Charles Shaler, and their new partner, Theobald Umbstaetter, to carve them off a portion of the society's broad holdings. Stanton argued the case, presenting Nachtrieb as the victim of an abusive, dictatorial, and manipulative Rapp, who was then near ninety. Nachtrieb admitted having grown disillusioned with the society, but claimed that Rapp threatened to expel him from the community altogether, and at the prospect of being left without a farthing he accepted the $200. When the case made it to the Circuit Court for Western Pennsylvania, Stanton found Justice Grier sitting there, too, and he was just as receptive to Stanton's arguments as he had been in Philadelphia, on the bridge case: he ordered the society to pay Nachtrieb $3,890—equaling the surviving members' average share of their total worth. Recognizing that Nachtrieb's victory might encourage further costly defections, the trustees appealed, and their case eventually reached the full Supreme Court, which found Stanton's brief deficient. He had provided no evidence of the tyranny with which Rapp had allegedly treated Nachtrieb, and none that Rapp's management would have been "repugnant to public order." These omissions left the justices with no choice but to rule according to the provisions of the altered contract that Nachtrieb had signed. After more than seven years of litigation, Grier's colleagues overturned his decision and ordered Nachtrieb to pay the trustees' legal costs.[12]

That was an extremely rare lapse for Stanton, who usually erred on the side of presenting too much evidence, rather than too little—let alone providing none at all to support his position. With relatively little money at stake, he probably took the case in the belief that he had only to sway a jury, or perhaps a judge, without anticipating that the issue would mean so much to the trustees that they would fight him to the bitter end. Stanton may have hoped to win it in the early stage through his increasingly close relationship with Grier, and new evidence would have been difficult to introduce once the appeals began.

Whether it earned him a fee or not, each case he tried before the Supreme Court enhanced his reputation and attracted more business. The bridge case resumed there on December 8, 1851, and he remained in Washington through much of the winter, seeming to take little enjoyment in the national capital. Watching the legendary Daniel Webster argue for a lady in court, Stanton cringed at the tired and "haggard" orator, who broke down in the middle of his argument and bungled his client's case. "Bunkum" speeches and dull lectures afforded the only intellectual stimulation, he complained. With precious few good-looking women in the city, Stanton noted with wry amusement that the provocative dancer Lola Montez had captivated all Washington, and that she refused to see even the illustrious Sam Houston until she could greet her admirers from the stage, "at $1.50 per head."[13]

Late in the spring Stanton made another trip to Washington to represent his Ohio riverboat acquaintance of several years before—the slaveholding Floridian David Yulee. A quorum of the Florida legislature had reelected Yulee to the U.S. Senate in January of 1851, but a majority of sitting legislators had not supported him. Two days later the absentees had returned, forced a second election, and cast a majority of votes for Stephen Mallory, who was seated. Yulee's protest had taken nearly a year and a half to reach the Senate. On June 10, 1852, Stanton appeared with his client before a select committee, evidently expecting an associate counsel to present the case, but that lawyer had fallen ill and left the job in his hands. Stanton threw everything into an argument that a quorum had existed in the legislature the day Yulee was chosen, and that a majority was all that was necessary for a selection, which left no vacancy for Mallory to fill in the subsequent election. With the Nachtrieb defeat fresh in his memory, this time he cited abundant examples, from the constitutional convention of 1787 through the contentious presidential elections of 1800 and 1824, all to no avail. The committee sided with Mallory, and Yulee had to await the next vacancy.[14]

During his prolonged visits to Washington, Stanton wrote occasionally to old Judge Tappan, imparting news of Democratic intrigues along with his own acerbic observations about would-be presidential candidates like Cass and Buchanan. Those were the last letters they ever exchanged, for the tension between Oella and her husband erupted violently the next spring, leading to a permanent estrangement between the two families. Eight days before Judge Tappan's eightieth birthday, on Friday, May 17, 1853, Oella and the children moved in with Pamphila and her family in Akron. "I suppose they will not get together again," the judge told one of his younger brothers. "It is better for both."[15]

Stanton came home to Steubenville in the middle of summer, about the time Oella filed a petition for divorce, asking for support and alimony. Almost certainly she did so on the advice of her brother, who always hovered protectively over his family. Benjamin had never accumulated much property in his own right, and Judge Tappan—who now blamed Stanton for the breakup of his son's marriage—had already secured his own estate against any claims by his daughter-in-law, rewriting his will with that danger in mind. For his part, Dr. Tappan went to bed and stayed there for months, complaining of a vague illness that was probably his excuse for retreating from society and dosing himself with spirits. One of his uncles back East heard that the doctor had been "intemperate," but Judge Tappan flatly denied it. He characterized it as a rumor Stanton had initiated and spread to Boston "to be out of the way of contradiction."[16]

Tappan still spoke of his forty-one-year-old son as though he were not yet a grown man—acknowledging his impulsiveness and hoping that he might yet learn some of life's lessons—but he genuinely seemed to doubt the alcoholism for which his namesake was best remembered by others. When one of Steubenville's long-standing ministers came forward in the divorce trial to swear that he had seen Benjamin stumbling drunk in the street, Judge Tappan presumed that the "Rev. gentleman" had perjured himself, but Benjamin's later behavior fully corroborated the testimony.[17]

Enough evidence surfaced to prove Oella's charge of extreme cruelty. When the hearing opened on October 10, 1853, Dr. Tappan asked for a change of venue, which itself seemed to reflect his poor reputation in the community, but the judge denied the motion and eventually granted Oella everything she asked: complete custody of the children, thousands of dollars in alimony, and hundreds a year in support. Benjamin ducked most of the support and alimony by retiring to bed again on the plea that he could not walk. A year after the initial separation his father arranged passage for him to the Pacific, but instead Dr. Tappan went to Cincinnati in search of medical treatment, and talked of going to Paris for an operation.[18]

With so deftly delinquent an ex-husband, Oella had to depend heavily on her brother. The oldest child of Oella's unfortunate union, thirteen-year-old Benjamin Tappan III, took his father's side and refused to live with his mother, in defiance of the court decree. That appears to have been the end of him for the Stantons—or at least for Edwin—but the boy may not have fared very well with his father, either. Dr. Tappan's wanderlust persisted for years after the divorce, and Judge Tappan's death in 1857 finally gave him the wherewithal to travel at will, while his son remained in the care of a half-literate Irish woman whom that willful boy would not obey.[19]

Immediately after his sister's divorce, Stanton returned to Pittsburgh to defend a man in a breach-of-promise suit in which he again astounded observers by making no defense at all. His most obvious mistakes surfaced in his lesser cases, to which he may not have devoted enough attention; his record seemed better in the more profitable contests between well-heeled litigants.[20]

One month after that strange lapse, Stanton turned thirty-nine, and the imminent approach of another decade appeared to initiate a consideration of matrimony. He admitted that the notion appealed to him, and the recollection of seven happy years with Mary must have fed that appeal, but enduring grief over his buried bride could have only impeded the development of any new relationship. By the summer of 1851 he had apparently taken an interest in a popular and pretty young lady from Pittsburgh whom he mentioned to Reuben Walworth, the Supreme Court commissioner in the bridge case, but by winter she had begun to show more attention to an army officer. When Walworth inquired good-naturedly about her, Stanton shrugged off the defeat and attributed it to his preoccupation with legal work.[21]

By now, Stanton and his partners had begun to follow cases to the Pennsylvania Supreme Court with some regularity, collectively losing a few more of them than they won. Most of that litigation entailed liability for damages to steamboats, disputes over business partnerships, and wrangling over estates involving anywhere from several hundred to a few thousand dollars. Once, Stanton defended Pittsburgh omnibus driver William Johnston all the way to the highest state tribunal over a $4 fine for having labored on the Sabbath. He must have intended to overturn the law against working on Sunday, and he argued that if it was legal to travel on the Sabbath then it must be legal to accommodate travelers on that day, but three good Christian judges were not persuaded.[22]

As Stanton's fortieth year unfolded, railroads began providing the corporate legal work that he evidently preferred. Two weeks before Christmas he appeared in U.S. District Court for Western Pennsylvania for the Erie & North East Railroad, which had run into public resistance as its workmen changed the width of the track to conform to the standard gauge between Buffalo and Cleveland. Like the Wheeling bridge, that simple modification ignited smoldering jealousies among rival municipalities, for the incompatible track widths forced all passengers to stop at least long enough in Erie to change trains, and made it a central port for steamers on Lake Erie. If all the rail lines radiating from Erie used uniform track widths, that city would lose its advantage as a destination point and become a mere way station. The city of Erie disputed the legality of the railroad's charter, and the mayor deputized Erie citizens to tear up the track. As counsel for the Erie & North East, Stanton obtained a preliminary injunction, but several of the railroad's more militant opponents continued their work. Early in January a U.S. marshal went up to Erie to arrest four of them and carried them back to Pittsburgh on a special train provided by the railroad.[23]

At a hearing a few days later the federal judge ordered the four held until their portion of the damage had been repaired. Stanton filed contempt citations against Erie's mayor, Alfred King, whose lawyer raised technicalities in the case, challenged the motivation behind the arrests, and complained that the entire proceeding amounted to the railroad's effort to punish and intimidate those who disputed its legitimacy. The intercession of the railroad to facilitate the initial arrest underscored that argument, and at the end of the second hearing the judge discharged King and the other four as well. That concluded only the first skirmish in what became a two-year struggle for Stanton, and ultimately he defended the Erie line against legal assault by the attorney general and the state legislature. One petition charged the railroad with the same offense that Stanton claimed against the Wheeling bridge company—that it obstructed other traffic—and the legislature finally revoked its charter. After numerous interim defeats, Stanton—the erstwhile foe of such chartered monopolies—finally won the war for his clients.[24]

Occasionally he engaged in suits between railroads, and rarely against them. In 1852 he fought the Pennsylvania Railroad's petition to force another rail line to carry its cars, and won with the argument that corporations did not necessarily enjoy the same rights as individual people. In the spring of 1854 he sued the same company on behalf of a German immigrant over the deaths of his wife and child. The little family had made an arduous winter journey to Pittsburgh on a poorly heated train, once spending three days and nights in an unheated building: the woman died on the last leg of the trip, and the child succumbed a few days later. Stanton, who had lost a wife and child himself, may have conducted the case out of a rare sympathy for his client, obtaining $3,000 for the immigrant widower.[25]

The westward flood of immigrants facilitated the spread of diseases into the new homeland, sparking outbreaks that sometimes grew into epidemics. Cholera struck with renewed virulence in 1849, originating in the immigration centers of New York and New Orleans and spreading into the interior over the next year. By the middle of summer, 1850, it had returned to Columbus and taken root in the crowded industrial neighborhoods of Allegheny City and Pittsburgh, prompting Stanton to leave the city for the relative safety of Steubenville. Four years later the disease resurfaced in Pittsburgh, raging simultaneously in numerous localities "with dreadful malignity," and sheer panic erupted. Associate Justice John McLean, of the U.S. Supreme Court, sent his own preferred cholera cure for the edification of Pittsburgh's Board of Health, and Stanton thanked him personally in one of the gratuitous letters he occasionally wrote to men whose acquaintance could be valuable.[26]

Partly because the most active partner was so often absent in Washington on those appeals, Shaler, Stanton & Umbstaetter took the son of a recent Pennsylvania governor on as a student (and Stanton wrote the father a letter lauding the boy's diligence and intelligence). The prominence of the firm and the affluence of its clientele inevitably brought Stanton into contact with Pittsburgh aristocrats, and somewhere along the way he encountered the wealthy Hutchison family. Lewis Hutchison, a native Kentuckian in his early sixties, had come to Pittsburgh decades before and made a fortune as a commission merchant; his building sat on the Monongahela waterfront, a short walk from the hotel where Stanton boarded. As the century passed its midpoint Stanton considered himself reasonably successful and comfortable, with real and personal property worth $8,000, but at that same juncture Hutchison's worldly estate approached a quarter of a million dollars: he kept a palatial home on Penn Street, with three maids and a driver.[27]

Stanton's connection with the family must have grown close, for by the summer of 1854 he was writing to the older of Mr. Hutchison's two daughters, Ellen, about the Fourth of July picnic he had taken in a vale near Steubenville with his mother, Oella, his son, and Darwin's widow. As the city's last cholera scare dissipated that autumn, he began calling regularly on Miss Hutchison. They may already have been friendly for some time. Years later the pastor at St. Peter's Episcopal Church remembered Stanton taking the pew behind the Hutchison family, where Stanton later told him he first developed an interest in her. Ellen struck casual acquaintances as refined and reserved, but in private she revealed a searing temper. She may have been the young lady Commissioner Walworth had alluded to nearly three years before, whom Stanton believed he had lost to a young soldier, for Stanton's earliest surviving letter to Ellen sympathized with her sadness over a shattered romance and her claim that her heart had grown "cold and dead." That letter was written less than three weeks after her twenty-fourth birthday—an age at which her peers might have begun to wonder whether she would ever marry. In the wake of her birthday Ellen gave notice that she feared as much herself, commenting that it had been an unhappy occasion; as though testing his intentions, she added her conviction that no man falls in love after the age of twenty-five. Stanton hinted broadly that it was not true, and early in their exchanges he confided to her that when illness forced him to lie idle in his room at the Monongahela House he passed the time by thinking of her.[28]

Comparing his economic situation against that of the Hutchisons may have given Stanton the first moment of doubt about his career choice, and it very likely came when he pondered the reaction of Ellen's parents to any proposal of marriage. In the short interval between his first two letters to Ellen he told a young cousin who had asked his advice about studying law that an aspiring attorney could not count on making a comfortable living. Even in a flourishing practice, he warned, the fees would prove "much smaller" than most people probably believed, and he rendered that opinion as though in regret, when his own income was higher than ever before.[29]

Stanton could thank the Wheeling bridge case for much of the income he did have, from the fees it had generated directly and from the new clients who had been drawn to him by its publicity. Early in December he interrupted his courtship to go to Washington for another hearing on the bridge before the Supreme Court, but he assured Ellen that he would think of her often, and proved it by writing a letter every other day or so. He described the justices arriving at the opening of the congressional session, sweeping in with their robes fluttering behind them, and noted that they took an early recess so they could parade upstairs and hear President Franklin Pierce address the two houses of Congress. The bridge case did not come up for another week, and when it did Stanton faced the renowned constitutional lawyer Reverdy Johnson of Maryland. At least in the account he prepared for Ellen he acquitted himself well, parrying motions here and objections there, but he refrained from offering too detailed a rendition of the courtroom combat out of fear it would only bore her. He did offhandedly mention that he noticed his youthful lust for victory waning, so long as he felt he had served his clients well.[30]

Stanton may have mistaken his amorous distraction for waning combativeness, because he never betrayed the slightest indifference to the outcome of important personal or professional contests. Now that Congress had authorized the bridge, he must have sensed ultimate defeat in the weaker elements of his constitutional argument, and may have been preparing Ellen for so conspicuous a failure by downplaying his concern over it. Even more likely, he may have hoped to make himself seem more appealing as a partner by suggesting that his notorious pugnacity had begun to moderate, for in the early stages of their relationship she complained of his irascibility and insisted that he curb the habit.[31]

When he was not occupied in court Stanton toured the capital with the federal marshal for the district, stopping at the city court where he had argued the McNulty case and dropping in on President Pierce. He enjoyed a social supper with the Supreme Court officers and congressmen, but Washington held less interest for him this time. By Christmas he was back in Pittsburgh, interviewing clients at 81 Fourth Street right through the holiday, and as the year drew to a close he seemed to dread leaving for a visit to Steubenville. From Washington he had, perhaps unwittingly, revealed a trace of jealousy when he admitted wondering where Ellen was at any given moment. Was she at a party, or at home; if she was at home was she alone, or with someone—and if so, whom? His curiosity evidently curdled as he realized that he was doing most of the writing, while she remained reticent about her activities, or fell altogether silent. He had already begun to profess his love for her, admitting that he hungered for hers in return, but his portion of their premarital correspondence leaves no doubt that she left him waiting many months for any reciprocal acknowledgment, and that she held the reins of their affair in a gentle but firm grip.[32]

His romance may have helped to direct his political future. Ben Wade, a former Whig from the Western Reserve, held a U.S. Senate seat that would open in 1857, and Stanton was being solicited to challenge him by the beginning of 1855. The fragility of his new relationship with Ellen probably only heightened his aversion to running for office, which would have forced him to reveal his position on the most volatile issues. Besides, if he did marry her he would have to change his official residence, for he must have known that she would never consent to live in provincial Steubenville. Within the first few weeks of the year his erstwhile political opponents in Steubenville learned officially that he would not seek the Democratic nomination for Wade's Senate seat. While other hopeful Democrats started their jockeying for it, Stanton went back to Pittsburgh to work on a couple of real estate cases.[33]

The first case came to trial in Pittsburgh's district court on January 22, 1855. It gave Ellen a convenient opportunity to see her suitor in action as he waded into a warm dispute between two factions of the city's Reformed Presbyterian Church. The congregation had split twenty years before over a matter of doctrine, with the more liberal body retaining the land and buildings that belonged to the church. In the intervening years property values had appreciated significantly, and the evicted orthodox members filed suit in hopes of reaping some of the windfall. Stanton represented the defendants—the "New Siders" who occupied the property. The trial lasted several days, with witnesses and spectators pouring in to see tables piled high with ancient books and papers. Stanton's lengthy introduction of the facts involved a quarter-millennium history of the church, down to the schism of 1833. The plaintiffs' attorney characterized the "New Siders" as heretics and backsliders who had abandoned their faith and lost all rights to any portion of the church's property, but Stanton replied that district courts were not equipped to rule on matters of faith. His clients held possession of the property, he pointed out, and had for some time; the "Old Siders" could offer no better title to it. The judge helped at the last moment by instructing the jury that the evidence and the law lay with the defendants, effectively awarding them the decision. The victory must have been especially sweet for Stanton, with his new local audience.[34]

Rising Pittsburgh real estate values also drove the other property case he litigated in 1855, involving a city lot overlooked in the will of a wealthy Allegheny County resident. Stanton won the original case in the U.S. Circuit Court for Western Pennsylvania, and when the executors appealed to the Supreme Court the following winter he prevailed there, too.[35]

The most engrossing case for Stanton that year—and the most conspicuous he had yet undertaken—carried him into the unfamiliar field of patent law. The astonishing acquittal he earned for Caleb McNulty lay in the forgotten past, and interest was even flagging in the Wheeling bridge case as railroads superseded river travel, but *McCormick v. Manny* would reestablish Stanton as a legal celebrity.

Cyrus McCormick, inventor of the harvesting machine that bore his name, embodied the rare combination of mechanical genius and business acuity, and he accentuated both traits with a fiercely combative spirit, relentlessly challenging competitors for patent infringements. He developed the prototype of his reapers at his home in Rockbridge County, Virginia, but he moved west to manufacture them—first to Cincinnati and then to Chicago, right on the edge of the broad, flat prairies where his reapers would be most practical. As patents expired, others imitated his machine, but their impatience to improve the efficiency of their reapers sometimes impelled them to adopt attachments or modifications for which McCormick still held patents, and he sued whenever he detected a potential infringement. Late in 1854 he filed suit against John H. Manny of Rockford, Illinois, who had already sold several thousand reapers. A violation of patent law had to be tried in a federal circuit court, and with both parties operating from northern Illinois it seemed logical that the case would be heard in Chicago, where Thomas Drummond would preside.

An old maxim in the legal profession holds that it is better to know the judge than to know the law.[36] Manny's principal attorneys, who were all from the East, were certainly thinking of that when they considered trying a case in a court they had never visited, before a judge they had never seen. Thus did Edwin Stanton first make the acquaintance of a gangly lawyer from Illinois named Abraham Lincoln.

Manny's patent agent, Peter H. Watson, lived in Washington, and George Harding, who had collaborated with Stanton on the Wheeling bridge case, came from Philadelphia. Stanton joined Manny's team late in the game, but even he had never practiced west of Columbus. Watson's first choice for a local Illinois lawyer lived in Chicago, but he declined, and someone next recommended Lincoln, who knew Judge Drummond well enough. In June, Watson traveled to Springfield and interviewed Lincoln at his home, offering him a $400 retainer to serve on the case. A month or so after Watson's visit, Lincoln wrote to him for the original petition and the answer, and for the depositions in the case, all of which Watson had promised to send as they were prepared. When he visited the court at Chicago on other business, Lincoln obtained his own copies of the filings and learned that the trial had been rescheduled at the U.S. District Court in Cincinnati on September 20. Watson still sent no depositions, or any reply to Lincoln's letter, and on September 1 Lincoln wrote to Manny & Company, explaining that he had been given none of the depositions and asking if the case would still be heard on the appointed day in Cincinnati.[37]

That much is clear from surviving correspondence and documents, which also demonstrate that Lincoln never represented Manny in court. Obviously Lincoln was awkwardly dropped from the case, but exactly how remains hidden behind the double veil imposed by recollections of recollections, the most important of which survive in two regurgitated renditions that both originated with George Harding. The two versions surfaced independently, but they were not entirely consistent, while the sole contemporary source was Stanton himself, who made no mention of Lincoln at all.

More than two decades afterward Harding told the tale to a young associate, who then waited nearly half a century longer to pass it on to a Lincoln biographer. According to that associate, during an 1876 carriage ride Harding admitted that Watson approached Lincoln primarily for the influence he might have with Drummond, and gave him the retainer despite doubts about Lincoln's capacity for so complicated a case: it was better to have him as an ally, Watson had reasoned, than to insult him and risk having that local influence swing to the other side. The removal of the case to Cincinnati eliminated their need for Lincoln, and they seem to have hoped he would simply go away. Harding had seen Stanton in action on the bridge case, which probably recommended him, but the new location for the hearing may have made Stanton even more desirable because the judge at Cincinnati would be Justice McLean of the Supreme Court, whom Stanton had cultivated personally. It could hardly have been the prevailing reason, for Stanton would have only enhanced Harding's own influence with McLean, who was his father-in-law.[38]

Harding went on to say that when he and Stanton met Lincoln on the stairway of Cincinnati's Burnet House on the morning of September 20, they found him every bit as ungainly and provincial as Watson had described him. They barely acknowledged his greeting, Harding said, and when Lincoln suggested that they walk to the courthouse together Stanton muttered unpleasantly and drew Harding away, leaving the rangy interloper on the step. Harding described Stanton making introductory courtroom remarks that left Lincoln out of Manny's legal team, leading Lincoln to withdraw from the case. Harding also claimed that Lincoln made such a poor impression that in 1860 he was disgusted by Lincoln's nomination as president, and Harding said he did not revise his opinion until later in the war.[39]

Every source for this legend shows signs of embellishment or invention, but Lincoln's unanswered inquiries about the case prove that his smug Eastern colleagues did ignore him after the change of venue made his assistance superfluous. Harding supplied the only testimony for the Cincinnati encounter that could be considered firsthand, and Stanton's curt and contemptuous affront is perfectly credible: he behaved with noticeable deference toward those he viewed as his superiors and often exercised a dismissive impatience with equals, subordinates, and social inferiors. Yet if the stairway slight happened Stanton never informed Ellen of it; he never even alluded to Lincoln, although he wrote at least two detailed letters to her during the ten-day trial.[40]

The arguments in the McCormick suit began in an improvised courtroom over the store of Moore, Wilstach & Keys, on Fourth Street, on September 21, and the newspapers listed Lincoln as part of the defense team. Edward Dickerson, McCormick's principal lawyer, took three days explaining the similarities between Manny's machine and McCormick's patented original. Among other imitated improvements, he complained particularly about the "raker's seat," where a man sat to sheave up the cut grain, and the "divider"—a projection from the front of the reaper that separated the grain to be cut from the grain to be left standing, and reduced the potential for jamming. To illustrate his argument he produced flurries of drawings and a caravan of models that littered tables at the front of the courtroom.[41]

Not until Tuesday, September 25, did Manny's lawyers have an opportunity to respond. Harding filled Dickerson's role on Manny's team, and the defense strategy required him to speak first on the mechanical and scientific issues that were his specialties. Stanton confessed that Harding proved much more effective on that subject than he would have been (and his effectiveness could not have been impaired by his marriage to Justice McLean's daughter). Harding needed three days to deliver his presentation, during which he refuted Dickerson's allegations on the grounds that the only similarities between the competing reapers involved inventions for which McCormick's patents had expired, or for which he had not made a broad enough proprietary claim.[42]

Stanton argued all of one day, making a characteristic assault on the plaintiff. He began by reviewing the intricacies of patent law, then ridiculed McCormick's medals from the London Agricultural Exposition, accusing him of using the unpatented creation of an inventor named Hussey to perfect the balance of his machine with the position of the driver's seat. "Why did this plaintiff stand up here and charge these defendants with being cheats," Stanton asked, "when they did no more than he did, to use public property? Nothing but the blindness produced by success, the dimness produced by those medals that have dazzled his imagination, could induce him to suppose there was any infringement; or to set up this claim, which was nothing more nor less than to get a construction which the government had refused to grant him—a monopoly of the reel and the raking machine—and failing to get it from the government, he rushes into Court to get the same monopoly, by the most remarkable, the most dangerous construction ever heard of, in support of an exclusive privilege against the public right."[43]

Reverdy Johnson's summation and rebuttal took two more days. Noting that the seat of Hussey's machine had proven impractical, and that McCormick had modified it, Johnson delivered what should have been the haymaker blow by pointing out that in winning his London medal McCormick had beaten Hussey himself, who had been one of the competitors. Johnson added that Stanton was merely distracting from the relevant issues of the cutter bar and the grain divider, and slandering the plaintiff in the process.[44]

After several months of deliberation, McLean ruled in Manny's favor, awarding substantial legal costs. McCormick, who seemed more intent on

Manny's practical infringement of his reaper than on the legal technicalities by which he had missed a favorable decision, almost immediately appealed the decision to the Supreme Court. Meanwhile, in other cases, infringements of the same nature were decided wholly or partly in McCormick's favor, including one in which the losers hired Harding and Stanton for their Supreme Court appeal.[45]

The technical gymnastics employed to save Manny's case may not have been limited to Stanton's glib statutory interpretations. Thirty years after that first hearing in Cincinnati, a young man working on a biography of Stanton stumbled across a seamier side to Manny's defense when he interviewed Albert E. H. Johnson, who had clerked for Stanton during the Civil War. Johnson had previously served in Peter Watson's office, and he suggested to Stanton's aspiring biographer, Frank Flower, that he inquire of William P. Wood about the reaper case. Johnson knew that something unsavory had happened, but it was many more years before Flower could get the story out of him.[46]

Among other occupations, before the war Wood had been a machinist and a model maker for patent applicants. Watson often hired him, and for the reaper suit Wood said that Watson sent him to find evidence helpful to Manny. He began by looking at every original McCormick reaper he could find in Maryland and Virginia. To nullify the complaint that Manny had infringed on McCormick's machine-mounted raker's seat, Wood found an old tag-along seat fashioned by McCormick's original manufacturer, after McCormick moved his operation west. According to Wood, Watson patented that clumsy device for Manny's use: then he prepared to argue that one raker's seat was the same as another, because Manny's reapers already used McCormick's seat, which balanced more easily and relieved the strain on the horses. The real trickery, as Wood explained it, involved his purchase of an old McCormick reaper, on which he straightened out the curved divider bar to suggest that Manny had developed the more efficient curved divider, and then masked his modification by treating the reworked iron with vinegar and salt to accelerate rust. Wood told Flower that he brought the doctored machine to Washington, where it became an exhibit in the Supreme Court appeal, in which McCormick was defrauded.[47]

Just as he had been reluctant to say anything at all at first, Wood initially seemed to shield Watson, Johnson, and everyone else involved in Manny's defense. In an 1897 affidavit he acknowledged having modified the old reaper, but insisted that he had done so on his own initiative, and he never divulged the changes that turned it into valuable evidence. Flower showed Johnson that document, whereupon Johnson signed a statement confirming that Wood had altered the machine, that it was used as an exhibit at the

Supreme Court hearing, and that the ruse was known throughout the firm. "I know that the changing of this machine was held as a secret in Mr. Watson's office," Johnson wrote, "and that the change was such as to make this McCormick machine divider a decisive element in his [McCormick's] defeat." Only in 1903, when Watson was dead and Wood learned that Johnson had revealed his knowledge of it, did Wood give Flower a supplementary affidavit implicating Watson and Johnson in the scheme. Johnson later refused to notarize a typewritten copy of his manuscript statement, citing justifiable concern that it might damage his reputation at the Patent Office, where he still worked, and that it would offend Watson's surviving family. He asked for the return of his handwritten copy, but Flower put him off, and it survives among Flower's papers.[48]

In some circles Wood appears to have been regarded as a disreputable character, and his hometown obituaries list a serried cavalcade of adventures that defy credulity, so his statement about his subterfuge on behalf of Watson's client invites skepticism. One historian thought Wood probably sold Flower "a bill of goods," besides deeming the deception unnecessary on the grounds that the decision of Judge McLean supported Manny "in every particular." If Wood duped Flower, however, he did it with the active connivance of Johnson, who had been a confidential clerk to both Watson and Stanton. Johnson had good reason to deny Wood's account, yet he corroborated it, which tainted them both with dishonesty, either in the falsification of evidence or in the manufacture of a pointless myth. The Supreme Court did not sustain McLean's opinion unanimously, either, but rendered a split decision in the case. The dissenting opinion alluded to the slight differences in Manny's divider, calling them "mere disguises" that "were indispensable to shelter the possession of property evidently pirated from the rightful owner." The principal mechanical difference noted in that dissent was the curve in Manny's divider, which comports with Wood's alleged doctoring of that fixture.[49]

Flower had evidently pursued Johnson's lead with a view to clearing Stanton of any complicity in a blatant fraud allegedly perpetrated through Watson's office. Neither Wood nor Johnson indicated whether Stanton knew about it, and it would have been natural for Watson to try to keep any such shenanigans as tightly within his own circle as possible. That would not speak well for Stanton's associates even if he remained ignorant of it himself, but they would have had to keep the juicy secret from him all during the ensuing war, when they all worked closely with him. The moment Stanton took over the War Department he appointed Watson assistant secretary of war, took Johnson in as chief clerk, and appointed Wood superintendent of the Old Capitol Prison, where he eventually ran afoul of superiors for his "irregularities" in the handling of prisoners.[50]

Events in Steubenville after the reaper trial may have provoked haunting memories of Stanton's first marriage just as he contemplated another one. Growth had finally crowded out the last of the city's original cemeteries, and for a year the trustees of a new association had been preparing forty-eight acres for a community burial ground on the slopes of a farm west of town. By October the first grave had been filled, and in January, when the weather had turned cold enough to reduce the stench, workmen began the grue-some task of removing the bodies from the old town cemeteries. Among the graves exhumed that winter were those of Edwin Stanton's father, sib-lings, daughter, and wife, which were all carried to the new family plot on a plateau near the edge of a ravine. Most of their coffins and all of the bod-ies would have been badly decayed. Stanton was occupied in Philadelphia through part of January, and February found him in Washington, at the Supreme Court, but the reverence he was said by numerous acquaintances to have later shown for Mary's gravesite implies that the disturbance of her remains would have troubled him even at a distance. Such a reminder of the romantic ideal he had described for Marie Bates many years after Mary's death might have been expected to ignite a sense of conflict at some level of consciousness between his new affection for Ellen and his long-cherished memory of Mary.[51]

He reached Washington on February 13, hoping to stay no more than a week, and went directly to the Supreme Court, where he showed much ir-ritation at the slow pace of the proceedings. That evening he grumbled that the court's time had been wasted by Reverdy Johnson and a Free Soil lawyer from Maryland named Montgomery Blair, who were making speeches in "a slave case that ought not to have occupied more than a couple of hours." With such impatience did Stanton dismiss the first hearing in Dred Scott's appeal for freedom.[52]

By mid-March Stanton was back in Pittsburgh. The next week, he be-came the target of bitter accusations in an anonymous letter in Pittsburgh newspapers that criticized the city's attorneys for losing the long, expen-sive, and ultimately fruitless Wheeling bridge suit. The case had brought acclaim for Pittsburgh's champions after the early victories, but the final defeat excited reproach, and of the attorneys who had been involved it was Stanton whose name had been permanently linked to the case, at least in Pittsburgh. Stanton could afford to ignore the attack, for he had associated himself with the triumph in the reaper case, and locally he had just won a dramatic reversal in an estate suit. Early in April he learned that he had also won his most recent Supreme Court appeal, including a judgment for costs. The old bridge case served only to mark Stanton's migration to the smoky, bustling city, and to the service of the business barons who controlled it. By 1856, he appeared to represent a preponderance of wealthy clients, often against poorer defendants, suggesting that his distance from his Jacksonian political roots had widened.[53]

His marriage to Ellen Hutchison in 1856 would complete Stanton's alliance with Pittsburgh's industrial aristocracy, but it would not happen without a test of wills. Ellen had upbraided him early in his courtship for irritability and a nasty temper, and he had promised to change, but at some point he resorted to his old ways and she brought him up short in an angry note. He was cold to the feelings of anyone who could not contribute to his "selfish gratification," she wrote, and occasionally he acted unkindly even toward those who could. Hers was a perception that many others observed in her fiancé during his lifetime, but she had both the nerve and the position to make him suffer for it. He admitted the fault quickly and contritely enough, but he soon turned the tables on her, asking how she could have been so harsh and unkind as to deny that he had changed when he had conformed to her wishes for so long, and had lapsed only once "under peculiar circumstances." She refused to see him for days, during which his epistolary apologies became more abject, and when he cut short an office appointment on a Sunday evening to appear in her parlor she sent down word that he could go away. She may have been reconsidering the decision to marry her churlish suitor, or merely trying to determine whether she could control him, but eventually he humbled himself enough to win absolution. It was probably then that he mailed her an awkward contract stipulating that in case of future "differences" they would not part "without a kiss of forgiveness and reconciliation." He urged her to sign it and keep it, and she did, although it seemed to place the burden of forgiveness on her.[54]

That saved the engagement from unraveling on the brink of its consummation. It seemed an odd match, with Ellen so young and attractive and Stanton so gruff and grizzly, but there may have been a bit of calculation in it for both of them. With Ellen, perhaps he never felt the deep emotional attachment that he had with Mary, who had waited patiently and devotedly through three years of absence during their courtship and then bore his long sojourns at Columbus. Such prolonged separation would sorely test his second marriage, for Ellen apparently lacked the patience and the sweet disposition that he and Pamphila had recognized in Mary: a presidential secretary would later find Ellen "cold . . . as marble," while Washington socialites would complain of her "freezing manner and repellent address." On the other hand, Ellen's youth and beauty would have appealed to him, both personally and as a source of social pride. Against Stanton's own resources and experience, too, the Hutchisons were fabulously wealthy and well connected, and—until he experienced the greater seduction of political power—Stanton always aimed for the financial security that had escaped his family in his youth. Combined with his salary, Ellen's share of the Hutchison fortune would make them very comfortable. For his part, Stanton made a practice of cultivating powerful connections, which Ellen appears to have found appealing: she perhaps considered her interests outside the realm of romance, including the prestige that might accrue to the wife of a nationally prominent attorney. After investing several years in two courtships, she may also have pondered her own narrowing prospects for a better bargain as she approached the age of twenty-six.[55]

Both of them must have concluded that the advantages would outweigh the potential discord of two strong natures. Still hampered by the leg fracture that had never healed correctly, the stocky bridegroom limped into St. Peter's, on the corner of Diamond and Grant Streets, on Wednesday evening, June 25. Ellen followed after an appropriate delay, armored in a heavy satin gown, and Reverend Edwin Van Deusen married them in a ceremony that the affluent Hutchison clan considered modest. The next morning the newlyweds departed for a lazy, weeks-long honeymoon tour of Canada and New England. By the time they returned to Pittsburgh, Ellen was pregnant.[56]

5

THE CALIFORNIA MISSION

The Stantons' honeymoon coincided with one of the most volatile seasons in American politics. Slavery had come to dominate public debate, especially after 1854, when Senator Stephen A. Douglas introduced the Kansas-Nebraska legislation. Driven by visions of a transcontinental railroad from the Pacific coast to his Chicago doorstep, and by his own presidential ambitions, Douglas had recklessly sacrificed the sectional truce over slavery reached four years earlier. To build the railroad, the unorganized land between Missouri and Utah would have to be carved into territories, and to win Southern support in Congress Douglas raised the prospect of admitting more slave states. The hard-fought Compromise of 1850 had left the territories of Utah and New Mexico to decide their own fate when they applied for statehood, and Douglas's legislation extended the same privilege to Kansas and Nebraska. That concession secured the Southern votes, but it simultaneously alarmed legions of Northerners who had been content with barring slavery's expansion. This shocking reversal lent credence to the abolitionist specter of a grasping slave power, and that in turn initiated a widespread reshuffling of political loyalties. Salmon P. Chase, Ben Wade, and other antislavery senators seized on Douglas's bill as proof of Southern aggression: Chase, who worried that the dispute over slavery might actually subside, seemed to welcome the new controversy.[1]

Douglas's deal with the devil launched an immediate struggle for Kansas. At the urging of Eastern abolitionists (and with their financial help), hundreds of free-state settlers moved into the territory to ensure that popular sovereignty produced an antislavery constitution for congressional consideration. Migrants from slave states did not come in sufficient numbers or with enough enthusiasm, so Missourians, seeking a buffer state to the west, crossed the border to stake their own claims or to simply cast votes for a constitution that would permit slavery. The contest led to rampant election fraud, violent assaults and rioting, occasional murder, a general arming of the factions, and periodic warfare. A posse of Missouri "border ruffians" descended on the free-state center of Lawrence, destroying two newspapers, a fortress-like hotel, and the home of a free-state leader. An abolitionist zealot named John Brown retaliated by slaughtering five unarmed and perfectly innocent Southern emigrants.[2]

In Washington, just before the last of those atrocities, the towering senior senator from Massachusetts, Charles Sumner, rose to deliver a blistering speech on affairs in Kansas. During his lengthy screed he repeatedly insulted slaveholders, the slave system, Senator Douglas, Senator Andrew P. Butler of South Carolina (who was absent from the chamber), and the state of South Carolina generally. Sumner's language shocked and outraged many Northern senators and all of those from the South, bringing Lewis Cass and Douglas to their feet the moment Sumner concluded. Douglas wondered aloud whether Sumner were trying to provoke one of his colleagues to "kick him as we would a dog in the street, that he may get sympathy upon his just chastisement," and three days later a South Carolina congressman fell into that very trap. Preston Brooks strolled into the Senate chamber the following Thursday, announced himself as a relative of Senator Butler, and struck Sumner over the head repeatedly with a hollow gutta percha cane. It was a poor substitute for a bludgeon and soon broke in half, but the blows opened two bone-deep cuts in Sumner's scalp, each of which required two stitches. Brooks desisted only after Sumner dropped to the floor and others intervened.[3]

When Brooks laid his cane over Sumner's head he gave the new Republican Party a handy martyr. Sumner rested throughout the summer of 1856 (while Edwin and Ellen Stanton made their leisurely way up the St. Lawrence River and down through New Hampshire's White Mountains to the Massachusetts seashore). First he recuperated on a Maryland estate just outside Washington, then on the New Jersey shore, and finally at a mountain resort in Pennsylvania, where he went horseback riding every day. Sumner enjoyed a brief recovery, just in time to make an appearance at the Massachusetts State House—where, a few weeks later, the legislature reelected him almost unanimously. Then he suffered a relapse, and his continued absence from the Senate helped to inspire the party faithful: his empty desk spoke more eloquently than he could have of the violence with which the South would punish its critics. Sumner raged over the inevitable suspicion that he was shamming for political effect, but in the end his recuperation dragged on more than three years, beginning with an extended tour to Europe that a sympathetic biographer called "an exhausting round of visiting and sightseeing."[4]

The assault on Sumner suddenly elevated the senator and his supporters in the popular imagination, casting Northern slave foes as civilized warriors of the pen and slaveholders as brutal proponents of the bludgeon. During the early months of his long recovery, Sumner's party gained such strength from Northern Whigs, Know-Nothings, and antislavery Democrats that it posed a great challenge to the party of Jackson. Instead of two parties contesting for the presidency, the exclusively Northern Republican Party initiated a sectional struggle, and Southern newspapers began calling it "warfare." In Kansas, it did become warfare again, with free-state militia mobilizing to meet another expected attack from the border ruffians. Northern dissatisfaction with Franklin Pierce's presidency, especially in his handling of the Kansas troubles, had cost the Democratic Party dearly. The Western explorer John Charles Frémont, the Republican Party's first presidential candidate, might have won had ex-president Millard Fillmore not run a third-party campaign on the Whig and American, or Know-Nothing tickets. As it was, Pennsylvanian James Buchanan, a career politician who had tried three times previously for his party's nomination, secured the last Democratic victory in a generation.[5]

Buchanan's home state was one of those doubtful Northern prizes he had to have. When Pennsylvania's October elections gave promise of a Democratic triumph for him, party loyalists in Pittsburgh wheeled out a cannon to celebrate. Lawyer Stanton may still have been in town to hear it booming, but he and his bride had packed up to leave the city. According to his sister, he gave Ellen her choice of permanent residence and she chose Washington, but professional opportunities and political outcomes may have had more influence than family tradition suggests. Stanton had business before the Supreme Court in the December term, first to argue Joshua Nachtrieb's futile appeal against the Harmony Society at the beginning of the term, and a few days later he and Harding had to defend another of Cyrus McCormick's patent pirates from that doggedly vigilant inventor. He made one last visit to Steubenville, and when it was time to return to the capital he took Ellen with him.[6]

Stanton maintained his ties to Shaler & Co., leaving his law library in their office, and the move to Washington may have begun as an extended vacation scheduled around Stanton's appearances at the Supreme Court. It was then still a city of stark contrasts: magnificent government buildings in white marble loomed over scattered, low, wooden houses, and in many quarters livestock roamed at large. "It has a southern country air that pleases me," said a Philadelphian who visited Washington in 1853. "It is not a city. There are open spaces in all directions and from all points a look out into fields & woods." Diplomats, congressmen, and socialites shared the streets with crowds of free black residents and slaves, whose public presence suggested far greater numbers than the official census. A Northern boy who had never encountered slavery and had first seen the capital six years before remembered much later that "the brooding indolence of a warm climate and a negro population hung in the atmosphere heavier than the catalpas."[7]

At first Stanton and Ellen took rooms at the National Hotel—a sprawling five-story establishment that dominated the corner of Pennsylvania Avenue at Sixth Street, between the White House and the Capitol, where Southern congressmen and their more conservative Democratic allies preferred to stay. As 1856 gave way to 1857 those men were the country's principal powerbrokers, which may have influenced Stanton's choice of lodging, for he always gravitated toward those who wielded the greatest political might. James Buchanan chose the National for his preinaugural headquarters, giving Stanton an opportunity to make his acquaintance, and the stocky Senator Douglas represented the best known of the dignitaries who came there to welcome the president-elect. The perpetual cavalcade of illustrious characters would have appealed to Stanton's bride, and to Stanton himself, for that matter, but illness marred their sojourn. Late in January a virulent gastrointestinal malady struck guests at the National, killing a few and felling scores of celebrities, including Buchanan, who went home to recuperate. The discovery of arsenic in the stomach of one victim ignited rumors of an abolitionist plot to poison as many slave-power sympathizers as possible, but the earliest accounts more plausibly hypothesized that a sewer backup from a frozen pipe carried into the hotel's kitchen.[8]

The National Hotel epidemic probably hastened Stanton's search for a more permanent residence, and he found a suitable house to rent at 365 C Street Northwest, not far from the National and Judiciary Square. He may have become aware of the rental through Gamaliel Bailey, editor of the city's struggling antislavery newspaper, the *National Era*, whom Stanton knew well enough that he lent him nearly $5,000 a few weeks after he moved into the new house. He was not sufficiently familiar with Bailey to forgo substantial collateral for that loan, however, and until principal and interest had been repaid Stanton took a deed of trust for a half-lot that Bailey and his wife owned nearby, fronting on C Street.[9]

By the third week of February Stanton was planning on staying in the house long enough that he sent home to his Steubenville gardener for grape vines. Once they had settled in, Stanton brought his son, Eddie, and nephew David to visit, so they could see the new president inaugurated. They all gathered at the Capitol to witness that event late on the clear, chilly, and windy morning of March 4, and that evening Washingtonians celebrated the event with a grand ball in a huge temporary structure on Judiciary Square, a couple of blocks from the Stantons' new residence. "Almost 'everybody as is anybody' was present," observed a reporter, including the bachelor president and his niece, who would act as White House hostess, along with the new vice president, thirty-six-year-old Kentuckian John C. Breckinridge. Stanton wrote that the boys enjoyed the inauguration immensely, but he failed to mention Ellen. She would certainly have relished such a congregation of the nation's luminaries, but she was well along in her pregnancy.[10]

During the winter, Buchanan's recuperation at his Pennsylvania home slowed the composition of his cabinet, and it was not until he had taken office that he appointed Jeremiah Sullivan Black to be attorney general. The ascent of Black, a resident of western Pennsylvania, greatly enhanced Stanton's connection to the administration, because Black came to the post from the Pennsylvania Supreme Court, where Stanton had often appeared before him. Stanton had evidently made friends with the judge already, and he capitalized on Black's new position with a letter of congratulation and an invitation. Several times in the first few days after Black's arrival Stanton dropped by Willard's Hotel, two blocks from the White House, hoping to catch him at the bar or in his room. He stopped at the attorney general's office, too, without success, and finally resorted to leaving a note, expressing delight that Black was a member of the new cabinet and mentioning that nothing would give him greater pleasure than to be of service. Quoting a character from *Little Dorrit* (which Stanton, the ardent Dickens fan, was obviously reading in its initial serialized form), he added Ellen's reminder that the attorney general could always expect "a knife a spoon and an apartment" at the Stanton home. Black replied that he had been overwhelmed by visitors and by applicants for office, but confessed his need for "a confidential friend of the highest professional ability" to talk with, and Stanton instantly offered to fill that role, promising to come to him whenever Black indicated "by note, signal, or message." From that moment their correspondence became regular, and Stanton soon found that he could influence not only Black's appointments but the president's, as well.[11]

In February of 1856, Stanton had impatiently witnessed the introduction of Dred Scott's petition for freedom at the Supreme Court. In December of that year the same case had returned for reargument only days after Stanton appeared in the McCormick case. Scott, a Missouri slave who had belonged to an army officer, had sued for official release after spending years living with his master in Minnesota Territory, where the Missouri Compromise of 1820 had precluded slavery. As Stanton had complained when Scott's suit first delayed his own case, there were numerous reasons the case might have been disposed of faster than it was, but as the proceedings dragged on it became increasingly clear that Scott's circumstances presented the potential for a landmark decision on the extension of slavery into the territories. Whether it could be introduced in those territories posed one of the most explosive issues Buchanan would face as president, and that led him to intrude on the court's independence to press privately for a definitive ruling. On the same day the new president appointed Black attorney general, Chief Justice Roger B. Taney announced his decision in the Scott case, and it brought Buchanan all the conflict and controversy he had hoped to avoid. In his most provocative legal aside, Taney declared the Missouri Compromise unconstitutional because Congress had no right to prohibit slavery in any unorganized territory belonging to the United States. That implicitly invalidated the Ordinance of 1787, which had forever forbidden slavery in the Northwest Territory above the Ohio River, and Taney seemed to imply that slaves might have to be tolerated in states where that institution had already been abolished, or had never been legal.[12]

Taney's reading of his momentous decision immediately preceded the justices' order to compensate their court clerk for managing the money deposited for the Wheeling bridge suit. Some of that money came to Stanton, whose fees had composed a hefty portion of the costs awarded by the court.[13] Through the early part of 1857 he represented at least three other clients before the high court, including the Erie & North East Railroad, and all that summer he busied himself with preparation for McCormick's appeal against the corporate heirs of John Manny. The reaper case required an occasional trip to Philadelphia to consult with Harding, and Stanton tried to plan time for a visit to Steubenville, where Oella had taken charge of his house at Third and Logan. By April he had begun to talk of selling the four-acre garden spot across Third Street, where his gardener lived. He had bought the "patch" as a horticultural refuge and natural buffer just before setting up shop in Pittsburgh, and Stanton had never returned long enough to take much pleasure in it; he must have rooted rather quickly in Washington to consider letting that land go so abruptly. Obviously he and Ellen both enjoyed their new home, where his illustrious acquaintances might come for afternoon visits and informal dinners, even as she grew heavy with child.[14]

The Steubenville journey met successive delays as Ellen's pregnancy approached full term. Oella traveled to Washington to attend the birth, and on May 9 Ellen delivered a girl, whom they named Eleanor Adams Stanton, after Mrs. Hutchison. The baby fared well enough, but within days Ellen returned to bed with the abdominal pain and fever of puerperal sepsis, and for a week or ten days Stanton had to wonder whether tragedy would strike again. If, as Pamphila intimated, Ellen did not quite meet the romantic ideal of Mary in her husband's estimation, the fear of losing her may have helped to tighten the new bond. Two weeks after Ellie's birth the danger seemed to pass, and by early June, when he found a nurse to care for Ellen and the child, Stanton felt it safe to travel. It was nearly two months before Ellen started washing and dressing the baby herself. The new mother seemed to chafe under the nurse's injunctions, feeling well enough to take long carriage rides and call on sick friends, while Stanton tended to business in Pittsburgh, Steubenville, and elsewhere.[15]

At least twice during his first year in Washington, Stanton endured significant illness himself. His health was "low," he admitted, for several weeks when he first arrived in the capital. By mid-February he was on the mend, but in August he took to his bed again for several days. He described no specific symptoms either time: his habitual use of modest euphemism in discussing his health defies a posthumous diagnosis for most of his acute maladies and injuries. He may have suffered from one of the intestinal ailments that seemed endemic in the city, but comments he made six months later leave it more likely that the two episodes involved his chronic asthma.[16]

With the humidity that usually accompanies it, the heat in Washington often becomes intolerable throughout the summer. That, and fears of deadly fevers lurking in the district's swamps and sewers, drove anyone out of the city who did not have to stay. Later in the summer, when Ellie could travel conveniently, Ellen joined this seasonal migration, evidently on a long visit to her family in Pittsburgh. Her husband remained behind, and Eddie may have gone to see his grandmother and one of his two Ohio aunts; he did not stay in Washington, at any rate, and his father would have been disinclined to leave him among the relative strangers in Pittsburgh when he was so near blood relatives. During that bachelor summer Stanton's asthma showed some improvement, and he endured at least one sweltering trip to Philadelphia. The return through steamy Baltimore left him especially glad that Ellen and the baby had not come along. The rail connections at Baltimore consisted of two widely separated depots, between which horsecars carried the continuing passengers: in that oppressive heat those shuttles were jammed as tightly as the people could be packed, and the seats in the train waiting at the other depot were full already. Stanton came home to find all the windows closed, and the house suffocating, although it was already past the middle of September and Southerners were flocking back from their Northern havens.[17]

By then the Panic of 1857 had begun in earnest. Three weeks before, the Ohio Life Insurance and Trust Company had failed, precipitating a string of other bank failures, a sudden loss of confidence in paper currency, and a run on surviving banks as depositors demanded all their money in gold and silver. Railroads had created new economic ties between the East and the corn belt of the old Northwest, and those ties only spread the shock. Bank failures and the suspension of specie payments leapfrogged eastward from Ohio to Philadelphia, Baltimore, and finally to New York. With the suspension of payments at every bank in New York the panic sank deep, and the crisis blossomed to a new level as businesses began to go bankrupt. With the speculative impulse curbed in New York, the price Virginia planters could ask for their abundant new tobacco crop suddenly plummeted, and thousand-acre plantations in the Piedmont went on the block, complete with slaves, as the toppling dominoes of debt radiated farther outward.[18]

It was at the height of the panic, with fortunes disappearing daily and business at a standstill, that Stanton received a letter from Attorney General Black offering a lucrative government assignment. In such uncertain times he obviously wanted the job, but it would require him to sail for California, where President Buchanan wished to challenge what the administration believed were fraudulent claims to some of the most valuable land on the Pacific coast.

In seizing about half of Mexico's territory in 1848, the United States had agreed to recognize the titles of landowners who had received their grants under Mexican authority. It would have been easier to determine who those landowners really were if federal authorities had conducted an immediate census, but that probably seemed unnecessary until the discovery of gold in California: after that, the demand for land soon put the promise to protect Mexican grantees in jeopardy as thousands of Americans started posting squatters' claims. One of the more brazen instances of fraud involved Jose Limantour's claim to a Mexican grant on both sides of the Golden Gate— encompassing the city of San Francisco, Point Tiburon, and all the islands in the bay. President Buchanan had not long held office when Black learned that Limantour's claim suffered from serious flaws, and shortly after that he heard from Auguste Jouan, a former employee of Limantour's, who volunteered that he had helped fabricate the grant. That had convinced Black to investigate, because if Limantour's claim could be invalidated the federal government would resume title to land where it had constructed or wanted to build numerous federal buildings.[19]

The disputed California land had already attracted Stanton's talents. The rich New Almaden quicksilver mine, south of San Francisco Bay, lay at the center of a four-way suit involving three potential owners, two competing mining companies, and the United States government. Barron, Forbes & Company operated the mine under the aegis of a Mexican mineral claim filed by Andrés Castillero, while a neighbor named José Berreyesa insisted that the mine fell beneath land he had been granted. A third disputant, Charles Fossat, challenged the validity of the Castillero rights and argued that the claim lay under land that had been granted to Justo Larios, from whom Fossat acquired it. Barron, Forbes & Company bought out the Berreyesa interests, so that company's rights depended on both the Castillero mineral claim and the Berreyesa land grant, while Fossat became a figurehead for a gaggle of investors who would eventually identify themselves as the Quicksilver Mining Company. The Quicksilver people hired Stanton, who appeared before the Supreme Court around the first of the year and tried to help legitimize the Larios land grant that Fossat had purchased.[20]

Black may not have known that Stanton was on retainer from Fossat's corporate backers when he offered him the job, for that hearing had not yet been held. Stanton responded to the offer after returning from a couple of weeks in smoky Pittsburgh, where he had taken Ellen, Eddie, and the baby. Black had evidently prodded him to leave immediately to investigate the land cases, but Stanton balked, explaining that he still had clients before the U.S. Circuit Court and the Supreme Court. He actually had few pending cases that could not have been postponed or handed off to Shaler and Umbstaetter, but Stanton may have hoped to disguise any desperation until his fee had been determined. He did have a couple of pressing cases before the high court, however: both the Fossat case and the McCormick patent-infringement appeal against the Manny heirs had been scheduled for the December term. The reaper trial remained his best known victory, overshadowing his ultimate defeat in the bridge case, and he would have wished to confirm Manny's triumph on appeal for the sake of his own reputation as an attorney, apart from the remainder of his fee. Stanton estimated that he could leave for California no earlier than the first of the year; as that was barely seven weeks away Black assented, sending him numerous files to study while he waited.[21]

Before Stanton departed for the West Coast, Kansas again seized the public's attention, and Washington became the vortex of the tension. Pro-slavery delegates chosen in a farcical election had convened at the hamlet of Lecompton, on the Kansas River, where they adopted a state constitution and sent it to Congress before giving territorial voters a chance to approve it. When they did submit it to Kansans for ratification, the referendum offered only the choices of accepting the constitution with slavery or accepting it without slavery: there was no provision for rejecting it altogether, and even the "antislavery" option allowed those who already had slaves in the territory to keep them. Buchanan, who had earlier insisted on a popular vote before sending any Kansas constitution to Congress, inexplicably changed his mind, and in his first annual message to Congress in December of 1857 he asked for its approval. Stephen Douglas, whose efforts to supplant the Compromise of 1850 had stirred up this hornet's nest in the first place, broke completely and publicly with Buchanan by sticking fast to the principle of popular sovereignty. When the issue reached the Senate floor on December 9 Douglas met it with a sarcastic denunciation of the president and the Lecompton convention, declaring that he would not allow "a small minority of the people in Kansas to defraud the majority," and that he would fight to the bitter end. Thundering applause erupted from the galleries when he finished.[22]

Douglas's speech marked the beginning of the great rift in the Democratic Party that would lead it and the nation to disaster three years later, but for the moment Douglas enjoyed a blizzard of commendation and congratulation from Northerners of an antislavery bent. His mail included a curiously noncommittal letter from Stanton, whose impending contract with the attorney general's office might have been compromised by any suggestion of pleasure at the president's discomfiture, and perhaps that accounted for Stanton's decision to send an accolade so ambiguous that Douglas may have wondered why he bothered: Stanton merely remarked that the "day has not yet come when an American Senator may not boldly speak what he truly believes." He added that he would have preferred to deliver the compliment personally (the better to impress the Senate's best-known Democrat, no doubt), but he pleaded that illness had kept him away.[23]

Ultimately McCormick's appeal to the Supreme Court was not heard until well into February of 1858, and the journey to California had to be put off that much longer. Stanton and George Harding faced Reverdy Johnson and Edward Dickerson again for several days, going over such items as Manny's curved divider and perhaps examining William Wood's doctored reaper—if such an implement ever existed. When the last of the defendants' arguments had been heard Stanton went home and wrote his own contract for the California mission, naming a fee of $25,000, with $5,000 of it in advance and $5,000 for initial expenses, and on February 17 he brought that draft to the attorney general's office. Black initialed it without question and sent a note to the secretary of the Interior Department, asking him to supply the $10,000 right away, because Stanton wished to leave in the morning.[24]

With that Stanton returned to the house on C Street to pack his trunks and carpet bags for himself and his fifteen-year-old son, Eddie. He invited Ellen, but she refused to make the long journey with a nine-month-old child, or to leave the baby behind. At his own expense President Buchanan had sent along his unemployed nephew, James Buchanan Jr.: the president personally handed Stanton $250 for the young man's fare. Perhaps because of the potential naval value of San Francisco Bay, Buchanan had also dispatched a greying navy lieutenant, Horace N. Harrison, to act in whatever capacity Stanton found useful; Harrison had just survived a court of inquiry and drew the assignment in lieu of a command.[25] The four of them took the train for New York, where they put up at the St. Nicholas Hotel for two nights during a snowstorm, and in bitter cold on the morning of February 21 they scrambled aboard the *Star of the West*, a sleek side-wheel steamer with a walking-beam engine projecting above the bulwarks. Once he and Eddie had stowed their bags in a chilly stateroom, Stanton stood looking out the window as New York Harbor drifted into the distance, taking him from his twenty-month bride and a daughter not yet old enough to miss him.[26]

Six hundred souls crowded the vessel. To lessen the risk of a fire at sea the ship had but one stove, in the main cabin on the lower deck, but women and children had taken complete possession of that space, so Stanton and his companions clustered together in his stateroom to capitalize on their collective body heat, wrapping their feet against the cold. It must have seemed an ominous start for Stanton, who had undertaken the journey in part because he hoped it would reduce the symptoms of his asthma. They ran into rough seas that first night, and the next day's rain dampened everything aboard ship. By the third night out Stanton started wheezing and straining for breath, and his condition grew only worse through the following day, aggravated by the cigars he admitted smoking continually. He confessed to Peter Watson, if not to Ellen, that it was the worst spasm he had ever suffered. A doctor among the passengers dosed him with ipecac and lobelia, in the then-common assumption that making him vomit would somehow improve his respiration, but while green-gilled passengers darted for the lee rail all around him Stanton felt not the slightest twinge of nausea. Lieutenant Harrison and Eddie both kept their sea legs, too, but young Buchanan could not stir from his bunk.[27]

Once in the Caribbean, however, Stanton reveled in the climate, with the bright sun, cool breezes, and brilliant sky. At night he lay on the upper deck and gazed at the silver coin of moon and glimmering planets, dreaming uncharacteristically of the sailor's luxurious life until, at last, he began to feel selfish about enjoying that paradise without the "chosen & sole companion" of his heart. Once he told Ellen that he felt lazy, as he had during their honeymoon, but any who knew his nervous and intent character would have had to see him in that state to believe it. Only enforced isolation from the tools of his profession seemed to leave him idle long enough to begin to appreciate a moment of lassitude, and he could not well work aboard ship. It was all he could do to write a letter in his cramped quarters, with a satchel as a lap desk, and that was only made possible by the recent invention of the fountain pen, which allowed him to keep his ink bottle capped and secure most of the time while the ship rolled and pitched. He wrote every day, straining his practical vocabulary to find new ways to express his loneliness and to assure Ellen that she—rather than any idealized image of domestic perfection from his first marriage—was his "beloved idol."[28]

The *Star of the West* (which would capture national notice three years later) put into Kingston, Jamaica, on the last day of February. Stanton took his son ashore as soon as the gangplank dropped, and since it was Sunday they attended a couple of different church services. Most of the residents showed some trace of African blood, and at a Wesleyan chapel the white congregants segregated themselves in a balcony, but at the Episcopal church blacks and whites mingled in the pews, except for the more prestigious government officials and army officers, who occupied a railed dais. Women did most of the work that he could see—including replenishing the coal bunkers on the steamer by balancing tubs full of coal on their heads as they filed up to the ship. By midafternoon the last passenger had returned, the coaling was finished, and the bowsprit turned toward the Isthmus of Panama.[29]

Asthma continued to afflict Stanton, discrediting the curative claims he had heard attributed to sea air, but his attacks diminished in severity, turning more frustrating and uncomfortable than alarming. On March 3 they reached the steamship port of Aspinwall, on the isthmus, where every man, woman, and child spilled out of the *Star of the West* and streamed toward the train that would carry them forty miles through the jungle to the Pacific. The train followed the route of the canal that would supplant it, taking the gaping Easterners past knots of scantily clad native women and children who sold fruit whenever the cars slowed to a stop. That afternoon the six hundred pilgrims emerged near the ancient, decaying city of Panama, where the two Stantons and their companions dined at a French restaurant before boarding the tug that would deliver them to their next steamer. At nightfall they had found new staterooms aboard the more spacious *Sonora*, and during the night the ship cast off, nosing out of the Gulf of Panama.[30]

As their ship started up the west coast of Central America and Mexico, Stanton busied himself writing down his oral arguments in the recent reaper hearing. Otherwise, the days passed in the invariable routine of strolling, lounging, and smoking. Each of their staterooms had cost the equivalent of a day laborer's annual wages, but the bunks were so short that even the stocky Stanton could not stretch his legs to their full length. Lieutenant Harrison encountered a servant on the *Sonora* who had once sailed with him; on the basis of their former acquaintance this steward started bringing them tea in their staterooms each evening, but even with such civilized amenities the life at sea that had seemed so appealing to Stanton in the Caribbean offered only "annoyance" after three days in the Pacific. In another week ocean travel would become an absolute "humbug."[31]

A gale blew them off course as they passed the Isthmus of Tehuantepec, tossing the ship violently. After the storm abated the *Sonora* put in at Acapulco for coal, and Stanton went ashore to mail his collection of letters to Ellen. Stanton's party pushed through dark streets crowded with vendors of food and homemade trinkets, none of which they stopped to buy, but they did find another restaurant run by a woman he described as "part French, part Indian and a good deal Yankee." On the way back to the ship they secured a supply of fruit and produce from the clamoring vendors, whom Stanton evidently included in his general conclusion that the people of Acapulco were "ignorant, degraded, lazy and worthless." A stop at Manzanillo, the next day, seemed long enough for Stanton to judge the inhabitants of that town equally shiftless.[32]

The *Sonora* fought its way up the coast in the face of a stiff northwest wind, a week behind schedule, and Stanton ran out of clean clothes. The aroma of seven or eight hundred travelers in the same plight may have contributed to the worn and fretful expressions the passengers began to wear. Noticing the misery among the women, and especially those with children, Stanton conceded that Ellen had known best when she declined to come with him. He kept to his stateroom most of the time, and when he finished the transcript of his reaper argument he dove into a Spanish grammar. One last storm, and the worst yet, tossed the ship about for two days along the coast of California, consigning young Buchanan to his bunk again, but Stanton and his son still escaped nausea. They were not immune to some anxious moments, however, when seas began breaking over the decks and dashing in the portholes to drench the staterooms. Finally, on March 19, the wind subsided and the sea settled into a vast mirror, blemished only by the leaping of porpoises and the occasional spouting and sounding of a pod of whales, and that evening the ship passed into San Francisco Bay. They docked at ten o'clock, and such a crowd met the ship that it took two more hours for Stanton to get ashore, but despite the late hour he led his little entourage into the city and checked into a room at the International Hotel, sprawling gratefully, at last, in a bed long enough for him.[33]

The next day, a Saturday, Stanton introduced himself to U.S. District Attorney Peter Della Torre as the attorney general's special counsel for land claims. Writing to Ellen that evening, he warned that Della Torre had described so many complicated cases that he thought he might have to linger in California longer than the four weeks he had estimated for Ellen: with an optimism that his understanding with Black did not seem to warrant, he had told her to expect him home about the first of May, but after his discussion with Della Torre he said he would not be able to even start back by that date.[34]

Stanton's letter to Ellen left San Francisco on March 22. It would have reached 365 C Street about the third week of April, and it was only a few days longer before Attorney General Black heard from Ellen that her husband planned to return so soon. Black, who had obviously expected the task to consume many months, wrote impatiently to Stanton about the confidence he had placed in him, and about the consequences—to Black as well as to Stanton—of his failure. "You must succeed," he wrote, "or be able to prove that success was utterly impossible." He made it clear that by coming back prematurely Stanton would let the government down and embarrass Black, who had assured the president of Stanton's tenacity. He demanded that Stanton give him "due and timely notice" before he thought of coming home, but he also appealed to Stanton's pride, adding that President Buchanan ("The Squire," as cabinet members called him) and his advisers "must continue to think that the smartest thing they ever did in their born days was to get you to look after the affairs of the parish."[35]

That last consideration interested Stanton intensely, and he submitted without a murmur when Black's letter arrived. The chronology of their triangular communication leaves the distinct impression that Stanton had told Ellen one thing and Black another—softening Ellen for the long separation by characterizing it as a matter of weeks, although he must already have implied his willingness to meet Black's expectation of a lengthy sojourn on the West Coast. Stanton reminded Ellen that his mission directly affected his "future professional employment," alluding either to his general opportunities to serve as government counsel or specifically to the dozens of California land cases that were already passing through the Supreme Court. He mentioned in particular the familiarity he was gaining with Mexican history and legal traditions, which would prepare him to serve one client or another in that expensive and seemingly interminable litigation. As a subsidiary benefit, he added that the climate appeared to have reduced his asthmatic attacks.[36]

At first he reported that he was working "night and day" on the land cases, telling Ellen that he rose at seven, ate breakfast at eight, and reported at the archives room of the U.S. Surveyor's office at nine, where he worked until five or six o'clock; then he would eat dinner before resuming work in his room at the International House until Eddie implored him to go to bed, at ten or eleven o'clock. He told Watson and Black that he worked ten hours a day in the archives, from 8:00 A.M. to 6:00 P.M., with Lieutenant Harrison, Buchanan, and often Eddie helping him sift through the records; as they put them in order he hired some clerks and bookbinders, but for all his own study of Spanish he still wanted translators. Harrison fairly gushed over Stanton's energy and diligence, remarking to the attorney general that he was "a man indeed in whom is no guile"—a statement with which some of Stanton's later associates would have particularly disagreed. Young Buchanan also praised him as "a kind hearted and companionable man," and twice in quick succession Stanton made certain to apprise the bachelor president, through personal letters, of his favorite nephew's many virtues.[37]

Most of Stanton's labors entailed collecting and organizing the voluminous, scattered archives of the land office, and under Black's instructions he attempted to compile a complete archive of legitimate claims. In his fifth week he, Eddie, and Della Torre ventured to the onetime state capital of Benicia, across the bay, to collect records that American soldiers had deposited there after the conquest, and among those boxes he would find several of the keys to his case against Limantour. More of the dispersed records turned up in San Jose, which had served as the first capital of the state, and Stanton sent Buchanan to Los Angeles to search for documents in southern California.[38]

Bribery of government officials remained common in California: in 1860, another special counsel in San Francisco reported to Black that he could have become independently wealthy that way.[39] If anyone offered Stanton illicit emoluments, then or later, it never came to light, but he did enjoy a little vacation, not to mention employment before the Supreme Court, at the expense of mine owners whose land titles and leases he never questioned. James Eldredge, who was an acquaintance of his and Ellen's (as well as a client in the Fossat-Quicksilver faction of the New Almaden case), had put Stanton in touch with Henry Laurencel—Eldredge's partner in the Guadalupe quicksilver mine near San Jose, which they operated as the Santa Clara Mining Company of Baltimore. That introduction led to an invitation for a four-day excursion around the perimeter of San Francisco Bay. Stanton left with Eddie the day after they returned from Benicia, and Laurencel whisked them down to San Mateo in a two-horse carriage for a night at his house. After breakfast the next morning they continued on to Santa Clara, where Stanton had his first (and perhaps only) glimpse of the immensely profitable New Almaden quicksilver mine, in which Laurencel had once been a partner. Eldredge and his Quicksilver cronies persisted in their efforts to seize New Almaden through court action, and later in the course of that contest both Stanton and Black would realize generous fees themselves. Eldredge also resorted to bribes if necessary, and it did not repel Black when Eldredge admitted as much to him. Within weeks of his sojourn on Eldredge's spread, Stanton submitted a report recommending that Black pursue litigation to wrest New Almaden from its operators, and that suit would eventually eliminate all the competing claimants, delivering the mine to the Quicksilver syndicate in the end.[40]

The Stanton men and their host ate lunch at a hotel in San Jose, passing the heat of the afternoon under the trees there, and that evening they reached the home of Eben Faxon, the superintendent of Eldredge's Guadalupe mines. Faxon had come to California in 1855 with instructions to spy on the New Almaden mine, to hire only Spanish-speaking Mexicans (who would not understand the operators' conversations), and to establish squatter rights over the Guadeloupe property, which then lay between the Santa Clara holdings and New Almaden. He would soon serve his own company's interests and earn an additional government fee himself by aiding Stanton's campaign to seize the competing mine. Faxon put Stanton and his son up for three nights in his picturesque hacienda, and on Monday morning, April 26, Laurencel's carriage took them up the east side of the bay to Oakland, from which they ferried back to the International Hotel.[41]

Back in Washington, the attorney general fought for the rest of the money to pay Stanton and his team of researchers. He warned that one man alone, meaning Limantour, had claimed land worth $10 million or

$12 million, while others demanded property worth nearly as much, with up to $150 million in property at stake throughout the state. The appropriation he had requested was the least his office would need to operate against such extensive claims, he noted, adding that the California land-grabbers had "agents, accomplices, and spies" in the capital waiting to see whether the government would defend itself. Yet even as Congress balked at funding the investigation, it passed laws to aid it. With abundant complaints of forged claims from Californians (in addition to Stanton's suspicions), Black proposed criminalizing the practice: Congress obliged, and eventually relented on the funding, too.[42]

Auguste Jouan had revealed that Limantour's grants were all forged on blank, officially stamped state paper that Governor Manuel Micheltorana had signed years after he left office. In the boxes of documents from Benicia Stanton found letters from Micheltorana to officials in Mexico City, from the same period as the reputed grants, in which the governor complained about the absence of the very stamped paper on which those grants had been forged. Stanton hired a team of transplanted New England "daguerreans" to photograph the documents, including examples of the gubernatorial signatures (both genuine and suspect), and particularly the seals: the seals differed on Limantour's grants from those that could be found in the index of land grants—an index that Stanton also discovered in those dusty boxes of records from Benicia.[43]

The Board of Land Commissioners had certified the Limantour claim, but with all the new evidence District Attorney Della Torre appealed that certification in the federal court for northern California. The trial opened in July of 1858, with Stanton sitting as associate counsel. Pablo de la Guerra, the mayor of Santa Barbara, testified that he had worked at the customhouse from his youth until the American takeover, and knew only one seal to have been used the entire time. Next, Stanton introduced those letters from Micheltorana, dated January 9 and March 15, 1843, concerning the lack of government paper with the official seals anywhere in California, after which he produced the original of one of Limantour's purported grants from Micheltorana—dated in February of 1843, on the sealed paper that was not then available. One witness testified that Limantour had admitted that his grants were all in his own handwriting.[44]

The keeper of the archives for the surveyor general told the court that he could find no evidence of a grant to Limantour, and with Jouan's testimony about the falsified grants the evidence against him seemed complete. The government closed its case against him on September 21, and Stanton presented two days of oral argument in the middle of October. The court sided with the government, and Stanton prepared a 700-page record of the testimony, documents, and photographs in case he had to argue it again before the Supreme Court. More than a year later Black reported to Congress that Limantour had filed no appeal, and would probably never dare to do so. Not all the disputed cases offered such conclusive proof of fraud, but Stanton's successful prosecution of Limantour appears to have prejudiced public opinion against almost anyone who claimed land under Mexican grants.[45]

As the summer of 1858 wore on, Ellen grew impatient for her husband to return, lamenting that he was missing most of the "firsts" in Ellie's development and worrying that he would grow distant from the child—if not from her mother. Loneliness, both for the society of her husband and for the social schedule she could hardly keep without him, would have been aggravated by the particularly intense heat and humidity of Washington that summer, which she found unbearable. Sensing her worsening disquiet, Stanton tried to reassure her with an increasing volume of reflection on the joy of returning to her arms, where he might lie with his head on her bosom and bask in her "sweet & gentle love." He insisted that she and their daughter mattered more than anything in the world to him: his son by Mary remained conspicuously absent from those professions of family devotion, and Stanton never—ever—mentioned Mary, as though Ellen were a little tender about the dead wife's idealized image. His frequent, fervent allusions to Ellen's love seemed designed as much to solicit her affection as to reflect his confidence in it, but at least Ellen had no cause for the jealousy that serial excuses for extended absences would have provoked in other wives: a philanderer would hardly have taken his teenage son along. Yet, in contrast to Mary's understanding and admiring attitude toward his wish to make a name for himself, Ellen clearly accused him of putting his own ambition ahead of his family responsibilities, for he denied that very suggestion in an August letter. Barely four months after he had reminded her how directly the California assignment would influence his "future professional employment," he reversed course in the face of his wife's simmering displeasure, denying that he had traveled so far and remained away so long for the sake of personal ambition. Contradicting his earlier statements to her and to Peter Watson, as well as his response to Black's stricture about staying on until the job was done, he told her that he had only come to California because he thought she would be happier if his health were improved by the climate.[46]

Certainly he had not changed his mind about the importance of the California mission to his career, yet in his zeal to soothe Ellen's anxiety and anger he had probably forgotten that he had already recited those career considerations to her. Her pleas nevertheless exerted some influence, because when the Limantour claim went to court Stanton asked Black whether he might take the steamer scheduled to leave September 20, by which time that case should have been concluded. Black sympathized, but he preferred Stanton to stay on during the government's challenge to the grants behind the New Almaden mine, cajoling him with the opinion that Stanton's presence would add great strength to the presentation of the case. Besides, his extended stay would allow him to compile a complete record for the inevitable Supreme Court appeal—similar to the 700-page volume he filed for the Limantour suit. Reluctant as always to disappoint a superior, Stanton complied. Instead of leaving on September 20, he wrote Ellen on the night of September 19 to convey the depth of his regret that he could not yet start for home.[47]

The title behind the lease on the New Almaden quicksilver mine seemed less obviously fraudulent than Limantour's claim to the gems of San Francisco Bay, but it was not without its challengers. The New Almaden mine abutted the land of the Santa Clara Mining Company, owned by Stanton's friend Eldredge and his California partner. The ownership of the mining rights depended, first, on the precise location of the Castillero, Berreyesa, and Larios grants and, second, on the validity of those various grants. Disputes over boundary descriptions served as red herrings, as they may have been designed to do, and those side squabbles clouded the issue of validity. Stanton must have suggested to Black that all the grants might be fraudulent, for the attorney general instructed him to take immediate steps to "give the Government possession of" the mine, or "at all events to secure the proceeds," which amounted to more than a million dollars worth of mercury a year. Under Black the federal government had appealed the land commission's decision certifying the Castillero and Berreyesa grants, and Black informed Stanton the appeal would not be dismissed in light of Stanton's report. He assured Stanton and Della Torre that they had "full authority" to do whatever was necessary "to vindicate the government's rights in the New Almaden quicksilver mine."[48]

Working on Stanton's advice, which was based on Black's wishes, Della Torre asked for an injunction to halt the extraction of quicksilver until it could be determined whether the land actually belonged to the government. Noting that none of the original grantees came forward to deny the various accusations of fraud, the circuit court issued the injunction, and production stopped at the richest mercury mine in the country. Eben Faxon, Stanton's host and the superintendent of James Eldredge's other mine, acted as an agent of the district attorney a week later when he submitted a report on New Almaden's capacity and facilities. With New Almaden closed, the price of quicksilver soon soared, as did the profits of Eldredge's company.[49]

Henry W. Halleck, a former army captain, a lawyer, and the superintending engineer for Barron, Forbes & Company, had already been examined at length in the case before Stanton entered it. As a witness for the mine operators Halleck corroborated the Castillero claim, which Stanton sought to discredit by impeaching Halleck's evidence and testimony. Stanton may not have really believed Halleck guilty of perjury, but he handled the operators and their allies quite roughly, at least for dramatic effect in the courtroom, and District Attorney Della Torre did insinuate that Halleck must have been lying. When Stanton and Halleck came together under different circumstances three years later, Stanton thought first of the unpleasantness over the New Almaden case.[50]

More than two years after Stanton left California, the federal court in San Francisco confirmed the Castillero grant, thereby rejecting the arguments and evidence Stanton had submitted. That decision jeopardized James Eldredge's plan to take over New Almaden through the Fossat suit, but by then Stanton had become attorney general in Buchanan's cabinet, and he acted immediately to counter the decision: the moment he heard the rumor of a ruling in the case—and with no chance to confirm it, let alone to read the decision and learn the rationale behind it—Stanton instructed his successor as the special counsel for California land claims to file an appeal against the Castillero claimants. Whether he intended it or not, that restored Eldredge's hopes.[51]

There were those who suspected high-level corruption in the selective prosecution of land claims in California—like the controversial Santillian claim, encompassing half of modern San Francisco. Herbert Bancroft, an early California historian, described that case speeding through the land board and the federal district court "almost unchallenged, to a complete confirmation," until Black appealed it to the Supreme Court and had the original decision overturned. Bancroft quoted a judge who insisted that the attorney general—meaning Black, it seemed—was "deeply interested" in that claim. California newspapers published while Stanton made his way home pointed to both him and Black.[52]

Suspicions of corruption clung particularly to the New Almaden mine because of the involvement of Stanton and Black on both sides of the case. At one time or another they each represented the Quicksilver camp that coveted New Almaden, and as agents of the government they challenged the Castillero and Berreyesa claims, thereby benefiting the covetous Quicksilver investors they served privately. Switching sides in the case left them looking inconsistent, as well as devious, because they had to pursue contradictory lines of argument to represent antagonistic parties. While suing to seize the New Almaden mine for the government, Black and Stanton had to declare that it did not lie on a valid grant of land, but Fossat's interests required an assertion that it lay on the valid Larios grant, and they had to float between those incompatible positions as the needs of their different clients dictated. Nor did it pass without notice that Black had appointed Stanton as his well-paid special counsel to conduct the early stages of the New Almaden suit, and that as attorney general Stanton later appointed

Black to a similar position, to carry it on. In their public capacities, both of them also continued to file government appeals to every decision in the case until their private clients in the Fossat faction won. No documentary evidence suggests active collusion between Black and Stanton, but Stanton's close relationship with the unscrupulous Eldredge, and his indirect services to Eldredge's interests as special counsel, create a distinct appearance of impropriety. That was enough for a public that had grown cynical over the proliferation of corruption in public life.[53]

Neither is there any indication that Stanton accepted any lavish gifts from the Quicksilver interests beyond a few days of vacation, but over the next three years he would earn the largest fees of his career, and mostly as counsel in the California cases. Rather than suggesting that he had taken a direct bribe, as some associates later insisted, his Quicksilver connection probably reflected his career-long preference for serving the wealthiest or most powerful men within his sphere for whatever legitimate fruit those associations might yield. No breakdown of Stanton's income by client has ever surfaced, but excessive fees shrouded a great deal of that era's graft.[54]

In October, having made his motion for an injunction against the New Almaden mines, Stanton again promised Ellen that he would start for home on the next steamer, early in November. The day before that ship sailed, he wrote once again to explain that he still could not go—this time because Eddie had come down with a fever. Eddie's fever had actually begun several days before Stanton's October promise, but it had not abated over the two intervening weeks, and they dared not leave. Hearings were being held just then over the appointment of a receiver for the New Almaden mine, and with nothing else to do Stanton likely dropped in on them. He was fully aware how lucrative the case would be: it would later yield Black, in particular, a small fortune in private fees.[55]

In the wake of each new shattered expectation of his return Ellen replied with expressions of increasing "pain and disappointment," as her husband acknowledged it, but after seven months of continued extensions and delays her impatience may well have been approaching the boiling point. Still, the accumulating consequences of her serial disappointments did not dissuade him from sending new assurances of his impending departure by each of the steamers that left for Panama City on the fifth and twentieth of every month. The first letter in each packet would insist that the next ship would bring them home, while the last letter bore a new and more abject apology beneath the San Francisco dateline. At each additional postponement he tried to console her with an assessment of how much his own health had improved during his long absence.[56]

Just as the November 20 steamer was about to leave, Stanton wrote Ellen that Eddie's fever had persisted for thirty-two days, and that the doctors had considered him in grave danger until the thirty-fourth day: he added that the boy wished to send Ellen his love and felt terribly guilty at "being the cause of detaining me." They should finally be able to leave by December 5, he predicted, or at least by December 20, but Christmas found them still at the International Hotel, and no letter survives to offer an excuse for them missing both those deadlines. Not until January 5, 1859, did they board the *Golden Age* with their trunks, bags, and an assortment of souvenirs from the beaches. Stopping at Acapulco on January 14, they reached Washington by the first weekend of February, two weeks short of a year from the day they left—and fully four times as long as Stanton had told Ellen he would be away. His prolonged absence had evidently created no serious rift, or at least not a permanent one. His persuasiveness may have served him as well at home as it did in the courtroom, and within two months Ellen was pregnant again.[57]

The California mission fully met Stanton's expectations for enhancing his "future professional employment." He came home forty-four years old, well established in the national capital, and closely connected with the nation's leading men, which ought to have eased his old terror of poverty. Lingering diffidence over his incomplete education, for which his brash and brusque manner may have reflected overcompensation, should also have begun to fade with his growing prominence in the legal profession. Still, his intimacy with the Quicksilver syndicate betrayed an uncertainty about himself, as though he doubted his capacity to survive without rich and powerful patrons, however doubtful their integrity.[58]

6

AN HONORABLE MURDERER

Samuel F. Butterworth, a creature of New York's Tammany Hall, had enjoyed more than one appointment at the hands of Democratic presidents, beginning with the post of U.S. Attorney for the northern district of Mississippi, under Martin Van Buren. President Pierce had made Butterworth superintendent of the New York Assay Office, and Buchanan had decided to retain him. Butterworth appears to have learned the value of various minerals from the new state of California, and especially the New Almaden mine, and eventually he allied himself with the Quicksilver syndicate's attempt to seize that property. That was probably what had brought him to Washington toward the end of February, 1859. During his visit to the capital he lodged at the home of California's senior senator, William Gwin, as did former senator and Treasury secretary Robert J. Walker. Gwin in particular was fiercely pro-Southern: both were Democrats who had served in Congress from Mississippi during Butterworth's term as U.S. Attorney there, and both were involved in the Fossat camp's quest for ownership of New Almaden.[1]

Late on Sunday morning, February 27, a messenger came to Gwin's house with an urgent note for Butterworth signed by his old Tammany friend, Congressman Daniel Sickles, asking that he come to the mansion Sickles rented on the west side of Jackson Square, within sight of the White House. Butterworth learned from a distracted Sickles that his wife, Teresa, who was barely half her husband's age, had confessed to an affair with Philip Barton Key—Washington's district attorney and the son of Francis Scott Key. Sickles had coerced Teresa into writing an extraordinarily detailed confession, requiring her to add a disclaimer denying any duress from him, and he had asked the servants to endorse it—a strangely precautionary demand for someone in such allegedly extreme agitation as Sickles. In Butterworth he had summoned an especially friendly witness, who advised him that he had but one "honorable" recourse. Shortly after this—according to the story that Sickles and two sympathetic observers survived to tell—Key appeared in Jackson Square and signaled the house with his handkerchief before strolling away toward the National Club, on the other side of the square.

Butterworth later denied that he conspired with Sickles, but he walked outside and had a few pleasant words with Key while Sickles armed himself with some pistols and followed by another route. Sickles came upon them from the opposite direction, and Butterworth retired while Sickles bellowed that Key had cuckolded him, firing one pistol after another until he had inflicted a fatal wound. Bystanders carried the unarmed Key into the club, where he soon died.[2]

Sickles reported the shooting to Attorney General Black, who lived a few blocks away on Franklin Square. Then he returned to his own home—an extravagant manse clearly beyond the reach of a congressman's salary. There city authorities arrested him, lodging him that afternoon in the decrepit city jail at Fourth and G streets.[3]

The coerced confession of the errant wife, the requested presence of a sympathetic witness, the convenience of multiple loaded pistols, and the teamwork in chasing down the victim all suggested premeditated murder. When initially asked whether he had anticipated Key being shot, Butterworth avoided a direct answer; later he claimed that he did not expect violence that day, and did not think Sickles left the house armed, but he contradicted himself when he excused his failure to interfere on the belief that both men were armed. According to Butterworth, Key had reached ominously inside his coat, suggesting that Sickles was guilty only of well-prepared self-defense, but all Key produced was a pair of opera glasses. Reading New York newspaper reports of the murder from his Gramercy Park parlor, George Templeton Strong found it difficult to sympathize with Sickles because he was such an "unmitigated blackguard," but he thought even worse of Butterworth: with no reason for vengeance or anger himself, Butterworth had nevertheless gone out to delay Key until his murderer could overtake him, and Strong felt that Butterworth "clearly deserves hanging." A friend of Key's deplored the adultery, but pictured Sickles waiting in ambush for his victim.[4]

Stanton, just back from California, probably learned about the shooting before nightfall. His rented house lay only four short blocks from the jail, and nearer still to the courtroom in City Hall. Key's home, where the body was eventually brought, sat even closer by, right on C Street. Two days after the shooting Stanton met with President Buchanan, who had bestowed an avuncular affection on Sickles since taking him to London as a secretary in the American legation during the Pierce administration. That visit to the White House on March 1 may have included the question of whether Stanton would act as counsel for Sickles: the direct or indirect involvement of Butterworth, Walker, and Black in the tragedy could have spawned the idea of hiring the lawyer who was proving so effective in California cases like the New Almaden claim.[5]

Sickles had already retained the services of some of his more illustrious New York colleagues, who happened to be among the nation's best criminal lawyers. The lead attorney, James T. Brady, had a reputation for extreme courtesy, profound logic, and a winning record in capital cases, while John L. Graham's forte seemed to be mesmerizing oratory. Thomas Francis Meagher, a bibulous young Irish revolutionary, acted as consulting counsel and general cheerleader for Sickles. For local talent, in addition to Stanton, the team added Daniel Ratcliffe, Allen Magruder, Samuel Chilton, and former congressman Philip Phillips, while the highly regarded Reverdy Johnson appeared a few times to offer advice. The *Washington Evening Star* observed that Sickles was collecting a lot of lawyers for a man whose defenders did not expect the jurors to leave their box before acquitting him.[6]

The defendant had good reason to expect mercy from a jury. The *New York Herald* thought the public would be "almost unanimous" in its sympathy with him, and doubted that a grand jury would indict him. Even if he were indicted, *Harper's Weekly* presumed that no jury would convict him of manslaughter if the adultery were proven, which it considered a foregone conclusion. Horace Greeley's *New York Tribune* reflected that with Key dead, the true story behind the affair might never come to light because all the survivors had "a common and obvious interest in putting him as deeply in the wrong as possible."[7]

In private, some doubted that Sickles had suffered from the sudden passion that he claimed, and a few newspapers insinuated as much. The curiously precise confession he extracted from Teresa certainly implied calculation, and it seemed even more suspicious because the illicit romance had been a matter of long-standing Washington gossip, which had already sparked one confrontation between Sickles and Key, months before. It was more than hinted at the time that he had allowed his beautiful young wife to associate freely with other men for the sake of his own political and social connections, but those were the mutterings of scrupulously respectful advocates of civil order and propriety, who inhabited the loftier strata of society: they might deprecate Key's conduct, but they also pitied him and Teresa. Contemporary attitudes toward women suggest that working-class people, and especially men, more often sided with Sickles to the extent of condoning the murder, or applauding it: one Washington visitor confirmed as much, later, by his observations of talk on the street and sympathetic behavior in the courtroom.[8]

It was this plebeian response that the defense team planned to capitalize upon, striving to bring Sickles to trial before that sympathy dissipated. Barely three weeks after the murder Stanton and most of the Sickles defense team trooped into City Hall in the belief that the grand jury would hand down an indictment that day. They were disappointed, but two days later Stanton returned with a motion asking the prosecutor to inform him when the indictment would come, and Robert Ould, who had stepped up to the position of district attorney when Key died, presented the indictment that afternoon. Stanton then started pressing for an immediate trial, requesting it for Monday morning, March 28, only four days away. Ould said he could not be ready so soon, but Stanton replied that Ould had the benefit of witnesses who were all close at hand, and complained that delaying the trial might cost Sickles the testimony of defense witnesses who had to leave town. No doubt hoping to have Sickles judged before indignation over the extramarital affair subsided, Stanton contended that justice in the case required as early a trial date as possible.[9]

It may have been Stanton's idea to try the case in the newspapers, as well. The *Washington Star* had already chastised the *New York Times* for attempting to justify the killing with false statements surrounding the case. News coverage was so extensive that reporters were certain to monitor the trial closely, and their stories would further inflame public opinion. The defense strategy would consist entirely of reversing the relative roles of Sickles and Key by putting the dead man on trial for having made a victim of the defendant, and the New York press prepared the public for just such an emotional appeal.[10]

The *New York Times* illustrated that tactic again on the morning the trial opened, effectively pushing for an acquittal when the editor supposed that no jury had ever before been asked to judge a man who killed his wife's paramour, "that seducer being the guest of his roof, the declared friend of the husband, and the assumed protector of the wife." The paper noted with apparent approbation that the threshold for juror bias was much lower in Washington than it was in New York.[11]

A crowd packed the courtroom on the morning of April 4 for the first day of jury selection, during which the opposing counsel clashed over the differences in class perceptions of the crime. For three days a parade of prospective jurors were turned away, disqualified over admitted bias—for nearly everyone in Washington had heard of the shooting and had formed an opinion—but finally on April 6 one man said he felt no bias and had made no prejudgments. Ould then asked him how much property he owned, and the man said he was worth "less than nothing," at which point Ould asked to have him disqualified. Stanton, who took the lead in jury selection for the defense, leaped to object, and Ould explained that jurors in the District of Columbia were required to meet a minimum property qualification of $800. Stanton knew that jury sympathy with his client would increase as the net worth of the jurors decreased, and he bellowed that he had been practicing law in Washington for fifteen years without ever hearing of that restriction, charging Ould with having dredged it up out of "oblivion." Ould replied that the rule had been in place since before the District was carved out of Maryland, and Judge Thomas Crawford evidently sustained him.[12]

As the trial progressed, reporters quickly deduced that Ould was outmatched as well as outnumbered, but he did not have to work entirely alone. The Key family had hired an attorney to join the prosecution, much as the Allegheny factory barons had hired Stanton to help convict their rioting operatives. They chose James M. Carlisle, with whom Stanton had worked in 1845 in that very courtroom, before the very same judge, to free Caleb McNulty.[13]

At the end of the first day of juror examination, Stanton complained that the dock where Sickles sat stood too far in the rear of the courtroom for his attorneys to communicate with him, or for him to hear the proceedings in so dense a crowd, and he asked that the accused be allowed to join them at their table. Judge Crawford refused, but so persistently did Stanton argue the point that the judge finally agreed to have carpenters move the dock itself closer to the front of the room. The next day the well-dressed defendant sat much closer to his lawyers, the judge, and—perhaps most important of all—the jury. When the trial began Stanton started hovering right alongside his client, ostensibly to consult with him, but they were still so far back from the bench that when Stanton addressed the court he often had to shout to be heard.[14]

The jury that finally gathered consisted of a dozen respectable farmers, businessmen, and tradesmen, but not a single "gentleman" in the occupational sense. Ould opened the prosecution's case with an account of the shooting, questioning a number of eyewitnesses for their recollections of the incident. Those witnesses included Cyrus McCormick—who, lodging in an adjacent house during one of his patent-infringement cases, had watched from a second-story window as Sickles fired the fatal bullet. Stanton vehemently objected when Ould called several of those same witnesses back to the stand to have them reiterate that Key had been unarmed. The prosecutor lingered on the point that the two men were only a few feet apart when Sickles fired each shot, and that he ignored the most plaintive pleadings of his victim.[15]

Ould closed the prosecution's case with surprising speed, which helped to fuel accusations that he had deliberately fumbled the case. Defense attorney Daniel Ratcliffe rose to demand why Ould had not at least called Samuel Butterworth as a witness: intent, probably, on impressing the jury with an air of disorganization and confusion on the part of the prosecution, Ratcliffe noted that Sickles had been jailed on Butterworth's testimony. Ould replied that Sickles's lawyers knew very well why he had not called Butterworth, suggesting that he would like to have done so. Butterworth had been conspicuously absent from Washington since the shooting, and he was such a close friend of Sickles's that Ould might have considered him a better witness for the defense than for the prosecution, but there hovered a suspicion that President Buchanan had played a part in hobbling the prosecution. Sickles had been a favorite of Buchanan's during the mission to Great Britain, and it was the president who appointed—or removed—the U.S. Attorney for the District of Columbia.[16]

John Graham opened for the defense with a long, emotional speech in which he argued that a man has as much right to protect himself from an adulterer as from a burglar. At one point he took up a book that he identified as *Dean's Medical Jurisprudence* and recited a passage that cut to the core of the defense team's strategy: the "state of frenzy" argument. "If a man's will is maddened," Graham read, "it cannot be contended that he is a free moral agent." He spoke for much of Saturday afternoon and Monday morning, and when he finally desisted Brady started calling a cavalcade of character witnesses, many of whom testified that the defendant appeared to suffer intense anguish and agitation on the day of the killing.[17]

Robert Walker, the former senator, secretary of the treasury, Kansas governor, and aspiring owner of the New Almaden mine, took the stand on April 12. He, Senator Gwin, and Butterworth had all been at the Sickles home just after the shooting, and Walker described the defendant shrieking, weeping, and wailing; Sickles had emitted some perfectly inhuman sounds, Walker added, and he seemed to grieve especially over the disgrace that had been visited on his daughter. As Caleb McNulty had done in the same room years earlier, Sickles responded as though on command with a renewal of that tearful demonstration, collapsing in the dock with violent, heaving sobs. Stanton, who had been standing beside Sickles, shouted to the judge for a recess so his client could compose himself. "Certainly," said the judge, and two Tammany Hall acquaintances leaped up to take their friend by the arms as he staggered slowly out of the room, followed by his father, while the spectators and members of the jury stared, or brushed away a few tears of their own.[18]

Stanton may have hoped for another lachrymal performance that day when his colleagues tried to introduce the confession Sickles had had the foresight to badger out of Teresa, but Judge Crawford disappointed them. Ould objected that the confession amounted to the wife testifying for her husband, which was forbidden within the District, and Crawford concurred. Not to be robbed of that wrenching testimony on behalf of their client, the defense lawyers allowed a copy of the confession to make its way into the newspapers the following day, in case anyone (including jury members) still doubted whether Teresa and the murder victim had been intimate with each other. In addition to publishing the text of the confession, *Harper's Weekly* also produced an enlarged copy of it in facsimile form.[19]

The defense wanted to call the owner of a little house on Fifteenth Street where Key and Mrs. Sickles were wont to meet, but Ould objected that the witness could not testify under District law because he was black. Again the judge agreed, but the defense seemed satisfied to arouse the prejudice of the jury with the race of Key's landlord, which might throw an even more unseemly light on his philandering. Locksmith Jacob Wagner admitted changing the lock on the Fifteenth Street house a week after the killing, under the eye of Key's brother-in-law, and Stanton asked if the prosecution had taken part in this "destruction of evidence." That raised an angry objection from Carlisle, but in a blaring voice and violent manner Stanton accused the prosecution of a "monstrous" attempt to suppress evidence in its zeal for the defendant's blood. Stanton's scornful sneer at "private prosecutors" seemed aimed at Carlisle, whom the Key family had hired, although Ould interpreted it as an affront to himself. Judge Crawford reprimanded Stanton, who apologized for having to shout, but Crawford warned him that the nature of his question had inflicted more offense than the volume of his voice.[20]

With Stanton "looking thunderbolts" at him, Ould denied the allegations and denounced them as a "disreputable rant," and he characterized Stanton as the defense team's "bully and bruiser." Indeed, the reporter for the *Washington Star*, in recalling Stanton's performance in the McNulty trial, observed that "his weapon in attack is more the sledge hammer than the rapier," and the correspondents for two other newspapers described Stanton's "sledge-hammer earnestness." Remarking that Ould would evidently rather send Sickles to the gallows than allow exculpatory testimony from a witness of the wrong color, Stanton cited a parallel North Carolina case in which the court gave the defense a chance to prove the innocence of a black defendant by allowing evidence similar to that excluded in the Sickles trial: all he wanted, Stanton added, was for his client to be accorded the rights granted to a North Carolina slave. Carlisle countered by observing that his learned opponent seemed to be making an antislavery speech. Stanton disavowed any such intention, and to convince the jury of his soundness on the subject of slavery he replied that the blood of slaveholders filled his own veins, through his paternal ancestors in North Carolina and his mother's family in Virginia.[21]

Perhaps remembering antislavery hints Stanton may have dropped during their 1845 collaboration, Carlisle said he hoped the courtroom stenographers would take down that statement, too, so it might be included in Stanton's biography when it came to be written, along with the doctrine of justifiable homicide that he now favored for his client. Stanton shot back that a defense of homes and families would stand as the proudest legacy he would convey to his children. This ringing assertion brought a thunder of stamping feet from the audience, the feelings of which were probably not lost on the jury.[22]

The judge sustained Ould's objection, but a series of white witnesses reported watching the lovers over the autumn and winter. A busybody named Nancy Brown, who had noted the couple each time they entered and exited their rendezvous on Fifteenth Street, gave Sickles another chance to demonstrate how deeply his wife's infidelity had affected him. Stanton, who still stood within whispering distance of his client, called to the judge again as Sickles burst into tears, asking that he be allowed to leave the courtroom while Mrs. Brown testified: it was simply too much for the defendant to bear. The next day Sickles broke down again when another of his friends testified, and again Stanton brought the attention of the judge—and the jury—to the uncontrollable agitation of the wronged husband. By means of such histrionics Sickles testified to his extreme mental distress without risking the danger of cross-examination on the stand.[23]

On February 27 Ould called some witnesses who refuted the portrait of a crazed Dan Sickles. Abel Upshur, a Treasury Department official who had seen Sickles on the day of the murder, considered him quite self-possessed. Even a friend and near neighbor testified that the defendant had seemed "extremely calm" that day.[24]

The reporting of the proceedings foretold the eventual outcome, to the sorrow of more staid readers. Benjamin Brown French, a perennial Washington officeholder who knew Key, regretted the depravity of "frail humanity" and reflected that while the defense attorneys attempted to prove temporary insanity they had actually proven that Key and Teresa had been subject to a more tenacious variety of the same derangement. Philadelphian Sidney Fisher, who considered Sickles "a low democratic politician" and Key "a gentleman by birth & education," dismissed the trial as a sham undertaken to certify the prejudice of popular opinion. George Templeton Strong recorded his disgust with the popularity of the Sickles defense several days before the jury reached a verdict. "As the law now stands," Strong observed, "Othello can shoot Cassio at sight and be sure of acquittal, because he did so on his best information and belief derived from Iago."[25]

All the testimony and evidence had been submitted by Saturday, April 23, and on that morning a bigger crowd than usual poured into the courtroom while one of the most vicious gales in memory whipped through Washington. The week had been unusually cold and raw, with several days of sharp, chilling rain, but on Saturday the wind tore down tree limbs and swamped schooners anchored in the harbor. Senator Stephen Douglas settled into a seat to hear the summations of the opposing counsels. Speaking for the prosecution, Carlisle raised the specter of social chaos if citizens were allowed to exact their own vengeance, and insisted that the defense had failed to prove that Sickles was insane at the time of the murder. That, he concluded, gave the jury no choice but to find the accused guilty of premeditated murder.[26]

Stanton's duties thus far had consisted of shouting objections, demeaning the prosecution, acting as drama coach, and bringing the greatest possible attention to his client's emotional breakdowns. Summing up for the defense, he argued that protecting one's domestic harmony meant more than the recognized principle of self-defense because the marital bond was more important than life or property. Since the law of the District of Columbia prescribed no redress, Stanton said, the victim of adultery had no choice but to "protect himself." Stanton boldly portrayed Sickles as the heroic protector of his daughter and "the mother of his child," and characterized Key's death as "a cheap sacrifice" toward that end. At first Stanton departed from the claim of momentary insanity to suggest that Sickles had obeyed a moral compulsion to save his soiled wife from the lecherous Key, whose charms had dragged her daily through the streets to "gratify his lust." He conjured the image of Key signaling to Teresa in front of the house, "drawing her from the side of her child . . . , from his roof, from his presence, from his arm, from his wing, from his nest." Catching him "in that act" justified the killing, Stanton proclaimed, obviously suggesting that it was tantamount to catching him in "the" act, and he implied that society should approve of the summary execution, rather than simply forgive it. Resorting to the emotional appeal he always made when law or logic worked against him, Stanton even called on "the Lord who watches over the family" to send the bullet unerringly to its target, and the applause that punctuated his remarks betrayed their effectiveness. Such arguments, Stanton knew, easily swayed men of modest means and education, like the jurors. The same strategy prompted him to attack the precedent on which the prosecution had demanded a conviction—the "Manning" case, in which a British husband had been punished for killing his wife's lover. Stanton stigmatized it as a relic of Stuart England, when "courtiers and corrupt men . . . might pursue with impunity the wives and daughters of the people."[27]

Stanton had wandered far from the temporary-insanity defense, so on Monday, the morning after Easter, James Brady resurrected that subject, leaning heavily on those tearful performances Sickles had offered in the courtroom more than a week before, when witnesses reminded him of the circumstances that had supposedly cost him his reason.[28] To this Ould blandly replied that while adultery was "a horrible thing," the court had been convened to try Sickles for murder. Because the homicide itself was not denied, he pointed out that the jury's only recourse was to decide between premeditated murder and manslaughter—which might have been appropriate had Sickles caught his wife literally in the commission of adultery.

The evidence instead demonstrated premeditation, he said. As for the ploy of temporary insanity, he mentioned how easily and readily a man might pretend to be deranged if he were on trial for his life. With that he ended the District's involvement in a case that evidently "gave him the headache," as one reporter said of the lackluster prosecutor. The judge then addressed the jurors and issued equivocal instructions that left the possibility of acquittal wide open. He even gave them license in that direction: to acquit him, they had to be satisfied beyond a reasonable doubt that Sickles was insane at the time of the murder, but they were also bound to give the defendant the benefit of any doubt they did have. One of the few New York newspapers unfriendly to Sickles snidely remarked that no member of Congress could be convicted of a crime while Judge Crawford sat on the bench.[29]

With no psychiatric profession to conduct an examination and offer a report, the jury had to rely on intuition to decide the question of sanity. In the absence of clinical evidence the defense team had done its best to prove the point through thespian performances, but lawyers on both sides probably understood that the formal defense amounted to nothing more than an excuse for acquittal on the tradition of male marital dominance. Stanton had said as much: the body of a man's wife belonged to him, and he had the right to defend it with lethal force. That attitude played well among men who rarely wore collars on their shirts, and no betting man would have put money on Sickles going to the gallows.

The jury finally withdrew on Tuesday afternoon, April 26, but spent barely an hour sequestered before filing back into the courtroom to announce a verdict of "not guilty." The room instantly descended into chaos, with Stanton so excited that he leaped to thank the jury before the verdict had been recorded. The judge chastised him, and Stanton apologized, but he danced around enough to attract notice, and a few seconds later he shouted a request to discharge the prisoner. City police surrounded Sickles, who was being mobbed, and he emerged from the courthouse a conquering hero, to cheers from a crowd that had gathered on that cool, rainy day. That evening he and his attorneys and friends enjoyed a massive victory celebration at the National Hotel. Back in Baltimore, friends of the Key family meditated bitterly on the "tenderness" and "delicacy" of the prosecution by Ould, whose appointment depended on the president, while Sickles "was a fast friend of the highest officer in the nation."[30]

With the conclusion of this unexpected opportunity for nationwide acclaim—or notoriety—Stanton gathered up his family for a trip back home. The day after the trial ended he wrote to one of the U.S. District Court judges in San Francisco, lamenting the dullness of Washington in what may have been either deep sarcasm or the collapse of manic energy, and he mentioned that he would be taking advantage of the lull to visit relatives for "some weeks." Two days after that they were on their way, with Ellen so newly pregnant that she may not yet have realized it, and on the last day of April they arrived at the Hutchison home, under the incessant canopy of Pittsburgh smoke.[31]

They did not return to Washington until June 19, and so long a sojourn could not have passed without a side trip to Steubenville or Akron, or both, to see his mother, Oella, the Wolcotts, Darwin's widow Nancy, and the troupe of nieces and nephews. Rather than traveling there by steamboat, as in the old days, they would have ridden the Pittsburgh & Steubenville Railroad, in which Stanton then held $5,000 in stock. By the end of June he was back in Washington, preparing reports for Attorney General Black that advised continued prosecution of some of the California land claims—including opposition to the Berreyesa appeal by the operators of the New Almaden mine, whose tenancy Stanton's off-and-on Quicksilver clients wished to see quashed.[32]

Payment for the government service in California came slowly. Twice in May, Eben Faxon had written to inquire about compensation for his report on New Almaden, and it was September before Black approved the balance of Stanton's fee for the West Coast mission, let alone compensation for his further services as special counsel since his return. Still, Stanton hardly wanted for money. Besides his considerable savings and the steady remittance of past-due fees, when he returned to Washington he found several thousand dollars waiting for him from the repayment of Gamaliel Bailey's loan. The belated remuneration for his California work must have reminded Stanton that he did not yet own a home in the capital, where his future evidently lay, and in October he bought a vacant lot from a George-town couple in what the city plan designated as Square No. 248. The long, narrow, 3,675-square-foot parcel lay at what was then calculated as 320 K Street Northwest, between Thirteenth Street and Fourteenth—just across from Franklin Square, and within sight of Black's front door.[33]

Ellen, just entering her third trimester and embracing the prospect of owning her first home with all the enthusiasm of a nesting mother, immediately began drawing up plans for the new house. She finished a sketch within three days, and her husband mentioned it to his father-in-law in a faintly patronizing tone, warning that Ellen wished to impress him with her "architectural skill." He and Mr. Hutchison would talk it over on his next trip to Pittsburgh, Stanton wrote, but he explained that Ellen was hoping her father would oversee the construction according to her plans, if she were "permitted" to proceed. There would presumably have been adequate room in the C Street house for Mr. Hutchison to stay with them during construction, for they had recently sent seventeen-year-old Eddie to Ken-yon for his first semester of college, but the invitation represented a liberal exercise in wishful thinking, because Mr. Hutchison had turned gravely ill and was then thought to be dying.[34]

It would be spring of 1860 before they even began digging the cellar of the new house, and most of another year before they could move in. Their home would rise as a blocky, three-story brick house with a flat roof, a little less than thirty feet wide but considerably longer, with its western side sitting right on the property line, where another house would later share the same wall. The eastern side allowed barely enough room for a narrow, gated walkway. The only exterior ornamentation consisted of arched lintels over the doors and windows, a crenellated cornice, and a slight projection in the central third of the front wall, creating shadow lines on either side of the doorway and the middle windows. Between broad K Street and the front door lay only a narrow sidewalk, although paving and curbing would later constrict the street, yielding a few square yards of lawn and a walkway three or four paces long. Everyone on that block kept their horses and carriages behind their houses, driving them out through alleys running crosswise and lengthwise down the middle of the block, opening on K and L streets. The basement would accommodate a coal furnace that heated the entire house by passive conduction, although multiple flues betokened numerous fireplaces. The comfort in which Ellen was raised and the property values of the Stantons' 1860 census entry attest to more opulent finishing and furnishings on the interior of the home than the plain façade betrayed.[35]

While Eddie began his studies at Kenyon and his father dickered for the K Street lot, events along the Potomac River brought the debate over slavery to a white heat that would not cool until the institution had been extinguished. John Brown—a perpetually scheming, occasionally dishonest, and invariably unsuccessful businessman—had diverted his talents to a murderous brand of social reform late in life, and he devoted his final months to a crackbrained plot to foment a slave revolt in Virginia. Leading nearly a score of equally zealous followers from his Maryland hideout into Harper's Ferry on Sunday night, October 16, Brown seized the United States arsenal and gathered some hostages, whose slaves he conscripted into his little army. By Monday morning word of the revolt was speeding upriver and down, bringing contingents of militia and volunteers who quickly trapped the would-be liberators inside the arsenal. Making a little bastion of the facility's fire station, Brown tried vainly to negotiate an escape while he and his men grew steadily more hungry, thirsty, and exhausted, but dozens of Marines arrived from Washington; Colonel Robert E. Lee of the U.S. Army came up to command them from his plantation opposite Washington, where he was passing a long leave of absence. On the second morning of the insurrection Lee ordered a few of the Marines to attack the station house, where they broke down the doors and killed or captured most of the insurgents.

Brown was captured alive, which only aggravated the ensuing political tensions. Had he been killed, the incendiary effect of his desperate gambit might have been dampened, but he used all of his remaining forty-five days to justify his actions and sanctify the cause of abolition. To the inevitable terror that his conspiracy had spread through the slave South, his hanging on December 2 added the indignant fury of a new crop of Northern admirers, whose tributes helped confirm exaggerated Southern fears of widespread Northern plans to destroy slavery.[36]

Stanton's sister remembered decades later that her brother visited her in Akron the winter after Brown's raid—presumably soon after Brown's hanging, for Stanton appeared regularly in the U.S. Supreme Court from late January through April. Pamphila and her husband, Christopher Wolcott, were both ardent opponents of slavery, but Wolcott was then serving as attorney general for the state of Ohio. He explained to Stanton that he would have offered his services in Brown's defense, except that he feared his official position would worsen the sectional antagonism. According to Pamphila, her brother added that he, too, would gladly have served as Brown's counsel, had he been asked. She may have included that memory to support her obvious effort to associate Stanton with the cause of emancipation, but his choice of clients and his courtroom rhetoric indicated that if he felt any indignation over slavery he still suppressed it. Perhaps he spoke as his sister remembered, but defending Brown need not have implied any sudden zeal for abolition. His animated defense of Dan Sickles did not, for instance, demonstrate that he approved of Barton Key's murder, or that he believed Sickles had been the least bit insane at the time. Then there was the perplexing question of Stanton's candor. Too many of his acquaintances recorded irreconcilable versions of what he had said to each of them in private to avoid the conclusion that he routinely presented the face he thought different people wanted him to wear, at least until his own interests dictated that he declare himself more openly. That unpleasant failing would become most obvious—or at least would be recorded more often—in the last decade of his life, which was then beginning. Subsequent controversies over those embarrassing inconsistencies may have moved his adoring sister to protest all the more earnestly that "Edwin Stanton was never false—to a principle of truth, justice, or honor!"[37]

Pamphila's devoted defense of her brother reflected his devotion to her, as well as to his other siblings and his mother. Family relationships obviously mattered the most to him, but when he had to choose between family members he always sided with the closest relative. Christopher Wolcott's father had bought the last house Lucy Stanton owned before her son moved her into his own home, but the elder Wolcott died before settling the mortgage, and on his mother's behalf Stanton sued the estate for the balance. He hired another firm to prosecute, probably to reduce the family friction, but the petition asked for money for his mother at the expense of his brother-in-law's inheritance, and Stanton showed considerable impatience when his attorneys let the case languish.[38]

The December term of the Supreme Court brought Stanton back to Washington, where he first argued an appeal by bondholders of the Cleveland, Zanesville & Cincinnati Railroad who had won a judgment against the company. Their efforts to seize enough company assets to meet that judgment had been blocked on a technicality by the U.S. Circuit Court in Cleveland, and Stanton appealed on their behalf. It may have been this case that took him to Ohio that winter to visit the Wolcotts, for he lost the appeal and his clients might have wished to continue their suit from a different quarter. He had better luck representing California ferrymen, whose vessel he may have ridden from Oakland to San Francisco at the end of his tour around the bay. A competitor who claimed to have secured an exclusive right to that passage across the bay sought to force Stanton's clients out of business, and appealed an adverse decision from the same San Francisco court where Stanton had prosecuted his land cases. The Supreme Court quickly affirmed the circuit court decision.[39]

Ellen gave birth to their first son on January 12, 1860. They named him Lewis Hutchison Stanton, after his grandfather, who had survived his autumn illness but remained in declining health. Again Ellen endured what was probably postpartum infection, and her husband neglected his office for ten days until she was out of danger. Doctors may have plied her with the deadly "blue mass" so popular at the time, or with some other mercury-laden mixture, for her hair began falling out a few weeks later.[40]

Two of Stanton's pending Pittsburgh cases reached the Supreme Court late in January, occupying him until the end of the month. In February he began representing the United States in dozens of California land cases, at times also representing private clients, so he appeared as often as five and six times a day until the middle of March. A facet of the New Almaden case came before the high court on April 2, but Attorney General Black handled that one himself. In the waning weeks of the term Stanton, the bank-hating Locofoco of the 1840s, prosecuted at least one citizen for the Bank of Pittsburgh.[41]

While Stanton argued the last of his California cases in March, warm debate flared in the House of Representatives over a resolution offered by Congressman John Covode. The House had spent the afternoon disposing of a series of bills for the "relief" of certain citizens (including Samuel F. Butterworth) when Covode, a Pennsylvania Republican, proposed the appointment of a committee to investigate whether the president had used bribes of cash or patronage to influence legislation or elections. The vague language of the resolution raised the hackles of Democrats loyal to Buchanan, who recognized an election-year fishing expedition, but Republicans and alienated Douglas Democrats joined forces to pass it. The hearings dragged on through the spring of 1860, offering one Buchanan enemy after another an opportunity to bring whatever evidence or innuendo would do the most harm. The spoils system had flourished for decades, no matter which party held office, so embarrassing details and inconsistencies inevitably emerged, further dividing a Democratic Party already splintering over how aggressively to protect slavery. The party convened in Charleston, South Carolina, late in April to nominate a presidential candidate, but delegates could not agree on a nominee to replace the discredited Buchanan. The convention's failure cast a deep gloom over the Democratic faithful of official Washington. Writing to Ellen, who was relaxing at her mother's home in Pittsburgh with Ellie and little Lewis, Stanton seemed to share that somber mood. To drive it away, he fled the bachelor confines of the C Street house to join Ellen for a week or two. While in Pittsburgh, he advised his failing father-in-law on the disposition of the considerable estate that would soon be left to Mrs. Hutchison and her children.[42]

As Democratic Party leaders organized a new convention, the president worried that one of his most bitter foes would take his vengeance before the Covode committee, and one Sunday in June, with only a few hours' notice, Buchanan called on Stanton for help. John W. Forney, who had worked for Buchanan's election, expected a generous reward for his services, and he had exploded in fury when Buchanan responded with no more attractive offer than the naval office at Philadelphia or the consulate at Liverpool. "I am no applicant for position at your hands," Forney had fumed in 1857, complaining that after devoting his money and the best years of his life to Buchanan's career he had suffered only "deep and bitter humiliation." Forney later delivered a public speech in which he had proposed assailing Buchanan precisely as the Covode committee was about to do, and the president suspected that Forney would perjure himself liberally. "God knows what he might swear," Buchanan told Stanton. "If he should tell anything like the truth, I have nothing to fear." He asked Stanton to attend the hearing the next morning, and to cross-examine Forney before the committee.[43]

Forney, who had been elected Clerk of the House of Representatives just before that body authorized Covode's investigation, may have proposed the inquiry. Having failed to obtain a suitable cabinet or diplomatic post, or a sufficient share of the lucrative government printing contracts that successive administrations had used to attract editorial support, Forney let fly as Buchanan had anticipated. He told the largely Republican committee that Buchanan had offered him enormous emoluments in return for supporting the Lecompton constitution, self-righteously insinuating that he had been insulted by so inappropriate a suggestion. The Saturday after Forney's appearance, and two days before Democrats reconvened in Baltimore, Covode's committee offered its own profitable morsel for cooperative printers when it ordered immediate publication of 50,000 copies of its report on corruption in the Pierce and Buchanan administrations.[44]

At Baltimore the Democrats fell into worse discord than they had at Charleston, and Southern delegates began bolting in droves to meet in another venue. Those who remained nominated Stephen Douglas, who had lost the South over his opposition to the Lecompton fraud. The rump convention chose Buchanan's vice president, the courtly John C. Breckinridge of slaveholding Kentucky. With that rupture and the further fracture of John Bell's bid as a Constitutional Union candidate, the November election was bound to go to Abraham Lincoln, whose victory would virtually assure secession.

Stanton made no public statement that might have intimated his own preference. To his Democratic friends he grieved over the dissension in their ranks, likely in sincere partisan anxiety, but his only surviving written comments on the 1860 campaign involved his logical prediction that the disintegration of the Democratic Party assured Lincoln's election. His sister later tried to mold that into an expression of Lincoln's acceptability, but others recalled only harsh words from Stanton about the Republican nominee. The recollections of those who knew him or his family concur that, contrary to his later professions of lifelong aversion to slavery, and despite the anger he had expressed over congressional concessions to the South, Stanton gave his support to the obvious candidate of the militant, slaveholding South. Jeremiah Black, with whom he was intimately connected at that time, insisted that Stanton "was out and out for Breckinridge," and "regarded the salvation of the country as hanging upon the forlorn hope of Breckinridge's election." Stanton's boyhood friend John Oliver reported encountering Eddie as he passed through Steubenville on his way back to Kenyon that autumn, and the boy volunteered that his father was going to vote for Breckinridge. When Stanton was confirmed as secretary of war under Lincoln, a Massachusetts newspaper also reported that he had supported Breckinridge in the election. A generation later, Senator John Sherman told a reporter that he had known Stanton since he was "a Breckinridge Democrat." If Stanton did not finally vote for the candidate of slaveholding Southerners, he must have whispered far and wide that he would, or had.[45]

Black said that Stanton bitterly criticized Stephen Douglas for creating the "unreasonable and mischievous schism" in their party, yet that schism had begun with Douglas's tirade against the Lecompton constitution, late in 1857, which Stanton had so cautiously complimented. If Black's later antagonism did not lead him to outright falsehood, Stanton again seemed bent on pleasing two incompatible factions, for Black swore that Stanton had stood with the Buchanan administration throughout the Kansas controversy. As Black remembered it, Stanton sided with Democrats in blaming Republicans for voting down a bill that might have ushered Kansas in as a free state—implicitly suspecting them of deliberately perpetuating the struggle for political capital.[46]

If Stanton did follow the administration line on Kansas, and if he advertised his allegiance to Breckinridge, he may have done so with a touch of calculation. Buchanan favored the young Kentuckian, whose succession he hoped would vindicate his own presidency, and it would have been in Stanton's nature to support "the Squire," with whom he enjoyed such cordial, useful, and occasionally profitable relations. He may have gone too far in that regard, for Buchanan noticed it. In a private note to his niece less than a year after leaving the White House, Buchanan described Stanton as a "clearheaded, persevering & practical lawyer" who was, he thought, "perfectly honest" (presumably in regard to money). Stanton did suffer from certain deficiencies, Buchanan admitted, and he had one particularly troubling habit: "He was always on my side," Buchanan complained, "& flattered me ad nauseam."[47]

Stanton's increasing tendency to associate with the more conservative elements of his party may have inspired Philip Phillips to approach him that summer about forming a partnership. Phillips was a Deep South transplant to the capital: he was born, raised, and educated in Charleston, where he practiced law and served in the state legislature before moving to Alabama. After one term in Congress he settled in Washington, opening a law practice, and he was one of the panel of lawyers retained by Dan Sickles. Fifteen months after that trial, with the rest of the city preoccupied by disunion, Phillips wrote Stanton to propose merging their practices, suggesting that such a union might reap mutual benefits and convenience. The partnership never developed, but as attorney general Stanton would hire Phillips to prosecute at least one government case for him. The two spent enough time together in the final year of the Buchanan administration that in a manuscript memoir, Phillips—who had reason to feel nothing but gratitude to Stanton—wrote that Stanton sounded more sympathetic to the South than Phillips himself was. John Lee, whose brother had married into the less friendly Blair family, told of a night at his house when Stanton argued all the practical advantages that secession might bring.[48]

Ten years later, soon after Stanton's death, James E. Harvey, a Southerner who had served as ambassador to Portugal, mentioned the political soirées that took place in Stanton's house after the slave states started to secede. In that informal salon Stanton seemed the most strident of all in defense of Southern rights, and he waxed so warm on behalf of the departing states that Harvey's friends took him for an outright secessionist. Shortly after Stanton died, Senator Henry Wilson revealed that Stanton had been reporting to prominent Republicans on secessionist leanings within Buchanan's cabinet, and that evidently prompted Caleb Cushing to recall that at the same period Stanton was telling perfectly contradictory stories to two conservative Supreme Court justices. As Harvey told it, Cushing—a Massachusetts man who had also enthusiastically backed Breckinridge—remarked that Stanton must have been a "duplex character." At least a couple of other men, both Southerners, remembered that during the secession crisis Stanton's sympathies had approached actual encouragement for disunion. Biased as they may have been, these men made claims that bore the ring of truth, for Stanton had seemed inclined to present a false face for much of his political life. Like other pairs of antagonistic correspondents after them, Jacob Brinkerhoff and William Allen might have deduced as much before the Mexican War, had they compared their respective letters from Stanton.[49]

That false face may have intruded marginally even in his domestic life. By all indications Stanton remained perfectly faithful in the physical sense, but if all who mentioned it spoke truthfully, he disguised a lingering emotional attachment to his first wife. In September he headed to Steubenville for Oella's wedding to a man from the far side of Ohio, traveling alone again on the excuse that the younger children showed signs of whooping cough. Eddie came from Kenyon to meet him. Together they drove up the hill west of town to the new family lot in Union Cemetery, to visit Mary's grave, and there—according to Pamphila—her brother told Eddie that he wanted to be buried beside Mary. It seems odd that he would confess such a wish to Eddie, whom he encouraged to accept Ellen as his mother. He even referred to her as "your mother" in letters to the boy, and the habit stuck: although Ellen was not a dozen years older than Eddie, he alluded to her as "Mother" even after his father's death. Stanton may have conditioned his son to that practice to save Ellen the aggravation of feeling that she had to compete with the heavenly perfection of her predecessor, but Pamphila would not be the only witness to her brother's wishes for his own burial.[50]

With the term over at Kenyon, Eddie spent several weeks at home in Washington. His father may have joined him for the return trip, in October, for he had court business in Cincinnati about the time classes resumed, but before Stanton left for Ohio he received one of President Buchanan's eternally polite messages asking him to stop by the White House "if quite convenient." Stanton probably exaggerated, later, when he ascribed the summons to the president's desire for constitutional advice, claiming that they engaged in a two-hour discussion on the impending presidential election, its potential consequences, and the chief executive's legal options in the event of secession. Buchanan was greatly preoccupied by the outcome of the vote: barely two weeks before, he had written a Pennsylvania friend to impress upon him the importance of their state's allegiance to Breckinridge—who would surely win the South, but needed New York and Pennsylvania to carry the presidency and avoid Southern secession. In the interim, Pennsylvania's state elections had shown it turning thoroughly Republican, portending ultimate victory for Lincoln. That in turn raised the question of the slave states leaving the Union, and what the federal government could do about it.[51]

Buchanan's note to Stanton came the day after newspapers reported the ominous election results in the Keystone State. It would therefore have been natural for them to discuss the consequences, but it seems improbable that Buchanan originally called him to the White House for his opinion on the subject, as Stanton later said he had. Buchanan's cabinet members observed that "the Squire" took too aristocratic a view of his executive responsibility to seek outside advice before coming to a decision; one of them complained that he only consulted his department heads on subjects that fell within their bailiwicks. Still, part of the Stanton legend (and thus the Buchanan legend) revolves around Stanton's self-serving depiction of his two-hour struggle to convince Buchanan that the president had every right to wield military force against a state that tried to secede, and that it was his duty to do so.[52]

Perhaps their conversation drifted to the topic, and Stanton offered an interesting interpretation of federal authority over refractory states, which may have prompted the president to ask him to reduce his thoughts to writing. Six months after the Sickles acquittal Buchanan did, after all, believe that Stanton "has not his superior as a lawyer in the United States," and a few weeks after his October interview with Stanton the president mentioned to his niece that "Mr. Stanton's opinion is conclusive." The chronological context of this reference implies, faintly, that the opinion may have had something to do with secession, but whether that opinion supported, undermined, or even mentioned the right of federal coercion remains unknown. Any formal brief has disappeared, and no hint of the subject survives except through Stanton's own assertions. Until Buchanan was dead, Stanton seems to have only circulated that story clandestinely, beginning several crucial months afterward, among a coterie of Republicans whose favor he was then courting. Stanton's colleagues in Buchanan's cabinet heard him say nothing in favor of coercion after he became attorney general, although he insisted ever afterward that he had persistently done so. His habit of obsequious deportment before superiors, and Buchanan's reputation for lofty insistence on the dignity of his office, combine to challenge the credibility of Stanton's tale of battling for two hours with his foremost political patron over the federal government's right to keep a reluctant state in the Union by force of arms. Stanton's self-portrait as the heroic Unionist persistently and militantly confronting a hesitant and timid chief magistrate would recur in the stories Stanton peddled privately, some of which later leaked out from various sources and excited the scornful refutation of other witnesses.[53]

Four weeks later, the national election confirmed the accuracy of the portentous Pennsylvania results, and Lincoln secured a plurality of votes without winning a single delegate south of the Ohio River. Within hours the secession chant began to echo, with the loudest reverberations emanating from South Carolina, and at that point President Buchanan did begin casting about for what legal remedies he might exercise against such a threat. He asked Attorney General Black for a formal opinion on his constitutional authority to enforce the laws and defend public property in a state where the federal officers or courts no longer functioned, and whether he could essentially wage war against a state under the Militia Act of 1795. Black replied that he could, certainly, respond with troops at the request of federal marshals who faced resistance too strong for suppression by a posse, and he could use force to repel an attack on U.S. military installations. However, in a state where no federal officials were left to request aid, the federal government had no right to invade. "The States are colleagues of one another," Black wrote, "and if some of them shall conquer the rest, and hold them as subjugated provinces, it would totally destroy the whole theory upon which they are now connected."[54]

This opinion directly contradicted the one Stanton later claimed to have offered Buchanan at the beginning of that month. Black said he showed it to Stanton—who, according to Black, made one minor alteration but otherwise "applauded it enthusiastically." This was the opinion that guided the president in his December message to Congress, and that single emendation to Black's draft may have spawned Stanton's assertion that he wrote some of Buchanan's message. If the recent advice from Stanton that Buchanan had found so "conclusive" had actually supported his right to wield military force against a state, it was exceedingly strange that Black's opposite opinion prompted no question or dispute from either Stanton or the president.[55]

The *Constitution*, a conservative Washington newspaper that some regarded as the administration organ, editorialized against meeting secession with force, and it published similar counsel from both Franklin Pierce and his own former attorney general. Buchanan not only incorporated Black's opinion in his last annual message to Congress but—apparently at the conciliatory behest of Secretary of State Lewis Cass—he emphasized the unconstitutionality of federal coercion. Anticipating with good cause that such an allusion to the government's legal quandary might be received as an invitation to secede, Black objected. A week later his entire opinion appeared in the newspapers, gratifying those who took an even dimmer view of federal power but infuriating those who looked for another Andrew Jackson to crush what they considered abject treason: these latter saw Black as the source of Buchanan's lassitude.[56]

It may not have been long after Buchanan's message came under attack before Stanton began privately circulating the story that he, rather than Jeremiah Black, had written the popular part of the speech, in which Buchanan pronounced the Union perpetual and secession illegal. The more timorous interpretation of federal impotence in the face of secession had been the work of someone else, Stanton averred, for he had belabored the president into adopting the theory that he could wield all the force he wished to subdue a rebellious state. If those to whom he imparted such tales of his own patriotism repeated them accurately, Stanton claimed that the unfortunate changes to the annual address were the work of certain anonymous "traitors," presumably within the cabinet.[57]

As the leader of the only remaining national party, Buchanan had appointed a geographically diverse cabinet. Four of his seven ministers hailed from the slave South, including two—Howell Cobb and Jacob Thompson—from Deep South states that would soon elect delegates to a secession convention. Treasury Secretary Cobb, whose brother was already preaching disunion in Georgia, resigned on December 8, initiating a disintegration of Buchanan's cabinet that distracted him from the political crisis. Once the press started hammering the administration for its restraint, Lewis Cass, the dropsical secretary of state, submitted his own resignation. In his official letter Cass tried to shroud his retreat in an atmosphere of principled unionism by citing petty differences over the reinforcement of the army garrison in Charleston Harbor. As Black obviously suspected, Cass seemed more interested in avoiding his share of public outrage over a policy he had fully supported until it became unpopular, and he did not even deliver his resignation personally. Instead, he presented it to the rather disgusted attorney general, who relayed it to the president on Saturday evening, December 15.[58]

Buchanan used that opportunity to elevate Black to the State Department, and as Black accepted the portfolio he virtually insisted on Stanton for his replacement as attorney general. Stanton had been working on the California land claims right along, Black argued, and he could readily handle the Supreme Court appeals that consumed so much of the attorney general's time. Buchanan acquiesced without hesitation. Black telegraphed Stanton to return immediately from Cincinnati, where he was attending the U.S. Circuit Court before Judge Humphrey Leavitt—for whom Stanton had once expressed such contempt in a letter to Leavitt's rival, Judge Tappan. Leavitt would eventually prove himself more devoted to the preservation of national authority than to protection of the Constitution, and in a private conversation Stanton gratified that firm federalist with so unequivocal a Unionist rant that Leavitt remembered it five years later. Stanton, who may have deduced what Black's telegram involved, boarded a train for the capital as soon as he could wrap up his court business.[59]

THE COURT SPY

A decade after Stanton entered Buchanan's cabinet, Jeremiah Black admitted that some people had tried to caution him about the new attorney general, and one of those people was Black's son-in-law, James F. Shunk, who had gone to California to help prosecute land-grant fraud. Shunk wrote regularly about affairs there, usually sending his dispatches by the biweekly steamer from San Francisco but occasionally via Pony Express, which cut delivery time in half. His letter of November 23, 1860, marked "strictly private," traveled overland by pony at five dollars per half-ounce, reaching Black on December 12. Knowing that his father-in-law was a friend and admirer of Stanton's, Shunk tried to warn him about ill feelings Stanton had left behind in San Francisco, where few remembered him kindly. Nearly two years after Stanton departed, many of those in the force of clerks, translators, and photographers he had employed to overturn the Limantour claim had still not received all the compensation he had promised them. While he was in California, Stanton had also used Black as a scapegoat for unpleasant department policies—including some that Stanton had recommended—and then distanced himself from those unpopular demands with the assertion that he knew Black but little. Shunk, who reminded Black that he had seen Stanton "puff his cigar upon your sofa for an hour at a time without alluding to business," thought this representation of Stanton's "rather disingenuous," adding that one of the other government prosecutors "says in good plain English that Stanton *lies*." With that dim view of the former special counsel so widespread, Shunk cautioned that Black's trust in Stanton was certainly misplaced. Black may have been thinking of Shunk's warning years later, when he recalled somewhat ruefully that he had permitted no "tale-bearer" to undermine his confidence in Stanton.[1]

The next letter Shunk opened from the department came over Stanton's signature: the Senate had confirmed his appointment as Black's successor in the final moments of business on December 20, the very day that South Carolina delegates voted to secede from the Union, and the new attorney general went right to work. Stanton spent much of Christmas Eve writing letters devoted to California cases, most of which involved presumed federal property under the domain of the Interior Department: he began by asking Interior Secretary Jacob Thompson for $5,000 for the special counsel in the northern district, explaining in another missive to the U.S. Marshal in San Francisco how he wanted the money disbursed.[2]

That same day, newspaper headlines heralded two disturbing bits of information from the president's cabinet: the disappearance of $870,000 worth of Indian bonds from the Interior Department, and the planned shipment of scores of heavy guns from the Allegheny arsenal near Pittsburgh to destinations along the Gulf Coast. On Christmas Day further reports connected the vanished Indian bonds to Buchanan's secretary of war, John B. Floyd. A War Department contractor had pressured Floyd into signing receipts for millions of dollars in materials not yet received, and the contractor had accepted the bonds in payment from an Interior Department clerk who was related to Floyd. Taken together, the irregular vouchers, the bonds, and the arms shipment to Southern states made the Virginian Floyd look faithless to his oath in more ways than one. Even if he did nothing worse than exercise extreme imprudence in both cases, so great an appearance of disgraceful conduct ended Floyd's usefulness to the beleaguered administration, and Buchanan looked for his resignation.[3]

Floyd found a seemingly honorable excuse to resign before the week ended. As soon as the ordinance of secession had passed, the governor of South Carolina sent three commissioners to wait on President Buchanan. They arrived on the evening of December 26 and took a house on Franklin Row, expecting to negotiate for the transfer of public property in Charleston Harbor, where the federal government still owned three forts, an armory, and the customhouse. Fewer than six dozen soldiers represented the U.S. Army there, under Major Robert Anderson, who had collected them all at Fort Moultrie, on the northern rim of the harbor. State authorities had not molested any of the forts in anticipation of a peaceful resolution, but Major Anderson had instructions from Buchanan—through Floyd, in fact—to put himself in a position for defense "to the last extremity." He felt vulnerable from an attack by land at Moultrie, and in the dark of night he ferried his little force out to unfinished Fort Sumter, on a man-made island in the middle of the harbor. Seen through the myopic lens of South Carolina hauteur, Anderson's withdrawal to a better defensive position reflected aggression, and that impression influenced the three commissioners who had come to Washington to treat with Buchanan as though they were foreign emissaries. The president had agreed to see them on Thursday, December 27, the day after they arrived, but word of Anderson's removal to Sumter reached him that day and he postponed the appointment until Friday so he could discuss that development with his advisers.[4]

That emergency begat Stanton's first cabinet meeting. He had just said good-bye to his brother-in-law, Christopher Wolcott, who was leaving for New York after a business-related visit, when he returned to his new office and found a message calling him to the White House. As he told it, he entered the cabinet room to see Floyd sitting on a sofa between the front windows, defending his request that Buchanan remove Anderson's garrison from Charleston altogether. Contending that Anderson had acted without orders, and against the president's policy of maintaining the status quo, Floyd insisted that returning Anderson to Moultrie would not be enough to regain the confidence of the South Carolinians. Floyd had not embraced secession, and most of his argument comported with the conciliatory, dilatory policy Buchanan had pursued thus far, but his insistence on complete withdrawal may have had its roots in a wish to pose an impossible demand that might allow him to leave the cabinet on a pretext of principle.[5]

The discussion of December 27 dragged on into the evening. The details of this and the other cabinet meetings in the remaining days of 1860 made their way into the newspapers and into the early history of the secession crisis with a tenor that portrayed James Buchanan as a feeble coward who would have crumbled before secessionist demands but for the unwavering patriotism and moral courage of his new attorney general. After a century and a half, it is now clear that most of those details—so derogatory of Buchanan and so complimentary to Stanton—came from Stanton himself. The standard description of the December 27 meeting entails a violent confrontation in which Stanton apprised the president that his administration was fast losing public confidence, after which he dressed Floyd down over the missing Indian bonds and his deference to the South Carolina secessionists. His tirade ostensibly concluded with the bold assertion that "no administration, much less this one, can afford to lose a million in money and a fort in the same week." That was the story told by Abraham Lincoln's most ambitious biographers of the nineteenth century, John Nicolay and John Hay, and it came directly from Stanton, who related it to Lincoln and Nicolay when they met in that same room, fourteen months later, to make a major general out of Ulysses S. Grant.[6]

It could only have been Stanton who leaked the December 27 cabinet debate to the *New York Times*, using Senator William Seward, Lincoln's senior cabinet designee, as an intermediary. By New Year's Eve the public knew Buchanan's official household had divided over whether to keep Major Anderson at Fort Sumter, to require him to return to Fort Moultrie, or to evacuate his troops from Charleston. In the newspaper accounts, Stanton, Black, and Postmaster General Joseph Holt of Kentucky emerged as champions of the Union, persuading Buchanan to leave Anderson at Sumter. "I found treason with bold and brazen front," Stanton would say of his tardy arrival at the meeting, "demanding the surrender of Fort Sumpter. . . . What followed is now history." In telling Lincoln and Nicolay of that night, he claimed that Buchanan's cabinet "had had high words, and almost come to blows in our discussion over Fort Sumpter."[7]

Stanton's image of himself as the paladin of national unity, smiting secessionists hip and thigh while stiffening Buchanan's resolve, eventually grew too public to go unchallenged. Thurlow Weed, whose Republican coterie Stanton began to court in an early instance of disloyalty to the Buchanan administration, later passed Stanton's self-serving drama on to a British daily, complete with Stanton threatening to resign if Buchanan failed to back Anderson to the hilt; in this version, his outburst elicited similar promises from three other cabinet officers (including one who had not yet even been appointed). The *New York Herald* reprinted the article a few weeks later, causing Stanton some embarrassment when it began circulating among informed Democrats, but that did not deter him from continuing to peddle the story in private. A White House portrait painter claimed that in 1864 Stanton told him of a cabinet meeting in which Buchanan blanched "white as a sheet," and "so much violence ensued, that he had to turn us all out-of-doors." The artist's account was corroborated by Stanton himself, who had not stopped ornamenting the story in 1865, by which time he had reduced James Buchanan to "a miserable coward, so alarmed and enfeebled by the gathering storm as to be mentally and physically prostrated." For his new colleagues in Lincoln's cabinet, Stanton described Buchanan moderating his own cabinet meetings in an old dressing gown, crouching in a corner by the fire and trembling "like an aspen leaf" while Stanton told him he ought to be hanged if he abandoned Fort Sumter.[8]

Augustus Schell, a New York politician, finally asked for confirmation or denial of Weed's hearsay from the surviving members of Buchanan's cabinet. Only Black responded to Schell directly, calling the story "wholly fictitious," but Buchanan indicated that it was false as well, while Thompson later characterized it as "absurd." Holt's account of the cabinet meetings in the closing days of 1860 also contradicted Stanton's saga of bellicose antagonism and resignations offered en masse. According to Black, Stanton never spoke offensively to any of his colleagues in cabinet meetings, and never sought or achieved "ascendancy." Black, who was responsible for Stanton's appointment, later insisted that Stanton always told him he had accepted the post so Black could have two votes instead of one—in nearly the same words that Stanton apparently uttered to Seward, just over a year later.[9]

Buchanan had decided before the next cabinet meeting, two days later, against withdrawing Anderson from Charleston, for by then his decision had prompted Floyd's resignation. Buchanan received it with an air of good-riddance, thinly veiled by his usual courtesy. He gave the War Department to Postmaster General Holt—the second promotion the Kentuckian had accepted at Buchanan's hands since 1857, when the president had saved him from the specter of insolvency with an appointment as patent commissioner. The postal department went to Holt's chief assistant, Horatio King of Maine. That left only two in the cabinet who harbored any patience with secession: Thompson of Mississippi and Philip Thomas of Maryland, who had replaced Howell Cobb at the Treasury Department. With vociferous nationalism Holt decided to stick with the government that had been feeding him for three years, so his elevation to Floyd's place alerted the more insightful insurgents at Charleston that Buchanan had turned against them, however delicate his communications. Secretary Thompson then tendered a letter of resignation, assuming that Holt's appointment betokened the adoption of a hard-line policy on reinforcing Fort Sumter, but Buchanan mollified him by promising that the cabinet would discuss any policy changes before they were implemented, and Thompson withdrew the letter.[10]

The South Carolina commissioners posed Buchanan's next challenge. He met with them on December 28, by which time they had spun themselves into a fury over Anderson's occupation of Fort Sumter, and they presented him with a demand for the complete withdrawal of Anderson's little battalion from Charleston, as Floyd had asked the evening before. Buchanan took their letter, and during the night drafted an official response to their memorial, which created the next crisis of his administration.[11]

The text of Buchanan's draft was lost forever in the tempest that followed, but its basic thrust could be gauged by the reaction of his advisers. He read it to the cabinet on December 29, and it struck Black in particular as offering too much legitimacy to the would-be ambassadors, besides sounding far too timid about the federal property in Charleston, much of which the South Carolina forces had seized after Anderson retreated to Fort Sumter. Buchanan may have offered to order Anderson back to Fort Moultrie, but certainly he did not even suggest removing the garrison from Charleston entirely, for Floyd had already resigned over that. Black objected to Buchanan reiterating his own legal opinion that the federal government had no constitutional right to "coerce" a state into remaining in the Union, which the president had evidently included as a subtle assurance that he planned no hostile action: Black evidently feared that the reference revealed the government's weakness and perhaps invited aggression.[12]

As Black saw it, his own objections, along with those of Stanton and Holt, failed to sway the president, and worry over the consequences kept Black awake most of the night. He was closer to Buchanan than any other cabinet member, owing him the most prestigious offices of his career, and he seemed to expect a Supreme Court nomination before they parted. The notion of challenging the president therefore affected him both personally and professionally, at a time when he was already sliding into economic distress. The next day he nevertheless went to the home of the secretary of the navy, Isaac Toucey, at the earliest hour he dared on a Sunday morning, to tell him that he could not remain in the cabinet if the letter to the commissioners were delivered as written. Then he went to Stanton and repeated his decision, at which Stanton said he would go out with him. Finally Black went to argue his case with the president, and to his surprise Buchanan handed him the letter with permission to revise it as he saw fit, rather than lose his most trusted cabinet officer after three resignations in three weeks.[13]

From the White House, Black strode over to the attorney general's office, where he and Stanton met to compile a list of suggested revisions. Two manuscript copies of the resulting memorandum survive—one of them in Stanton's handwriting and one in Black's—but it was Black's draft that went to the president that evening. Black, after all, held the influence with Buchanan, and it would only hurt the president's pride to learn that the newest member of his cabinet also knew the president's arm was being twisted. Both men would claim to have been the sole author of the suggestions: Stanton did so the same day—but only in a private communication to a prominent Pittsburgh citizen. If that letter is faithfully transcribed, Stanton melodramatically described "treason all around us," hoping that Buchanan might be guided by "the written objections *which I have just prepared.*" Yet four years later, before the authorship of the memorandum became a matter of public doubt, Black incidentally asked Stanton to "recollect how fully you concurred in the opinion I wrote on the subject, before I left the Attorney General's office, and how unreservedly you endorsed another paper afterwards which embodied the same views." Writing to Stanton alone, Black portrayed him as little more than an approving observer to the communications with the South Carolinians. Stanton's letter to his Pittsburgh acquaintance reflected a violation of cabinet confidentiality that would become habitual with him, but it also illustrated his tendency to exaggerate his own participation and influence. Allowing prominent outsiders to believe that his chief had essentially accepted the secession of South Carolina, Stanton predicted that the Union would soon pass beyond saving if the president's course were not reversed.[14]

In another cabinet meeting on New Year's Eve, Black presented the memorandum to Buchanan, who readily assented to all the changes and directed the preparation of a new draft reflecting Black's concerns. Holt considered the amendments mainly stylistic and designed to avoid misunderstanding by the commissioners, rather than a substantive revision that required Buchanan to shift his policy, and he suspected that more anguish had been wasted on it than the situation required. Jacob Thompson found

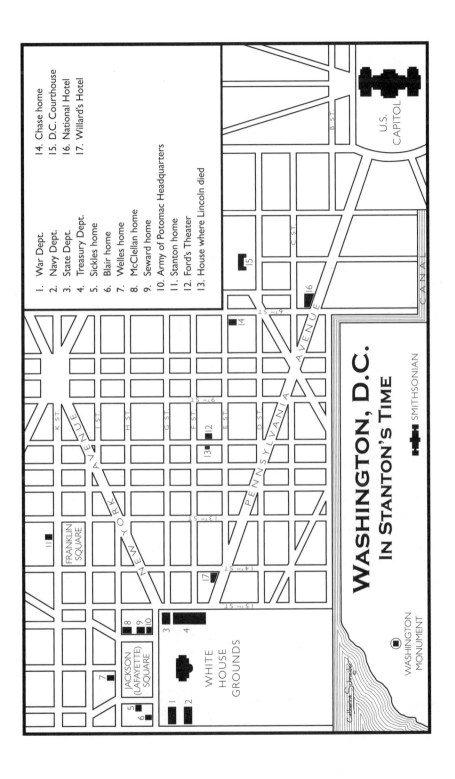

WASHINGTON, D.C.
IN STANTON'S TIME

1. War Dept.
2. Navy Dept.
3. State Dept.
4. Treasury Dept.
5. Sickles home
6. Blair home
7. Welles home
8. McClellan home
9. Seward home
10. Army of Potomac Headquarters
11. Stanton home
12. Ford's Theater
13. House where Lincoln died
14. Chase home
15. D.C. Courthouse
16. National Hotel
17. Willard's Hotel

SMITHSONIAN

WASHINGTON MONUMENT

WHITE HOUSE GROUNDS

JACKSON (LAFAYETTE) SQUARE

FRANKLIN SQUARE

U.S. CAPITOL

NEW YORK AVENUE

PENNSYLVANIA AVENUE

CANAL

K ST.
I ST.
H ST.
G ST.
F ST.
E ST.
D ST.
C ST.
B ST.

15TH ST.
14TH ST.
13TH ST.
9TH ST.
6TH ST.

Catharine Schmidec

the second draft of the letter more radical, perhaps because it lacked the diplomatic acknowledgment or conciliatory gestures implied by the first draft, but Buchanan insisted that the letter would be delivered as it had been revised.[15]

Despite Stanton's professed anxiety, from that point forward there appeared to be no question of Buchanan giving in to the demands of the South Carolinians. Indeed, the president's determination to stand firm may have been developing since the cabinet council of December 27, when he sided with Black, Toucey, Holt, and Stanton against those who would have been more accommodating to the secessionists. A Virginia senator who saw Buchanan on the afternoon of December 30 found that he had already decided to sustain Anderson at Fort Sumter. Stanton's admirers have emphasized that Buchanan's attitude toward secession underwent a noticeable transformation from the moment Stanton entered the cabinet, and Stanton tried diligently to promote that perception, but Stanton's debut coincided with Anderson shifting his garrison to Fort Sumter, which appears to have led to Buchanan's changed attitude. That, and the subsequent seizure of the other public property in Charleston, forced Buchanan to either react apologetically or proceed authoritatively. He opted for the latter course, following it as persistently as he could within the context of his belief that he could not legally make war on an individual state—and, as Joseph Holt pointed out, Abraham Lincoln initially observed the same constitutional scruples. Rather than Buchanan responding to Stanton's unionism, it was more likely that Stanton merely concurred in the prevailing opinion.[16]

On the last day of the year, the president sent his reply to the three "private gentlemen" from South Carolina, refusing to recognize them as emissaries of any government, or to remove Major Anderson from Fort Sumter. He closed with a reference to the defensive nature of Anderson's mission, as though to disavow any aggressive intent, but it was evident from his tone that any rumors of executive acquiescence to South Carolina's withdrawal were mistaken. The would-be commissioners replied with heat and implied threat, accusing him of having "probably rendered civil war inevitable." If two-decade-old reminiscences can be credited, when the commissioners' reply was read at the next cabinet meeting everyone present decided that it could not be formally received, including the Southerners Thomas and Thompson.[17]

Buchanan might try to avoid offensive military action, especially since he had no effective force or fleet to deploy, and he might be happy to hand the entire crisis over to the Republicans whom he felt had provoked it, but he stubbornly maintained the principle of federal authority even as secession fever spread to the Mississippi and the Rio Grande. Meanwhile, the more enduring vignettes of Buchanan wringing his hands and whimpering helplessly over the national troubles sprang from the furtive whisperings of his most faithless cabinet officer, Stanton, who betrayed him in ways those who went south never did.[18]

Stanton had not served as Buchanan's attorney general a full week before he began communicating secretly with the administration's political enemies in the North, to whom he routinely revealed the confidential discussions of the president's inner circle. The inside details of his first cabinet meeting appeared in the *New York Times* four days after that marathon session, courtesy of Seward, who maintained a close relationship with Henry Raymond, the editor of the *Times*: a decade afterward Seward revealed that Stanton had no sooner taken office than they met at Seward's home on Jackson Square, in the old clubhouse where Philip Barton Key had died. Seward was friendly with Peter Watson, Stanton's colleague in the patent suits, whom Stanton sent to Seward to offer daily reports of the treason, malfeasance, and incompetence within Buchanan's official family. Seward naturally accepted, apprising the president-elect on December 29 that he had "gotten a position in which I can see what is going on in the councils of the President." The flavor of Stanton's information is reflected in Seward's lament that "things there are even worse than we understood." Stanton's espionage began the following day, and continued every day until the inauguration.[19]

Stanton had long resorted to duplicity for personal advantage in uncertain circumstances. That was probably why he had played both sides of the fence over abolition, and it appears to have been his motive for betraying Buchanan. The secession crisis, after all, had thrown Stanton into an awkward political and economic situation. Since the Panic of 1857, his private practice had subsisted primarily on government contracts procured through the Buchanan administration—with the renowned Sickles case perhaps coming his way incidentally through the same association. The only significant client Stanton had secured on his own in recent years was his old nemesis Cyrus McCormick, who had hired him to extend his reaper patents, and he lost that case. Had Stanton resigned in protest over Buchanan's policies, and especially if Black had resigned with him, the well of remunerative government litigation would have dried up. Besides, Stanton had privately declared the Democratic Party as good as dead, and most people (including Seward himself) expected Seward to be the power behind the throne in Lincoln's administration. It made perfect sense for someone who solicited government employment to find common cause with those who might control the dispensation of that patronage for the foreseeable future.[20]

Had pure nationalism underlain Stanton's infidelity to Buchanan, his behavior in cabinet councils would presumably have leaned more toward the bellicose, demanding manner that he described in his private fables—which even his friend Holt failed to corroborate. He might also have been expected to stand on those same principles before secessionist sympathizers, instead of pretending to agree with them, as numerous witnesses testified that he did. It may be true, as Black's biographer supposed, that even in the face of his expressed contempt for the president-elect Stanton was angling for one of the open cabinet posts under Lincoln, but with so many prominent Republicans demanding a spot he must have understood how long a gamble that would have been. More likely, he sought friends high in the new administration from whom he could expect further work, as he had so obviously done when Buchanan took office. If that was his plan, it worked well. Along the way, he also distorted the historical image of President Buchanan, who still believed Stanton "perfectly honest" even after it became clear that he had cast his fortunes with the political opposition.[21]

In the December 30 memorandum to Buchanan, Black had advised dispatching warships to Charleston, with reinforcements for the garrison. Even as that document was being written and copied, the commanding general of the U.S. Army sent a message to the president asking permission to do that very thing. Winfield Scott, hero of both the War of 1812 and the Mexican War, remained fairly combative at the age of seventy-four and the weight of about three hundred pounds. He sought executive permission to bypass the War Department altogether and secretly order about five companies of recruits from New York to Charleston aboard a cutter and a sloop of war. To this request he received no immediate reply, but by the second day of 1861 he drafted instructions for the embarkation of two hundred men, arms, and ammunition, along with provisions for three months, aboard a private steamer contracted for the purpose. Three nights later, the two hundred men filed out of Fort Columbus, in New York Harbor, and boarded the *Star of the West*, on which Stanton had sailed to Panama.[22]

With a nominal destination of New Orleans, the *Star* left New York on Saturday evening, January 5. That same day, a five-day-old letter from Major Anderson arrived at army headquarters in Washington, noting the apparent construction of hostile batteries but remarking that he could command the harbor as long as the government wished to keep it. That, and his comment that "we are now where the Government may send us additional troops at its leisure," persuaded the president and Holt to call off the relief effort, rather than risk another incident. A telegram to New York arrived after the reinforcements and supplies had left, so Holt appealed to the secretary of the navy for a vessel to intercept the steamer. Toucey sent the twenty-two-gun *Brooklyn* from Hampton Roads, but that powerful warship only put to sea late in the morning of January 9. By then the *Star of the West* had already tried to dash into Charleston with the U.S. flag flying, only to be driven back by artillery fire from the works Major Anderson had spotted under construction barely a week before. Those batteries would only grow stronger over the coming days, and the opportunity for safely reinforcing or supplying Fort Sumter had already passed.[23]

The guns that fired on the *Star of the West* awakened a martial spirit in the North. Editors advised the president that there was only one possible response, calling on him to back up Major Anderson with the "whole power of the navy and army" and advocating the reinforcement of Fort Sumter "at any cost." The insult stung deep, arousing intense nationwide indignation, but calmer spirits recognized the fragility of the situation in the South, where any armed reaction by the federal government might have pushed all the slave states into secession.[24]

As it was, conventions in Mississippi, Alabama, and Florida voted those three states out of the Union by the time the *Star of the West* returned to New York. As he descended the steps of the U.S. Senate for the last time, Senator Albert Gallatin Brown of Mississippi met Attorney General Stanton coming from the Supreme Court, and Stanton bid him a friendly farewell. In a speech to the Confederate Congress on January 30, 1865, Brown claimed that Stanton had congratulated him on sticking to his principles, and assured him that the South was in the right. That accusation soon found its way into Northern newspapers, eliciting no denial from Stanton.[25]

Jacob Thompson did not wait for Mississippi to go out before leaving the cabinet. He had tried to deter secessionists from a preemptive attack on Anderson's garrison with the assurance that no troops would be sent against South Carolina while he remained in the cabinet, and he felt Buchanan had duped him by sending them on the sly: incensed, Thompson violated cabinet confidentiality himself by telegraphing a warning that the *Star* was coming. Philip Thomas, who had entertained an even friendlier view of secession than Thompson, quickly followed him. Buchanan appointed John Adams Dix of New York to fill Thomas's slot at the Treasury Department, but he left the Interior, like the Post Office, with the chief assistant in charge. Except for the Kentuckian Holt, an all-Northern cabinet now reflected the sectional rift in the nation.[26]

That did not stop House Republicans from creating another committee to look into the conduct of the administration, and specifically into communications between officers of the executive branch and Southern secessionists. Chairman William A. Howard later voiced a belief that Stanton had written the resolution that spawned his committee, and he said Stanton had supplied it with an endless stream of information about his fellow cabinet officers and, presumably, the president himself. Howard and Henry Dawes, another Republican member of the committee, insinuated that Stanton secretly conveyed a belief that Secretary of the Navy Isaac Toucey, of Connecticut, warranted surveillance or arrest for treasonable activities.[27]

Such wild accusations bespoke disproportionate paranoia, besides illustrating Stanton's perfidious conduct toward colleagues who advocated administration policies that Stanton himself at least pretended to support. His correspondence from the period suggests that his nerves, fluctuating between optimistic calm and intense anxiety, were no more trustworthy than his political loyalties. On January 15 he assured his brother-in-law that the secession fever would burn itself out by the inauguration on March 4, and that peace would again prevail, with greater prosperity than ever. Eight days later he wrote to Salmon P. Chase, freshly returned to the U.S. Senate and a candidate for Lincoln's cabinet, to warn that secessionists planned to seize Washington as their own capital, and that they would probably succeed. Such rumors had been buzzing around Washington since early in the month, seemingly emanating from the highest authority: General Scott had appointed Charles P. Stone, one of his Mexican War staff officers, to muster in militia for the District of Columbia as early as January 2, and Stone began culling suspected secessionists by imposing a nationalistic mustering oath. Rumors of a rebel coup took a particular edge late in January, but while Stanton seems to have said little about such fears in cabinet discussion he arranged secret meetings in the dark of night with prominent Republicans to divulge his undocumented expectations of impending treachery. He saved all of his most provocative rumors for the ears of those who belonged to the party that was about to take power.[28]

Charles Sumner, recovered finally from his 1856 caning, had returned to the Senate to represent Massachusetts and the abolition cause that James Buchanan held responsible for the nation's troubles. Buchanan and Black believed the entire cabinet shared that opinion, but if Stanton deplored abolitionists in cabinet meetings, he pursued them for clandestine interviews. He called Sumner to his office on January 25 and led him through six different rooms looking for one unoccupied by clerks. In a secluded alcove he told the senator that secessionists filled the government, so they would have to meet secretly somewhere else. Two nights later they talked until after midnight in Sumner's room, where the excitable Stanton proffered a sufficiently exaggerated version of confidential White House discussions to convince Sumner that secessionists were plotting to capture Washington: Stanton also told two other Massachusetts men that Southern traitors would attack Washington between February 4 and 15. In his conclaves with Republicans, Stanton seemed closer to hysteria each day, concluding finally that secessionists did not so much intend to leave the Union as to conquer and dominate it—to "govern the North as well as the South."[29]

In his sudden, specific frenzy over the security of the capital, Stanton was again following the lead of Jeremiah Black, although with characteristically amplified anxiety. With so many states dropping out of the Union, or considering it, it seemed probable in the second half of January that all the slave states would eventually go, and that would leave the capital of the United States surrounded by hostile territory. With no evidence of treasonable designs against Washington, Black nevertheless advised the president that possession of the city would represent the ultimate triumph for a new confederation of slave states, adding "if they *can* take and *do not* take it they are fools." Black's argument certainly did not lack reason—Senator Judah P. Benjamin of Louisiana had envisioned such an outcome early in December—but while Maryland and Virginia remained in the Union the danger seemed remote. Black claimed only circumstantial evidence of such a conspiracy, and no further evidence has surfaced since, but after the seizures of federal forts and arsenals he naturally doubted secessionist assurances, and rabid Southern editors had already advocated seizing Washington. Black recommended that Buchanan increase the military presence at the seat of government, pointing out that if his apprehensions proved groundless, no harm would be done. The president still doubted the likelihood of such an uprising, but he bowed to Black's reasoning and ordered as many troops into Washington as could be spared on short notice. In the process he aroused curiosity in the House of Representatives, where some members wondered if the president held disturbing information unknown to Congress.[30]

The only commotion around the government departments on February 4 consisted of the gathering of more than ten dozen delegates from twenty-one of the remaining states at Willard's Hotel, within carbine range of the White House. These elder statesmen, including congressmen, senators, and former president John Tyler, hoped to imitate Henry Clay's feat of 1850 by offering a compromise to secession through a menu of congressional legislation. Most of the proposals involved restoration of the elements in the Compromise of 1850, and at a rally at Steubenville in the middle of January Stanton's former neighbors adopted resolutions supporting those measures; when Stanton's old friend John Oliver informed him of it, Stanton responded with satisfaction. "If the resolutions of your meeting were sanctioned by the Republican party in Congress," Stanton replied, "I think that the troubles that now disturb and endanger the country would speedily be removed." About the same time—perhaps the same day—Stanton gave Senator Sumner precisely the opposite opinion about the peace conference, telling him that the compromise effort amounted to nothing: it was all a ploy to gain time for secession in the border states, and for the capture of Washington.[31]

Stanton's erstwhile law partner, George McCook, had attended the Steubenville rally, and a couple of weeks later he visited Washington. Stanton gave him a much more optimistic picture of the situation in the capital than he was circulating among Republicans, as well as a far more comforting impression of the relations between the president and General Scott. Those two were kind and cordial toward each other, Stanton attested, and were quite capable of defending the city. Buchanan intended to finish out his term there, and would use all the power at his disposal to sustain the government until then; only if Virginia and Maryland seceded might they face trouble. Furthermore, Fort Sumter was not about to be surrendered. It was as though McCook's confident friend were a completely different person from the attorney general who muttered such frantic midnight alarms.[32]

Georgia, Louisiana, and Texas left the Union by the first of February, creating a solid tier of nominally independent states, and the process of forming a new alliance began. Before that month ended, the Confederate States of America had a constitution, a provisional congress, and a president, yet for all his agitated audiences with Republicans Stanton appears to have remained otherwise calm. He may even have relaxed his secret agent's caution enough to join Seward in his home at the former clubhouse for a dinner with the actress Pauline Cushman, soon to be celebrated as a spy in her own right.[33]

Early on the morning of February 23, Abraham Lincoln evaded a rumored assassination plot by slipping into Washington on the train from Baltimore with two companions. After breakfast and a nap he proceeded to the White House with Senator Seward, to pay a courtesy call on President Buchanan, whom they caught during a cabinet meeting. Buchanan introduced Lincoln to the assembled department chiefs, including Stanton, who would have long since deduced that the president-elect was the same country lawyer from the reaper trial in Cincinnati. If Lincoln had not yet associated the name of the new attorney general with that experience, surely on entering the cabinet room he recognized the spectacles and the distinctive whiskers of the lawyer characterized by one observer as "pig-faced." If either of them alluded to their earlier encounter no one recorded it, but during the denouement of the old administration and in the early months of the new one Stanton reportedly still held Buchanan's lanky successor in contempt. In 1870, while members of Buchanan's official family and other acquaintances were still alive to dispute it, Jeremiah Black published an image of Stanton damning Lincoln "with bitter curses" and calling him "contemptuous names, and with *simian*, if not with 'swinish phrase.'"[34]

During the final fortnight of the Buchanan presidency Stanton applied himself primarily to California land-grant appeals and pardons for criminals, most of whom were serving time for counterfeiting, mail theft, or assault. Three pardons involved homicide, and one killer had not reached the age of sixteen when sent to prison, while another was said to have been insane at the time of the crime—which may have seemed an especially effective plea to the onetime defender of Daniel Sickles. Stanton had just about enough time left in office to receive, if not respond to, a letter from James Shunk warning about "gangs" of witnesses who had begun appearing to challenge the government's suits against California land claimants. Stanton assured one of his special prosecutors in California that he had mailed him checks for $7,500 between December 4 and January 5, adding that he could not imagine what had become of the money, and he forewarned the printers who had published the record of the New Almaden case that their bill for almost $5,000 had been approved, but the appropriation fell short. He asked Peter Della Torre to stay on as special prosecutor to the new district attorney for northern California, explaining that he had requested the acting secretary of the Interior Department to pay him $5,000 for that service. He even saved a tidbit for Jeremiah Black, perhaps in consolation for the dashing of Black's Supreme Court hopes. Buchanan had sent Black's name in for confirmation, but so many Southern Democrats had resigned that the Senate refused to consider the nomination, and on that very day Stanton offered the outgoing secretary of state a portion of the special-counsel booty from California.[35]

The morning of March 4 broke with rain, but cooler air soon drove the clouds away, and a little after noon President Buchanan appeared at Willard's Hotel in an open barouche, to collect Lincoln and escort him to the Capitol. They disappeared into the bowels of that marble edifice, where Vice President Breckinridge turned the chair of the Senate over to Hannibal Hamlin, after which Lincoln and Buchanan emerged on the front steps. Chief Justice Roger Taney administered the oath of office, and Lincoln began to address the crowd. He remarked on the attempt at disunion, but refused to acknowledge it as accomplished, contending that one party might violate a contract, but all parties had to agree before it could be dissolved. Most of his speech argued against the legality of secession. Then he broached the subject of compromise, even advocating a constitutional amendment perpetuating slavery. Finally, he vowed to continue the policy of peaceful resistance Buchanan had followed, cautioning his "dissatisfied fellow countrymen" that the question of civil war lay with them. "The government will not assail you," he promised. "You can have no conflict without yourselves becoming the aggressors."[36]

Lincoln closed his first utterance as president with what may be the most eloquent appeal to nationhood ever written in the English language. "The mystic chords of memory," he hoped, "stretching from every battle-field, and patriot grave, to every living heart and hearthstone, all over this broad land, will yet swell the chorus of the Union, when again touched, as surely they will be, by the better angels of our nature." The parade marshal for the day, an old Democrat, positioned himself where he could hear the address clearly, and he thought it nearly perfect: "peaceable—but firm." He supposed it would appeal even to Southerners. Nearby, Stanton felt no such confidence. Not only did he doubt that Lincoln's speech would do anything toward resolving the crisis, he suspected it would only aggravate the situation. In a private letter to Della Torre he announced that the latest news from the South was the worst yet. That may have cast a pall over a little farewell party the cabinet enjoyed that night at the home of District Attorney Robert Ould, whom Stanton had faced—and insulted—in the Sickles trial.[37]

The bad news Stanton referred to came in a recent communication from Fort Sumter. At the final gathering of Buchanan's cabinet on the morning of March 4, Holt had brought a disturbing letter from Major Anderson dated the last day of February, in which he reported that Charleston Harbor was now so thoroughly covered by Confederate artillery that it would take at least 20,000 disciplined troops to subdue them and relieve the garrison. That posed a dire immediate problem, with provisions in Sumter growing short, because there were not 20,000 men in the entire U.S. Army. Anderson had mentioned in December that the South Carolinians had prohibited him from buying food ashore, and his superiors at Washington ought to have been able to deduce that rations might be a problem nearly two months after the last unsuccessful supply mission. Periodic reports of the expanding batteries encircling the fort might also have suggested the increasing difficulty of forcing an entry into the harbor, but Holt expressed complete surprise at both the staggering estimate of troops and the shortage of food in the fort. Until the new secretary of war could be confirmed, Holt remained on duty, and the morning after the inauguration he strode into Lincoln's office with a lengthy letter that explained Anderson's plight and simultaneously denied any personal responsibility for that disturbing development. With glib bureaucratic logic, Holt threw all the blame on the besieged Anderson, whose brave messages of continued defiance Holt used to justify excessive optimism in his War Department. Lincoln forwarded Holt's letter to General Scott, who turned the criticism back on Buchanan and his cabinet for dallying until it was too late.[38]

While the new president grappled with the prospect of having to give up the foremost symbol of federal authority in the seceded states, Stanton also lingered in his office, waiting for Edward Bates to be confirmed as attorney general. On the afternoon of March 5, Stanton, Holt, and Isaac Toucey met at the Washington rail station to see the former president off to his Pennsylvania estate. The next day, at Lincoln's request, Stanton provided him with a nomination for John J. Crittenden to the Supreme Court, on the assumption that there would be a resignation, and then he turned the attorney general's office over to Bates. Before leaving, Stanton escorted Bates to Capitol Hill and introduced him to the staff at the Supreme Court, offering any assistance that might be needed in the future. In a letter to Buchanan a few days later, Stanton admitted having met with Seward to secure the appointment of a Buchanan friend as a federal judge. Holt, he understood, might be selected for the judgeship instead of Buchanan's friend, and Stanton saw no hypocrisy in observing that Holt "appears now to be the chief favorite of the Republicans"—those "red blacks," as he contemptuously called them. Stanton would later regale Lincoln insiders with his own heroics in the name of Union, but he let Buchanan believe that he scorned Holt's effort to court the new administration at Buchanan's expense: he alluded to Holt selling himself as the stout nationalist who had helped reverse Buchanan's destructive course, predicting with implied distaste that Holt would secure an exalted judicial nomination on the strength of that claim.[39]

Soon after the inauguration, Stanton took dinner again at the home of Secretary of State Seward, along with Seward's mentor and patron, Republican sachem Thurlow Weed. For all the disdain Stanton supposedly harbored for Holt's self-congratulatory assertions when he related them to the former president, he gave Weed a glowing account of his own part in saving the nation from the treacherous Floyd, Thompson, and Toucey and the "imbecile" Buchanan. Stanton took particular credit for "thwarting" a plot to capture Washington that existed mainly in paranoia propagated in part by himself, but when a similar alarm surfaced in April he discounted it as "groundless."[40]

Stanton's surreptitious services to the incoming administration did not go entirely unappreciated. Weed suggested that Seward offer Stanton the diplomatic portfolio at Constantinople, since "something must be done" for him. That suggestion went nowhere, but Lincoln had to appoint a new federal attorney for the District of Columbia when Robert Ould decamped for Richmond, and Seward proposed Stanton. Asked for an opinion on his fellow Washingtonian, Postmaster General Montgomery Blair reported having learned of an impropriety during Stanton's brief tenure as attorney general. He insisted there was no mistake about it: Stanton had taken a bribe to drop an appeal—perhaps in one of those California land claims, in which Stanton showed so little concern about the appearance of conflicts of interest. The charge shocked Lincoln and the cabinet. It was apparently never investigated, and probably was not true, but the president deferred to Attorney General Bates, who preferred someone else.[41]

Business could not have overwhelmed Stanton in the weeks after the changing of the guard, for his personal correspondence grew more prolific than at any previous time. To his former colleague John Dix, still a solid Democrat, he blasted Lincoln and his advisers for equivocation in dealing with secessionists and for a lack of firm policy—the same faults he later ascribed to Buchanan, in his conversations with Republicans. He wrote to

Buchanan every couple of days at first, describing the uncertainty of the new president, division in the cabinet, and the assurance (almost certainly conveyed by Seward) that Fort Sumter would be evacuated. Then, early in April, he sent new tidings that Sumter might be reinforced, in spite of all the cabinet talk about giving it up.[42]

Indeed, the cabinet had initially leaned toward removing Major Anderson's garrison from Charleston before his provisions gave out, and Seward had injudiciously confided that knowledge to a new set of Confederate commissioners, to deter them from any rash action before the crisis could be peaceably resolved. Montgomery Blair had balked at what he deemed a craven surrender, helping to stiffen the will of his beleaguered chief magistrate. Then Lincoln sent two envoys to Charleston to assess local attitudes, and late in March they returned with the prediction that any vessel trying to reach Sumter would be attacked, even if it brought only food. That may have reminded Lincoln of the national furor over the firing on the *Star of the West*—and, with editorial sentiment turning toward letting the seven states go in peace, Lincoln may have reflected on resurrecting such useful public indignation. Once the Senate adjourned from its special session, the president began to contemplate a new relief expedition, although behind his back Seward was still promising that the place would be abandoned.[43]

Two weeks after the cabinet had lopsidedly voted to remove Anderson's troops, opinion had swung in the opposite direction, and only Seward remained opposed. Lincoln planned with his military advisers to send troops and supplies to Fort Sumter and also to Fort Pickens, in Pensacola Bay, and the first ships left New York for Florida on April 2. The fleet bound for Charleston departed on April 8 and 9.[44]

The grass in Franklin Square, across from the Stantons' new house, had turned a luxuriant green and the trees were leafing out when reports of those first troop and ship movements stirred Washington gossip on April 6. No one on the street knew where they had gone, but it was certain they would appear at one of the disputed Southern forts, and no one could deny how provocative their arrival would be. A drizzle set in the next morning, thickening to steady rain that fell for three days, in torrents at times, while offices and homes in the capital city hummed with growing speculation over the consequences of another confrontation. At least one of the president's secretaries expected little more than a passing skirmish, without significant repercussions. Stanton supposed it would put an end to the uncomfortable truce, but he anticipated an early conclusion to any fighting. In a letter written on the sodden Monday that the first steamers left for Charleston, Stanton confidently advised the 1812 veteran John Dix that "a round or two often serves to restore harmony."[45]

On the fortieth morning of Lincoln's presidency, Washington learned that the batteries around Charleston Harbor had opened fire on Fort Sumter before the little fleet even arrived. Lincoln had sent a messenger announcing that he was shipping provisions and reinforcements to Major Anderson, but that he would withhold the reinforcements if the food were allowed into the harbor unmolested. The president had remarked almost wishfully on the public reaction if the Confederates fired on a vessel bringing only food to hungry men, but the resupply effort completely contradicted Secretary Seward's promises of imminent evacuation. That apparent breach of faith only infuriated the civil and military authorities in Charleston and destroyed any trust in Lincoln or his government, driving them to the fatal indiscretion Lincoln likely wanted. Once the Confederate commander at Charleston received Lincoln's notification, he demanded Anderson's immediate surrender, but the major refused, and before dawn on April 12 artillery erupted in a flaming crescent around the brick bastion. With his barracks blazing and ammunition running low, Anderson hauled down his flag the next day.[46]

The attack played into Lincoln's hands, giving him the excuse he had been waiting for. Under the same militia law that had governed George Washington, he called upon the states to raise 75,000 troops for ninety days of service, to quell the rebellious "combinations" within the so-called Confederacy. He distributed the quotas of troops among all the states that had not yet seceded, anticipating perhaps that the insult to the flag would reignite national sentiments in the eight remaining slave states. Lincoln was grievously mistaken on that point: his appeal portended coercion, bringing absolute refusal from most of the Southern governors and provoking a new round of secession.[47]

Probably without thinking of the public-debt burden that would ensue, Stanton had mentioned to Dix that the "vast consumption" of war matériel would restore prosperity to a nation that had been suffering months of recession. With advance notice that must have come from Seward, Stanton knew of Lincoln's call for troops before it was issued, and he immediately advised his brother-in-law in Pittsburgh on the variety of goods and services that would be required, so the Hutchison warehouses and transportation system could be the first to take advantage of the sudden opportunities. Noting that many of his neighbors were packing up to leave Washington in anticipation of civil unrest, Stanton declared that he would take his chances in the capital, where all his economic interests lay. He professed "firm faith" in the survival of the government despite a foreboding that Virginia and Maryland would secede, but lest his own finances suffer he had already used his inside information to sell off his government bonds.[48]

After April 15, the day Lincoln called out the militia, life in Washington grew even more uncertain. Wild rumors of a subversive plot reverberated through the city, and District of Columbia militia roved the streets and guarded the public buildings. Five companies of Pennsylvania volunteers reached the capital on the night of April 18, unarmed and clad in variegated local uniforms. They had been escorted between Baltimore's two disconnected rail stations without incident a few hours before, but as the 6th Massachusetts changed cars there the next day a hostile crowd challenged what Southern sympathizers regarded as an unconstitutional mission of conquest. Unlike the Pennsylvanians, the Massachusetts men carried muskets, and they responded to brickbats with close-range volleys that killed men, women, and children. Police waded into the fray, separating the protesters from the soldiers, a few of whom had fallen victim to a paltry return fire, mostly from pocket pistols. The bloodied regiment finished its fateful journey to Washington that evening, but Baltimore officials begged that no more troops be sent through their tinderbox city. When assent to that urgent request came too slowly, they sent Maryland militia to dismantle the railroads leading into the city and to burn the railroad bridges Northern reinforcements would have to cross. That effectively blocked any more militia from Pennsylvania, and prevented the passage of any from New York or New England except by water. A detour by sea brought the next contingent to Annapolis after some delay, but the railroad had been torn up between there and Annapolis Junction.[49]

Stanton described outright hysteria in Washington. Certainly anxiety prevailed in most quarters, and some citizens had been sleeping alongside loaded revolvers for months, but few showed worse panic than Stanton. When the interrupted rail lines caused a shortage of produce in the street markets, Stanton foresaw famine. Despite the absence of any visible threat from belligerent factions in Virginia and Maryland, the confident, defiant Stanton of early April gave way to despair by April 23. On that date he wrote John Dix that the situation in Washington was "desperate beyond any conception," and warned that "any shadow of hope to preserve this government from utter and absolute extinction" required the immediate arrival of help from New York.[50]

For nearly a week the interruption at Baltimore also stopped regular mail service to and from Washington. Stanton wrote to Buchanan on April 20 and 23, but those letters never reached Lancaster. He dubbed April 23 "Blue Tuesday," reflecting the gloom in a city defended by no more than 4,000 soldiers, Marines, and militia, and that day evidently did mark the depth of his own despondency. Then, on April 25, the aristocratic dandies of the 7th New York Militia disembarked at the Washington rail station in their grey overcoats and white cross-belts, having themselves repaired the railroad as far as Annapolis. This bandbox regiment would be called out three times over the next couple of years and would never fire a shot, but suddenly everyone seemed to feel safe again from the legions of invisible insurgents. With the seaborne route via Annapolis well established, a small flood of New York troops quickly followed, but mad rumors maintained that rebels as strong as 50,000 or 60,000 were gathering in Virginia to seize Washington. Stanton renewed his predictions of an attack on the city, and persisted in them for weeks.[51]

No rebel invasion or sympathetic fifth column drove Stanton from his home, but the Northern militia pouring into the city did. They occupied every public building that could offer shelter—from the city hotels to the sprawling Patent Office—and soldiers even bedded down in the echoing halls of Congress. Then they began spilling into the public squares to camp and drill, including Franklin Square, across K Street from Stanton's new house, where their staccato shouts and collective chatter combined with the constant clanging of pots, pans, and equipment to disturb sleep at night and annoy the residents all day. Worse yet, the army established temporary hospitals nearby, bringing the additional threat of contagious disease. In the middle of May Stanton moved Ellen, Ellie, and Lewis to a rented house in a quieter neighborhood on H Street, closer to the White House.[52]

By May the hordes of office-seekers who had packed Washington's hotels after the inauguration had either found employment or given up hope, although a steady stream of new federal supplicants perennially meandered in and out of the capital. The more resourceful applied to friends who held important posts themselves, or had done so recently enough to still wield influence, and some approached Stanton. He did what he could through acquaintances in the new administration, sending notes to Seward, Secretary of War Simon Cameron, and Interior Secretary Caleb Smith as well as dropping the names of Republican senators Ben Wade and Zachariah Chandler when necessary. He complained to Buchanan that Lincoln had made only a few token appointments among Democrats, after which all the choice patronage had gone to "Black Republicans," despite the administration's appeal for nonpartisan resistance to secession. Dix had drawn a commission as major general, but he felt so effectively shelved that he was already talking about resigning. Stanton tried to see his old friend Chase, now head of the Treasury Department, to land some government work for himself, but an officious assistant kept him waiting. Stanton then resorted to a letter, making a pitch for another special-counsel assignment that might revive his legal reputation at the White House.[53]

Private law practice had virtually ground to a standstill amid such tumultuous events. While Stanton sought Chase's aid, Judge Black solicited a substantial fee from Buchanan for writing a two-volume biography of the retired president, noting that legal work had dried up for the present. The cash-strapped Black had to accept a position as recorder for the same

Supreme Court to which he had recently been nominated as an associate justice: not until the Fossat claimants hired him to continue their quest for the New Almaden mine would his personal finances recover. Joseph Holt, another lawyer without a practice, may have drawn some compensation from a pro-Union speaking tour—an enterprise that was often supported by private committees. He collected some income from temporary government assignments, but real security only returned a year and a half later, with a permanent appointment to a senior staff position in the army.[54]

In that same stagnant legal atmosphere, after corresponding with Chase and some of the other department heads (presumably including the grateful Seward), Stanton found some government employment. First, he resumed his duties as special counsel for the United States in those endless California land cases, writing orders on behalf of the attorney general for the federal attorney in San Francisco and paying particular attention to the New Almaden mine. He floated from the land cases to counseling other federal departments on short-term contracts such as he had sought from Chase, and he went out of his way to befriend the general in chief, Winfield Scott. Stanton's skill as an adviser may have been overrated, but his influence at the Supreme Court warranted consideration, and he had not hesitated to use his cabinet position to cultivate that influence with favors for the justices.[55] Presumably on the authority of the attorney general's office, he occupied two rooms in William W. Corcoran's new, unfinished art gallery at the corner of Seventeenth and Pennsylvania. Corcoran was one of the founders of Riggs & Company, where Washington's wealthiest citizens and most government officials, including Stanton, did their banking. Because of Corcoran's supposed Southern sentiments, the army simply commandeered his property inside and outside the city.[56]

Two months after his prediction that demand for military resources would enrich the North, Stanton was raving about corruption in military procurement and sounding the alarm about the prospect of national bankruptcy. "On every side the government and soldiers are pillaged," he complained to Dix, in June. "Arms, clothing, transportation, and provisions are each and all subjects of peculation and spoil." In his correspondence with Democrats hostile to the White House he adopted the *New York Herald's* favorite pejorative for Lincoln and his administration—"imbecile"—but his evident contempt did not deter him from seeking favors and employment from members of Lincoln's cabinet.[57]

Through May and June Stanton remained in the city. With most of his limited work involving assignments from different government departments, he had no need to travel on business, but he also put off personal visits on the excuse of anxiety over an armed uprising in, or an attack on, Washington. Apprehension heightened as Confederate armies gathered at

Harper's Ferry and Manassas Junction, and by the middle of July political pressure forced General Scott to mount an attack on Manassas Junction. He sent Brigadier General Irvin McDowell with about 30,000 men: they and the rebels at Manassas both lacked training, but inexperience impedes the aggressor more than the defender. McDowell sallied across Bull Run on the morning of July 21, and by that evening his battered divisions came spilling back to Washington in unseemly haste. Five days later, in the last letter he would ever write to Buchanan, Stanton described the army as completely defeated and demoralized. Still convinced that the Confederates actually wanted the Union capital, he expected Washington to be captured at any moment.[58]

The three-month terms of the militia regiments had already begun to expire before the battle at Bull Run, and some regiments had started home on the eve of the fight. The War Department had begun insisting on three-year enlistments by May, forcing many eager volunteers to either muster in for three years or go home without a taste of field service. That had created some confusion among the recruits, and after Bull Run a private in the 1st Minnesota petitioned in federal court for his discharge on the grounds that he had been duped into a three-year commitment. By August Stanton was becoming the cabinet's legal handyman (perhaps thanks to Seward), and Secretary of War Simon Cameron hired him to defend the government in that test case. Appearing before Justice James Wayne at the Supreme Court, Stanton argued that the pertinent army regulations did not apply to volunteers. After casting some aspersions on soldiers who wanted out of the army, he added the emotional appeal that he usually employed when the law weighed against him. If the Minnesota man were released, he said, then his entire regiment would have to be discharged, followed by the whole army, whereupon the very building where they stood would fall to Confederate forces. That seemed to impress Justice Wayne, who returned the soldier to his regiment.[59]

While striving to keep reluctant soldiers in the ranks, Stanton saw to it that his own son remained a civilian. Eddie lived at home until late August, hesitating to return to Kenyon amid the expectation of an attack on Washington, and like many young men that summer he longed for a little martial glory. The prospect of carrying a knapsack and rifle dissuaded him from enlisting as a private, so he asked his well-connected father to solicit a commission for him, as he had done for others. Stanton refused, admitting finally that he did not want his son going into the army.[60]

Stanton's activities on behalf of the government did not prevent him from serving its apparent enemies. Eugenia Phillips, the wife of Stanton's would-be associate Philip Phillips, landed in the Old Capitol Prison with two of her daughters late in August for suspected communication with Confederate agents. For all Stanton's loyal talk among Unionists, Philip Phillips later described him preaching devout state-rights doctrine to Southerners like himself, and Stanton worked so vigorously on behalf of Mrs. Phillips that she referred to him as "our noble friend." With the aid of Reverdy Johnson and Justice Wayne, he gained her release.[61]

To rebuild the army, the War Department called in a young general with a good reputation in the antebellum service and a record of minor victories against ragtag rebels in western Virginia. Major General George B. McClellan, a Pennsylvania native and recent resident of Cincinnati, arrived late in July, and Stanton began courting him almost immediately; that acquaintance may have helped yield him the test case on volunteer enlistments. McClellan had served on General Scott's staff in the campaign to capture Mexico City, and in 1861 "Little Mac" was still less than half the age of the commanding general, but their similar egos and the disparity in their notions about military matters created early tension. Then came a disaster on the Potomac at Ball's Bluff, outside Leesburg. Brigadier General Charles P. Stone, inspector general of the District of Columbia militia during the secession crisis, lost a bloody affray that McClellan blamed indirectly on Scott, telling some Radical Republican senators as much. That brought the differences between McClellan and Scott to a head. If Stanton did not help persuade McClellan to challenge Old Fuss and Feathers for command of the U.S. Army, he at least aided the ambitious young general in the clandestine preparation of his bid for overall control—allowing him to use the Stanton home as a hideaway through much of October 31, where he composed a lengthy report to Secretary Cameron that served as his argument for taking complete charge himself. Stanton even wrote the preamble to the report, which concluded with a request that it be laid before the president. It was, and the next day Lincoln retired General Scott, elevating McClellan to the chief command.[62]

A two-week-old child stirred occasionally at the Stanton house while McClellan scribbled. Like all Ellen's children, James Hutchison Stanton was named for a member of her family. His parents decided at that juncture to vaccinate him against the smallpox that sometimes lurked in the nearby military hospitals, but the precaution carried its own dangers, and not long afterward a reaction set in, spreading a rash over the baby's entire body that persisted through the autumn and into the winter.[63]

Early in November Captain Charles Wilkes of the U.S. Navy created a crisis for the administration when he stopped the British steamer *Trent* in the Atlantic and removed two Confederate diplomats bound for Europe. Britain angrily demanded their return, and McClellan glumly assumed that apologies must be made. Attorney General Bates thought otherwise, and when McClellan dropped in on Stanton for his interpretation he came away with the gratifying opinion that Wilkes's action was perfectly defensible. McClellan's colleague in an Ohio railroad company—Samuel L. M. Barlow, a New York attorney and fervent Democrat—consulted with Stanton on that topic. Barlow found Stanton a firm Democrat of the Breckinridge-Buchanan stamp, who thought the war should have been avoided and blamed Northern abolitionists for it as much as Southern secessionists. On the *Trent* affair Barlow tended to concur with Stanton, against the prevailing sentiment among more prominent members of the New York bar, and when he returned to New York he sent Stanton articles on the subject, with records of case law. Meanwhile, as though in recognition of his usefulness, Cameron offered Stanton a full-time position as special counsel to the War Department, giving him the same two rooms in the Corcoran gallery that he had used while working on the California land cases. Stanton's optimistic view of the *Trent* case failed to win over Lincoln, however, and with most of Europe and many American jurists against him the president followed his inclination to swallow national pride and surrender the insurgent emissaries to British authorities.[64]

Upon his formal appointment as a federal advocate, Stanton at last informed the Quicksilver investors that he could no longer represent their New Almaden interests against the government, and they turned to the underemployed Jeremiah Black. Stanton's reluctance to continue handling the New Almaden case may have involved a fear of over-commitment rather than a conflict of interest: he still accepted the case of one private citizen against the United States that Christmas, while Judge Black prosecuted for the government.[65]

It was already apparent to James Buchanan that some of his former department heads had begun defecting to the Republicans—who now insinuated that Buchanan had been complicit in aiding secessionists, despite his public support for Lincoln's war. Joseph Holt had offended "the Squire" with a published letter in which he had depicted secession leaders greeting Buchanan in festive camaraderie: having originally known Holt as an office-seeker, the former president suspected the motive behind that letter when he learned of Holt's appointment as a special commissioner for the War Department. Before Stanton's first permanent position in the new government had become official, Buchanan had also already noted his former attorney general's growing intimacy with the same "Black Republicans" whom Stanton had so vilified in his private letters. The retired president warned Horatio King not to be surprised in the near future to see his portrayals of the erstwhile cabinet officers published somewhere. "I think I know them all perfectly," he said of them, "unless it may be Stanton."[66]

8

METAMORPHOSIS

Simon Cameron knew he was in trouble less than six months into his term as secretary of war, by which time complaints of his incompetence and crony-ism circulated broadly. Stanton's brother-in-law, Christopher Wolcott, went to New York City that summer and found Salmon P. Chase there, seeking loans for his Treasury Department from New York bankers. Having heard the worst about Cameron, Navy Secretary Gideon Welles, and others in the Lincoln cabinet from Stanton, Wolcott advised those bankers not to lend a dollar until Lincoln had fired the secretaries of war and the navy. Secretary Chase returned to Washington in mid-August with promises of $50 million in credit, but the bankers included a resolution requesting cabinet changes, especially at the War Department. Two weeks later one of Cameron's former colleagues in the Senate warned him of secret lobbying in that body for his removal. While Cameron seemed fully aware of the campaign against him, he had no idea that his sternest critics included Stanton, his legal adviser.[1]

Cameron's enemies multiplied as the year progressed, and in trying to appease them he only made more. In a cabinet meeting on November 15 he brought up the idea of arming male "contrabands"—as the government had begun to call the escaped slaves who were pouring into Union lines—and his suggestion jarred both Caleb Smith and Edward Bates into vehement opposition. Their dispute carried over to private dinner parties and into the newspapers, much to the embarrassment of a president who could not yet entertain such radical ideas. Toward the end of the month Cameron began preparing an annual report in which his recommendation for enlist-ing black soldiers figured prominently, and years later he claimed he shared the document with Stanton for comment. Cameron said that Stanton failed to warn him against so explosive a policy proposal, and even revised a pas-sage to increase its impact. Then, in what may have been a calculated sally to win the favor of Radical Republicans, Cameron distributed the report before submitting it to the president. Therein lay the seeds of his downfall, for the press pounced on the provocative topic and presented Lincoln with a choice between infuriating either conservatives or Radicals. The president dressed Cameron down in the next cabinet meeting, requiring him to delete the objectionable passage, and Welles considered Cameron's days as secretary of war numbered.[2]

If Stanton did amplify Cameron's argument for arming slaves (and Cameron waited until Stanton was dead to make the claim), he may have meant to ingratiate himself with Cameron, or to compromise Cameron's position with Lincoln. Either result could have borne fruit: Cameron was then his principal employer, and was responsive to flattery, while Stanton's own close relationship to key cabinet members and his status as a former attorney general made him a logical replacement if Cameron's presence became embarrassing to the administration. That line of thinking may have motivated Stanton's background murmuring against both Cameron and Welles, and through strategic deception he had made himself palatable to senators of all political persuasions, which would greatly ease his confirmation if he were nominated. As the stars aligned against Cameron, Seward grew increasingly willing to press Lincoln on Stanton's behalf. Christmas nevertheless passed and 1862 began with no changes in the cabinet, and on January 7 Postmaster General Montgomery Blair unburdened himself to Massachusetts governor John Andrew about negligence in the War Department. As Blair put it, there was at that time effectively no secretary of war.[3]

Rectifying that problem appears to have required collaboration between Seward and the president, but neither of them ever told the story, and others were left to guess. Cameron attended the cabinet meeting of Friday, January 10, and it passed without any particular reference to him, but the next day the president addressed a short note to him announcing that he could offer him the mission at St. Petersburg in order to satisfy Cameron's purported wish to resign from the cabinet. Seward and Lincoln spent the entire morning together on Sunday, January 12, evidently considering how the politically powerful Cameron could be nudged out without turning him into a political enemy. Gideon Welles thought it was Seward's idea to mollify Cameron by offering him the recently vacated Russian portfolio, and to propose it through Cameron's last friend in the cabinet, Secretary Chase. Seward had already primed Chase on the subject, and had apparently also mentioned Stanton as a possible successor. Chase grew so enthusiastic about it that he thought it was his idea, and Cameron soon felt the same. The credit belonged to neither of them, for when Montgomery Blair complained to the president about Stanton, still believing he had taken a bribe, he asked who had forwarded the name. Lincoln, who apparently did not credit the bribery accusation, told him it had been Seward alone. Stanton's intrigues of the previous winter had finally produced a significant dividend.[4]

After conferring with Cameron, Chase dropped him at Willard's while he drove back to Seward's to announce that the exchange would be acceptable. Although Seward had alluded to Stanton the night before, he allowed Chase to suppose he was managing the negotiation, and asked—still innocently—who should take Cameron's place. Chase named Joseph Holt and Stanton, and discounted Holt because he was a slave owner. Just then Cameron burst in with the president's curt letter, which he took as a peremptory dismissal, but Seward and Chase assured him there was no intent to offend. While driving Cameron home, Chase advised him to see Lincoln in the morning, agree to the exchange, and urge Stanton's nomination, ostensibly to replace one Pennsylvanian with another.[5]

Thus did Cameron come to insist that he had won the honor of choosing the man who would replace him, in addition to the pleasant opportunity "to go abroad." He must have complained to Lincoln about the note hinting for his resignation, because the president prepared a more complimentary version backdated to January 11. In a letter for the record also dated January 11, Cameron responded with affected grace not unmixed with gratitude. Even his fellow cabinet members heard nothing of the change until rumor carried the story through the city on January 13, by which time Stanton's name and Cameron's ambassadorial nomination had both been sent to the Senate.[6] Stanton had seen the president about the appointment, and obviously agreed to take it.[7] Justice Robert Grier heard the news as he left the Supreme Court, and that night three other members of the high court told him they all thought it would revive confidence in the government and restore credibility to the conservative cause. A friend of Seward's reported that the people of New York City seemed to welcome Stanton's appointment as a token concession to conservative opinion and a promise of more efficient and honest management. Cameron, at least, had previously served as adjutant general of Pennsylvania, but Stanton's lack of experience and aversion to all things military seem to have caused no concern.[8]

The resignation of so many Southerners, and the expulsion of others deemed too sympathetic to secession, had concentrated Republican strength in both chambers of Congress, with Radical Republicans becoming the most powerful faction in the Senate. Most of them still knew Stanton as a bitter Breckinridge Democrat, despite the friend he had made in Charles Sumner, and many may have heard of his aspersions on the administration and the ruling party. To smooth the way, Chase sent his driver through fresh snow and freezing temperatures on January 14 to fetch Senator William Pitt Fessenden, of Maine, for a chat with the nominee. Stanton was suffering from a bad cold and had refused to make a requested call on Jeremiah Black, so Fessenden may have met them at Stanton's house. Fessenden, who leaned to the Radicals at the time, found Stanton entirely satisfactory.[9]

Family lore holds that Ellen Stanton opposed the appointment. Under ordinary circumstances the position brought prestige enough, with social rank below only the presidency and the State and Treasury posts, and nine months into the nation's greatest conflict the secretary of war wielded—or could have wielded—more practical power than anyone except the chief executive. That should have appealed to a society-conscious young woman, but after a taste of cabinet life Ellen may have dreaded more controversy, long days alone, and late-night emergency meetings, especially with her youngest child suffering a serious reaction to his vaccination. The family would face a reduction in income, too, although they would trade the uncertainty of self-employment for a regular salary that most cabinet members found adequate.[10]

If Ellen objected, Stanton ignored her wishes. Friends and family maintained that he accepted the appointment from purely patriotic impulses, and a desire to further the national interests may well have influenced him, for his professional success in recent years had been tied to the reach of federal authority. There was also the status of the office, and its power, which he would immediately seek to expand.

Major General McClellan initially greeted Stanton's appointment as comforting evidence of the administration's aversion to Radical policy, for in the presence of conservatives Stanton exuded political sympathy. McClellan (who came to hate Stanton) described the nominee agreeing to go into the War Department only if McClellan thought he could help him win the war, but Stanton had said something equally complimentary and self-effacing to Seward—and earlier to Black, when going into Buchanan's cabinet.[11] Stanton's seeming admiration for McClellan switched to antagonism too quickly to have reflected the discovery of genuine ideological differences or an abrupt realization of incompetence, leaving political calculation as his most likely motive for turning against another benefactor he no longer needed.

For several weeks McClellan had lain seriously ill with typhoid, and Stanton's efforts to win his confidence apparently included a warning that the general's enemies were already vying to replace him on the assumption that he would die. In his anxiety over the army's inactivity, Lincoln had called a conference with several cabinet members and some generals, including Irvin McDowell, whom McClellan saw as his chief rival. Stanton's innuendo brought the pale and haggard McClellan to the White House, and may have contributed to the sullen attitude with which the general met the apparent executors of his military estate. When pressed for information about his plans, he declined to reveal them to so diverse a group, lest they leak into the newspapers.[12]

That was Monday, January 13—the day on which Lincoln nominated Stanton. McClellan's concern over the press revealing his plans did not prevent him from courting his own journalistic favor, and apparently at Stanton's instigation. While Stanton declined to risk the nasty weather on

Tuesday to visit Judge Black, he seemed happy to do so that evening to introduce *New York Herald* correspondent Malcolm Ives to McClellan at his home on Jackson Square. McClellan still felt weak, but his illness had put an edge on official and public impatience with the army's inaction, and he welcomed a chance to defend himself. Stanton made a friend of the reporter by arranging the interview, and he used their meeting to further that relationship. For Ives's benefit, both the general and the secretary-designate disparaged the misrepresentations of the rival *New York Times*, and Stanton promised that if he were confirmed he would cleave to the *Herald*. To seal their secret bond, he gave Ives permission to take his editor some juicy background tales from the Buchanan administration. Stanton departed early, inviting Ives to come to his house the next day and leaving the general to make his own case.[13]

Senator Fessenden returned a highly favorable report on Stanton to Capitol Hill. Henry Wilson of Massachusetts, the Republican chairman of the Committee on Military Affairs, had doubtless been primed about Stanton by Sumner, and at the end of Senate business on Wednesday, January 15, Wilson called for an executive session. When the gavel fell and senators spilled outside into a sleet storm, Stanton had been confirmed by a vote of 38-2: only Republicans James Grimes of Iowa and Samuel Pomeroy of Kansas demurred. Most senators wanted Cameron removed, and knew that his departure depended on Stanton's confirmation, as well as passage of Cameron's Russian ministry appointment.[14]

The wife of the assistant postmaster general heard a band serenading Stanton the evening of January 16, which may have been the night he joined the president at the opera. An aristocratic New York artillery officer saw them there, commenting on Lincoln as a "gawk" and on the new secretary as "a long-haired, fat, oily, politician-looking man." Ellen made a better impression, striking the postal official's wife as "very handsome," with an "easy dignity."[15]

From retirement, James Buchanan could not comprehend the appointment of Stanton to undertake the most burdensome and responsible position in the government. He assumed that McClellan, whom he considered Stanton's friend, had recommended him with the expectation of controlling military affairs himself. The Squire had evidently moderated his once superlative opinion of Stanton: he told his niece that he had only appointed him attorney general because of his familiarity with the California land cases that were just coming to a head, and although Stanton had proven a good lawyer he had not shown particular talent in "public, commercial or constitutional law." Buchanan firmly doubted that Stanton was corrupt, but in complaining of his persistent flattery and air of eternal loyalty, he accused Stanton of studied insincerity. Buchanan bridled when Joseph Holt published a letter praising the new secretary by insinuating that he and Stanton had saved the country from a weak chief magistrate. The former president also cringed to learn that two of Cameron's cronies would stay on at the department.[16]

Stanton made his debut at the War Department a week after his appointment, and Cameron continued in the office until then, but Stanton's first real business took place at his house, after breakfast on Sunday, January 19. Ben Butler, a cross-eyed major general from Massachusetts, dropped in to discuss transporting an army from Boston to Ship Island, Mississippi, from which he proposed a campaign into Texas. Butler shared Stanton's recent political sympathy with Breckinridge Democrats, and he had already converted to the Radical Republicanism that Stanton would soon espouse.[17]

Stanton's metamorphosis began the very next day. Cameron signed his last order the morning of January 20, and Stanton passed for the first time beneath the sign reading "Office of the Secretary of War." McClellan, still looking wan and weary, treated him to a formal reception, introducing two or three hundred generals and field officers in full uniform, and Stanton had a friendly word with each. Then, that same evening, Stanton invited McClellan's worst enemies for a private conference, in which he appears to have given them some tips about stalking their prey. Senator Ben Wade and his Joint Congressional Committee on the Conduct of the War, consisting of Senator Zachariah Chandler, three other Radical Republicans, and two token War Democrats, sat with Stanton from eight o'clock Monday evening until late that night: Senator Andrew Johnson of Tennessee, one of the Democrats, would come to know Stanton much better. They must have spent more time examining Stanton's views on politics and the war than on official business, because he could not have given them much information about the massive department he had overseen for only a few hours, and the note Chairman Wade addressed to Stanton the following morning implies the direction of their conversation. Wade requested two specific pieces of information aimed directly at McClellan: did statutory authority exist for McClellan's role as "commander-in-chief of the army of the United States," and did the law allow for any rank higher than that of major general?[18]

Those were telling questions, indicating that the previous night's conversation had leaned heavily in the direction of either abolishing McClellan's position as general in chief or promoting someone else over his head. That a committee so preponderantly hostile to McClellan had only then thought to examine such questions six weeks into its official existence further suggests that Stanton may have provided those hints. Treachery to his former friend and presumed patron would have comported with Stanton's tendency to simulate concurrence with those whose cooperation he needed, and he could feel relatively safe solidifying his new position by sacrificing his friend to the committee because the members had bound themselves to at least temporary secrecy.[19]

As though nurturing the spirit of this clandestine combination against McClellan, on January 27 Stanton resumed the secret communications he had conducted during the Buchanan administration, slipping Senator Wade a "most confidential" copy of a surprise executive order dictating that McClellan put the nation's armies in motion by George Washington's birthday—an order that Stanton himself had urged on the president. At 7:30 that evening, Stanton welcomed the three most fervent Radicals among Wade's inquisitors into his home, where they presented him with a packet of dubious testimony they said painted Brigadier General Charles P. Stone as a traitor. With the same collegiality he had shown Wade for the past week, Stanton obliged his subcommittee by promptly issuing an order for Stone's arrest.[20]

General Stone was precisely the sort of soldier Wade and most of his committee members sought to undo. Like McClellan, he was a West Point graduate, a talented engineer, but—most important of all—a Democrat who seemed inimical to abolitionists. On the upper Potomac he had lost the spectacular little battle at Ball's Bluff, near Leesburg, but his real crime seems to have been obeying the fugitive slave laws, under which he returned runaway slaves to loyal Maryland masters. That had wrung a sarcastic rebuke from Charles Sumner, who ridiculed Stone's military ability and smeared him as a slave-catcher. Alluding to the beating Sumner had taken so meekly on the Senate floor, Stone reciprocated in a private note by calling the senator a coward. The Ball's Bluff defeat, which had produced the congressional impetus for Wade's committee in the first place, had also spawned much talk about Stone being a secret secessionist who had lost the fight deliberately. Hostile witnesses from within his division testified to those rumors, dressing them up with accusations that Stone was well respected by the enemy across the river, and with tales of letters passing between him and his counterpart on the other side, under flags of truce. Packets of private letters had also crossed the lines.[21]

It was Stone's responsibility to read any private letters that passed to or from the enemy, to ensure they contained only personal matters and to glean any useful military intelligence they might convey; envelopes came to him unsealed for that purpose. It was also necessary for him to communicate under flags of truce occasionally, especially after the battle, and he had cultivated operatives on the Virginia side who sometimes sent him letters. None of that incriminated him in the least. Confederate regard for him stemmed mainly from his gentlemanly behavior and his disinclination to make war on civilians: the rebels had no doubt about Stone's loyalty to the Union. The rest of the "evidence" consisted of rumors and malicious innuendo, and most of it came from a single New York militia regiment that had given Stone a lot of trouble. As a defense lawyer, and especially as a former prosecutor, Stanton should have spotted the flaws in that accusation at the outset, but he insisted on an arrest, maintaining the committee had presented sufficient evidence. McClellan held off for eleven more days, asking Senator Chandler to give Stone a chance to answer questions, but when the committee did hear from Stone again they refused to cite specific allegations that he could refute, purportedly out of worry that he might retaliate against the subordinates who had accused him.[22]

Finally, a suspicious refugee who was caught slipping across the Potomac from Leesburg provided more testimony against Stone, apparently by answering leading questions. When McClellan received the report of that interview he forwarded it to Stanton, who returned peremptory orders for Stone's arrest, using the illness of Lincoln's sons as an excuse for not telling the president about it. In the middle of the night a guard detail seized the astonished general, and the next day he was taken to Fort Lafayette, in New York Harbor, where he remained six months without charges or trial. Over the next seven weeks McClellan repeatedly reminded Stanton of Stone's plight, lobbying for a trial—but Stanton, whose friends and allies always depicted him as a champion of justice, kept putting him off on the excuse that the committee was still collecting evidence. In fact, Stone had been under arrest only nineteen days when the "investigation" ceased altogether, and thereafter he remained a prisoner at the whim of the secretary of war. It took an act of Congress to finally secure his release: in what would be difficult to interpret as anything less than vindictiveness, Stanton refused to free him until the last day of the congressional deadline.[23]

Stone was only the first victim of the new secretary's animus. At the same time Stanton imprisoned the general, he had Ives, the *Herald* man, thrown into the Old Capitol Prison—apparently for taking up the cause of another state prisoner in the new political prison at Fort Lafayette, and for trying to collect on Stanton's promise of favored journalistic status. Later, Ives went to Fort McHenry as a "prisoner of war."[24]

The fawning hanger-on of 1861 became the grasping bureaucrat of early 1862, assiduously concentrating his power, and less than a month into his tenure he secured full control over the government's civilian arrests. Until then Seward had exercised that authority, but Stanton apparently persuaded both Seward and the president to let him decide who would go free or remain in custody. Stanton himself signed Executive Order Number 1, which took the backhanded form of a general release of all whose liberty Stanton did not consider "incompatible with the public safety." That qualifying clause announced the first major transfer of executive power to the secretary of war, and the next day Seward sent his chief detective over to

Stanton, since the State Department no longer needed him. Stanton appointed two of his own friends as a panel to review each case, assuming his new authority with a deceptively magnanimous air, but six months later his agents would be rounding up so many citizens for political dissent and other "crimes" that he made the Seward regime seem lenient by comparison.[25]

Stanton's word, rather than army regulations, became the new law at the War Department. Colonel Clement A. Finley, a Pennsylvanian nearing his sixty-fifth birthday, had served as an army surgeon since the Madison administration, and he had held the position of surgeon general for eight months when Stanton took office. He was rather an old fogey, and a civilian observer who called him "ossified" saw no way to get rid of him. Stanton found a way. A Pittsburgh acquaintance of Stanton's accused a Philadelphia physician of malfeasance as an employee of the medical bureau, and Stanton passed the allegation on to Finley, evidently expecting him to dismiss the employee without a hearing. Instead, Finley gave the doctor a copy of the informant's letter, and the would-be defendant sued the Pittsburgh man for libel. That brought Stanton's wrath down on the surgeon general, who pointed out that he had merely followed department policy, but Stanton sent Finley into exile, arbitrarily choosing Boston. After a couple of weeks waiting for orders there, Finley saw the light and applied for retirement.[26]

The removal of Finley might have been regarded as an injustice exercised in the interests of efficiency had Stanton not sinned far worse against Finley's very capable successor. Before filling the vacancy, Stanton called in the senior officers of the Sanitary Commission—roughly the equivalent of the modern Red Cross—to seek their opinion on a replacement for Finley. At the top of their list stood Assistant Surgeon William A. Hammond, who had spent a decade as an army surgeon before the war. The entrenched cronyism of the Medical Bureau had required him to start from the bottom when the war lured him back into service, but Hammond showed talent, ability, and an extremely forceful personality that had not endeared him to his superiors, including Simon Cameron. The Sanitary Commission consisted of some powerful celebrities whom Stanton hoped to win over: his first official letter had requested a meeting with the board's general secretary. In front of that delegation Stanton seemed not to object to its choice, although he later claimed to have objected very much. He apparently told them the president preferred the next senior surgeon, Robert Wood, who was known to detest Hammond, but that seems not to have been true. Lincoln himself chose Hammond, whose career Stanton would later try to destroy.[27]

Less than a week after his purported pledge of exclusivity with the conservative *New York Herald*, Stanton conveyed his compliments to the Radical *New York Tribune*, soliciting the support of editor Charles A. Dana with a long letter of appreciation. In another letter at the end of the next week,

Stanton invited Dana's collaboration in the struggle, referring to "the task before us—I say us—because the Tribune has its mission as plainly as I have mine." He offered implicit criticism of McClellan with the remark that his army would have to "fight or run away," and declared that there would soon be an end to "the champagne and oysters on the Potomac." Stanton wrote to Dana an average of once a week initially, defining his views in a manner the influential newspaperman was likely to find most agreeable. He expressed perfect concurrence with Dana's military theorizing, asserting that McClellan should be sending a hundred thousand men westward to rid Kentucky and Tennessee of treason and rebellion "with fire & sword," and complaining that "we have had no war; we have not even been playing war." Still, Dana wondered about Stanton's profuse concurrence at first, inquiring of Senator Sumner whether the new secretary really shared their attachment to abolition.[28]

While he maligned McClellan to his new Radical friends, Stanton pleased them further with kind words about Major General John C. Frémont, whom Lincoln had relieved of his command in Missouri the previous November. Frémont, the Republican Party's first candidate for president, had become the darling of Radical Republicans in the summer of 1861 with an order emancipating the slaves of all Missourians he suspected of complicity in the rebellion. To placate conservatives, the president had revoked that order when Frémont declined to rescind it. Finally Lincoln had removed the general, whose administration in Missouri had included considerable corruption in the channels of supply and transportation. Lincoln had appointed a commission that included Stanton's college classmate David Davis and Holt (his still-conservative former colleague) to look into the claims against Frémont and his quartermaster, Justus McKinstry: the commission would soon report that Frémont and McKinstry had exercised an "orientally despotic power" that had turned St. Louis into the "El Dorado of Army contractors."[29]

Knowing that this report was coming, and perhaps what its results might be, Wade's committee undertook a conspicuously sympathetic investigation of that corruption. Testimony did not begin until February 5, and Wade told Charles Dana on February 3 that it would take a long time to complete, yet he had already prejudged the case: Frémont was innocent of any wrongdoing, Wade insisted, and had been sacrificed "by a weak and wicked Administration." With the first witness yet to be heard, Wade confided that he intended to appeal to the new secretary of war to restore Frémont to command—specifically mentioning that he had influence with Stanton. Wade spoke the truth at least about that: Stanton took no official action until Wade's committee had gone through the motions, but he informed Dana before the committee even began its work that he intended to give Frémont another chance in the field, and a few days later Frémont handed him a plan for a campaign into Texas. Yet only four days previously, after a question apparently suggested by Frémont's case, the eager Ives of the *Herald* had told his editor of Stanton's stated opinion that all "blundering and abolitionist generals" should be "dropped."[30]

Another political controversy arose in the West over an expedition proposed by Senator James H. Lane of Kansas, who had secured a commission as brigadier general from the president, along with permission to take a division of cavalry and infantry south from Fort Leavenworth. The object of the campaign remained vague—it probably aimed to disrupt Confederate forces in Arkansas—but the plan was wrecked by the colliding egos of Lane and Major General David Hunter, who commanded in Kansas. Lane and Hunter both wanted to lead the column, and their contending appeals bothered everyone up the chain of command. In his plea to Stanton, Hunter asked for a free hand with his troops and for the latitude to establish district policy on slavery, as Frémont had in Missouri. Hunter may have heard rumors from the Radical side of Stanton's political persona, and hoped to seduce him, but Stanton referred the tiff to Lincoln, who reminded Lane that if he did not wish to subordinate himself to Hunter he could decline the assignment.[31]

Lincoln replaced Frémont with Henry Halleck, who thought Stanton still held a grudge against him over the New Almaden mine case. A few weeks later Colonel Ethan Allen Hitchcock, who knew Halleck from the old army, came into the War Department as an adviser to the secretary, and when Stanton learned of Hitchcock's friendship with Halleck he volunteered that his antagonism to the New Almaden operators had been purely professional. It was his "partner" who had maligned Halleck, Stanton said, meaning perhaps Peter Della Torre. Hitchcock relayed the explanation, as was evidently intended, although Stanton's spontaneous recollection of the incident cast some doubt on his denial: McClellan later claimed that Stanton described Halleck to him as a scoundrel and liar, while Halleck said the same of Stanton. Halleck nevertheless took Hitchcock's missive at face value and pointed out that he, too, had merely been working as an employee of the mining interests, and had never owned a dollar's worth of stock.[32]

Stanton retained Cameron's assistant secretary of war, railroad executive Thomas Scott. Thanks to a bill pushed through by his new friend Wade, he also quickly appointed two more assistants—John Tucker, who had been helping Cameron arrange army transportation, and Peter Watson, John Manny's patent agent in the McCormick suit. Samuel Butterworth, the New Almaden intriguer and confidant of Daniel Sickles, gratified a contractor friend when he predicted that Stanton would keep Tucker, for that contractor expected Tucker to prove as receptive to his business proposals as Scott had.[33]

Then, Stanton hired Watson's assistant, Albert E. H. Johnson, as the chief clerk of the War Department. Johnson and another clerk remembered Stanton respectfully in print, but their private remarks cast doubt on the sincerity of their published statements, and both men were evidently prone to invention. Johnson lauded Stanton with particular zeal in a public address decades later, and Charles F. Benjamin published a friendly postwar article. Johnson called Stanton a "tyrant," but added a flattering explanation. Benjamin used the same word half a century after he met Stanton, in a letter that contradicted the complimentary flavor of his earlier article: he seemed to resent Stanton's arrogance, and said it was imitated by the "petty tyrants" Stanton chose for his assistant secretaries later in the war, including Charles Dana, formerly of the *Tribune*.[34]

In addition to his assistant secretaries, Stanton brought flocks of new employees into the War Department with him. The day after his nomination, the Senate amended an old bill to allow fifty-two new clerks and messengers in the War Department and ten new places in the adjutant general's office, all to be named by the new secretary. While this reinforced staff tackled daily business, Stanton scoured the disorganized department files. At first he worked late every night, insisting that all official business take place at the department, and for many weeks that rule consigned him to long hours in his second-floor office facing the White House. That pace continued unabated until Saturday night, February 8, when he suddenly collapsed, unconscious, on the floor of his office. He returned to his desk on the Sabbath despite feeling a little less hearty, but it was nearly a week before one of his cabinet colleagues could report Stanton "quite restored to health." For a time afterward he imposed limits on War Department access, with the public's business to be conducted only on Mondays, while Tuesday through Friday would be devoted to military matters, and Saturdays were reserved for members of Congress.[35]

Department business remained slow and uncertain for some time after the installation of the industrious new secretary, who had to familiarize himself with his new domain and, probably, confront a backlog of correspondence. A week after Cameron left, the president sent over a request to elevate a Regular Army captain to brigadier general, but the note was mislaid in the pile of paperwork on Stanton's desk. Lincoln had to repeat the demand three weeks later, but more than another month passed before Stanton issued the commission.[36]

On his first day as secretary, after the dress uniforms had drifted away from his reception, Stanton asked his assistant secretary, Tom Scott, to prepare a report on the quantity and quality of army transportation. Three days later Scott submitted a preliminary report, with recommendations. From his own examination of records in the Ordnance Bureau, Stanton had already contemplated some changes there, as well, and he dispatched Scott on an inspection tour of arsenals and transportation facilities in the West. On January 29, with Watson and Tucker both on duty, Scott started west, where he detected frauds in the quartermaster department—especially by Reuben Hatch, chief quartermaster to Brigadier General Ulysses S. Grant, at Cairo. Grant had already arrested Hatch, whom he suspected of extensive graft, particularly in the realm of river transportation. Only personal connections to the president saved Hatch's hide.[37]

Stanton's preoccupation with transportation reflected the widespread impatience for the nation's armies to move against the enemy. McClellan contemplated shifting some eighty thousand men from the Potomac to Kentucky late in January, after George Thomas's timely victory over a ragtag Confederate division on the upper reaches of the Cumberland River at Mill Springs, Kentucky—about the same time that Stanton claimed the idea as his own, in a letter to Dana. Mill Springs gave encouragement disproportionate to the numbers involved by producing the first rout of Confederate forces since McClellan's campaign in western Virginia, in the first weeks of the war, and by compromising the eastern flank of the long Confederate defense line across Kentucky. Virginia's roads remained too soft for the passage of vast armies, but the navigable rivers in Kentucky and Tennessee beckoned Union forces deep into the Confederate heartland. In the first cabinet meeting after his fainting spell, Stanton surprised some of his colleagues by proposing out of the blue that Congressman Frank Blair—the brother of the postmaster general who thought so little of Stanton—be appointed a brigadier and given command of an expedition to open the Mississippi River. Attorney General Bates suspected that someone else had put Stanton up to it, and the president dismissed the idea, remarking that the grandest goal of all required "the highest general in the region."[38]

That general was already using those rivers. General Halleck had authorized Grant to move up the Tennessee River and cut the long Confederate defense line there, sending him reinforcements for the purpose. Grant put 15,000 men on transports early in February, leaving with a few gunboats under Commodore Andrew Foote and aiming for Fort Henry, just inside the Tennessee line. Fort Donelson, a bigger bastion a few miles away on the Cumberland River, also lay in Tennessee, so Halleck asked McClellan to add Tennessee to his department, taking it away from Don Carlos Buell's Department of the Ohio. Grant's troops were still working their way around Fort Henry on February 6 when the gunboats opened up, and the place capitulated an hour later, after most of the garrison had escaped. With that Grant marched his army overland to Fort Donelson while Foote steamed down the Tennessee to the Ohio and then back up the Cumberland, but when his gunboats arrived the batteries at Donelson handled them rather

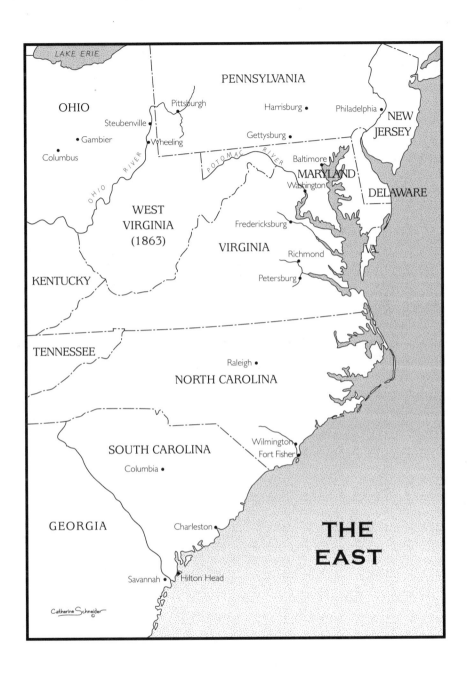

LAKE ERIE

OHIO

PENNSYLVANIA

Pittsburgh

Harrisburg •

Philadelphia •

NEW
JERSEY

Steubenville •

• Gambier

Wheeling

Gettysburg •

Columbus

Baltimore

MARYLAND

Washington

DELAWARE

WEST
VIRGINIA
(1863)

Fredericksburg •

VIRGINIA

Richmond

VA.

KENTUCKY

Petersburg •

TENNESSEE

Raleigh •

NORTH CAROLINA

SOUTH CAROLINA

Wilmington

Fort Fisher

Columbia •

GEORGIA

Charleston •

**THE
EAST**

Savannah •

Hilton Head

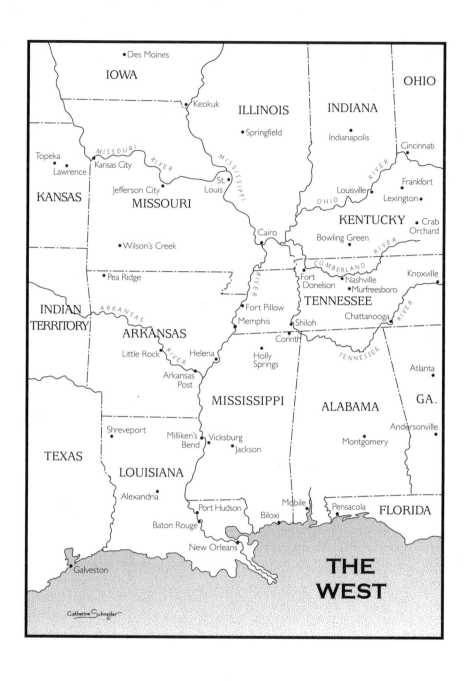

THE
WEST

roughly. Nearly as many troops defended the place as Grant had brought with him, so he awaited more reinforcements. On February 15 the garrison tried to break out, crumpling Grant's right flank and opening an escape route, but irresolute Confederate generals failed to grasp the opportunity and Union troops counterattacked, driving the rebels back into their works. Commanding the fort was John B. Floyd, secretary of war under James Buchanan, who must have wondered whether the noose awaited a cabinet officer who engaged in rebellion. Floyd slipped away with his portion of the garrison, and the next ranking general followed his example, leaving Grant's friend from the old army, Simon Buckner, to accept Grant's demand for unconditional surrender the next morning. As these tidings came in to Washington by telegraph, McClellan tried to capitalize on that rupture in the rebels' defensive network, wiring back to Halleck and Buell for a coordinated advance on Nashville. Apparently without consulting Stanton or McClellan, the president dropped by and sent a telegram to Halleck, adding his own suggestions.[39]

While Grant wrestled with the forts on the parallel rivers, Brigadier General Ambrose Burnside pursued another element of McClellan's grand strategy with an amphibious operation against Albemarle Sound, in North Carolina: Roanoke Island fell to him on February 8. Having had nothing so exciting since Thomas's triumph in Kentucky, Northern newspapers bellowed the news of Fort Henry and Roanoke as bookend victories, giving Lincoln something to brighten his fifty-third birthday. Word of Donelson's surrender added a slightly delirious touch to the air of celebration when it reached Washington on the morning of February 17, with Stanton exuberantly calling for three cheers from the War Department staff.[40]

When Stanton left the War Department that night he went straight to the White House, bustling into the president's office with a commission for Grant as major general. Lincoln was busy with his private secretary, John Nicolay, but he immediately signed the commission, voicing a general compliment to the soldiers of the West. At an expression of regret that Floyd had eluded capture, Stanton muttered that he wanted to catch his former colleague and hang him—just as Floyd seemed to fear. Then Stanton recited his melodramatic version of Floyd's last cabinet meeting, in which he said Buchanan's ministers had "almost come to blows" over Major Anderson's withdrawal to Fort Sumter. He depicted himself as the champion of the Union cause, chastising Buchanan for the failures of his administration while accusing both Jacob Thompson and Floyd of embezzlement and graft, and he seemed to take credit for forcing Floyd to resign. None of the original witnesses would ever remember the incident Stanton's way, but his own rendition of his performance impressed his White House audience quite favorably.[41]

Stanton habitually embellished his own utterances in the retelling, but he bristled when others did so for him. Soon after regaling Lincoln and his inner circle with his fierce patriotism, Stanton addressed a Washington conference on the army and the railroads, at which an Associated Press reporter portrayed him as giving generous credit to McClellan for the recent victories. The correspondent had not been present to hear what was said, but he wrote that Stanton expressed complete confidence in the young general, "whose military schemes, gigantic and well matured, are now exhibited to a rejoicing country." That account conflicted with the low opinion Stanton professed for McClellan within Radical earshot, and when Charles Dana sent a clipping of the story to him Stanton called it "a ridiculous and impertinent effort to puff the General by a false publication of words I never uttered." Dana published that denial in the *Tribune*, offering the first indication that all was not well between the secretary of war and the commander of the national armies, and conservative sheets quickly deduced that Stanton meant to put McClellan "in the shade." To confirm Dana's faith in his aversion to McClellan, Stanton ridiculed the general's efforts to ensure effective cooperation between Halleck and Buell, describing "a certain Military hero in the telegraph office at Washington last Sunday organizing victory, and by sublime military combinations capturing Fort Donelson *six hours after* Grant . . . had taken it sword in hand & had victorious possession."[42]

Stanton ultimately traced the story of the railroad conference to McClellan's friend Samuel Barlow, whose account of the meeting the reporter had embroidered to convey the "general terms" of Stanton's speech. Barlow had clearly read too much into Stanton's remarks, and the episode forced Stanton to lend some authority to one or the other of his contradictory poses. Neither McClellan nor his friends could miss the secretary's disavowal of his reported expression of confidence in the commanding general.[43]

For McClellan, the turnabout came as no surprise. On February 19, the day before the railroad conference, Ben Wade and Andrew Johnson had called at the War Department on behalf of the Committee on the Conduct of the War to complain about the relative isolation of Washington. Rebel batteries blockaded the lower Potomac, and Confederate troops in northern Virginia controlled the Baltimore & Ohio Railroad, impeding transportation and supply from the Chesapeake and the western states. Wade had earlier parried a committee resolution on this very matter to avoid even implied criticism of Stanton, for he and the secretary were now firm allies. He also owed Stanton a great favor: Wade's antagonism to the president's management of the war had caused the Ohio legislature to balk at giving him another term in the Senate, but Stanton had let the legislature know that he would consider it "a great national calamity" if Wade were not reelected.[44]

The blockade of the Potomac and the railroad had to be addressed somehow, and in his interview with the two senators Stanton expressed perfect agreement, melodramatically describing "his cheek burning with shame at this disgrace upon the nation." He diverted the responsibility for those embarrassments to McClellan, whom he went to fetch from another room. Wade angrily grilled the general about the two logistical problems. As Stanton might have explained, had he felt the least bit supportive of his general, McClellan was planning an operation to restore traffic on the Baltimore & Ohio: he told Wade he hoped to accomplish it within days, after building a pontoon bridge over the Potomac to provide an avenue of retreat, if one should be necessary. Wade impatiently replied that if his troops had to come back across the river they might "come back in their coffins." Less than three weeks before, Wade had confronted General Stone with suspicions of treachery based largely on the accusation that he had sent his troops over the Potomac without adequate means of withdrawing or reinforcing them, but McClellan made no reply to this rank hypocrisy save, perhaps, an angry stare. Stanton endorsed Wade's every remark, and if McClellan entered the room with any doubts whether his onetime friend had taken sides with the Radicals he left those doubts behind when he walked out the door.[45]

Willie, the president's twelve-year-old son, died of typhoid fever on the afternoon of February 20, and Lincoln all but abandoned his duties for most of a week, neglecting correspondence and avoiding official visitors. In a strange contrast, considering his customary reaction to family tragedy, Stanton buried himself in work at the same time, while his own son James lay at home with no great hope of survival. It seems improbable that he felt less for the boy than he had for his first child, two decades before. Instead, he may have found that his overwhelming new duties distracted him from the grief that might completely overcome him if he gave in to it. He alluded to the baby's anticipated death almost incidentally in a letter to his sister, admitting that he threw himself so completely into department business that Ellen sometimes did not see him for days at a time, and had to endure the ordeal essentially without him.[46]

While the president mourned, Stanton communicated indirectly with the western generals by sending Tom Scott his "general impressions" of the movements they should undertake. He issued no order, merely telling Scott that he hoped to persuade McClellan to transfer fifty thousand men to Halleck and Buell, but Ben Wade had badgered McClellan about beginning operations in Virginia only two days previously. Stanton complained that the commanding general now feared sending troops to the West, lest it inhibit or delay the campaign in the East, although Stanton maintained he had plenty of men for any plan. Stanton may have embraced his western schemes for the potential to diminish McClellan's stature as much as for strategic advantages, and he was already beginning to deprecate the general within the department.[47]

    At this juncture Stanton composed an order in his own hand, citing executive authority for peremptorily taking "military possession of all the telegraphic lines in the United States." The day after Willie's funeral a subdued Lincoln resumed work, holding a cabinet council in which Stanton must have convinced him of the need for such an autocratic imposition. The order went out that day under Stanton's signature. It named Edward Sanford, president of the American Telegraph Company, as "military supervisor of telegraphic messages throughout the United States," and Sanford's first act announced Stanton's prohibition against publishing any intelligence about military operations, which he distributed privately to the editor and publisher of every major newspaper.[48]

    Seizing formal control of wire traffic assured more certain communications with commanders in the various departments, and it reduced expenses: Stanton had already cautioned Assistant Secretary Scott about the cost of his telegrams, and the government could not be charged for messages transmitted by army operators over their own or commandeered lines. Those benefits would have constituted the public argument for the takeover, but the inaugural order from Sanford, and Stanton's later abuse of the authority he had assumed, highlight the profound political control it also gave the secretary of war. Stanton could not but have foreseen the power to dictate what information reporters might send, and to encourage positive coverage of his department and the administration through selective application of that power. His appropriation of the telegraph system soon made him the main conduit of information for all the most important government business, and his habit of withholding news even from cabinet colleagues demonstrated how much he prized that role. His refusal to delegate authority over the telegraph service to department commanders often impeded and frustrated military operations, but he seemed to prefer control to efficiency.[49]

    It was also Stanton's aim to control McClellan. Under Cameron the army had essentially run itself, and McClellan had exercised a remarkably free hand, especially when a diffident commander in chief hesitated to interfere. McClellan had all but removed the secretary of war from the chain of command, bringing the adjutant general of the army into his own headquarters, while Cameron was reduced to a liaison to the governors and contractors who provided troops and equipment. When Stanton spoke of having to persuade McClellan on matters of broad military planning he revealed that the general's independence persisted, and betrayed his unhappiness with it. Stanton intended to reassert the authority of his office, interposing himself between the president and the general, and the easiest way to achieve dominance over someone like McClellan might be to orchestrate his removal, at least as general in chief. Stanton may have begun working toward that end from the day he assumed his duties as secretary, and his efforts were about to come to fruition.[50]

While the army around Washington had indeed done little over the winter, the poor road conditions offered some excuse. More frequent frosts and thaws worsened the potential for mud, which the larger armies of the East could churn into a quagmire, and without the longitudinal rivers of the West a drive to the south posed a logistical nightmare through early spring. Using the water routes he did have, McClellan planned to concentrate an army near Annapolis, carry it down Chesapeake Bay on steamers, and land it at Urbanna, fifty miles east of Richmond on the lower Rappahannock River, where warmer weather and sandier soil seemed to promise less mud. That route would bypass the Manassas works and the batteries on the Potomac, forcing the Confederates to give up both as they raced from Manassas to save their capital, which McClellan hoped to reach first by shorter, drier roads; his cavalry would burn bridges and deprive the rebels of the railroad. Lincoln instead directed McClellan to move a few miles south from Alexandria, cross the Occoquan River, and seize the railroad below Manassas, forcing the rebels into an abrupt retreat or a fight for life; that shorter route would not only be faster but would keep McClellan's army closer to his own capital.[51]

Missing the tactical ingenuity of Lincoln's proposed flanking maneuver, McClellan objected that the Occoquan route gave the enemy the chance to resist his advance at every step from highly defensible positions, making it bloody and time-consuming: when Union forces finally did reach Richmond, it would already have been heavily fortified, while a dash from Urbanna should find the city unprepared. His pitch for that plan foresaw the grueling campaigns of other generals who would try the direct route to Richmond, and with Joe Johnston in command of the rebel army McClellan's anxiety warranted consideration, especially under the traditional theory of war as a contest for capitals. Lincoln's concern for Washington implied adherence to the same theory from the defensive perspective, but the offensive aspect of the president's Occoquan plan took a more modern view of the rebel army as the proper objective.[52]

By forcing a Confederate withdrawal toward Richmond, the Urbanna movement would theoretically have stopped the raids on the Baltimore & Ohio and allowed for its rapid reconstruction. Lincoln's hesitation to approve the plan, along with Radical indignation over the inconveniences in transportation, persuaded McClellan to mount a rapid drive to restore that railroad. He had long since notified Halleck of the desire for a general offensive by February 22, in accordance with the president's directive, and

Halleck's initiative had already been productive. McClellan had also ordered operations begun against New Orleans and coastal Florida, Georgia, and South Carolina, and the operation on the B&O would represent the opening stroke for the Army of the Potomac.[53]

The program called for a pontoon footbridge across the Potomac at Harper's Ferry, with a flotilla of canal boats as the foundation to a stronger bridge, for the passage of supply trains, ammunition wagons, and heavy artillery. With those spans in place, a sizable force could march into Virginia and seize Winchester, where Major General Thomas J. Jackson had spent the winter with a small but troublesome Confederate army. Engineers laid a pontoon bridge on Wednesday, February 26, allowing thousands of troops to cross into Virginia, and in a driving rainstorm that night McClellan sent back a report of glorious success. The boats came up the Chesapeake & Ohio Canal, arriving the next morning. In howling winds the first of them turned toward the lift lock passing into the river, but it was narrower by several inches than the regular locks along the canal and would not admit the long line of waiting boats. After lunch McClellan wired his chief of staff in Washington to send no more troops for the present, but by the middle of the afternoon it was evident that no solution could be found, and he had to admit the failure to Stanton. He would have to rebuild the railroad bridge, he explained, which would take some time, and until then "Stonewall" Jackson might remain at Winchester.[54]

Stanton would have received McClellan's good-news telegram of Wednesday night by the time he began work on Thursday morning, but he went all day without sending that encouraging information to the president. Not until word of the mortifying roadblock came over the wire, around the dinner hour, did he hurry over to the White House, burst into Lincoln's office, and melodramatically lock the door. Finding the president with Nicolay again, Stanton read Wednesday's auspicious telegram first, as though to build their hopes: then he read the second one, describing the impossibly narrow lift lock, and Lincoln asked what that meant.

"It means that it's a damned fizzle," Stanton spat. "It means that he doesn't intend to do anything." That excessively bleak and accusative assessment, conveyed with the amplified air of indignation that had swayed many a jury, elicited a furious reaction. Lincoln called in McClellan's chief of staff (and father-in-law), General Randolph Marcy, reprimanding him in place of McClellan in a tone and vocabulary especially harsh for the habitually kindly chief executive. "Lincoln swore like a Phillistine," claimed a correspondent of the *Chicago Tribune*, who may have gotten the details from Stanton, and it seemed that McClellan stood on the brink of removal. In the course of his tongue-lashing, the president repeated the phrase Stanton had suggested, telling Marcy that it was becoming a common belief that McClellan "does not intend to do anything." When Marcy stammered out an explanation Lincoln cut him off, dismissing him abruptly when he tried to continue.[55]

The canal-boat fiasco came up the next day in a cabinet meeting, and Senator Sumner found Lincoln still agitated about it the day after that. Such anger seemed unwarranted, because reconstruction of the B&O began immediately, and Winchester fell to Union soldiers two weeks after that first pontoon bridge spanned the Potomac at Harper's Ferry. McClellan learned of the president's fury when he returned to Washington, but Stanton used a lie to stop him from seeing Lincoln about it, telling the general that "upon learning the whole state of the case the President was fully satisfied." That was March 1, while Lincoln was still fuming, and Stanton—who had fanned the president's anger—certainly knew as much. He would misrepresent the episode again seven years later, in an interview with a historian of the war, exaggerating the consequences of the blunder and claiming, falsely, that he had tried to calm Lincoln's rage. With that sly trick Stanton set the precedent of denying McClellan direct access to the White House, and in the process he tarnished the general's image a little further in the president's eyes.[56]

Cheering military news poured in from across the country as winter came to an end, with far-flung armies winning victories every few days. Grant captured Clarksville, Tennessee, on February 19, and Buell marched into Nashville six days later. The last rebel soldier left Kentucky when Columbus, their "Gibraltar of the West," fell into Union hands on March 4, and Federal troops thrashed a Confederate army in northwest Arkansas during the first week in March, clearing that corner of the state. Instead of redounding to the glory of George McClellan as commander of all the armies in the United States, those victories seemed to reflect badly on McClellan the commander of the Army of the Potomac, whose progress seemed slow and insignificant.[57]

While McClellan's light faded, Stanton gained in influence with the president, who granted his wish to make Andrew Johnson military governor of Tennessee. Tom Scott was testing the pulse of moderate Tennesseans in Nashville, and he pleaded with Stanton not to appoint the polarizing, uncompromising Johnson, but Stanton seems not to have apprised Lincoln of Scott's objection.[58]

McClellan turned next to his Urbanna plan. On March 7 he held a council of war with his eleven division commanders and his chief engineer, asking them to decide between attacking Manassas and slipping behind Johnston's army downriver. He stood out of the decision, and by a two-thirds majority they opted for the Urbanna landing: McDowell, Edwin Sumner, Samuel Heintzelman, and the chief engineer, John Barnard, voted to move against Manassas, while the other eight favored the amphibious operation. Seven of the eight were admirers and allies of McClellan. Evidently counting McClellan and General Marcy as well, Stanton complained that the council showed ten generals who were "afraid to fight," and he may have pressed Lincoln to promote those generals most objectionable to McClellan. The next day, March 8, the president issued an order, the original of which was written by Stanton, organizing the Army of the Potomac into four corps commanded by the three "fighting" generals of the March 7 council and by Erasmus Keyes, a Republican in the anti-McClellan clique who had given the most equivocal support to the Urbanna plan. The largest of the corps, with four divisions, went to McDowell, the Radicals' favorite soldier after Frémont. Those happened to be the four senior generals, yet the same document named another inexperienced but reliably Republican political general, James Wadsworth, to command the defenses of Washington. In a separate order Lincoln required McClellan to begin his movement within ten days, but stipulated that he could not have more than fifty thousand men for it until he had subdued the batteries blockading the lower Potomac. McClellan still thought the batteries could be eliminated without loss of men or time by flanking them with the landing at Urbanna, but those guns seemed a particular bugbear for congressional Radicals, especially on Wade's committee, and they had enlisted Stanton in their cause.[59]

To McClellan, the order naming corps commanders posed the worst intrusion. He protested that he wanted to choose his own corps chiefs once they had been tested in the field, but Radicals suspected he would select his personal favorites. The Committee on the Conduct of the War had already stressed to the president the importance of the corps organization, and requested an interview with him immediately after an especially friendly evening conclave at Stanton's home, where the secretary pledged his loyalty to the committee "in every respect." In their conference with Lincoln, Wade and the other members told him that Stanton shared their sense of urgency, but the topic ranged so far beyond the scope of their authority that they probably approached the president at Stanton's behest, to add pressure. The order was almost certainly his idea, and he may well have been the source of the suspicion that McClellan would appoint men who would serve him faithfully and strengthen his position. That was Stanton's own habit, after all, as his War Department appointments demonstrated, and he would have been on the lookout for it. Lincoln told the committee members that he did not share their anxiety about it, but he finally consented to approve the very detailed order Stanton had prepared. Pedestrians ambling along Pennsylvania Avenue past McClellan's headquarters that night saw him staring reflectively out the window toward the White House, as though pondering his dwindling independence.[60]

The next day came reports that the Confederates had abandoned their batteries on the Potomac and Johnston's army was retreating from its works at Manassas. McClellan rode over the Long Bridge into Virginia in the afternoon to investigate with his entire army, but the divisions he was supposed to organize into corps were still camped indiscriminately, and he wanted to send them off in order of their proximity to the enemy. He asked Stanton if he could suspend the order to form corps for the moment, but Stanton, who had likely instigated that order, replied uncooperatively that it was "the duty of every officer to obey the President's orders." He relented only when McClellan explained that such insistence would delay the pursuit of Johnston, and that the responsibility would be Stanton's; even then, Stanton deceptively alluded to the corps structure as "a policy which the President has ordered."[61]

Before McClellan left to lead the army forward, the White House lapsed into a panic over information that the Confederate ironclad *Virginia* had steamed out of Norfolk on March 8 and attacked the U.S. fleet at Hampton Roads, sinking the 50-gun *Congress* and the 24-gun *Cumberland*, and grounding the 47-gun *Minnesota*. A break in the underwater cable delayed any report from Fort Monroe; the message had to go by boat to Cape Charles and then be relayed by telegraph through Wilmington, Delaware. It reached Washington on the forenoon of Sunday, March 9, just after the president summoned Senator Orville Browning and his family for a social visit. Browning, an old friend of Lincoln's from Illinois, stepped into the executive office to find the president and two of his private secretaries there, along with an agitated Stanton, who was waving a telegram with the latest news. Nicolay described Stanton stalking back and forth "like a caged lion," while the other secretary, John Hay, thought him "fearfully stampeded." Stanton raved that the ironclad would sink or capture the entire fleet, seize Fort Monroe, and appear before Washington by dark. He scoffed at navy secretary Gideon Welles's comforting explanation that the Union ironclad *Monitor* was on its way with two big guns, and Welles described Stanton as "almost frantic." The president showed a little excitement himself, and left for the Navy Yard with Browning to see Captain John Dahlgren, whom Lincoln regarded as an expert on naval technology. The president seemed calm when he arrived there, but Dahlgren aroused his apprehension by concluding that the *Virginia* drew little enough water that it might reach Washington, or for that matter New York. Welles suggested that it would be well if the ram did climb the Potomac, for it would be easier to trap, but he observed that it could not attack both Washington and New York at once, and he doubted it would threaten either.[62]

The supplies and transports gathered at Annapolis for the Urbanna expedition suddenly seemed at risk, and the presence of an invulnerable enemy warship in the Chesapeake banished any notion of an amphibious operation. Then the *Monitor* fought the *Virginia* to a draw, and the Tidewater seemed open to navigation once more, but the news that Johnston was pulling back toward Richmond scotched the Urbanna operation, because that brought the enemy as close to Richmond as McClellan would be at Urbanna. McClellan, however, had already formulated an alternative plan, farther down the Chesapeake.[63]

That afternoon Senator Browning returned to the White House. Stanton was still there, talking wildly about having sent to New York for a powerful ironclad steamer to be built immediately, "at whatever cost," to come down and destroy the *Virginia*—as though it were within his jurisdiction and could be done overnight. Stanton interfered in naval affairs enough to order his quartermaster general and Captain Dahlgren to load a fleet of old canal boats, colliers, and transports with stone and sand for scuttling in the channel should the *Virginia* start upriver. The boats were collected, but when Welles got wind of it he objected to Stanton meddling in his department, so Stanton offered the vessels to the navy, for the same purpose. Welles quipped that it would be a pity for them to close the river themselves when they had just been freed from the Confederate guns that blockaded it. Then he added that Stanton's decrepit armada might better be sunk in the channel of the Elizabeth River, to trap the *Virginia* at Norfolk. The army would first have to carry a battery covering the mouth of the river from Sewell's Point, he said, and Stanton jumped on that suggestion next, pursuing the idea for days.[64]

The visibly distraught secretary of war also disturbed Browning with disparaging remarks about McClellan that revealed his utter lack of confidence in the country's top general. Stanton said that Lewis Cass had suggested trying one general after another, until he found someone satisfactory, adding that he wanted to do just that, and the unimaginative inspiration from Cass may have been what brought Stanton a visitor the following day. Late on Monday morning, March 10, with cavalry and artillery clogging Pennsylvania Avenue and infantry filling Fourteenth Street all the way to the Long Bridge, an old soldier made his way from the Washington train depot to Stanton's office. The secretary was out, and Peter Watson suggested that the old man wait for Stanton at Willard's. He did as Watson advised, but at the hotel he developed a severe nosebleed and had to send for a doctor, who put him to bed in one of the rooms.[65]

The patient was Colonel Ethan Allen Hitchcock, grandson of the Revolutionary hero whose name he bore. He had left the army several years before, almost four decades after graduating from the military academy, and his career had included conspicuous service on the staff of Winfield Scott. Halleck had suggested promoting Hitchcock and assigning him over the various brigadiers in Tennessee, to reconcile conflicts in seniority. Stanton had wired Hitchcock at his home in St. Louis the previous Friday, calling him to Washington for an interview, and for all his nearly sixty-four years Hitchcock had complied, arriving within seventy hours of reading the telegram. Stanton showed up in his room at six o'clock that evening, acting his most courteous, sensitive, and solicitous self, and offering to take Hitchcock to his house to be nursed. With the subservient mien he had nearly abandoned since ascending to the war office, Stanton struck Hitchcock as "civil beyond expression," offering to do "anything" for him: he offered to make him a major general, since his advice was crucial even if he could not take the field. The old man demurred on all fronts, declining to disturb Stanton's home and hesitating to accept the commission, but he did agree to offer advice informally.[66]

Considering the juncture at which he had chosen to ask Hitchcock to the capital, Stanton was manifestly anticipating McClellan's departure on the Urbanna campaign, when the War Department would lack his military expertise. Stanton was also probably preparing to argue that McClellan should be relieved as general in chief when he went to the front, and if the president acquiesced it might be prudent to have a qualified candidate to fill the vacancy, lest Lincoln think later of reinstating McClellan.

At the cabinet meeting on March 11 Stanton submitted a report on the expenses and administration of the army, eliciting concern at least from Attorney General Bates over the inefficiency, disorganization, and "reckless extravagance" it revealed. Stanton blamed McClellan, complaining that his subordinates filed their reports with the general, while McClellan reported nothing to the War Department. After only fifty days in office Stanton could not reasonably have been held responsible, but his report and explanation led directly to the end he had seemed to pursue from the start: the cabinet and president agreed that McClellan should be relieved from the top command while in the field with the Army of the Potomac, and any reports from army commanders would go directly to the secretary of war. The decision arrogated to Stanton the responsibilities for which McClellan's passion for planning and organization best fitted him, leaving him with the field command he was least competent to wield. Stanton again wrote both the rough draft and finished copy of the order, indicating that it was likely his proposal, and that evening Lincoln called Seward and Chase to hear him read the order before endorsing it. Seward suggested that Stanton sign it, to assert his authority a little more forcefully, but Stanton came in just then and objected. As with the assignment of corps commanders and the conditions imposed on the Urbanna operation, Stanton preferred to remain nominally aloof, lest he corroborate the rampant allegations that he had it in for McClellan.[67]

On advice he had received from Hitchcock that day, Stanton used the same order to give Halleck command of the entire West, from Knoxville to Kansas, in accordance with a plan Halleck had been pushing for a month. Keeping his early promise to Charles Dana, he also persuaded Lincoln to create the Mountain Department between Halleck's bailiwick and McClellan's, and to put John Frémont in charge of it. Stanton's part in granting the assignment to Frémont would be evident to Ben Wade, who would share that knowledge with other Radical Republicans, but sending the order out under the president's name saved Stanton trouble with Democrats.[68]

The first inkling McClellan had of his reduced position came from his father-in-law, General Marcy, who read of it in the morning edition of the *National Intelligencer* on March 12. Lincoln had meant the blow to fall more softly: he sent a former Ohio governor over to McClellan's camp to explain the reasoning personally, and comfort the general with assurances that he still owned the president's confidence and affection. That sensitive gesture succeeded in spite of the unsettling surprise, bringing the young general to an apparently sincere expression of gratitude for Lincoln's kindness. No such tact infected the chief of the War Department, who oversaw the transfer of administrative responsibilities with cold efficiency.[69]

The order removing McClellan as general in chief named no successor, allowing him to consider it a temporary measure, as the order implied. The duties he had assumed from General Scott fell on the inexperienced Stanton, aided by what advice he could gather from professionals like Hitchcock. Two days after securing McClellan's demotion, Stanton convened the first meeting of a "war board" consisting of himself, the adjutant general, quartermaster general, commissary general, and the chiefs of ordnance and engineers. Consulting daily with them, he assumed the duties of general in chief, so the United States dispensed with an overall military commander on the same day that the Confederate States adopted one.[70]

Johnston's army had settled into new positions beyond the Rappahannock River, halfway to Richmond. Pursuit seemed pointless, if the costly overland campaign to Richmond were to be avoided. McClellan had adopted the compulsory corps organization by then, and on the morning of March 13 he sat with the four new corps commanders at Fairfax Court House to discuss what should be done next. They concluded by formal votes that McClellan's substitute plan for the obsolete Urbanna movement posed the best chance of success: to sail down to Fort Monroe and strike for Richmond along the peninsula between the York and James rivers—presuming the *Virginia* could be contained by the *Monitor*. With five days left before the deadline in the president's March 8 order, McClellan conveyed the results of the war council to the War Department by the hand of General McDowell, but Stanton telegraphed late that afternoon that the paperwork included no discussion of a plan. Perhaps Stanton merely wanted more details, but McClellan quickly replied that McDowell should have given him the plan. Having learned that Stanton did not want to appear to be slowing things down, McClellan hinted once again that any nitpicking would only delay the offensive: if the proposal met with Stanton's approval, it could begin the next morning, and the secretary's "speedy action" would facilitate it. Stanton must have hurried to the White House for a quick discussion about it, and he sent word back the same night that the president approved, so long as Washington were left "entirely secure," and the army moved somewhere, right away.[71]

On Friday, March 15, as the Army of the Potomac marched back toward the docks at Alexandria, McClellan returned to Washington for one last weekend at home. When he arrived at his headquarters on Jackson Square, that night or the next morning, he found his telegraph office denuded of equipment and records. While the general was out in the field Stanton had ordered the wires, keys, files, and operators removed to the War Department, where he installed everything in the second-floor telegraph room connecting to his own office. Stanton had assumed authority over all telegraph lines in the country less than three weeks before, and the creation of a central telegraph office would have been a logical next step, especially with McClellan bound for the front, but it lent an air of permanence to McClellan's removal as general in chief. It also boded ill for their future relations that Stanton waited until McClellan went away for a few days to seize everything, without a word of notice before or after the fact.[72]

The appropriation of McClellan's headquarters telegraph began the active phase of Stanton's effort to edge the general out of the limelight. McClellan knew he had enemies working diligently against him in Washington—and primarily Ben Wade's joint committee, which sent a delegation to Manassas on March 13 to investigate accusations that McClellan had long ignored an obvious Confederate withdrawal. Stanton, too, seemed unmistakably hostile. Sam Barlow had begun to doubt Stanton's professed friendship for the general, and claimed that he had said so to the secretary.[73]

Those fears were fully justified. When a partially recovered Ethan Allen Hitchcock showed up at the War Department again, on March 15, Stanton bluntly asked him if he would take McClellan's place as commander of the Army of the Potomac. "I was amazed," Hitchcock admitted that evening. "I told him, at once, that I *could not*." Long-established executive usage did not endow the secretary of war with authority to unilaterally order so significant a substitution: Stanton may have pretended otherwise, but Abraham Lincoln would not have been inclined to waive his prerogative in the appointment of army commanders. Inevitably Stanton knew, as he offered the post to Hitchcock, that he would have had to persuade Lincoln, but he had succeeded remarkably in that enterprise of late. Hitchcock rejected the proposition in absolute dismay, so Stanton asked if he would take control of the army's Ordnance Bureau, but he wanted nothing to do with that, either. Whispering that Lincoln was under great pressure to remove McClellan, Stanton took Hitchcock over to the White House, where the president confirmed as much by producing a fresh letter from a citizen who had demanded McClellan's dismissal as a traitor. Lincoln, whom Hitchcock judged frank and approachable, explained that although he held constitutional authority over the nation's military he knew nothing about it, by which he seemed to hint at having Hitchcock serve as general in chief. After relentless pushing from Stanton (who, Hitchcock thought, "hardly knows what he wants, himself"), the old veteran agreed to accept an appointment as major general if he could serve only in an advisory capacity under the secretary of war. Stanton allowed him to write his own orders for that duty.[74]

That very evening, someone overheard Stanton calling McClellan "a dead failure," but McClellan had ridden back to the city that night, and Stanton's campaign against the general turned more covert again. He took the precaution of closing his office door before regaling Hitchcock with a catalog of anecdotes illustrating McClellan's incompetence, but next he comforted McClellan's chief engineer, John Barnard, with the patently insincere assertion that he was the general's best friend. Then, on the eve of the president's final date for the offensive, Stanton told Barnard that McClellan should not move until he was absolutely ready—as though encouraging him to miss the deadline. Fortunately for McClellan that ploy came too late: he had the first of his anticipated 130,000 men on the water by March 18, the last of those ten days. On the evening of March 24 Stanton summoned Wade's committee to his office to lament his inability to have McClellan ousted, and incidentally to take personal credit for persuading Lincoln to remove the general from the overall command. Unless he played it very close to the vest Stanton must have stopped looking for someone to take over the army while the general remained within riding distance of the capital, but McClellan started south on April 1. The next day Stanton resumed his hunt for a replacement, and he apparently accelerated his covert efforts to undermine McClellan.[75]

While taking Senator Browning home in his carriage the night of April 2, Stanton asked him to intercede with the president on behalf of Napoleon Bonaparte Buford, the fifty-five-year-old colonel of an Illinois regiment. Buford had graduated from West Point in 1827, but his antebellum military career was limited to eight years as an artillery lieutenant. In the spring of 1862 Buford's regiment was wading through swamps along the Mississippi: how he came to Stanton's notice can only be surmised—perhaps the martial name itself had drawn his attention—but Stanton suggested promoting him to major general over the head of every brigadier in the service, and giving him command of the Army of the Potomac.[76]

Stanton and Browning had just come from speaking with the president, where Stanton had read them a letter he had been given by a prominent person he refused to name. It may have come to him through Ben Wade, who had just received it from a constituent. According to that correspondent, before the war McClellan had been inducted into a secret, largely Southern society called the Knights of the Golden Circle by the secession apostle William Yancey. As in the case of General Stone, Wade wasted no time passing the unsubstantiated allegation along to Stanton, who made haste to convey it to the president without any investigation of his own. Browning remembered Stanton substituting Jefferson Davis's name for Yancey's as he read the letter, and purporting that the Confederate president still commanded the general's loyalty. Lincoln rejected any suggestion that McClellan was disloyal, and Stanton quickly added that he concurred, but contended that many others questioned the general's loyalty, which damaged public confidence in him. Later, in the carriage, Stanton told Browning a completely different story, admitting that he did believe McClellan was guided by Davis's influence, and that he thought the general should have been removed from command long before. Stanton had evidently hoped to sway the president with the accusative letter, but on finding Lincoln unreceptive he had lapsed into his perennial tone of artificial agreement. While the secretary of war thus strove to disparage him far and wide, McClellan gathered his forces at Fort Monroe for the most ambitious military campaign the United States had ever seen.[77]

9

BEST FRIEND TO ALL

When Stanton presented the cabinet with his preliminary report on the army, on March 11, 1862, his estimate of the number of men under arms came as a shock. His war board had calculated 672,878 men, while no one, including Stanton, had anticipated more than half a million. Rather than yielding a sense of security against the presumably smaller Confederate army, the revelation provoked alarm at the enormous expense. Stanton had found only $200,000 left in appropriations for the Quartermaster Department, but quartermaster requests totaled $76.5 million. Financial observers in New York predicted that by spring the nation would demand an end to the war just to avoid bankruptcy, and Stanton's report kindled the same fear among cabinet members.[1]

Two weeks before, the president had signed the Legal Tender Act, forestalling federal insolvency by authorizing the sale of $500 million in twenty-year bonds, the printing of $150 million in paper money that Stanton would once have raged against, and the imposition of $150 million in new taxes. Paying for the equivalent of Napoleon's Grande Armée would require still more government borrowing, or worse yet the inflationary printing of more treasury notes. Secretary Chase gauged the daily cost of the war at $1.5 million, and the War Department alone had accounted for more than $21 million in outstanding requisitions on the day Lincoln's signature certified "greenbacks" as money. The army, Chase warned Stanton, already exceeded the size allowed by statute, and its payroll cost the treasury $325,000 or more per day.[2]

A spate of Union victories cast a bright light on the financial situation, bringing hope that the rebellion might soon be crushed and federal expenses restored to normal. After the fall of Fort Donelson, Captain Dahlgren guessed that the rebellion would collapse within another sixty days, and events were keeping pace with that schedule. On March 1 *Harper's Weekly* reported "the beginning of the end," and as early as March 12 the *New York Times* went a step further and declared "the end of the rebellion," pointing to victories in Tennessee and at Pea Ridge, Arkansas, as well as Johnston's evacuation of Manassas. The abandonment of Manassas in particular impressed the editor as "a confession by the rebels that the war is ended." Two days later the *Times* announced that the rebels at Winchester, Virginia, had decamped, and the day after that a special supplement detailed the retreat of Confederate forces from their Mississippi River bastion at New Madrid, Missouri, describing it as "another victory, or what is the same thing, another evacuation by the rebels." Then Burnside captured New Bern and Beaufort, North Carolina, while Thomas Sherman's troops seized St. Augustine and Jacksonville, Florida, finding pockets of Union sentiment. Rebels had also been driven out of New Mexico. Union armies moved to besiege coastal forts in Georgia and North Carolina, and Island Number 10 in the Mississippi. "Victory is crowning the U.S. movements on every hand," rejoiced a Pennsylvanian living in Canada. Headlines announced the capture of New Orleans a little prematurely, but Butler's expedition and a fleet under David Farragut were on their way up the Mississippi. Even Stonewall Jackson, who had gained fame at Bull Run, met defeat at Kernstown on March 23, and it began to look as though all those boys in blue might be home for the harvest.[3]

The sister of Postmaster General Blair and Frank Blair, whose father chatted frequently with Lincoln, foresaw the complete suppression of the rebellion by the Fourth of July, and such predictions grew shorter by the day. On the last Saturday of March, with the Army of the Potomac winding down its namesake river to presumably deal Richmond a fatal blow, at least one Washingtonian expected the next week to decide the war. By Thursday, April 3, it was generally understood that McClellan had landed a hundred thousand troops on the tip of the Yorktown peninsula, and aristocratic New Yorkers were betting he would dine in Richmond by the following Sunday.[4]

Ten weeks of virtually unbroken military success intoxicated Unionists across the North, and Stanton imbibed that euphoria himself. Late in March he alluded to "this hour of apparent victory" in a private letter, and a few days later he gave official confirmation of that same optimistic illusion. On the third day of April he directed all army recruiting officers to close up shop, sell whatever government property remained, and proceed to their regiments with any detailed soldiers and all their recruits. Weeks later, when it became obvious that this had been a stupendous blunder, Stanton would claim that his order had only been temporary, to tally up how many troops the nation had accumulated, and that he planned to keep replenishing the ranks. That would be easier to believe had he not waited eleven days, during which a tremendous battle in Tennessee discredited the notion of a quick victory, before he dunned the governors for an accounting of the troops they had sent. Years later, his Radical friend Henry Wilson reiterated that Stanton merely meant to "suspend" recruiting for the sake of economy and troop consolidation, but his April 3 order referred to it as "discontinued," with no hint of resumption. Closing all the rented offices and selling the furnishings bespoke finality, and administration propaganda confirmed as much. William Stoddard, who served as another of Lincoln's private secretaries, wrote opinion pieces for the weekly *New York Examiner* in which he offered positive interpretations of government policy, and in the April 10 edition he explained that the end of recruiting meant "the army is large enough to carry to full completion all the plans and purposes of the Government." Soldiers in the ranks read it that way, too.[5]

Stanton's order to end recruiting may have emanated from nothing more sinister than excess optimism on his part, mingled with bad judgment and impulsiveness—or possibly from a concern for expense, although that troubled him little during the remainder of the war. Looking back on it years later, McClellan thought the order may have been intended to hobble him, by precluding the raising of any more troops to reinforce his army. That view seems far-fetched and consistent with McClellan's tendency to find scapegoats, but Stanton had shown a propensity for complicated intrigues as early as 1840, when he tried to deprive the Colliers of the postmaster appointment at Steubenville. This trait became more pronounced after his first cabinet appointment, and it reached an apparent peak in the contest with McClellan. Stanton had, for instance, called Senator Wade's joint committee into his office on the night of March 24 for an evident strategy meeting on the undoing of McClellan, when no other acute issue hovered in the air. According to George Julian's fairly candid memoir of that meeting, Stanton betrayed frustration that he could not persuade the president to unseat the general, and he appears to have assembled the committee members to determine how they could manage it themselves. If they did not conspire that evening to hamstring McClellan, their actions over the next ten days proceeded with incredible coincidence toward that end, beginning the very next morning when the committee decided to formally investigate "the late movements of the army of the Potomac." Then came the transfer of ten thousand men from McClellan to Frémont, for which Stanton and his Radical collaborators had pressured the president. Next, Stanton tried to besmirch McClellan's loyalty before the president and Senator Browning, even as he was choreographing a complaint about the safety of Washington for the express purpose of keeping McDowell's corps away from McClellan.[6]

In the polarized and paranoid atmosphere of the day, most of the energy directed against McClellan arose from anxiety over Washington's supposed weakness and the suspicion that traitors—including perhaps McClellan—meant to see the city captured. As preposterous as that was, many Radicals genuinely feared it. Stanton cannot easily be credited with so sincere a motive, for his conversion from McClellan's friend to the Radicals' servant had been too abrupt for anything less than a preconceived strategy: if he was to keep the support of his new Radical patrons, he had to play the part. Besides, foiling the wily McClellan might permanently relieve Stanton of his foremost competitor for control of the department.

Some suspected an even more malignant purpose. Many Democrats believed the Radicals hoped to delay victory on the battlefield until they could force emancipation through individual confiscation or a universal proclamation. Horace Greeley, Charles Sumner, and their coterie had discussed such a hope privately, as Stanton may have known through Sumner, and he might have been glad if his action appeared to accommodate them, whether he intended that result or not. As it happened, the dearth of recruits that summer did contribute to setbacks in the field that persuaded Lincoln to revive the war spirit by proclaiming emancipation.[7]

Even as War Department clerks were copying Stanton's order in Washington, forty thousand Southern soldiers gathered in their camps eight hundred miles away to disprove the theory of waning Confederate determination. That afternoon they marched in four corps from Corinth, in northeastern Mississippi, to avenge a season of humiliation and heartbreak. On a Sabbath morning three days later, near the banks of the Tennessee River, they burst out of the woods around a Methodist meetinghouse called Shiloh Church and caught Ulysses Grant's recumbent army almost completely by surprise. In a succession of ferocious and costly attacks they drove Grant's Westerners two miles over twelve bloody hours, grinding up more than a quarter of each army and amassing the most appalling casualties the continent had ever known. By nightfall Grant's survivors had fallen back into a defensive arc near Pittsburg Landing, awaiting reinforcements from the far shore: they came, mostly from Buell's Army of the Ohio, and the next day Grant counterattacked the weakened Confederates, regaining all the ground he had lost. He did not pursue the retreating rebels, who returned to Corinth with their commander killed and their hope of reversing the tide of Union victories shattered. Embellishing the results of Shiloh and combining them with the capture of Island Number 10, Northern editors added two more victories to their tally, initiating a three-year tradition of periodically predicting "a speedy winding up of the rebellion." Still, some of those who had seen the field at Shiloh drew a different lesson from the battle. The courage, fury, and persistence of the Confederate assaults clashed violently with the imagined malaise and defeatism in the Southern armies: no men could have charged repeatedly into such withering volleys of musketry and artillery for a cause they considered lost.[8]

For all the talk of ultimate victory, Shiloh resurrected lingering distrust in Grant. General Hitchcock noted soon after the battle that official Washington regarded Grant as "absolutely disgraced and dishonored" for being surprised and caught unprepared. That opinion had evidently arisen from the complaints of Hitchcock's friend and Grant's superior, Henry Halleck, who tattled privately, for War Department consumption, that he "never knew a man more deficient in the business of organization" than Grant.[9]

Stanton must have heard such talk through Hitchcock or other War Department gossips, but he left the management of Halleck's subordinates to Halleck, declining to interfere much in the affairs of the armies beyond the Alleghenies. Even when Halleck had submitted serious, official complaints about Grant before Shiloh, Stanton had intervened only at the president's behest. As general in chief, McClellan had kept in close touch with Halleck, Buell, and other department commanders, requiring daily reports and communicating frequently with them about strategy and intelligence. When Stanton assumed that role, those routine communications dropped off: lacking the military background and the sense of scale that McClellan had shared with Halleck, he tended to avoid strategy, telegraphing instead about defensive precautions, technical details, or political subjects. Stanton might inform Halleck about progress in building steam rams for a Mississippi flotilla and the shipment of armaments, or he would pass on Andrew Johnson's concerns about the security of Nashville. As Halleck was gathering his forces to move on Corinth, Stanton apparently asked him to round up disloyal Tennesseans in his vicinity, and Halleck essentially refused, reminding the secretary of war that "we are now at the enemy's throat, and cannot release our great grasp to pare his toe nails."[10]

Commanders in the field beyond the Mississippi did not communicate directly with Stanton; instead, they reported to an assistant adjutant general in St. Louis. Even after McClellan had been deposed as general in chief, Stanton allowed him to correspond with Burnside, in North Carolina, as though he were attached to the Army of the Potomac. Only in matters affecting Virginia did the secretary intrude very often, trying once to peel troops away from Halleck to build up Frémont's nominal force in the mountains, but he focused primarily on operations along the Potomac and Chesapeake. Stanton usually exchanged several telegrams a day with or about McClellan, partly because that general could be so verbose and demanding, but partly, too, because the secretary watched his performance so closely, out of genuine mistrust or something less admirable.[11]

The day after Stanton called a stop to recruiting, McClellan issued his first orders for what would go down in history as his Peninsula campaign. Originally he had expected the navy to aid his march to Richmond, following him up the James and York Rivers to assure the safety of his supply line and provide significant artillery support, but with the *Virginia* lying at Norfolk the navy dared not navigate the James, while Confederate batteries on the York River momentarily closed that route. The first step, then, was to open the York, and McClellan moved directly on Yorktown, expecting to capture it in a stroke, gather his legions, and plunge on toward the "great battle" before Richmond.[12]

Gloucester Point, opposite Yorktown, had been fortified, and as his troops moved against the Yorktown defenses on April 4 McClellan wired McDowell that some of his corps should land behind those batteries and capture them. Then, supposing McDowell had already departed for Fort Monroe, McClellan telegraphed William Franklin to take the Gloucester Point batteries with his division. Not until the evening of April 5 did a telegram from the War Department reach McClellan with the "astonishing" information that McDowell's big corps would not be joining him.[13]

Hours before he left Washington, McClellan had reluctantly acquiesced to Lincoln's decision to deprive his army of Louis Blenker's 10,000-man division, which the president had decided to reassign to Frémont under what he characterized as great pressure. The pressure Lincoln spoke of involved no manifest military necessity. It emanated instead from Radicals who wished to see Frémont endowed with a force equal to their estimate of him, and Stanton had pressed Lincoln most directly about it, against the recommendation of General Hitchcock. At the importuning of Frémont, Stanton began "vigorously urging" the president to transfer Blenker from McClellan, and also to send Joseph Hooker and 9,000 men of his division to Frémont. Lincoln did hope to equip an expedition to cut the Virginia & Tennessee Railroad, deep in Virginia, but Hitchcock also advised against using Frémont for that: Buell was better situated to sever the rail link between the Confederate armies at Richmond and Corinth, Hitchcock argued, while Frémont should cover McClellan's right flank. Hitchcock's opinion probably reached the president through Stanton: perhaps because of it, Stanton told McClellan that Blenker could be kept in the Shenandoah Valley until McClellan thought it safe to release him—technically on McClellan's right flank, supporting Nathaniel Banks against the lingering threat of Stonewall Jackson. That leaves the impression that Stanton had secretly instigated Blenker's detachment as a mere matter of appearances, to salve Frémont's pride and satisfy Radical demands. After all, similar considerations had motivated the very creation of Frémont's department.[14]

The withholding of McDowell's corps, numbering nearly 40,000 men, arose from the fear that McClellan had left Washington too thinly protected, and Stanton helped promote that anxiety. In the council McClellan had called with his corps commanders, back on March 13, three of them had concluded that 25,000 troops were enough to keep the capital safe, in addition to the garrisons of the forts, while old General Edwin Sumner had put the figure at 40,000. Just before he started for Fort Monroe, McClellan had submitted a report indicating that he would leave more than 55,000 troops behind, in addition to 18,000 under James Wadsworth, who commanded the District of Washington. McClellan had been gone only one day when Wadsworth—a Republican political appointee and McClellan critic—complained to Stanton that, while he had 19,000 new, untrained troops for duty around the city, McClellan wanted nearly a third of them for distant posts. He also feared the other 55,000 were too far away from the capital in their camps at Manassas and in the Shenandoah Valley. Stanton gave Hitchcock and Adjutant General Lorenzo Thomas all the correspondence, asking them to judge whether McClellan had complied with the president's orders to leave the city "entirely secure." The war board, including Stanton, Thomas, and Hitchcock, had seemed to conclude on March 27 that the troops at Manassas and in the Shenandoah counted as part of the city's defenses, but after a cursory review of the paperwork on April 2, Thomas and Hitchcock replied that McClellan had not "fully" complied with either the president's instructions or the advice of the corps commanders. They obviously based that verdict on the location of 35,000 of those troops in the Shenandoah Valley, although they professed "no opinion" whether that force should have been included. A third of the 55,000 troops did not exist, for McClellan had duplicated units in his hasty tally, or had anticipated recruits prematurely; thousands of other troops had been sent even farther away, to Frémont, but Thomas and Hitchcock seemed only to detect those errors after submitting their conclusions.[15]

With the judgment of two career soldiers to back him, Stanton hurried to Lincoln with Wadsworth's complaint, overlooking the discrediting inconsistency between the findings of his war board on March 27 and the April 2 opinion of Thomas and Hitchcock. At the same time, or perhaps even before, he had notified Ben Wade, for that same day the Committee on the Conduct of the War sent a request for a meeting with Lincoln on the evening of April 3. They simultaneously scheduled an interview for the morning of April 3 with General Wadsworth, who presented them with an underestimate of the troops McClellan had left behind. Perhaps further agitated by the call of Wade's committee, the purpose of which he probably divined, Lincoln told Stanton to order either McDowell's corps or Sumner's to remain at or near Manassas until further notice. Stanton chose to keep the bigger corps, that of the more Radical-friendly McDowell, ostensibly because part of Sumner's had already embarked for Fort Monroe. Adjutant General Thomas notified McClellan that McDowell had been retained "by order of the President." Explaining the order to McClellan more fully two days later, Stanton used the passive voice that he employed whenever he wished to veil his own role in an unpleasant decision. He alluded to the detachment of more than a quarter of McClellan's expected force as though it were an incidental detail, glossing the news over with praise of the general for his rapid advance on Yorktown and closing with the hope that he would soon be in Richmond.[16]

It was probably not McDowell's politics that persuaded Stanton to retain him but the size of his corps—the largest in the army. Certainly it would provide the capital with ample security: that its absence might hinder McClellan concerned Stanton less, for the secretary would have grieved little over anything that dimmed the glow of the general's reputation.

The Yorktown operation had actually ground to a halt several hours before McClellan learned that McDowell would be withheld. Impeded more by his own preternatural caution than by a shortage of troops, McClellan balked at the sight of ambitious works defending Yorktown and called up his siege train, the very mention of which carried an ominously dilatory connotation.[17]

McClellan begged the president to relent on the McDowell decision, or to at least send him Franklin's division of that corps—and, with his habitual inclination to please, Lincoln did give him Franklin's troops. The loss of 30,000 men still dug deeply into the numerical superiority that contemporary military wisdom required for offensive operations, leaving McClellan closer to equal numbers than he would have preferred—besides convincing him that he might actually be outnumbered. In almost the same stroke, the president had created two new departments, assigning McDowell to the Department of the Rappahannock and Nathaniel Banks to the Department of the Shenandoah, with the troops already serving there. The administrative change in Banks's case had no effect on the numbers before Yorktown, but officially it took another 35,000 men from McClellan's control.[18]

The sense that he was steadily losing power and prestige could have only heightened McClellan's natural tendency to caution, and it worsened the insecurity that seemed to grip him whenever he came within reach of the enemy. The tone of his appeals to the president suggests that McClellan still felt some friendship and sympathy from the White House, but Stanton was another matter: it leaked back to the general that Stanton had privately characterized the retention of McDowell (and presumably the official detachment of Banks) as a "blow" aimed at McClellan. After Stanton's abrupt shift in personal and political demeanor over the previous eleven weeks, McClellan naturally suspected the secretary of aiming that blow himself. Along with Democrats generally, McClellan came to believe that Radicals like Stanton, Wade, and Wadsworth had conspired to deprive him of enough troops to assure his failure—either to orchestrate his removal or to prolong the war until it turned into a crusade against slavery. Surviving evidence documents Stanton's clandestine antagonism toward McClellan and surreptitious efforts to undermine him; it also shows the more overt contempt that Wade and other Radicals harbored for the general—all of which lends the appearance of conspiracy. If no plot existed, it was understandable that the McClellan clique believed it did.[19]

Hampered by McClellan's perpetual fear that the enemy had the advantage over him, and by the atmosphere of administrative hostility that helped augment it, the taking of Yorktown required a full month, instead of the two days the general had expected. During that month, the navy captured New Orleans, and Ben Butler occupied the city with the same exaggerated antagonism for his former political bedfellows that Stanton had been exercising more discreetly. Henry Halleck led all three Union armies in west Tennessee toward Corinth, in a campaign so glacial it would probably have provoked the president and secretary of war to new demonstrations of frustration had they not been so preoccupied with McClellan's creeping pace in Virginia. Before Halleck even issued his orders for the march, it was already common knowledge that the Confederate Congress had passed a law conscripting white men between eighteen and thirty-five, and forcing Confederate soldiers of those ages to remain in the service: this should have aroused appreciable Northern alarm, both for the additional soldiers it would bring into Confederate ranks and for the degree of determination it represented among Southern leaders. Having taken the responsibility for terminating Union recruiting when martial enthusiasm was still running high, Stanton may have felt more than his proportionate share of that alarm.[20]

Most newspapers emphasized the good tidings that spring, and through his new authority over communications and travel Stanton encouraged that trend. He could put an individual reporter out of business by refusing him access to the scenes of active operations, or he could hobble an entire newspaper through the denial of wire services, and he began early to employ those powers against the unsupportive press.

William Russell, the war correspondent for the London *Times*, had engendered great wrath in the army and administration with his acerbic account of the debacle at Manassas, soon becoming known to one and all as "Bull Run" Russell. The piece had helped foster Southern sympathy among the British upper crust, and it may have irked Stanton that Russell was friendly with General McClellan. Stanton had treated Russell cordially enough in the middle of March, at a function in the British minister's residence, but when McClellan started his army toward Fort Monroe, Stanton established a pass system for travel there. Russell appeared at the War Department late on the morning of March 27 with a request for a pass while Stanton was in the next room at a war board meeting. Stanton returned a scrawled refusal, explaining that he had stopped all passes in that direction except for U.S. officers. That may have been true, although he obviously granted exceptions, as he did to a correspondent of the friendlier *Baltimore American*, but he would not allow the *Times* man to go. To soften Stanton up, Russell wrote an appreciative piece about him in the *Star* a few days later, naively describing him as McClellan's powerful and trustworthy ally against the critical Radical "cabal," and with that presumed favor to his credit he tried again the day after McClellan departed. The general had left behind his blessing for Russell's presence, and a signed pass from General Marcy, but Stanton still withheld his permission. Realizing that the secretary intended to impede him as much as possible, Russell gave up and sailed for home.[21]

Once the Army of the Potomac took to the field, Stanton started enforcing his privately circulated February 25 admonition against "publishing intelligence in respect to military operations." The original message had specified no penalties, and it purportedly applied only "for the present," but it soon became obvious that Stanton regarded it as a permanent decree. He had already persuaded the president to invest him with Seward's former authority to make "extraordinary arrests"—which was to say arrests without legal cause, and imprisonment without due process—and he did not hesitate to use that vast, unprecedented power. His increasingly suspicious colleague in the Navy Department believed he relished it above all things: "Mr. Stanton was fond of power and of its exercise," wrote Secretary Welles. "It was more precious to him than pecuniary gain, to dominate over his fellow man."[22]

Senator James McDougall, a California Democrat, came to a similar assessment. Criticizing the arrest of General Stone and the peremptory treatment of Surgeon General Finley, MacDougall reminded the Senate that Stanton was "the recipient of large professional bounties at the hands of the last Administration," and that as a friend of Buchanan he "fought under the banner of Breckinridge in 1860," before embracing the Lincoln administration after it came into office. "He is an energetic, active, efficient man," MacDougall admitted. "He acquires a place of power. Now, I say he is no Democrat if I know what a Democrat is; he is no Republican if I know what a Republican is. Sir,"—and here he raised his voice sharply—"he *belongs to the party in power*."[23]

Stanton's use of his consolidated authority did nothing to dispel such opinions. Before the first transport left Alexandria, Stanton ordered the publishers and printers of the *Washington Sunday Chronicle* arrested for reporting too precisely on the army's jaunt to Manassas, contrary to the vague caution that he now called his "order." The *Chronicle*'s owner, John Forney, saw to it that the paper gave the administration relentless support, so no punishment followed; the arrests may not even have been carried out. Initially Stanton found the suspension of telegraph privileges sufficient to keep most newspapers in line, but the president had given him great arbitrary authority, and within six months his War Department would start wielding that authority to punish political criticism.[24]

Broadly interpreted, Stanton's dictum would have hamstrung the reporting of war news, for even inadvertent transgressions would have been difficult to avoid. The *New York Times* detailed General Banks's movements in the Shenandoah Valley, and published an article outlining McClellan's "plan of the war," but Republican editor Henry Raymond suffered no repercussions. Raymond's paper, along with others, frequently published maps showing troop positions, and Stanton's supervisor of telegrams pointed out that the April 19 edition of *Harper's Weekly* described the juxtaposition of the opposing armies before Yorktown, but no arrest orders followed. A year later the *Chronicle* leaked medical information that revealed the strength of the various corps in the Army of the Potomac just as it prepared to do battle, but Stanton failed to issue even a token arrest order. The *New York Times* never endured the secretary's arbitrary wrath throughout the war, even after publishing the secret plans of generals just opening their campaigns. It would be the opposition press that had the most to fear when Stanton's War Department decided to make an example of a newspaper. Editors who wished to report freely on operations employed rhetoric more supportive of administration policy than sincerity might have warranted.[25]

That was surely not an unintended consequence. Stanton might have liked to enforce censorship more widely, if not more equitably, but he found it impossible. His ban would have created yawning gaps in news coverage had it been strictly observed, and to replace the proscribed information he supplied a stream of bulletins on the progress of the war. Those bulletins were designed to reflect the administration's perspective rather than to ensure accuracy: one of the earliest War Department press releases addressed the criticism that was leveled at General Grant for failing to pursue his beaten enemy at Shiloh, refuting it with the misleading claim that his orders prevented it.[26]

In the middle of April General Hitchcock traveled down to the peninsula on an inspection tour for Stanton, who had charged him with investigating McClellan's claims that he needed more men, supplies, and ordnance. Hitchcock concluded that McClellan had about as many men as he could effectively handle on the constricted topography, and needed nothing beyond steady supplies and some heavy ordnance, which was on its way to the front as he prepared to return to Washington. The roads there were far worse than McClellan had predicted in his early arguments for this line of operations, but they were drying out when Hitchcock arrived. McClellan seemed confident, and justifiably so, said the old general, who returned to the capital more hopeful about the results than he had been when he started.[27]

After weeks of perfecting his artillery positions, McClellan was about to initiate a massive bombardment against the long line of Confederate works when, on May 3, he reported the enemy "unusually quiet." The next morning they were gone. McClellan sent cavalry after them and followed up with infantry, but rain softened the roads again and he only managed to tangle with Johnston's rear guard at Williamsburg, on May 5.[28]

With Yorktown taken, Stanton suggested that he and Lincoln go down to the peninsula and organize the troops at Fort Monroe for a movement on Norfolk, to deal with the *Virginia* he so dreaded. The president invited others, and he, Stanton, and Secretary Chase met at the Navy Yard on the afternoon of May 5, where Brigadier General Egbert Viele joined them. At 6:00 P.M. the four of them boarded the revenue cutter *Miami*, and the little steamer started down the Potomac in a drizzle, but thick fog forced them to anchor until just before dawn. They entered Chesapeake Bay around noon, but choppy water slid their lunch dishes around the table and knocked their glasses over, leaving the president and his war minister too queasy to eat. The crew shook the sails out and they were still scudding southward when darkness fell. Stanton, who had sailed to California without a qualm, remained seasick until they dropped anchor off Fort Monroe late in the evening. They sent a message ashore, and General John E. Wool, the local commander, came out in a boat with several staff officers despite the hour. A tug then ferried everyone to the towering *Minnesota*, where they climbed a precarious ladder to the deck for a late-night chat with flag officer Louis Goldsborough, the commander of the squadron at Hampton Roads, about his plans for disposing of the *Virginia*. He explained how he had made a ram out of the huge steamer *Vanderbilt*, given to the navy by Cornelius Vanderbilt, and he described the capabilities of his own two ironclads—the *Monitor* and a new armored steamer called the *Naugatuck*. The dignitaries began to believe that Goldsborough could handle the Confederate monster, and they retired to their bunks on the *Miami* after midnight.[29]

On Tuesday the seventy-eight-year-old General Wool climbed into the saddle, provided horses for the president and Secretary Chase, and put Stanton in a carriage with John Tucker, leading his guests on a ride through his soldiers' camps and the incinerated village of Hampton. After reviewing Wool's troops, the White House delegation went back to work. Stanton, whom General Viele recalled particularly for his hostility to Mc-Clellan, telegraphed routine congratulations for the exaggerated victories McClellan claimed. Apparently acting on the advice of Governor William Sprague of Rhode Island, who was traveling with McClellan, Stanton wired Peter Watson to prepare McDowell's corps for an advance on Richmond from Fredericksburg. Lincoln, meanwhile, called a council at headquarters. Stanton proposed that Goldsborough send three gunboats up the James River to support McClellan, and the president endorsed that suggestion.[30]

That night Lincoln and Stanton slept at the fort. On Thursday morning Stanton telegraphed Ellen about the nice weather there, wishing she and the baby could escape the heat of Washington, but the peace of that day was about to be disturbed. Stanton followed Lincoln out to the shore to meet Chase, Viele, and Goldsborough, whom the president ordered to send his ironclads and bigger steamers across Hampton Roads and engage the batteries on Sewell's Point, at the mouth of the Elizabeth River. "Things are moving now," Stanton told Watson, and Lincoln intended to borrow the army and navy long enough to capture Norfolk and its dreaded ironclad. When the ships lurched into motion, the executive contingent jumped in a tug bound for Fort Wool, a mile off Fort Monroe. The guns there bore on Sewell's Point, three miles farther off, and when the ships opened on the point so did Fort Wool. Their combined firepower soon silenced the Confederate battery, and the Union guns turned on another fort farther inland. At midafternoon the squat, intimidating form of the *Virginia* took position at the mouth of the river. The president and his ministers had started back for the fort by then, and reached shore just as the rebel ram started back up the river and the shelling died away.[31]

With the *Virginia* covering the point there could be no landing there, so—again at the urging of Stanton—Chase volunteered the *Miami* for reconnoitering. Venturing out on Friday, while the *Monitor* guarded against another sally by the *Virginia*, Chase and General Wool scouted a promising location at Ocean View. The president wanted to land closer to Norfolk, and commandeered a tug to make a foray of his own with Stanton. They came in close enough to send a boat, but before it reached the beach some horsemen rode into sight on shore. That evening encounter gave Stanton, if not Lincoln, the closest contact he would ever have with an armed enemy.[32]

Wool loaded several regiments on steamers during the night, ferried them over in the dark, and landed them at Ocean View early Saturday morning. Despite his years, Wool rode along, asking his orderly to surrender his horse to Chase when they landed. Lincoln and Stanton accompanied the flotilla, and Stanton went ashore, but his old knee injury kept him afoot. Chase moved ahead with the army, acting as an aide to Wool, while Stanton served as a scrivener for the president, writing orders and dispatches. The defenders of Norfolk had abandoned their entrenchments, and the mayor drove out to surrender the city. The next morning, as the politicians prepared for their return to the capital, they learned that the *Virginia* had just been scuttled. The president insisted on swinging across to have a look at the smoldering remains. On Stanton's suggestion, Lincoln had cut through the administrative snarls that often foiled military operations directed from afar, and had orchestrated the destruction of the only impediment to the irresistible, naval-assisted campaign McClellan had originally envisioned.[33]

While Chase and Wool were surveying the amphibious advantages of Ocean View, a telegram had come in from McClellan, asking again for permission to reorganize the corps structure that had been imposed on him. The fight at Williamsburg convinced him that the "utter stupidity & worthlessness" of the corps commanders had nearly lost the day. The men commanding the corps under him just then—Edwin Sumner, Samuel Heintzelman, and Erasmus Keyes, had all been in the army three or four decades, but McClellan preferred younger, modern soldiers like himself. From his own observations at the front Governor Sprague wired Stanton, just before the Confederate evacuation of Yorktown, that McClellan had effectively made the corps commanders subordinate to Fitz John Porter, William Franklin, and William F. Smith, all division commanders in their late thirties who had attended West Point around the same time as McClellan.[34]

There was truth in Sprague's observation. In the initial advance to Yorktown with his untried army, McClellan generally led with Porter's and Smith's divisions, and when he decided to lay siege he named Porter "director of the siege." During the pursuit from Yorktown, he communicated directly with Porter, Smith, and Franklin as much as with Sumner, Heintzelman, and Keyes. When McClellan's telegram reached Fort Monroe in the wee hours of May 9, asking to rearrange the corps, Stanton showed it to the president. He must have mentioned Sprague's comment about McClellan's favoritism, for in a friendly response to McClellan Lincoln admitted having heard that his chief confidants were Porter and perhaps Franklin. He approved the reorganization in the end (although Stanton referred to it as a temporary arrangement), but Lincoln cautioned that McClellan risked losing support and confidence if he removed Sumner, Keyes, and Heintzelman at a stroke. McClellan acted on that judicious hint, retaining the three original corps commanders, but he created two new corps and appointed Porter and Franklin to lead them. That voluntary compromise suggested how much better Lincoln might have managed McClellan without Stanton's intercession.[35]

McClellan was not the only major general repelled by Stanton's manner. The steamer *Baltimore* returned Lincoln, Chase, and Stanton to Washington on the morning of May 12, and the next day General Hitchcock submitted his second resignation in two weeks. He had already offered one on April 28, after Stanton—who had been growing increasingly abusive toward subordinates and lesser visitors—finally snapped at him.

"My *sweet* temper has been dreadfully tried here," Hitchcock wrote, just before his first resignation. Hitchcock characterized Stanton as narrowminded, bullying, and impulsively judgmental. He used coarse, insulting language toward those beneath him, flinging his arms about in infantile tantrums ("like a wild man in the dark") and habitually indulging spontaneous, unjustified prejudices against people over whom he held authority. "He has not yet departed from propriety in his intercourse with me," Hitchcock assured his nephew on April 25, adding that he would do it only once, but Stanton offered some unspecified affront the very next day. Hitchcock tendered the resignation, but withdrew it when Stanton pleaded that Hitchcock's departure would "destroy" him—meaning, probably, by confirming his reputation for rude conduct. In his second resignation letter Hitchcock cited persistent ill health, flatly denying that his desire to leave bore any reflection on Stanton's deportment—an odd remark that seemed to suggest the very problem. At that the secretary turned importuning and obsequious once again, mollifying Hitchcock with a long leave of absence rather than have the entire department, and undoubtedly the whole administration, know why he really left.[36]

A more public allegation against Stanton made it into the newspapers a few days after he returned from Fort Monroe. Massachusetts senator Henry Wilson, chairman of the Military Affairs Committee, published a letter in which he acknowledged and replied to a rampant suspicion that he, Sumner, and Stanton were interfering with and impeding McClellan's plans. Wilson defended Stanton in particular, whom he characterized as more deserving of McClellan's commendation than his condemnation.[37]

Those suspicions extended beyond McClellan's Democratic friends. Judge David Davis, who had managed Lincoln's election campaign, recognized the universal belief among Illinois Democrats and conservative Republicans that Stanton had "allied himself with the Abolitionists" and abetted them in "crippling McClellan." Davis seemed to believe it himself and cited some reasons, observing that the abolitionist press was striving to weaken support for McClellan and seemed to hope for the defeat of generals who did not share its extreme views. He knew, too, that Stanton had restored Frémont to a field command against the president's inclination. Davis had been told that Frémont admitted having "not as good a friend in the world as Secretary Stanton"—a turn of phrase that Stanton used with indiscriminate insincerity. Davis had also heard that the most extreme abolitionist of all, Wendell Phillips, had praised Stanton as the most "earnest" member of the cabinet. Then there was the Radical feud with conservative generals, exemplified by Stanton's persecution of General Stone, and the winter-long Radical demand that McClellan get his army moving—followed by the springtime insistence, also driven by Radical pressure, that he leave much of that army before Washington. As though foreseeing the tempest of opposition that would arise from the conversion of nationalist goals to abolitionist purposes, Davis concluded that "if we are disappointed in Mr. Stanton, the confidence of conservative men will receive a terrible shock."[38]

It is now evident that Stanton did secretly cleave to the Radicals from the moment he entered office, ingratiating them by embroidering his private professions of antislavery sentiment into a fantasy of lifelong abolitionist ardor.[39] It seems unlikely that he deliberately stymied McClellan so the Radicals could engineer some means of emancipation, but he did obviously sacrifice his relationship with the general to secure Radical support and to consolidate his authority. Observers of all political persuasions might understandably have interpreted Stanton's words and deeds as evidence that he sincerely favored Radical motives and strategies. Nor was it outrageous, in light of Stanton's behavior toward him since January, for McClellan to see Stanton's fingerprints on any executive orders, actions, or inaction that seemed to foil him.

While Lincoln could not miss the antagonism between the secretary and the general, he seemed to ascribe it to misunderstanding and to differences in personality, and he perhaps assigned more blame to McClellan than to Stanton. Before another year passed, the president would show some distaste when he heard Stanton utter little falsehoods to his fellow cabinet members, but he may never have fully appreciated his war minister's capacity for duplicity. As Lincoln's old friend Joshua Speed observed, the president was too honest to conceive of such dishonesty in another without undeniable proof.[40] The profitable jaunt to Norfolk may have fostered disproportionate confidence in Stanton, whose idea it was, and it was convenient for a president who had to tiptoe through the competing factions on Capitol Hill that his secretary of war enjoyed the support of a powerful congressional coalition.

Senator Wilson's letter brought one of Stanton's college friends out of the woodwork. On the day the letter appeared in the New York press, Reverend Heman Dyer, a Kenyon College faculty member from Stanton's era, wrote the secretary from New York with an implicit offer to defend him against the accusations that he was thwarting McClellan's operations. Many people had expressed their belief in the allegations, Dyer wrote, although he always replied "that Mr. Stanton was incapable of any political intrigue, . . . or of any intentional wrong to any person or party." Characterizing Stanton as "an old and highly esteemed friend," Dyer hinted he would be glad to have any information that might satisfy the doubts of his skeptical acquaintances.[41]

Stanton, who described his duties as so onerous that he sometimes did not see Ellen for days, pounced on Dyer's offer and immediately prepared a fifteen-page brief for his own defense, taking it through at least two drafts that must have required several hours to prepare. First he castigated his critics as jackals comprising two odiferous classes: "plunderers" of the public treasury whom he had driven from the department (like Jesus clearing the Temple), and "scheming politicians, whose designs were endangered by an earnest, resolute and uncompromising prosecution of this war as a war against rebels and traitors." He recounted the points of contention with McClellan—most of which he portrayed as the result of presidential decisions, without admitting his own part in encouraging or instigating them. He also employed strategic inaccuracy to improve his case, telling Dyer that

McClellan's February campaign to Winchester was "abandoned," which was untrue: it had been completed within two weeks. Stanton withheld the specific reason behind the delay in the Harper's Ferry operation as though it were a state secret—perhaps because so few people knew about the undersized canal lock that revealing it might betray him as the source of the information. He insisted there had never been "a shadow of difference" between him and McClellan until the dispute over McDowell's corps, in April, yet their relations had begun to unravel the day Stanton took office, and by mid-March his hostility to McClellan was being widely discussed. He disparaged the Peninsula campaign as "the most expensive, the most hazardous, and most protracted" plan McClellan could have presented, adding that McClellan's views contradicted those of the best military minds, suggesting that he wasn't much of a general.[42]

All of this had to be "strictly confidential," Stanton insisted, on the grounds that it would do much damage to public confidence in the commander of the largest national army. By that he meant that Dyer could not publish the letter: he could broadcast its contents by word of mouth or other means, for Stanton made no objection when Dyer replied that the secretary's explanations would serve to answer those who had been so critical of him. A defense distributed privately posed less risk of embarrassing rebuttal, and Dyer was not the only conduit Stanton used to broadcast it. A month later, through Congressman Samuel Hooper, Stanton denounced McClellan in the same "confidential" fashion to the editor of the *Boston Evening Transcript*, Horatio Woodman, who used the information to take Stanton's side editorially.[43]

This strategy fit the Stanton pattern, in which whispered slurs belied the official pretense of loyal support. Not even Lincoln escaped Stanton's backbiting, as Captain Dahlgren of the Navy observed: on the evening of May 21 Dahlgren took dinner with Stanton, Chase, and Senator Sumner at the home of Congressman Hooper, whose son had recently been rescued from a Confederate prison through a special exchange arranged by Stanton. The dinner was clearly a Radical confab (before the soup came, Sumner handed Stanton a private letter from Wendell Phillips), and Stanton and Chase directed some unspecified satirical barbs at the president, to the surprise of Dahlgren. According to McClellan's chief engineer, Stanton had made another sneering remark about McClellan "organizing victory"—a phrase he had been ridiculing since Fort Donelson in his correspondence with Radicals. With such tokens of contempt from Stanton leaking back to McClellan through his staff, the general's paranoia seemed justified.[44]

One abolitionist congressman did offer McClellan what the general considered a supreme compliment. Owen Lovejoy, an Illinois Radical, opened the day's proceedings in the House on May 9 with a resolution tendering the thanks of Congress to McClellan "for the display of those high military qualities which secure important results with but little sacrifice of human life." It passed, and McClellan received it as a "very handsome" acknowledgment of the quality he valued most in a general: the night before Lovejoy spoke, McClellan had commented proudly that his maneuvering had saved ten thousand lives. His frequent appeals for more troops may have arisen as much from his goal of forcing a bloodless retreat as from his own inner doubts and exaggerated estimates of enemy numbers, which he put as high as twice his own field strength. Through the middle of May he continued to press the secretary of war for more men, reporting that Johnston was drawing reinforcements from the Deep South. He asked General Wool for some of his command, too, but Wool apprised Stanton of McClellan's "desponding" calls for troops and assistance, and Stanton told Wool to ignore them. Having learned to mistrust Stanton, McClellan assumed the secretary stood behind every refusal of reinforcement.[45]

Fearing that Stanton might be withholding dispatches, McClellan wrote to the president directly, asking for all the men he could spare, sent down by water. Thanks to the interruption of recruiting there were no new troops to send, and Lincoln still did not want to empty out the lines around Washington, but on May 18 Stanton told McClellan that the president had finally consented to send McDowell's corps, but by land rather than by water. With 35,000 to 40,000 men, McDowell would march south from Fredericksburg, staying between the Confederates and Washington to address both McClellan's desire for support and the anxiety over the safety of the capital. The president took responsibility for determining the land route, and Stanton conveyed it as Lincoln's decision, but it had come after consultation with most of Stanton's war board.[46]

Later, General Scott would also advise sending McDowell down on steamers, rather than overland, but McClellan's insistence on water transportation may have had less to do with speed than with control. If McDowell came by land, he would begin his march independent of the Army of the Potomac, and McClellan feared he might remain so, operating more as a cooperating commander than a subordinate. Assuming that this had been the idea behind Stanton's orders, perhaps to groom McDowell for the overall command, McClellan raged privately over Stanton's sneaking character until he expressed a sanitized version of that fear to Lincoln. The president assured McClellan that he would have the overall command, and the general relaxed again.[47]

Thanks to Stonewall Jackson, McDowell's corps never took a step toward Richmond. After the fight at Kernstown, late in March, Jackson had retreated south, up the Shenandoah Valley, followed eventually by Nathaniel Banks while Frémont tried to work his army around Jackson's left, from the fringe of the Allegheny Mountains. As McClellan's army closed in on Yorktown, late in April, the Confederate equivalent of general in chief, Robert E. Lee, arranged to reinforce Jackson with a division from Johnston under Richard Ewell, so he could distract the enemy by wreaking havoc in the valley. While Ewell occupied Banks, Jackson hurried his own troops to the town of McDowell, where he repelled two of Frémont's brigades and drove them back on their comrades, chasing them north. Once those Yankees were on the run, he faced about and retraced his steps to rejoin Ewell. Pushing his men at a grueling pace, he turned back down the valley with Ewell and struck Banks at Front Royal on May 23, nearly cutting him off from his line of retreat. After slicing up the Union rear guard at Middletown, Jackson fell on Banks again outside Winchester on May 25, crumpling his line and driving Union soldiers through the town in full retreat. They never stopped running until they reached the Potomac, and once there they spilled across the swollen river, taking refuge in Maryland while Jackson veered toward Harper's Ferry.[48]

Jackson had routed two separate armies before they could combine against him. He also achieved much of Lee's greater goal by sparking panic among Union generals across northern Virginia and politicians in Washington, thereby distracting the Lincoln administration from McClellan's campaign along the James.

Stanton and the president were not in Washington to hear the first rumblings from the valley. They had slipped away together on Thursday night, May 22, to see McDowell about his campaign to Richmond. With Captain Dahlgren they landed at Aquia Creek early in the morning, where McDowell met them with his train. On the way back to camp McDowell stopped the train to show them an enormous trestle army engineers had built over the Potomac Creek ravine, and Dahlgren later recorded how the adventurous Lincoln proposed that they walk across it on the narrow catwalk between the rails. The president boldly led, followed by the others, but—wrote Dahlgren—Stanton of the lame knee grew dizzy and froze halfway across, forcing the captain to slip around him and take his hand to steady him the rest of the way. After outlining their expectations for McDowell's march to Richmond and his junction with McClellan, they all rode out to review Marsena Patrick's brigade, beyond Fredericksburg. Stanton's knee again kept him out of the saddle, but the president cantered comfortably past the troops against the setting sun. The demise of Richmond seemed imminent when they started back to Washington that evening. Their boat docked at the Navy Yard at three o'clock on Saturday morning, but the passengers slept until five, when the president and Stanton went looking for breakfast. Late in the morning Stanton found telegrams from Banks at the War Department, reporting that he was falling back and asking for help.

Peter Watson had evidently sent a wire in Stanton's name to General Dix, the night before, to send Banks what men he could spare from Baltimore by rail, and had ordered a regiment to plug Thoroughfare Gap, between Front Royal and Washington.[49]

By the time Stanton reached his office things seemed more desperate than earlier, and Lincoln joined him at the War Department. Before noon Stanton telegraphed McDowell to leave an extra brigade at Fredericksburg when he marched south, in case Banks needed it. Less than six hours later the president himself addressed a wire to McDowell, telling him to put the Richmond movement aside altogether and send half his corps to Banks— one division up the Potomac, and another overland. His aim was not only to bolster Banks but also to cut off Jackson's retreat, for which Lincoln sent instructions to Frémont. McDowell complied promptly, but told the president that the most direct route from Fredericksburg to the valley was longer than Jackson's road to the same point, leaving it unlikely that his reinforcements would arrive in time, while a great advantage would be lost at Richmond. To another general McDowell openly belittled his orders, accusing the administration of falling into a "flutter" and wondering where Blenker's ten thousand had gone. If Jackson could so frighten them with minor attacks at different points, McDowell warned, "he will paralyze a large force with a very small one."[50]

That was precisely what was happening. With his 16,000 Confederates, Jackson had already occupied the full attention of 60,000 Yankees under Banks, Frémont, and McDowell, and Stanton tried to throw as many more into that sideshow as he could squeeze from coastal garrisons and state governors. He had evidently already sensed the criticism that might come his way for closing the recruiting offices, and on May 19—the day after Lincoln decided to release McDowell to McClellan—he had instructed the adjutant general to ask the state governors how soon they could each raise between one and six new regiments. Francis Peirpoint, the putative chief executive of Virginia's rump Union legislature, had illustrated the folly of the order ending recruiting with his immediate reply: he could not raise a regiment in any reasonable time because, "having discouraged all idea of further volunteering among the people, they have engaged in other pursuits for the season." The governor of Minnesota expressed similar doubts. Other governors responded with more hope than foresight, supposing they could meet their quotas in anywhere from a few weeks to ninety days, and on May 21 Stanton had begun authorizing them to proceed. With the bad news from Banks he wired frantically for the governors to rush forward those new troops, and he started asking for state militia, too. Montgomery Blair was probably the source for a description of a dreadfully panicked secretary of war trying to "affright the world," but a Republican congressman from Massachusetts laughed at Stanton's appeal for the governors "to call the Clerks out of the stores," ridiculing it as "the flurry of a girl who meets a cow in the street."[51]

Stanton so lost his composure at this juncture that he was taken in by a malicious prank. On a recommendation in a letter signed with the name of prominent Philadelphia lawyer Horace Binney, Stanton began accepting more of the three-month militia that had proven so costly and ineffective in 1861. Three days later, after Stanton had authorized more than a score of such regiments, Secretary Chase reminded him that the three-month levy was no longer legal. The regiments Stanton authorized had already begun recruiting, and rather than admit his mistake he allowed them to fill up and serve out their terms, but he deliberately misinformed Binney that Chase had opposed his idea because of expense and "other evils incident to short enlistments." He only found that he had been duped when Binney denied ever having written to anyone on that subject.[52]

Judging by the governors' estimates of the time it would take to raise new regiments, and the rate at which they had been sending them forward when Stanton closed down volunteering in April, the army should have been able to gain fifty thousand men in the intervening seven weeks. That equaled McDowell's corps and Blenker's division combined, which was every man McClellan had ever called for from the peninsula. Between Stanton's March report on troop strength and the end of June, attrition had reduced the army by fifty thousand, instead of seeing it grow by the same amount through recruiting.[53]

Studiously ignoring the impact of his recruiting blunder, Stanton blamed McClellan, and to some extent so did the president. Stanton's mother-in-law was visiting just then at the K Street house, where the baby's condition and Ellen's anxiety steadily worsened, but Stanton and Lincoln remained at the telegraph all day Sunday, May 25. In the evening Seward, Senator Sumner, and Senator Browning joined them there to hear the latest. As usual, Sumner seemed to absorb Stanton's more strident view of the underlying problem. "The whole trouble," Sumner informed Massachusetts governor John Andrew, "is directly traceable to McLellan," whom he accused of having taken too many troops with him "*so as to leave Washington defenseless.*" In a candid letter to McClellan, Lincoln himself noted that Banks came to grief after he had been deprived of James Shields's division, for McClellan's benefit. Lincoln never suggested that McClellan had actually removed too many men from Washington, let alone that he had done so with the treacherous intent of sacrificing the capital, but he did remind the general that he would have taken too many troops with him had Lincoln allowed it: it had been the fear of something like Jackson's attack that had moved Lincoln to let Stanton retain McDowell, rather than any "unwillingness to sustain" McClellan. The president misinterpreted Jackson's drive as a "general and concerted" movement of the rebel army, instead of the calculated diversion that it really was, and in a second wire later that day he even broached the subject of McClellan giving up his campaign against Richmond and coming to save Washington, if he did not soon initiate an attack on the rebel capital. That discouraged message demonstrated how close Jackson came to far greater success.[54]

During the panic over Stonewall Jackson, Stanton issued an order taking "military possession" of all the country's railroads in the name of the president, just as he had done with the telegraph system. He may have assumed that extraordinary authority to ensure the availability of the Baltimore & Ohio Railroad, or perhaps that was merely his excuse: he corresponded over the next couple of days with the president of that line about the transfer of troops. Sunday and Monday passed in a tempest of telegraphic messages, with exaggerated reports from perennial alarmists like Brigadier General John Geary, who told his wife he was outnumbered twenty to one and officially reported tens of thousands of rebels in the Shenandoah Valley. Then, as suddenly as it had risen, the Confederate tide ebbed. By Tuesday afternoon Shields reached Manassas, on his way back into the valley, and he found evidence of so few Confederates in that vicinity that he characterized the reaction to Jackson's incursion as a "shameful stampede."[55]

Without McDowell, McClellan worried about his right flank—especially after the Confederates below Fredericksburg disappeared, presumably toward Richmond, and Fitz John Porter brawled with enemy forces north of the city. McClellan prepared to cross the Chickahominy River toward Richmond, expecting a fight at any moment if his orders to the troops were any indication, and he haggled with General Wool, Stanton, and the president over small garrisons in his rear, asking that Wool replace them and free his troops for the coming battle. Wool declined to send a single regiment, so McClellan appealed to Lincoln, noting that he was losing three hundred men a day from disease and casualties. Stanton finally satisfied the want with three regiments from New York, and promised others if they were needed. McClellan expressed his thanks, and might have seen the exchange as an attempt at a goodwill gesture—but, having endured Stanton's duplicity in the past, he may not have credited it. His mistrust of the secretary of war was trickling down to the men in the ranks now, too.[56]

As May neared its end McClellan passed on the report of a runaway slave who said that Confederate General P. G. T. Beauregard had arrived in Richmond, bringing troops with him. Beauregard, the hero of Fort Sumter and Bull Run, had led Albert Sidney Johnston's army back from Shiloh to Corinth after Johnston was killed. Halleck's armies had converged on him in another campaign carried on at a snail's pace, and Beauregard had finally slipped away just as the trap was about to be sprung. Now,

McClellan suspected, Beauregard had come to reinforce Joe Johnston before Richmond.[57]

It was not true, but for weeks to come the specter of Beauregard reinforcing Richmond would periodically bedevil either Washington or McClellan, beginning a few days after he passed that incorrect intelligence along to Stanton. On May 31 the Army of the Potomac lay separated by the Chickahominy River, with three corps north of the river and two south of it; the latter two were camped along the Richmond & York River Railroad that served as a supply line from the base at White House Landing, on the Pamunkey River. The Chickahominy ran high with recent rain, and Johnston saw a chance to overpower the two isolated Yankee corps. Early in the afternoon concentrated rebel brigades swept out of the woods between Seven Pines and Fair Oaks Station, flushing Silas Casey's division out of its works and into headlong flight. A couple of hours intervened before anyone outside the immediate vicinity realized the extent of the onslaught, and Heintzelman brought up some reinforcements to blunt the assault, but he was driven back to within a mile of the next station on the line. Sumner managed to bring a couple of divisions over the river on precarious bridges, and by dark the Confederate drive had lost its momentum. The next day the Yankees took back most of the lost ground by the bayonet. Stanton forwarded to McClellan two dispatches from Halleck, demonstrating that Beauregard and his troops were almost certainly still in Mississippi, and McClellan declared that he was satisfied on that point.[58]

Stanton reassigned General Wool to Baltimore, transferred John Dix from Baltimore to Fort Monroe, and gave McClellan control over Wool's former department. Dix, Stanton's friend and former cabinet colleague, took offense at being stripped of an independent command and made subordinate to McClellan, but Stanton declined to revise an exchange that appears to have been Lincoln's idea. That order went out to McClellan under Stanton's name, without the note that it was "by order of the president," with which Stanton usually qualified more unpleasant instructions. If by that Stanton hoped to persuade McClellan of his friendship, the president nullified the effect with a handwritten note revealing that the decision had at least been a joint one.[59]

Whoever had conceived of the order, McClellan wasted no time putting it to use. The day after Dix arrived at Fort Monroe, five thousand of his troops shuttled to White House Landing on transports. The enemy had drawn in even closer to Richmond than before, and McClellan grew extremely confident of the outcome. Lincoln himself had remarked while the fighting was winding down on June 1 that he thought the worst of the task was finished. In fact, the worst had only begun, for Southern casualties on May 31 had included Joe Johnston, wounded by a piece of shell: Jefferson

Davis chose Robert E. Lee to replace him, and Lee's succession would soon reverse Southern fortunes.[60]

Lee's eldest son had inherited the small plantation house from which White House Landing had taken its name. It now sat amid McClellan's supply base—but, because the house was said to have once belonged to George Washington, McClellan had placed guards over it and left it unmolested. Stanton informed the general that he had heard wounded men were being denied shelter there, along with more vicious rumors that they were forced to buy so much as a glass of water. McClellan instantly and bitterly replied that the historic little frame house could accommodate only two dozen wounded men even if it were devoted to their use, while the allegation about having to buy water was simply ridiculous, because there was so much available.

"I cannot believe that you will regard this a cause for rebuke or censure," he concluded. Stanton replied that he was merely forwarding the complaints of others, so McClellan might respond, and he promised that he would "labor" to squelch the rumors with McClellan's answers. He did not labor at it very hard, however, for when the House of Representatives instructed Speaker Galusha Grow to ask for an official explanation, Stanton refused to supply the correspondence—ostensibly at Lincoln's direction. He said only that the surgeon general had since designated the Lee home at White House Landing for hospital purposes. That unnecessary secrecy only aroused even more suspicion among congressmen, some of whom evidently believed a worse rumor that McClellan had made a pact with General Lee. McClellan and his friends supposed that Stanton had planned it to happen that way, and that the only plausible reason for withholding the correspondence was to disguise Stanton's pettiness or McClellan's indignation at the accusation.[61]

A copy of the new surgeon general's formal request to appropriate White House, along with the letter conveying it to McClellan, both appeared in handwriting that was new to War Department communications. Tom Scott had expressed a wish to return to his railroad business, and Stanton promptly replaced him with his own brother-in-law, Christopher P. Wolcott, who was then unemployed. With Peter Watson as his other principal assistant and A. E. H. Johnson as his clerk, Stanton had now fully packed his office with friends and relatives. Only John Tucker remained from the old guard, and Stanton kept him in the field. Writing home to Pamphila after his first day's work in the War Department, Wolcott reflected Stanton's open contempt for McClellan when he remarked that the general was "utterly unfit for the position he holds."[62]

Government officials frequently employed friends and relatives in that era. Secretary of State Seward's son, Frederick, acted as his assistant secretary, for example, and no one thought twice of that. The difference in Stanton's case is that he purportedly shunned such habits to avoid the slightest hint of impropriety, yet he was one of the greater offenders in the cabinet. His defenders cite his refusal, a couple of weeks previously, to give his nephew a Regular Army commission, but that nephew, Benjamin Tappan III, was the pariah of the Stanton family because of his disloyalty to his mother, Oella. Early in the war Benjamin had enlisted as a private in the 8th Ohio. His father, Dr. Benjamin Tappan Jr., served as surgeon of that regiment until he was sent home for drunkenness the following spring, whereupon his son joined the Regular Army as a hospital steward. In May of 1862 young Tappan tired of his duties, or his wages, and sought a lieutenancy in the Regular service, but Stanton rejected the application. Lincoln directed him to make the appointment anyway, if the boy's only disqualification consisted of being the nephew of the secretary of war, but Stanton still refused, claiming it violated a rule against granting commissions except for "meritorious service." The secretary's stubbornness in that case reflected his vindictive side, rather than any aversion to hiring relatives, and he proved as much by taking Pamphila's husband in as his assistant. Stanton did later hesitate to appoint a cousin for whom Ben Wade solicited a commission, but he had no scruples about asking the president to appoint Pamphila's son to West Point. He also took his own son into the War Department later in the war, rather than see him go into the army, although he seemed to authorize a convoluted ruse to make it appear that he had not done the hiring himself. Stanton engaged in nepotism and cronyism as readily as any bureaucrat of his day; he merely denied it, and disguised it better.[63]

By the time Wolcott entered the office, Stonewall Jackson had moved farther up the Shenandoah Valley, and Washington turned calm once again. Lincoln began sending reinforcements to McClellan by steamer, starting with ten thousand men under George McCall, from McDowell's corps. Five regiments went to him from Baltimore, and two from Washington. When Jackson finally slipped away from his pursuers, Stanton let McClellan know that McDowell would be ordered down to him again, and still by land. McClellan argued again for sending him by water, offering a litany of practical reasons. Unsatisfied with the help coming his way so freely, he mentioned another report that Beauregard was on his way to Richmond, and while he largely discounted it he asked Stanton about sending him part of Halleck's army.[64]

In his reply to this message Stanton tried to dispel McClellan's belief in his antagonism, which was inciting the Democratic press to clamor for Stanton's removal. Rumors of his replacement sprouted everywhere, and Samuel Barlow ventured the hopeful opinion that "Stanton has no longer a friend anywhere." Stanton, perhaps thinking that he might reverse those rumors at their source and reduce the furor against him, closed a routine telegram to McClellan with a long sentence gushing with his devotion to the general's interests. He assured McClellan that "there never has been a moment when my desire has been otherwise than to aid you with my whole heart, mind, and strength since the hour we first met." Denying the aspersions of those who thought him the general's enemy, he vowed that "you have never had, and never can have, any one more truly your friend, or more anxious to support you." Stanton wrote this only days after he gave the editor of the *Boston Evening Transcript* all the dirt on McClellan's failures as general in chief, the better to pillory him in print for Stanton's vindication. The very ardor of Stanton's claim evidently betrayed its insincerity to McClellan: he had not been privy to most of Stanton's behind-the-back statements, but he had surely heard enough to be wary. In a letter to his wife the next day, McClellan ornamented Stanton's profession of eternal affection with an exclamation point, and described the telegram as "wonderful," in a tone of incredulity. The mistrust Stanton had engendered in the early weeks of his tenure worsened the jealous nature of the egotistical young general, infecting his relationship with Lincoln, whose patience and candor better suited a wary subordinate like McClellan. A Washington bureaucrat assured McClellan on June 12 that the president still resisted the aspersions of Radical critics, but within another week McClellan suspected that Lincoln had "again fallen into the hands of my enemies."[65]

In addition to the suspicions engendered by Stanton, McClellan suffered from poor intelligence supplied by Allen Pinkerton. From the eve of Yorktown's evacuation, Pinkerton's spies had always seen two Confederate soldiers for every one before them, and they applied that same duplication to the reinforcements streaming into Richmond. Late in June Pinkerton calculated that Lee had more than 180,000 troops, and he doubted even that figure as "considerably short of the real strength of their army." McClellan rounded that off at 200,000, or nearly twice the size of his own army, and seemed to believe it. As he prepared for his assault on the city he sought help from every corner, asking Burnside how many he might send from North Carolina and flavoring his messages to Stanton with frequent, sidelong allusions to the "overwhelming forces" he faced. Again he attributed the growth of Lee's army to Beauregard, sending Stanton a clipping from the *Richmond Dispatch* of June 21 reporting that Beauregard was on his way to Richmond from Alabama with "a large portion of the Army of the Mississippi." Reports gathered at Washington tended to corroborate these inflated estimates, giving Jackson alone 40,000 men, and the sense that he was so vastly outnumbered persuaded McClellan to devote much precious time to the building of earthworks, in case he were repulsed and counterattacked.[66]

The tale of Jackson's 40,000 troops probably amounted to disinformation. McClellan might reasonably have suspected the same of Beauregard's reported transfer, but he seemed convinced that a preponderance of the Confederacy's forces lay before Richmond, awaiting his attack. More than once before had he succeeded in pressuring Stanton to grant his requests by insinuating that the responsibility for failure or disaster would fall on the war minister for refusing to cooperate, and as his troops undertook the first step in his planned assault McClellan tried once again to coerce more troops from the secretary of war. On the evening of June 25 he telegraphed another report of Jackson's presence on his right flank, adding that he had so frequently reported his "great inferiority in numbers" and "the necessity of re-enforcements" that he considered himself "in no way responsible for it." He melodramatically promised to do all he could with his "splendid army," and if it were "destroyed by overwhelming numbers" he could "at least die with it." Accurately predicting that he would be attacked on the morrow, McClellan closed with the snide observation that he considered it useless to ask again for reinforcements.[67]

Stanton passed that telegram on to the president, for whom it was not intended, and Lincoln took it personally, frankly expressing his hurt feelings and insisting that he had given McClellan all he could. For once Lincoln was not being fair, although he may not have recognized it—but perhaps he should have, for he had just returned from a lightning visit to West Point to confer with General Scott on the situation in Virginia. Scott had examined the positions of the various troops and concluded that the president had erred in his own arrangements and opinions, while McClellan had been correct. With the garrisoned forts, the detachment at Manassas, and the armies of Frémont and Banks, Scott considered Washington safe from any detachment the enemy could spare. Meanwhile, he said, "the force at Fredericksburg" was too far away to be of use to anyone, and it would be better to send it to McClellan, whom he deemed capable of capturing Richmond from his present position. The fall of Richmond at that relatively early stage of the rebellion would, Scott believed, bring it to an effective finish. In an unintended final blow to the president's military thinking, the old general added that if McDowell's troops were sent to aid McClellan they would move faster and more certainly by steamer up the York River, as McClellan had requested, than they would by land. In the mind of old General Scott (the best natural soldier the United States had ever known), McClellan had been right on virtually every count.[68]

10

THE CABAL

Lincoln's visit with General Scott represented but the latest in a series of consultations he had sought as part of his military education. Even a social breakfast on June 18 had turned into a debate over military strategy. He sent his carriage for Senator Browning that morning, and at Willard's Hotel Browning picked up retail tycoon Alexander T. Stewart for the ride out to the Soldiers' Home on Seventh Street, where the Lincolns spent the steaming Washington summers. Their conversation quickly focused on the war, and particularly the Virginia theater, with Stewart pronouncing McClellan a great humbug, and suggesting John Pope as his replacement. Pope had made a name for himself with the capture of Island No. 10 in the Mississippi, and he had led one of Halleck's armies to Corinth, where Halleck had credited him with wildly exaggerated accomplishments. The subject seemed forgotten when the presidential carriage took everyone back to the city, but the next day Stanton telegraphed Pope in St. Louis, where he had gone on a brief furlough to see his family. Stanton had found him through Pope's father-in-law, an Ohio congressman, and he told the general he would like to see him in Washington if his orders allowed further absence from his command. Pope asked permission of Halleck, who expressed reluctance, but Pope may have sensed advancement and told Stanton he would leave in the morning.[1]

Stanton had no sooner wired Pope than he and Lincoln hopped on a steamer to Alexandria and boarded a special train to Manassas, where General McDowell was recovering from a nasty fall from his horse. They arrived early in the afternoon, conferred with the general for a couple of hours on unknown subjects—the move to Richmond, perhaps, or something altogether new—and left that evening.[2]

Then came Lincoln's lightning rail journey to West Point. When he returned, Pope was waiting for him. The president had finally understood that he had made grave mistakes in shaving Virginia into departmental slivers to separate Banks from McClellan (and to accommodate Frémont)—mistakes for which Stanton shared great blame, since he heavily influenced those decisions. Lincoln, however, never flinched from admitting an error of his own, or from accepting the responsibility for someone else's, if it would smooth the waters. Stanton may have hoped that Lincoln had summoned Pope to replace McClellan, but the president wanted him to command in northern Virginia, where he would consolidate the uncoordinated forces of Frémont, Banks, and McDowell into a single army. In the orders that announced the formation of the Army of Virginia, Lincoln gave Pope the mission of defeating and driving away the Confederates under Jackson and Ewell, threatening Charlottesville, and vaguely aiding McClellan to capture Richmond. There was no mention of sending McDowell to the peninsula, as Scott had urged.[3]

For Lincoln, Pope's appeal may have been how well the president knew him. He and Pope's father had been friends; they shared Kentucky kin. The president then had no other professional soldier with whom he could consult, and Pope seemed like someone he could trust. Moreover, Pope was a Republican—a rarity in the Regular Army, and he could avoid the political hostility McClellan had encountered among congressional Radicals.[4] That became clear when Pope saw Wade's Joint Committee on the Conduct of the War a few days later, and talked the Radical line for them. He told them he intended to march his army sixty miles from Washington, leaving even fewer and worse-trained troops to defend the capital than McClellan had, but the Radicals who dominated the committee uttered not a word of reproach—nor did Stanton, who had virtually accused McClellan of treason for pursuing the same plan three months before.[5]

The clause in Pope's orders that best revealed the degree to which mistrust had distorted communications between Washington and McClellan was the instruction to "attack and overcome the rebel forces under Jackson and Ewell." Based on surprisingly accurate information from a deserter and other intelligence, McClellan had been telling Stanton since noon of June 24 that he suspected Jackson had left the valley and was sneaking up on his right flank, with an attack planned for June 28. Stanton dismissed it as a hoax, designed to disguise a plan to strike Washington once McClellan launched his assault on Richmond. On June 26 General Pope assumed command of his new army, but instead of taking the field he took rooms at Willard's Hotel, where he interviewed his new corps commanders while they chose their staffs. Only Banks and McDowell came to him. Haughty Frémont asked to be relieved rather than serve under a junior officer, and the secretary of war obliged him, vicariously rebuking him for his example of unpatriotic selfishness: Stanton made sure to say that the president had directed him to convey that displeasure. The assorted audiences with Pope and the organization of the various corps headquarters were concluded by the second day of July, but by then George McClellan and the Army of the Potomac had been battered and bloodied.[6]

As McClellan had feared, Confederates fell on his right flank at Mechanicsville on June 26. Stonewall Jackson was not among his assailants that day, but he was right behind them, and Lee had amassed so much manpower by stripping Richmond's defenses that he seemed to wield the massive force McClellan believed. Lee struck again on June 27 beyond Gaines's Mill, where Fitz John Porter arranged a defensive crescent on a low ridge south of Old and New Cold Harbor. That evening, repeated Confederate charges broke through Porter's line and forced him to retreat south, across the Chickahominy toward Savage's Station, on the York River Railroad. Missing a chance to smash through a thin cordon on his left and seize Richmond, McClellan also withdrew that part of his army to Savage's Station. There Lee's columns converged, while McClellan abandoned the railroad and started his troops south, away from his huge supply base at White House and toward the James River. On June 29 the rear guard fought off Confederate attacks at Savage's Station, but McClellan insisted on flight and led the retreat. He fixed his eye now on reaching a new base of operations on the James—a move he had contemplated earlier and would later claim to have been his intention all along. Another rear-guard action at White Oak Swamp on June 30 and the repulse of a flank attack at Glendale allowed the Union army to reach Malvern Hill, a broad plateau overlooking the James. On July 1, with McClellan again too far away to control the battle, his reunited divisions finally made their stand, staving off successive waves of rebel infantry that swarmed desperately up the slope after them. That ended the fighting in what became known as the Seven Days. McClellan, still thinking himself vastly outnumbered, took refuge within a defensive perimeter at Harrison's Landing, five miles downstream, and began pleading for impossible numbers of reinforcements: a hundred thousand more men would not be too many, he suggested, estimating his remaining effective force at no more than fifty thousand.[7]

After midnight on the last night at Savage's Station, an exhausted McClellan had written a defensive, disingenuous, and somewhat irrational report to Stanton about Porter's fight above the Chickahominy. The battle had been lost, he contended, because his force was too small, and he seems to have believed as much, but Porter had been badly outnumbered only because McClellan kept most of his men on the other side of the river, falling for Lee's bluff against fewer than half their numbers. In setting the scene for Stanton, McClellan alluded to "the sad remnants of my men," and swore that he could take Richmond if he only had ten or twenty thousand fresh troops—which, although he claimed not to have "a man in reserve," he might have drawn from the three corps that had done little or no fighting. If he were to reverse the tide of defeat, he said, he needed the heavy reinforcements he had been requesting, and he must have them immediately. Thus far he had only written the letter that any bureaucrat would have composed to justify his own mistakes and lay the blame for failure at someone else's door, but as the message grew longer, the hour later, and the bleary-eyed general more fraught, he tentatively suggested that he felt the government had not sustained him. He must have sat there for a time, stewing over that notion, nourished as it had been by Stanton's now-apparent duplicity on other occasions. Stanton's antagonism explained for McClellan the unanswered portion of his appeals for more soldiers, especially in conjunction with the suspected abolitionist motive of postponing victory, and the thought of it drove the dejected general to a moment of insubordinate rage. "If I save this Army now," he added, at the end of the sheet, "I tell you plainly that I owe no thanks to you or any other persons at Washington—you have done your best to sacrifice this army."[8]

This was the last Washington heard from McClellan until the first of July; Confederates cut the telegraph lines later that day. When that dramatic final message finished clicking in over the War Department wire, Stanton took it to the president and reminded him that every time he had ordered troops sent to McClellan, or withheld them, it had been on Lincoln's authority. That was true enough, although Stanton occasionally helped to sway the president's thinking, but McClellan's history with Stanton very likely led the general to believe that Stanton exercised his persuasiveness more often and more arduously than he may have done. Having evidently little knowledge of the darker side of the relationship between those two men, Lincoln thought it "very harsh" of McClellan to accuse Stanton of being "the author of the disaster."[9]

When General Hitchcock gave Ben Wade's Committee on the Conduct of the War copies of the War Department's correspondence with McClellan, the transcription of the June 28 telegram ended with McClellan's admission that he did not "feel" the government had sustained him: the more personal and direct accusation against Stanton had been deleted. Not until McClellan published his final report, in 1864, did the telegram appear publicly in its entirety. In 1887 McClellan's literary executor, William Prime, accused Stanton of having mutilated the dispatch to protect himself against suspicions that the accusation might be true. Not until 1907 did a Stanton admirer publish an alternative explanation: in a memoir that appeared that year, former telegraph operator David Homer Bates wrote that Stanton's clerk, A. E. H. Johnson, showed the inflammatory message to Colonel Edward Sanford, Stanton's supervisor of telegraphic messages, who censored the offensive passage because it was "false." According to Bates, the War Department copy never contained the final sentence, and Stanton did not alter it to censor McClellan's accusation. Bates apparently did not write from personal experience, however. He seems to have heard the story from Johnson himself, who repeated it in his own address to the Columbia Historical Society in 1909. In that address Johnson insisted that Stanton's copy never contained the controversial words, as though he could recall its original wording forty-seven years later.[10]

In a footnote to Bates's book, Johnson also claimed that General Hitchcock testified to the same thing at a court of inquiry for Irvin McDowell, early in 1863, but that was not true. Hitchcock could not have known whether the original June 28 message had been edited, because he was still on convalescent leave in New Jersey when it arrived at the War Department. In April Colonel Sanford had told Stanton he did not feel at liberty to withhold anything addressed to the secretary of war: why he would dare do so in June, depriving Stanton of an incriminating, insubordinate comment from McClellan, is nearly as compelling a question as how he could have managed to keep it secret from the secretary, especially if department employees as far down as Bates and Johnson already knew of it. Equally curious is that those two employees, both friendly toward Stanton, kept silent for more than twenty years after Prime's conspicuous indictment. The popularity of war stories in the 1880s would have offered innumerable opportunities to correct Prime with their own tale, had it been true. Instead, it appears to have been a late-life invention by Johnson, who admitted being complicit in the production of fraudulent evidence in the reaper case—or had helped falsify that tale of fraud.[11]

Lincoln's reaction indicates that he saw the complete telegram: his comment that McClellan had been "very harsh" on Stanton, and blamed him for everything, would not have been justifiable had the final remark been removed. Without that direct accusation, the telegram became a more general criticism of the entire administration, employing "you" in a way that could easily have been interpreted as plural. In the insecurity of his first six months in office, Stanton would have been the only one with an interest in deleting that sentence from subsequent copies of the telegram. The battle between his friends and McClellan's had grown so bitter and uncertain by then that Stanton would almost certainly rather have kept McClellan's acerbic comment from the public than save it as an exhibit for a court martial.

McClellan's reverse and his discouraging telegrams produced another panic in Washington, implying as they did that he was about to be overwhelmed. Ostensibly at the president's behest, Stanton dashed off a telegram to Halleck, at Corinth, to send 25,000 men immediately but to continue his planned movements toward Chattanooga and East Tennessee. The blithe expectation that Halleck could hold his ground and still advance with a reduced force suggested a frantic atmosphere in the capital. Stanton may have substantially aggravated that anxiety, recognizing as he did the widespread belief in his direct responsibility for McClellan's plight. His ailing infant took a turn for the worse at that juncture, and his old colleague Peter Watson urged him to "take some rest," but after a hasty visit to the child's bedside he returned to work. Due, perhaps, to the arrogant independence of telegraph operators whom Stanton had made subordinate to no one but his own superintendent, his telegram took more than two days to reach Corinth. In the interim, he and Lincoln had heard encouraging observations from a newspaperman just back from White House Landing. Even then Stanton expected Halleck to send reinforcements, but the president relented rather than lose ground in Tennessee, so Stanton stripped troops from the Carolinas. Everyone had to go to McClellan's aid, he insisted—everyone, it seemed, but Pope.[12]

Public focus on the antagonism between Stanton and McClellan reached its peak about then. A few days after the Army of the Potomac settled into a new camp at Harrison's Landing, Zachariah Chandler rose in the Senate chamber to chastise his hometown newspaper, the *Detroit Free Press*, for an editorial in the July 3 edition that held "Stanton, Wade, and Chandler" responsible for McClellan's setbacks on the peninsula. "It is well known," Chandler asserted, "that the press for weeks has been filled with denunciations of the Secretary of War." The *New York Herald* considered Stanton the mere tool of "our radical disorganizers" and "the author of defeats," calling openly for his removal. Commenting on the all-out attack on the secretary of war, even the supportive *New York Times* suggested General McClellan as a replacement for Stanton.[13]

Private condemnation of the head of the War Department turned even more acerbic. Frederick Law Olmsted, the architect of Central Park, knew Stanton through his duties with the Sanitary Commission, and by the height of summer Olmsted had come to absolutely despise him. Olmsted chastised the managing editor of the *New York Tribune* for offering "special pleading" on behalf of a man Olmsted considered "the meanest kind of small[,] cunning, short sighted, selfish politician . . . the worst kind of hypocrite, [who] trades in prayer and devotion, and is habitually the grossest possible blasphemer . . . a bully and a liar. He is, I judge, a political confidence-man." Characterizing Stanton as a "canting impostor," Olmsted reminded the president of the Sanitary Commission how the secretary of war had pretended extreme friendliness to McClellan in front of the visiting officers of the commission and "what a business he made of taking us in." Six weeks later, Olmsted had abbreviated his opinion but had not softened it, summing Stanton up as "a bad man, a coward, a bully and a swindler."[14]

Nor was Olmsted alone in his contempt. Under such concentrated opprobrium Stanton evidently thought it best to seek détente, and he wrote McClellan another personal letter appealing to his sense of justice and trying to elicit his sympathy, citing the domestic distraction of his dying child and what he called "the cloud that wicked men have raised between us for their own base and selfish purposes." Again he assured the general that no one ever had "a truer friend than I have been to you and shall continue to be." With a young child of his own, McClellan may have felt a twinge of actual sympathy: he reminded Stanton of the unusual intimacy they had shared until he became secretary of war, but since then Stanton's behavior had been "marked by repeated acts done in such manner as to be deeply offensive to my feelings and calculated to affect me injuriously in public estimation." McClellan agreed to begin again nonetheless, and Stanton suddenly seemed willing to give McClellan anything he asked for—"no matter what."[15]

The rapprochement did not last long. The very morning after Stanton appealed for a truce, he spent several hours in his office with Senator Chandler, who came away from that meeting more disgusted with McClellan than he had ever been before. Apparently influenced by a discussion with Stanton that could have contained none of the friendliness Stanton claimed to harbor for McClellan, Chandler concluded that the general should be shot, and he seemed to mean it literally.[16]

On July 11 Lincoln bade Stanton call Henry Halleck to Washington to take up the vacant post of general in chief, which McClellan had supposed he could resume once his campaign succeeded. Pope had recommended Halleck as the president's adviser, if not as general in chief, and Lincoln probably judged that they might work as well together in the East as they had in the West. Secretary Welles assumed this was all part of a plan Stanton and Chase had hatched to depose McClellan, but as pleased as they may have been at the prospect, it appears to have been pushed by Pope, who perhaps saw Halleck as his own potential ally against McClellan. In a rushed visit to Harrison's Landing, however, Lincoln seemed to gain McClellan's approval of Halleck's appointment, too.[17]

It took Halleck over a week to report, but Stanton never told McClellan he was on the way, and as soon as McClellan's friend Samuel Barlow heard the news he interpreted it as a "direct slap in the face to McClellan." McClellan doubtless shared that opinion, although an ordnance officer in the War Department thought Halleck's appointment amounted to Stanton's admission that he could not manage everything himself. Then McClellan found evidence that Stanton was reading all his private telegrams, which had to pass through the room next to Stanton's office. The secretary tried to mollify McClellan once more by having an intermediary relate an apparent fantasy to Barlow about Stanton twice saving the general from removal by the president, but by then it was too late. Having spoken to Tom Scott and Montgomery Blair, Barlow had finally lost all trust in Stanton, and he warned McClellan that no one of reasonable intelligence who really knew Stanton could fail to detect that he was "the greatest hypocrite alive." McClellan told his wife, who also hated Stanton, that he would not be deceived again.[18]

It did not help Stanton's public image that while Lee's soldiers were chasing McClellan to the banks of the James the president made another backhanded effort to raise troops, because that only highlighted again Stanton's misjudgment in closing down recruiting three months before. For those who credited McClellan's view of the secretary, that mistake offered firm evidence not only of a disinclination to support McClellan but of an active effort to deprive him of manpower. "Thank Heaven," a New York man exclaimed in his diary, "the President has called for a few hundred thousand volunteers to reinforce the army, at last. Would he had invoked them three months ago!"[19]

While Lincoln was aggressively seeking volunteers, he was also doing his best to make it look as though he wasn't. In an unconvincing charade designed to downplay the terror that had gripped the administration for the second time in five weeks—and perhaps to save face for Stanton—Seward was visiting and telegraphing Northern governors and persuading them to "offer" troops to the president without a formal call. Lincoln initially suggested that they pretend to volunteer 100,000 men altogether. In discussing it with the governors, Seward raised that number to 150,000, but the next day, after a desperate telegram from McClellan pleading for "large reinforcements," Lincoln asked if Seward couldn't squeeze 200,000 out of them. Stanton proposed 300,000, and in the end it was unclear to the governors just how many men they were to "offer," although Lincoln finally settled on 300,000. He told the governors that he would not need nearly that many if he had them at hand then and there, but the time it took to raise them would increase the number needed. "If I had fifty thousand additional troops here *now*," he wrote Governor Edwin Morgan of New York, "I believe I could substantially close the war in two weeks."[20]

That statement would have made more sense on May 25 than on July 3. When the order came to stop recruiting, the states were still organizing an average of 30,000 new troops a month: that would have given Lincoln his 50,000 men by late May, probably with enough of them in Washington to mitigate the psychological impact of Jackson's drive down the valley. Then McDowell might well have been allowed to move against Richmond with most of his corps, backing Joe Johnston into the trap he dreaded most. That timely opportunity to overwhelm the primary symbol of Confederate independence, and to confront the principal rebel army with greatly superior force, was lost through panic over the shortage of troops in and around the capital. Stanton's recruiting blunder had contributed significantly to that shortage, and thus to the lost opportunity.[21]

The greatest advantage of McDowell coming down by land was that with the largest corps in the army he might have operated with a little independence. The belief that Lee had assailed McClellan with overwhelming force prevailed in the army and in the public, and so did Lincoln's speculation—that if McClellan had only had 50,000 more men, or even 20,000, he would have won the day and seized the rebel capital. This belief was mistaken, for McClellan already fielded more men than he seemed capable of handling under the stress of battle. Such an insight into the general's shortcomings required more perspective than anyone enjoyed in July of 1862, however, and every suspicion that McClellan had been deprived of enough men carried an implicit rebuke to the secretary of war. So widespread was the din against Stanton that when Halleck left Mississippi for Washington, his camps around Corinth and newspapers in the Northwest buzzed with rumors that he was leaving to take over as secretary of war.[22]

Stanton played along with the subterfuge of the state-offered troops, meanwhile collaborating with congressmen to initiate a bill for the first nationwide conscription law in American history. Through Charles Sumner, Stanton had grown chummy with Henry Wilson, the chairman of the Senate Committee on Military Affairs, and Wilson was preparing an amendment to the Militia Act of 1795 that would give the president authority to call out several hundred thousand more men for as long as nine months, and to demand them from the states: should any state fail to provide its quota, the president would be authorized to order a draft of its citizens. Wilson presented the bill on July 8, defending it for a week against complaints that it gave implied authority for the enrollment of "persons of African descent" and offered them freedom for their service. It finally passed in the Senate on July 15 and went to the House on July 16, on the last day of the session. Enamored as he must have been with the provision on even limited emancipation, Radical Thaddeus Stevens moved for an immediate vote, but his fellow Pennsylvanian Charles Biddle objected that it was too important an issue to pass so hastily. Congressmen anxious to go home handily rejected Biddle's argument, and the bill sailed to victory on a voice vote. Lincoln signed it the next day.[23]

During the doomed reconciliation between McClellan and Stanton, little James Stanton breathed his last. Ellen and the children had moved three or four miles west of town, into a house in a cooler, more bucolic setting that they rented from a navy captain on sea duty. Stanton remained at the K Street house most of the week. His last visit to his family ended on Monday, June 30, when the baby seemed to be improving, but on Saturday, July 5, a message came to the War Department that the child was dying. Stanton rushed out of the office, and it was that evening at the summer cottage, while the infant rallied, that he wrote the letter in which he again declared himself McClellan's best friend. The boy was still alive in the morning, but began sinking again a few days later. Lincoln hurried away that week to Harrison's Landing, to talk with McClellan, and Stanton stayed home: the story was credited in Washington that he might not be safe in the presence of the Army of the Potomac. The president returned to work on July 10—the same morning a *New York Times* editorial advised that McClellan might make a better war secretary than the incumbent—and that day the Stantons' baby died.[24]

The following morning Stanton returned to his office, at least long enough to send the telegram calling Halleck to Washington. Faced with another family member to bury, he bought a lot on a ridge in Georgetown's rolling Oak Hill Cemetery. He, Ellen, and the children drove there the next Sunday, followed in another carriage by the president, Seward, Welles, and Seward's son Fred. Observing the traditionally slow walk of a funeral cortège, they had some time to themselves, and Lincoln took the opportunity to broach the subject of emancipation. He had been considering it as a war measure, he said, either to threaten wavering rebels into submission or to deprive the Confederacy of as many agricultural and military laborers as possible. He surprised Welles, at least, because until then Lincoln had evinced the conservative attitude of most of his cabinet, recoiling from federal interference in what they saw as a state issue. Lincoln conceded that he had mentioned it to no one, but said he had been mulling it privately for some time. The two cabinet members both thought it might be justified, and feasible.[25]

Conservatives began to see the military advantage that slavery gave the rebels. On the morning of July 22 Francis Cutting, a prominent New York Democrat who had turned "at least half-Abolitionist" when the war began, dropped in on Stanton to talk about emancipation as a war measure. Given Stanton's notorious hostility to casual visitors, Cutting must have arrived with an influential introduction. He and Stanton seemed to agree entirely on the need to proclaim an end to slavery, at least in the rebellious states, for the same reasons Lincoln had raised during the drive to Oak Hill Cemetery. Stanton took his visitor over to the White House and left him with Lincoln, and Cutting thought he convinced the president, partly through an argument that abolitionist volunteers would replenish the armies.[26]

In the cabinet meeting that afternoon, Lincoln presented a draft of a proclamation freeing rebels' slaves in accordance with the second Confiscation Act, which he had signed at the end of the congressional session. Stanton jumped on that, advising the president to issue the order immediately, and old Edward Bates, from the slave state of Missouri, sustained him. Seward argued against it: thinking of diplomatic ramifications, he suspected that foreign manufacturers were so dependent on cotton that this threat to the Southern crop might hasten intervention; he also feared it could damage the nation's cotton trade "for sixty years"—presumably through the development of other sources for cotton. According to Stanton's notes on the meeting, the veteran abolitionist Chase also hesitated, calling it "a measure of great danger" exceeding anything he had ever recommended, and that it might lead to universal emancipation. The war secretary's brother-in-law and new office mate, Christopher Wolcott, claimed that during the night he (and Stanton, he implied) harried Chase diligently about the opportunity that had presented itself. Wolcott, who had served as Ohio's attorney general when Chase was governor, was known by some as a "pet" of the treasury secretary: his lobbying may account for Chase's diary entry taking credit for giving the measure "cordial support," as well as a proposal to arm those freed slaves. Seward plied the president with contradictory arguments, Wolcott told Pamphila, and that may have been true, for at Willard's Hotel the next day Cutting encountered Thurlow Weed, who told him he had undone whatever persuasion Cutting had worked on the president. In the end Lincoln's July 25 proclamation avoided any overt reference to emancipation, warning only that any persons who had not returned to their "proper allegiance to the United States" within sixty days would be subject to penalties, including the loss of their property.[27]

The idea of arming slaves still interested Lincoln, despite his reservations. Two days later he showed Senator Browning a map of the counties bordering the lower Mississippi where slaves outnumbered whites by about four to one. He was determined that the river should be reopened for navigation, and if it were necessary he would "take all those negroes to open it, and keep it open." A desire to gauge the political repercussions of emancipation or the mobilization of black men may have inspired the president to call on Stanton for a tally of the volunteer troops who had come forward from the loyal slave states, to see how many soldiers might be offended by such a change in policy.[28]

Courting the Radicals as he was, Stanton lost nothing by his strident advocacy for emancipation, especially in the confidentiality of the cabinet room, but the prospect infuriated McClellan. During the president's visit on July 8, McClellan had handed him a letter impertinently advising him on policy—the infamous Harrison's Landing letter, in which he disapproved of arbitrary arrests, confiscation, and above all the abolition of slavery by federal decree. That evening, in a conciliatory reply to Stanton's July 5 missive, McClellan told Stanton to ask the president to let him read that letter. Stanton probably never saw it, but its contents would have come as no surprise to him, for he was already familiar with McClellan's position. In his former guise as a Breckinridge Democrat, after all, Stanton had portrayed such a conservative himself, and McClellan told him that the views he expressed to Lincoln were merely the ones he and Stanton had agreed upon so cordially the previous summer.[29]

At the July 22 cabinet meeting, Stanton also proposed using the new draft law. He asked for permission to call up fifty thousand militia under that authority, and Seward suggested that they double it to a hundred thousand, explaining later that he anticipated a greater danger from his constant chimera—foreign intervention—if the country were slow to strengthen its armies. Lincoln hesitated, having just tripled the number of men he had asked of the governors, and wrote Stanton after the meeting to say he thought it best to ask for no more troops. The administration had already shown too much evidence of panic to risk reinforcing that impression.[30]

While Lincoln's cabinet discussed such momentous topics, two generals in blue and grey met at Haxall's Landing, on the James River, to agree on terms for exchanging prisoners of war. Prisoners had been piling up on both sides for more than a year, with deleterious effects to their health from long confinement, and the families of officers in particular had been lobbying heavily to have their men released. Negotiations between General Wool and an officer from Richmond had begun early in the spring but had stalled over Stanton's refusal to exchange Brigadier General Simon B. Buckner. Stanton may have wished to hang Buckner, in lieu of John B. Floyd: Buckner's fellow Kentuckian Joseph Holt had asked Stanton to subject the general to what Holt called "the halter." Over such spite the prisoners from Bull Run languished months longer. Not until July 22 did Confederate general Daniel Harvey Hill and Union general John Dix conclude their articles of agreement on prisoner exchange. Under the terms, all prisoners would be released on parole within ten days of capture after they promised not to take up arms again until formally exchanged for enemy prisoners of equal rank. Then they would be transported to either Aiken's Landing, on the James, or to Vicksburg, on the Mississippi, for repatriation. Whoever held more prisoners would turn them all over, but the surplus men would be prohibited from returning to duty until their own armies had taken new prisoners to offer as equivalents. By such arrangements thousands of men would be saved from the inevitably unhealthy conditions of crowded prisons; if there were a dispute, the system was not to be interrupted while the parties resolved the difference through negotiation.[31]

July 22 ended with yet another significant development. Henry Halleck arrived at the Washington rail depot that night, and the next day he reported to the War Department and White House for duty as general in chief of the nation's armies. A friend of Secretary Seward's wondered whether the meeting between Halleck and Stanton could have been very cordial, remembering Stanton's "published report to Judge Black that Halleck the lawyer had perjured himself in the New Almaden case!" A few days after Halleck's arrival, Wolcott betrayed to his wife what Stanton was probably thinking. Halleck was not Wolcott's "pattern man," he wrote, but he thought the promotion a great improvement not only because it would restore command unity but because it "substantially degrades McClellan into a mere subordinate." He probably also echoed Stanton when he hoped the appointment would deprive the president of any further excuse "for interfering in the conduct of the war"—although Lincoln had "interfered" often enough when McClellan was general in chief, and would continue to do so while Halleck held the position.[32]

By the time Halleck arrived, Ambrose Burnside had already been in Washington a couple of days, fresh from delivering two divisions to Newport News, near Fort Monroe. Burnside and McClellan had been friends at West Point, and McClellan had given him a railroad job when the Panic of 1857 and the failure of a government contract forced Burnside to liquidate his business assets. So successfully had Burnside secured the North Carolina sounds that everyone thought very highly of him in July of 1862, and Lincoln sent him down to Harrison's Landing with Halleck and Quartermaster General Meigs, to determine whether McClellan would make another lunge for Richmond or bring his army back to Washington and start over.[33]

At McClellan's headquarters Halleck said he could promise no more than twenty thousand reinforcements (which seem to have included Burnside's seven thousand) if McClellan wanted to attack Richmond again: otherwise, he should join Pope's army along the Rappahannock. McClellan preferred to take the reinforcements and resume his campaign, and he met with Burnside and his corps commanders to discuss it. When they emerged, most of them agreed with McClellan, so he informed Halleck that he would accept the twenty thousand troops and move directly against Richmond.[34]

Lincoln had assured Halleck that McClellan would never fight, and that if he were given another hundred thousand troops to match Lee's reported two hundred thousand he would soon relay new information that the rebels had four hundred thousand, and wail for more reinforcements. Halleck's steamer had not yet reached Washington when McClellan seemed to confirm Lincoln's prediction, reporting on ominous Confederate troop movements from the Atlantic coast and the Southern interior toward Lee's army. In response, he suggested sending all U.S. troops from the Carolinas, Georgia, and Florida to his own army. In addition, he asked if Halleck could not *possibly* draw 15,000 or 20,000 men from the West to reinforce me temporarily?"[35]

He sent this message only hours after being told that the original twenty thousand would be his outside limit on reinforcements. Throughout July 27 and 28 the frustrated president and Stanton pressed Burnside to take command of the Army of the Potomac, but the affable, loyal, and generally humble Burnside declined to supersede his friend. McClellan alone, he said, owned the administrative capacity to lead so large an army. That saved McClellan from immediate removal, but he pleaded for reinforcements several more times over the next few days, even after Burnside warned him, through an intermediary, of the attempt to replace him. When Halleck heard reports of Richmond being evacuated and asked McClellan to reconnoiter, the general crept so timidly toward the rebel capital that Halleck abruptly ordered him to start bringing his army up to Aquia Creek, to strengthen Pope along the line of the Rappahannock. There would be one more pointless skirmish to retake Malvern Hill, but McClellan's grand campaign was over.[36]

John Pope's campaign, meanwhile, was just beginning. From the comfort of his Washington hotel room he had forwarded a bombastic greeting to his new Army of Virginia, telling men he had never seen that he came to them from the West, "where we have always seen the backs of our enemies." Deploring the common use of such terms as "lines of retreat" and "bases of supplies" in the Eastern army, he advised his troops to consider only their opponents' lines of retreat "and leave our own to take care of themselves." Pope's announcement struck one brigadier as "very windy & somewhat insolent," and its pretentious assertions would echo with intense irony for the veterans of an army that would be remembered for its defeats. If John Pope could be believed, Stanton composed the worst of that rodomontade. Many who knew Pope might have hesitated to believe him, but the rhetorical style and choices of phrase did reek of Stanton's blowhard manner, and the address carried more implied insult to George McClellan than Pope probably would have chosen to offer the man who might assume command over him.[37]

Pope's field orders also betrayed the flavor of Stanton's vengeful side, as well as his ignorance of the demoralizing effects of looting and rapine on an invading army. No longer would troops be detailed to guard private property, Pope decreed, and the army would subsist on the country where it operated. Soldiers naturally took that as their cue to pillage at will: at least one elderly, unarmed Virginian was killed in broad daylight as he tried to defend his family against a Yankee cavalryman intent on forcing his way into the house—and this more than a week after Pope issued an admonitory order against just such interpretation of his original directive. A West Pointer from McClellan's army who joined Pope's forces behind the Rappahannock thought discipline in the Army of Virginia had evaporated.[38]

Burnside ferried his partial corps from Newport News up to Aquia Creek, sending most of those men to Pope under a subordinate who did not outrank him, as Burnside did: Pope had already assumed command over two corps commanders whose dates of rank preceded his, and that seemed to be enough of an affront to seniority. McClellan nevertheless feared that, even as the more senior general, he might be required to take orders from Pope, or that his troops would simply be given to Pope. Beset by apprehension on that account, he dawdled at Harrison's Landing with his army, blaming his plight on the secretary of war, whom he accused of turning against him without cause. At the same time, Pope could reasonably wonder whether McClellan would not take charge of the whole if he brought his troops with him.[39]

While Halleck tried to coax a reluctant McClellan to board his men on steamers, the president's advisers wore down his reservations about calling for more new soldiers. The same day that Halleck ordered McClellan to leave the peninsula, he dropped in on a cabinet meeting where he submitted a recommendation for an immediate draft of 200,000 militia. Stanton did not attend the meeting, but he had already seen Halleck's memo, along with his further advice to raise the 300,000 volunteers from the July call as soon as possible, and to fill up the old regiments first. Lincoln had begun distancing himself from military affairs, allowing Halleck to make the decisions, and Halleck's opinion appeared to persuade Lincoln to at least demand the 200,000. In the wake of the criticism he drew for shutting down recruiting, and the accusation that he had deliberately starved McClellan's army for men, Stanton had forgotten his concerns about the expense of an oversized army and characteristically forged ahead in precisely the opposite direction. The day after the cabinet meeting, he issued a call for 300,000 militia to serve nine-month terms, warning that any state failing to produce its quota within the impossibly short span of eleven days would be subjected to a draft.[40]

President Lincoln alluded to the controversy over Stanton and McClellan at a Union rally in front of the Capitol on the evening of August 6, where he discredited the competing allegations and tried to reconcile the two men's supporters. With two troop levies totaling 600,000 men just behind him, Lincoln told the assembled crowd that McClellan must wish to be successful in the field, and that Stanton must also wish it because McClellan's failure would be Stanton's. The dispute over how many men McClellan had been given was argued, he said, by different partisans who used different figures to prove their points—with McClellan's enemies citing the grand total of troops that had been sent to him, and Stanton's enemies counting only those left who were fit for duty. He admitted that "McClellan has sometimes asked for things that the Secretary of War did not give him," and he conceded that McClellan was not at fault for requesting what he needed, but neither did he see how Stanton could be blamed for not giving what he did not have. The president concluded with the declaration that Stanton had never withheld anything from McClellan that it was in the executive power to give, and Lincoln took all the responsibility for anything Stanton had kept back from the general.[41]

The *New York Herald* considered that account less than credible but typically generous of Lincoln, whom the paper suspected of throwing "the mantle of charity" over Stanton, as he had done with Cameron. McClellan and his friends had already anticipated Lincoln's assumption of blame, and rejected it. Barlow predicted that history would point the finger of blame only at Stanton, who had flattered McClellan before he became secretary and thereafter relentlessly disparaged him to the president and "the meanest lick spittles that hang round his Department." Barlow, who had believed in Stanton until the evidence of his treachery became overpowering, felt certain the secretary worked hard to persuade Lincoln that McClellan was incompetent or, worse yet, disloyal. The president had made honest mistakes, Barlow supposed, but he was forced to rely on the facts as they were presented to him. With Stanton "to *invent* the facts," Barlow wrote, "the conclusions are irresistible": To McClellan's champions, it seemed further evidence of animus that Stanton undertook strenuous efforts to raise new legions only after the general had been defeated and all but deposed.[42]

Under the implied excuse of what would later be styled "national security," Stanton quickly followed his draft decree with two supplementary orders in which he nullified much of the Bill of Rights. Citing no authority but his own, on August 8 he "authorized and directed" all U.S. marshals and chiefs of police—over whom he could claim no constitutional authority whatever—to arrest and imprison anyone who "may be engaged, by act, speech, or writing, in discouraging volunteer enlistments, or in any way giving aid and comfort to the enemy, or in any other disloyal practice against the United States." In a single sentence Stanton abolished the First Amendment, overrode the Fourth, ignored the Fifth, and eviscerated the Sixth. He essentially criminalized every citizen's right to criticize the government. Republican officials would quickly embrace his order as an opportunity to treat criticism of the Lincoln administration and its political supporters as a form of treason, and to punish Democrats—almost exclusively—for daring to voice disagreement. Under Stanton's order officers were not required to bother with arrest warrants before they seized dissident citizens—or, in consonance with the conditional "may" of the order, before they imprisoned citizens who were merely suspected or accused of dissidence. Then those marshals and police might (and did) hold those prisoners in custody indefinitely, with no need to inform them of the charges against them or allow them to confront their accusers, because those rights had already been routinely abrogated in political arrests.

Stanton added another sentence that also eliminated the right of the accused to receive a public trial before a jury of his peers in the county where the offense was supposed to have occurred. He appointed a special judge advocate, Major Levi Turner, to try those droves of new political prisoners before military commissions, should the government ever try them at all. In 1845 Stanton had flattered Caleb McNulty's jurors with the reminder that they represented the Sixth Amendment's guarantee of the most cherished safeguard of a free society—trial by jury—but in 1862 he blithely expunged that very guarantee. His order effectively seized much of the power to administer justice from the judicial branch and delivered it to the executive department in which he had won so much control. Meanwhile, he transferred the determination of guilt or innocence from independent judges to army officers, whose professional future depended in large measure on Stanton's own fickle favor.[43]

Five days after his initial order, on the eve of his threatened draft and with the connivance of Seward and Halleck to sway the president, Stanton prohibited American men of military age from leaving the country, and effectively declared them paroled prisoners in the counties where they then resided. Any draft-age man who attempted to leave his county or state without a pass was to be arrested, delivered to the nearest military post, and "placed on military duty for the term of the draft." With what may have been deliberate ambiguity, Stanton did not clarify whether the duty should involve manual labor or armed service, or whether "the term of the draft" extended only through the period of draft selection or the entire nine months of service for which men were to be drafted. As an additional humiliation, those detained transients were ordered to pay the cost of their arrest and transportation, and a $5 bounty to the arresting officer. To shield himself and his agents from any civil application of due process, Stanton's order suspended the writ of habeas corpus nationwide for arrests made under it, as well as in the cases of those who were imprisoned under his August 8 order.[44]

For the moment, the United States government lapsed into virtual dictatorship, with Stanton exercising authority to impose fiat law, either exacting punishment without trial or establishing a trial process in which he could control the outcome. Republican U.S. marshals took immediate advantage of his order to begin rounding up dissident newspaper editors, judges, and other citizens, either on their own initiative or upon complaints filed by other administration appointees and supporters. Many prisoners were dragged halfway across the country for incarceration at Washington—much as British colonial authorities had hauled American defendants all the way to Halifax to answer charges, in the very practice that inspired the Sixth Amendment. One coffle came from Iowa and Illinois, including newspapermen like Dennis Mahony, the Irish editor of the *Dubuque Herald*, who had been annoying Marshal H. M. Hoxie for weeks with his editorial appeals for peace. Hoxie arrested him as soon after he received Stanton's August 8 order as he could collect the necessary affidavits. Mahony was not released from the Old Capitol until autumn, and like most of his fellow prisoners he was kept imprisoned until he consented to sign a waiver of his right to sue his captors for false arrest. Faced with bankruptcy and the loss of his newspaper, he signed.[45]

In New Hampshire, Dr. Nathaniel Batchelder had opposed the war from the start, and at an August recruiting rally he had the temerity to accuse prospective recruits of enlisting solely for the bounties their town offered, adding that nothing but death and damnation awaited them in the army. For that audacity he spent nearly two months in the bowels of a coastal fort, coming home only after posting heavy bonds against a promise never to utter such opinions again. On August 12 Charles Bush interrupted a war meeting in Fond du Lac, Wisconsin, promising that if he were drafted he would desert, because there no longer seemed to be any government or laws to defend: the U.S. marshal arrested him, and he languished in a Milwaukee jail until at least the middle of October, even though he had promptly signed the oath of allegiance. Stanton cast an old acquaintance, Dr. Edson B. Olds, into Fort Lafayette for making uncomplimentary remarks about the Lincoln administration in a speech during his bid for the Ohio legislature. Congressman William J. Allen, an Illinois Democrat seeking reelection, was also arrested on the campaign trail. Suddenly it was almost impossible to utter any effective criticism of the war, or the administration, without at least the threat of arrest.[46]

Prisoners started coming in from all over the country, often on the flimsiest evidence of guilt, even when measured by Stanton's inventive interpretations of what constituted a crime. His new judge advocate began fielding reports on hundreds (and ultimately thousands) of American citizens taken into custody for the exercise of what had been considered inalienable rights in July, but became crimes in August by virtue of executive dictum. A young Kentuckian became one of the earliest victims when Stanton's last order found him in northern Ohio, where he was searching for a college he could afford to attend. He was arrested on the way home, and imprisoned in Toledo for the new offense of leaving his home county without a pass. A Philadelphian of local Democratic renown landed in federal custody when he denounced similar arrests in his city, and boldly predicted that Democrats would throw Lincoln out of office at the next election. The governor of Maine reported a member of the Coast Survey directly to the secretary of war for expressing political opinions that might tend to "discourage enlistments." A discharged lieutenant from Illinois went to jail when he remarked, apparently in casual conversation, on his disdain for the Radical agenda and anyone who would fight for "damned abolitionists." Nor were these particularly extreme cases of injustice under Stanton's crackdown.[47]

The arbitrary arrests under Stanton's order may have made more enemies for the administration than anything since Lincoln's decision to oppose secession with military force, including perhaps the militia draft itself, from which the reluctant and unsupportive soon found other avenues of escape. The idea that the opposition could no longer criticize policies that seemed so wrongheaded went down hard, and such widespread arrests of dissident citizens, legislators, and even congressmen contributed substantially to the sharp backlash in the state elections of October and November. Stanton could not have expected otherwise, but with ardent partisanship he kept jailing critics, painting all who disagreed as traitors, and the president allowed him free rein. Before the sands of September ran out, Stanton evidently persuaded Lincoln to lend more legitimacy and permanency to his August orders by reissuing them from the White House in a declaration of martial law to hover over the heads of American citizens "during the existing insurrection"—at least for the specific "crimes" Stanton had outlined.[48]

These measures followed logically from Stanton's persistent efforts to consolidate as much power in his own official person as the hierarchy of the government allowed. That same purpose obviously underlay his appointment of military governors in conquered portions of Confederate states, for which he obtained the president's previous consent, and it particularly explained his haste to install his then-friend from the Committee on the Conduct of the War, Andrew Johnson, against the urgent advice of Assistant Secretary Tom Scott. Within six months of entering the War Department Stanton had named military governors in Tennessee, North Carolina, Louisiana, and Arkansas, and he hoped next to install one in Texas. These administrators theoretically reported to him, rather than to the president, and that allowed Stanton great latitude in dictating rudimentary Reconstruction policy; only in conspicuous controversies would Lincoln interfere.[49]

If the military governors were not all more tractable than civilian governors in the Northern states, they were at least technically subordinate to Stanton, and he had evidently grown so accustomed to deference that he found gubernatorial independence hard to bear. Reinforced by the nationalist implications of the Militia Act amendments, Stanton stubbornly assumed federal dominance over the loyal states, too, which promptly bred tension between Washington and some state capitals—both by the direct effect of his condescending tone and the indirect impact of his resentful complaints. By blaming War Department shortcomings on the governor of Illinois, Stanton precipitated a rare exchange of unpleasant messages between that official and the president, and Stanton himself managed to insult the governor of Wisconsin twice in two weeks.[50]

With the edicts of August and September, Stanton wielded nearly as much power in the loyal states as he did in occupied territory. He could unilaterally deprive any citizen of freedom, needing only an unproven accusation. Nothing illustrated his willingness to take advantage of groundless allegations better than his continuing persecution of Brigadier General Charles P. Stone, whom he had arrested in 1862 on vague suspicion but was forced to release days after issuing his orders of August 8 and 13. Less than a month into Stone's imprisonment, Senator James McDougall had inserted an amendment into a military pay bill requiring charges to be presented within eight days after an officer's arrest, with his trial or release to follow within thirty days: the eight-day rule already existed under the seventy-ninth Article of War, but Stanton ignored it from the start. McDougall also introduced a resolution demanding accountability from the secretary of war; Radical Henry Wilson, however, amended it to require information about Stone's arrest from the president, who knew only what little Stanton told him. On nothing better than Stanton's advice, Lincoln declined to offer any charges or specifications. The pay bill limped its way through the session, finally passing muster during early July, but the president only signed it on July 17, in a flurry of other last-minute legislation.[51]

Stone had already been imprisoned more than five months when Lincoln signed the bill, and if Stanton ever intended to charge him with anything, let alone try him, he ought to have been ready to do so by the middle of July. There had not been any credible evidence, however, and the only charge that might have been accurately leveled against Stone was that he had insulted Stanton's secret Radical ally, Senator Sumner—who had insulted Stone first, and unfairly. In as blatant an example of spite as he could have offered, Stanton kept Stone confined until the last hour allowed by the new legislation, as though marking the days on the calendar. On August 16 he ordered Stone's release, pretending that he only did so because a court martial could not be convened within the time prescribed by the statute. Stone left close confinement for the first time since February 8, but suspicion had permanently smeared his reputation, and without the vindication of a trial it would remain forever tarnished. Even one of Stanton's military courts would have been hard-pressed to find any credible evidence to justify his long imprisonment, which is probably why Stanton never convened one.[52]

It was, furthermore, Stanton's habit to finish off a wounded enemy. Having sacrificed Stone to please his new Radical friends, he dared not grant the general any important assignments, and left him awaiting orders for six more months. In the meantime, Stanton ignored or denied all requests for Stone's services before finally allowing him to take a staff position under another general. Later, without cause or excuse, he summarily mustered Stone out of his volunteer rank of brigadier general, and a dejected Stone finally resigned his Regular Army commission as well, realizing that Stanton would bar him from any promotion. To the president's discredit, he let that injustice continue uncorrected, despite a petition from hundreds of prominent Massachusetts men and a plaintive personal appeal from Stone himself. This was the most conspicuous instance, if not the most egregious, in which Lincoln allowed Stanton to inflict undeserved suffering through the extraordinary powers he had vested in his secretary of war. Nineteenth-century historian and Lincoln supporter Alexander McClure alluded to such injured innocents when, even in the glow of post-assassination reverence, he noted Lincoln's complicity in Stanton's excesses. "It will be regretted by the impartial historian of the future," McClure wrote, "that Stanton was capable of impressing his intense hatred so conspicuously upon the annals of the country, and that Lincoln, in several memorable instances, failed to reverse his War Minister when he had grave doubts about the wisdom or justice of his methods."[53]

The attention Stanton paid to keeping Stone incarcerated until the last possible day seems all the more malicious because the secretary was dealing with so many other urgent issues at that juncture. Along the Rappahannock, Pope faced Confederate forces under Stonewall Jackson, and Lee was moving north with the rest of the Army of Northern Virginia; McClellan, meanwhile, dawdled on the peninsula, taking his own good time obeying the orders to send his men to Pope's aid. Since Halleck's promotion, coordination in the West had also begun to suffer without a single overall commander, and Confederate armies started to stir in east and middle Tennessee, cutting behind General Buell's advanced position and aiming for Kentucky, where isolated Union garrisons began to worry. A Confederate army attacked Baton Rouge early in the month, and Butler evacuated the city, pulling back toward New Orleans. Indian war was about to erupt on the prairie, although Stanton appeared to regard that as an annoyance unworthy of much attention or resources.[54] Then there was the daily administration of the army, made all the more onerous by the raising of new levies and the preparation of instructions and regulations for the new federal draft. Drafting had originally been scheduled for August 15 within those states that had failed to meet their quotas, making department business especially hectic through the first half of that month.

Innumerable questions and decisions attended this mobilization, and some of them involved the entirely new topic of uniforming and arming black men. Stanton, it seems, had been complicit in attempting to outfit "contraband" slaves on the sly since the very week he shut down the recruiting offices. The Radical courtier David Hunter, freed from his assignment at Fort Leavenworth and dropped into South Carolina to command the southeast coast, wrote Stanton a cryptic letter on the very day the secretary suspended recruiting, asking for fifty thousand arms for "such loyal men as I can find in the country." In case there were any doubt who those fifty thousand loyal men in South Carolina might be, he hinted that scarlet pantaloons would be the only uniform he required for "these people." Stanton gave him no direct, written answer, but a couple of days after that letter would have arrived in Washington the *New York Times* reported that its correspondent in the capital had learned Stanton was considering using black soldiers as garrison troops in forts down in the torrid latitudes. The secretary did seem to favor the idea, but his refusal to act openly caused much wasted effort.[55]

Hunter suffered the same fate as Frémont had when he tried to combine a promise of emancipation with his efforts to lure slaves into the ranks. The president revoked his presumptuous order with some indignation over the trouble it caused, leading Stanton to curse Hunter for grabbing headlines with such a public display. "Damn him," Stanton was heard to mutter, "why didn't he do it and say nothing about it?" Hunter did emulate the secretary's covert style at least in the recruiting of his red-legged regiment, but when he sent a large portion of his white troops to McClellan in July he beseeched the president to allow him to enlist loyal persons "without regard to complexion." Lincoln showed that dispatch to the cabinet, and Stanton, Chase, and Seward applauded the idea, but the president refused to endorse it. Hunter continued to organize his contrabands, and on August 4 he asked Stanton for authority to commission officers for a completed regiment. Stanton failed to reply, still preferring tacit understandings and probably hoping Hunter would press on surreptitiously, but six days later the general reported that he had finally disbanded the regiment because he had "failed to receive the authority which I expected."[56]

Kansas senator (and brigadier general) James Lane informed Stanton on August 5 that he had recruited enough men to fill four white regiments and two black ones. To this, also, Stanton made no reply. Fifteen days later, when the governor of Kansas asked whether he could commission officers in Lane's black regiment, Stanton answered that he could send the names to Washington and instructions would follow, but a month after that Stanton finally told Lane he was only authorized to recruit "loyal white men."[57]

Ben Butler likewise alerted Stanton in mid-August that he intended to raise a "Colored Brigade" from the Creole veterans of several Louisiana regiments that the Confederate army had rejected because of their African ancestry. Butler had engaged in a rancorous dispute days before with a subordinate who wished to organize black soldiers, but then—ever the political chameleon—Butler underwent a sudden change of heart. On the last day of July, Secretary Chase wrote to him about the evolving public attitudes on emancipation, describing the president as showing less resistance to the idea and implying that the same might be true about putting slaves into uniform: Butler would have to judge the wisdom of that, Chase advised, but he added that Butler could "hardly go too far to satisfy the exigency of public sentiment now." Chase hurried that letter to the New Orleans steamer, and it may have inspired Butler's August 14 proposal to Stanton, who again kept a judicious silence that avoided discouragement for Butler or responsibility for himself. Butler understood that game better than Hunter did, and when more than a week passed without a response he issued an order for reactivation of the antebellum Native Guards, consisting of the "free colored citizens" who had been recognized as part of the state militia before the war.[58]

The secretary's own attitude about arming black men remains as inscrutable today as it did then. In the presence of Radicals, including family members like the Wolcotts, he apparently stood firm for emancipation and mobilization of the freedmen, but before conservatives he deplored the very notion of black men under arms. In the confidentiality of cabinet councils, he showed a preference for the Radical line, but whether he did so from personal conviction or internal strategy can only be guessed. His vigorous recruiting among freedmen later in the war may also have reflected pragmatic politics at least as much as principle.

During congressional debate over Stanton's conduct in early July, Charles Wickliffe of Kentucky denounced him as an ally of the abolitionists. Fellow Kentuckian Robert Mallory rose to contradict Wickliffe, relating a personal encounter with the secretary of war "two or three weeks since," when Mallory and two other congressmen were about to leave Stanton's office. The secretary called them back to his desk and showed them part of a letter from an officer seeking permission to raise a black regiment, asking the conservative Mallory what the reply should be. Mallory answered that black men should never be allowed to bear arms, especially against whites. With those members of the House and his own staff within earshot, Stanton obligingly announced that he had not only returned a refusal but had ordered the officer arrested—which was almost certainly a gross exaggeration, an outright lie, or a clever deception. No one challenged Mallory's intended defense of Stanton, or asked him to produce his witnesses, but Thaddeus Stevens immediately voiced his surprise and, in a frank admission that said a great deal about the integrity of Lincoln's secretary of war, confessed that Stanton had given him just the opposite impression. Stevens made it clear that Stanton had told him he was sending arms and equipment to generals in the field for the use of any loyal men in the South. "I regret to find that I was mistaken," Stevens said, perhaps acknowledging distaste for the duplicity that Mallory's encounter revealed.[59]

Somehow Stanton managed to explain away his conflicting personas, at least to the satisfaction of the chief Radicals. Perhaps he had ordered the arrest of the unnamed officer who made the request, but not for the implied reason. Had any soldier suffered such an indignity for simply asking to raise black troops, congressional Radicals would have leaped to defend him, yet no motion for congressional inquiry followed.

The changing attitudes that Salmon Chase had observed, and especially the evolution of the president's thinking, coincided with (and may have spawned) Stanton's willingness to officially authorize black soldiers. Two days after Ben Butler outlined his plan for Louisiana's Native Guards, and the day after an annoyed David Hunter asked to be relieved from command, Brigadier General Rufus Saxton sought permission to raise up to five thousand black men "as laborers" in Hunter's department. He also wanted to arm them to protect that haven for escaped slaves, arguing that the hordes of refugees gathering there deprived the Confederacy of both agricultural and military labor. Like Hunter, Saxton based his plea on the relatively defenseless state of the southeast coast after heavy reinforcements had gone from there to reinforce McClellan; unlike Hunter, he suggested he might need no official appointment of officers for the recruits, and he hesitated to characterize them as soldiers. It must have come as a surprise when, after Stanton granted the request for five thousand laborers, he added explicit authority for another five thousand "volunteers of African descent" to be trained in military drill and armed.[60]

That constituted the first official sanction for black soldiers. Stanton wrote those orders only four days after his ambiguous reply to the governor of Kansas, stalling on the naming of officers for Lane's regiment. In the interim Lincoln had written his legendary response to Horace Greeley's "Prayer of Twenty Millions" editorial, in which he declared that any action he took on emancipation would bear on whether he believed it would contribute to restoration of the Union: whether he freed some, none, or all of the slaves depended on whether it would further his goal of reunion. No cabinet meeting fell between August 20 and 25, but the publication of Lincoln's letter in the *New York Tribune* of August 25 may have initiated some discussion between him and Stanton about the direct and indirect military value of slaves to the Confederacy, and that in turn may have led to at least a tacit understanding based on Saxton's proposal. At the July 22 cabinet council Lincoln had indicated a willingness to have fugitive slaves unofficially armed "for purely defensive purposes," and Saxton's request envisioned precisely that, but at the same meeting Lincoln had made it clear that he disapproved of their formal organization into military units. That was essentially what Stanton had authorized, and as eagerly as he might wield the inherent or vested powers of his office, he had watched (and purportedly abetted) Simon Cameron's downfall on that very issue; he would never have dared intrude overtly in such an arena of executive policy without some license from the president—even if it were only a verbal exchange on which he could plead a misunderstanding. There appeared, however, to be no misunderstanding.[61]

The political and martial tensions of August culminated late that month in another disaster on the Bull Run battlefield. McClellan had finally begun shipping his troops up from the peninsula, and Halleck started them toward Pope from Aquia Creek and Alexandria, where McClellan arrived to a virtually empty camp on the evening of August 26. That same night, Stonewall Jackson slipped behind Pope and burned his supply base at Manassas Junction, after which he disappeared into nearby woods until Pope's retreating army passed that way up the Warrenton Pike. Jackson struck him broadside on the twenty-eighth, engaging him that afternoon and all the next day, until Lee came up with Longstreet's half of the army. While Jackson occupied Pope on August 30, Longstreet slammed into him from beside and behind, ultimately sending the Army of Virginia scurrying back toward Washington. One more sharp clash in a driving thunderstorm hastened Pope's flight to the safety of the forts around Washington.[62]

While Jackson lay waiting to strike at Pope, Stanton looked for a way to drive McClellan out of the army. On August 28 he presented Halleck with a list of questions designed to indict McClellan on charges of disobedience, asking if the general had moved from the peninsula as promptly as Halleck thought appropriate, and whether he had started Franklin's corps marching toward Pope from Alexandria as quickly as possible. Probably Halleck had already answered those questions verbally, for Stanton's formal request seemed intended to accumulate evidence for a court martial. Despite the developing crisis on the battlefield near Bull Run, Halleck devoted considerable time to the collection of the correspondence and the composition of his formal reply, indicating that he had been "by no means satisfied" with McClellan's alacrity.[63]

With the Army of the Potomac and the Army of Virginia coming into contact with each other, Stanton feared that McClellan's seniority might persuade Halleck to give him overall command, or at least allow him to have his own, larger army. The chain of command then being recognized would have made it awkward for Stanton to overrule Halleck, especially since the president was trying to avoid interfering with Halleck's discretion. Tradition prescribed the respective authority of the president, secretary of war, and general in chief, fluctuating within certain bounds according to the inclination of the sitting president and within Lincoln's own evolving development as commander in chief. Under Lincoln's successor Stanton would manipulate a cooperative Congress into legislating his virtual independence of—and even superiority to—the military powers of the president he served, but in matters so significant as the appointment of an army commander or a general in chief, President Lincoln regarded the secretary of war only as an adviser, and not always an especially privileged one.

Stanton did have the authority to level charges, and he also had the right and the cunning to appoint a court that would probably convict McClellan of disobedience in the face of the enemy: David Hunter had just come home on leave, and he owned enough rank—and rancor—to preside over the trial of his former general in chief. For the moment, the crisis necessitated a more immediate solution, lest McClellan resume command by default, and Stanton went to work on a cabinet demand for his dismissal by the president. Before Halleck even returned his response to the incriminating questions, Stanton appeared at Chase's house to seek his assent, knowing that the treasury secretary was next among McClellan's cabinet critics. The two of them then went looking for the attorney general, but Bates was not at home. Bates visited Chase the next morning, offering his support for a cabinet petition, and later Chase saw a strongly worded draft that Stanton had drawn up, accusing McClellan of utter incompetence and disobedience of orders that jeopardized the safety of the armies as well as the "national existence." Chase suggested a few modifications, and Peter Watson drafted a new copy, which Chase and Stanton both signed, whereupon Chase carried the paper over to Gideon Welles at the Navy Department. Welles would not sign: it was, he said, inappropriate to go behind the president's back, rather than having an open discussion about it.[64]

Sometime Saturday afternoon, August 30, Stanton invited the president and John Hay to his house for what Hay called "a pleasant little dinner." Seven weeks after the death of Ellen Stanton's baby, Hay described Ellen as a "pretty" woman, but "as white and cold and motionless as marble, whose rare smiles seemed to pain her." Stanton spent the meal berating McClellan for failing to reinforce Pope quickly enough, and he suggested a court martial on that charge, which could have carried the death penalty. If the president said anything in reply, Hay failed to record it.[65]

That evening, word reached Washington of Pope's defeat. Hay found that Stanton had clogged the roads to Manassas with "a vast army" of volunteer nurses, consisting mainly of government clerks, half of whom left the city roaring drunk and caused immense trouble for those trying to hurry troops to Pope. Agitated by Halleck's hand-wringing admission that Washington might fall, Stanton remained at the War Department late into the night, and after dinner Welles came in to learn if there was anything new. Quickly introducing the subject of McClellan, Stanton tried to persuade Welles to add his name to their petition with a protracted recital of McClellan's failures and failings, beginning from the time Stanton took over the War Department. Welles still declined to sign, although he agreed with the thrust of the argument.[66]

On the last day of August McClellan beleaguered General Halleck with discouraging intelligence and advice, complaining that he had no command of his own. Halleck finally wired back, asking for McClellan's help and promising that he would have charge of all the troops "not temporarily belonging to Pope's army in the field." The next morning the two generals met at headquarters, and in the evening McClellan was summoned to Halleck's home, where the president grilled him about his apparent lethargy in responding to Pope's plight—then asked him to take charge of the defenses. While those three talked at Halleck's house, Edward Bates finally saw Stanton's petition and thought it too severe, rewriting it himself in a milder tone and signing it at the bottom. Stanton put his signature nearest the body of the petition, followed by Chase and then the Interior secretary, Caleb Smith.[67]

The next morning—Tuesday, September 2—Halleck and the president arrived at McClellan's Washington residence, at the corner of H Street and Madison Place, catching him at breakfast. The president's intense anxiety over the danger to the capital that day drove him to order all the government employees in the city organized into companies and battalions, and supplied with ammunition, even as tens of thousands of soldiers poured in from the front. Feeling that no one could inspire and reorganize the refugees from Bull Run as quickly as McClellan, and knowing how hostile Stanton had become to the general, Lincoln had decided to sidestep the secretary and ignore his objections: expanding on Halleck's orders, he gave McClellan control of not only the defenses but of all the troops straggling in from the battlefield. That effectively restored him to the command of the Army of the Potomac and reinforced him with Pope's entire command.[68]

The cabinet met Tuesdays and Fridays, and that Tuesday Stanton had planned to present the modified declaration—which no longer charged McClellan with negligence and disobedience, or asked for his dismissal, but did assert that a majority of the cabinet considered it unsafe to give him command of any army. William Seward did not attend that day, sending his son, the assistant secretary, in his place, but most of the other department heads had gathered in Lincoln's office when he arrived, late, followed shortly afterward by Stanton, whom the president had probably been briefing on his decision to put McClellan back in charge. Evidently Lincoln was called from the room again for a moment, and Stanton took the opportunity to whisper, in a quavering voice, that McClellan had already been reinstated. A flurry of surprised responses still buzzed through the room when Lincoln returned and caught the drift, admitting that it was true. He downplayed the significance of the decision, contending that no other general commanded such confidence within the army. The ministers protested seriatim, with Stanton arguing that the president had effectively absolved both Halleck and McClellan of responsibility for defending the capital: McClellan could point to Halleck holding the overall command, while Halleck could honestly claim that he had not made the decision to assign McClellan. Chase complained that McClellan had practically been made general in chief again. Most of the rest voiced their lack of confidence in the general, including Welles, and even Blair made no attempt to defend him.[69]

Early in the discussion someone handed Lincoln the signed objection, and it worsened the anguish he already felt at such unanimous opposition from his cabinet. While the document contained no threat of resignations, it carried that implication, and indeed Chase had presented it to Welles with the remark that "either the Government or McClellan must go down." Lincoln said he felt so distressed he was "almost ready to hang himself," or resign, knowing how sincere his advisers were, but he made it clear that he had seen no other choice in the emergency. Chase replied that there was Joe Hooker, or Burnside, or Edwin Sumner, while trusting the safety of the capital to McClellan amounted to surrendering it outright, but the discussion finally abated without conclusion. Sympathy with the president's predicament precluded anyone from forcing the point, and, even with the rare agreement of the entire cabinet, Stanton's hope of manipulating the commander in chief vanished as the ministers drifted out of the room.[70]

Stanton invented a more personal and dramatic version of the incident for private audiences, in which he heroically bid the president to "gird on the sword" himself and be the commander in chief the Constitution made him. He said Lincoln only turned pale, fled the room, and soon afterward gave McClellan command of the army again.[71]

The president probably expected to satisfy his cabinet by finding someone besides McClellan to actually lead the army back into the field, and Chase's suggestion of Hooker, Sumner, or Burnside may have reinforced that hope. Chase favored Hooker, but he held only division command, and his elevation over so many officers would inevitably have caused hard feelings. Sumner, a stubborn fighter and obedient soldier, was born during the administration of George Washington, and his talents were limited. Burnside presented the best alternative, because he outranked everyone but McClellan, Halleck, Banks, and McDowell, and he had already done extremely well in independent command.

Pope's retreat left Burnside cut off, and he spent the next couple of days preparing to abandon Aquia Creek. Burnside began forwarding troops to Washington with all the supplies and equipment he could save, and around midnight on September 4 he boarded a steamer for Washington. On arrival the next morning he must have reported to Halleck, who either was in conference with the president already or directed Burnside to the White House. There was no time to waste, for the previous evening reports had come in that the rebels were threatening to cross into Maryland at Leesburg and upriver, and someone had to lead an expedition against them. Lincoln again asked Burnside to assume command of the consolidated armies and go after Lee, but again Burnside refused, recommending McClellan above all others. With that, Lincoln and Halleck repaired to McClellan's house again, ordering him to take the army in pursuit of Lee.[72]

This news caused no further stir in the day's cabinet meeting, but Chase likely echoed the thoughts of his colleagues when he said, on September 2, that McClellan's appointment to command the defenses would make it difficult to have anyone else lead active operations. The main topic of cabinet conversation on September 5 was Pope's report, which Welles characterized as a "manifesto" when Pope read it to him the night before. Pope accused Fitz John Porter of failing to obey orders, and offered evidence that McClellan had interfered to keep Franklin from the battlefield. Stanton, who had been fuming over McClellan and his dilatory devotees for days, probably suggested that Porter, Franklin, and lesser partisans be relieved from command and investigated for possible prosecution, and the president assented.[73]

Contending that they were indispensable to the pursuit of Lee, McClellan asked to have Porter and Franklin restored to their commands, and in appealing to the president he claimed that Stanton had promised to "cheerfully agree" to it. The suspended generals resumed their places, but as willing as Stanton might be to feign cheerfulness toward McClellan, there was one soldier he could not return to duty without alienating his Radical friends in Congress. As McClellan prepared to leave the city he asked for the services of General Stone, as though to test the authenticity of Stanton's cooperation, but the secretary never replied.[74]

Zimmerman Tavern, Stevensburg, Virginia. Here, early in 1862,
John Murray Forbes learned the local gossip about Edwin M. Stanton's ancestors.
(photo by Clark B. Hall)

"Fairfield," the Virginia home of Stanton's grandfather, Thomas Norman,
under Union occupation in the winter of 1864 (Library of Congress)

George McCook (from Joseph B. Doyle, *In Memoriam: Edwin M. Stanton*)

Stanton's birthplace in Steubenville, ca. 1900 (from Frank A. Flower, *Edwin McMasters Stanton*)

Kenyon College, as Stanton might have remembered it (Library of Congress)

Edwin M. Stanton and Edwin L. Stanton, ca. 1853 (Library of Congress)

Jackson Square (now Lafayette Square) in Washington, ca. 1858
(Library of Congress)

Jeremiah S. Black (Library of Congress)

San Francisco about six years after Stanton's sojourn there (Library of Congress)

New Almaden quicksilver mine, Santa Clara County, California
(Library of Congress)

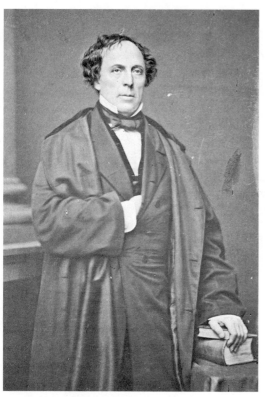

John B. Floyd (Library of Congress) Jacob Thompson (Library of Congress)

Left to right: John Bingham, Joseph Holt, and Henry Burnett
(Library of Congress)

Ethan Allen Hitchcock (Library of Congress)

Thomas Eckert (Library of Congress)

Ellen M. Stanton during the Civil War
(from George C. Gorham, *Edwin M. Stanton*)

Edwin M. Stanton in the summer of 1865 (previously unpublished;
courtesy of the New Hampshire Historical Society)

Left to right: Edgar Welles, Robert Todd Lincoln, and Edwin L. Stanton,
the sons of President Lincoln and his secretaries of war and the navy
(Library of Congress)

Lewis Hutchison Stanton, ca. 1900 (courtesy of Frank Mevers)

The Stanton family lot
at Oak Hill Cemetery
in Washington, D.C.
(photo by the author)

Seven-cent postage stamp
dedicated to Stanton
(Smithsonian National
Postal Museum)

Stanton statue outside the Jefferson County Courthouse
in Steubenville (photo by the author)

11

THE WAR WITHIN

McClellan rode out of Washington at the head of his entourage on Sunday, September 7, 1862. He may not yet have cleared the district line before the president opened a letter from Senator Garrett Davis of Kentucky, who warned that Stanton was still "so hostile to Genl. McClellan that he cannot possibly give him a proper support." Stanton had, in fact, chosen the man who would help him smash the McClellan coterie, and Davis was well acquainted with that man. Amendments to the Militia Act adopted the previous July had included the creation of an enhanced post of judge advocate general, with the pay of a colonel of cavalry and a network of assistants, to investigate and prosecute soldiers and civilians before courts martial and the new extra-constitutional system of military commissions. In the hands of the right—or wrong—secretary of war, the judge advocate general could be made to serve as the War Department's grand inquisitor. Stanton was that secretary: the man he preselected for the post, Joseph Holt, proved amenable to Stanton's ultimate intentions for the office as an agency for the enforcement of political doctrine and the dissemination of partisan propaganda. As soon as the enabling act surfaced from congressional debate, Stanton alerted Holt that he would like to see him at his office, and the day after Lincoln signed the bill Holt visited the War Department for an afternoon interview.[1]

Stanton and Holt had come to know each other in the Buchanan cabinet. Until each of them accepted office in the Lincoln administration, each played the role of a conservative Democrat of nationalist sentiments, and Holt persisted in that vein at least through the war's first winter. When Stanton entered the War Department, Holt had suggested that he adopt a more moderate tone toward the rebels, and had recommended David Davis, Stanton's conservative Kenyon classmate, for appointment as another assistant secretary. In February he had also urged Stanton to press Lincoln for a public statement denying any ambitions toward emancipation.[2]

Holt understood Southerners' fear of abolitionists. He was a Kentuckian who had inherited, bought, and sold plenty of slaves himself. In a college debate he had apparently taken the "anti" side in a formal discussion on slavery, which some have mistaken for heartfelt early evidence of abolition sympathies, but what prosperity Holt had ever enjoyed, either through the family fortune or his own endeavors, had emanated from the slave-based wealth of Kentucky and the Vicksburg region of Mississippi. Any genuine antipathy he entertained toward the institution arose after he had divested himself of most of his own human chattel and found a living independent of the plantation economy, in government service. Sometime between Holt's February letter to Stanton and their July interview, Holt appears to have adopted the Radical perspective.[3] For former conservative Democrats like Stanton and Holt, after all, only the most exaggerated expressions of political reliability could avert potentially ruinous suspicion.

Because of their close association during the rest of the war, it bears noting that Holt could be just as duplicitous as Stanton. His later career was speckled with controversies that strongly suggested the dishonesty of one party or the other, most of which were followed by Holt's persistent efforts to exonerate himself, and usually he left the impression of protesting too much. More than once over the next few years he would appeal ostentatiously to Stanton for a court of inquiry to clear his name after some scandal, only to have Stanton obligingly declare Holt's integrity beyond question. Despite such protestations of probity, at least twice during his second marriage Holt engaged in clandestine dalliances with women to whom he wrote in French, to conceal the content of those missives. Both of his wives complained of his habit of leaving them at home for long periods while he sought a livelihood elsewhere, but it was Margaret, his second wife, who pleaded most pitiably for him to either come see her or allow her to join him while he was fending off similar demands from a mistress.

Until a few months before Margaret's death Holt wrote weekly, and often more frequently, to a woman he met in Washington on March 4, 1859. Signing as "Aglai Lapsley," and later as "Amelie," she responded letter for letter, applying increasing pressure for him to come see her again. She referred to Holt as "my tender lover" eleven days after their first meeting. "I await you with impatience," she hinted, on April 11, and on May 8 she addressed him as "Dear but cruel lover." A week after that one of her letters began with "Come[,] come . . . oh come." On October 22 she described herself as "your Darling, who loves and thinks of no one but you." Most of her letters came marked "free," for Postmaster General Holt had evidently provided her with a supply of franked envelopes, while Margaret was forced to stamp her mail at three cents per letter. When his wife entered the final stages of her illness, Holt finally began ignoring his new coquette, diverting his energies to "My precious Maggie" once more. In December he suspended his letters to Amelie, responding finally to one of hers three months after Margaret's death, but she replied with a coolness that heralded the end of that affair. This would not, however, be Holt's last illicit amour.[4]

Even if Holt had not been as willing to revise his political principles as readily as he redirected his personal affections, as a perennial candidate for public employment he might have found a potentially permanent government post difficult to refuse. After years of apparently unproductive leisure in the South, during which his finances had declined precipitously, Holt had come perilously close to the specter of poverty by the late summer of 1857. His situation had grown so desperate that his wife enlisted her sister to solicit a job for him in her brother-in-law's legal firm, and Holt was only saved from that humiliation by a timely civil appointment from President Buchanan, who named him commissioner of patents in September. Holt accepted the post reluctantly, as though it were beneath him (and his father-in-law appears to have agreed), but he took it for the salary. If the job offered little prestige, it soon led to better things: Buchanan immediately chose Holt to replace the deceased postmaster general in March of 1859, and in the final nine weeks of his term shifted him to the War Department. Thereafter Holt resided in Washington, conveniently available for appointive office. He served on government commissions under the Lincoln administration, for which Stanton, in his letters to Buchanan, had initially cast Holt as a turncoat. Stanton had no sooner gone over to the "Lincolnites" himself, however, than he assigned Holt to another commission, on which he spent the spring and early summer of 1862 auditing contracts the War Department had already signed—taking longer than anticipated, but persuading several contractors to accept reduced compensation. Each of these assignments paid Holt more than the annual salary he had drawn as patent commissioner, and on September 3 he accepted his last, longest, and most remunerative government billet, as the army's judge advocate general.[5]

The position had become necessary by September because so many citizens had been arrested as a result of Stanton's August 8 order. Most of them appear to have been apprehended by overzealous marshals and constables for exercising their First Amendment right to political expression, or for "violations" as ridiculous as laughing at Home Guards on drill, or being "very saucy" to them. Numerous doctors, for some reason, were accused of criticizing the effectiveness or the morality of the war, including one Illinois physician victimized by a deliberately false accusation that seems to have gone unpunished. That doctor spent at least seven weeks in confinement, although his brother-in-law, Brigadier General John A. Logan, vouched for his patriotism. It was perhaps partly to address such politically damaging abuses that Stanton called Holt in, four days after Logan wrote to the president about that outrage; four days after that, Stanton rescinded the indiscriminate authority to make arrests without authorization from him, state governors, or military commanders. Certainly he did not name Holt judge advocate general from any excess concern for civil liberties, as illustrated by the ordeal of Nathaniel Batchelder, the New Hampshire doctor imprisoned for accusing prospective recruits of enlisting for money rather than patriotism. Six days after his appointment, Holt reviewed Batchelder's record and reported that if any case deserved prosecution, it was his. Holt would merely provide a semblance of order and method to Stanton's arbitrary system of political enforcement.[6]

In his nominal duties and in the collateral benefits Holt could provide through the exercise of those duties, he soon proved that Stanton had chosen well. His appointment came the day after Stanton's attempt to have McClellan dismissed, and only two days before he relieved Porter and Franklin of their commands, to answer Pope's charges. It was probably no coincidence that Holt's service to the secretary of war began with a decisive assault on the McClellan camp, but Lincoln's resurrection of McClellan postponed this crusade.[7]

Within a week of leaving Washington McClellan had found the Confederates, or at least some of them, and fought a battle with Lee's rear guard at South Mountain, Maryland, beyond Frederick. Lee had boldly divided his army into several detachments on both sides of the Potomac River to capture a garrison of twelve thousand men at Harper's Ferry, and while the Confederates occupied that vulnerable position an Indiana soldier serendipitously discovered a lost copy of the orders directing those scattered elements. As usual, McClellan considered himself outmanned when he actually outnumbered Lee nearly two to one, and that overestimate of enemy strength persuaded him to proceed too cautiously to destroy the isolated detachments in detail. The delaying action at South Mountain allowed Lee to concentrate all but one division of his army near Sharpsburg, and McClellan attacked him there on September 17 in three major assaults that he failed to coordinate. Lee shifted troops to meet one attack after another: just when Ambrose Burnside's corps started to bend the rebel line backward, that last Confederate division under A. P. Hill showed up to cave in Burnside's flank, ending the bloodiest day of the war. After staring his foe down one more day, Lee began a hurried but orderly retreat across the Potomac into Virginia, resuming a position little different from the one held by Stonewall Jackson the previous winter and spring. McClellan's only effort at pursuit consisted of having Fitz John Porter throw some troops across the ford behind Lee at Shepherdstown, Virginia, which led to a bloody repulse.[8]

Washington had been saved, Maryland had been rescued, and Robert E. Lee, who had become such a terror to Union generals over the past twelve weeks, had been forced to retreat. Lincoln and Halleck nevertheless both seemed dissatisfied with the fruits of Antietam—Halleck doubting whether

McClellan had really won a battle and Lincoln frustrated that Lee had escaped unmolested. The biennial congressional elections would all take place within the next six weeks, and a decisive victory would have favorably influenced them, which no doubt further aggravated the president.[9]

Stanton did not even wait for the results of the battle. Zachariah Chandler had written from Michigan in a fury on September 10, as soon as he heard that McClellan, Porter, and Franklin had been restored to duty, moving Stanton to reply with complete concurrence—and with the excuse that he was "powerless" to prevent it. By shifting the responsibility to the president Stanton absolved himself before the Radicals, and by allowing Halleck to manage McClellan he hoped, probably, to silence the allegations that he had been deliberately hindering the general: the frequent communications between the War Department and the Army of the Potomac had dropped off sharply, once Halleck entered army headquarters. While McClellan chased the invaders, Stanton even attended to long-neglected business from his California mission, using his connections with Chase's department to secure disputed compensation for Peter Della Torre. The accusations of interference with McClellan lingered nonetheless, and from Sanitary Commission headquarters in Washington Frederick Law Olmsted broke into another rant. "Of all the damned infernal scoundrels that the Almighty for our sins' sake curses us with," he assured a New York friend, "Stanton is the hardest to bear." Incredulous that so many seemed unable to "see through his veil of godliness & patriotism," Olmsted blamed Stanton for painting the Peninsula campaign as a failure, and pointed out that McClellan had accomplished much with relatively few casualties and made no drastic mistakes. To Olmsted, Stanton was "a liar, a gambler in armies, who had bet heavily against McClellan, who prays with clergymen and never ceases with Genl McClellan's subordinates to call him 'a God damned fool.'"[10]

As flawed as Lincoln deemed the victory at Antietam, it came close enough to suit the purposes of his contemplated emancipation decree. Had he issued his proclamation with his armies in retreat from Manassas, it would have conveyed nothing but weakness and desperation, but with the rebels driven back into Virginia he dared announce it. No greater triumph appeared to be in the offing, after all, and on September 22 he authorized Secretary Seward to announce that all the slaves would be considered "forever free" in any state that had not forsaken rebellion by January 1, 1863. The document appeared in newspapers the next morning, allowing exactly one hundred days for each state to make its decision.[11]

The Emancipation Proclamation attracted such retrospective sympathy that it came to overshadow the president's next proclamation. On September 24 Lincoln declared that martial law would apply not only to rebels and their agents but also to any citizens "discouraging volunteer enlistments, resisting militia drafts, or guilty of any disloyal practice, affording aid and comfort to rebels against the authority of the United States." In such cases, he also suspended the right of habeas corpus, perhaps anticipating the retroactive congressional approval he ultimately received for similar orders of doubtful constitutionality.[12]

This proclamation may have created as much discontent among loyalists as it did among the disloyal elements it was meant to suppress, and by its nebulous definitions of new crimes it effectually created disloyalty where there had been none. Secretary of the Navy Gideon Welles heard no discussion of it in the cabinet, and he clearly regretted executive decrees that tore so deeply into the heart of constitutional liberties, but Stanton eagerly embraced the latest document because it echoed his own order so closely that he may have written it. It lent executive authority to Stanton's own edict of August and placed the responsibility on the president: victims had already started suing Stanton as the author and agent of their incarceration.[13]

Emancipation and the draft promised to inflame the political rhetoric of the approaching elections as well. Stanton inadvertently gave Illinois Democrats a volatile issue when, a few days before the proclamation, he authorized the commander at Cairo to ship contrabands deeper into the state as domestic servants. State law prohibited the introduction of free blacks, and workingmen resented the competition.[14]

The threat of martial law could be used to curb such embarrassing criticism of the administration: Stanton's original proclamation had already demonstrated how easily it could be molded into a tool for political intimidation. Arrest for inflammatory speech had silenced Illinois congressman William J. Allen's reelection campaign and Dr. Edson B. Olds's bid for the Ohio legislature—although both won their races from prison. Lincoln's Kentucky friend, James Speed, complained that "we are rapidly tending towards a military despotism," and only his personal appeal against the arrests of civilians in Louisville moved the president to have Stanton reprimand the commander there. In wielding their new power to control the political debate, federal officials would soon begin jailing their own supporters over well-meant remarks or letters to the editor that were mistaken for partisan censure. Such arrests exerted a chilling effect on commentary even among the faithful: an Indiana lieutenant warned his loyal father against making any public statements. It may not have been Lincoln's conscious intention to wield his proclamation as a bludgeon against dissent, but Stanton quickly put it to such use, and the president interfered seldom enough to imply approbation with—and share responsibility for—the oppressive effect. So extensive were those first roundups that they tended to diminish the administration's apparent repression when the arrests abated to what should still have been objectionable levels.[15]

Muzzling administration opponents only worsened discontent among them and augmented their ranks, as the fall elections would show. The proximity of those elections may have heightened the president's interest in an expedition down the Mississippi, and specifically one led by a prominent Democrat. The suggestion came to him from John McClernand, a major general, six-term congressman, and lawyer whom Lincoln knew from Springfield. The expedition itself carried a certain appeal as an antidote for public dissatisfaction with McClellan's inactivity along the Potomac, but McClernand was also a strategic political choice for the command. As a talented orator and a Democrat popular among Westerners of that stripe, he made a most effective recruiter, and placing him in command of a significant operation could dispel fears of the administration undermining Democratic generals. Stanton and the president therefore moved very quickly on McClernand's detailed plan for a riverborne expedition, which he outlined on September 28. In telling Chase about it on October 7, Stanton took the credit for having made the proposal, which was not true, and said the president liked the idea, which was true. Two weeks later the president gave McClernand orders to repair to Illinois and begin gathering troops, promising that he would command those forces independently and would report only to Halleck. Five days after that, and more than a week before the elections, McClernand had arrived in Springfield to raise the great Democratic army of the West, with which he expected to seize Vicksburg and reopen the Father of the Waters.[16]

Once the election was over, Stanton seemed to forget about the independent command, or to allow Halleck to overlook it. McClernand sent dozens of new regiments down the river to his rendezvous at Memphis, but in mid-November, when he saw that General Grant was taking his troops from Memphis, he appealed to Stanton for redress. Stanton passed the inquiry on to Halleck, who assured McClernand that the location of the troops made no difference to his ultimate command. A month later McClernand was still waiting for orders, unaware that Grant had just given thousands of his recruits to William T. Sherman for an assault on Vicksburg. Stanton claimed that Halleck was supposed to have addressed McClernand's situation, but it was not until McClernand sent simultaneous telegrams to Lincoln and Stanton, complaining that he seemed to have been superseded, that Stanton did really interfere. Even then, Halleck only told Grant that the president intended McClernand to assume immediate command of one corps of Grant's army. Montgomery Blair brought the issue up in cabinet a few days before Christmas, questioning why McClernand seemed to have been "set aside," and when Lincoln bristled at the suggestion Stanton said he and Halleck had just resolved the command dispute in McClernand's favor that day. The explanation brought Stanton an implied rebuke from Lincoln, who said he thought the matter had been settled long before.[17]

For all the promises and protests, McClernand finally did lose the independent command through no fault of the president, who evidently saw more talent in him than others did and acted in good faith. McClernand blamed his troubles on Halleck's dislike of volunteer generals without a West Point education; Stanton, however, harbored no special regard for West Pointers, and he could have reversed any effort by Halleck to reduce McClernand's role. The secretary's ambiguous replies to McClernand's complaints and his failure to overrule Halleck imply some guile on Stanton's part. Perhaps politics prejudiced him—Democrats who resisted the administration on policy posed a political threat if they gained prominence on the battlefield—but Stanton and Halleck may also have begun to hear, through General Sherman's connections, how little Grant valued McClernand. The following winter Sherman's father-in-law, old Tom Ewing, was in Washington defending some Ohio men from kidnapping charges for arrests made under War Department authority: after seeing Stanton, Ewing informed Sherman that neither Stanton nor Halleck had any confidence in McClernand, whose "toadying" had won over the president. "You could not desire to stand higher in the estimation of any one than you do with Stanton & Halleck," he assured his son-in-law, relaying gratuitous flattery and turns of phrase characteristic of Stanton.[18]

Democrats with double stars on their shoulders found the administration much less patient with them as November approached. Don Carlos Buell, commander of the Army of the Ohio, suffered from the same timid caution that infected George McClellan, and when two Confederate armies invaded Kentucky at the end of summer he showed much more enthusiasm for retreat than for confrontation. Only when he had backed up against the Ohio River and collected the scattered elements of his command had he started after Braxton Bragg's wing of the invasion. By then, orders had been sent for George H. Thomas to replace him, but Thomas generously objected that Buell was about to begin his pursuit. Like McClellan, Buell won a qualified victory against an army half the size of his own at Perryville, on October 8, but he, too, sat down to rest and resupply his troops while Bragg retreated into Tennessee. At the end of the month Governor David Tod of Ohio, whom Stanton knew from the bank fight of the 1840s, reported that Ohio soldiers seemed unanimous in their wish for Buell to be removed. Stanton replied in a conspiratorial but not-quite-truthful note that he had been trying to remove Buell for two months, and had ordered it once, only to have the president revoke it. He added that William Rosecrans had been sent quietly to Kentucky to replace him a week previously, although he had heard nothing yet of Rosecrans's arrival. The impending election in Indiana, Buell's home state, had probably dictated the secrecy of the change, and Buell only learned of his rumored replacement through newspaper gossip.

He acknowledged his receipt of the orders on Saturday, November 1, too late for the news to exert much more effect on the elections in the West.[19]

McClellan felt the pressure, too. More than five weeks after Antietam, and less than two weeks after J. E. B. Stuart rode his Confederate cavalry completely around the Army of the Potomac, McClellan complained to Halleck that his horses were all suffering from fatigue and debility. Halleck, already impatient with McClellan's procrastination, handed that telegram to the president, who replied to McClellan with unwonted sarcasm, wondering "what the horses of your army have done since the battle of Antietam that fatigues anything." Stanton, too, ventured into biting irony, which was more to his nature, but he did it in the course of creating another dossier against McClellan just as the next military campaign began. The general had finally started moving his army over the Potomac on October 26, only to be beset by a vicious storm that lashed the columns with chilling rain as they marched and tore down their tents when they camped. The next day, while the gale persisted on the upper Potomac, Stanton asked Halleck for an official response about the supply deficiencies McClellan had claimed, and whether they should have delayed the army from marching in early October, when the general was first ordered to move. Halleck assured Stanton that the army was well stocked, and could have begun a campaign weeks before. "Having waited 3 weeks after peremptory orders to move," Stanton ominously commented, "it is strange that he should have just now discovered that his army wanted shoes & could not move till supplied."[20]

October had been dismal for Republicans generally, but especially for Radicals. Governor Oliver P. Morton of Indiana had visited Washington earlier in the month, meeting Stanton at Chase's house, where they lamented the nine lives Democrats like Buell and McClellan seemed to enjoy. Brigadier General James Garfield, a guest in Chase's home that fall, found it odd that Stanton, Lincoln, and Halleck all wanted to get rid of McClellan, yet none of them did. Stanton was not allowed to, Garfield inferred, while Lincoln feared the effect on the border states and the army, and Halleck was simply afraid to take the responsibility. Buell's replacement had been on his way to Louisville when Stanton asked Halleck for the incriminating information on McClellan—probably in hopes of prodding the president to remove him, too.[21]

The last state elections that year fell on November 4, and the administration took a beating in them, as it had in most of the others that fall. Having absorbed the defeat, and with little else to lose, Lincoln decided to dispose of General McClellan once and for all. On November 5 he wrote an order relieving the general from command and putting Burnside in his place. Although giddy at the downfall of his erstwhile friend, Stanton credited wild suspicions that McClellan would lead the army against Washington rather than relinquish command, and he arranged an elaborate choreography to deprive him of the chance. The orders were to be carried by Brigadier General Catharinus P. Buckingham, onetime professor at Kenyon College and another "special duty" general Stanton had brought into the War Department. Buckingham would see Burnside first: if he again refused to supplant his friend, Buckingham was to return to Washington without alerting McClellan; if Burnside agreed, they would go to McClellan together to deliver the news. Burnside did hesitate again, but this time the president had issued him an order instead of making a request, and to tip the scales Buckingham confided that the next choice would be Joe Hooker, whom Burnside mistrusted. Burnside and Buckingham rode fifteen miles in the middle of the night through a howling blizzard, finding McClellan still awake and working. For all the Radical anxiety, McClellan surrendered the command instantly. Informing his wife the next afternoon, he at least pretended to feel more sympathy for Burnside than regret for himself.[22]

The same stroke that concluded McClellan's military career opened the way for McClellan's enemies to end Fitz John Porter's. Ostensibly at the president's direction, but probably with Stanton's urging, Joe Hooker took over the Fifth Corps so Porter could report to Washington. Everyone knew this meant a court martial on Pope's old charges.[23]

Charles Wainwright, the chief of artillery for the First Corps, thought it certain that Porter would be convicted, "whatever the evidence before the court may be," both to provide a scapegoat for John Pope's "blunders" and to hurt McClellan by punishing his friend. The selection of officers for the court validated Wainwright's cynical suspicion, and although it was created under Halleck's name Stanton obviously dictated which officers would compose it. For president he chose the man who would become his favorite headsman, David Hunter. Hunter thought Stanton "not sincere," and admitted that "he wears two faces," but he had been advertising his Radical impulses to the secretary since he entered the War Department. General Hitchcock sat next in rank: in his diary and in family letters he might pretend to be independent of Stanton's influence, but he did bend to the secretary's bullying, as his reluctant acceptance of his commission illustrated; Secretary Welles thought Hitchcock showed "little moral courage." Six brigadiers and one brevet-brigadier filled out the rest of the court, including three men with personal reasons for condemning Porter: James Ricketts and Rufus King had fought under Pope at Second Bull Run, and Porter's conviction could deflect blame from their portion of the army, while Silas Casey could be depended on to bear a grudge against McClellan for censuring him over the collapse of his division at Fair Oaks. Napoleon Buford—the onetime colonel Stanton had impulsively thought of promoting to command the Army of the Potomac—was the brother of John Buford, who had led Pope's cavalry at

Bull Run. James Garfield, the house guest of Salmon P. Chase that autumn, had already admitted his prejudice against McClellan (and, by inference, against Porter), if only in private notes on his October interviews with Irvin McDowell. From meeting Garfield at Chase's home, Stanton knew his position within the army's factions.[24]

At least a solid majority of the officers on the court could be expected to weigh any evidence with a jaundiced eye. Numerous other idle generals could have been found to sit, but notwithstanding their availability the order detailing the members of Porter's court bore the routine assertion that no officers except the ones named could be spared "without manifest injury to the service." Porter wrote to McClellan to ask what he knew of the officers, but because he feared that no letter could reach Porter "unopened" McClellan did not respond in time, and when he did he could only warn that General Hunter "is an enemy of mine." Porter surely detected the design behind the panel that would judge him, but with no tangible evidence to support a protest against any of them he declined to enter an objection that might inspire further malice against him.[25]

If there were any remaining doubt about the court's eventual decision, Joseph Holt erased it by serving as judge advocate in the case, rather than assigning an assistant. Porter was allowed to have attorneys present in the courtroom, and he chose two—one of whom was the formidable Reverdy Johnson—but the prestige and talent of his counsel would avail Porter little. The admission or rejection of evidence, and the ultimate verdict, would be decided by a court that stood firmly behind the prosecutor.[26]

Strictly speaking, the judge advocate at a court martial was supposed to oversee the rights of the accused even as he prosecuted him, but Holt made no such effort. He had been a private attorney, and he had been a county prosecutor: having been trained in the adversarial tradition, he had to choose one or the other, and days before the trial began an editorial from Holt appeared in New York newspapers that effectively announced which way he intended to go. Written under the date of October 25, it was supposedly meant as a letter to Hiram Barney, a stranger to Holt whom Lincoln had appointed to the lucrative post of collector at the port of New York. Holt's screed reflected the flair for political propaganda that had made him so popular on the lecture circuit the year before, and it confirmed that Holt (like Stanton) had revised his political principles upon taking a position with the administration. In coded phrases he justified the president's recent proclamations on emancipation and "disloyal acts" as legitimate war measures, diagnosing disloyal speech that provided "aid and comfort" to the enemy as the product of discouragement over the "inaction of our armies." Eight months before writing the letter he had hoped to see Lincoln disavow any intention of interfering with slavery, but now he declared his willingness to see slavery die in order to save the government. His subtle conciliatory tone of the previous spring had disappeared, and with it the conservative spirit he had shared with McClellan, Buell, Stone, and Porter. Now he doubted that the sensibilities or reputation of any "General in the field" meant much alongside the preservation of the Union, and he pleaded for a campaign to crush the enemy "while an October sun is yet shining." No one would misunderstand his allusion to the indolence of McClellan and Buell, but by the time his comments appeared those two had been deposed, and Holt's belated assent to the publication of his letter betrayed an intent to turn public opinion against such generals, as his conduct in the Porter court martial would attest.[27]

An October sun no longer shone, but the armies east and west had begun to stir. Attempting to satisfy the administration's undeniable anxiety for activity, Burnside held a conference with Halleck and Quartermaster General Meigs as soon as he took command: within a few days, he started marching his columns down the Rappahannock toward Fredericksburg on a new campaign, moving rapidly enough to reveal the wisdom in McClellan's mania for preparation. His plan depended entirely on surprise, and that required pontoon bridges to be waiting for his leading divisions when they came opposite Fredericksburg. Halleck and Meigs had assured him that the pontoons would be there, but those assurances proved invalid, and when Burnside arrived he could only watch, day after day, as more Confederate legions settled in on the other side of the river to contest his crossing. Halleck, feeling pressure from the War Department, had told Burnside to fight a battle as soon as he could, even if he lost it, and Lincoln had also betrayed some disappointment with the pace only ten days after Burnside's first man stepped off. The president showed a different side when he met Burnside at Aquia Creek on November 26, finding it necessary for once to advise an aggressive general against haste: when Burnside mentioned Halleck's demand for action, Lincoln replied that he, and not Halleck, had the last word. Lincoln proposed a flanking maneuver, offering another fifty thousand troops from the new levies to be landed below Fredericksburg, to cut off Lee's retreat. Burnside feared that would take too long, and Halleck said the same when Lincoln laid it before him. That put an end to such strategic ingenuity, and could only have impressed Burnside further with the need to act quickly.[28]

Since taking over Buell's army at the end of October, Rosecrans had moved down into Tennessee, but the most spectacular news from that front had been the surprise and almost complete capture of one of his brigades, just as Burnside was preparing to bridge the Rappahannock. That only aggravated the thirst for success on the battlefield, and Burnside felt increasing pressure to do something significant, and soon. All the while, Joe

Hooker was slipping private letters to Stanton—starting with legitimate business, then tattling on Burnside for discouraging the bold operations Hooker proposed, and finally lobbying for his own promotion. Ever receptive to illicit intelligence, Stanton did nothing to remind Hooker of the chain of command.[29]

With an impetuosity born of desperation, Burnside threw his army over the river in two huge columns, the larger of which crossed to a plain below Fredericksburg under William Franklin while the other poured into the city with old Edwin Sumner in command. Franklin was to seize a low ridge crowned with artillery at the extreme right of Lee's line and then turn his right flank by marching beyond it, down the Richmond Stage Road. Once Lee seemed to be falling back, Sumner would assail the more elevated position at Marye's Heights, a mile behind the city and nearer Lee's left, hoping to catch the troops there in the middle of their withdrawal. Perhaps dreading to make a mistake—or, some thought, hoping to confound Burnside—Franklin launched his assault late and languidly. Slow communications and misinterpreted messages turned failure into disaster: Burnside mistook a report of Confederate troops moving down the ridge toward Franklin's fight as evidence that Lee was weakening his left, so he unleashed Sumner's divisions against Marye's Heights late in the morning. The result was a bloodbath. Brigades one after another dodged various obstacles, re-formed their ranks, and swept up the largely open hillside into a storm of shell and sheets of musketry. The slaughter continued all afternoon and into the dusk. Franklin, with more than half the army, may have been considering the consequences his West Point classmate, Charles Stone, had suffered after losing the fight at Ball's Bluff. Instead of plunging back toward the woods where his first assault had been repulsed, Franklin insisted that he could barely hold his own against Stonewall Jackson, whom he heavily outnumbered. Two days later Burnside withdrew from that hard-won ground and had to report the loss of nearly thirteen thousand men, to no purpose.[30]

The astounding losses, greater than at Antietam, stunned and alarmed Northerners and provoked outrage. Critics of the administration laid into the president, but friends of McClellan blamed Stanton on the assumption that he had ordered the cataclysm. Although Stanton seemed the most popular scapegoat, he had virtually abandoned discussions of strategy with any of his army commanders since Halleck became general in chief, and particularly after friends warned him of popular outrage over his perceived hindrance of McClellan. It was Halleck who had pushed Burnside hardest, although he may have done so at Stanton's urging. When Burnside learned of all the press criticism he prepared a letter for publication that absolved the president, Stanton, and Halleck, instead taking the responsibility on himself, and he went to Washington for permission to publish it. Touched by such generosity, Lincoln assented, but Stanton got wind of the letter and eagerly anticipated it in the next day's paper. Burnside was still in Washington on the morning of December 22, having slept at Willard's after revising the letter, and he had already mailed it to the *New York Times* when Stanton called him to the office and curtly observed that the promised epistle had not appeared. Burnside snapped back that the matter concerned only himself and the president. The letter came out in the December 23 edition; many assumed that Burnside had been urged to publish it to protect the administration, and in Stanton's case that carried a kernel of truth.[31]

Stanton's rudeness to Burnside was not uncommon for him, but he may have grown especially testy because he had just endured a fairly exhausting week of cabinet intrigue. It all began with a caucus of Republican senators on December 16, which Lyman Trumbull opened by remarking on the great public agitation over the devastating and fruitless casualties at Fredericksburg. Other Radicals immediately blamed the trouble on the presence of a conservative like Seward in the cabinet, and they proposed a resolution declaring their lack of confidence in him. As William Pitt Fessenden of Maine described the scene, he told his colleagues that a member of the cabinet had complained to him of "backstairs influence" with the president, which everyone regarded as a reference to Seward's predominant role: Fessenden's narrative suggested that his cabinet informant may have been Chase, but Stanton had cause to create a diversionary spat, and would have had no scruples about such backbiting against his foremost cabinet ally, if it would improve his own image among Radicals.[32]

Orville Hickman Browning blamed the Radicals who engineered the caucus for having discredited Lincoln with the country by pressing him for the confiscation bills and the Emancipation Proclamation, and he supposed they were attacking Seward to divert public indignation from themselves. Ira Harris, who held Seward's former seat in the Senate, suggested amending their resolution to advise a less specific reorganization of the cabinet. John Sherman objected to that idea, fearing it might be misconstrued as a proposal to dump Stanton, against whom there was already a widespread popular outcry over Fredericksburg. A very similar resolution passed nonetheless, and on Thursday evening, December 18, a committee of the senators presented it to Lincoln in his office. When it had been read, Ben Wade jumped in to say that the president had left the war to men (like Seward and McClellan, presumably) who lacked sympathy with its aims—by which he must have meant emancipation, although he did not say it. Fessenden noted that antislavery generals like Frémont and Hunter had all been disgraced or displaced. As it happened, old Francis Preston Blair had sat in the same office the day before and accused "Ultra-abolitionists" like Wade of trying to destroy Lincoln by associating him with Stanton, whom Blair said had "lent himself for a time to the Ultras." Blair, once a close confidant of Andrew Jackson, had advised the president to reinstate McClellan and replace Stanton, and he asked Senator Browning to speak to Lincoln about how rapidly Stanton and Halleck were "ruining the country."[33]

With those conflicting viewpoints in mind, Lincoln said nothing in reply to Wade, but the next day he asked the senators to return in the evening. When they filed in at 7:30, minus Wade, who had taken his joint committee to Falmouth to investigate the Fredericksburg disaster, they found all the cabinet members waiting for them except Seward, whose resignation sat in the president's pocket. Lincoln gave the delegation his answer, denying their complaints that he left his cabinet out of policy discussions, or that he consulted exclusively with Seward. Chase disappointed the more Radical senators by corroborating him. Montgomery Blair and Bates both remarked that a president was not required to bow to his cabinet's opinion, or even to seek it. Lincoln frankly admitted that he feared the senators' initiative would lead to "a general smash-up" of the administration, with Seward's resignation precipitating Chase's, and he said it had "been intimated that Mr. Stanton would do the same." This confrontation between the extremes of the Republican Party dragged on until one o'clock in the morning, but Stanton sat perfectly silent through it all.[34]

After a few hours of sleep Stanton went first to Seward's home on Jackson Square, evidently to recount the senators' demands. When Gideon Welles arrived at the president's request to urge Seward not to resign, Seward was expostulating with Stanton and warning that he would be the next victim. That suggestion seemed to awaken Stanton's anxiety, and while Welles tried to dissuade Seward from leaving the cabinet Stanton remarked that he was busy, excusing himself to go to the War Department.[35]

Soon after Stanton reached his office, Senator Fessenden showed up. Stanton flattered him with the observation that the previous evening's long meeting had been "the most impressive scene he had ever witnessed, and that he was particularly struck by the dignity and propriety exhibited by the senators." He added that he was "disgusted" with the cabinet, and particularly ashamed of Chase, whose corroboration of the president he characterized as untruthful. As though fishing for confirmation, Stanton said he thought Senator Harris had offered the more general resolution of dissatisfaction with the cabinet to throw the suspicion on the War Department, with an eye to removing him as secretary, but he cryptically remarked that he "did not mean to be driven out of the cabinet by Seward." Stanton mentioned that he had not offered to resign, as the president had implied.[36]

Fessenden went away convinced that the problem did not lie with the cabinet so much as with "our good Abraham," whom he judged lacking in order and vigor, however "earnest and true" he seemed to be. The senator evidently liked the president very much, but found him too weak to be efficient. "His attachment to individuals, and his tenderness of heart are fatal," Fessenden confided to a cousin. He supposed Lincoln might do well enough if he were surrounded by stern, resolute men, and he may have been thinking of Stanton, especially after hearing Stanton's derogatory comments about his colleagues.[37]

Later that day Stanton went to the White House, where he and Chase were both waiting when Welles showed up to report that he had succeeded in persuading Seward to retract his resignation. Lincoln walked in, asked Welles if he had "seen the man," and on learning of Seward's assent he mentioned that he had called Chase there to settle the matter. Lincoln had, perhaps, intended to ask Chase to submit his own letter of resignation, so he could act on them together, but Chase apprised him first that he had brought it with him. The president reached his long arm across the table, saying "Let me have it." Fairly snatching it from Chase's fingers, he skimmed it and remarked, "This cuts the Gordian knot," while Chase twisted uncomfortably in his chair to glance at Welles.

Stanton reminded the president that he had offered to resign "the day before yesterday" (his denial to Fessenden notwithstanding), and said he wished the president to consider that document already written and in his possession. "I don't want yours," Lincoln said, still transfixed by his good fortune, telling Stanton that he could go back to his department. "This is all I want," he added, dangling Chase's resignation in the air. When he told them he would detain them no longer Welles and the discomfited Chase took the hint and started out, but Stanton hung back at the door, saying something to Lincoln that he evidently did not want the others to hear. Whatever it was died with the two of them.[38]

Chase's gambit allowed Lincoln to preserve his cabinet without seeming to offend either extreme of his party. He rejected both resignations, thereby paying backhanded tribute to each faction, but the public doubts about Stanton remained unrelieved. Postmaster General Blair, who had already grown to hate the war secretary and would not even speak to him about cabinet business, admitted to Welles that he thought Stanton had choreographed the senators' intrusion to divert attention from himself— and Welles found it credible, although he also suspected that Chase and Caleb Smith may have had a hand in it. When the cabinet tempest waned, critical attention swung back to the War Department, and rumors of Stanton's departure multiplied. It was then that Burnside's public assumption of responsibility for the debacle at Fredericksburg suddenly seemed important enough for Stanton to press him for it.[39]

As with many other incidents within Lincoln's administration, the main source for the December cabinet crisis is the diary of Gideon Welles, an opinionated conservative who grew to dislike Stanton intensely during the seven years they served together. Historians have long discounted the image Welles left of Stanton because of his personal distaste for his colleague, but in editing his diary Welles took no pains to worsen the portrait, except perhaps in the first chapter, which amounts to a memoir: the revisions evident in the published diary are more often stylistic than substantive. Furthermore, Welles's distaste becomes more complimentary to himself than discrediting if Stanton acted only occasionally with the duplicity Welles documented through all three volumes of his diary. Numerous other observers corroborate that this was Stanton's nature—including otherwise friendly witnesses, and surviving correspondence confirms it.[40]

Edward Bates and Orville Hickman Browning both kept diaries during their respective service in the Lincoln and Johnson administrations, and those two conservatives also left disparaging portraits of the secretary of war: Bates thought him a bullying coward, while Browning considered him insincere, hypocritical, and malicious. Seward, no stranger to deception and intrigue himself, remained friendly with Stanton even after their politics diverged and Stanton seemed less than true to him: perhaps Seward clung too long to the promise of solidarity Stanton had made to him, but even he would finally come to distrust Stanton. Chase usually reflected the generous views of the secretary of war held by the Radical faction to which Stanton last hitched his political star, but he also remembered Stanton as a conservative Democrat whose persistent avoidance of antislavery activism had belied his professed sympathy for that cause. Among the cabinet officers, only Blair hated Stanton enough to seriously undermine his reliability as a witness, and that intense hatred says something about Stanton, too. Welles, Bates, and Browning each differed with Stanton politically, but they often managed to remain respectful of others with whom they disagreed, and their consistently negative appraisals of Stanton deserve more credence than they have been accorded.[41]

More sympathetic portrayals of Stanton, meanwhile, rely primarily on memoirs. In particular, two War Department clerks offered amusing or touching stories to illustrate how much Lincoln loved and respected his secretary of war, or to illustrate virtues that were contradicted by Stanton's documented conduct. Albert E. H. Johnson denied Stanton's favoritism to friends, relatives, and business associates, although he was an example of it himself; Charles Benjamin strove to show that Stanton respected the right of army officers to hold dissenting political beliefs, despite Stanton's vindictiveness toward those who revealed differing political sympathies. Both clerks repeated what seem to have been Stanton's own exaggerated or altogether invented renditions of his intimate interactions with Lincoln. Benjamin, who credited himself with more exalted positions in the army and the department than he ever held, also portrayed Stanton and his department cronies in a more positive light in his published recollection than he did in private.[42]

Several postwar stories circulated that seemed to illustrate very intimate relations between Lincoln and Stanton. One involved a delegation of officials who had secured from Lincoln an order exchanging certain military units between Eastern and Western theaters, but when they presented the order to Stanton he refused to honor it. They reminded him that it came from the president, and he supposedly responded that if Lincoln had issued such an order he was a "damned fool." Returning to the White House, they apprised the president of Stanton's comment, to which Lincoln replied that if his secretary of war had called him a damned fool he must be right, because he usually was. "I will step over and see him," he was said to have responded. Even Congressman George Julian, who told that story in his memoirs, implied that it might be apocryphal: if it were true, it could be interpreted as Lincoln using humor to disguise his embarrassment at having a cabinet officer who would act so insubordinately.[43]

In a very similar tale, a speculator prevailed on Lincoln for a pass to bring cotton out of the Confederacy, and the president gave him his card, with a note introducing the man to Stanton. The speculator reportedly met with the same refusal by the secretary, who tore the card up and threw it in a wastebasket. Angered by the rebuff, the man came back and told Lincoln what Stanton had done, eliciting only the observation that "that's just like Stanton." Doubtful authenticity also attends that twentieth-century anecdote, which appeared in a memoir replete with unconvincing or controvertible stories, but if it really happened it might illustrate the accommodating president's habit of allowing Stanton to take the blame for unpleasant decisions.[44]

More reliable, probably, are the contemporary observations of those who had access to the president, his war secretary, or their respective staff members. Noah Brooks, a correspondent for a California newspaper, revealed to a friend his confidential views of the executive department just before Christmas of 1863, describing Stanton (in addition to Blair and Halleck) as "a great drawback" to Lincoln because he was so unpopular; he supposed Stanton would have been far more popular "if he were not so domineering and so in love with the beauties of military law." In a confidential letter to a friend, Brooks wrote that "Stanton is coarse, abusive, and arbitrary; decides the most important questions without thought and never reconsiders anything, and abuses people like a fish-wife when he gets *mad*, which is very frequent; nevertheless he is industrious and apparently devoted to the interests of the Government." Since the interests of the government and those of the administration were then difficult to distinguish, Brooks can be forgiven for missing that Stanton worked for whichever better served his own interests. Years later, Brooks reflected that he had seen in Lincoln "a certain diffidence about any attempt to thwart the Secretary in any way," remembering that the president "dislikes to contradict or interfere with the Secretary if it could be avoided."[45]

Peter Watson assured Julian that Stanton "was never imperious in dealing with Mr. Lincoln," but that does not comport with the sharp rebuke Stanton gave the president during one late-night conference over moving troops to Chattanooga. Stanton showed temper as a bluff, and Brooks hinted that the president shrank from crossing his volatile war minister as though he were afraid to provoke him—much as the mild-mannered president avoided conflict with his temperamental wife. As some have suggested, Stanton gladly enforced unpopular policies, giving the president political cover, but even Lincoln could suffer from the imperious attitude he allowed his secretary to cultivate.[46]

Whether from his abundant store of trust or from a desire to avoid discord, the president usually let Stanton have his way—sometimes to his political disadvantage, and to the detriment of his historical image. In the case of Charles Stone, for instance, Lincoln must have initially accepted Stanton's side of the story without question, for the least examination ought to have exposed the gross injustice: perhaps Lincoln did not feel comfortable admitting, even to himself, that his secretary of war had unjustly destroyed a loyal general. After Stone had been released, and after he had finally been returned to duty, he sent Lincoln an anguished personal plea for some word of exoneration or confidence. The president began to draft an awkward reply, but after he admitted thinking that the evidence against Stone did not seem conclusive he did not finish the letter; perhaps it was painful to recognize that he ought to have questioned the judgment or motives of his war minister. He must have mentioned Stone's request to Stanton, because Stanton chose that very moment to muster Stone out of the volunteer service, stripping him of his brigadier's star without warning, cause, or the possibility of appeal. Again the president allowed Stanton's spite to rule, although he clearly doubted that Stone was guilty of anything deserving such treatment.[47]

The president's refusal to intervene in other, later prosecutions tainted with malice offered similar digressions from Lincoln's fair and generous nature, and his inaction may also reflect Stanton's influence, which was buttressed by the concurrence of Stanton's close ally, Holt. Lincoln's evident surprise when he caught Stanton speaking falsely to other cabinet members suggests tardy comprehension of the war minister's notorious habit, and in Lincoln Stanton may have quickly recognized and exploited the same innocent honesty that the president's old friend Joshua Speed regarded as such a liability. Stanton still mixed his approach with a little pandering at first, but his chief's legendary humility and patience moved him to bolder behavior than he had ever dared exercise outside a courtroom, and once his position seemed secure his manner became intolerable even to many of his colleagues. The War Department operated with less-than-perfect efficiency during the war, notwithstanding occasional feats of supply and transportation, but by dint of long hours, a large staff, managerial tyranny, and enormous expense Stanton avoided the paralysis of the Cameron era. That made Stanton seem indispensable to Lincoln, who may have tolerated his secretary's unpleasant traits in the belief that few could have kept the War Department functioning even as smoothly as it did.[48]

Welles also faulted Stanton for hypocrisy, which figured to some extent in cabinet debate over the bill on West Virginia. Radicals welcomed the opportunity to create another free state, but conservatives frowned on it as a violation of the Constitution. Depending on the interpretation of a semicolon in the first part of Article 4, Section 3, new states either cannot be formed from the territory of an existing state or, if so formed, the division requires the consent of that state's legislature as well as that of Congress. The latter was probably the intent, although English grammar implies the former. Even under the more generous interpretation, only the rump Virginia legislature had approved the action, and it represented merely a fraction of the state. Attorney General Bates, whose opinion should have guided the policy, found it unconstitutional and inexpedient, but the president asked the entire cabinet for written opinions. Smith had just resigned, and Blair and Welles objected on practical and legal grounds, while Seward, Chase, and Stanton favored it. Stanton, ignoring the illegitimacy of the token Virginia government, denied any conflict between the bill and the Constitution. Time would reveal that his opinion arose from situational motivation rather than legal principle: at the close of hostilities the same Radicals who had recognized the rump legislature's authority to approve the partition of Virginia ignored its legitimacy as a state government, and Stanton would be the first to reveal that inconsistency when it became politically convenient.[49]

Lincoln had no sooner signed the West Virginia bill than Burnside returned to Washington, fuming. Still feeling pressed for military action by army headquarters and the War Department, he had arranged a flanking maneuver and had just issued orders for it when William Franklin allowed two of his generals to go to the president and disparage the plan. Lincoln let that insubordinate ploy succeed, requiring Burnside to call off his latest offensive, and that brought the justly indignant commander of the Army of the Potomac back to the White House. Arriving on the morning of December 31, Burnside met early and privately with the president, pleading either to be allowed to begin his campaign or to be removed from command. The

Fredericksburg debacle had ruined the country's faith in him, he conceded: he ought to be replaced, and in his view the same was true of Stanton and Halleck. The president wanted to talk it over with those two, and he agreed to meet Burnside again the following morning. The general stayed up well after midnight at Willard's Hotel, putting his opinions on paper, and early on New Year's Day he handed his letter to the president with Stanton and Halleck standing alongside. "The Secretary of War has not the confidence of the officers and soldiers," Burnside wrote, with reasonable accuracy, "and I feel sure that he has not the confidence of the country." He applied similar censure to Halleck, for his eternal evasion of responsibility and a failure to coordinate the operations of different armies. Lincoln read the letter and returned it, as though to say that no one would be removed just yet.[50]

Stanton could not have been oblivious to the accumulating flurries of editorial condemnation that boded ill for him in the battle between Radicals and conservatives. That may have occasioned his impatient note to General Hunter on the first Monday in 1863, urging him to hurry up with the trial of Fitz John Porter. The court had been sitting for more than four weeks, Stanton noted, and should wrap up its proceedings in short order. "The state of the service imperatively demands" it, he explained, as though the officers of the court were needed on duty, but he gave no such instructions for haste to the court of inquiry that was judging the performance of Irvin McDowell: those generals had been sitting for more than six weeks then, and (perhaps because it was necessary to retain control over McDowell until he testified against Porter) they would meet for another month with no prodding from the War Department. Instead of "the state of the service," it was probably the state of Stanton's reputation that demanded immediate action, in the form of a conviction for General McClellan's foremost ally in the army. David Hunter interpreted Stanton's demand for haste literally: he read the message to the court on Tuesday, allowed the government to recall Generals McDowell and Pope that day to seal the case for the prosecution, and declared an end to further testimony.[51]

As Porter had predicted a week before, the verdict was a foregone conclusion. Even if "those high in power" had not directed the court to return a guilty verdict, as Porter suspected, he and McClellan had enough enemies among the members to predispose them to do so. As though to illustrate the blatant prejudice that permeated the court, one of the supposedly impartial members, Rufus King, had left the bench to take the stand against Porter.[52]

For all the complicated testimony and correspondence submitted to the court about the positions of Union and Confederate troops at Bull Run, the crux of the prosecution's case consisted of Porter's telegrams to Burnside, in which he disparaged Pope's military competence and expressed a wish to get out from under his control. As judge advocate, Holt had submitted several of those telegrams dated on the eve of the battle and during the early fighting. In one, Porter remarked that all Pope's "talk of bagging Jackson, etc., was bosh," and he lampooned the tactical intelligence in Pope's camp, remarking sarcastically on the erroneous claim that Longstreet had been cut off. Joking presciently, he told Burnside "I expect the next thing will be a raid on our rear . . . by Longstreet, *who was cut off*." This was all the evidence Holt could find to suggest that Porter's failure to attack on August 30 had represented anything more sinister than reasonable discretion, and he stymied Porter's attempt to introduce similar telegrams from a couple of days earlier that tended to mitigate and explain the apparent contempt for Pope and his army. After clearing the room, the members of the court concurred with Holt, denying any evidence so threatening to the government's case.[53]

The court heard Porter's written defense read aloud on January 10. It ran to thirty-seven printed pages, and when that formality had been observed Holt told the court that preparing a written reply for the prosecution would produce a delay that was "most important to avoid." The reading must have consumed the greater part of the day, but there seemed to be plenty of time left to clear the court again for what the recorder characterized as deliberation, after which the court promptly found Porter guilty of disobeying orders and misbehavior before the enemy. With that they sentenced him to be cashiered from the service and barred from any further position of profit or trust under the U.S. government. Pending presidential approval the decision remained secret, and reporters who had covered the trial and heard all the evidence confidently predicted acquittal. Even the *New York Times* opined that neither Porter's trial nor McDowell's court of inquiry had illuminated any "startling and terrible crimes."[54]

On January 12 the president asked Holt to review the trial record. This elicited the report Holt should have submitted to the court before the verdict, had Stanton not been goading him for a speedy conclusion, and under military law it was supposed to be an objective analysis of all the evidence, pro and con. Holt instead returned a searing summation for the prosecution that Porter would have no opportunity to rebut. He pretended to consider the evidence in Porter's favor, then discredited it, and with scathing sarcasm he excoriated the defendant over omissions for which the court had not even convicted him. He focused heavily on Porter's "sneering" allusions to General Pope, whose father was known to have been a friend and benefactor to the young Abe Lincoln. He returned this one-sided analysis to Lincoln on January 19, passing it to the president through Secretary Stanton—who, at least theoretically, learned only then what the outcome had been. For him it had come none too soon, for the *New York Herald* was proposing that Lincoln fire both him and Halleck in favor of McClellan, who could presumably do the work of both, and better.[55]

It could have been no coincidence that Stanton waited until that very day to send Holt's commission as judge advocate general to the Senate for confirmation, along with nominations for the promotions of four members of the court: Silas Casey's promotion to major general was backdated to May 31, as though to transform the rout of his division at Fair Oaks into a meritorious achievement. David Hunter's reward consisted of immediate restoration to command of the Department of the South. James Ricketts and Rufus King earned no overt recompense, but their army had found an excuse for its defeat. Irvin McDowell, who provided the most useful government testimony against Porter by his convenient inability to remember exculpatory details, escaped censure for his second defeat at Bull Run. With his fealty to the McClellan-hating Chase and his demonstrated preconception of Porter's guilt, James Garfield needed no special recognition. Old General Hitchcock went back to his nebulous duties at the War Department after dropping a curiously cordial note to Holt as their "official relations" came to a close.[56]

Joseph Holt had only completed his official duties in the case, however. There yet remained the exercise of his new, de facto post as Stanton's chief propagandist. He had partially fulfilled that role with the verbosely deceptive review of the case, which he had obviously styled for public consumption. Then, with Stanton's implicit approval, if not at his explicit direction, Holt began releasing the government's side of the case for publication while the trial was still in progress, and the finished product was already printed and bound by the time the president endorsed Porter's conviction and sentence: it carried only the testimony of the prosecution witnesses, as though Porter had made no defense. Before the week was out, Holt's jaundiced review appeared in the *Washington Chronicle*, the administration's friendliest newspaper, and from there it spread across the country in pamphlets published by the *Chronicle* at government expense. Stanton distributed bundles of them to field officers in the Army of the Potomac, as though in warning. The secretary of the navy, who bore little sympathy for Porter, frowned on those publications, regarding them as ex post facto efforts to justify a decision that he seemed ready to question. Holt's diatribe nevertheless had the desired effect on many readers, including personal friends of Porter. George Templeton Strong, at whose Gramercy Park residence Brevet Major Porter had first dined a dozen years previously, consigned his old acquaintance to equal infamy with Benedict Arnold after perusing Holt's deceptive denunciation.[57]

The excitement over Porter's dismissal was still reverberating in Washington when General Burnside returned to the city and informed the president that if Hooker and a squad of other generals were not cashiered, à la Porter, he could no longer lead the Army of the Potomac. He had finally tried to undertake another flanking maneuver after Lincoln had canceled his last one, only to have the heavens open up and turn the landscape to mud, and Hooker was now criticizing him openly, as were some of his corps and division commanders. At last Lincoln agreed that Burnside probably could no longer command the army effectively, and decided to replace him with Hooker. He had apparently made the decision after consulting with at least Stanton and Halleck, who seemed resigned to the change, although concerns about Hooker's drinking and judgment worried Secretary Welles. Many people disliked Hooker, among them Generals Franklin and Sumner, both of whom the president had relieved in consequence. Senator Browning reminded Lincoln that the army had greater confidence in McClellan than in anyone, and the president acknowledged as much, but lamented that McClellan "would not fight."[58]

The debacle at Fredericksburg and Burnside's notorious Mud March of January had driven discouragement deep into the warp of the Army of the Potomac, but those military failures were not the sole cause of plummeting morale, and a flagging spirit was not peculiar to the army on the Rappahannock. Depression and discouragement tinged letters home from soldiers posted all over the South. Most men in the army came from the modest end of the economic spectrum, and since the Treasury Department had shifted to paper currency their families were suffering from an inflation that increased the cost of everything while leaving their military pay stagnant. A private's monthly compensation of thirteen dollars depreciated steadily in value, and between them the Treasury and War departments made matters worse by neglecting to pay the troops in order to reserve enough funds to satisfy military contractors: when Congress finally insisted on bringing soldiers pay up to date, the Treasury simply printed another $100 million in shinplasters, which immediately sent the worth of that money plummeting even further. Repeated defeats and the periodic replacement of army commanders seemed to promise perpetual, unavailing conflict, and had bred a sense among the public that the physical and financial sacrifices would only worsen. On top of all that, the specter of emancipation had angered many who had gone to war solely to quell the rebellion and save the Union and had no intention of engaging in an antislavery crusade.[59]

All this contributed to an epidemic of desertion—the worst of it in the battered Army of the Potomac, from which tens of thousands absconded, but spectacular instances of desertion and mutiny afflicted the Western armies, as well. Grant's department leaked streams of deserters, especially from Illinois: 40 percent of one regiment from southern Illinois deserted before Christmas, and all but a handful of the rest refused to turn out for the defense of Grant's supply base at Holly Springs, Mississippi, instead surrendering en masse when the enemy appeared. Eighty percent of another regiment deserted on its way to join Grant's army, and he disbanded it altogether.[60]

Grant's troops on the Mississippi, under Sherman and later McClernand, suffered terribly from disease, probably because so many of them were kept for long periods aboard steamboats, drinking river water. Whole regiments came down with fever, and muddy graves dotted the riverside. Disease and desertion had weakened the armies far more than casualties on the battlefield, and as 1863 opened the need for manpower grew crucial. To stem the flood of desertions the cabinet considered a proposal, likely from Stanton, that one offender should be selected for execution. Stanton evidently proposed a candidate, but the administration had not yet developed the stomach for such brutality unless it could be inflicted on someone of higher rank than private. General Hooker established a system of furloughs that helped to improve morale in his army, and toward the end of the winter the president issued an amnesty that brought some deserters back into the ranks. Absenteeism slowly began to shrink, but by the end of spring thousands of two-year regiments would be going home for good, and right behind them would come the first flood of some 90,000 nine-month troops who had responded to Stanton's August levy, most of whom would not reenlist after a taste of the worst the army could offer.[61]

To compensate for this attrition, Stanton lobbied for a more comprehensive draft law than the previous summer's amendment to the Militia Act. In his first annual report (from which he omitted any mention of his halt to recruiting), he complained of "serious defects" in the militia law, and indicated that he would send his recommendations for a new system to Congress. On January 28 Henry Wilson, who chaired the Committee on Military Affairs, entered a new bill for amending the Militia Act, and Stanton had clearly helped him to prepare it, if he did not write it entirely. The Senate referred the bill to Wilson's committee, and Wilson returned it a week later, ready for debate. Stanton shared it with no one in the cabinet, much to the annoyance of those members who would later see their departments stripped of essential employees by the first levy. He may not have brought even the president very deeply into the discussion.[62]

Stanton's preponderant influence on the bill was reflected in the provisions that awarded most of the authority for regulating and enforcing the draft to the president, presumably through his secretary of war. Senator John Carlile, who had been elected by that vestigial Unionist government of Virginia, considered the bill inconsistent with the basic theory that the government belonged to the people, rather than the other way around. William Richardson of Illinois warned that it gave the president "more power than belongs to any despot in Europe or anywhere else." If passed, he said, it would let the executive make law unilaterally, affording him "the absolute power to take every man into the service who may differ with him in political sentiment." Only two seasons previously, the Radical *Chicago Tribune* had ridiculed Confederate conscription, insinuating the illegitimacy of a government that could not maintain its army by volunteering. Even Secretary Seward deemed it inconsistent with the spirit of the United States government to force men to fight, and he seemed to blame emancipation and Stanton's arbitrary arrests for depleting the armies and discouraging recruiting.[63]

Through February the two chambers argued and amended the bill, which originally encompassed all male citizens between eighteen and forty-five. Ultimately the lower age limit rose to twenty, probably to exempt enough healthy young men so they could enlist as substitutes for drafted men who could afford to pay them: that was an old tradition in the militia and the army. The congressmen also added commutation to the bill, allowing a drafted man to buy his way out of a single draft call for—as they finally decided—$300. This would become known as the "$300 swindle," and it would serve as the principal evidence that the draft law was meant to apply mainly to poor men, because the cost of commutation represented the wages a laborer might expect during the course of an entire year. The clause had actually been inserted to help keep the price of substitutes down, for the benefit of the working classes if not for the downright poor. A great many common citizens would take advantage of it, as would whole communities.[64]

Stanton disliked commutation and would eventually recommend its repeal. His passion for administrative control, meanwhile, was reflected in a provision of the draft law creating a network of provost marshals throughout the country. These officers, with whatever assistants and troops they needed, would administer the draft and, incidentally, monitor the population for loyalty, with authority to make arrests for acts or speech they considered "treasonable." That inspired considerable but ultimately insufficient resistance in the House of Representatives, where a few liberty-minded congressmen complained that the new executive powers and the political police force would turn the entire country into a military camp, with presidential whim assuming the force of law. Stanton's old courtroom and rostrum foe from Harrison County, John Bingham, dismissed such concerns with authoritarian tones of his own, welcoming the military punishment of dissident speech and expressing a preference for summary execution. His comment aroused applause in the House that illustrated the majority's intolerant temperament, and the bill passed at the end of the session, early in March.[65]

The draft could secure no immediate recruits, because eligible males would first have to be tallied in a canvass requiring the time and effort of a census—for which the War Department had to appoint hundreds of enrolling officers, in addition to provost marshals, assistants, and medical examiners. For more immediate replenishment of the armies, Stanton turned to the legions of contrabands who had fled their masters in the occupied territories along the Mississippi, where Lincoln had looked so covetously on the black majorities the previous summer. As early as Christmas, Stanton had confided to Charles Sumner that he anticipated twenty thousand black recruits before summer, and late in March he sent the army's adjutant general, Lorenzo Thomas, on a tour of the armies in the West, directing him to try organizing troops from the contraband camps in Grant's department. Thomas, who feared that Stanton wanted to "get rid" of him, found the secretary of war almost always rude, and he was surprised at Stanton's unusual kindness when he proposed this faraway mission. Thomas failed to recognize that sudden, unaccustomed kindness was a bad sign from Stanton: according to Colonel Edward Townsend, who spent the rest of the war as the acting adjutant general, Stanton disliked Thomas, and had concocted the tour to dispose of him without the bother of displacing him. Yet Stanton also seemed genuinely interested by then in the object of Thomas's assignment: that same day he telegraphed General Banks, at New Orleans, to immediately begin raising new regiments among Louisiana's recently freed slaves. He named a general to command them, and said he expected to see a brigade completed within a month.[66]

Stanton had first offered General Frémont command of this hypothetical new black army, but Frémont declined on the grounds that he wanted more active service. Stanton told Sumner that he considered appointing officers for prospective regiments, and sending them down South, to recruit their commands to full strength. The mania for black troops arose not only from the desire to reinforce the shrinking and rather demoralized white armies, and from the Radical hope that the mobilization of freedmen would discourage any backpedaling on emancipation, but also to intimidate rebellious Southerners with a slave society's most dreaded threat. In attempting to persuade slave owner Andrew Johnson to recruit from Tennessee's black population, the president predicted that "the bare sight of 50,000 armed and drilled black soldiers upon the banks of the Mississippi would end the rebellion at once." In the event, the sight seemed to have the opposite effect on Southern determination, but there was still the basic demand for reliable soldiers of any color, and Stanton soon saw the chance to establish a vast new federal army, independent of the states and under the sole command of the president and his war secretary. Senator Sumner mentioned someone else's suggestion for a new Bureau of Colored Troops within the War Department, to nurture such a praetorian phalanx, and Stanton first replied that he lacked the authority to create more bureaus; then, after giving this appealing prospect a week's thought, he exercised that very authority and created the Bureau of Colored Troops. The 1st U.S. Colored Infantry began advertising for recruits in the city of Washington that week, and within six months most of the president's fifty thousand black soldiers had donned blue uniforms.[67]

12

ORGANIZING VICTORY

When Stanton sent Lorenzo Thomas on his recruiting mission in March of 1863, he urged him to impress on General Grant's officers that resistance to the raising or use of black troops would not be tolerated. Reluctance would run high among professional soldiers, Stanton knew. He also seemed to harbor other reservations about Grant, perhaps partly over Halleck's lingering distrust of him for having been taken by surprise at Shiloh, but probably even more because of the recurrent stories of Grant's weakness for alcohol. General Hitchcock had known Grant in the old army and in St. Louis, and after Shiloh he confided to a friend that Grant had "been little better than a common gambler and drunkard for many years." That pungent observation doubtless reached Stanton's ear, and it seems revealing that Stanton retained in his files copies of formal charges made early in 1862 by Captain William Kountz, a quartermaster in Grant's army who reported the general drinking heavily—including one bout with Confederate officers, during a truce.[1]

The conflict between Grant and General McClernand resurrected the concern over Grant's capacity and conduct. When the self-important McClernand snatched his troops away from Sherman and descended on Arkansas Post, capturing it with an overwhelming force, Stanton sent congratulations and promised him whatever he needed—implying, in a very roundabout way, that he supported McClernand's quest for an independent command. In a War Department interview with Captain Kountz, Stanton—most likely employing some deception—convinced Kountz that he was friendly to McClernand. Then came more reports of Grant getting drunk, including another accusation from Kountz, endorsed by McClernand. Stanton, after lobbying by Thomas Ewing, nevertheless appears to have been wondering by the end of winter how to certify Grant as the right man for the army at Vicksburg. Grant and McClernand, meanwhile, submitted their grievances to Halleck and Lincoln, respectively, ignoring the secretary of war.[2]

It may have been to reassert his own prerogative that Stanton concluded to send a confidential agent. Charles Dana had quit the *New York Tribune* after a spat with Horace Greeley, and Stanton had employed him for some months on one of the commissions with which he favored friends, giving him twice the pay of an army captain plus expenses. When that job ended, Dana reminded Stanton of his usefulness by warning that New York City's district attorney was trying to indict the secretary over some of his arbitrary arrests, suggesting that Seward's alter ego Weed was behind it: Seward and Weed seemed to be turning against them over emancipation, he confided. Then Dana tried to bring some cotton out of the Confederacy, going down to Memphis with a fellow investor just as Grant tried banishing such troublesome speculators from his department. The venture availed Dana little, but he made the most of it by writing Stanton again in a strained tone of righteous patriotism, advising the abolition of the very cotton trade from which he had hoped to gain. In March, Stanton made Dana a special commissioner again under his direct authority, providing him with written orders for nominal duties and verbal instructions for a more covert mission, with an advance of $1,000 on a generous new salary. Dana left for Cairo on a pretext of inspecting paymasters' services in the Western armies, but once there he opened a letter from Stanton telling him to report fully on "the real condition of things at Vicksburg and on the Mississippi," as they had discussed privately in Stanton's office. Dana was to essentially decide between Grant and McClernand, for the latter of whom neither Dana nor Stanton bore any great love.[3]

When Dana reached Grant's headquarters, weeks later, Grant's staff immediately suspected his role as a "confidential agent of the War Department."[4] Sharing Stanton's habit of grasping the coattails of upward-bound men, Dana promptly aligned himself with the more promising general, even keeping silent when he saw Grant indulge his predilection for alcohol, and insisting, in public and private, that Grant did not drink at all: he evidently withheld the secret from Stanton, as well.[5] Relying primarily on the pejorative interpretations of Grant's coterie, Dana reported critically on McClernand, who was both the lesser general and more troublesome, but Dana's assessment was not based on direct observation. As he was prone to do with information that confirmed his prejudices, Stanton let that first impression rule his opinion. Dana's dispatches satisfied his (and Dana's) political preference, for while McClernand may have been a War Democrat, the emphasis fell on Democrat. It did not hurt Grant's image in Stanton's eyes (or Dana's) that he responded positively to the Radical program of arming freedmen.[6]

Dana's assignment as a special commissioner came in lieu of an appointment as assistant secretary. One of Stanton's first requests as secretary of war had been for two additional assistant secretaries to help him gain control over a disorganized department, but that authorization expired on

January 21, 1863, and Stanton told Peter Watson that he would not ask for a renewal. John Tucker's appointment ended that day, and Watson wished to return to his more lucrative occupation as a patent agent—not to mention that his health had suffered. Christopher Wolcott, meanwhile, had the better claim for retiring on the excuse of health. He suffered from tuberculosis, and had been weakening since the previous summer. Stanton offered him a sinecure in North Carolina, but on January 23 Wolcott resigned, returning to Pamphila and their two boys early in February. According to a letter Pamphila inserted in her memoir, Watson claimed that Stanton pleaded with him to stay on in the one remaining authorized position, insisting that he would perish without the help of the only friend he had left whom he could trust. Without either Watson or Wolcott, Stanton said, he would not be able to "*carry out the great scheme of emancipation* so as to overcome the rebellion." Watson said Stanton asked him "How would you feel, if seeing me go down you could not deny that your aid might have kept me up?" Then he switched course and threatened to resign if Watson would not remain with him. Watson finally consented—"finding that I could not say nay."[7]

Stanton may have been leading Watson down the primrose path: he had already asked to extend the terms of the additional assistant secretaries, and Congress had agreed, as well as authorizing a War Department solicitor. Stanton then declined to take advantage of the extra assistant on the excuse of frugality, and said he would try to get along with one. Appointing Dana a major in the adjutant general's office circumvented that restriction.[8]

Stanton's family and friends would later insist that ceaseless labor destroyed his health, but work did no more to kill him than thirty-five years of smoking did. Nightly attacks of asthma made sleeping difficult, and probably contributed to his penchant for late hours, but marathon days were partly a choice. Stanton's conniving nature nourished an instinctive distrust of others that manifested itself in an unwillingness to delegate important tasks to any but close, tested friends. For that reason he installed relatives and longtime business associates as his assistant secretaries, and his motivation may have made him sensitive to a habit that was common in his day: it would have been otherwise needless for someone who surrounded himself with cronies to deny that he did. He took Dana on after more than a year of close acquaintance had shown him to be loyal—to Stanton. Later, when Peter Watson resigned, Stanton did not replace him, having perhaps exhausted his stable of reliable associates. Gradually he assigned some of the duties of an assistant to his oldest son, although he avoided giving him the title and apparently resorted to subterfuge to explain how Eddie was hired. He seemed unwilling to lose his grasp on any more of the department's business, or to trust others with much of it.

To compensate for the lack of assistants, Stanton made gradually more use of the adjutant general's office and other staff officers. He appointed discreet senior officers who screened his visitors and correspondence, disposing of as much business as they could and only burdening Stanton with those matters he would have insisted on handling himself. Career soldiers tended to be more tractable than civilians, since Stanton could seal their professional destinies, and he could inflict his occasional rages on them with less danger of losing their services, thereby ensuring closer adherence to his explicit wishes. Colonel James Hardie acted as his chief intermediary during the final year of the war, exercising even the power of arrest under Stanton's name.[9]

Through such delegation Stanton could clear his schedule for extracurricular duties, and during the winter of 1863 he diverted much of his attention to manipulating the state elections of March and April. The autumn of 1862 had found him busy with the militia draft, and he had applied little energy to the elections in the West beyond suppressing vocal dissent through arbitrary arrests. Only in the two rural, highly conservative lower counties of Delaware had he deployed federal troops to "monitor" the elections, and even there the predominant anti-emancipation, Southern-sympathizing faction had taken the election, if by a narrower margin than it might have otherwise.[10]

The disastrous results in the fall elections of 1862 may have provoked Stanton to take more direct action as 1863 began. New Hampshire's annual election, held during town meetings on the second Tuesday in March, amounted to something of a bellwether for the rest of the country. To reverse the losses of the previous autumn, Stanton applied department resources to subdue or subvert the will of the Granite State's conservative electorate, and his first ploy proved to be the most effective: he sent a New Hampshire delegation to the president with a proposal to make Colonel Walter Harriman of the 11th New Hampshire a brigadier general if he would run as a spoiler in the gubernatorial election. The president acceded, and Harriman, an old Democrat, ran under the banner of the Union Party. His campaign saved the day for Republicans, who would otherwise have lost easily. Democratic nominee Ira Eastman still defeated his Republican opponent, Joseph Gilmore, by six percentage points, but Harriman siphoned off just enough ballots to keep Eastman a few hundred below a majority of the total vote. Therein lay the wisdom of the tactic, for without a majority the decision went to the legislature, which still held a significant Republican majority from the 1862 election: the representatives voted along party lines to install the loser of the popular vote.[11]

Even with Harriman's distracting candidacy, New Hampshire had seemed all but lost to the administration on the eve of the election, and Stanton took further precautions. In late February he ordered the 2nd New Hampshire Infantry back home for unspecified duty under Colonel Gilman Marston, who had recruited the predominately Republican regiment. Marston, a sitting congressman himself, distributed the various companies near their home counties, and just before the election he declared several days' furlough for everyone. At least a few of the soldiers may have served as thugs as well as voters, and after the election a mob composed of men from that regiment was dissuaded only by a heavy cordon of police from sacking the office of the conservative *New Hampshire Patriot*. Whether they voted for Harriman or Gilmore, their numbers increased the majority Eastman needed, and in appreciation for its electoral help the whole regiment was allowed to remain at home until the end of May. Stanton impulsively recommended Marston for a brigadier's star on the day the colonel agreed to the scheme, and that intrusion on state patronage appears to have scuttled Harriman's promotion.[12]

While he rewarded soldiers who backed the administration, Stanton punished those who exercised any other political viewpoint. Lieutenant Andrew Jackson Edgerly belonged to the 4th New Hampshire, which had been raised among the faithful by a Democratic politician, and Edgerly, who was home on recruiting service for his regiment that spring, clung to the party descended from his namesake. The political activities of Harriman and Marston must have led him to suppose that an American soldier enjoyed a right to participate in electioneering. He saw nothing wrong with distributing Democratic tickets among prospective voters, but someone reported him—perhaps one of Marston's officers or men—and that was the end of his military career. Three days after the election, War Department Special Order 119 summarily dismissed him from the service "for circulating Copperhead tickets and doing all in his power to promote the success of the rebel cause in his state." "Copperhead" served by then as the Republican slur for Democrats who disagreed with administration doctrine.[13]

Connecticut came next. Republicans there needed help, too, and Stanton assured Governor William Buckingham that he would do anything necessary to help defeat Democratic challenger Thomas Seymour. A canvass of the state predicted that Buckingham would lose by two or three thousand votes, so with the War Department's help he embarked on a complicated ruse to bring home that many Republicans in uniform. As the man who had appointed every officer in the Connecticut regiments, Buckingham could depend on the loyalty of most of them, and his agents instructed them to hold mock referenda among their troops on a resolution to continue the war to the last extremity. An affirmative vote indicated a reliable Republican or a War Democrat who could be expected to reject Seymour's antagonism toward administration policies, and—after the voting on the referendum—the officers of each company were told to choose ten voting-age men from those who had supported the resolution to go home during the election; the bigger companies in the heavy artillery were to send twenty men apiece. Their comrades viewed their departure as a furlough, but that would have sparked jealousy in the Army of the Potomac, where furloughs were hard to come by, so they took their arms with them when they boarded transports for Connecticut: Stanton had ordered them to "duty" in their home state via government transportation, as he had the New Hampshire soldiers. With the example of Lieutenant Edgerly fresh in the newspapers, few of those soldiers would have been likely to support Seymour even if they had eluded the filtering process, for there was nothing secret about the ballots they cast. By Buckingham's own reckoning, he would have lost the election without the votes of those handpicked soldiers.[14]

The Committee on the Conduct of the War supplemented Stanton's stratagems by rushing into print with reports on its partisan investigations. The committee heard witnesses as late as March 28, and Burnside had submitted additional exhibits on April 3, but three days later soldiers were reading the published version in their camps. It appeared in three bound volumes, with transcripts of all the testimony taken during the once-secret hearings. Most of the questions posed during the previous sixteen months had been framed to elicit responses favorable to the Radical viewpoint, and the "ultras" who dominated the committee had been remarkably successful. To drive the theme home, they also drafted the summative reports, acquitting all their favorite generals without exception while damning McClellan and all others of a conservative turn. To credulous readers, the publication discredited all conservative politicians who championed those generals.[15]

The Saturday before the Connecticut vote, Stanton lost the third member of his family in nine months. Christopher Wolcott had sought rest too late, and he died at home on April 4, moving Stanton to take his first break from department duties in nearly fifteen months. His newly remarried sister Oella had died suddenly at the end of July, 1862, two weeks after his baby son and just as he and Lincoln were first trying to supplant McClellan with Burnside, but he had sent the ailing Wolcott to attend Oella's funeral in his place. Stanton boarded the train on April 7, and President Lincoln, who had gone down to review the Army of the Potomac, sent Watson authority to act as secretary in the interim.[16]

The burial took place in Union Cemetery, on the bluffs above Steubenville. Eddie may have come out from Kenyon College, where he was finishing his senior year, and it was the first time Stanton had seen his mother or his youngest sister since Oella's wedding, in 1860. He returned to Washington within a week, asking the president to appoint Pamphila's sixteen-year-old son to West Point. The boy did not report and was dropped from the rolls, but Lincoln reappointed him and in September he entered the class of 1867.[17]

The day Stanton returned to his office, Joe Hooker's cavalry left its camps in the initial stage of a grandiose plan to force Lee out of his Fredericksburg burrow and trap him as he fled toward Richmond, but torrential rain that night forced a postponement. Rain continued off and on for several days, and every streambed filled its banks or overflowed. Fretting over the delay, the president took Stanton and Halleck down to Aquia Creek on April 19 for a conference with Hooker. The general intended to follow his original notion of sending his cavalry in a wide arc around Lee's left flank, but now with a heavy force of infantry to strike him from behind, so the nervous politicians returned to the capital to wait through another week with the army idle. The terms of the two-year regiments began to run out, and a few minor mutinies erupted when mustering dates conflicted with enlistment dates, leaving some toughened veterans satisfied that their time had expired.[18]

Then, four days before April trickled out, the great blue host began to stir and separate, with half of it slipping secretly up the Rappahannock and half sidling down opposite Fredericksburg and below town, where Franklin had failed four months before. The plan called for another assault on Marye's Heights, to hold the Confederate army in place long enough for the upstream force to cross the Rappahannock and Rapidan rivers, swing back toward Fredericksburg, and slam into the rebel rear. May had begun before Hooker's players had all taken their places: four corps waited near the stage stop called Chancellorsville, west of Fredericksburg; a fifth sat at a ford nearby, and two lay before the city. On Friday, May 1, Hooker started forward from Chancellorsville, only to fall back under a heavy attack, for Lee had deduced his intentions and shifted most of his army to meet the flanking threat. Leaving a skeleton force to defend the Fredericksburg line, Lee sent Jackson's entire corps on its own sweeping flank march the next day, and on Saturday afternoon Jackson struck Hooker from behind, putting much of the Eleventh Corps to flight and throwing the attackers on the defensive. Back at Fredericksburg, Yankees finally burst over Marye's Heights and rolled west to clamp Lee between the converging halves of Hooker's army, but Lee reversed his tactics, leaving a holding force at Chancellorsville and turning back with the rest to bloody the Fredericksburg column. Four days of fighting killed and maimed 30,000 men in blue and grey, but even with twice as many effective troops as his opponent Hooker could take advantage of neither the favorable odds nor his superior position. Too confused and shaken to grind the enemy to dust in open combat, he shrugged off the appeals of his more aggressive corps commanders and, with provisions running low, withdrew across the Rappahannock, leaving his cavalry to find its own way back from behind Confederate lines.[19]

Washington knew nothing of Hooker's retreat until the afternoon of May 6. The only hint of fighting had come from hundreds of Confederate prisoners, clad mostly in variegated homespun, who passed beneath Attorney General Bates's window—among them the son of Senator Albert Gallatin Brown, of Mississippi, who claimed that Stanton had encouraged his secessionist impulses in 1861. Secretary Welles drew his first inkling of a repulse around noon, when a telegram passed through his office addressed "Headquarters near Falmouth" from Admiral Dahlgren's son, Ulric, who was on Hooker's staff. Within the hour Welles saw Senator Sumner bemoaning defeat, so he stepped across to the War Department, where Stanton and Seward had been sitting together most of the morning. Welles asked Stanton if he knew where Hooker was.

"No," Stanton snapped. Welles scowled at him, and Stanton relented enough to confirm the defeat, admitting that Hooker was back on his side of the Rappahannock. Lincoln plunged into despair over the unavailing carnage. The only consolation lay in reports that Lee's smaller army had suffered proportionately worse than Hooker's, and that Stonewall Jackson had been shot, but Union losses exceeded those suffered at Fredericksburg. The endless casualties and sequential defeats were seriously eroding Northern will.[20]

That flagging spirit had already manifested itself in the need for trickery to elect Republican candidates in New Hampshire and Connecticut. Even worse disaffection infected Ohio, where an overtly antiwar candidate took the hustings late in April. Clement Vallandigham, the state's most prominent dissenting Democrat, had been gerrymandered out of his congressional seat the previous autumn, so he ran for governor. Ambrose Burnside had already assumed command of the Department of the Ohio, which included most of Ohio and four other states, and he had issued an order prohibiting a variety of activities, including expressions of "sympathy for the enemy." If enforced, that edict could have effectively prevented opposition candidates from campaigning for office, and Vallandigham went out of his way to ridicule the order in a speech at Mount Vernon on the first of May. Burnside planted spies in the audience to record the address, and a few nights afterward a squad of provost marshals broke into Vallandigham's home to arrest him. They carried him off to department headquarters at Cincinnati and, in compliance with the president's proclamation of martial law for "disloyal" persons, immediately put him on trial before a military commission.[21]

The court consisted of Burnside's subordinates and staff officers. As expected, it found Vallandigham guilty of violating the general's order and sentenced him to a federal dungeon for the remainder of the war. The president and his cabinet, except perhaps Stanton, thought the arrest of Vallandigham unwarranted and imprudent, but felt obliged to sustain Burnside in his misjudgment. Although they accepted the court's decision, they all preferred seeing Vallandigham expelled into the Confederacy. Most of the cabinet (except Stanton, again) may have regretted the case because it illustrated the potential abuse that had made Lincoln's martial-law proc- lamation so dangerous and repugnant in the first place. Burnside had ar- rested a political opponent of the sitting president on the campaign trail for crimes that did not exist, and tried him before a military court because the civil justice system would almost certainly have dismissed the case.[22]

Vallandigham did submit a motion for habeas corpus, but it went to the U.S. District Court in Cincinnati, before the aging Humphrey Leavitt. Con- gress had finally granted the president authority to suspend habeas corpus whenever and wherever he deemed it necessary, and Stanton advised doing so now. Lincoln considered it, but he relished authoritarian rule far less than Stanton, and he spoke first with Seward and Chase, both of whom argued against it. Chase knew Leavitt better than Stanton did, and believed he would side with the government, so Lincoln waited, and his restraint bore fruit. In a rambling discourse Leavitt argued essentially that rebellion justified the imposition of military law over the civilian population. Betray- ing his political bias with a denunciation of Vallandigham and his "class of mischievous politicians," the judge virtually authorized dictatorial execu- tive control under the president's constitutional authority as commander in chief. Despite acknowledging the Constitution's attention to the separation of powers, he concluded "it would be an unwarrantable exercise of the judi- cial power to decide that a co-ordinate branch of the Government under its high responsibilities had violated the Constitution in its letter or its spirit by authorizing the arrest in question." In a final allusion to his own weakness and his court's impotence, Leavitt confessed that he was reluctant to issue a writ that military authorities would likely only ignore. With the ailing Chief Justice Taney absent, the Supreme Court refused to hear the case on a tie vote. Until the high court ruled otherwise, three years later, the extent of military domination over American political life would be limited largely by the personal restraint of the chief magistrate.[23]

Military commissions had been used to try civilians earlier in the war, but under Stanton they became widespread. He recognized that fiat law required a dependably compliant judiciary, and cooperative tools like Judge Leavitt did not preside over all courts. Stanton had finally hired a War Department solicitor—William Whiting, a personal friend of Senator Sumner—who was just then overwhelmed with appeals for habeas corpus; as Peter Watson complained to Joseph Holt, "This Dept stands no chance in a game of shuttlecock with the lawyers before disloyal judges." In March Congress had passed the Habeas Corpus Act, authorizing the president to suspend the writ but also prohibiting him from trying civilians before military courts. With the help of Holt and Stanton, Lincoln ignored the restrictive second part of that law, disingenuously denying that those ar- rested by the military were subjected to punishment: he instead insisted that they were merely incarcerated to deter them from committing crimes. The Habeas Corpus Act required the War Department to submit lists of civilian prisoners to federal judges, but when Holt finally submitted those lists to Stanton he offered numerous excuses why they were incomplete, including an admission that he deliberately omitted "a considerable number" of the prisoners. In fact, he appears to have ignored most of them, probably to keep their cases out of the hands of "disloyal judges," and it would have been consistent with Stanton's nature and practice if Holt did so with the secretary's tacit approval, to provide what a later generation would characterize as plausible deniability. Stanton, knowing that the lists were incomplete, did not require Holt to comply more fully with the law.[24]

If the president were going to flaunt congressional authority and impose military justice on the civilian population, that system could be sustained only as long as the executive branch absorbed and retained the function of the courts. Stanton had lent his military trials a semblance of legitimacy through his Senate ally Henry Wilson when he suggested the enabling legislation for a judge advocate general; this measure established a nominal review process that helped quell public outcry against executive usurpation of judicial powers. It also improved the efficiency of military law, facilitating an extension of its reach. Most important, it kept defendants out of the civil system. Thenceforward Stanton never hesitated to use the threat of military arrest against a citizen, anywhere in the country, until a federal judge's ruling in a false-arrest suit opened the possibility that he might be held personally accountable for his actions.[25]

Stanton found further justification for military rule in Francis Lieber, a professor at Columbia who was already known for subordinating individual rights to the citizen's duty to the nation that protects those rights. A native of Berlin, Lieber had been raised in a culture that, in defining freedom, did not stress personal liberty. By 1863, his impatience with rebellion seemed to overcome any caution against the repressive effects of excessive executive power and his own emphasis on the importance of an independent judiciary. In a letter to his old friend Halleck, Lieber proposed a commission to codify the rules of war to guide armies in the field on—among other things—the imposition of martial law and the treatment of prisoners. Stanton appointed Lieber, Hitchcock, and three other generals to a board for that purpose, but Lieber composed most of the document himself. Halleck sent it to Stanton, supposing the secretary might turn it back to the war board for amendment. Instead, Stanton published it unchanged as a general order, allowing a Prussian nationalist to stand as his ex post facto authority for overriding the Constitution and congressional law.[26]

Whether one supported Stanton's brand of justice depended as much on partisan affiliation as principle, and many did support his extraordinary arrests. One Philadelphia Republican, although quick to seek his Democratic cousin's release from arrest for criticizing the administration, nonetheless approved of the government's right to detain him, even without proper authority. A Yale student with a war record advocated a temporary dictatorship, and vocal proponents of war to the bitter end often seemed content with arbitrary government power, perhaps because they entertained little fear that they themselves would ever become its victims. Partisanship and vulnerability also often determined editorial defense or condemnation of routine constitutional infringements: dissident sheets of Democratic persuasion like the *Chicago Times* regularly denounced unconstitutional tactics that might be (and were) used against them. Soldiers generally applauded Stanton's excesses against peace advocates, but perfectly loyal officers who cherished constitutional liberties cringed at the explosion in arbitrary arrests, hoping it would provoke an electoral rebuke of the administration. Some prominent Republicans voiced opposition to military arrests in the loyal states of the North, including most of the cabinet, and Lincoln hinted that even he often found them more troubling than his secretary of war did, although he stuck to his perennial, questionable claim that they were necessary.[27]

The furor over the bloodshed and lost opportunity at Chancellorsville took some of the edge off public reaction to the Vallandigham case. A predictable cry for Hooker's removal arose: old Francis Preston Blair, the sage of Silver Spring, wrote again to Lincoln, urging him to make use of McClellan. Blair had heard that the president only removed McClellan because Stanton misrepresented nearly all the corps commanders when he said they asked to be relieved from duty under him: Blair understood that Lincoln had been forced to choose between his general and his secretary of war. "The result has been a succession of disasters," he reminded the president. "From first to last, under the immediate auspices of Stanton & Halleck, our army has met defeat." The public blamed those two for the disaster at Second Bull Run, he maintained, and praised McClellan for saving the capital and driving Lee from Maryland. He characterized Stanton as the ever-willing political turncoat who stuck by Buchanan through the Lecompton fraud but regained office with the support of the Radicals, who seemed to be Lincoln's worst enemies. Would the two-year and nine-month veterans reenlist under such leadership? Could conscription be forced on the people? Replace Stanton, "Father" Blair implored him. It was not clear if he wanted McClellan restored to the Army of the Potomac or put into the War Department, where his abilities might be more valuable and his failings less visible.[28]

Hooker had become the latest darling of the Radicals, and they tried to hold him blameless for Chancellorsville. Senator Chandler assured his wife of his full confidence in Hooker, although he acknowledged there was "a deep laid conspiracy for his removal." Stanton knew that the weight of McClellan's admirers applied the pressure against Hooker, and he mentioned to War Department solicitor William Whiting that it might be time to start highlighting McClellan's opportunism in the newspapers. Horatio Woodman had previously published the unadulterated Stanton perspective in the *Boston Evening Transcript*, Stanton noted: he must have stopped short of specifically instructing Whiting to recruit Woodman, but Whiting took the hint and passed it on.[29]

It was nevertheless true that nothing had seemed to go right since McClellan's departure. Eight months had passed since the last Union victory in the East, and the army that had reached the left bank of the Rappahannock when McClellan yielded command of it still sat on the left bank of the same river. If McClellan had squandered most of February and March before moving against the enemy the previous year, Hooker had let most of April pass as well, and since November 32,000 men had fallen before Lee's guns, or been spaded under the mud in the pestilential camps around Falmouth.[30]

Prospects were nearly as bleak in the West. Like McClellan, Buell had driven his opponent from the field in the autumn and then allowed him to escape. As December turned to January Rosecrans had staved off an attack by Braxton Bragg's Army of Tennessee at Stone's River, below Nashville, and the president embraced that limited success as a the only victory he was likely to see anytime soon. Grant had known nothing but serial failure in his campaign to take Vicksburg, open the Mississippi, and divide the Confederacy. Late in December a combined thrust had come to grief when a raid on Grant's supply base stymied his wing of the operation, leaving Sherman to assault the powerful Confederate position at Chickasaw Bluffs alone, and Sherman had lost eighteen hundred men in the attempt. Then General McClernand had come along and commandeered Sherman's troops for the successful enterprise at Arkansas Post, early in January, but since then nothing had worked. An ambitious effort to channel the river away from Vicksburg came to naught; two ironclad gunboats sent down past the city to dispose of the little rebel fleet were both captured; another canal cut well upstream, to let gunboats into the Tallahatchie and Yazoo rivers for an attack on Vicksburg's northern defenses, availed nothing beyond trapping the gunboats and requiring the army to extricate them.

With the stubborn determination that would bring him military renown, Grant decided to march most of his army below Vicksburg on the Louisiana side of the river, crossing to the Mississippi shore under cover of a naval flotilla that ran the Vicksburg batteries. To divert attention from his main body he sent a cavalry brigade on a raid down the middle of Mississippi from end to end, and left Sherman north of the city with enough troops to threaten an attack from that quarter. While Hooker was crossing his river to move on Chancellorsville, Grant ferried thirty thousand men over the Mississippi. Taking most of his provisions from the countryside, he started northeast toward the capital, Jackson, luring more of John Pemberton's army out of Vicksburg. Two weeks later Union soldiers drove Joe Johnston, Pemberton's department commander, out of Jackson with his pitifully small conglomeration of rebel troops, and then Grant turned toward Vicksburg, smashing Pemberton's weaker army at Champion's Hill, punishing him again at the Big Black River, and chasing him right into Vicksburg. Twice in four days Grant hammered at the entrenched Confederate perimeter with frontal assaults, but they cost too many casualties and he began digging in for a siege, churning the hills and gullies around the city into a maze of earthworks and infantry obstacles. Halleck had wanted General Banks to join Grant from New Orleans, but logistics never allowed their cooperation, so Halleck reinforced Grant with troops from Kentucky and Missouri.[31]

Apparent stalemate on all fronts and appalling casualties reduced enthusiasm for continuing the struggle, but the harbingers of conscription transformed discouragement into anger. By June, citizens working by contract for the newly appointed provost marshals of their congressional districts had begun roaming their counties as enrolling officers, taking down the names, ages, and addresses of every male resident they found. Many of them encountered resistance, and some were met with violence. Enrollers in Maine, New York, Pennsylvania, Ohio, Indiana, and Illinois were driven away with threats and assaults; in Milwaukee, the wives of eligible conscripts beat enrolling officer with clubs or doused them from upper windows with boiling water; in Chicago, one was beaten nearly to death. In western Pennsylvania and central Indiana, enrolling officers and provost marshal employees were killed from ambush.[32]

Governors and state adjutants general appealed to Stanton for help. In Ohio, David Tod asked permission to expand his "Governor's Guard" into a full regiment, presumably for use against dissident citizens. Stanton agreed, but he left most of the work to the provost marshals and the military commanders. Always ready to close an iron fist on dissent, Burnside—who had just been chastised for shutting down a major opposition newspaper— asked permission to impose martial law in one Indiana county. Busy soliciting troops in the East to repel another advance of Lee's army, Stanton offered no objection, and he seemed to trust that Burnside's methods would quell the unrest.[33]

If he felt confident that the potential for actual revolt in the West could be handled by military force, Stanton took a dimmer view of the situation before Washington. It may only have betrayed diminishing confidence in Hooker, but toward the end of May Stanton began fretting anew over the safety of the city, grumbling to General Hitchcock that he and Halleck had both brought the capital's defensive deficiencies to the president's attention without result. It could have been no comfort when a Southern informant appeared at the War Department with a wild story about a Confederate scheme to send a brigade of cavalry into Washington, dressed in captured Union uniforms, to kidnap Lincoln, Seward, and Stanton himself. Then General Meigs brought more specific rumors of a cavalry raid on Alexandria, and Stanton called in General Heintzelman, who commanded the defenses, but outposts had reported no suspicious activity and Heintzelman scoffed at Meigs for stampeding so easily.[34]

Stanton also complained about the president interfering in the chain of military command, and giving orders to Hooker directly. When Hooker reported to Washington he went straight to the White House, ignoring the secretary of war and Halleck, against both of whom he nursed grudges dating back to their days in California. Halleck sulked and whined, and Stanton seethed at the snub.[35]

Early in June Lee began slipping away from Fredericksburg for another foray across the Potomac. Hooker, who seemed intent on avoiding another clash with the Confederate chieftain, proposed making a dash at vulnerable Richmond, but all the high-level clucking over the security of Washington had impressed the president more than Stanton may have supposed: Lincoln told Hooker that Lee's army ought to be his target, instead of the Confederate capital. Hooker brought his army trudging back up toward Washington in torrid heat and swirling dust, spreading it out before the city in a broad front from Manassas to Leesburg while Lee's lean veterans strode steadily northward, gobbling up much of a sizable garrison at Winchester and threatening Harper's Ferry again as they entered Maryland.[36] When Lee lunged still farther north, Hooker chased along behind, while newspapers at home and soldiers in the ranks longed for McClellan to come lead the army again.[37]

Ten thousand Union soldiers occupied Harper's Ferry and Maryland Heights, across the Potomac. The previous September detachments from Lee's army had captured a division left there, so Hooker wished to abandon the place and reinforce his army with the garrison. Halleck wanted Harper's Ferry defended, but the president had given Hooker control of everything in Maryland east of Cumberland, and Hooker ordered the Harper's Ferry troops to pack up and join him. Halleck countermanded that directive, and Hooker asked to be relieved. Lincoln made no effort to talk him out of it: Hooker had begun sounding too much like McClellan, the president told his cabinet, by grousing over his orders and asking to strip other points to augment his army. Ignoring Hooker's good sense about Harper's Ferry, Lincoln chose a successor without much consultation: if he even mentioned it to

Stanton he met with no objection, for Hooker had begun to infringe upon Stanton's hegemony within the War Department, which he had achieved only after a long struggle with McClellan. Halleck's attitude often reflected pressure he felt from the president and secretary, and the disdain for Hooker evident in Halleck's dispatches may have echoed Stanton's annoyance with Hooker's own arrogance.[38]

At three o'clock on Sunday morning, June 28, after coming up to Frederick, Maryland, by a special train from Washington, Brigadier General James Hardie found the encampment of the Fifth Corps outside town and woke Major General George G. Meade, from a sound sleep to announce that he was the newest commander of the Army of the Potomac. By then Lee's troops were in Pennsylvania, headed generally toward Harrisburg. Meade hoped that Major General Darius Couch—who had given up command of the Second Corps to take charge of Pennsylvania's militia—might stall the enemy below the Susquehanna until the Army of the Potomac could catch up and fall on the rebels from behind.[39]

As the army skirted Washington toward the end of June it picked up other units that had spent the winter in the outer defenses of the city, including numerous big, untried regiments of nine-month militia that had nearly completed their terms without a taste of enemy fire. One entire brigade of Vermonters, as large as a veteran division, would start going home in barely a week, but that might be time enough to get some use out of them, so they marched into Maryland with the rest of the army. They half expected to be asked to stay a little while beyond their muster-out dates, and thought they might exercise their right to refuse: the War Department routinely angered its veterans by keeping them long past the expirations of their individual enlistments, but the regimental mustering date was still sacred.[40]

Several nine-month Maine regiments dropped out in Washington because they were due to be mustered out at the end of June. Those men were frantic to get home, and there was nothing the government could do to make them stay except beg, which is essentially what Stanton did.[41] Lee sat poised to sidle around Meade and strike at Baltimore or Washington from the north, and J. E. B. Stuart's cavalry had ridden between the Army of the Potomac and Washington, cutting off communications with Meade and raiding nearly to the district border. Stanton gave way to the desperation that always afflicted him in the face of more direct dangers to the capital. He asked a former Maine congressman to address his homeward-bound brethren to stay on for the "emergency," promising proper acknowledgment, and he seemed willing to give anything. Most of them flatly refused, and boarded trains for home. Only a portion of the 27th Maine, amounting to a couple of hundred men, responded to the most plaintive exhortations of their colonel, and in return Stanton promised every one of them a Medal of Honor. So taken was he with that form of tribute that he authorized a Medal of Honor for anyone who agreed to remain beyond his time, and for that matter to any of the tens of thousands who turned out with the militia in Maryland or Pennsylvania. The Maine volunteers lingered in camp less than a week longer before going home to await their medals, while all but a handful of those who grappled with Lee's army received no such decoration.[42]

Instances of pure fright like this had already earned Stanton a national reputation for panic. Those at the White House had seen it after the depredations of the CSS *Virginia*, and Congressman Henry Dawes had ridiculed it in the wake of Stonewall Jackson's attack on Banks, thirteen months before. Stanton had been stampeded again during the first bad news from McClellan, at the end of the previous June, and each time he had momentarily infected Lincoln with his terror. His fragile nerves precipitated frantic appeals for troops, undermining confidence in the administration's judgment and discouraging volunteering at critical junctures, until conscription had become necessary. Charles Farrar Browne, who published vernacular satire under the pseudonym of Artemus Ward, reflected widespread public opinion when he caused his alter-ego to remark that "E. Stanton has apeerently only one weakness, which it is, he can't allus keep his undergarments from flying up over his hed."[43]

Meade finally met Lee at Gettysburg, taking a beating on the first day and losing ground on the second, but the third day decided the contest. On the afternoon of July 3 Lee sent nearly a quarter of his remaining army across a mile of open fields in an effort to pierce the Union center on Cemetery Ridge, but artillery had already weakened the attack significantly by the time it came within musket range, and the infantry finished it. The nine-month Vermonters played a prominent role, and dozens of them lay dead on the field when the remnants of Lee's attack receded into the woods on the opposite ridge. The two armies faced each other for another day, but then Lee turned his army homeward under the muffling effects of heavy rain, trailing a long, tragic train of wounded. Meade followed cautiously, and when Lee reached the Potomac a few days later he found it too swollen to ford. In haste he churned the landscape from Hagerstown to the river into imposing earthworks, settling in behind them to face down his pursuers for a week, until his engineers could extemporize a bridge. Continued rain seemed to promise Meade plenty of time to plan carefully, and he hoped to deprive Lee of a chance to even the score of Gettysburg. Only when he ordered everyone forward on the morning of July 14 did he discover that those intimidating works were empty: using a makeshift pontoon bridge and one deep ford, the rebels had slipped away during the night.[44]

Meade's report reached Stanton at the War Department, while the president was holding a skeleton cabinet meeting with Welles and John P. Usher, who had replaced the ailing Caleb Smith in the Interior Department. Stanton rushed in and asked Lincoln to step outside with him, where he told him Lee had gotten away. The president looked so distressed when they reentered the office, and Stanton seemed so agitated, that Usher asked if he brought bad news. Stanton denied it, as though Usher were not fit to know such inside information, and when someone else repeated a rumor that Lee was back across the Potomac Stanton retorted that he knew nothing of it. Welles recorded that the president turned to Stanton "with a look of painful rebuke" for the lie. "*I do*," said Lincoln, repeating what Stanton had just told him. The president may have overlooked his war secretary's disingenuous nature most of the time, but he could not have claimed to be completely unaware of it.[45]

Meade's stock abruptly tumbled. The soldiers who would have had to storm Lee's entrenchments, many of whom had battered themselves against similar works before, breathed a collective sigh of relief and counted Lee's flight as a sufficient victory; those who had not been there, and faced none of the danger, deplored Meade's failure to crush his foe. Back safe from Vicksburg, Dana blamed Meade for missing a chance to end the war. Lincoln felt the same, and Halleck apprised the new army commander of the president's "great dissatisfaction," so offending Meade that he asked to be relieved of command. Lincoln wrote a kindly explanation of his reasoning, meanwhile expressing his appreciation for the victory at Gettysburg, but he never sent the letter and Meade went on feeling wounded despite Halleck's assertion that no censure had been intended.[46]

As usual, Stanton laid on the sharpest criticism, but he applied it indirectly. While cannily negotiating with a Pennsylvania newspaperman for a share of government advertising in return for favorable editorial treatment, he informed the editor that no man had ever let such an opportunity to save his country slip through his fingers "since the world began," as Meade had below Hagerstown. To a staff officer known for his pseudonymous newspaper commentary, Stanton characterized it as "the greatest mortification of the war," and suggestively complimented that soldier on his writing.[47]

Fatigue may have aggravated Stanton's discourtesy to Usher, for he had been up much of the previous night. A department messenger had awakened him after midnight in his K Street home with a report that New York City was "at the mercy of a mob." Riots rocked the city in response to the government's first attempt to impose the new draft law. Recent victories exerted no immediate effect on the impression of the conflict as interminable and unwinnable. Meade's triumph at Gettysburg had coincided with Pemberton's surrender to Grant at Vicksburg, but the consequences of Vicksburg required the perspective of time to appreciate. Lee's survival contributed substantially to Northern discouragement, because citizens above the Potomac had come to consider him nearly as indestructible as those below that river did. Defeatism and desperation bred violence among those who expected to be drafted.[48]

Horace Greeley had virtually predicted the riots a month before. The same spirit of "individual sovereignty" that fueled the demand for emancipation would resist the draft, warned that quixotic reformer: instead of forcing men to fight in a manner so obnoxious to a free society, he advised the government to do what private employers had to do when labor grew scarce, and increase the compensation it offered to soldiers. Raise the pay of the private from $13 per month to $25 or $30, he wrote, and let the cost of the war fall where it belonged, instead of on the poor soldier. Drafting men into the army "oppresses the masses" as much as imprisonment for debt, he contended, and conscription deserved abolition as much as slavery did. The mob that tried to destroy the office of Greeley's Radical newspaper on the first day of rioting might have desisted had it been known that he opposed the draft as earnestly as anyone who tossed a paving stone at his building.[49]

Most of the militia in New York had mobilized for the invasion of Pennsylvania and was not available to confront the rioters. Police with nightsticks, partially disabled soldiers of the new Invalid Corps, and some army recruits fought the mob ineffectually, but chaos reigned until troops from the Army of the Potomac arrived. Fresh from denouncing Lee's evasion of Meade as something akin to a devastating loss, Stanton informed the mayor of New York that Lee's retreat had turned into a complete rout, "with his army broken." He promised battalions of veterans to quell the mayhem in Gotham, and sent whole brigades for the purpose. Organized troops started clearing the streets on the fifth day of violence, and by July 18 relative calm had returned. Another riot had flared in Boston, and had been more quickly subdued when besieged soldiers fired directly into the crowd. After a few weeks with veteran regiments camped in New York City's parks, the draft resumed with nothing more than administrative objection from Governor Horatio Seymour.[50]

The New York draft riots, along with a minor Confederate raid, provided an excuse for martial law in Kentucky just in time for the army to control ballot boxes in the state elections there.[51] The riots also muffled an embarrassing fiasco that emerged in California newspapers in the middle of July. The story reached the East by early August, implicating the president and his associates in a shady deal involving the New Almaden quicksilver mine. Suspicion fell mostly on Stanton, because of his involvement on two conflicting sides of the case, although he seems to have been innocent in this episode.

It all began with a Supreme Court ruling in the December term that invalidated Andrés Castillero's mineral claim, on which Barron & Forbes had founded their mining operation. The decision leaned on an assumption of fraud based, probably, on prejudice engendered by Stanton's 1858 prosecution of the unrelated Limantour claims. Without Castillero's right to the mineral resources, the title relied on ownership of the land—a point not fully understood by at least one justice—and vague topographic descriptions left some doubt whether the grant of José Berreyesa or that of Justo Larios encompassed the mine. Barron & Forbes owned the old Berreyesa grant, while the Quicksilver Mining Company backed Charles Fossat, the current proprietor of the Larios land.[52] Only if the New Almaden mine was found to lie beneath neither grant would the ownership devolve on the United States, but wily Quicksilver investors evidently orchestrated a premature seizure of the property by the government, hoping to lease the mine from the Interior Department. Daniel Sickles's friend Samuel Butterworth, the president of Quicksilver at the time, secured a valuable ally in Leonard Swett, a close friend of Abraham Lincoln. Quicksilver principals offered Swett an exorbitant reward if he could gain control of the mine for the company, and he evidently approached Interior secretary Usher, who had some experience selling out to corporate interests. Early in May, Usher, Swett, or both, persuaded the president to sign a writ expelling the Barron operators under an obscure 1807 law meant to protect public resources. They either lied to Lincoln or relied on the complicated nature of the dispute to disguise from him the inapplicability of the law in the New Almaden case, since it had never been (and never would be) declared public domain. On May 24 Swett and Butterworth sailed from New York to seize the mine, with Swett acting on Lincoln's authority as an agent of the government.[53]

They reached San Francisco early in July, proceeded to San Jose, and enlisted the U.S. marshal and a detachment of cavalry to enforce the president's warrant, if necessary. The collector of the port of San Francisco telegraphed to Washington that the seizure would give Democrats powerful ammunition in the imminent elections, because it posed a threat to all the state's influential mining interests, and Lincoln replied with instructions to avoid "a riot." Halleck telegraphed the commander at San Francisco that the secretary of war had issued no order for the takeover of the mines, and that any purported order must have been "surreptitiously obtained." He used the same phrase in a telegram to his law partner in California, who still represented New Almaden and published the wire in local papers—creating the impression that Stanton had "surreptitiously obtained" the writ, as though still trying to secure New Almaden for the Quicksilver syndicate.[54]

That was an understandable assumption among those who knew the history of the case, as a Democratic newspaper remarked early in the San Francisco furor. Under the headline "Black and Stanton—Stanton and Black," the editor described Stanton coming to California under a generous retainer from Attorney General Black and serving as Black's "cat's paw" to wrest New Almaden from its rightful owners for the sake of Robert Walker, Butterworth, and others. Then, when Stanton became attorney general, he hired Black in turn, until the Quicksilver owners engaged him to finish the job. All this was essentially true, and the editor did not even mention that Stanton had also served as a lawyer for the Quicksilver investors at least before and after his tenure as opposing counsel for the government. That stunk sufficiently even in 1863 to spawn a suspicion that Stanton had engineered the illicit seizure, and that insinuation enjoyed particular popularity among Democratic newspapers that already doubted the honesty of the secretary of war. Underhanded dealings in return for generous emoluments may also have seemed to explain the description of Stanton that had appeared in the *Sacramento Union* only a few weeks before, alluding to his expensive sartorial taste, his "gorgeous way of living," and the "handsome style" in which he supported his "little, aristocratic wife."[55]

Yet Stanton was blameless for the writ of seizure: the culprit was Swett, who served as another example of how blind Lincoln could be to the duplicity of his close associates. Apparently with good cause, the *New York World* accused Swett of misrepresenting the meaning of the Castillero decision to Lincoln. Swett and Butterworth were in cahoots, the *World* reported, and Swett's financial interests dictated his opinion. The president may have been catching on when, after he countermanded the order, Swett argued persistently for its implementation. Telegrams were pouring in pleading for suspension of the warrant, Lincoln told Swett, "while you are the single one who urges the contrary," and Attorney General Bates noted months later that Swett was responsible for the whole "shameful arrangement." The writ was never enforced. The mine remained in the hands of the original operators until the Fossat claimants prevailed over the Berreyesa grantees, in the spring of 1864, giving the mine to the Quicksilver syndicate that had thrown a decade of effort and a great deal of money into gaining possession of it.[56]

As the recipient of quite a bit of that money, Stanton cringed at the publicity that followed Swett's scheme. In an August cabinet meeting, after clippings from California newspapers reached Washington, Bates and Usher complained of Halleck's published allusion to the "surreptitiously obtained" warrant: Bates felt genuinely insulted, and Usher probably squirmed self-consciously over his own part in assisting Swett. To their protests Stanton added no little croaking, in cabinet council, over the abuse and lies he had suffered at the hands of the newspapers and "distinguished men"—turning away from Blair with those words, as though to include him among the libelers. Blair had often impugned Stanton's honesty, insisting that he was lining his pockets on government contracts. No evidence supports that allegation, and the gradual decline in Stanton's financial position while he was in the War Department leaves it doubtful. Nor was it likely that he had accepted private payment for services rendered as a public official, although representing litigants antagonistic to the government while he was acting as the agent of the government tainted any decision he might have made that benefited his private clients: whatever fees he collected from those clients, meanwhile, might also have been interpreted as bribes, and clients as shady as some of the Quicksilver partners perhaps viewed them that way. For someone like Blair, Stanton's long association with such characters may have engendered early doubts about his integrity, and Stanton's undeniable duplicity in other matters would have only corroborated those suspicions.[57]

The New Almaden ruckus reached the Atlantic coast just in time to be overshadowed by resumption of the draft. Politicians and citizens of all persuasions ignored much else in their sudden anxiety to complete their various state, county, and town quotas with as little personal sacrifice as possible. The lists of drafted men whose names had been drawn from lottery wheels created an enormous scramble for substitutes—and for money to pay commutation fees. All that attention distracted the press and public from the imputations against the president and his ministers.

The first implementation of the draft caused a stir within the cabinet itself. Both Chase and Welles bridled at the clerks and artisans conscripted from their departments, blaming Stanton for failing to exempt essential government employees when he and Senator Wilson prepared the legislation. Welles wondered whether Stanton had omitted such a suggestion deliberately, so fellow secretaries would have to come hat-in-hand to him for relief. When they asked him to exempt the other departments wholesale he refused, insisting that drafted employees should come to him individually. Welles recorded that Chase refused to even talk to Stanton about it, saying he "had no favors to ask of the War Department." To the exasperated Welles, Stanton declined even to grant blanket exemptions to sailors in the U.S. Navy, who might fail to report because they were serving overseas, or in hostile waters: Welles fumed that Stanton would have him come begging on behalf of each drafted sailor. Such stubbornness promised inefficiency in every afflicted department, and would only have heightened the administrative burden Stanton already complained about, leaving Welles convinced that the war secretary was trying to assert his dominance within the cabinet. Stanton, the navy secretary complained, "seems gratified that such power should have been placed in his hands by Congress."[58]

There was, however, one young man whom Stanton would not see drafted. His son Eddie, who had been inducted into the Phi Beta Kappa fraternity, graduated from Kenyon that summer with both baccalaureate and master's degrees, and so bright and accomplished a lad was not to be wasted in uniform. There seemed no shame, after all, in the nation's highest officials protecting their sons from a danger they imposed on most other young men. President Lincoln's draft-age son was sitting out the war at Harvard, and Stanton made room for his own boy in the War Department.[59]

He never seemed embarrassed at this most obvious instance of taking care of his own, but someone found it compromising enough to offer an unconvincing explanation. Stanton's clerk, A. E. H. Johnson, claimed that Eddie worked without pay until the telegraph chief, Thomas Eckert, secretly put him on the payroll. Charles Benjamin, another clerk, seemed to follow Johnson's late-life reminiscence when he repeated the story, but Eckert would not likely have dared to undertake such a ploy unless Stanton himself inspired the charade. After installing his friend Watson, along with Watson's confederates Wood and Johnson and his brother-in-law Wolcott, Stanton might well have worried about charges of favoritism, and it would have been characteristic of him to bring his son into the department through a back door.[60] Shortly before Eddie graduated from Kenyon, and again a few months after he began work at the War Department, Stanton refused a staff commission to his cousin William Stanton—again basing the refusal "entirely on the ground of relationship"—but Eddie's appointment (and Wolcott's before him) contradicted that. Eventually, too, Stanton gave cousin William a cozy spot as paymaster, relationship notwithstanding. The porous fantasy of Stanton's aversion to nepotism seemed designed to disguise the extent to which he practiced it.[61]

With the capture of Vicksburg, and the surrender of Port Hudson a few days later, the Mississippi River had theoretically been reopened, although an observer remarked that he would not have cared to lead an excursion downriver to New Orleans just then. That seemed like the right time to begin another bifurcation of the Confederacy east of the Mississippi, and early in August orders started coming to Rosecrans, in Tennessee, and to Burnside, in Kentucky, requiring immediate movements by each of them into east Tennessee. Those orders came under Halleck's name, but they carried a curt, demanding tone echoing Stanton's voice. Rosecrans was to drive Bragg out of Chattanooga while Burnside came over the mountains with a small force to take Knoxville. Burnside was still short of men, having loaned most of the Ninth Corps to Grant, and both he and Rosecrans took umbrage at Halleck's sudden peremptory orders. Each of them rebuked the general in chief independently for instructions that seemed to deny them any discretion, and that was very much unlike Halleck, who customarily avoided the responsibility for anything like a direct order. Without much doubt, he was probably only relaying directions from the secretary of war, whom Secretary Chase watched grow increasingly impatient. Still, another ten days passed before either Rosecrans or Burnside could accumulate enough food and forage to embark on their expeditions. Burnside's route would take him beyond the reach of any railroad, and his was the more precarious operation, but he started first, on August 15, and Rosecrans moved the next day.[62]

By then, Washington withered under a long, steamy heat wave. Ellen was pregnant again and Stanton had sent her and the children out of the city, as he always did in summer: this year she had gone to Bedford Springs, in the mountains of southern Pennsylvania. The president had the use of the Soldiers' Home, near the district boundary, at federal expense, but through 1863 Stanton paid for Ellen's lodging, and at the springs she considered her accommodations "wretched." Such routine expenses produced the impression of Stanton's "gorgeous way of living" that the California reporter had noticed: they quickly ate through his government salary, and began chewing into his savings, but after ten straight days of stifling heat he felt grateful that Ellen and the children did not have to bear it. Their comfort, or at least their absence, allowed him to concentrate on work, but he and the president had been talking about going up to Bedford together for a few days to escape the oppressive atmosphere themselves. Something always intervened for one of them, but finally Stanton did slip away for a long weekend. He left the office on Friday afternoon, September 4, leaving Watson in charge again, and the following Sunday Lincoln telegraphed to say that Burnside had captured Knoxville. By the time Stanton returned to work on Wednesday, Rosecrans had also occupied Chattanooga.[63]

George Meade had returned the Army of the Potomac to the upper reaches of the Rappahannock, where he attempted to curb desertion with an array of executions while incorporating the first levies of conscripts into his army. As they lolled in the enervating humidity of August and September, the veterans of that army occupied themselves with a number of tributes to their longest-serving generals. By subscription, the members of John Sedgwick's old division presented him with an inscribed sword, an ornate saddle, and a sleek new horse; Dan Sickles, who had lost a leg at Gettysburg, received a rugged field carriage and team from the officers and men of his corps; the Pennsylvania Reserves, which General Meade had originally commanded, bought him a Tiffany sword, and Governor Andrew Curtin came down to present it. The sword presentation attracted great publicity, earning full coverage in the *Washington Chronicle* and in Pennsylvania and New York papers—some of which reported complimentary remarks that Meade had actually declined to make about Governor Curtin, who was up for reelection. None in the administration could have failed to know of the elaborate presentation, but no one complained of it, or of any of the other testimonials to distinguished generals. Such initiatives technically conflicted with Paragraph 220 of the General Regulations of the Army, which forbid all soldiers from "conveying praise, or censure, or any mark of approbation against their superiors in the military service," but because the presentations nurtured good morale the regulation had never been enforced.[64]

That changed when Meade's generals began planning a fund drive to show their continuing esteem for George McClellan. General Sedgwick proposed it among the corps commanders, and everyone (apparently including Meade) thought it such a good idea that a circular made the rounds offering enlisted men and junior officers a schedule of graduated contributions, from ten cents per private to twenty dollars for a major general. This posed no practical violation of Paragraph 220, because McClellan remained unassigned and should not have been considered a superior of anyone on active duty. To McClellan's enemies in the administration, the morale of the troops or the fair and consistent application of regulations meant nothing against their desire to quash any token of respect for the man they had come to see as a political rival. Radical Carl Schurz, an astute politician and a less-than-mediocre general in the Eleventh Corps, forwarded a copy of the circular to Secretary Chase, whom he knew despised McClellan, and Chase showed it to Stanton. Veneering their personal prejudice with a pretense of official propriety, they concurred that such a demonstration amounted to "an insult" to the president, who had deposed McClellan. Chase gave the circular to Lincoln, who probably comprehended how petty it might seem to object to a sincere tribute for a general from his fellow veterans, but he also saw the political implications. With the ever-crucial fall elections on the immediate horizon, Republicans could not bear to have soldiers complimenting the country's most prominent Democrat. When Chase admonished the president to "see" Stanton about it he did so, leaving the matter in the hands of his perennial enforcer.[65]

Stanton called Meade to Washington that day, September 22, and Meade arrived near midnight by train from Culpeper. The McClellan testimonial must have been part of the discussion that night and the next day, because the day after Meade returned to the army he reported that the effort to honor McClellan had been abandoned. He sent out a new circular announcing that the intent of the subscription had been "misconstrued," but those who read the Radical newspapers knew what had happened. Stanton waited a couple of weeks to have Halleck issue a general prohibition on the basis of Paragraph 220, to disassociate it from the McClellan effort and to mask its arbitrary enforcement.[66]

The generals who proposed the subscription may have considered themselves lucky when they learned how spitefully Stanton treated any soldier who revealed admiration for McClellan. The following summer, West Point superintendent Alexander H. Bowman and two officers on the faculty invited McClellan to deliver the commencement address at the military academy. As the foremost unassigned graduate of the institution, McClellan seemed the perfect choice, but the graduation ceremony coincided, unfortunately, with the effective start of the 1864 presidential contest, which Bowman may have overlooked in his concentration on academy affairs. When Stanton learned of McClellan's appearance he summarily dismissed Bowman, who was himself an 1825 alumnus of the institution, and reassigned the other two to minor posts where they would have no opportunity to distinguish themselves any further.[67]

The McClellan testimonial, while vexing to Stanton and perhaps the president, took second place in Meade's discussion with those two on Wednesday morning, September 23. They and Halleck spent most of his brief visit questioning him about the feasibility of sending a detachment of the Army of the Potomac to reinforce Rosecrans, who had gone into Georgia and been mauled by Bragg at Chickamauga Creek, just below Chattanooga. Reinforced by two divisions of Longstreet's corps from Lee's army, Bragg had sent most of the Army of the Cumberland spilling back into Chattanooga in full retreat. Lincoln himself had raised the topic of sending men to Rosecrans before they even knew of the setback at Chickamauga; the president wondered whether the advantages of defensive warfare would not allow Meade to hold his ground against Lee and send tens of thousands of men elsewhere, for offensive operations. Stanton had evidently been promoting that idea, but when he, the president, and Halleck proposed it to Meade on Wednesday the general argued against it, leaving Washington just after noon convinced that the president had been persuaded not to deplete the nation's principal army.[68]

Meade did not reckon on the obstinacy of Stanton, who remained at his desk late that night. Near midnight John Hay came into the War Department, looking for an orderly to deliver some dispatches to President Lincoln at the Soldiers' Home, and he found Stanton preparing to go there himself. Some telegrams had come in from Charles Dana, who was now keeping a critical eye on Rosecrans. One message arrived at 10:00 P.M., telling of Bragg advancing slowly against Chattanooga that afternoon. Another came in an hour later, attributing the defeat to greatly superior Confederate forces and the failure of Major General Alexander McCook to deploy his corps properly; Dana added that McCook and another corps commander had fled the field ahead of their troops, found lodgings in Chattanooga, and gone to sleep. General McCook was the younger brother of Stanton's friend and former law partner, George McCook, and when Hay came into the room Stanton was disputing that analysis. "No, they need not shuffle it off on McCook," Hay heard the secretary say. Rejecting the opinion of his own camp spy, Stanton concluded that McCook was not accountable and blamed it instead on Rosecrans, who had also left his army behind in his haste to return to Chattanooga.[69]

Stanton asked Hay to go to the Soldiers' Home and fetch the president. This was the first time his secretary of war had ever called for him in the middle of the night, and as Lincoln rose from bed to dress he worried that the ultimate disaster had overcome Rosecrans, and just before the October elections. At the War Department he found that Stanton had also gathered Halleck, Seward, Chase, Peter Watson, a brigadier in the adjutant general's office, and the War Department's director of military railroads.[70]

Stanton explained that he had called them together to decide whether anything was going to be done to relieve Rosecrans, whose situation he considered perilous, and he asked Halleck how many men Burnside could send him. Halleck, who evidently did not understand Burnside's effective force or situation, replied that he could spare twenty thousand men and get them to Chattanooga in ten days "if not interrupted," or he could send twelve thousand in eight days. Sherman could bring twenty thousand or more, but not in less than ten days, and they would have to come from Vicksburg or Memphis. Stanton, concluding that no troops would be likely to reach Rosecrans in time to help, sprang the idea that he had apparently borrowed from Lincoln: put Hooker in command of twenty thousand men from Meade and speed them to Chattanooga by rail. The Army of the Potomac seemed likely to remain inactive for a while to come: the Eleventh and Twelfth Corps could march for Washington in the morning, and as they began arriving at night they could board railroad cars that would take them to Nashville in five days.[71]

"Why, you can't get one corps into Washington in the time you fix for reaching Nashville," the president replied, telling a story to drive the point home. Stanton snapped at the congenial Lincoln in a way he would never have dared to do to James Buchanan, informing him that it was no time for jokes. Seeming to admit defeat, Stanton invited the group to adjourn to the next room, where he had had a little food prepared, but during the meal he continued to lobby. Chase, and then Seward, took up his cause. When they returned to the conference room everyone but the president seemed to favor the idea, and even he finally relented, agreeing to have Halleck telegraph to see if Meade had any aggressive movement planned: if not, the troops would be taken.[72]

Stanton had apparently put great faith in his ability to persuade the president, for he had already telegraphed several railroad executives, including his former assistant Tom Scott, summoning them to the capital. At two-thirty in the morning Halleck wired Meade to prepare the two corps for departure—provided he had no immediate offensive plans, and he had not. The railroad men arrived the next day to orchestrate the movement, closing their lines to commercial traffic and collecting scores of rail cars from their various branches. The preponderance of rolling stock would consist of seated cars accommodating as many as three dozen men apiece, but the unlucky had to crowd onto the oak floors of baggage or stock cars, with a few open flatcars here and there.[73]

The first contingent of two thousand men from the Eleventh Corps pulled out of Washington in two trains on the evening of September 25, reaching Camden Station in Baltimore that night. A few cars were dropped from each train there, to ease the strain on the engines over the mountains, and the locomotives left half an hour apart, traveling about ten miles an hour. For three more days trains kept steaming into the capitol, the last of the Twelfth Corps boarding cars on the afternoon of September 28. By then the head of the Eleventh Corps had crossed the Ohio and rattled on toward Columbus, Indianapolis, and Louisville. Between dawn and noon of September 29 the first four trains pulled out of the station at Louisville, and a continuous stream of men passed through that city for the next week. Infantry came first, followed by the horses and the artillery. Here and there a man sleeping on a flatcar or on the roof of a baggage car would tumble off: even at such low speeds that caused a few serious injuries, but the trains kept their pace, and the first four arrived at Bridgeport, Alabama, on the final evening of September. From there steamers would take them up the Tennessee River toward Chattanooga. The tail of the Eleventh Corps left Louisville during the night, and the leading elements of the Twelfth Corps rolled out on the first of October; Hooker went to the head of his new command on October 3. Trains were still leaving Washington then, laden with guns and horses, but the last of the infantry had come in by October 6, thirteen days after Stanton's conference.[74]

Hooker did not beat the time Halleck so optimistically thought Burnside could have made, but he relieved Burnside from having to abandon east Tennessee. He had also brought eighteen thousand men within supporting distance of Rosecrans before Sherman could have supplied a soldier. Hooker had traveled three times as far as Longstreet had to reach Bragg, and the individual units had required less time to move from army to army over exterior lines than Longstreet's movement had taken on interior lines. Thanks to the lethargy of Braxton Bragg, they had arrived with time to spare. For the first time since proposing the excursion to Norfolk, Stanton had personally initiated a conspicuously productive feat, and it would contribute to a more spectacular achievement less than two months hence. It was perhaps his greatest single contribution to ultimate victory.[75]

The operation had not been conducted without political motives, however, and it may have served the administration in ways no one had anticipated. Opposition sentiment had dwindled since the victories at Gettysburg and Vicksburg, but those gains had been offset by the surprising defeat at Chickamauga, only eleven weeks after the Confederacy had seemed finished. Stanton's sensitivity to political interests probably alerted him to the impact of that reverse, and to the importance of avoiding any disasters at Chattanooga so near the October elections in Ohio, Indiana, and Pennsylvania. In his preoccupation with influencing elections, Stanton may even have calculated the benefits that might accrue from sending a thousand carloads of men and matériel through the heart of Ohio and Indiana, where the greatest number of people could see them. The entire transfer was supposed to be secret, but the news traveled far enough ahead that throngs waited at each stop along the way. Women pressed desserts on the passengers when the trains stopped, and the cars creaked along so slowly that pedestrians could talk to soldiers leaning out the windows. As small as Hooker's force might have seemed in comparison to the field armies by 1863, its route through the heartland still provided civilians with an impressive image of the strength and determination of the government.[76]

How much that helped could never be estimated, but it certainly did no harm. The administration's supporters fared well in all three elections, including Indiana, where Stanton's provost marshals had angered even the Copperhead-conscious governor Morton with unwarranted arrests of perfectly loyal citizens. Republicans did particularly well in Ohio, where the exiled and discredited Vallandigham lost by a landslide, and the party recovered from the drubbing it had taken in 1862. Stanton's efforts to tip the Ohio vote had been superfluous, but by sending soldiers home and granting leaves to officers with oratorical talent and administration sympathies he may have helped win at least local Republican victories in Maine's September election, and in New York in November. In Pennsylvania, even Republicans believed they had triumphed through a combination of soldiers' votes and fraud.[77]

13

PRISONERS OF CIRCUMSTANCE

Hooker's movement fulfilled only part of the program to relieve Chattanooga. Stanton belatedly gave the president the telegram from Dana disparaging McCook, and the president showed it to Welles and Seward, remarking that he was being urged to remove Rosecrans; Stanton's mutterings on the night of September 23, 1863, hint that he was the one doing the urging. Welles proposed George Thomas, who had saved the army on the second day at Chickamauga, but more comprehensive plans already appear to have been developed. The next day Halleck telegraphed Grant, at Vicksburg, that Rosecrans needed all the troops he could spare, and suggested that Grant go to Nashville to oversee the transfer. Grant had recently suffered severe bruises and sprains when his horse fell on him during a visit to New Orleans, and his name might not have come so readily to mind in Washington had it been known that witnesses to the accident considered Grant drunk.[1]

Not content with Halleck's indefinite and seemingly advisory instructions, Grant waited for orders. They were two weeks coming, and carried a tone of mystery, directing him to Cairo, where he would receive further orders; at Cairo he was instructed to go on to Louisville with his staff, to await the arrival of a War Department official. Still hobbling about with a crutch, Grant left right away, around noon on October 17, and as his train pulled out of the Indianapolis depot in the evening a messenger stopped it for that anticipated officer of the War Department—none other than Stanton himself—who had raced out from the East on a special train in a little over a day. Accompanied by portly John Brough, the new governor of Ohio, the secretary of war came aboard and met his most successful general for the first time. As they proceeded to Louisville, Stanton told Grant he was to have an immense new command called the Military Division of the Mississippi, entailing his old Department of the Tennessee as well as Rosecrans's Department of the Cumberland and that of the Ohio, under Burnside. Stanton carried two copies of the order assigning the new department to Grant, both signed by the president, but one copy relieved Rosecrans of duty and replaced him with Thomas. Since Grant would have to manage

305

the commander of that army, he was allowed to choose between the two. He chose the orders appointing Thomas without hesitation, and only after Grant wired acknowledgment of his orders did Lincoln learn who would head the army at Chattanooga.[2]

Stanton and Grant took rooms at the Galt House in Louisville. Grant continued on to Nashville and Chattanooga after a couple of days, to assess his new task and find a reliable supply line. Stanton loitered in Louisville, conferring with Tom Scott and Andrew Johnson about a new railroad from Nashville. He started home on October 22, warning Peter Watson that he would not be returning with the same haste in which he had departed. His route took him within thirty miles of Steubenville, where his mother still lived in the house at Logan and Third, and after a six-day journey that included a detour there he resumed work in Washington, where hangers-on at the White House seemed to understand that Stanton, rather than Grant, had deposed Rosecrans.[3]

Just before leaving for Indianapolis and Louisville, Stanton attempted a special prisoner exchange for Major Harry White, a Pennsylvania state senator: since the recent election, the Republicans held a one-vote majority in the state Senate, and White represented that one vote, so his presence could prove crucial to Pennsylvania's support of the war. Unfortunately for Keystone Republicans, the exchange cartel had begun to disintegrate. It had suffered a setback at the end of 1862, after Jefferson Davis issued a proclamation authorizing the summary execution of Ben Butler (if he was captured) and halting all paroles for Union officers until federal officials punished Butler for the hanging of a New Orleans citizen. In the same pronouncement Davis had decreed that captured black troops and their officers should be turned over to the civil authorities and tried for servile insurrection. Stanton stopped the exchange of Confederate officers in turn, but under pressure from his exchange commissioner he rescinded that order, and the enemy reciprocated.[4]

Butler's initial brutality in New Orleans colored the rest of his rule there, leaving even his successor to suspect that his administration had been corrupt. His heavy hand provoked Davis to devote most of his proclamation to Butler's crimes, but Davis's objection to the Corps D'Afrique would ultimately provide the principal excuse for disrupting prisoner exchanges. In a region where racial supremacy dictated both economic and physical survival for white citizens, the concept of arming black men would never be tolerated, and the Union government's insistence on recognizing them as soldiers should have dictated an abrupt and permanent end to the entire exchange system. Certainly it jeopardized the process, especially after the Confederate Congress passed a resolution reiterating Davis's threat to U.S. Colored Troops and their officers, but Union authorities overlooked the principle of racial equality and continued to trade captives until the preponderance of prisoners shifted back to them.[5]

The U.S. government's enthusiasm for prisoner exchanges seemed to fluctuate with the balance of prisoners. Stanton embodied that equivocation, and he appears to have been at least partly responsible for it. When he entered the War Department the Confederacy held a couple of thousand prisoners from the early battles, while few rebel soldiers had been captured: a handful of privateers held as pirates constituted the most conspicuous captives in Union hands. The Union prisoners in Richmond, Charleston, and Tuscaloosa inspired flurries of letters from worried relatives, and especially the Massachusetts prisoners from Ball's Bluff, who represented a disproportionately influential community, at least for a secretary of war anxious to please the Radical constituency. Stanton's first communication on the subject involved his selection of two North Carolinians for use in a special exchange of Union officers who included the son of Congressman Samuel Hooper of Boston. Four days later, on February 11, 1862, Stanton instructed General Wool to arrange for regular exchanges of prisoners, who would all be released soon after capture on parole, promising on pain of death not to fight again until they had been formally exchanged for prisoners from the other side. The system would parallel a cartel observed by the United States and Britain during the War of 1812.[6]

Then came Fort Donelson, yielding about thirteen thousand new Confederate prisoners. Stanton immediately ordered the captured rebel generals withheld from any exchanges, confining them separately in basement cells at Fort Warren in Boston Harbor—while speciously denying that they were held in "dungeons." His refusal to exchange them sabotaged Wool's efforts. When those complications forced Wool to report that negotiations had ground to a halt, Stanton seemed perfectly satisfied to let them remain so, remarking on March 13 that he had "exhausted all the means in a fruitless effort to establish a just and liberal system of exchange." Thus skirting responsibility for the continued suffering and deteriorating health of Union prisoners, he hung on to the significant new surplus of captives until after the Seven Days fighting: when Lee captured more than six thousand of McClellan's men and lost fewer than a thousand himself, Stanton's interest in exchange revived. The balance of prisoners had nearly leveled again, and with a little pressure from the president Stanton directed the new commander at Fort Monroe, General Dix, to negotiate a cartel. Within ten days it was done, implying how quickly it might have been accomplished had Stanton insisted on it himself.[7]

Through the rest of 1862 that cartel saved thousands of men from long-term captivity in crowded, often unsanitary conditions, and the practice continued into 1863 except for the three-month interruption in the exchange of officers. Field commanders could still trade captive officers and men with their antagonists after a battle, and they often did, but then in early July nearly forty thousand rebel prisoners fell into Union hands. Stanton soon began to assail the entire exchange system again, this time concentrating on the parole process, which required the captors to deliver their prisoners to either of two exchange points: at Aiken's Landing on the James River, or at Vicksburg. Because Union troops usually played the role of occupiers, their garrisons had been vulnerable to rebel raids, and often the raiding forces had found it convenient to parole their prisoners on the spot, to carry on with their operations. Thousands of Union soldiers had surrendered to cavalryman John Hunt Morgan and to invading Confederate armies in Kentucky, late in the summer of 1862, going free on parole; Stonewall Jackson had paroled the entire garrison of Harper's Ferry that same season. Those paroles had all been observed, but Morgan was making another raid through Kentucky, Indiana, and Ohio when Halleck issued a blanket reminder that soldiers could not be considered legitimately captured unless the enemy held "actual possession" and could deliver them to the exchange points. Henceforth, he warned, such paroles would not be regarded as valid.[8]

The day after Halleck's reminder, knowing nothing about it, General Grant paroled John Pemberton's entire army on the spot where he captured them, primarily because a shortage of river steamers prevented the transport of thirty thousand rebels to Northern prisons. Technically, he presented his captives at one of the specified exchange points—Vicksburg—but his possession of the place prevented the enemy from receiving them, so he failed to deliver them to Confederate officials. It seemed inconsistent to demand equivalents for them while simultaneously revoking the paroles of Union soldiers released by Lee on his retreat from Gettysburg, but that was the position taken by Stanton's War Department, and it soon aggravated a growing disagreement over how many prisoners each belligerent had delivered. That confounded the effort to free Major White. Stanton found an excuse to offer a Mississippi major in return, exempting him from the prohibition on a dubious technicality, but that partisan mission remained unfulfilled when Stanton left for Louisville.[9]

The hard line on prisoner exchanges, like the War Department's hard line on most subjects, came from Stanton. Lincoln told a New York delegation that he did not wish to disrupt exchanges, even to protect his black soldiers, because of the misery it would cause all prisoners. His visitors supposed that only heavy pressure would prod the president to reverse his position on that issue, and—if Ward Hill Lamon spoke the truth—Stanton applied much of that pressure. A quarter of a century later Lamon described Stanton admonishing the president for his sensitivity to the prisoners' plight, and urging him to stop exchanges on the entirely practical ground that it would reduce Confederate manpower, with no reference to threats against captives from the Colored Troops. Lamon could be a very inventive story-teller, but the record tends to corroborate this account. Army headquarters did finally call an end to exchanges, officially citing loftier principles about black prisoners, but as general in chief Grant revealed that the order was motivated by the wish to tie up rebel manpower. Grant may have supported or even recommended it for that reason, but that sort of policy was the re-sponsibility of the secretary of war, or the president.[10]

Richmond remained the center for prisoners of war in the Confederacy, with Union officers confined primarily in warehouses like Libby Prison, enlisted men on an island in the James River, and the sick in an assort-ment of impromptu hospitals near the waterfront. These accommodations had already grown squalid and inadequate by the autumn of 1863, and the introduction of thousands more prisoners from Chickamauga and east Tennessee seriously strained their capacity. The concentration of so many citizens, refugees, and Confederate soldiers in the rebel capital made it dif-ficult to feed the teeming prisoners, and on the same day Stanton returned from his jaunt out West a boatload of Union prisoners came down to Fort Monroe for release who appeared to be starving. They undoubtedly were malnourished and certainly hungry, but the worst cases probably reflected chronic intestinal disorders. Solomon Meredith, the exchange commis-sioner who received them, instead suspected deliberate deprivation, and he proposed reducing the Confederate prisoners to the same paltry rations reportedly issued in Richmond. General Hitchcock, the chief overseer of exchanges just then, advised against it. Stanton told Meredith to go ahead anyway, and issued a written order to that effect, but Hitchcock warned that if they imitated the meager rations purportedly distributed in Rich-mond it would provoke an uprising in the Northern prison camps.[11]

In his annual report, submitted a couple of weeks after Hitchcock's warn-ing, Stanton promised retaliation if it were necessary for the protection of Union prisoners. Months later, Richmond authorities unconditionally re-leased one boatload of especially sick prisoners, including some in advanced states of emaciation. Equally cadaverous patients were quite common in Union hospitals and prison camps, too, but Stanton allowed the illustrated newspapers to reproduce photographs of the frailest of the returned prison-ers. He also notified Ben Wade immediately, so his joint committee could look into it, and lobbied the president for retaliatory reduction of the rations supplied to Confederate officers in Union prisons. The commissary general of prisoners prescribed a menu smaller than the U.S. Army issue and Stan-ton approved it, making it the standard prison diet for the rest of the war. Captives on both sides suffered intensely from negligence, inefficiency, or graft, and especially those in the Confederacy, but Stanton was the only senior authority in either government to officially withhold available food from enemy prisoners for any extended period.[12]

While Stanton advocated retaliation mouthful for mouthful, Confederate prison authorities reported alarming shortages of food in Richmond, and expressed similar fears of a revolt. For some fourteen thousand men they found barely enough meat to issue a quarter of a pound to each on November 10, and the next day they had not an ounce left to give. The Confederate commissary general of prisoners, John Winder, worried that if those men were not fed they might well try to break out, and he evidently doubted his ability to stop them. Two weeks later Stanton's counterpart in Richmond, James Seddon, authorized the construction of a prison in southwest Georgia, where provisions and security might be easier to provide, and General Winder chose his son Sidney to undertake the mission. Before November ended, Captain Winder and a young commissary department agent from Americus, Georgia, climbed in a buggy and drove ten miles out of town to examine a tract of land near a station on the Southwestern Railroad called Andersonville.[13]

Some of the Union soldiers who would fill the stockade prison at Andersonville, or the cemetery nearby, began their long journey to that place even as Sidney Winder surveyed the site. By late November Grant had determined on a program to pry Braxton Bragg out of his imposing position atop Missionary Ridge and Lookout Mountain, and Bragg aided him by detaching Longstreet with a sizable force to drive Burnside out of east Tennessee. Burnside lured Longstreet into besieging him in Knoxville, keeping him occupied while Grant attacked Bragg. Hooker assailed Lookout Mountain on Bragg's left, which fell with relative ease, and then Sherman attacked Bragg's extreme right, at the lower end of the ridge, where by dint of savage fighting the rebels held him at bay until George Thomas made for Bragg's center at the base of Missionary Ridge. Thomas's men were supposed to stop there, but with a spontaneous impulse from the lower ranks they swept up the precipitous slope toward the artillery that crowned the crest, breaking the tenuous Confederate line there and chasing the fugitives over the other side. The division fighting Sherman backed away to mount a rear-guard defense on the Georgia side of the state line while the rest of the Army of Tennessee fled south, taking along a few unfortunate Yankees who would wither or die in captivity.[14]

The Army of the Potomac made another stab at Lee the morning after Grant's triumph. It had been an inauspicious autumn for Meade, with Lee flanking his shrunken army at Culpeper and forcing him into a hasty retreat, after which Meade crept back toward Culpeper, rebuilding a ruined railroad as he went, until he regained the line of the Rapidan River. On

Thanksgiving, November 26, he pushed his five remaining corps over the Rapidan in an effort to skirt Lee's right flank and separate him from his direct supply line. It nearly succeeded, despite some egregious bumbling by William French and his Third Corps. After three days of fighting around a tributary of the Rapidan called Mine Run, Meade arranged a powerful two-front assault for the morning of November 30, but the overnight construction of earthworks persuaded Major General Gouverneur K. Warren to call off his part of the assault, and a sorely disappointed Meade was barely able to cancel the other attack in time. As he led his troops back over the Rapidan, Meade assumed that this would end his tenure at the head of the army, for he revealed to one of his West Point classmates that both the president and secretary of war had warned him to fight, whatever he did. Stanton, he said, had told him it would be better to leave eighteen thousand men lying on the field, with no gain, than to come back without a fight. Meade, perhaps recalling Fredericksburg, disputed that logic.[15]

While Union soldiers scaled the face of Missionary Ridge or prepared to cross the Rapidan again, Stanton and Eddie headed west on the Baltimore & Ohio Railroad. The proclamation for Thanksgiving fell that year on Lucy Stanton's seventieth birthday, and on his October visit to Steubenville her oldest son must have promised a little celebration. Eddie had just returned from Gettysburg, where he had listened to Mr. Lincoln deliver a little dedicatory speech at the unfinished soldiers' cemetery. Ellen remained in Washington with the other children. After a night or two in the old house with his mother, Pamphila, and her boys, Stanton hurried back, resuming work the day of the aborted attack at Mine Run.[16]

On his return, Stanton found the president sick with varioloid—a mild form of smallpox. Congressmen were pouring back into Washington for the next session by then, and in his discomfort Lincoln was working on his annual message. Toward the end of that message, he unveiled a new proclamation offering amnesty to broad swaths of citizens and soldiers in the Confederacy if they would merely swear future allegiance to the United States. Worse still, from the perspective of the Radicals on whom Stanton most relied now for political support, Lincoln included effective restoration of ordinary relations, with the right to form a new government in any state where 10 percent of those who voted in 1860 took that oath. His characteristically lenient offer collided violently with the rising Radical intention of reducing the seceded states to conquered provinces when, and if, Confederate armies could be swept from the field. Unsatisfied with Lincoln's resort to emancipation and his organization of a new black army, the disciples of Ben Wade meant to crush their antebellum foes in the halls of Congress, or any who might imitate them in the future, and to replace them with a constituency of Republicans recruited in large measure from the former slave population. The war between Congress and the White House that had subsided the previous winter reopened, throwing Stanton back into the fray as a clandestine combatant.[17]

He apparently tried to engineer a coup for the Radical cause in the late summer, after the military governor of Louisiana presented him with a petition from loyal citizens who wanted to adopt a new constitution and reenter the Union. They had submitted a plan for a convention of "every loyal free white male citizen," and Stanton showed it to Chase, who suggested removing the color barrier. In his instructions to the governor, Stanton revised the wording ambiguously, authorizing a convention of "all the loyal citizens," and Chase observed that the governor was also supplied with the attorney general's opinion that free black men were citizens. Chase gave Stanton so much credit that he may have suggested the plan, which allowed the administration to deny issuing any explicit order to give freedmen the vote: the method certainly bore his brand. Whether the president was even aware of the change is not certain. He had never supported the idea before, and when Nathaniel Banks objected to any introduction of black voting Lincoln gave him full discretion on the matter, but in March of 1864 Lincoln did field a fruitless suggestion for token black suffrage among soldiers and "the very intelligent."[18]

The Radicals who might have most appreciated that suggestion, had they known of it, would nevertheless have denied Lincoln's right to allow the convention. Their disappointment with him encouraged Chase in his own ambitions for the presidency, for which he was already cultivating secret support through his broad network of friends and Treasury Department staff. Stanton found it consistent with his allegiance to the Radicals to show a certain warmth to Chase and his presidential promoters: he took particular pains to extend furloughs and arrange preferential assignments for the son of Henry Ward Beecher, whose newspaper touted Chase as a successor to the president. A couple of weeks later, he requested that Chase serve as godfather to his and Ellen's fourth and last child, Bessie. Conservative observers saw his shift of War Department patronage from moderate Republican newspapers to Radical organs as evidence that he wished Chase to take the nomination from Lincoln. It was Stanton's habit to play both ends against the middle, which would have behooved him to remain cordial and implicitly conspiratorial with a serious competitor for the White House, but Chase's home-state rivalry with Ben Wade dictated discretion, lest he alienate his powerful friends in the Wade circle. On December 6 Stanton invited one of the more prominent members of the Chase team, James Garfield, to dine at the K Street house: he had recently persuaded the president to grant a major general's commission to Garfield, who promptly resigned to take his seat in Congress, but Stanton promised to keep the slot open for him in case he should wish to return.[19] Banker Jay Cooke, the master sales agent for treasury bonds, served as one of Chase's more generous backers, and his newspaper support included the *Ohio State Journal* of Columbus. The half-owner of the *Journal*, Francis Hurtt, was also an army quartermaster whose corruption had brought him to public grief, and, after Burnside arrested Hurtt, Stanton had convened a court martial. Holt assigned the case to another rising star in the judge advocate general's office, Henry Burnett, but the charges against Hurtt leaked into the newspapers, complete with reference to Jay Cooke and Company as parties implicated in the schemes. Stanton took direct control of that indiscretion, rebuking Burnett and eliciting his admission that he did not consider the Cooke firm "criminally connected," except in one minor detail.[20]

The underlying animosities of the presidential race were not Stanton's only distractions. He had also had to devote substantial attention to an essentially personal struggle with Surgeon General William Hammond, whom he thought he had deftly disposed of. Stanton had honed his skills and accumulated an impressive arsenal in the arena of administrative combat, making Hammond a poor match, but Stanton had found it wise never to underestimate an opponent, and to plan carefully for an overwhelming attack. That was the spirit that led him to try to ruin the young doctor.

Hammond had greatly enhanced the efficiency of the medical service, and would have done more but for a lack of War Department support. He proposed an independent ambulance corps, but Stanton refused to endorse it on the ground that army trains were already too long. When Hammond remonstrated with him, Stanton had Halleck belittle the idea by comparing the army's efficiency in removing the wounded with that of the Confederates, who had far fewer ambulances and no organized hospital corps. A bill for such a corps nevertheless went to Congress, probably through Hammond's friends in the Sanitary Commission, but with Stanton's opposition it came to nothing. Then Hammond asked for 150 mules and drivers, for employment of the French cacolet—a chair to transport wounded men, suspended from either side of the mule; Stanton also refused that. Hammond's determined, demanding nature clashed with that of the secretary of war, who would brook no challenge from an underling. Barely a month into his tenure Hammond's friends in the Sanitary Commission started complaining that Stanton was "paralyzing" the new surgeon general through his lethargy in appointing more medical officers, and Hammond must have carried that complaint to them. Stanton detected or deduced as much, and he soon began showing his teeth to the commission, launching a feud with Hammond less than a year after his appointment.[21]

On May 4, 1863, Hammond denounced the heavy doses of calomel administered to victims of dysentery, and ordered the drug stricken from the supply list. That provoked a storm of protest from old-army surgeons and the American Medical Association, which pronounced Hammond's accusation of "wholesale malpractice" unjust. Calomel and "blue pill," two favorite compounds for the treatment of intestinal diseases and fevers, contained heavy concentrations of mercury, and they probably caused more deaths and long-term debility than any other Civil War medicine, but Hammond's assault on their use gave Stanton the excuse he had sought to destroy his troublesome bureau chief.[22]

Stanton immediately started forwarding Hammond complaints against his bureau, and began building a case for dismissal. In July he appointed another new commission to look into Hammond's conduct in office. To chair it he chose Andrew H. Reeder, a former territorial governor of Kansas, whose plan to appropriate the farm of a Kansas settler Hammond had foiled nearly a decade before, when he was a surgeon at Fort Riley: in company with then-captain Nathaniel Lyon, Hammond had interceded against the governor. Reeder's committee never called for Hammond, although it evidently did collect evidence and testimony of a damaging character, and Stanton ignored Hammond's request for a copy of Reeder's final report. Next Stanton sent Hammond on an inspection tour of posts on the southeast coast and in the West; in the meantime, the secretary installed his own personal physician, Joseph Barnes, as the acting surgeon general, purportedly only for the duration of Hammond's absence. Hammond recalled that when he left the War Department on that mission Stanton shook him by both hands, which official Washington had learned to interpret as the secretary's substitute for the kiss of death.[23]

The Hammonds rented a house in Washington on the same street as the Stanton home, and at one point "the pretty Mrs. Hammond" (as the Sanitary Commission treasurer called her) asked Stanton about her husband's apparent demotion. He reportedly replied that he "never dreamed of ousting her husband from the Surgeon-Generalship," but while the good doctor was absent in the West someone ransacked his Washington office and made away with a portion of his records. Then Hammond received an odd reprimand from the adjutant general, at the instigation of the secretary of war, for issuing an order to a medical purveyor after he had been relieved of his responsibilities as surgeon general. Hammond responded directly to Stanton, reminding him that he had issued those orders at Stanton's own directive, but that letter elicited no reply. Concluding that Stanton was trying to provoke his resignation, the combative young man wrote to the president, noting that Stanton had launched an investigation that had no legal basis, and had deprived him of his position without benefit of a trial or a court of inquiry. He asked to be restored to his position, but Lincoln took the matter up with Stanton's ally, Joseph Holt, who ominously suggested a trial.[24]

Hammond's trial would be typical of the tribunals under Stanton and Holt, with a Stanton-friendly officer appointed to preside, and a majority of officers who were either malleable or clearly prejudiced against the defendant. Richard Oglesby, an Illinois Radical, sat as president, while three of the other members were lifelong soldiers over sixty years old, who would be well acquainted with the aged surgeons who almost unanimously despised the upstart Hammond. Stanton's personal friend John Slough, who had proven reliable in the Porter court martial, was called back for this trial. Albion Howe, who was being pushed out of division command in the Army of the Potomac to oversee the artillery depot at Washington, would feel the weight of official disapproval and probably act accordingly, while John Starkweather later enjoyed more favor with Stanton than his competence merited. Of the nine officers on the court, Hammond would later compliment three for their fairness and attention to the evidence; the rest Stanton seemed to have judged correctly, either in their prejudices or their pliability.[25]

Holt did not act as judge advocate, instead assigning a new assistant in his office. John Bingham, Stanton's old Whig foe from Cadiz, had lost his congressional seat in the 1862 electoral massacre of Ohio Republicans. It was likely Secretary Chase, a longtime friend, who tried to secure Bingham a federal judgeship that did not come to fruition, but Stanton may have recommended him as an assistant judge advocate.[26]

The months-long trial eclipsed the more embarrassing concurrent prosecution of Quartermaster Hurtt. Hammond's charges were all dredged up from events in 1862, carefully arranged to create an air of calculated graft and embellished by the evident perjury and forgery of Dr. George Cooper, whom Hammond had removed as medical purveyor in Philadelphia in the fall of 1862. Cooper produced a letter he said he wrote to Hammond under the date of June 15, 1862, accusing the surgeon general of buying shoddy blankets from a contractor as a reward for political support. The prosecution also produced correspondence, out of context, to support its claim that Hammond had insisted on paying exorbitant prices for those blankets, all to defraud the government. Another charge involved unbecoming conduct, based on Hammond's allegedly false explanation to Cooper that he was being removed because General Halleck wanted the place for Louisville purveyor Robert Murray.[27]

When Hammond supplied letters contradicting the claims of malfeasance, the court refused to introduce them, apparently including one rebutting the testimony of a witness then on the stand. Hammond demonstrated that Cooper's accusative letter had to be a forgery, and he produced Cooper's own certificates that the supposedly overpriced, poor-quality blankets were acceptable and sold at the usual rates. He supplied documentation showing that direct purchases had been the custom among his predecessors (as it would remain the habit of his successor), but the court refused to enter it; neither were letters deemed admissible showing Stanton had known of his direct purchases from the outset, and that he had once approved the practice.[28]

Bingham accused the defendant of rejecting a lower price for blankets with a letter offering a moderate discount, although that letter could not have reached Hammond by the time he ordered the more expensive ones. Despite letters from Halleck and Dr. Murray fully corroborating Hammond's assertion that Cooper had been removed to make way for Murray, Bingham harped instead on Halleck's inability to recall telling Hammond that he wanted Murray in Cooper's place. Through misrepresentations and manufactured suspicions, Bingham cultivated only the faintest impression of culpability, but that was all Oglesby's court needed, and in the end Hammond was found guilty. The findings implicitly rejected evidence that Hammond's actions had been justified or authorized in nearly every instance, but the court at least did not confirm the imputations of deliberate fraud and personal gain.[29]

Hammond's defense closed early in May of 1864, and should have led directly to Bingham's reply and the court's deliberation, but the decision did not emerge until late August. Before learning the verdict, Hammond so doubted the impartiality of the court that he and his wife asked to see the president, to present rejected evidence that a fairer mind might find valid. Lincoln refused to see Mrs. Hammond and never responded to her husband's request. Stanton's own enforcers therefore succeeded in having Hammond dismissed, and Lincoln kept clear of the evidence, approving the findings based entirely on Bingham's rebuttal and Holt's one-sided review of the case. In all likelihood the president never even saw the 2,400-page transcript of the proceedings. The portion of the transcript that included Hammond's defense statement is now the only missing segment of the record, and it may have been removed to prevent executive perusal: Holt was specifically accused of a similar ruse in another case, less than a year later.[30]

As he had with General Porter, Holt turned the Hammond trial into a propaganda coup for his chief, countering criticism of Stanton's behavior toward Hammond by portraying the late surgeon general as a callous profiteer. With ready authority from the War Department he published Bingham's reply in a long pamphlet at government expense. Releasing the charges for newspaper regurgitation, Holt included the original allegations that the goods Hammond had bought were of inferior quality or unfit for use, that he bought them knowing as much, and that he had done so to enrich himself through kickbacks from his suppliers. Perhaps to enhance public indignation, he allowed a decimal point to slip two places to the right, inflating the cost of the disputed items from $35,314 to $3,531,400. Holt then falsely announced that the court had found Hammond guilty on all counts, ignoring the acquittal on all charges of fraud and corruption. Alluding to Hammond's "spoliation of the Government treasury," he claimed it was "in part accomplished by the purchase of inferior medical supplies and stores, thus compromising the health and comfort and jeopardizing the lives of the sick and wounded soldiers suffering in the hospitals and upon the battle-fields of the country." Holt's review of the trial appeared in the accommodating *Washington Chronicle* of August 21, and served as Hammond's first notice that he had been convicted and dismissed. Hammond noted that it contained plenty of abuse and misrepresentation, but "not one single jot or tittle of the evidence for the defense." What Hammond called Holt's "*ex parte*" treatment of the entire case mirrored Holt's perversion of the judge advocate's role in his review of the Porter court martial.[31]

In one final, malicious blow, Stanton let it be known that the solicitor of the War Department had ordered the erstwhile surgeon general prosecuted for recovery of the proceeds of his "frauds." As Stanton knew very well, such an order would have been void on its face, because all the evidence of fraud had been rejected, but he seemed determined to create a false impression that would annihilate the doctor's reputation.[32]

The self-righteous tone permeating Holt's review of the Hammond case echoed throughout the trials of army quartermasters and civilian contractors whom Holt and Stanton prosecuted for swindling the government. The hypocrisy of those two emerges with the revelation that they conspired to wring kickbacks out of army contractors for partisan political purposes less than a month after Hammond's conviction. Stanton had long since promised to help Lincoln's friend Joshua F. Speed establish a "loyal" newspaper in Louisville, which is to say a newspaper loyal to Lincoln, and for such projects he was happy to divert advertising funds, but in the final stages of the campaign he also devised a scheme in which quartermasters would choose contractors based on their willingness to pay premiums that amounted to campaign contributions. Stanton issued the instructions to those quartermasters, but Holt appears to have been the manager of this particular extortion in Kentucky. The quartermaster at Louisville tactfully mentioned how illegal that process was, but then offered an alternative that demonstrated his familiarity with ways of skimming money: to meet the requirement that such contracts be publicly advertised, he suggested advertising for much less of a given product than the government wanted, and buying the balance from suppliers who were willing to pay the graft. General Rosecrans participated in the scam, and reported his success directly to Holt.[33] The Kentucky scheme apparently represented only a fraction of the campaign funds extorted from contractors under Stanton's authority.[34]

Having eliminated Hammond, Stanton promoted his friend Barnes to brigadier general and appointed him surgeon general. Barnes had worn his uniform for a quarter of a century, and would retain his new post for nearly twenty more years, but while he was barely eleven years Hammond's senior he represented the old school. Enjoying the support that Stanton had withheld from Hammond, Barnes carried through some of his predecessor's initiatives—leaving his name on the voluminous medical history of the war, for instance—but he also supported and prolonged the outdated methods Hammond had tried to reform. After the war, Barnes disparaged Hammond's "unlucky circular" attacking the use of mercurial medicines, instead defending them with studies and conclusions of 1817 vintage, so army surgeons continued to kill and cripple their patients with heavy metals for years to come. Stanton's vendetta against Hammond stripped the Medical Bureau of a young director whose energy and innovation might have inspired a generation of steady modernization, rather than permitting the regression to harmful traditional practices that Barnes allowed.[35]

In the spring of 1864 a White House visitor observed that Stanton had effectively abdicated as secretary of war, becoming "civil manager of the details of the Department," and his immersion in those details had become habitual by the end of 1863. During periods of relative inactivity he took up the most menial tasks, monitoring everything from the supply of the entire army to furloughs and discharges for individual soldiers. In the latter role he showed himself unduly susceptible to social and political influence: for the soldier-kin of his childhood friends, wealthy bankers, literary lions, Supreme Court justices, senators, or members of powerful newspaper families, Stanton thought nothing of extending a furlough, revoking unpleasant orders, offering an assignment near home, or arranging a special prisoner exchange. If the request were too much to ask, he might present another option: when Radical Thad Stevens asked Stanton to appoint his namesake nephew a sutler for the dismounted cavalry camp near Washington, Stanton went one better and appointed the boy provost marshal over a Pennsylvania district. For such personages Stanton seemed to enjoy dispensing favors, and usually he attended to them personally, making certain that the recipient of the favor knew it.[36]

The poor and friendless saw much less generosity from Stanton. Common folk seeking the discharge of underage runaways met routine refusal, even if they had already sacrificed sons in the war, and those wishing to have a loved one released from captivity were told that the rebels refused further exchanges, or that "special exchanges are not approved." Even battle-scarred generals of suspect politics felt the war minister's impassivity: one brigadier with a faint scent of McClellanism sought reimbursement for medical bills incurred while he was home recovering from wounds, but Stanton refused, sending the wounded officer limping away thinking the secretary of war "a mean fellow." The softhearted president approached Stanton about a poor widow whose son had been fined heavily by a court martial, asking that the boy be allowed to reenlist instead, to reap some benefit from the bounty, but Stanton declined. The raucous fourth-classmen at West Point found the secretary more understanding when their collective misbehavior brought them all to the brink of court martial: he interceded to save them from punishment, perhaps because those plebes included his sister Pamphila's son, whose reinstatement he had already arranged once before.[37]

Stanton's minute involvement reflected his choice not to reappoint either of his additional assistants when their terms expired. Instead, he used military officers for many duties, and commissioned his confidant Charles Dana as an adjutant general, assigning him to special missions. Late in 1863, with Peter Watson glancing covetously at an opportunity in the railroad line and complaining again of his health, Stanton brought Dana in from the field. A clerk later characterized Dana as one of Stanton's "petty tyrants," but he eased the office burden sufficiently that Eddie took a month's vacation with his grandmother and his Aunt Pamphila. In January of 1864 Stanton asked for and received authorization for a second assistant secretary at $3,000 a year, claiming the attempt to do without one had failed, but he simply gave the appointment to Dana, for whom the legislation only formalized the position and offered a pay raise.[38]

Stanton enjoyed much more clerical help than his predecessor. He brought so many new people into the War Department that it required the slapdash addition of third and fourth floors to the department building on Seventeenth Street. Under him the department created several new bureaus, while the existing ones expanded significantly. At the end of 1863, for instance, the chief of ordnance recommended nearly quadrupling his complement of civilian employees.[39]

The superannuated chiefs of War Department bureaus may have aggravated Stanton's burden. Commissary General Joseph Taylor had been a commissioned officer before Stanton's parents met. The chief engineer, Joseph Totten, turned seventy-six in the spring of 1864, and when pneumonia carried him off Stanton installed Richard Delafield, who had entered West Point before Stanton was born. Taylor died before July. The chief of the Ordnance Bureau, James Ripley, and the paymaster general, Timothy Andrews, were both born in 1794. Ripley was forcibly retired in September of 1863, after reporting adversely on the performance of a breech-loading carbine manufactured by George Opdyke, the Radical Republican mayor of New York City: Opdyke complained directly to Stanton, who replied that he was "not satisfied" with Ripley's report, and cryptically assured Opdyke that his assistant, Watson, would make a "more careful examination."[40]

Colonel George Ramsay succeeded Ripley, after some scheming by Stanton. The president insisted on Ramsay, who stood next in rank, while Halleck preferred a certain major and Stanton championed Major Alexander Dyer. In one of his administrative sleights of hand, Stanton installed Lincoln's favorite, but assigned Captain George Balch as Ramsay's chief clerk, using Balch as his surrogate. Ramsay appears not to have demonstrated so much of the instinctive subservience common among the oldest soldiers, and he chafed so at Stanton's imperiously demanding manner and at what he considered Balch's meddling that he, too, departed within a year. Then, finally, Stanton replaced him with Major Dyer—the man he had wanted from the outset.[41]

Like Hammond, Quartermaster General Montgomery Meigs was sent off on a tour of inspection in the West in September of 1863. Charles Halpine, an officer awaiting orders in Washington, wondered why so many bureau heads should be scattered about on errands that could be handled by lesser officers; he concluded that Stanton was shuffling and "guillotining" those just below him to excuse his department's shortcomings. Another of those periodic public cries for Stanton's removal had arisen in the *New York Herald*, and Halpine composed an anonymous newspaper article accusing him of sacrificing his subordinates to save himself. It was the secretary's "last dodge," Halpine suggested.[42]

The chief of the army's new Signal Corps also ran afoul of the secretary of war that autumn. Albert J. Myer, the founder of the corps, committed the faux pas of competing with the U.S. Military Telegraph, which operated under Stanton's direct authority. In September, when Myer advertised for telegraphers, Stanton issued a severe reprimand. Six weeks later the superintendent of Stanton's telegraph service advised either abolishing the Military Telegraph or transferring to it all the telegraphic duties and equipment of the Signal Corps; Colonel Myer immediately followed up with a report emphasizing the services and promise of Signal Corps telegraphers. Barely a week after the dueling reports reached him, Stanton called Myer in for a blistering rebuke, removing him as chief of the corps and sending him into exile at Cairo.[43]

As spring approached, Stanton had to remind his grizzled bureau chiefs to provide enough provisions for an additional half-million troops called for by the president. The previous October Lincoln had appealed for three hundred thousand men, to be drafted if they did not come forth voluntarily by January 5, 1864, and they had not come. Rather than impose an immediate draft, Lincoln had issued a second proclamation on February 1, demanding a total of five hundred thousand men but extending the draft date to March 10. After prodding his quartermaster and commissary generals to calculate the food and supplies that would be required for so many new soldiers, the secretary warned Senate finance committee chairman William Pitt Fessenden that these new levies would quickly deplete the congressional appropriation for the War Department, and that precipitated a joint resolution for another $25 million in April.[44]

That huge draft call came exactly a fortnight after Indiana's governor, Oliver Morton, had warned Stanton that "considerations of the most vital character demand that the War shall be substantially ended within the present year." Morton probably meant that if the war still seemed undecided by the quadrennial election of November, the Democrats would inevitably field a peace candidate and prevail. Raising another five hundred thousand troops in time for the spring campaign must have seemed certain to overwhelm the enemy in both major theaters, and the startling February 1 proclamation had represented Lincoln's answer to Morton's concern.

The March 10 draft deadline threatened to influence the closely watched New Hampshire election of March 8, so Stanton undertook another heroic effort to secure a Republican victory through War Department manipulation. Added to arbitrary arrests and federal interference with earlier elections, the draft had aggravated New Hampshire's traditionally conservative voters, giving the administration even more cause to worry about losing the state in 1864 than in 1863. Defeat there would have encouraged dissent elsewhere, so—in concert with Governor Joseph Gilmore—Stanton concocted a scheme to neutralize the impact of the draft call in the Granite State. He declared that every man recruited since July would count against the half-million-man call of February 1, essentially forgiving the July draft quota, and the surplus recruits would be applied toward what Stanton now characterized as a 200,000-man draft of February 1. Three weeks before the election Gilmore alerted the New Hampshire press that the state had met its quota, which turned out to be false even under Stanton's contorted formula. That contradicted the understanding of Lincoln's proclamation in other states, and seriously impeded recruiting nationwide. Rhode Island's governor asked for a similar indulgence, and Vermont's adjutant general also pointed out the discrepancy, complaining that the news had all but stopped recruiting and the raising of local bounties in his state. Eventually Stanton had to reinterpret the February 1 draft proclamation for all states, and reduce their quotas accordingly.[45]

To supplement the draft-quota artifice, Stanton again flooded New Hampshire with as many loyal Republicans as he could find in uniform. The repression of dissident opinion in the army and persistent administration propaganda had vastly improved the reliability of soldier votes, but Stanton still felt the need for careful selection. Governor Gilmore's sly son-in-law, William E. Chandler, visited Stanton to ask about furloughs for New Hampshire soldiers: Chandler fully understood that the War Department distinction between "well-behaved and viciously inclined soldiers" in distributing that privilege served as the code for political reliability. Stanton furloughed swarms of troops from guard duty at Point Lookout military prison, in Maryland, and from hospitals in New England. A plan to reenlist willing veterans for another three years included the offer of a thirty-day furlough, and the furloughs of most of New Hampshire's reenlisted veterans were scheduled to coincide with the election: Stanton extended the time for one regiment, to carry them a couple of days beyond the election. On top of that, Chandler conspired with the captains of two heavy artillery companies at peaceful Fort Constitution to identify and furlough all the Republican voters in the garrison, sending them home for the election while the "Copperheads and minors" remained behind to guard Portsmouth Harbor from nonexistent naval threats. One newspaper warned readers that Republicans were also printing fraudulent Democratic tickets with the name of the gubernatorial candidate cleverly misspelled, so they would be invalidated if cast as ballots.[46]

"The Granite State has uttered her voice in favor of the war policy of the Government," Gilmore informed Stanton on March 9. This time a comfortable margin showed that all the precaution had not been necessary, including the subterfuge about draft quotas, but the awkward recalculation required by the detection of Stanton's trick forced an entire new draft. Pressed by Stanton, with the help of Seward, the president reluctantly issued yet another draft proclamation on March 15 for two hundred thousand troops, to make up for most of those shaved from the previous call in consonance with Stanton's ploy. Freshly reelected, Gilmore made a hasty trip to Washington to consult with Stanton on how to avoid admitting that the state's draft quota suddenly fell short, and he returned with permission to raise a regiment of cavalry, offering special state bounties. His quota would be satisfied when he completed the 1,200-man 1st New Hampshire Cavalry, and Stanton did not badger him about the balance.[47]

On the afternoon that New Hampshire citizens and soldiers went to the polls, the train from Relay House pulled into the Washington rail depot and disgorged three rumpled officers, bleary-eyed after a four-day journey from Chattanooga, No one had been sent to the station to meet them, but General Grant and his two staff officers made their way to Willard's Hotel—where, that evening, someone came to fetch them to a grand reception at the White House. As Grant already knew, Congress had resurrected the full rank of lieutenant general, dormant since George Washington shed his uniform at the close of the Revolution. Since then no general but Winfield Scott had worn the three-starred epaulettes even by brevet—and, as Grant also knew, he had been the presumed recipient throughout the debate on the bill. He enjoyed broad support for his victories at Vicksburg and Chattanooga, the Radicals embracing him all the more over his enthusiasm for raising black troops. When Grant entered the reception room a crowd formed, and through it waded Abraham Lincoln, who took him by the hand. After a dizzying swirl of introductions and congratulations, Lincoln sent for Stanton.[48]

The president had thought of bringing Grant east months before, fearing only jealousies like those John Pope had initiated in the Army of the Potomac, but as general in chief Grant would likely surmount those regional antagonisms, especially if an Eastern general continued to command that army. Dana had returned from Chattanooga lauding him more enthusiastically than ever, and Stanton had sent General Hunter to Chattanooga in December for a second opinion on Grant's character. Hunter had come back in December, full of praise. Impelled perhaps by the accident in New Orleans, rumors had carried north again about Grant's continued drinking, but Hunter claimed—as inaccurately as Dana, but perhaps with less intent to deceive—that he didn't drink at all. Halleck, who went down in history as Grant's subversive critic, knew that Grant's promotion would displace him: he had nevertheless assured the War Department's intellectual-on-retainer, Francis Lieber, that Grant was "a fine man and a good officer" and he must have given similar opinions to the secretary of war and the president. The Senate debate demonstrated that Grant had retired all administration doubts by February, and early on the afternoon of March 9 Grant accepted his commission in an awkward little ceremony in the cabinet room.[49]

With the arrival of Grant, Stanton retired again (and finally) from the realm of military operations. Grant recognized the differing roles of the secretary of war and the general in chief, and he observed those distinctions, so he posed no threat to Stanton's control of the department and (at least for the present) he excited none of the hostile rivalry that McClellan had. Unlike Halleck, Grant never hesitated to make decisions, so neither did he require prodding. He came to Washington with no intention of remaining at army headquarters, wishing to avoid political interference with his authority, and while he always considered and tried to accommodate the wishes of his civilian superiors, and acknowledged their legitimate oversight, he preferred to conduct operations without their intrusion. That left Stanton in comfortable command of his domain, and gave him the additional time to engage in the peripheral political intrigues that seemed to attract him.

One of those intrigues involved a reorganization of the Army of the Potomac. Still seeking an active assignment after several brief missions, General Hunter came to see Stanton before Grant's arrival and asked if he might have a corps in the Army of the Potomac. Stanton replied that Meade resisted the appointment of anyone outside "his own particular set," and while it would have been his preference to impose "a complete and radical reorganization" on that army he encountered too much resistance. Hunter replied that the Army of the Potomac appeared to be as much under the command of McClellan as ever, adding that it served mainly as a promotional machine for a McClellan presidency. Stanton suggested telling that to the president, and Hunter later claimed that he did. That may have softened the resistance Stanton had mentioned, and he called Meade into Washington to discuss the reorganization. Perhaps Stanton also spoke to Ben Wade about how to purge some of the more entrenched McClellan partisans, for a few days later one of Meade's corps commanders told Wade's Committee on the Conduct of the War that the Army of the Potomac had too many corps: it was too difficult to find five good corps commanders, said General Warren, and too cumbersome to wield five corps in battle. Less than two weeks after Warren spoke, a general order went out to Meade's army, breaking up the First and Third Corps and distributing their divisions among the Second, Fifth, and Sixth. John Newton and William French, the commanders left without corps, were both survivors of the McClellan circle, as was George Sykes of the Fifth Corps, which went to Warren. Morale in the two broken corps plunged momentarily, but—despite the political motivation behind it—the consolidation boosted overall competence in corps command.[50]

Stanton, who had recently held a "very satisfactory" strategy meeting with Wade's committee members, may also have offered support for the Radical assault on General Meade himself. Stanton knew which of Meade's former subordinates held the stoutest grudges against him, and the committee called his worst enemies first. Dan Sickles, Stanton's fast friend, bore Meade's blame for exceeding his orders on the second day at Gettysburg and creating near-fatal havoc on the left flank; Abner Doubleday, an industrious Radical, resented Meade for removing him from corps command; Albion Howe, who was faithfully meeting expectations as a member of Surgeon General Hammond's court martial, had just been deposed from division command in Meade's army. Those three supplied the anticipated testimony against Meade, and at the close of Howe's second day of testimony Wade and Senator Chandler convened with the president and secretary of war to demand Meade's replacement. They suggested restoring Hooker, which Meade thought Stanton might resist, but apparently he did not.[51]

It happened that Meade was in the city that day, and had heard all the charges made by Sickles and Doubleday. The "whole town" was talking about it, he found. Wade had been content to condemn him without a hearing, as he usually was in the case of those who differed with him politically, but he could hardly dispute the justice of at least pretending to hear him out. On Saturday, March 5, Meade met Wade alone, for a three-hour interview about his tenure at the head of the army, at the end of which Wade asked if he had anything to add. Meade replied that he might have a lot more to say if he knew what the witnesses against him had told the committee. Wade denied there were any allegations against Meade, and revealed nothing; he remarked only that his questions had covered all the controversial points. Before Meade went back to the army he saw Stanton, who apprised him of "much pressure from a certain party" to eliminate him in favor of Hooker, as though to absolve himself of any association with the effort.[52]

Radical newspapers persisted in flailing Meade for lethargy and timidity in the aftermath of Gettysburg, repeating Sickles's accusations in particular. The following Friday Meade returned for a second round of testimony, again finding only Wade, who wished to see Hooker reinstated; some of the committee had shown signs of sympathy with Meade, and Wade pretended to be friendly himself, but by meeting the general alone he could later misrepresent the tone and flavor of his testimony. Afterward Meade saw Stanton, who had already talked with Wade about the latest interview. With the superlative vocabulary Stanton always seemed to employ at his most insincere, he assured Meade that Wade had described his testimony as "the clearest statement that had ever been made to the committee," and "perfectly satisfactory." Three more weeks of hearings demonstrated the falsity of that statement, as did the unrelenting newspaper campaign, which betrayed leakage of the criticism heard by the committee. When the *New York Herald* published an account of Gettysburg that obviously came from Sickles, Meade asked for a court of inquiry, but Stanton refused, contending that "no attention should be paid to such a person as Sickles." Stanton can well be imagined speaking derogatorily of a friend to one of his antagonists, but it is just as likely that he sought to guard Sickles from the embarrassing revelations an inquiry might provide.[53]

Meade worried that Grant would replace him, but the generals Grant knew came mainly from the West, and he still wished to avoid a regional clash. In his third week as lieutenant general he did order Charles Stone up from Louisiana to await orders at Cairo, and he evidently entertained a notion of putting Stone to use in the Army of the Potomac. Stone had gone with Nathaniel Banks on his ill-fated campaign up the Red River, and by the time he received Grant's order Stanton had intervened, arbitrarily mustering Stone out as a brigadier general of volunteers and reducing the importance of any assignment Grant might give him. As with Surgeon General Hammond, when Stanton had wronged someone that badly he seemed to think it necessary to destroy him—to remove his victim from the arena and deprive him of any opportunity for vindication or vengeance.[54]

While Grant prepared the various armies for a coordinated campaign against the enemy in all theaters, Stanton stockpiled ammunition for a similar offensive against political opponents, whom he would collectively stigmatize as traitors during the presidential campaign. The furloughs of reenlisted veterans had sparked a rash of mob actions north of the Ohio, with soldiers sacking the offices of Democratic newspapers, threatening violence against Democratic officeholders, and assaulting citizens who supported them. Partisan confrontations had led to numerous shooting incidents, with occasional fatalities, and the War Department painted all of them as Copperhead uprisings, even when soldiers had clearly provoked the mayhem. Through the sprawling network of provost marshals, Stanton had learned of a roving organizer of secret societies by the name of Phineas C. Wright, who was boarding at a hotel in Detroit from which he was ostensibly plotting to foment another uprising across the Old Northwest. On April 20 Stanton ordered the arrest of Wright, who went quietly into a cell at Fort Lafayette, but that mendacious dreamer provided the material for an ornate charade that would pay political benefits for more than a year.[55]

Like George Bickley, who had originated the antebellum Knights of the Golden Circle as a spontaneous brotherhood of dues-paying members, Wright appears to have been part vagabond, part charlatan, and part megalomaniac. He, too, tried to spawn his own secret fraternal order from time to time, and the political repression of 1862 and 1863 finally allowed him to sell the idea of a clandestine organization. Wright's "Order of American Knights" amounted to little more than a Democratic version of the Union League chapters springing up across the country—politically harmonious social clubs, in which a few may have hoped to imitate the Union Leagues' propaganda function. The core of the order consisted of a handful of schemers who imagined more ambitious ventures but could never agree on them, and it had already collapsed as an organization when the provost detail seized Wright.[56]

The political repression that lent the would-be brotherhood what popularity it did enjoy survived long after the dissolution of the Order of American Knights. Wright's own lengthy incarceration, without formal charges or hearing, illustrated the ease with which Stanton's prison system could swallow a citizen, suppressing and ignoring his every protest and plea; military commissions conducted the trials anyway, with the results effectively predetermined. Holt simply filed Wright's request for a jury trial and apparently intercepted his outgoing letters, thereby controlling his communications with any counsel. Less controversial prisoners with influential friends might move the secretary of war to reconsider, or they could appeal over his head, but even that frequently failed. One of Stanton's former law students wrote from Wheeling, seeking the release of a cousin who had been arrested by the governor of West Virginia: the man's only crime consisted of vocal disagreement with the administration, but that was enough to brand him "disloyal," and Stanton refused to let him go. The arrests usually bore a decidedly partisan flavor. The only Republicans taken into custody were generally arrested by mistake or through misunderstandings and were quickly released, but even the most exalted Democrats had to watch their tongues. A friend of Samuel Barlow's who worked in the Interior Department and heard much inside gossip warned that Stanton's detectives considered Barlow and Democratic Party leaders fair game for "summary acts," hinting that even George McClellan ought to be careful what he said and did. Barlow complained to Postmaster General Blair that someone in the post office routinely opened his mail.[57]

Union prisoners in Southern hands gave Stanton more trouble than anyone he held in custody. Remembering the ban on officer exchanges from late in 1862, Union officers confined in Libby Prison already blamed him for their prolonged incarceration, and he was beginning to feel their relatives' smoldering anger. In December of 1863 that pressure had persuaded him to abandon his pretended principle and authorize Halleck to offer Lee an exchange for everyone then held at Richmond, but Lee would not consent without agreement on the disputed exchanges from Vicksburg and Port Hudson.[58]

Some weeks later, Ben Butler, commanding then at Fort Monroe, learned that the Richmond prisoners were about to be sent to the new camp at Andersonville, and he proposed sending his cavalry dashing up the James River into Richmond to free them. Along the way, his raiders would torch as much of the industrial capacity of the Confederate capital as they could, and swing down Clay Street to seize Jefferson Davis. Butler undertook this raid with the knowledge and approval of the secretary of war, and perhaps of the president as well, for Lincoln had commented nine months before, with evident favor, on a suggestion of burning at least the government portion of Richmond and taking Davis prisoner. The Army of the Potomac cooperated with Butler by launching a diversion along the Rapidan at the cost of 270 men, but Butler's horsemen retired as soon as they met unexpected resistance. Butler reported that a deserter had forewarned the rebels. "Perhaps there will be better luck next time," Stanton replied.[59]

The next time came within days. One of Meade's cavalry commanders, Judson Kilpatrick, suggested making a raid on Richmond from the Rapidan, with a view to springing all the Richmond prisoners. The president called him to Washington, had a chat with him, and sent him to Stanton to discuss the operation in detail. The plantation house called Fairfield, where Kilpatrick's division quartermaster made his headquarters during the winter encampment at Stevensburg, was the home of Stanton's grandfather, Thomas Norman—where Stanton had visited in his youth; the subject may have come up during the interview. Kilpatrick proposed descending on the Confederate capital with a strong mounted column and splitting his force to assail the city from both sides of the James River. Thousands of enlisted men shivered on Belle Isle, in the middle of the river, while the officers' prison at the Libby warehouse stood near the waterfront on the left bank; these he hoped to liberate, besides doing some damage to the enemy's communications and transportation. Stanton would almost surely have raised Butler's idea of capturing the Confederate president, and his contempt for his enemies may have allowed some discussion of the easier task of outright assassination, but he would never have recorded that part of the program on paper. Enthralled at the thought of freeing the prisoners, or disposing of Jeff Davis, Stanton ordered Kilpatrick to submit a detailed plan. Meade's cavalry chief doubted the raid could succeed, but during one of Meade's visits to Washington Stanton divulged his and the president's anxiety about the prisoners, so Meade felt obliged to accept Kilpatrick's wild idea.[60]

The raid promptly came to grief. Meade arranged an infantry demonstration on Lee's left, allowing Kilpatrick to slip around his right flank and ride for Richmond with 3,600 troopers. Secrecy deluded even corps staff officers into supposing he was headed all the way to Georgia, although some enlisted men knew he would strike for Richmond to free the prisoners. All went well until Kilpatrick split off a few hundred men under twenty-one-year-old Colonel Ulric Dahlgren, son of the admiral, who was to cross the James west of Richmond while Kilpatrick attacked the city from the north, on the Brook Turnpike. Rain had raised the river too high for Dahlgren to ford, but when he heard the firing on Kilpatrick's front he made his own feeble attack from the west, only to be discouraged by a collection of local militia. He turned to join Kilpatrick, who had already given up and run for it himself. In his haste, Dahlgren led his vanguard at such a pace that those behind lost them in the darkness, veering off in another direction and cutting their way to the east, where they finally reached Kilpatrick. Dahlgren, who was already missing a leg from the Gettysburg campaign, picked his way over back roads at the head of a hundred men until he rode straight into an ambush, and when he showed fight Virginia militia shot him out of the saddle, dead. Most of his followers surrendered. In his own flight, Kilpatrick had suffered losses, as well, and a surly George Meade learned that the raid had cost his army 340 men, 583 horses, 644 breech-loading shoulder arms, 516 revolvers, and a long list of other equipment, with nothing to show for it.[61]

Political embarrassment added a bitter touch to the affair. Handwritten orders found on Dahlgren's body suggested the capture or killing of "the rebel leader Davis and his traitorous crew." An unsigned order issued as though in preparation for the raid explained that once Dahlgren's men had entered Richmond "it must be destroyed and Jeff. Davis and cabinet killed." The discovery threw Richmond into a fury, provoking an indignant letter from Lee to Meade and frustrating rebel soldiers in the ranks who longed to "carry fire and sword" into Northern territory. Confronted by Meade,

Kilpatrick denied that Dahlgren had "published" any such address to his men. He insisted that the orders he approved had lacked the instructions to destroy the city and kill the Confederate leaders, and stressed that he had given Dahlgren no instructions of that sort. Neither had he received any such orders from his own superiors, Kilpatrick added.[62]

With many associates, including Holt and Dana, Stanton used personal interviews to convey those wishes he did not care to commit to paper. Such nebulous hints lent denial the grace of technical truth—not that Judson Kilpatrick had any aversion to an outright lie. Dahlgren's papers, and especially the unsigned address that might have been intended for oral delivery to four hundred men at the Richmond city limits, probably reflected the real spirit of the raid as it had filtered down from Kilpatrick's conversation with Stanton.

On the same day that Meade responded to Lee's inquiry, Stanton's stern attitude on prisoner exchanges surfaced in an order issued by Grant, prohibiting any further exchanges until the claimed deficiencies from the Vicksburg and Port Hudson paroles had been matched by repatriated Union prisoners; he also insisted on equal exchange privileges for black soldiers. Those impossible conditions effectively represented a refusal to exchange any prisoners at all. Grant's instructions intruded on a realm of policy that Stanton had jealously reserved for himself until that point, but it burdened the general with the responsibility for a decision that would kill many thousands of men.[63]

Grant stood at the brink of his spring campaign when he announced the end of prisoner exchanges, leaving his soldiers little hope if they fell into enemy hands. The burgeoning prison pens in the South cast a daunting shadow over the possibility of capture, and similar crowding beset Northern prisons. Before the Army of the Potomac even moved, eleven thousand rebel captives occupied the sand spit at Point Lookout. The same number of Union prisoners had already poured into the stockade at Andersonville, Georgia, with hundreds more arriving daily.[64]

One way to address the prisoner problem was to overwhelm the enemy and force a capitulation. Toward that end Stanton tried to bolster the Army of the Potomac with as many veteran troops for the spring campaign as he could find, and five governors in the West offered to raise tens of thousands of summer soldiers who might take over for garrisons in the rear. Governors always found short-term levies easier to fill, and if hundred-day prison guards and rear-echelon garrison troops could relieve a hundred thousand experienced soldiers for duty in the field, it seemed probable that the Confederate army would face an irresistible force when the shooting started. Stanton first asked Grant for his views, and he approved. With that opinion Stanton endorsed the plan, and on his recommendation the president accepted the proposal. Quartermaster General Meigs calculated that it would cost something under $19 million to pay and equip that many men for a season of soldiering, not counting weapons, and Stanton added some generous padding to that estimate, asking his friend Senator Wilson to push through another appropriation of $25 million. The money came, and soon the summer regiments began filling up. In Ohio, John Brough fulfilled his promise immediately by calling up some of his National Guard regiments. Although mobilization gave some of Ohio's upper crust an unpleasant surprise, in other states hordes of eager boys well below the age of military service welcomed the call.[65]

Thus far the army was supposed to have enrolled no one under the age of eighteen except musicians, and then only with the permission of a parent or guardian—although the mustering officer sometimes circumvented that requirement by signing as guardian for real or pretended orphans. The need for manpower had grown so acute by February of 1864 that Senator Wilson introduced a new bill, likely after consultation with Stanton, permitting boys as young as sixteen to enlist as private soldiers with parental consent. That precipitated a flurry of appeals from parents who asserted that their sons had enlisted against their wishes, most of which Stanton rejected or ordered rejected. So many boys under sixteen filled those hundred-day regiments, and began slipping into the volunteer regiments, that Stanton had to ask for a new law providing for the dismissal of any officer who mustered an underage recruit. That law may have driven many mustering officers to demand better proof of age or permission, for the stream of parental complaints dwindled, but the penalties for that offense had to be stiffened with a $1,000 fine and a two-year prison sentence at the next session of Congress. The sincerity of Stanton's desire for compliance may have been questionable, as well, for he finally lowered the army's minimum height requirement from five feet, three inches to five feet, even. A greater proportion of adult males may have fallen between those measurements then than later, but the reduction would more often have accommodated adventurous lads in their early teens. With so many potential soldiers hanging back from service, the army needed every man willing to fight, and perhaps every stripling.[66]

14

MINISTER OF PROPAGANDA

A lack of concert among far-flung Union armies had abetted the rebellion for three years. The summer campaigns of 1861 had flourished and flickered out independently, while hesitation, mishap, and disagreement prevented the largest army from taking the field with its smaller counterparts the following February. Two major offensives did begin together late in April of 1863, coinciding more by default than by design, but it was Ulysses Grant who introduced the concept of multiple, simultaneous incursions that would prevent Confederates from shifting their own forces.

Grant opened the 1864 campaign with coordinated offensives in nearly every theater. By the first of May Franz Sigel occupied Winchester, on his way up the Shenandoah Valley, while William Averell led a cavalry column out of Charleston, West Virginia, for a raid on the salt mines of southwestern Virginia. The following day George Crook started a division of infantry on a parallel course from West Virginia to cut the Virginia & Tennessee Railroad, and as Crook's men shouldered their knapsacks Ben Butler feinted up the York River toward Richmond. On May 4 Butler pulled that punch and began transporting his troops up the James River on steamers to City Point and Bermuda Hundred, ten miles above Petersburg and fifteen miles below Richmond. That same day the Army of the Potomac, with Burnside's recruit-heavy Ninth Corps in tow, crossed the Rapidan and swung west, hoping to cut Lee off from Richmond as Meade had tried at Mine Run. Two days later, in north Georgia, Sherman started maneuvering against Joe Johnston, who had taken over the shaken fragments of Bragg's Army of Tennessee.[1]

Meade ran into trouble when the head of his columns failed to clear the Wilderness by nightfall of the first day. This dense second-growth forest bordered both sides of the Orange Turnpike and Orange Plank Road west of Chancellorsville, where Joe Hooker had met his match. With an army barely half the size of Meade's, Lee struck the Yankees on both roads, holding them fast and even driving them back here and there on May 5 while he waited for Longstreet's corps, just back from Tennessee. The next day Longstreet launched a powerful assault on Meade's left, at the intersection of the plank road and the Brock Road, and the fighting turned as fierce as any the Eastern armies had ever seen. At the Brock Road, the Vermont brigade of the Sixth Corps was cut nearly in half: a man from the 2nd Vermont described his regiment's front line melting like wax, claiming that his regiment lost 364 men in less than half an hour. Longstreet's own men wounded him—the luckiest bullet of the battle, for the Yankees, and their line held.

Grant, who was traveling with Meade's army, waited through most of May 7 for another attack, and that evening he slipped to his left along the Brock Road, toward Spotsylvania Court House. Confederates beat him to that hamlet, and for two weeks he hammered at them in one entrenched position after another. On May 12 massed ranks of blue uniforms rolled out of the morning mists to swallow a protuberant salient in Lee's line, complete with two rebel generals and a couple of thousand of their men, but the long struggle at Spotsylvania began to look like a serious roadblock before it ended. The astronomical cost in human life only worsened the frustration, and Grant started stripping the big heavy artillery regiments from the Washington forts to replace his staggering losses. In his first month campaigning against Lee, he would accumulate more casualties than the Army of the Potomac had suffered under McClellan in all of 1862. One new battalion could muster only 130 of its original 700 men by the end of the first week.[2]

Butler fared no better. He missed an early opportunity to seize Petersburg, sending a cavalry raid in that direction to burn a bridge or two, but his infantry only threatened the city from the far side of the Appomattox, skirmishing inconsequentially with a much weaker force. While rebel reinforcements raced toward Petersburg from the Carolinas, Butler turned his attention to Richmond, his primary goal. Pierre G. T. Beauregard, commanding below the James, surprised the Federals at Drewry's Bluff on May 16, with three divisions sweeping out of a thick fog and putting them to flight, scooping up guns, flags, and hundreds of Yankee prisoners, including a brigadier general. Meanwhile, Petersburg's defenders fumbled a chance to thrash the smaller portion of Butler's Army of the James north of the Appomattox, but both of Butler's wings retreated to the safety of Bermuda Hundred, settling into an innocuous torpor.[3]

Down in Georgia, Sherman maneuvered Johnston out of his first stronghold, at Rocky Face Ridge, by distracting him in front with two of his armies while the third marched around Johnston's left, toward the rail town of Resaca, to cut his railroad communication with Atlanta. After repelling the frontal assaults, Johnston recognized the threat to his left and rear, withdrawing to a strong position between two rivers at Resaca. There he battled twice his numbers for two more days, but on the morning of

May 16 Sherman's troops pushed forward to find that the Confederates had decamped, after detecting another flanking movement.[4]

As of May 17, the news from the front that had reached Washington and New York offered plenty of gloom. Grant seemed locked in an endless struggle with Lee, and that contest preoccupied the public consciousness. Butler had been chastised and neutralized in spectacular fashion, and at last report Johnston was still successfully resisting Sherman's legions on the Rocky Face-Resaca line. The only other major offensive had been Nathaniel Banks's foray up the Red River in Louisiana, from which he had returned in much greater haste, with far fewer men than he had taken, having accomplished nothing. Along with that appearance of stalemate came stories of tens of thousands of men killed and maimed from the Rapidan to the Red, and the exodus of those well-trained heavy artillerymen from the forts around the capital left a feeling of insecurity there. It was at that juncture, on the morning of May 18, that the *New York World* and the *Journal of Commerce*, both conservative sheets, published a discouraging proclamation supposedly signed by the president and William Seward, conceding with heavy heart that Grant's "first Virginia campaign" was "virtually closed." Besides announcing yet another call for four hundred thousand troops, the decree appealed in solemn tones for a day of "fasting, humiliation, and prayer" over the defeats and delays. Most readers seemed taken in by the spurious proclamation, and it sent the price of gold soaring. Remarking on that result, Gideon Welles diagnosed the hoax as a conspiracy of rebels and gold speculators. He was half right.[5]

John Dix, in New York, telegraphed Secretary Seward to determine whether the suspicious announcement really was a fraud. Seward dashed into the War Department around noon to find out if anything like that had passed over the telegraph, but it had not. He asked if Stanton had closed down the two Democratic papers that had published the piece, but Stanton had just learned of it himself, and Seward urged him to have them suspended promptly. Stanton wasted no time, drafting an order for Dix to arrest the editors, proprietors, and publishers of the *World* and the *Journal*, and to post guards in the offices to prevent any further production. Lincoln dated and signed the order, and it reached Dix that afternoon. In the president's name, but perhaps without his knowledge, Stanton instructed Dix to take possession of the Independent Telegraph Company in New York and arrest its managers and operators, all on the unsubstantiated assumption that the company had been involved in the deception.[6]

The suppression of a newspaper did not disturb Stanton as much as it did others in the cabinet, or even as much as it usually troubled the president. Nearly a year before, General Burnside had shut down the *Chicago Times* over its strident editorial response to his arrest and trial of Clement

Vallandigham, and to the president's implicit approval of those proceedings. Welles thought the entire cabinet recoiled at the idea of closing a newspaper, and Lincoln had hinted broadly that he wanted Burnside to rescind the order. Stanton made that request, but he commended Burnside's motives and implied that he might do something similar again when "immediate action" was required—although he added that, when time allowed, the president wanted to know if Burnside felt the need to arrest citizens or suppress newspapers.[7]

Perhaps thinking of the impending presidential election, and the prominence the two New York papers would occupy in the opposition debate, Stanton stood ready to put them out of business, and to consign the editors to the tender mercies of military justice. The order he prepared for Lincoln's signature had specified that the newspapermen should be held in "close custody" until they could be tried before a military commission, and it was Stanton who would determine when that might be. He, too, might choose the officers of the commission. General Dix had already begun investigating the hoax, and he found that the newspapers in question, as well as the *New York Herald*, had all received a copy of the proclamation on foolscap-sized tissue paper like that distributed by the Associated Press: the telegraph did not seem to be involved at all. The *Herald* had printed a number of papers with the proclamation, Dix added, but had learned of the deceit before those papers went out. The editors of the *World* had also announced the fraud in their bulletin as soon as they knew of it, and offered a $500 reward for the name of the author. Dix expected to find the real culprits, and wondered whether the president might not want to suspend his arrest order.[8]

Stanton wanted to hear nothing of that sort. He refused to modify the order—or, apparently, to even apprise the president of Dix's discovery, let alone ask whether he wished to reconsider. He simply told Dix that he should have obeyed the directive instantly. Dix, a personal friend to Stanton's family, promised to comply, but Stanton responded with yet more reproof. The publication amounted to a treasonable act, he lectured, adding that everyone associated with the production of the offending newspapers shared equal guilt. "You were not directed to make any investigation," he went on, "but to execute the President's order; the investigation was to be made by a military commission." Stanton had composed that order, however, and may have pressed the president to approve such severe language—if he even did approve it. Stanton had already selected an officer to conduct an investigation, as it turned out, but four hours after Dix first alerted him to his discoveries Stanton's sleuth also concluded that the fraud had begun in Washington, without the complicity of the editors. Clearly disappointed that he could not use the incident to quash some of the more hostile newspapers in the nation, a sheepish Stanton let Dix know of the findings, adding that if that was also

Dix's understanding (which he already knew to be the case) he could suspend the arrests. The newspapermen and Samuel Barlow, who came under immediate suspicion for his interest in the *World*, were all released, but the perfectly innocent employees of the Independent Telegraph Company still went to Fort Lafayette for a couple of days.[9]

So long as the bogus proclamation seemed to originate with the Democratic press, Stanton denounced it as a "great national crime" and intended to prosecute it fully. He abandoned such hyperbole when it emerged that the forger had been a reporter for the friendly *New York Times*, who had planned to make a killing on the gold market: that scuttled the propaganda value of the incident, ending Stanton's interest in the case. The reporter, James Howard, followed the perplexed telegraphers into Fort Lafayette, lingering there three months. Henry Ward Beecher appealed for Howard's release, which the president wished to grant so long as Stanton was "satisfied," and at that gesture of executive deference Stanton uttered no objection. There the affair quietly ended.[10]

While Stanton hunted for ammunition to use against Democrats, congressional Radicals prepared for a struggle within their own party, turning their attention to the president himself. The generosity of the amnesty offer and Reconstruction plan outlined in his last message to Congress had alarmed them, and they bridled over his claim of executive authority to restore the seceded states to the Union. Henry Winter Davis, a Radical and freshman congressman from Baltimore who had attended Kenyon with Stanton, introduced a bill in the House that would have empowered Congress to readmit states. His position effectively recognized secession as an accomplished fact, rather than a legally void action, as Lincoln had always maintained. In Radical eyes, the rebellious states had relinquished their statehood, and once conquered they had to be readmitted like any new territory, with congressional approval.[11]

That contradicted the reasoning that had justified the war thus far—namely, that the states had no right to leave the Union, and had not done so: as conservatives saw it, insurgents had commandeered the governments of those states. Davis's bill instead implied agreement with secessionists who considered their states out of the Union, but it served the purposes of those who wanted to see a more punitive peace, as well as those who wished to ensure emancipation and establish a political presence among the freed slaves. Lincoln had insisted all along, with evident candor despite occasional appearances to the contrary, that his principal war aim was to restore the Union. His proclamation on emancipation had nominally freed most slaves in the Confederacy, but it had not declared an end to slavery nationwide, and Lincoln had always regarded outright abolition as the prerogative of the states, by individual initiative or constitutional amendment. Davis's proposal required any state seeking readmission to first adopt a constitution forever prohibiting slavery. He also barred anyone from voting or participating in a constitutional convention who had served in the government of the Confederacy or any of its states, and anyone who had voluntarily borne arms against the United States: former rebel soldiers would have to prove they had been forced to fight.[12]

The House passed the bill by a vote of 73–59 on May 4, just as Meade's troops began looking for campsites in the Wilderness. Pressed by Davis to "do something for emancipation," Ben Wade took it up in the Senate, but it was not until July 1 that he introduced the House bill to provide a republican form of government for "certain States whose governments have been usurped or overthrown." The very title of the bill refuted the claim of its sponsors, who denied the status of statehood to any portion of the Confederacy, and Gratz Brown of Missouri proposed an amendment that all but emasculated the legislation by restoring most of the Reconstruction authority to the president. Brown's amendment passed after long debate in stifling heat—John Carlile of Virginia called the Senate chamber a "furnace" that day—and with that dramatic change the bill passed. When the House took up the amended bill the next day, Davis secured a call for a conference committee, and late that afternoon, with hungry senators leaving the chamber and the bill's opponents clamoring for a dinner recess, Wade deftly moved that the Senate "recede" from the amendment and adopt the original House version. He won by a slim majority, 18–14, with 17 senators absent.[13]

On the Fourth of July the president and John Hay visited the Capitol. The House of Representatives had a tradition of reading the Declaration of Independence on the last day of the session, and Hay seemed amused when Samuel S. Cox, a conservative from Ohio, sarcastically objected that the Declaration was an "insurrectionary document" that would give aid and comfort to the enemy. The reading went on over his facetious protest, and while the clerk droned through it Lincoln entered his designated office to sign bills. Senator Chandler badgered him a bit to sign the Wade-Davis bill, but the president declined. He denied that Congress could constitutionally force abolition, and for that reason he suggested an amendment allowing the states to decide the issue. The idea that any states had left the Union he found particularly repugnant, because it presumed that states could legally and effectively dissolve their bonds with the nation. That had been the heart of the dispute from the beginning, and he did not want to discourage or rebuff the constitutions and governments that loyal citizens had already adopted in Louisiana and Arkansas, under the 10 percent plan of his December message to Congress.[14]

In this first skirmish over Reconstruction between the White House and Congress, Stanton may have lent some aid and comfort to the president's enemies. Early on he had installed military governors in the occupied portions of Confederate states, reflecting his fondness for direct control but also implying the right of presidential Reconstruction. To the extent that military rule accorded him predominate authority, Stanton evidently interpreted the restoration of state governments as an executive function, but that was before Radicals in Congress sought to wrest the authority from a president who appeared to be backsliding into conservatism. Concern for the opinion of his powerful Radical friends may have inspired Stanton to invite his old classmate, Winter Davis, to visit his home a few evenings after Davis's first attempt to introduce his Reconstruction bill—although Davis was also deeply involved in a plot to make trouble for Secretary Welles, for which Stanton was feeding him information.[15] Stanton and Davis had been conniving with each other for quite some time, in fact, and Davis thought Stanton was "with" him in general. Republican congressman and volunteer major general Robert Schenck resumed military command in Maryland just in time for the 1863 elections, and to ensure that Davis prevailed in his contest against the hated Blair faction Stanton had instructed Schenck to monitor the polls. That order promised to inhibit conservative voting, provoking a complaint to the president from the governor, but Stanton and Schenck claimed they considered violence almost certain and Lincoln refused to make more than a minor change to Schenck's orders. Having secured the right to intimidate the opposition, Stanton betrayed the partisan purpose of the charade by bidding Schenck to skin Blair's hide "and stretch it on a barn door."[16]

By the height of summer Radicals had lost any practical hope of running Chase for president. He had allowed supporters to tout him early in the year, creating an impression of disloyalty to his own president, but after some uncomfortable exchanges with Lincoln Chase claimed to friends that he was trying to give up all thoughts of the presidency. Still, his days in the cabinet were numbered: there had been much murmuring about Chase's Treasury agents and their lucrative special permits for bringing cotton out of captured Confederate territory; finally a controversy emerged over Chase's collector at the port of New York, Hiram Barney. That confrontation led Chase to offer another resignation, and this time Lincoln accepted it—having already won the nomination of the Republican, or "Union," Party. Chase's departure deprived Stanton of his oldest friend in the cabinet, and left him the most Radical member of the president's official family.[17]

As secretary of war, Stanton earned less than half the annual income of his last years in private practice.[18] Thanks at least in part to Ellen's dowry and her inheritance from her father's estate, they owed nothing on their home. His $8,000 salary represented several times the pay on which government clerks kept families in the city, but a houseful of servants and Ellen's appetite for entertaining appear to have depleted their savings substantially by the summer of 1864. That may be why, as the extreme heat of late June again suggested a shadier retreat for his wife and children, Stanton finally accepted the standing offer of a free cottage on the grounds of the Soldiers' Home, on a gentle rise north of the city, out Seventh Street. The president lodged his own family there through the summer, and usually joined them in the evenings. Stanton, with his habit of late nights at the War Department, stayed more often at his K Street house.[19]

Confederate soldiers threatened the Soldiers' Home early that summer. Victorious rebel armies came dashing down the Shenandoah Valley toward Washington for the third year in a row, throwing the city into another panic. David Hunter had finally found his active assignment, taking an army up the valley and making hard enough war on civilians and heavily outnumbered rear-echelon troops, but he had found equal numbers of Confederate veterans more challenging. In the middle of June, Lee had detached Stonewall Jackson's old corps, under Jubal Early, to drive Hunter away, and Early had done just that, hurling him back into West Virginia without either his artillery or his wounded. Then Early followed Lee's plan of feinting at Washington, in hopes of relieving pressure on the Army of Northern Virginia again.

By July 6, Early's men had crossed into Maryland at Shepherdstown and Williamsport, converging on the Monocacy River below Frederick. There sat Lew Wallace, with a few regiments gathered quickly from eastern Maryland. About half of his troops consisted of hundred-day men, including a Maryland regiment three weeks from home, but on July 8 the better part of two brigades reached him from the Sixth Corps, which Grant had sent up from the Army of the Potomac. Still outnumbered nearly two to one, Wallace put up a respectable fight the next day, but eventually his left flank caved in and grey-clad infantry swept across his direct road to Washington, capturing hundreds of Yankees and driving the rest through the woods toward the Baltimore Pike.[20]

Confederate cavalry chased the fugitives toward Baltimore, cutting the telegraph lines between there and Washington, and the sense of isolation sparked sudden apprehension in the capital. Stanton could tell colleagues nothing: no one knew where, or how many, the rebels were. Rumors credited Early with thirty thousand: he did not have half that many, but wild estimates of forty and fifty thousand floated here and there.[21]

One of the last telegrams to come into the War Department announced Wallace's defeat, and when Stanton passed that message along to the president he added a curious report that an unknown rider had been seen behind Lincoln's escort that evening, as he returned to the Soldiers' Home—a horseman in uniform, but not the standard issue of the U.S. Army. Apparently afflicted with some of the nerves that troubled him whenever the enemy neared the city, Stanton adjured the president to remind his escort to be extremely alert. His alarm continued the next day, when Early's skirmishers appeared north and west of the district, picking their way toward the Washington suburbs: at ten o'clock on the evening of the tenth, Stanton essentially ordered the president and his family back into the city, sending a carriage for them. By July 11 the rest of the city had spun itself into what Attorney General Bates considered "ludicrous terror," but the customarily frantic Stanton suddenly appeared to have contained his anxiety: he showed such exaggerated coolness that Gideon Welles thought him "dull and stupefied," and others commented on Stanton's seemingly dazed condition. Welles concluded that such unusual outward calm must be feigned, for Stanton was taking last-ditch measures to defend the city. In the absence of all those heavy artillery regiments sent to reinforce Grant, he had assigned a squad of idle generals to organize government clerks, employees of the Quartermaster Department and Navy Yard, convalescent soldiers, and civilian volunteers to man the fortifications. Drums beat the long roll throughout the day as the remaining garrison troops marched to the forts, and a few companies of the Veteran Reserve Corps filed out in their light-blue uniforms to confront the foe, whose approach raised ominous clouds of dust in the distance. Stanton called for the citizens of Philadelphia to come out under arms, and for New York to send its militia once again.[22]

If Washington suffered from a shortage of troops, there were so many major generals loitering about the capital that their very numbers led to confusion. General Halleck seemed to be little more than Stanton's adjutant, passing on his orders and questions. Christopher Augur held general responsibility for the city's defenses, and Alexander McCook took charge of the mobilized government employees. Stanton thought he had assigned Quincy Gillmore to oversee the sector around Fort Lincoln, along the Bladensburg Turnpike, but Gillmore knew nothing about it. Stanton may have added to the confusion by his own interference when General Augur commandeered the company of Pennsylvania Bucktails that served as the president's infantry guard to defend Fort Reno. Although that still left the troop of cavalry that followed Lincoln about the city, Stanton evidently objected to Augur's actions, again showing so heightened a concern for the president's safety that it seemed a bit theatrical.[23]

While his foraging details scooped up provisions and horses, Early lunged toward Fort Stevens, inside the district line on Seventh Street. The president went there to watch, climbing up on the parapet until a soldier gruffly ordered him down. The garrisons of all the forts in and outside the city stood to the alert. Around the entire circumference of Washington, including the far side of the Eastern Branch, near St. Elizabeth's Hospital for the Insane, civilians whose homes lay in the range of the fort's guns were ordered to pack up and be ready to leave, but the only real skirmishes erupted before forts Stevens and DeRussey. With so few men, Early knew he could never enter the city, and he dared not allow a general engagement to develop because it would reveal his relative weakness, so he contented himself with lying on the outskirts of the capital for a couple of days, to keep drawing more of Grant's men away. Besides sending the entire Sixth Corps, Grant also diverted the first steamers filled with the Nineteenth Corps, which he had just brought up from Louisiana to reinforce the Army of the Potomac.[24]

The first brigades of the Sixth Corps docked at Washington the evening of July 11, marching straight out Seventh Street, past the Soldiers' Home, to Fort Stevens. More boatloads arrived the next morning and throughout the day, and the troops hurried to Fort Stevens through sweltering heat. When Secretary Welles drove out there on the afternoon of July 12 he met Ben Wade, and together they found the president already in the fort, sitting in the shade by the parapet. One man in the fort had just been shot, and a few wounded passed through from the skirmish line, on litters. Government officials and hundreds of gawkers stood about in white dusters and crinoline, annoying the officers in the fort, but the secretary of war stayed at his desk all day, and he had ignored the regular cabinet meeting that morning. Thomas Eckert, chief of the War Department's telegraph service, connected an apparatus within half a mile of Fort Stevens, and Stanton remained at the other end of the line. Early's failure to attack soon convinced most observers that his force had been badly overestimated, and Stanton seemed more at ease with the Sixth Corps in the city and the Nineteenth Corps on the way. He assured the former Illinois senator, Orville Hickman Browning, that Washington was perfectly secure.[25]

By Wednesday morning, July 13, the rebel pickets had disappeared. Early had slipped away during the night, and eventually a long blue column lumbered after him. From their abandoned camps and reports from residents in the occupied neighborhoods, critics quickly understood that the invaders had not been so numerous after all, and that they had weakened themselves further by probing in widespread detachments, to create maximum consternation. Those tactics had flummoxed the War Department: General Halleck seemed particularly defensive when Welles challenged his estimate of Early's strength, but it was only at the War Department that Welles could find anyone who thought the rebel force had amounted to much at all. The president himself seemed to cling to the notion that Early had been formidable, but War Department paranoia appeared to feed that belief. The alarm among the generals and the administrators had made them look "contemptible," remarked the acerbic Welles. A soldier just arrived in the city with the Nineteenth Corps seemed to agree, finding the fortifications so intricate that Lee's entire army could not have taken the city. Stanton evidently shared Halleck's chagrin, for in briefing ex-secretary Chase on the raid he tripled Early's numbers to justify the panic. A few days later, after it became obvious how few rebels had actually threatened the city, Stanton began to turn on Halleck as the scapegoat.[26]

As embarrassing as it had been, Early's raid seemed less threatening to the president's reelection hopes than the Radical campaign for control of Reconstruction. With the Republican nomination in Lincoln's hands, Ben Wade and Winter Davis prepared to attack him in the press if he continued to insist on his authority to reorganize loyal governments in the rebel states. It may have been no coincidence that, while Wade and Davis conspired, War Department solicitor William Whiting dropped in at the home of Gideon Welles, preaching the doctrine of congressional Reconstruction.

Stanton had established the position of department solicitor in the winter of 1863 by asking Senator Fessenden to incorporate it into a Treasury bill in anticipation of the Conscription Act. Whiting was a patent attorney from Boston whom Stanton and Watson may have known from antebellum practice, and he numbered among the Radicals: Charles Sumner called him "my personal friend," and said the two of them agreed "in policy & object." The duties of the solicitor consisted mainly of supplying legal opinions on the exercise of federal authority over American citizens, and Whiting's opinions tended to fall as far on the side of maximum governmental power as Stanton might have wished. As Welles saw it, Stanton "used" Whiting, who in turn wrote letters and opinions "to order." Not being asked for an opinion on a particular subject did not stop the solicitor from writing one, either, and the year before he had published a letter outlining his views on Reconstruction, clinging to the more equivocal Radical opinion that Wade and Davis had advocated: he refused to recognize the right of secession, but he insisted that the seceded states had given up all their rights, and had to seek permission to reenter the Union, after first adopting new state constitutions prohibiting slavery. Welles, a more strict constitutionalist than Lincoln, observed that Whiting seemed to use international law and other arguments "outside of the Constitution to punish States inside."[27]

Whiting failed to budge the navy secretary. The record Welles left of the visit suggests that he considered Whiting a tool of Stanton, whom Welles may have suspected of having sent him. Had Welles known what Wade and Davis were working on—as Stanton surely did—he might have been even more certain of Stanton's involvement.

The Wade-Davis Manifesto, as it would be called, appeared at a critical juncture. Both major Confederate armies had been backed into effective sieges, but Northern patience had worn dangerously thin. Sherman, whose armies had pushed into the outskirts of Atlanta, seemed by the end of July to have stalled, although he had thrown back consecutive counterattacks. At Richmond and Petersburg things looked even worse, for an ambitious attempt to explode a mine under the Confederate lines and rush through the breach had turned to disaster when Union troops found themselves trapped in the mine crater: the fiasco caused four thousand Union casualties, with nothing gained. Early was still marauding along the upper Potomac, and the same day as the mine explosion his cavalry set fire to Chambersburg, Pennsylvania. On Friday, August 5, the *New York Tribune* carried a letter signed by Wade and Davis, accusing Lincoln of having created token governments in the rebellious states in order to count their electoral votes for himself. Such a victory might be challenged by his opponent, they hinted, or the votes of those skeleton states might help elect "an enemy of the Government"—meaning any conservative Democrat. They particularly resented the president's proposal to install military governors without Senate approval, branding it a "dictatorial usurpation," and they regarded the veto of the Wade-Davis bill as a "studied outrage on the legislative authority of the people."[28]

Committed Radicals embraced this letter as a declaration of war against the administration. As Wade and Davis must have hoped, abolitionists and advocates of retribution began almost immediately to talk about holding a new convention to nominate a more acceptable candidate, or to promote the candidacy of John C. Frémont, who had been nominated by a Radical fringe convention in the spring. There were even suggestions of an alliance with War Democrats to nominate someone like John Brough of Ohio. A serious third-party candidate posed the worst threat to Lincoln's reelection, as Republican National Committee chairman Henry Raymond fully understood: less than a week after the manifesto appeared, Raymond conceded to Fessenden (who had replaced Chase at the Treasury Department) that "it will be a work of great labor to reelect Mr. Lincoln." By August 22 Raymond warned Lincoln that in every state the tide was turning firmly against them, and on that same day Thurlow Weed wrote Seward that without prompt measures "all is lost."[29]

The next morning, convinced that his chances of reelection had all but evaporated, Lincoln prepared an odd document, admitting the probability of his defeat and expressing an intention to cooperate with the president-elect to save the Union between the election and the inauguration—adding that no one could defeat him except on a platform that would prevent him from saving it afterward. That he should ask the members of his cabinet to sign such a memorandum seemed as strange as writing it, but he went further and asked them to endorse it on the reverse, sight unseen, and none of them hesitated. Lincoln folded the paper, sealed it, and tucked it in a drawer of his desk.[30]

The paper made no reference to the fate of emancipation, which implied a presumption that it might have to be given up: even at that late date, restoration of the Union remained Lincoln's main object. Raymond had suggested making a peace offer to Jefferson Davis based solely on reunion, and the day after Lincoln asked his cabinet to sign the blind document he went so far as to draft an order for Raymond himself to go to Richmond. According to John Nicolay, the president was dissuaded from so rash a course by Seward, Stanton, and Fessenden.[31]

In the middle of August, Lincoln could hardly rely on his own cabinet members. Some of them surely doubted his electability, and one or two may have hoped he would give way to another candidate, if only to withhold the presidency from Peace Democrats, or any Democrat. Blair stood firmly behind Lincoln, then as always, and Welles joined him in that loyalty, probably in the expectation that he could still win. With the Radicals lending Lincoln a conservative aura, Attorney General Bates likely felt all the more comfortable with his chief, although he may not have been so sanguine. Usher, the Interior secretary, probably hoped against hope for reelection, if only to retain his office, both for its legitimate emoluments and for any gratuities from those seeking to exploit public lands. Fessenden showed a moderate bent despite his early sympathy with Radical Republicans, but his later attitude toward Reconstruction suggested that he may have differed with Lincoln's policy: perhaps he would not have grieved inordinately at the president's withdrawal from the contest, since he wished to avoid the Democratic triumph that Lincoln's candidacy then seemed to promise. Like his political mentor, Weed, William Seward also worried that Lincoln posed a grave danger to Republican victory, although he exerted none of his considerable influence to hint that the president should withdraw.

For all his apparent loyalty, Stanton seems at that moment to have been the least certain of Lincoln's supporters within the cabinet. Like Usher, he had grown fond of his position, but more for the unprecedented power it brought him than for the pecuniary rewards. Welles, who had once heard Stanton offer to resign, doubted that he ever meant it, supposing instead that he would be one of the last to quit—"and never except on compulsion." Stanton had nevertheless conspired covertly with Henry Winter Davis in his campaign against Welles, and had worked with Davis and others to weaken Blair's political base in Maryland. If he had so readily betrayed the colleagues who most fervently upheld the president, it seems unlikely he would have taken much pains to discourage or deflect Davis's concentrated assault on Lincoln's conservative conduct. Since entering the War Department he had invariably accommodated and gratified his Radical allies whenever possible, and it would not be surprising if he offered advice or information even in this instance—especially in light of his intimacy with

Davis, for whom he served as a pallbearer a little over a year later. Contributing to the demise of Lincoln's presidency might have cost Stanton his position as the effective viceroy of the United States, but Lincoln seemed bound for defeat anyway, and faithlessness to James Buchanan had brought Stanton enviable benefits in the succeeding administration.[32]

Sometime in August Jeremiah Black stopped to chat with Stanton outside his house. They talked about the odds for peace: Stanton apparently remarked that Lincoln's refusal to accept Confederate independence or continued slavery would cost him reelection, short of a turnaround on the military front. Black said he intended to travel to Canada to explore the possibility of peace and reunion with their former cabinet colleague Jacob Thompson, who was serving as a Confederate commissioner there. Stanton raised no objection, and may have offered encouragement. Black made the trip in due haste, meeting Thompson in Toronto on August 20 and leaving him with the impression that Stanton had sent him. Stanton would give him safe conduct if he would come to Washington, Black said. Their discussion came to naught, and Black reported as much to Stanton in a private letter, offering that Thompson characterized the Southern people as "unanimous" for peace but fearful of the insult and degradation of immediate, universal emancipation. Stanton did not reply until August 31, by which time the political situation had changed drastically, and he disavowed any connection to the visit. Black, evidently comprehending Stanton's anxiety, supplied him with a letter exonerating him from any unseemly scheming, but it would have been pointless for Black to have promised Thompson safe passage to the capital if Stanton had not shown some approbation of the mission. It seems likely that Stanton may have given at least equivocal assent: the president's own willingness to consider sending a peace envoy would have implied that the subject was no longer forbidden, and having Thompson come to Washington would have looked much better than sending Raymond to Richmond.[33]

Discouragement at the White House only deepened as August ground to a close. Military affairs still seemed unpromising, except for the navy's capture of Mobile Bay early in the month. Atlanta remained defiant, and Lee's army continued to hold its own around Richmond and Petersburg, fending off assaults on either side of the James; two days after Lincoln wrote his discouraging memorandum on his reelection prospects, Winfield Hancock's Second Corps—the cream of the Army of the Potomac, which had repulsed Pickett's Charge at Gettysburg—suffered a humiliating rout at Reams's Station, below Petersburg. Then, suddenly, the political skies brightened just as the Democratic convention opened in Chicago, and in part because of it. The Democrats gathered on August 29: the election lay barely ten weeks away, giving Radicals little time to arrange yet another convention and find another candidate. Repenting of his dalliance with the opposition, the mercurial Horace Greeley revealed privately on August 30 that while he had opposed Lincoln that summer he would stand behind him thereafter, for the sake of unity against a "Copperhead triumph" and "Pro-Slavery reconstruction." He apparently wrote that letter just after leaving a meeting with Winter Davis, Benjamin Butler, John Andrew, and other advocates of a new convention, who hoped to persuade Lincoln to withdraw. Thurlow Weed reported to Seward a few days later that the meeting marked the end of the "conspiracy" against Lincoln. The nomination of George McClellan on August 31 brought most of the rest of the renegades back into the fold, too. Charles Sumner, who had hoped as late as August 24 that Lincoln would graciously give way to another candidate, finally embraced the ticket of Lincoln and Andrew Johnson.[34]

It was not so much the choice of McClellan that pleased Republicans as the peace plank hammered into the party platform on August 30 by Clement Vallandigham, who had returned from exile without interference from federal officers. The president had probably welcomed his attendance at the convention, for his resolution calling for an armistice and a convention of all the states smacked of Confederate influence. Lincoln had said that the campaign would probably pit a Union candidate against a disunion candidate, and McClellan's chances were poisoned if he assumed the latter role. In accepting the nomination he repudiated that part of the platform, alienating devoted Peace Democrats, while Republicans saw him as the candidate who would squander three years of sacrifices. The platform cost McClellan immense prestige in the army, even among soldiers who greatly admired him: the hope it gave Republicans may have accounted for Stanton's sudden coolness toward Black's freelance peace mission in the reply he wrote on August 31. Peace-seeking had become odious.[35]

With the nomination of McClellan and the apparent collapse of Radical hopes for another contender, Stanton dove headlong into a herculean effort to ensure Mr. Lincoln's reelection. He intended to portray McClellan and his entire party as something much worse than craven quitters, and he had been accumulating material for that purpose for months, in accordance with a valuable propaganda ploy he had learned from Governor Oliver Morton of Indiana. In 1863 Morton had blunted the previous year's Democratic resurgence through the efforts of Henry Carrington, a political general whose primary purpose seemed to consist of cultivating a state of fear around imaginary or wildly exaggerated plots. Carrington had reported on a secret society of 92,000 armed Indianans waiting to rise up against the government, and at first Stanton doubted Carrington's competence, if not his sanity. Henry Halleck agreed, noting that Carrington lacked any field experience and owed his commission entirely to political influence: Halleck remarked that Carrington lacked both the "judgment and brains" for his post. Yet Morton soon turned Carrington's collection of hearsay, rumors, and innuendo into a published pamphlet exposing the supposed conspiracy of the Knights of the Golden Circle. Spreading paranoia through the army and the West, the myth quickly colored almost any disagreement with administration policy as treason, demonizing mainstream Democrats and contributing to a wholesale recovery of Republican strength in October of 1863.[36]

That service counterbalanced Carrington's deficiencies as a soldier, and his example was not lost on another Republican political appointee. In 1864 Colonel John P. Sanderson, an apostle of Simon Cameron who was serving as provost marshal for General Rosecrans, in St. Louis, portrayed the Order of American Knights as another vast seditious conspiracy. Inquiries by Carrington and Sanderson had led to the arrest of Phineas Wright in April, but they sought bigger game and saved their most alarming allegations for more timely release. Conducting, collecting, and perhaps embellishing or inventing interviews with anonymous prisoners of war and state, Sanderson alleged that this secret order had attracted two hundred thousand active members and up to a million sympathetic followers for an armed uprising. One informant he did name had the reputation of "a great rascal" with another provost marshal, who supposed the man would say anything to avoid prison. Sanderson put particular store by the flagrant rumors credulously relayed in what he called "An Anonymous Letter from a Lady"—which contained no reliable or verifiable information, and might well have been a forgery. Engaging a pair of paroled Confederate officers, whom he referred to only by aliases, Sanderson purportedly "infiltrated" the organization. Illustrating the political slant of the interrogation, one confused but zealously cooperative prisoner testified that the society consisted of "all Democrats who are desirous of securing the independence of the Confederate States with a view to restoring the Union as it was." Sanderson folded all that foolishness and fabrication into a long report for Rosecrans just before the Republican convention. His file kept expanding through the summer, and in late June he added his own interview with a woman who claimed that she had served in the garb of a man as an officer under Nathan Bedford Forrest.[37]

Rosecrans seemed bent on using that fat packet of papers to worm his way back into the executive confidence he had lost at Chickamauga. Writing directly to the president of "a plot to overthrow the Government," he asked permission to send the information by a staff officer. Lincoln told him to send it by express, but Rosecrans claimed it was too sensitive, and an annoyed chief magistrate finally sent John Hay all the way out to St. Louis. When Hay brought the OAK story back to Washington, Lincoln seemed to discount it as an elaborate fable.[38]

A couple of weeks later Henry Carrington produced a similarly trumped-up indictment against Democrats in Indiana. The enormous fifth column he had reported on in early 1863 had apparently evaporated after that year's election, but he found a new bugbear in the Sons of Liberty, part of a supposed conspiracy to take the states of the Old Northwest out of the Union. The Indiana elections were barely three months away when Carrington published his entire exposé in a Morton-friendly Indianapolis newspaper, implicating prominent Democratic political figures and newspaper editors. Four weeks later, and four weeks away from Missouri's state and national elections, a Republican St. Louis newspaper did the same with the gist of Sanderson's report.[39]

For Stanton, all this posed an irresistible propaganda opportunity for the presidential election, and he handed it to his most reliable collaborator in that genre. Joseph Holt's duties did not seem to include the investigation of secret societies, and his task of reviewing court-martial cases should have left him little time for such extraneous roving, but Holt could understand a political mission. Stanton dispatched him to Louisville to investigate subversive organizations there and in states north of the Ohio River; almost as an afterthought he bade Holt to assess "the administration of military justice" there, perhaps to give the assignment a semblance of relevance to his position. From Louisville, Holt would proceed to St. Louis and conduct similar examinations.[40]

The ostensibly imminent danger of an uprising did not dissuade Holt from making a leisurely journey of it. Forty miles from Louisville lay his family home, where his mother and his brother's family still lived, and he spent more than two weeks in that vicinity, on what bore all the earmarks of a vacation junket. Stanton's orders required him to do little more than speak to the governor and military commander of Kentucky, pick up their share of the subversive-society dossier, and then proceed to St. Louis, where he arrived soon after Sanderson's allegations had appeared in the newspaper. He could not have been in that city more than a day when he filed his Kentucky report, which gratified Radical readers by blaming the guerrilla depredations there on Lincoln's amnesty proclamation. He also gave Stanton the answer he sought about secret societies, assuring him that "careful investigation" had uncovered a treasonable conspiracy in Kentucky, Ohio, Indiana, Illinois—and Missouri as well, but he had not yet received Sanderson's latest sheaf of incriminating materials. He did not linger nearly so long in St. Louis as he had in Louisville, merely meeting with Rosecrans, Sanderson, and a few select officials before returning to Washington with the packet of testimony and accusations. Early in August he essentially reiterated his Kentucky report as his account of affairs in Missouri, attributing guerrilla activities to rebels who took the oath of allegiance and accepted amnesty before returning to bushwhacking and banditry. Again Holt endorsed the accuracy of Sanderson's voluminous case against several subversive fraternities, some of which sounded like nothing more sinister than political clubs for the promotion of Democratic candidates. He insisted that there was "no doubt" they had planned uprisings in March and on the Fourth of July, only to be foiled by "events." They were infiltrating the government, he charged, and taking control of communications through the telegraph service. Holt identified Vallandigham, the most conspicuous of the Peace Democrats, as the leader of those traitors.[41]

Sanderson submitted a supplemental report on August 20, including unproductive inquiries into a group he called the "McClellan Minute Men" and some scraps of penciled scribbling that he claimed were the minutes of OAK meetings. Stanton held onto it for a few days, but on August 31, with McClellan's nomination a fait accompli, he gave that installment to Holt and told him to compile a "detailed report" on the insurrectionary conspiracy—or rather conspiracies, because different groups were accused of different plots. Like Holt's reviews of the Porter and Hammond courts martial, this report was meant for publication, the better to smear McClellan and all his supporters with the taint of treason. Holt may have consulted with Henry Carrington, because Carrington mentioned only four days later that he was working on a history of the societies that he was going to give the president for public consumption. One month before the election, Holt presented his summary of the government's conspiracy theories, all boiled down to a diatribe against the opposition candidate for president, and Stanton rushed it into print for widespread distribution in pamphlet form. Yet he made no provisions to defend against the uprising the report warned about, and disapproved or discouraged all requests for troops and arms to prepare against such contingencies.[42]

A handful of would-be conspirators and confidence men did try to convince Jacob Thompson that they led an extensive network of dissidents who would engage in revolt, large-scale sabotage, or subversion at a given signal. At least some of them only sought to bilk Thompson out of the clandestine-operation funds he carried in gold coin, and all of them seemed prone to either willful or hopeful exaggeration. Stanton seemed to understand as much, because the only visible action he took against the supposedly pervasive and deadly threat was to stage another military trial.[43]

Harrison H. Dodd of Indianapolis, a political dreamer and huckster, had founded the Sons of Liberty and appointed "generals" to command its nonexistent military wing. To the detriment of Democrats generally, and Peace Democrats in particular, he persuaded Vallandigham to accept titular leadership of the national organization, which he viewed as the Democratic answer to the nationwide network of Union Leagues. After Dodd was arrested, Stanton appointed General Alvin Hovey to command the military district of Indiana, instructing him to work with Governor Morton—who got on very well with Hovey, and perhaps recommended him. Hovey's division had been known for extensive destruction of personal property in operations against Vicksburg, as well as widespread corruption in the confiscation and sale of cotton—and Hovey himself had been accused by the military governor of Arkansas of trading contrabands for cotton, returning them to slavery at the rate of two per bale. Hovey served nobly as Morton's ally, however: three days after his appointment (and less than a month before Indiana's election) he appointed a military commission to try Dodd and his Democratic associates for treason.[44]

Henry Burnett, the boyish judge advocate who was becoming a favorite with Holt and Stanton, managed the case for the government. He dragged out the prosecution testimony until the eve of the state elections, whereupon three of the defendants were convicted on every charge and sentenced to hang, but no verdict came for Dodd. Just before the conclusion of the trial he escaped from his hotel, where he had been held under a guard too light to be convincing.[45]

The trials served as Stanton's main contribution to the state elections in the West. After dinner on October 11, the night of those elections, the president and John Hay ambled through bright moonlight, dry leaves, and chill autumn air to the War Department, to read telegrams of the returns. Stanton had all but barricaded the building, locking the doors, but one of his messenger boys spotted the lanky Lincoln and guided the pair inside through a side door. Charles Dana came in and sat with them, and as they waited for the news Stanton puffed his cigars and the president reached into his pocket for a thin volume of dialectical humor, which he started reading aloud. Hay described them all chuckling over a talented rendition, but years later Dana remembered Stanton leading him into an adjoining room, where the secretary snarled profanely over the chief magistrate immersing himself and his staff in such drivel at so critical a time. Then, apparently, Stanton returned to the telegraph room and resumed his amiable pose, turning talkative as War Department telegraphers reported promising results from Pennsylvania, Ohio, and Indiana. In addition to the show trials, Stanton had furloughed thousands of sick and wounded soldiers from those states who could be expected to vote heavily Republican. He boasted to Hay of the Louisville quartermaster's aid to Republican campaign rallies—probably without mentioning his extortion among contractors. Stanton did say he demoted one staff officer out there and sent him to the front after that officer had reportedly placed a bet against Governor Morton's reelection. Stanton blithely promised to make a general of one colonel whose regiment had unanimously voted the Republican ticket, but while Hay doubted

Stanton's sincerity the night's news brought such bright portent for the November vote that it failed to sour the evening for him.[46]

The night after the October elections, Chief Justice Roger Taney died at the age of eighty-eight. He had not been well for months, and had sometimes failed to appear in court, but his tenacity had begun to frustrate his detractors and aspirants for the office. Ebenezer Rockwood Hoar, a Massachusetts judge who hoped to see his colleague William Evarts installed as chief justice, had admitted his disgust the previous February, when Taney recovered from an acute illness: when he survived a second bout in May, Hoar observed that Taney was "clinging to life in the most shameless manner." Taney's death launched a scramble for the post, with Governor John Andrew of Massachusetts promising to see the president personally on behalf of Evarts, while Attorney General Bates gauchely asked Lincoln for the appointment. Salmon Chase made his own bid by mobilizing his friends the instant he heard of Taney's demise. Supposing that Stanton would help him—and apparently without considering that Stanton might like the appointment, too—Chase let him know that he would accept the job if it were offered to him, and asked what Stanton thought about his prospects.[47]

As soon as he heard of Taney's death Stanton had telegraphed Chase and Justice Robert Grier, in Philadelphia. Grier, for whom Stanton had done many personal kindnesses, included in his reply the comment that Stanton may have been hoping for—naming him as the most logical and deserving successor to Taney. Stanton coveted the post for himself, for although it would have meant leaving the second-most-powerful position in the wartime government it represented a lifetime appointment at the acme of his profession, and with a salary equal to that of a cabinet officer. As willing as he might be to ask the president for favors on behalf of others, he evidently understood (as Bates did not) that requesting the appointment outright put the president on the spot and approached presumption. He entertained no qualms about the indirect approach, and he may have enlisted the aid of his charming wife. Erstwhile senator Orville Browning, still a friend of the president and a lobbyist in the capital, dropped by the Stanton home on the evening of October 16 to see Ellen—apparently at her request, since Stanton was away on a visit to Grant's armies outside Petersburg. She remarked that she, herself, very much wanted her husband to replace Taney, asking Browning to propose his name to the president.[48]

Browning, who knew of Chase's lust for the position and dreaded seeing him on the bench, complied with Ellen's request the next day. Lincoln seemed to agree with Browning's assessment of Stanton's qualifications, offering no hint of whether he might offer him the spot, but for a few weeks the likelihood of Stanton's elevation bred frenzied speculation over who might replace him, with Butler and Banks attracting the most bets. General

Grant made a special trip to Washington to avert the possibility of Butler going into the War Department, and he returned to City Point satisfied that it would not happen. A friend of Evarts's who seemed to have inside knowledge predicted, late in November, that the president would not give Stanton up as secretary of war. Lincoln probably said something like that, too, if only to save Stanton's pride, but he may also have preferred to keep his volatile war minister as a subordinate, rather than raise him to a position where he could challenge presidential policy if his nature so tempted him.[49]

Stanton's ambition for the post seemed well-known in some circles, despite his reticence. Hoar counseled Evarts to sit back and let the two main contenders fight themselves to a frazzle and pick up the pieces. "What I want is to have Chase and Stanton and the Kilkenny cats, and have you come in as the innocent third person," he wrote, but as the weeks passed Stanton's hope faded. When Lincoln won reelection, Stanton let it out that he did not want to be chief justice—probably to avoid seeming disappointed and humiliated at being passed over. The sun shone brightly on Evarts for a few days in late November, and both Holt and William Whiting surfaced as potential nominees. The president responded as generously to Welles's suggestion of Montgomery Blair as he had to Browning's hint about Stanton, but on December 6 he surprised his entire cabinet by choosing his troublesome former treasury secretary to head the court. Dana, who probably obtained his information from a discomfited Stanton, explained to a friend that Lincoln appointed Chase reluctantly, under intense pressure.[50]

Nine days after Taney's death, and eighteen days before the presidential election, Major Burnett resumed his prosecutions at Indianapolis, redundantly trying the three condemned men and two more of their compatriots on slightly different charges. That confirmed the political motive behind the trials, extending the proceedings for weeks and initiating more publicity to influence the national election. Burnett produced enough witnesses that no defense testimony could be heard, or reported on, until after the presidential contest had been decided. In any election, a certain percentage of citizens are gulled by histrionics like the Indianapolis treason trials, and inevitably that charade exerted some effect on the tallies. It may not have changed the outcome, but similar propaganda from Carrington and the impact of the Vallandigham trial had contributed heavily to the astounding reversal of Democratic fortunes in the fall elections of 1863. The extent to which the trials were motivated by a wish to manipulate public opinion was probably reflected in Joseph Holt's failure to forward the trial records to the president for approval of the sentences. He and Stanton may have simply thought the usefulness of the trials expended. After the assassination of Lincoln, those unexecuted sentences presented an additional opportunity for political exploitation, to further the Radical goal of associating dissident

Democrats with the president's murderers, so the findings and sentences went to Andrew Johnson while he still exhibited a vindictive spirit. Johnson's belated approval of the findings, if not the sentences, set in motion the Supreme Court case that declared the Indianapolis trials and most of Stanton's military commissions unconstitutional.[51]

William Sherman surely won more votes for the administration than the treason trials had when he captured Atlanta on September 2, just as the country digested the news of McClellan's nomination. Grant's favorite cavalryman, Major General Phil Sheridan, cemented that support with decisive victories against Jubal Early at Winchester, on September 19, and at Cedar Creek exactly a month later. With such tangible evidence of declining élan in the Confederate army, even a peace man might reason that the fastest route to that goal would be to press the fight to a timely finish. Still, 45 percent of voters opposed Lincoln on November 8, with the Confederacy clearly approaching military and economic desperation, and that testified to dissatisfaction with administration policies that included excessive government intrusion and the exercise of arbitrary authority. For many Americans, and some loyal Republicans, Stanton represented those obnoxious impositions more than Abraham Lincoln did, and not without justification: if Lincoln did not assume dictatorial powers during his presidency, his secretary of war strove to do so for him. George Templeton Strong, the Sanitary Commission treasurer and friend of the surgeon general whom Stanton had railroaded, likened Stanton's behavior to that of a dictator. "He is a ruffian and will always abuse the power of his great place to purposes of arbitrary, vindictive tyranny," Strong predicted, noting that he found it difficult to vote for Lincoln while he retained Stanton.[52]

The president's July troop levy came due in September, and Stanton seemed anxious to get it out of the way before the election. He informed Grant that Ohio, Indiana, and Illinois in particular were not sending forward any troops because, he supposed, the governors wanted the men at home to vote in the October state elections. That posed a dual problem, partly because it deprived the army of manpower at a critical moment and partly because those governors hoped to postpone the draft until after their elections, pushing it to the eve of the presidential contest. To appease war supporters, to attract the soldier vote, and to have it finished and forgotten well before the November election, Stanton wanted to hold the draft immediately: he may have supposed that the Indianapolis trials would compensate for any political damage from a draft. The morning of September 13, as soon as he learned of an administration landslide in the Maine elections, Stanton asked Grant to send him a telegram advising a prompt levy to fill up the army. The general complied, remarking that the "agony of suspense is worse upon the public" than the draft itself, and Stanton published it to justify his refusal to brook any delay. Stanton had perhaps learned a lesson from trying to sway New Hampshire's March election with his disastrous deception over the Granite State's draft quota.[53]

John Frémont withdrew sullenly from the presidential race in the second half of September, apparently in return for the resignation of Blair as postmaster general. The elimination of a third-party candidate eased anxiety at the White House, but Stanton took no chances with the personal threat of George McClellan on the opposing ballot. As in most elections, he furloughed thousands of soldiers, often concentrating on those certified as reliable by their officers, or whose circumstances suggested they would vote heavily Republican: when one lot of New York soldiers mostly voted against the administration, Thurlow Weed concluded that they had obtained their furloughs under "false pretenses." October returns had shown the states on the right bank of the Ohio to be safe, but in Wisconsin Republicans sought an extra measure of security by spreading bogus Democratic tickets again. Democrats in New York were accused of a similar tactic.[54]

Stanton paid particular attention to states with strong Democratic machines, like Delaware, where the Union Party governor asked for and received troops to monitor the polls—and furloughs, with government transportation, for all his state's volunteers and invalids. Stanton seemed especially trusting of hospitalized soldiers, whose wounds he may have interpreted as badges of Unionism. Several states had arranged for their soldiers to vote in the field that year, including New York, which adopted the most complicated method: the governor appointed commissioners to register soldiers and obtain their permission to have other voters at home cast their ballots as though they were "personally present at the general election." New York State leaned Democratic, and Stanton unleashed Joseph Holt on at least one of Governor Horatio Seymour's voter registrars, accusing him of fraud. With the tried-and-true Radical general Abner Doubleday in charge again, a military court performed with the partiality Stanton expected, while Henry Raymond, editor of the *New York Times* and chairman of the national Republican committee, dutifully reported the proceedings on the front page.[55]

Then Stanton learned that Seymour intended to call out his organized militia to monitor the voting on November 8. Suspecting that Seymour meant those state forces to discourage Republicans from voting (just as Stanton's troops had routinely discouraged Democratic voters in the border states), he hastened to detach other troops from the Army of the Potomac to perform the same duty. He asked Grant for five or six thousand of them, under "loyal, suitable officers," and when he insisted on an army officer being "loyal" he was clearly referring to party loyalty. He asked for Western troops, perhaps lest New York regiments bring eligible Democratic voters, but to be certain that they performed their duty with a Radical flavor Stanton brought Ben Butler up from Bermuda Hundred to command them. Under Butler at least some Democrats were denied the vote on ridiculous pretexts, including the prominent banker August Belmont: standing in the same line with him, George Templeton Strong saw Belmont refused a chance to vote on the irrelevant grounds that he had bet on the election.[56]

When the president and some of his inner circle convened at the War Department on the night of November 8, Stanton did not join them. John Hay had found him at home, in bed, on the previous Sunday, and illness kept him from his office for most of the next two weeks: he required even the president to come see him, rather than venture outside himself. A reporter heard that on the day of the election Stanton was "sick abed with chills and fever," and Dana described his chief as "quite feeble" until early December, speculating that only Stanton's health would prevent him from remaining in Lincoln's cabinet as long as he wished. After the acute fever symptoms abated, Stanton still suffered increasingly from worsening asthma.[57]

Heavy smoking aggravated his respiratory condition, and, in light of the then-unsuspected allergic origins of asthma, his long days in the War Department may have contributed more to his declining health than the fatigue this work entailed. Thirty years after the war, the same reporter who noted Stanton's chills and fever recalled the war office as a "musty old barrack," conjuring images of pervasive mold that would have tormented an asthmatic. An inspection early in 1865 found the building very poorly ventilated, and noted the soot that accumulated in the upper chimney flues. The rooms were heated entirely by fireplaces, and the poor draw of the choked-down flues on the third and fourth floors would inevitably have produced abundant smoke whenever someone kindled a fire in Stanton's second-story office, or in the telegraph room. The heating season had just begun when Stanton retired to his sick chamber, suggesting that asthma may have exacerbated whatever ailed him.[58]

Not until November 25 did Stanton attend another cabinet meeting. The president read a draft of his annual message to Congress, asking those present for their opinions, and Stanton offered some suggestions on Reconstruction that revealed an uncharacteristic air of conciliation. He advised reiterating the amnesty policy of the previous year, and continuing to invite rebels back to national allegiance without additional concessions, perhaps with a reminder that they would have been better off had they done so a year before. Regardless of whether he agreed with Welles on the subject of negotiating with individual states for their return to the Union, Stanton's favorable remarks on the 1863 message conflicted with the Radicals' hostility to the president's generosity. With Chase gone, perhaps Stanton felt less obliged to toe the Radical line in council. He had thus far served Radical interests surreptitiously, and the change at the Treasury had given cabinet discussion a slightly more conservative tone, which Stanton appeared to imitate.[59]

Attrition in the summer and fall of 1864 made Stanton one of the most senior cabinet members. Blair had left in September, and then, after the election, Bates resigned as attorney general. Stanton seemed so pleased at his retirement that he gave him an uncharacteristically warm farewell, offering to do anything he could for the two boys Bates had in the army. Stanton's good humor may have arisen from the possibility that his faithful ally Joseph Holt might come in as Bates's replacement, and the president made that offer, but Holt declined. Stanton had created the Bureau of Military Justice months before, putting Holt in charge, still as judge advocate general, but with a promotion to brigadier general—and, seven years after accepting his first federal office, Holt understood how much more valuable a permanent government post was than a temporary executive appointment. Like the head of the War Department, Holt was fond of control. He wielded more power and commanded more deference as judge advocate general than he ever would have realized as attorney general, and as the head of Stanton's alternative justice system he also appeared to enjoy unusual economic benefits. One of his amorous correspondents could not fathom his refusal of the president's appointment, but Holt had probably reached the limits of his ambition with a position he might hold indefinitely, and he chose employment security over further honors.[60]

Stanton had also attained the pinnacle of professional satisfaction. Seward called him the "Carnot of the war" and the "organizer of victory," and friends of the administration usually concurred, while some of Stanton's critics even offered grudging credit for his handling of the War Department. Still, he, too, would have preferred a lifetime appointment of equivalent status to his impermanent situation.[61]

Stanton's performance was often measured against the man who preceded him as secretary, and the comparison worked to Stanton's distinct advantage: the relative order he wrung from the chaos of Simon Cameron's tenure is generally and justifiably regarded as his principal contribution to the war. Stanton showed abundant organizational ability, to which he added marathon days and his churlish, intimidating manner to keep the cumbersome department operating steadily, if not altogether smoothly. No one is indispensable, however, and inevitably there were others who could have managed the position—or who could have grown into it, for in 1862 no one had any experience at the head of so massive and complex an organization, and least of all Stanton. McClellan, Halleck, Dix, and even Pope made better administrators than field generals, while some governors of bigger states—Edwin Morgan, Andrew Curtin, and Oliver Morton, for instance—demonstrated much administrative talent. None of those men ever assumed as vast and complicated a post as Lincoln's War Department, but neither had Stanton when he was first appointed. Probably no one could have done a better job than Stanton, however: he was available at the time and proved capable of "running the machine," as some phrased it. That explains much of Lincoln's reluctance to part with him, despite his unpleasant personal and political traits. For that matter, Stanton's reliance on duplicity and intrigue usually worked to Lincoln's immediate political benefit.

The efficiency of Stanton's department nevertheless suffered because he often tended to value compliance over competence, as he did with the surgeon general, the ordnance bureau, and the supply departments. That made his obsession with details all the more crucial, and crippling, since his preference for pliable subordinates left his general staff with enough weak spots that he felt compelled to devote more of his own attention to those areas. A better manager of people might have found the job a little easier. A less impulsive administrator would probably not have imitated Stanton's incomprehensible halt to recruiting, which contributed significantly to the reversal of the Union tide in Virginia during the spring and summer of 1862 and all but assured the divisive resort to conscription. That single grievous error probably helped to prolong the war, increasing the destruction to life and property and worsening future political strife and sectional animosities.

More importantly, another person might not have tread so heavily on civil liberties. Stanton's precedent-setting repression of the civilian population stood as his foremost legacy to the nation, and it seems particularly unfortunate that so much of it was so unnecessary, and so partisan. The extraordinary authority Stanton accumulated only whetted his appetite for control. As a young lawyer he had demonstrated a fondness for domination that was probably not confined to the courtroom. He also had a knack for cultivating influence, often through obsequious or devious deportment. Those traits bespoke a taste for power in progressively wider circles, and as the head of Lincoln's War Department, Stanton, next to the president, often wielded more power than anyone in the United States. His use and abuse of that power revealed much about his character, and little of it was complimentary.[62]

15

THE GIFT OF MARTYRDOM

The approach of Lincoln's second term raised intense speculation over which cabinet officers he would retain. Montgomery, Frank, and old Preston Blair, who remarked that Seward and Stanton "hang together and ought to hang together," wished the two of them would go "for the good of the country," but doubted Lincoln would dispense with either. Nor did they entertain much hope that Stanton would leave of his own volition, supposing—as Welles did—that he would hold out to the bitter end. Decades later, Ward Hill Lamon recollected Stanton expressing a desire to retire to private life as the war drew to a close, but he said that Lincoln graciously refused on the grounds that Stanton had been too good a friend and too faithful a servant for that.[1] Lamon appears to have taken this flattering story from Stanton himself, who described such an exchange in an unabashedly self-aggrandizing 1866 letter to an Ohio Radical. According to the war secretary's mawkish tale, Lincoln put his hands on Stanton's shoulders and, "tears filling his eyes, he said: 'Stanton, you cannot go. Reconstruction is more difficult and dangerous than construction or destruction. You have been our main reliance; you must help us through the final act.'"[2] Stanton's plea for the chief justiceship implies that he did not want to return to private life, but rather to secure life tenure in a government post.

As the heating season began, Stanton's worsening respiratory condition suggested a vacation, but he had probably resigned himself to several more months of suffering when General Sherman presented him with an inviting opportunity for salubrious respite. Sherman had led four corps out of Atlanta after the presidential election, abandoning his supply line and striking overland for Savannah, living off the land and leaving it barren in his wake. On December 18, the day before Stanton's fiftieth birthday, a message arrived from Ossabaw Sound, Georgia, announcing that Sherman had made contact with the navy there. He arrayed his troops for an assault on Savannah, but the badly outnumbered Confederates fled across the river into South Carolina, and on Christmas Day news reached Washington that Sherman was in the city, where his prizes included twenty-five thousand bales of cotton.[3]

The capture of Savannah left Wilmington, North Carolina, as the Confederacy's only Atlantic seaport, and Grant was moving to close it. With the assistance of a naval flotilla, he had sent an expedition from Butler's army down to attack Fort Fisher, near the tip of Cape Fear, but Butler had gone along to steal the glory and had made a botch of it—withdrawing all his troops and abandoning what Grant's chief engineer considered a near-certain chance to capture the fort and isolate Wilmington. Stanton made a feeble attempt to blame the navy, but even he could not defend Butler, and the year ended with a decision to make a second attempt in secret, to prevent Butler from joining in.[4]

On New Year's Day the president and cabinet officers usually received dignitaries and the general public at the White House, and later at their homes, but January 1 fell on a Sunday in 1865, so the receptions were postponed a day. The White House event began at noon. The commissioner of public buildings, Benjamin French, introduced visitors to the president, secretaries, and to Mrs. Lincoln ("such as desired it," French noted wryly). After an hour or two the cabinet members returned to their homes to greet callers. Stanton and Ellen had hardly opened their doors when he came down with chills again and retired early, but he had already decided on the trip to Savannah, and that afternoon he called Quartermaster General Meigs to his bedside to make plans.[5]

That same day, Sherman wrote Stanton that he was besieged by allegedly loyal citizens or neutral nationals claiming to own the cotton, and the general asked permission to ship it to New York for sale by the federal government, as Stanton saw fit. That letter may not have arrived by the time Stanton left, but bringing all that captured cotton north served as the nominal purpose of the journey, although any agent of the Treasury Department could have done that. Acting adjutant general Edward D. Townsend later remembered that it was actually Surgeon General Barnes who persuaded Stanton to take the trip, by recommending a sea voyage to improve the secretary's asthma.[6]

Stanton joined Meigs aboard the army steamer *Northerner* at the navy yard on the afternoon of January 5, bringing along Barnes, Townsend, and an assortment of civilians, including Hiram Barney's successor as the collector of the port of New York, Simeon Draper. Draper was also the cotton agent for New York, and Gideon Welles suspected another of the Treasury Department swindles that had so tainted Chase's tenure as secretary. As Welles put it, Draper had "more than any one honest man can do to discharge his duties as a collector faithfully," let alone to venture off on so profitable an enterprise as the Savannah junket.[7]

Running down to Fort Monroe that night, they laid over on January 6, transferring to the army transport *Nevada* the next day and starting for Port Royal, South Carolina, through heavy seas. The steamer rolled far enough toward her beam ends to keep the passengers awake and clinging to their bunks, but the wind subsided on the eighth, and the following morning they passed Charleston, putting in at Port Royal that afternoon to deliver commissary stores. At the dock Stanton saw a Jewish peddler whom he had earlier refused a pass to come south, and although the man had later obtained a valid pass from the president Stanton peremptorily ordered him jailed, which earned the secretary some criticism even from an officer who disliked the peddler. After midnight the *Nevada* turned for Savannah, reaching Sherman's headquarters that evening.[8]

Mr. Draper assumed control of Savannah's customhouse, post office, and other public buildings while Colonel Townsend wrote out Stanton's order for Meigs to take charge of the cotton and see that it was turned over to Treasury agents. Like Sherman, Stanton had assumed British nationals or other neutrals would claim it under "sham" titles, and when he inspected the mountain of white bales he ordered all the identifying marks obliterated, to prevent anyone from proving their title to it. A quarter of a century later General Sherman remarked that he had intended to ship the cotton back to a prize court in New York, so the ownership could be determined. Stanton's ruse worked against the government, Sherman asserted, because claims were later granted for three times as much cotton as had actually been captured, and the government had to pay for it all. Postwar War Department correspondence confirms that such claims were made.[9]

Before leaving Savannah, Stanton met with a gathering of Savannah's black religious leaders—some of them freeborn, some long free, and some only free since the arrival of the Union armies. General Sherman had become the target of complaints from Radicals over his efforts to keep runaway slaves from following his armies as he traversed Georgia. Having only enough transportation for his own men, and only enough food so long as they kept moving, he could not safely encumber himself with tens of thousands of refugees, but wild rumors credited one of his division commanders with having driven a crowd of those men, women, and children back on rebel cavalry, to be butchered. In his first dispatch from Savannah, Sherman had insensitively mentioned the need to "clear the army of surplus negroes, mules and horses," which had provoked a rebuke from Chief Justice Chase. Halleck warned that Sherman's critics had gained the ear of the president, alluding probably to Stanton, among others, and Stanton had shown annoyance at Sherman's policy before he left Washington—directing him to gather in contrabands as they approached his lines, and to expel the families of Confederate officers from their homes. When he reached Savannah, Stanton revealed that he had, indeed, believed that rebel cavalry had slaughtered contrabands, a conclusion that Sherman dismissed as a combination of misapprehension, exaggeration, and assumption. Sherman said he had as much trouble protecting freedmen from greedy Northern recruiters, who were snapping them up to serve as substitutes for drafted white men, as he did to protect them from their former masters. He seemed to think he had disabused Stanton "of that Negro nonsense," but the meeting with those black leaders may have been intended as much to instruct the general as to inform the secretary.[10]

The ministers traipsed up to the second floor of Sherman's headquarters, a private mansion on one of Savannah's lush squares, and the general joined Stanton for the interview. One of the eldest of the ministers, Garrison Frazier, acted as spokesman, demonstrating a sophisticated understanding of the politics of the war, for all his isolation in Confederate territory. He answered specific questions, beginning with the capacity of his people for self-support, and he said they most needed land on which they could support themselves. Assuming that prejudice would persist for years, he preferred colonization to integration, and all the rest agreed with him except a young Methodist Episcopal minister who had come down from Baltimore. Frazier assured Stanton that the former slaves would support the government, noting that only two from Savannah had left the city with the Confederates, and that thousands of young men would join the army as either soldiers or laborers. The subject of the franchise did not arise in the meeting, although Chase had advocated it in his letter to Sherman, but Stanton probably recognized that when Frazier spoke of the "government" he was referring to the Lincoln administration: he had no need to ask which way black men would vote if they could.[11]

Despite the altruism Stanton claimed, it seems unlikely that he harbored much genuine interest in the freedmen's welfare. His support for the Radical agenda probably reflected nothing more commendable than political strategy. Stanton too often treated administrative and social inferiors with indifference, arrogance, and even cruelty to believe him capable of much sympathy for the truly downtrodden. He showed his colors in the class struggle in 1849, when he prosecuted Pittsburgh's striking mill workers, who were sympathetically represented by "the whole bar" of that city. His secret claim of solidarity with Chase's abolition zeal, two decades before, rang no more true than his canting letters to prominent clerics, or his evident satisfaction with General Sherman's paternalistic condescension. Stanton had dodged or ignored Chase's every effort to excite him to any overt activity on behalf of the enslaved: Chase himself obviously doubted the extent of Stanton's antislavery devotion. Stanton's claims of a lifelong hatred of slavery were offered to no one but ardent abolitionists, and mainly after the cause had become politically popular and advantageous. A year later, in conversation with her husband and Chief Justice Chase, Ellen Stanton let slip a revealing glimpse into the Stanton home when she recoiled in horror at the suggestion of seating black people at her table. Unlike the secretary, Mrs. Stanton seemed not to frame her opinions to suit her listeners, but if her husband did not share her sentiments he betrayed no discomfort with them.[12]

In accordance with the majority wish of the gathered ministers, Sherman arranged for at least the temporary settlement of Savannah's freedmen on separate parcels of confiscated land. Northern abolitionists only denounced his order as further evidence of Sherman's prejudice, apparently looking on those settlements as internment camps. Embarrassed by indirect association with that program, Stanton sent the minutes of his interview to William Lloyd Garrison, the Boston abolitionist, gratuitously intimating that he, at least, did not consider Southern blacks "an inferior race." The better to quell any Radical doubts about his reliability on race, he also forwarded a copy of the minutes to Charles Sumner the same day, in the professed hope that Congress might adopt some measure to discharge the government's duty toward "the colored people of the South." He was probably referring primarily to the redistribution of confiscated lands, and he may also have been hinting at granting freedmen the vote, but he certainly seemed to imply now that Congress, and not the president, would have to do justice to the former slave.[13]

To the distress of the department staff officers at Hilton Head, who found Stanton "very bearish and boorish," he stopped there again on the way home. He stayed but briefly, and those at headquarters breathed a sigh of relief when the *Spaulding* carried the secretary away. He still left the Jewish peddler in close confinement: Lincoln later freed the man and, in a letter that began "About Jews," mildly chastised Stanton for the apparent anti-Semitism behind his treatment of the peddler and a Jewish officer whom he had summarily dismissed on some pretext. As his steamer rounded Cape Fear on January 16 Stanton ordered it within spyglass distance of Fort Fisher to see how the latest assault had fared, but all was still, and when the lookout distinguished the Stars and Stripes flying over the fort the *Spaulding* dropped anchor. Stanton made his presence known, and Alfred Terry, the commanding general ashore, came out to present him with the big garrison flag the Confederates had flown at the fort. Stanton hurried back to Washington with that trophy and the news, feeling quite hearty.[14]

Fort Fisher yielded more than two thousand Confederate prisoners. As they boarded U.S. transports for the prison at Point Lookout, General Grant asked Confederate authorities to allow three Christian Commission clerics access to Union prisoners in Richmond, so they could assess their condition. The illustrated weeklies had recently reproduced more photographs of returned prisoners, and the images of their naked, skeletal frames had infuriated a Northern public that blamed their condition on deliberate starvation, rather than on the chronic intestinal ailments that more likely caused it. The Confederate exchange commissioner, former District Attorney Robert Ould, conceded that Union prisoners were suffering, and he made another offer of exchange, man for man.[15]

The refusal to exchange prisoners had long brought the families of imprisoned men to censure the Lincoln administration over the obstinacy of its nominal reason for that refusal. Not many of the white prisoners in the South or their loved ones at home appreciated the new principle of racial equality enough to endure interminable imprisonment. Gideon Welles shared their impatience on that point: he seemed to doubt the sincerity of the purported indignation over the treatment of black prisoners and their officers, and with good reason. Both Grant and Stanton had admitted, or inadvertently revealed, that the objection to racial discrimination only served as an excuse to keep possession of an entire army of Confederate prisoners, nearly 67,000 of whom lay in Northern pens by February.[16]

Grant must have consulted with Stanton on Ould's offer in some message now lost, because his next known communication on the subject, on February 2, offered the abrupt report that he was arranging the exchange of three thousand prisoners a week, as though they had already agreed on the basic question of resuming the cartel. "This is as fast and probably faster than they can be delivered to us," he explained. The exchange of black soldiers posed no impediment to the process because it was not mentioned at all in the correspondence with Ould, although that dispute had supposedly been the central issue. Within two days newspapers deep in the Confederate interior proclaimed the revival of the cartel. One such sheet brought a welcome note of authority to the exchange rumors inside the palisade at Andersonville, where so many prisoners felt their government had abandoned them—and where cold, rain, and spitting snow had driven hundreds of them to cast their lot with an equally desperate Confederate recruiter. Within days steamers began shuttling prisoners between Point Lookout and Richmond, but the inmates of faraway Andersonville had weeks to wait. A train full of paroled Confederates rolled slowly past the prison early in March, fresh from the North, but no one left Andersonville until after the middle of the month. Soon Confederate surgeons would recoil at the frailty of some of their own paroled countrymen, but no photographers or reporters stood by to record their emaciation.[17]

Grant may have set aside the argument over black soldiers that had stymied exchanges because he sensed the impending collapse of the Confederacy, and realized that thousands of lives would be lost to further obstinacy. Stanton either approved or declined to interfere, perhaps at least in part to relieve himself of the mounting antagonism from prisoners' friends and relatives. He, too, foresaw the end—and not merely the end of the war, but of the old order. On the last day of January Congress passed the Thirteenth Amendment, abolishing slavery altogether; the next day Lincoln signed it, although his endorsement was not necessary before it went out to the states for the two-thirds ratification that would make it the law of the land.[18]

After Stanton departed Savannah, Sherman rolled across South Carolina and left it a wasteland wherever his troops passed. Meanwhile, Lee's celebrated Army of Northern Virginia began bleeding deserters by scores. Charleston, the defiant target of assaults and bombardments by the army and navy, fell to a lieutenant colonel in command of a regiment composed of former South Carolina slaves. General Terry moved up from Cape Fear and captured Wilmington a few days later, meeting a delirious welcome from the city's erstwhile slave population, and by the fourth day of March the head of Sherman's juggernaut had crossed into North Carolina.[19]

March 4, 1865, ought to have marked one of the more gratifying moments in Abraham Lincoln's public life, but things turned sour just before noon when Andrew Johnson took the oath of office as vice president in the Senate chamber. Braced against recent illness by a little liquor, Johnson stumbled into a maudlin, rambling disquisition on his common origins, the virtues of pure, plebeian democracy, and—in flagrant contradiction of Ben Wade's conquered-province theory of Reconstruction—on the contention that his home state of Tennessee had never left the Union. James Speed, a brother of one of Lincoln's oldest friends from Springfield and now the new attorney general, whispered to Welles that Johnson seemed "deranged," and Welles muttered to Stanton that he must be "either drunk or crazy." Stanton conceded that there was "evidently something wrong."[20]

After the outgoing vice president finally silenced his successor and administered the oath, everyone poured out onto the Capitol steps, which were still wet from the morning rain. The clouds dispersed and a warm sun broke through just as the president emerged, which almost everyone viewed as a hopeful portent, and in his lilting tenor drawl Lincoln recounted for the crowd the economic and political conflicts that had brought the war. Observing that everyone recognized slavery as somehow the cause of the war, he spoke of it as a thing of the past, without alluding to the abolition amendment. He justified the enormous sacrifice of blood and treasure in terms of divine retribution, fixing the responsibility on God's will, and concluded with an eloquent appeal for peace without rancor, as though to stay those who sought vengeance against their enemies.[21]

March brought the end of one political season and the beginning of another, heralded by the annual New Hampshire election. Republicans in the Granite State's congressional delegation solicited furloughs for voters among the War Department clerks, but peaceful portents made that superfluous, and the elections went well enough for the president and his administration to relax a little. The White House found time, finally, to address the Indian troubles in Dakota Territory, and Stanton allowed his recruiters to raise regiments for service against the Sioux from among the Confederate prisoners. The anthropologist Louis Aggasiz saw scientific opportunity in that conflict, confidently asking Stanton for a couple of Indian cadavers and a few severed heads, embalmed with an arsenic solution and shipped by express in barrels of alcohol.[22]

Warmer weather and the imminent spring campaign fostered interest among Washington's powerful in making inspection tours of the Army of the Potomac. All knew this might be the last season for such sights, and in the middle of March Stanton embarked for City Point with Ellen, Representative Samuel Hooper of Massachusetts, Hooper's beautiful, widowed daughter-in-law, and several other dignitaries and their wives. At City Point they boarded a car on the military railroad, shifting finally to ambulances for the ride to Meade's headquarters. A Regular Army major formed the headquarters guard for a review by their second-ranking civilian commander while Stanton's wife and the others stood by. As stern and dignified as the major may have seemed as he watched the proceeding from the saddle, he entertained a dry disdain for the honorable secretary, whom he likened to "the horse in the Bible, who smelt the battle from afar." Meade's staff turned out the Fifth Corps for a more impressive show, consuming the entire afternoon. When the visitors departed, the major cast a discreet glance the ladies' way as they lifted their petticoats and climbed back into their ambulance, revealing a good deal of what he called "jambons." He may have been referring to the Widow Hooper or to Ellen, whom men of any age always seemed to find attractive, when he added that "one *leg* was beautiful as far as it went, which was a little above the garter."[23]

The major's wry opinion of Stanton revealed a fairly common reaction among career soldiers who had seen much action. A few months later, when cavalry commander James H. Wilson learned from one of Grant's staff officers that Stanton had tried to thwart him, he responded with scornful irony. Hinting at Stanton's reputation for cowardice among men of arms, Wilson called him "the greatest civilian of his day," and he clearly regarded Stanton's contempt as a compliment. "I would rather be opposed by Edwin M. Stanton than by any man in America," Wilson sneered.[24]

If seasoned soldiers did not like Stanton, neither did he show much appetite for their company. A couple of days amid the bustle of City Point satiated both Ellen and her husband, especially given the primitive housing, and on the morning of March 18 they started back to Washington. Two days later General Grant invited the president down, hinting that they had some issues to discuss and suggesting that the rest might do him some good. Lincoln, who evidently enjoyed camp life far more than Stanton did, readily accepted, and he and Mary left the Washington arsenal the afternoon of March 23. Ellen Stanton and Mrs. Lincoln did not care much for each other—Mary Lincoln often seemed jealous of younger, prettier women— but in an apparent effort to improve relations the Stantons hopped into their carriage together and raced to the dock to bid the first family adieu, missing them only by minutes.[25]

Lincoln's visit was supposed to have lasted a couple of days, but it stretched into two weeks. After tying up overnight during a gale, the president's boat reached City Point late on March 24, and a grand review planned for his benefit the next morning had to be postponed when the Army of Northern Virginia launched its last offensive. Before dawn, Lee pierced Grant's works outside Petersburg, trying to force him to shorten his lines, or abandon them altogether, so he could hold those Yankees back with part of his army and send the rest to Joe Johnston. Commanding the remnants of the Army of Tennessee and the refugee troops from Georgia and the Carolinas, Johnston was backing northward toward Virginia with Sherman right behind him; in desperation, Lee hoped they could combine against Sherman, crush him, and then turn back to face Grant together. The Ninth Corps alone stopped the breakthrough before breakfast, cutting off a couple of thousand Confederates, capturing them, and covering the slope between the lines with rebel dead, but other fighting flared farther down the line the rest of the day.[26]

Two days later General Sherman steamed up to Grant's headquarters from North Carolina for a quick conference before he and Grant initiated their next campaigns. They joined the president in the stateroom of his steamer, the *River Queen*, where he outlined simple criteria for peace. Let no severity discourage surrender, he told the generals: the rebels need only lay down their arms and go home, recognizing federal authority once more, to resume their peaceful existence—and, implicitly, all the rights of citizenship. In a second gathering on the morning of March 28 he reinforced that magnanimous spirit. The next day Union troops were bearing down on Lee's extreme right flank, and the fighting continued for the following three days, through driving rain and deepening mud, until on April 1 infantry and cavalry under Phil Sheridan cracked the defenses and put a sizable portion of Lee's army to flight, scooping up thousands of prisoners. The next morning Grant opened his batteries all along the Petersburg line, breaking it in two west of town and fighting into the suburbs. Early on April 3 Union soldiers crept forward to find the Confederate lines empty. They poured into the city, and above the James other troops marched into Richmond, where the firing of warehouses had ignited a conflagration that swept uphill from the James River waterfront toward the heart of the city. Meanwhile, most of the Army of the Potomac and the Army of the James turned westward to head off the fragments of Lee's fugitive army, which were streaming toward a junction at Amelia Court House.[27]

The president toured Petersburg, following a Ninth Corps division into the city around noon. The next day he traveled to Richmond, stopping at Clay Street to visit what had been the home of Jefferson Davis until two nights previously. He sat at the desk where Davis had signed his executive orders, in the room where he had rejected the proposals of unofficial peace emissaries like Preston Blair. Lincoln spent the night in the city, and the next morning John Campbell—a justice of the U.S. Supreme Court before secession and Davis's assistant secretary of war until the moment of his flight—asked for a word, to inquire how Virginia might regain its place in the Union. In his happiness at the evident collapse of the rebellion Lincoln turned even more generous than usual: he told Campbell that if the Virginians who had "acted as" the legislature of Virginia would reconvene and vote to take their forces out of the rebellion, they would be allowed to do so, and he implied that it could lead to a speedy restoration of the state's privileges under the federal Union. He gave an order to that effect to Major General Godfrey Weitzel, who had been left to command the troops in Richmond, instructing him to allow the legislators to meet for the stated purpose but to disperse them if they attempted any hostile action.[28]

Back in Washington, William Seward had broken some bones in a carriage accident on the afternoon of April 5, and Stanton wired the president that he should probably come back. Lincoln remained a few days longer, reveling in the news that Sheridan had caught up with Lee's rear guard and captured much of it, along with a wagonload of generals, and he visited the hospitals, shaking hands with men who had been wounded in the final assault on Petersburg.[29]

Lincoln left Weitzel with the admonition to avoid "pressing little points" on the vanquished. He had not yet returned to Washington when Stanton, who seemed to take control of the government during Lincoln's absence, berated Weitzel for not forcing Richmond's ministers to invoke a prayer for the President of the United States. Charles Dana, who stayed behind in Richmond after Lincoln left, had inquired of Weitzel about the Sunday services, and as Dana told the story Weitzel had lied to him—telling him the prayer had been required when, Dana claimed, it had not been. Dana may have misunderstood Weitzel, or he may have been giving Stanton the excuse for complaint that he intuitively knew the secretary wanted, and indeed he did stir his boss to aggressive action. Stanton attended Episcopal services when he went to church, and prayers for those in authority were a standard part of the Episcopal ritual, so he demanded an explanation of Weitzel: when that explanation contradicted Dana's version of events, Stanton called it unsatisfactory, and insisted on imposing the prayer. The president supposed that Weitzel had merely acted in "the spirit and temper manifested by me," but the tempest illustrated how much Stanton's spirit (and Dana's) differed from Lincoln's.[30]

With a little better cause, Stanton also objected to giving Virginia's legislature permission to convene. The president asked Secretary Welles for his opinion about it, and Welles advised against it. As he argued a couple of days later, acknowledgment of the Richmond legislature conflicted with the formal recognition granted to Francis Peirpoint's rump government at Alexandria: Welles himself had not considered the Alexandria legislature legitimate, especially in granting the partition of West Virginia, but Lincoln had, so Welles thought it would be better not to become entangled with competing governments. That seemed to convince the president, who told Weitzel to send home any representatives who might have come. Stanton reported to Sumner that he had belabored the issue with the president, evidently taking credit for the reversal.[31]

Stanton apparently feared that Lincoln intended Virginia to resume practical statehood. Lincoln's order on the legislature had discouraged Senator Sumner, who heard of it in Richmond from Weitzel and then hurried back to confer with Stanton. The news caused the secretary of war intense anxiety, Sumner told Chase, that the fruits of Union victory might be lost. As Sumner and Stanton seemed to view it, the fruits of victory included the right to dictate to the beaten foe. Sumner had frequently fretted over the president's gentler approach, and evidently despaired of the future with so flexible and forgiving a man taking charge of Reconstruction.[32] As it happened, the need for any Virginia legislature to withdraw state forces from the Confederate army all but vanished on April 9, when Lee surrendered his army.[33]

At the next cabinet meeting, on April 14, Stanton proposed his own plan for restoring both Virginia and North Carolina to the Union, essentially subjecting the two states to his own authority through a single military governor. Welles again raised the problem of Peirpoint's skeleton government, and the president asked Stanton how he would handle Peirpoint, but Stanton's reply suggested that he had not thought of that. The plan struck Welles as undemocratic, and he did not care for lumping two states together under one administration, but since it was merely a draft they refrained from much argument over it. Stanton had arrived late for the meeting—as was his habit, noted Welles, who considered his grand entrances a deliberate affectation—and he proposed somewhat presumptuously that normal trade along the Southern coast should be resumed on an order issued in his own name. Welles, whose department would normally have enforced commercial restrictions at the ports, suggested that the president who had imposed the blockade should assume the authority for lifting it. General Grant was present for the meeting, his work done in Virginia, and all hoped for good news from Sherman, who had Johnston cornered in North Carolina. The president prophesied good tidings from that quarter, basing his belief on a dream he had had the night before.[34]

Down in Charleston Harbor, hundreds of soldiers and civilians clambered over the crumbling ramparts of Fort Sumter on a makeshift stairway the morning of April 14 to see Robert Anderson raise the same flag he had lowered four years previously. Stanton had planned the ceremony in the cradle of secession, and had hoped to attend as the chief dignitary, but the steamer *Arago* sailed with the assembled guests before the president returned from the James River. With Seward disabled and Assistant Secretary Dana in Richmond, watching over Weitzel, Stanton did not want to leave the capital.[35]

After dark that evening, while the president took his wife and another couple to see *Our American Cousin*, a crowd of soldiers gathered at Stanton's home and called for a speech, which he gave them. His audience dispersed sometime before ten o'clock, about the time John Wilkes Booth crept up the stairway to the president's private box at Ford's Theatre and put a bullet in the back of Lincoln's head. As Booth fled, theatergoers climbed into the box to attend his victim. A young clerk in the War Department claimed that he and an acquaintance ran the seven blocks from the theater to Stanton's home to apprise him of the shooting. A different messenger brought the news that Secretary Seward had been murdered, too, in the bed where he lay recovering from his carriage accident. Stanton proceeded to the Seward home, and when he forced his way through the crowd he found Welles, who lived only a few doors away. A brawny intruder had barged into the house, fighting off a medical attendant and two of Seward's sons to slash at the secretary with a knife, and he had stabbed a fifth man as he fled the scene. Welles found Seward lying on his blood-soaked bed with a couple of doctors bending over him, and was whispering with the doctors when Stanton came into the room, bellowing questions. One of the doctors silenced him with a finger to his lips. After stopping at the room of Seward's son Frederick, who had been beaten senseless, Stanton and Welles started for Ford's Theatre.[36]

The dying president had been carried across Tenth Street to a boarding house owned by one William Peterson. The whole street was closely packed with people, black and white. Inside, Welles found Lincoln lying diagonally across a small bed, and inquired quietly about the prognosis. A doctor assured him it would only be a matter of hours. Stanton went straight to work collecting evidence, issuing orders to the army and bulletins to police in the major cities, and sending dispatches to John Dix, in New York, for distribution to the newspapers. Speed, the attorney general, joined him in the back parlor. In his first telegram, started at 1:30 A.M. and transmitted at 2:15,

Stanton related the basic facts of Lincoln's mortal wound and the attack on the Sewards, but he also inserted a curious reference to the cabinet meeting of the previous afternoon, in which he mentioned that Lincoln "spoke very kindly of General Lee and others of the Confederacy." That apparent invitation to indignation at the ingratitude of a treacherous foe implied that he had already concluded the assassination was a Confederate plot, or that he wished it portrayed so to the public. Two hours later he made his first overt effort to link the murder to the fugitive government: a search of Booth's room had already produced a letter from one of the conspirators in an earlier plot to kidnap the president, advising him to determine first how such an action might be regarded at Richmond. Stanton immediately interpreted it as an appeal to coordinate the assassination with the Confederate government, or to seek official authority.[37]

Stanton's preliminary hints produced the desired effect. After his dispatches were published, the public's surprisingly profound grief for a president who had been so widely criticized turned to anger at the enemies who were presumed to have orchestrated the outrage. From soldiers, from women serving as nurses in the hospitals, and from citizens across the country came a keening wail against the Confederacy and the "serpent slavery." It would have been logical to consider enemy involvement a possibility, especially in light of the simultaneous attacks on Seward and Lincoln, but Stanton appears to have been the first government official to jump to that conclusion, and the first to encourage its widespread publication.[38]

A *New York Herald* story described Stanton sobbing uncontrollably at the Peterson house. A reporter from the *New York Tribune* attributed a similar breakdown to Charles Sumner, but the *Tribune* man also reported that as Lincoln died every member of his cabinet was "bathed in tears." Forty years later a young soldier who was there that night also remembered Stanton weeping in the moments after the president's death. Welles described pervasive sadness in the house, but did not mention shedding tears, or seeing anyone besides Mary and Robert Lincoln do so, until Saturday morning, when a grief-stricken Tad asked who had killed his father. Only at sight of the wailing Tad did James Speed give way to his emotions, and Speed had known Lincoln longer than any other cabinet member. Stanton must have developed a certain affection for so amiable a man as Lincoln over more than three years of close association, although perhaps not as deep a fondness as some have supposed, for Stanton appeared to mold his affections to his interests, and Lincoln was his political protector. That consideration colors the traditional evidence of Stanton's personal regard for the president and his personal safety. He managed to suppress most of whatever grief he felt, or to transform it into nervous energy.[39] Of all those present he was the most active and efficient, closing off the city with relative speed, calling General Grant back from New Jersey, and interviewing witnesses and informants in the company of the attorney general and a stenographer from the Veteran Reserve Corps. He showed none of the emotional collapse attributed to him when his first wife and his brother died.[40]

Stanton's emotional detachment and his domineering persona made him valuable that night, as others wallowed in anguish. Vice President Johnson stood by, but while Lincoln still breathed no one expected him to take charge. With the government headless and the capital paralyzed, it may have been one of the few appropriate moments in American history for dictatorial leadership, and Stanton assumed that role with alacrity. He conveyed an air of control and a semblance of order that staved off absolute panic, inadvertently giving the country his best few hours of service.

Lincoln died at 7:22 on Saturday morning, April 15. Long afterward, a few witnesses told conflicting stories of Stanton remarking "Now he belongs to the ages" at Lincoln's death, but no accredited contemporary account attributes it to him. That quotation first appeared in print a generation later in an article by Lincoln's two surviving private secretaries, one of whom was in the Peterson house, but they also tended to accept the stories Stanton told about himself, and to use them in their histories of the Lincoln administration. If Stanton actually uttered such a haunting and memorable phrase, it seems odd that no reporters quoted it at the time. He did draw the window shades closed.[41]

Andrew Johnson took the oath of office at ten o'clock that morning in the parlor of the Kirkwood Hotel, where he lodged, and Welles asked Speed to call a meeting of the cabinet at noon, in the office of the new treasury secretary, Hugh McCulloch. Johnson announced there that he wished the cabinet members to stay on, except for Usher, who had already submitted a postdated resignation. Stanton evidently took charge of the meeting. When Welles proposed that Speed administer the State Department until Seward recovered, Stanton insisted instead on the chief clerk, whom he knew. Welles then suggested that Johnson take Seward's office in the State Department until the Lincolns left the White House, but Stanton objected on the excuse that Seward's papers would be "disturbed," and persuaded Johnson to use a room McCulloch had offered, next to his own office. Welles, suspicious of Stanton by now, wondered if Seward's office held documents embarrassing to Stanton, or perhaps to Stanton and Seward together.[42]

Another cabinet meeting convened the next morning, Sunday, at the impromptu office in the Treasury building. Stanton came bustling in over an hour late, carrying a sheaf of papers on the Reconstruction plan he had introduced only two days before. He gave each cabinet member a copy of the proposal, with revisions that excepted Virginia and its nominal government, in deference to Welles's objection, but he advocated military rule in every other state in the former Confederacy. Again they discussed it little, merely taking the copies for later digestion, but as they moved to the general subject of how the rebels would be treated Welles observed that Johnson stiffened noticeably, and hinted that he would make examples of some of the leaders.[43]

Ben Wade had asked Johnson if he would meet with his old comrades from the Committee on the Conduct of the War, and Johnson granted them an hour that same day. Wade, Chandler, Julian, and two other Radicals filed in and found the new president a marked improvement over his predecessor. Wade represented those extreme Radicals who—like Henry Ward Beecher—thought Lincoln soft on rebels and indifferent to the rights of freedmen: when Beecher first heard of the assassination, he remarked that "Johnson's little finger was stronger than Lincoln's loins." Johnson gave Wade a fighting talk, damning treason as a crime that had to be punished, and Wade blurted out that he had faith in him. "By the gods," Julian remembered Wade saying, "there will be no trouble now in running the government!"[44]

That evening Welles stopped at the War Department to talk to Stanton. While he lingered, several more Radicals walked into the office, including Sumner and two of those who had seen Johnson earlier with Wade's committee. Welles felt it might seem rude to leave just as they came in: he also thought Stanton found it inconvenient to have him present, but when Sumner asked about his Reconstruction plan Stanton produced it and started reading it to them, with Welles listening. For some time Welles had believed that someone was leaking internal cabinet discussions to persons outside the circle, and Stanton's casual revelation of so delicate a piece of cabinet business "in embryo" confirmed his suspicion. Before Welles took his leave, Sumner interrupted the reading to ask what provision Stanton had made for granting freedmen the vote, and Stanton said it would be troublesome to include it at that time because of differences among "our friends." The discomfited Welles carried away the realization that Stanton was working behind the president's back. Published comments by Thurlow Weed and Tom Ewing the elder had already revealed that Stanton had also betrayed the secrets of the Buchanan administration, and Welles realized that he must have been doing the same during Lincoln's presidency.[45]

The days immediately after the assassination found Stanton busier than ever, managing the army, planning the president's funeral, trying to take control of Reconstruction, and investigating the assassination. On his orders provost marshals and their hired detectives were rounding up scores of suspects, witnesses, and those who would later be known as "persons of interest," a couple of whom actually had some complicity in the assassination. On April 16 detectives identified and arrested Samuel Arnold, the author of the letter to Booth, and he promptly volunteered the names of Michael

O'Laughlen, George Atzerodt, and John Surratt, who had been involved in the kidnap plot. O'Laughlen fell into police hands the next day, and that night army officers went to the home of Mary Surratt, on H Street, looking for her son; meanwhile, they arrested her and her daughter. While the officers lingered there, Lewis Powell, the man who had attacked Seward, came to the door and walked unwittingly into custody. Booth, his accomplice David Herold, and John Surratt remained loose, and on April 20 Stanton issued rewards totaling $100,000 for their capture.[46]

As he advertised the rewards, Stanton made the unilateral decision to try any defendants in the military court system, where the only appeal could be made to a president who had already implied that his agenda involved severe retribution. Stanton named Joseph Holt to oversee the assassination investigation, again stepping significantly beyond his constitutional authority to order all civilian police officers and magistrates to report to Holt, "and to observe his instructions." Holt, who had served Stanton's political purposes so well before, quickly adopted the secretary's theory of Confederate involvement in the assassination. To help spread the opprobrium for the crime to conservatives generally, Stanton gave Holt the assistance of Henry Burnett, who had so deftly handled the election-eve treason trials in Indiana and had just concluded another military commission in Cincinnati, where he had prosecuted the alleged conspirators in a plot to release rebel prisoners held in Chicago. Later Holt and Burnett were joined by John Bingham, the quondam congressman, who would serve as a "special" judge advocate for this case.[47]

By the time of Lincoln's death General Sherman had run Joe Johnston to ground in North Carolina, and the two put their armies into camp while they composed an intricate surrender convention for the approval of their respective governments. Sherman, who had waged war as viciously as any of the Radical generals he scorned, always maintained that his hostility would vanish the moment the rebels laid down their arms, and his agreement with Johnston confirmed that. Word of the assassination had not reached them when they first met, and the spirit of magnanimity that Lincoln had expressed during their interview aboard the *River Queen* seemed to overcome Sherman. With his Confederate counterpart he proposed nothing less than a blueprint for Reconstruction, including a general amnesty, the restoration of citizens' political rights, and the preservation of state governments. While Sherman and Johnston continued their cease-fire the paperwork traveled north, reaching Grant on the evening after Lincoln's body left the rotunda of the Capitol. He recognized immediately that Sherman had exceeded his authority, asking Stanton to call a special cabinet meeting.[48]

Stanton gathered the president and cabinet members that evening, and they unanimously rejected the agreement as intruding on the prerogatives of the chief executive—and on those of Congress, as any Radical might have argued. Stanton waxed especially vitriolic on Sherman, and later that night he composed an order for Grant to proceed to Sherman's headquarters and "direct operations against the enemy," thereby reducing Sherman to the anomalous position Meade had endured for the last year of the war. To this he added an unnecessarily public rebuke through another of his press releases to General Dix, citing in it a March 3 order that Sherman had never seen, prohibiting any political negotiations with Confederate generals. That public diatribe seemed tuned for the ears of Radicals, and he devoted most of it to criticism of Sherman, charging that the armistice had probably allowed Jefferson Davis to slip away with a fortune in Confederate gold. He even insinuated, albeit indirectly, that Sherman may have made a bargain with the rebel leaders so they could escape the country with their loot. Perhaps agitated by guilt over his blatant injustice to Sherman, Stanton grew frantic a few days later, suspecting that the general intended to lead his armies against the government. Stanton's raving seemed to infect his apparent new protégé, Speed, who even wondered whether Sherman might arrest his best friend, Grant, when he arrived.[49]

The ferocity of Stanton's attack on Sherman in the cabinet meeting seemed designed to convince the others that the generous surrender terms amounted to insubordination, approaching treason. If that was his intention, it worked on the president as well as on Speed. When Senator Chandler later broached the topic with Johnson, he was pleased to hear the president speak harshly of the convention.[50]

Looking back on Stanton's disproportionate alarm, Welles thought he regarded peaceful reunion with intense trepidation because, as a turncoat from the ranks of state-rights conservatives, Stanton—like Holt—feared a rapid restoration of the old Union. Reconstruction as Lincoln had imagined it, and as Sherman's convention conceived it, would likely restore the Democratic Party to power. For heart-and-soul antislavery politicians like Ben Wade, Charles Sumner, and Pennsylvania's Thaddeus Stevens, that would have spelled disaster because it would assure the defeat of their social-justice agenda, thus squandering what they viewed as the chief fruits of victory. For men like Stanton and Holt, who had learned to depend on government connections for their livelihood, restoration of the old political order would have exacted a more personal toll. Those two in particular also faced the potential of prosecution for the excesses of their military tribunals, and had they been subjected to the same version of justice they inflicted on others they would have had good cause for worry.[51]

Grant left Washington before that accusative telegram went out, joining Sherman in North Carolina and instructing him to offer Johnston the same terms as Lee had accepted at Appomattox: the rebels were to turn in their arms and go home on parole, and were not to be disturbed so long as they maintained good behavior. Johnston accepted without hesitation, and Grant did not inflict the intended humiliation of watching over Sherman; instead, he came directly back to Washington. Stanton had nevertheless aroused enormous animosity toward Sherman over the faux pas. Even the general's brother, Senator John Sherman, expressed his distress at the terms, although he pointed out that his brother was merely extending the generosity Grant and Lincoln had shown. He added that the incident was all the more painful in the wake of the assassination, and the vindictive atmosphere prevailing so soon after Lincoln's funeral may have explained the public's exaggerated anger, which Stanton's press release seemed designed to incite. Henry Halleck, by then assigned to Richmond, had joined in the clamor against Sherman, and directed Sherman's subordinates to disregard their commander's orders. Stanton had that edict published, too. Convinced that Stanton had acted maliciously—and it is difficult to believe otherwise—Sherman quietly nursed his grudge.[52]

Henry Burnett later reported that Stanton continued to direct the investigation into the assassination until it was ready for trial, and his correspondence confirms as much. Even with Holt in nominal charge, Stanton issued minute instructions, ordering Burnett to have innocent bystanders like the wardrobe manager at Ford's Theatre arrested, and instructing him to send for evidence as obscure as the undergarments of one of the actresses and the bass viol of one of the musicians. The secretary of war himself opened scores of letters gleaned from the Washington post office, forwarding Surgeon General Barnes a private letter from an assistant surgeon written in a tone that Stanton considered "unbecoming anyone in the employ and pay of the government."[53]

As he oversaw the investigation and the demobilization of a million-man army, Stanton still found time for propaganda. On April 25, while Lincoln's body lay on view in New York City, Stanton sent Dix another dispatch for publication, announcing that evidence indicated the assassination plot had been hatched in Canada and approved in Richmond. That evidence consisted initially of a statement offered by a deserter—Hans Henry Von Winkelstein—who had enlisted in the Regular Army at New York in 1861 but had decamped two years later and joined the Confederate army as Henry Von Steinacker. In the spring of 1865 he was confined at Fort Delaware: he bought his release with a fanciful tale of having met three mysterious civilians, including one named Booth, while he was roaming the Shenandoah Valley, alone, in the summer of 1863. According to Von Steinacker, the same trio later appeared in the encampment of his regiment, where they and his officers convened a meeting of a secret order dedicated to the assassination of Abraham Lincoln. Von Steinacker's officers had included John Yates

Beall, a Confederate operative who was hanged in New York seven weeks before Lincoln's death, so his fable dovetailed with Stanton's desire to link the assassins to secret societies and agents of the Richmond government.[54]

Encouraged, perhaps, by Von Steinacker's convenient story, Stanton asked Henry Burnett for a report on the secret societies and how they might have been involved in the assassination, and on May 2 Burnett replied that "many, if not all, the persons connected with the late assassination of the President were members of this resuscitated Order of Knights of the Golden Circle." That same day Stanton asked Holt for a list of Confederate officials for whom he had any evidence of involvement, and Holt produced it immediately. With those two documents Stanton composed a proclamation indicting Jefferson Davis, several of his agents in Canada, "and other rebels and traitors" in the murder of Lincoln, and he took it to a cabinet meeting at Johnson's Treasury Department office. Stanton evidently detailed none of the evidence, merely claiming that it existed, but Johnson signed the proclamation, and Stanton promptly sent it to the newspapers via Dix, as well. To his cabinet colleagues Stanton remarked that he wanted the conspirators tried and executed before Lincoln's remains had been interred at Springfield.[55]

By then, John Wilkes Booth was dead. He had fled through eastern Maryland, breaking his leg when his horse fell on that first night's wild ride, forcing him to stop briefly at the home of Dr. Samuel Mudd. Later he slipped across the Potomac into Virginia, and a cavalry detachment that had been on his trail caught up with him at a farm near Port Royal. Trapped in the barn, which the soldiers set afire, he was hobbling about with a carbine in his hand when one of the cavalrymen poked his revolver through a gap in the barn wall and fired at him. By chance the ball struck Booth in the neck, paralyzing him, and he died soon afterward on the porch of the house. Herold, who had accompanied him, gave up without a fight, and was brought back to the Washington penitentiary, where he joined the other suspects, including Dr. Mudd.[56]

While Stanton lay stretched out on the sofa in his house on the evening of April 26, with Ellen sitting nearby, a buggy pulled up in front of his house. His chief detective, a shady character named Lafayette Baker, fairly ran inside to announce the killing and capture. Baker also introduced Lieutenant Colonel Everton Conger, whose detail had run Booth down. Stanton rose from the sofa, and Conger presented him with a packet of articles he had taken from the assassin's clothing. Stanton poured the contents out on a table, including a pocket diary, and looked them over for half an hour or more before handing everything but the diary to Baker with instructions to give it all to Joseph Holt, whom he wanted to conduct the prosecution through the Bureau of Military Justice.[57]

Promising that the proof against the defendants was "clear and positive," Stanton had little difficulty persuading President Johnson to allow a military trial; he also wanted the trial held behind closed doors, apparently so he could release or withhold information as he pleased. Attorney General Speed, the aggrieved friend of Lincoln, provided a legal opinion that a military commission had jurisdiction under the proclamation of September 24, 1862, because the murder was purportedly meant to aid the rebellion; Speed's predecessor, Edward Bates, roundly denounced him for succumbing to the wheedling of Stanton, whom Bates saw behind the decision. "He believes in mere force," Bates growled, "so long as he wields it, but cowers before it, when wielded by another hand."[58]

Stanton appears to have had two main goals. The first was to ensure that the assassination case would be tried by a reliable team of military prosecutors and judges, and overseen by his trusted ally Holt.[59] The mere allegation of high-level Confederate involvement provided an excuse for a military trial, and the second goal—the political effort to associate the universally abominated crime with rebels and their Northern sympathizers—did not require actual proof. The longer the process dragged on, and the more innuendo it entailed, the more political benefits might accrue to the Radical cause.

It did not take Stanton long to capitalize on the popular fury against the moribund slave power that his own accusations had provoked. On the same day that the military commission first met, Stanton revealed in cabinet council that he warmly supported voting rights for freed slaves—which he had tried to persuade Charles Sumner not to press, barely three weeks previously. Gideon Welles saw that the tide was turning in the direction of suffrage, at least for "aspiring politicians."[60]

Opposition to the military trial of the suspected conspirators came loud and strong across the country, and from friendly as well as hostile sources. Sanitary Commission treasurer George Templeton Strong doubted the legality and the prudence of Stanton's course, which ultimately tainted the process with the distinct appearance of an orchestrated verdict. For once all the major dailies in New York City agreed—including Horace Greeley's Radical *Tribune* and Manton Marble's consistently conservative *World*— demanding that civil authorities try the case. So effective was the unanimous condemnation that Stanton took a bizarre step to punish what he viewed as Greeley's betrayal, and to pressure him to abandon his strident editorial position: on May 12, Stanton retained his friend Edwards Pierrepont to prosecute Greeley and the other owners of the *Tribune* in criminal court and by civil suit for "Greeley's persistent effort the last four weeks to incite assassins to finish their work by murdering me." Stanton's personal propagandist Horatio Woodman tried to soften criticism with a report in the *Boston Evening Transcript* that Stanton had originally opposed a military trial, but that was patently untrue.[61]

Two of General Grant's staff officers, Horace Porter and Cyrus Comstock, had been assigned to the commission. Comstock argued, perhaps for both of them, that the commission lacked jurisdiction, notwithstanding Speed's supportive opinion, which had been based on the presupposition that the defendants were guilty. Comstock complained as well about the secrecy of the trial, and of the manner in which all eight defendants were brought in hooded and shackled.[62] Stanton replaced the uncooperative Comstock and Porter the following day. He went out of his way to assure them that they had not been removed for any insidious purpose, leaving it all the more likely that he had done so precisely because of their opposition to the trial. He offered the unconvincing excuse that they were considered inappropriate judges because their chief, Grant, had purportedly been one of the intended victims: worse conflicts of interest had not prevented Stanton from assigning Rufus King and James Ricketts to Fitz John Porter's court martial, and he knew that Comstock and Horace Porter were members of Grant's staff when he named them to the court. A couple of days later Comstock went to the president to ask if he would open the trial to the public, and eventually Johnson agreed to allow at least some visitors into the courtroom, but Stanton held ultimate control over the passes. Most of them went to government officials, military officers, or their wives.[63]

The composition of the court reinforced the impression that a conviction had been designed from the start. David Hunter, the Radical opportunist who had served the same role in the campaign to ruin Fitz John Porter, sat as president. Major General Lew Wallace, a Democrat-turned-Republican, seemed to find it necessary to exercise the exaggerated loyalty of the convert that Holt and Stanton so prominently illustrated, and his performance on this court would lead Stanton to trust him as president of another show trial later that year. August Kautz, a major general by brevet, had led a division of cavalry under Ben Butler with marked mediocrity, which might have inclined many career soldiers to comply with the perceived expectations of their superiors, but Kautz maintained a measure of objectivity during the trial. Brigadier General Albion Howe had shown similar inefficiency on the battlefield, and had been consigned to the rear as a result, after which he had seen the light, voting for conviction in Surgeon General Hammond's court martial; at one critical juncture Howe would aid the prosecution by challenging the competence of a defense witness on a ridiculous excuse. Robert Foster, another brigadier, had served in the same regiment with Lew Wallace in the early days of the war: he showed no signs of partiality, but Brigadier Thomas Harris made up for him, siding with Hunter in a vicious personal attack on Mary Surratt's attorney and embracing the most obvious perjury as gospel. David Clendenin, a former schoolteacher, had joined the army in his thirties and held the volunteer rank of lieutenant colonel when the trial began: he would have been mustered out within weeks, but in apparent reward for his services in the trial he was jumped two grades by brevet to brigadier general only four days after the execution of the conspirators, and the promotion allowed him to make the Regular Army his career. The two who replaced Comstock and Porter also ended up as career soldiers with brevets as brigadier general, and presumably they entertained no qualms about depriving the defendants of their constitutional right to a jury trial; one of them joined General Howe in trying to silence a crucial defense witness, who would have discredited one of Holt's perjurers. Stanton could have depended on a slight majority of the original court detail, and a solid majority of the ultimate members.[64]

During the trial, cavalrymen occupied every open square between Pennsylvania Avenue and the makeshift courtroom at the penitentiary. A squad of mounted men escorted each member of the court and each judge advocate; defense counsel merited no such safeguard. Ostensibly for their own protection, Holt's three chief witnesses to Confederate involvement testified in secret, and it was only after the official court record of their testimony had been leaked to a Cincinnati newspaper that the real reason for court secrecy surfaced: all three were impostors and perjurers, who were exposed by the unintended publication of their accounts. Even after General Dix confirmed the foremost of them as an untrustworthy mountebank, Holt clung to all three. He produced three subtly incriminating letters that had all been "found" under mysterious circumstances, including one that supposedly washed ashore in North Carolina and another that was picked up on a streetcar in New York City, after it had allegedly been dropped by a man wearing a false beard and a hidden revolver. Holt's main witness to the Canadian Confederate connection turned out to be a professional confidence man—Sandford Conover, alias James Watson Wallace, alias Charles A. Dunham—whose mendacity stained the government's case and eventually raised a serious question of whether Holt had been gulled by Conover's perjury or complicit in it.[65]

A week into the trial, prominent Washington Radicals heard that Stanton was about to resign. That rumor surfaced just as newspapers began reporting that Sherman's army was nearing the capital on its way from Richmond, and the official snub Sherman had given Halleck on his way through that city suggested that he was coming with blood in his eye, intent on taking revenge against the author of his recent humiliation.[66]

When the soldiers who had marched through the Carolinas did arrive, they and their general went quietly into camp below the Potomac. No mutinous mob assailed the War Department, but a few days later even the trial of the conspirators had to pause as the soldiers took over the city. Washington spilled over with visitors who had come to see the last grand review of the Army of the Potomac and Sherman's ragged vagabonds. Before dawn on May 23 tens of thousands of cavalry, infantry, and artillery filed into the streets radiating away from the Capitol as crowds of civilians, convalescent soldiers, and Confederate deserters jostled each other for vantage points on both sides of Pennsylvania Avenue. A canopied reviewing stand had been erected where the avenue bent behind the White House, and there sat President Johnson, with Stanton on his right and General Grant on his left, along with a few other cabinet members, military officers, and ladies. At nine o'clock General Meade and his staff began the long ride between cheering crowds, followed by the cavalry and the Ninth Corps, with bands blaring. Spectators tossed bouquets from the sidelines. Artillery brigades squeezed in between the divisions, and gaps between the units created an accordion effect. A single division represented the Nineteenth Corps, but the Fifth marched with full ranks, as did the Second Corps, and it was well into the afternoon before the last caisson had rumbled past.[67]

The armies of the West took center stage the next day, marching in the loose-jointed fashion that had carried them across four states, bowing and turning to wave their acknowledgment of the onlookers' cheers. Some of them led mules burdened with pilfered cookware, atop which sat the occasional half-tamed critter collected along some Southern byway. A battalion of bummers—the undisciplined stragglers who had foraged so avariciously through the Carolinas—rode their commandeered horses and mules.[68]

General Sherman led the procession, saluting the president and Grant as he passed the reviewing stand. Once past, he consigned his horse to an orderly and climbed up to sit with the dignitaries. Johnson, Grant, and the others all stood to greet him, shaking his hand, but this was the first time he and the secretary of war had met since Stanton's tantrum over the Johnston convention. A Massachusetts congressman had seen Sherman two days before, finding him still extremely bitter over Stanton's savage dispatches, and when a hopeful Stanton extended his hand Sherman let him grasp the air with it, clapping his own hand to his side and merely nodding or bowing slightly. Across the avenue sat others who had been waiting for this very moment, many of whom had trained binoculars or opera glasses on the tall, florid general and the squat, grey bureaucrat.[69]

Stanton swallowed the insult. He may have begun to feel overwhelmed by the avalanche of criticism over trying the assassination suspects by military commission, and doubted his own popularity: even Radicals like Henry Winter Davis and Carl Schurz had expressed great distaste for Stanton's secret military trial. Sherman's soldiers, meanwhile, began showing overt contempt for the secretary of war in public, and Stanton dared not arrest them for fear of inciting violence—perhaps against himself. Two days after the review a drove of Sherman's officers poured into Willard's Hotel and started damning Stanton high and low; some of them would periodically jump up on the bar, call for "three groans" for the secretary, and then jump back down for another drink. Mrs. Sherman tried to heal the breach by making a social call on the Stantons herself: ex-Senator Browning inquired of Stanton, who welcomed the attempt and entertained Mrs. Sherman for "a very pleasant half hour," but the general remained obdurate, insisting that Stanton owed him an apology. The tense situation among Sherman's soldiers may have accelerated the process of mustering out the armies, and on May 29 the War Department ordered all white troops sent home whose terms of service would expire before October. U.S. Colored Troops would all remain on duty, partly on the logic that it would give them continued employment. They were also more susceptible to discipline than white troops, and could be relied upon to serve without such alarming displays of insubordination.[70]

16

AVENGING ANGEL

The trial of the accused conspirators resumed immediately after the grand review, consuming all of June. Many of the witnesses were lodged in the Old Capitol or other prisons. When each had testified satisfactorily, Stanton or Holt would recommend their release and pardon; sometimes Holt would have them furnished with transportation home, or even ask that they be paid for particularly incriminating testimony. Among them was Henry Von Steinacker, alias Von Winkelstein, one of Holt's early witnesses to official Confederate involvement. Von Steinacker had lied about himself and everything he supposedly knew, but considering the customary consequence for deserting to the enemy he could hardly be blamed for resorting to perjury.[1]

On June 27, after the various defense counsel had made their arguments. John Bingham began a two-day summation, spending most of the first day defending the jurisdiction of the court and denouncing defense attorney Thomas Ewing Jr.'s comparison of it to the Spanish Inquisition. To justify the military tribunal Bingham recounted the mutual corroboration of Sandford Conover and the battery of other impostors who had furnished the necessary accusations about Confederate agents, some of which had already been discredited. On the second day Bingham reviewed the evidence, casually misrepresenting crucial aspects of it in direct contradiction to the testimony, and especially as it related to Mrs. Surratt. The two witnesses who did her the most damage were both evident conspirators themselves, at least in Booth's early plan to kidnap Lincoln, but both were released from the Old Capitol prison to testify against her, and neither was prosecuted: at least one of them—Louis Weichmann—was later installed and kept in government office through the intercessions of Holt and one of the replacement judges, James Ekin.[2]

Bingham's misrepresentations were not intended to influence the court's decision, which was already fixed. As in all the other military trials he and Holt had conducted at Stanton's direction, his review was meant to mold public opinion toward the viewpoint Stanton wished to impose, and it was quickly published at government expense for distribution as a free pamphlet. The dense and disjointed trial transcripts, which showed some of the weaknesses in the government case, were only produced commercially by the court stenographer, for private purchase.[3]

Even outside the jaundiced atmosphere of that courtroom, the evidence against Powell, Herold, and Atzerodt would have left no doubt of their guilt. It was just as obvious that Arnold and O'Laughlen had participated in the kidnap plot. Less convincing was the testimony against Dr. Mudd, who had harbored Booth during his flight, but the cooperative Weichmann obliged the prosecution with enough incriminating testimony. Edward Spangler, a stagehand at Ford's Theatre and a friend of Booth's, appears to have contributed unwittingly to Booth's escape, but he was undone by a single witness who offered testimony that conflicted somewhat with the recollections of others. All eight of the defendants were convicted anyway. At least five of the nine members of the court met Stanton's expectations, voting for the death penalty in almost every instance, but the two-thirds majority required for execution was achieved only in the cases of Powell, Herold, Atzerodt, and Mrs. Surratt. Arnold, Mudd, and O'Laughlen all drew sentences of life in prison at hard labor; Spangler, who was essentially innocent, was given six years.[4]

In the tenor of the time, that result was probably inevitable: even the jury in a criminal courtroom would likely have shown little mercy amid the post-assassination hysteria.[5] Stanton would have sacrificed none of the political effect he sought had he remanded the eight to a civil court, and he would have avoided the distinct impression that he had deliberately manipulated the result through his internal judicial system.

General Kautz claimed years later that Holt, Bingham, and Burnett showed obvious dissatisfaction that some of the defendants had escaped the noose, and that five members of the commission wanted to present a petition asking the president to consider clemency for Mrs. Surratt because of her "age and sex." Certainly it did seem inconsistent that members who had imposed the death penalty had also recommended commutation of that sentence: at least two of the signers (almost certainly Hunter and Ekin) must also have voted for her execution, because a two-thirds majority was required. The signatures of Kautz and Foster were no surprise, as they were the two most independent of the judges, and the addition of David Hunter's name could be explained by his desire to shun responsibility for sending a woman to her death: his reputation already bore a sufficient stain for having made war on helpless civilians.[6]

The reference to Mrs. Surratt's age as a reason for clemency has puzzled students of the case for a century and a half. A nineteenth-century plea to save a female from execution is easily understood, but Mary Surratt was just beyond her middle forties at the time of the trial, which was not considered old even then. A new interpretation of the intent behind the petition emerges from reading the allusion to her "age and sex" collectively, as a euphemism for menopause, which was still popularly viewed as producing hysteria and occasional insanity. Two defense attorneys remarked afterward that Mrs. Surratt became savagely afflicted with menopausal symptoms throughout her imprisonment, consisting mainly of excessive, persistent menstruation that made her cell "scarcely habitable." Only after she had endured two months alone in a cramped cell, and eighteen days before her hanging, did Stanton authorize General Hancock to afford her more comfortable quarters and such "necessaries" as she required.[7]

What happened next has never been satisfactorily explained, but one interpretation does reconcile most of the conflicting testimony. John Bingham later admitted that he took the court's findings to Stanton and decried the clemency petition: it conflicted with an opinion the two of them evidently shared with Holt—that the sentences should not be mitigated, nominally for the sake of justice, but perhaps more to sustain the legitimacy of the court. President Johnson had fallen seriously ill and was confined to his room for the first week of July, but it was Holt's duty to make a report on the findings and sentences and present it to Johnson for approval. The petition for clemency was written on a different kind of paper from the long list of findings and sentences, which were bound together at the top with ribbon laced through three drilled holes. If it was attached to the papers that Holt carried to the White House on July 5, it was bound at the back of the packet in a fashion that would disguise it: the sixteen pages of findings were immediately followed by the notice of the court's adjournment, denoting the end of the record. Just below that, Holt wrote a paragraph signifying the president's approval of the sentences, flipping the entire document over to finish that paragraph. After some discussion, the ailing Johnson signed it in a shaky hand. The blank page on which Holt wrote the second half of the approval paragraph seemed to confirm that the record ended there, but beneath that page lay the petition, facedown, so that only by continuing to the next page and turning it over would Johnson have seen the body of the document. He insisted ever afterward that he did not see it on that occasion, while Holt maintained that in signing his name to the approval "the President's eye necessarily fell on the petition or recommendation in favor of Mrs. Surratt." If the pages were gathered in that manner, however, and the petition was folded over to accommodate his signature, his eye fell only on the top margin of that petition. Had he turned it over, he would have seen only two upside-down signatures on the bottom of the page, but considering his weakened condition he may not have turned it over at all, instead handing it back to Holt.[8]

Holt claimed later that he pointed out the petition, and he said Johnson read it, but the two of them were alone in the president's bedroom and

Johnson steadfastly denied it. Johnson's truthfulness came into some question a couple of years later, when Ulysses Grant insinuated that the president misrepresented an understanding between them, but Holt's reliability is even more doubtful. His pompous assertions of spotless honor are severely compromised not only by the numerous incidents during his career that challenged his veracity but by his penchant for illicit personal liaisons. Even as he indignantly defended himself against accusations that he withheld the clemency petition and suborned witnesses, he was carrying on a clandestine relationship with a woman who seems obviously to have been married.[9]

Stanton was under the weather himself in early July, but he still worked, and with their offices in the same building he and Holt surely discussed the findings, the petition, and probably the importance of avoiding clemency. Their opposition lends strength to the argument that Holt either did not include the petition or arranged it among the papers in a way that made it less likely Johnson would find it by himself. Had he left it out, and had Johnson called him to account for it, he might reasonably have pleaded oversight, since the paper seemed to be ancillary to the trial, but by carefully concealing it against ordinary perusal he could honestly have insisted that it was there: Holt's awkward remark that Johnson's "eye necessarily fell" on the petition may suggest a similar effort to mislead. Holt failed to mention the petition in his summary of the case, urging instead that the sentences were necessary to serve "the highest considerations of public justice," and his zeal toward that end does nothing to corroborate his later recollection that he mentioned it specifically. Johnson's irate response when the existence of the petition finally became common knowledge further supports his own contention, although at the time he had shown no disposition to leniency himself.[10]

Newspapers alluded to the rumored existence of a clemency recommendation when they reported the sentences—which were scheduled to be carried out within forty-eight hours of Johnson's approval—but the cabinet learned nothing of the petition, and Johnson was even less likely to hear or read of it from his sickroom. Not until John Surratt was captured and brought back to Washington for trial, in 1867, did the petition become notorious, whereupon Johnson called for the paperwork and found the petition attached—as Orville Browning phrased it when he saw it—"in such a way as to show that it had been subsequently done." Browning, who by then had joined the cabinet as Interior secretary, asked about it at the cabinet meeting of August 9, 1867, and everyone present—including Johnson, Seward, and Welles—denied having been aware of the recommendation until it was publicized in Surratt's trial.[11]

After that, memories of the incident divided along partisan lines, except perhaps for former Attorney General James Speed, who reported that he saw the record of the case in the president's office before the executions, with the petition attached. That may have been true, but if he did see the document it must have been because Holt specifically showed it to him. Johnson was not in his office all that week, and Holt necessarily took the signed papers back to his own office with him when he left the president's sickroom. Johnson later contended that Speed had seen the petition at the War Department, but even Speed's version offered no proof that Johnson saw it, and probably neither he nor the rest of the cabinet knew about it. As Johnson later pointed out, the clemency petition that Holt claimed to have shown him as part of the trial record was conspicuously absent from the record of the trial that Holt authorized for publication.[12]

The only testimony suggesting Johnson did know about the petition before the executions came eight years later, from Radical Republicans and friends of Holt who by then had become Johnson's dedicated political opponents. Responding to Holt's 1873 appeal for helpful testimony, John Bingham provided him with a suspiciously pat narrative that conflicted with what Welles and Browning had to say on the subject. Bingham claimed that he called at Holt's office after the executions, asked Holt for the trial record without saying why, and found the petition attached, just as Johnson said he did in 1867. Bingham, who may have wanted to shed any personal responsibility in Mrs. Surratt's death, then added that he asked Seward and Stanton if Johnson had known about the petition: according to his chronologically implausible tale, Stanton and Seward both assured him that the issue of clemency had been discussed and rejected in cabinet council before Mrs. Surratt went to her death. That last detail contradicted Holt's own claim that Johnson only saw the clemency petition in his bedroom. Furthermore, Johnson's illness had precluded any cabinet meetings between the trial and the execution. Seward, meanwhile—who was dead by the time Bingham made his claim—had been one of those who told Browning that he only learned of the recommendation for mercy in 1867.[13]

Former Interior secretary James Harlan, a fiercely Radical enemy of Johnson's by 1873, tried to rehabilitate Bingham's account by suggesting that he had heard the matter discussed in an informal cabinet gathering with only a few members, but he discredited his own version by including Seward—and "possibly" Attorney General Speed. Speed declined to corroborate this, but Johnson's personal secretary from 1865, another Radical, claimed that Johnson told him about the petition, although he was not certain when.[14]

Bingham insisted that he withheld this information when the storm first exploded because Stanton advised him to keep quiet about it. By the time Bingham came forward, Stanton was beyond denying that he had let Holt's name go undefended. Holt, who had already printed one self-exculpatory pamphlet about Sandford Conover's perjury scheme, published all the supportive correspondence on the pardon scandal in another one. "It seems almost incredible that he could have been guilty of such cold blooded meanness towards a friend," a Texas judge said of Stanton, after Holt sent him his latest *Vindication*, "but the evidence is absolutely conclusive against him."[15]

Stanton might well have squelched an effort to defend a friend, particularly if it might spawn an investigation into his own actions, but Bingham's excuse for not revealing the information is no more credible than the rest of his factually flawed account. He was another potential conspirator in withholding the clemency petition, and he responded a little too enthusiastically to Holt's request for exculpatory testimony, basing it on alleged statements from two men who were then dead. Holt's failure to solicit evidence for his exoneration until Seward and Stanton were out of the way also invites suspicion: he started seeking testimony soon after the second of them had died. If the accusation against him so troubled him, his long delay in making an inquiry suggests the opportunity their deaths offered to manufacture his own vindication without fear of contradiction. That evident readiness to deceive comports with the character of a man whose chronic philandering only hinted at the pliable ethics that he disguised with an aggressive air of exaggerated rectitude. It is no tribute to Holt's probity that he worked so closely, so long, and so harmoniously with the devious Stanton, whose posthumous reputation he seemed willing enough to sacrifice in order to salvage his own. The two were cut from the same cloth.

The clemency petition notwithstanding, Mrs. Surratt was hanged with her three codefendants on July 7, and they were buried at the foot of their gallows; Stanton even denied Mrs. Surratt's daughter her mother's body. The hasty execution outraged many who thought the military commission illegal, but the news of the hanging came almost simultaneously with the report of the court's decision and sentences, leaving no time for protest. Then, having exacted retribution for Lincoln's murder, Stanton sought to appease national anger over the sufferings of Union prisoners—anger that he had cultivated with those photographs of repatriated skeletons. In August Stanton appointed Lew Wallace president of a nine-member commission for the trial of Captain Henry Wirz, the Swiss-born officer who had served as commandant of Andersonville prison. For judge advocate Stanton appointed Norton Chipman—who, like so many of Stanton's War Department associates, had worked as a patent attorney.[16]

Through Charles Dana, Stanton had collected a vast trove of Confederate records in Richmond, for which he has long been credited with having performed a wonderful service to historians. No historical motive inspired him: he saved the records to find evidence that would incriminate Confederates in either the Lincoln assassination or in atrocities against Union prisoners. On April 5, while Richmond still smoldered, he ordered General Weitzel to collect all the correspondence and papers in the Richmond post office and other public buildings. Dana secured that material and every other Confederate document he could find, beginning with a cache of treasury papers that lay partially destroyed behind the railroad depot. When Henry Halleck assumed command at Richmond, one of his aides took charge of the Confederate archives, and Halleck mentioned their potential use as evidence against rebel agents "and their coadjutors, here and at the North." In sending the first ninety crates of documents, he told Stanton the papers might provide "some important links of testimony," and he had the homes of prominent Confederates searched for evidence against the officials Stanton and Holt were trying to implicate in the Lincoln assassination. Before he fled Charlotte, North Carolina, Confederate secretary of war John C. Breckinridge instructed his chief clerk to turn their department records over to the U.S. officer who assumed command there, so in May Halleck was able to notify Stanton that those archives were on their way to Washington.[17]

As soon as he learned of that discovery, Stanton wrote to his Boston newspaper ally Horatio Woodman, asking if he would come straight to Washington and examine them. Woodman could not leave home just then, and with no one to scour the Confederate archives the prosecution found no documentation for their claim of rebel culpability: only two pieces of purported official correspondence appeared as exhibits in the trial of the conspirators. Not until July 21 did Stanton create the Bureau of Confederate Archives, naming Francis Lieber as chief, and Lieber organized a systematic perusal of all the papers that had been preserved. Numbers of large, leather-bound ledgers had been sent up from Andersonville, where Captain Wirz delivered all the letterbooks, registers, rolls, and morning reports from the commandants' office to the Union officer who came to take him away, and these attracted particular notice. The delay in Wirz's trial partly reflected the time required to scan those books for incriminating material.[18]

The trial of the wretched Wirz provided an even more shameless example of injustice than that of the conspirators, most of whom were at least guilty of some of the charges against them. Wirz, a man of humble demeanor, owned no real responsibility for the suffering of Union prisoners under his care. He was the only Confederate officer who stayed with the remaining prisoners to the last, after hostilities ended and everyone else had abandoned their posts; the records he had preserved helped to document his attempts to mitigate the misery of those inside the stockade. It had simply been his misfortune to be the man responsible for confining and imposing prison discipline on tens of thousands of Union prisoners. His name and face were known to more exchanged and paroled Yankees than those of any other Confederate prison official. Worse luck for him, he had fallen into the hands of a government disproportionately influenced by a secretary of war who had lobbied strenuously against prisoner exchanges: even many Northerners and Union soldiers held Stanton responsible for the consequences of his policy. For many whose sons had died in rebel captivity, or had returned home broken in health, Abraham Lincoln and Edwin Stanton best represented the intransigence that had laid so many Union soldiers under the Georgia clay. Captured Union officers in particular knew that Stanton had posed the main obstacle when they sought release through special exchanges. Lincoln's assassination had absolved the former president of any sins in the public mind, and that left mainly Stanton to take the blame, until Wirz fell into his hands. The shocking photographs, the congressional investigation, and lurid newspaper accounts of the sufferings of Union prisoners—all part of Stanton's propaganda campaign—had ignited so much outrage that someone had to answer for it.[19]

Three days after Wirz was led away from Andersonville, other Union horsemen surprised the encampment of Jefferson Davis and his party near Irwinville, Georgia, barely fifty miles away. A delighted Stanton passed on the false rumor that Davis had been captured wearing his wife's clothing, and ordered him brought north in irons.[20]

Late in August, eleven weeks after his arrest, Wirz finally came to trial in Washington, crossing the street under guard from the Old Capitol Prison to a courtroom in the basement of the Capitol building. There sat another military commission, headed by Lew Wallace, who had not only voted to hang most of the defendants in the conspiracy trial but had refused to recommend clemency for Mrs. Surratt. General Wallace presided reluctantly, but not because of any aversion to the process: he was merely anxious to start for Mexico, to engage in a speculative mining operation. His first view of Wirz elicited a reaction that predicted the verdict. He described the prisoner as "nervous and fully alarmed," adding that he "avoids your gaze, and withers under the knit-brows of the crowd." Even before the charges had been read, Wallace found this scapegoat for the suffering of Union prisoners "well chosen for his awful duty."[21]

Former prisoners dominated the trial, peddling a litany of miseries real and imagined. Most of them blamed it all on the captain who had been charged with housing, feeding, and providing medical care for more than thirty thousand men without adequate materials or authority, and who had been responsible for preventing their escape with a garrison of guards he did not command. Hearsay flourished, and former prisoners who admitted never having witnessed Wirz inflict any cruelty were allowed to express their opinion that tales of heinous crimes were nevertheless true. Georgians who lived near Andersonville and had profited from the prison, or had accepted employment with the prosecution, offered testimony that close scrutiny might easily have discredited; they suggested other compliant witnesses, and were rewarded with cash and pardons. Meanwhile, Judge Advocate Chipman interfered directly to prevent the appearance of one defense witness by using his parole restrictions against him. The court continually overruled defense objections to rumors, hearsay, and patently fabricated exhibits, but habitually sustained prosecution objections to the introduction of exculpatory evidence or anything unflattering to Union officials or policy. Chipman successfully countered challenges to the veracity of former prisoners on the sole ground that their service in the Union army proved their truthfulness. Some of those prosecution witnesses turned out to be deserters and bounty jumpers, but Chipman instead ascribed those very crimes to innocent Union soldiers who provided defense testimony. One man came to tell how Wirz had allowed him and five others out of Andersonville to take President Lincoln a petition from a committee of prisoners, begging him to resume exchanges, but Chipman prevented that testimony by a sentimental appeal to the memory of the martyred president: that Lincoln (or Stanton) refused to see the petitioners implied a heartlessness that was unbelievable, he argued, and such a slander should not even be uttered. The court concurred, and the testimony was not allowed.[22]

Such one-sided proceedings posed an inviting opportunity for propaganda, but the volume of testimony threatened to overwhelm any attempt to publish the transcripts of the trial in any form the public was likely to read. Early newspaper coverage of the case disappointed Joseph Holt, and he suggested to Stanton that they find a newspaper of large circulation that might give the case its full attention. He proposed the *New York Times*, the editor of which had chaired the Republican National Committee during the 1864 election, and the *Times* promptly obliged with lurid enthusiasm.[23]

Not far into the trial the court's bias became so blatant that both of Wirz's lawyers attempted to withdraw in protest, remarking that they could clearly do nothing for him before such a tribunal. As president of the court Wallace happily dismissed them, but the doomed Wirz pleaded with them to remain and they consented, albeit with manifest hopelessness. The Bureau of Military Justice had collected a mountain of evidence and an army of witnesses over the spring and summer, and the court blocked almost every attempt to challenge the credibility of the government's case—more of which consisted of perjury or forgery than in the assassination trial. Reading the more preposterous testimony, including some from witnesses who lived near the prison camp, a Georgia newspaper suspected that the prosecutors were conducting a contest for "the most astounding tale of crime and horror." Even Lew Wallace's sister, who sat in the gallery, felt that "the whole power of the Govern't was put forth to crush one miserable worm."[24]

Although more credible witnesses acquitted Wirz of any cruelty or neglect, and his correspondence with superiors confirmed his claimed efforts to ameliorate conditions, the forces Stanton had put in motion moved inexorably toward the desired end. On October 24 Wirz appeared for the court's finding and sentence. A doctor had just testified that the prisoner's physical condition would have prevented him from inflicting much, if any, of the violence he had been accused of personally committing, but the good doctor might as well have remained at home: the court's next action was to declare Wirz guilty of murder and of deliberately destroying the health of Union prisoners—in collaboration with Jefferson Davis and an assortment of other Confederate officials. A gallows was built in the yard of the Old Capitol, and there he was hanged on November 10. His widow was also denied possession of his body, and he was buried alongside George Atzerodt.[25]

The trials only increased Stanton's unpopularity—and Holt's—in the South. Their efforts to implicate Confederate officials tended to demonize the entire South, driving a wedge between the sections and discouraging immediate restoration of the Union. The pair may have intended that very effect, and initially their actions seemed consistent with Andrew Johnson's vindictive rhetoric, but Johnson had begun to turn from the seemingly Radical path he had trod in the wake of the assassination. Barely three weeks after taking office he recognized Francis Peirpoint's Virginia government as the fastest route to restoring that state to loyalty. On May 29 he appointed a provisional governor for North Carolina, with instructions to organize a republican form of government with voting privileges for every man who would be qualified to vote under the state laws of 1861—excepting several classes of Confederate officers, officeholders, agents, and former soldiers whose property exceeded $20,000 in value. Through June he issued similar proclamations for Mississippi, Georgia, Texas, Alabama, and South Carolina, adding Florida on July 13. Louisiana and Arkansas had established loyal governments under Lincoln's wartime 10 percent plan, and Johnson had always insisted that his own state of Tennessee had never left the Union; the government he had presided over from 1862 still ruled that state. By the time Congress convened in December, Johnson had reason to hope that the entire former Confederacy would have been restored to the Union.[26]

During the long congressional recess, Radicals scribbled hasty notes to each other in an effort to intercede with what Thad Stevens called "the insane course of the President." Stevens had written a friendly, cautionary letter to Johnson in May, asserting the prerogative of Congress in Reconstruction, but he had already tried to rouse Radical indignation in private. Even before the president installed that first provisional governor in North Carolina, Stevens admitted to Charles Sumner that he feared Johnson would have "so be-deviled matters" before Congress convened that his course could not be reversed. With escalating concern, Sumner and Stevens began pressing through the summer for freedmen's voting rights, calling on correspondents to make speeches, write letters, and take convention action designed to reduce the states of the old Confederacy to territorial status. Meanwhile, the president and conservative members of his cabinet like Gideon Welles adhered to Lincoln's original contention that the states had no right to secede, and therefore had never done so. The differences between those theoretical interpretations accounted for the contradictory opinions about which branch of government held the responsibility and authority to oversee Reconstruction: if the state governments had simply been hijacked, the restoration of those states fell wholly within the law-enforcement powers of the president; if they had been dissolved, only Congress could determine when they might be readmitted.[27]

In July Ben Wade heard from an ally that the governor of Louisiana was turning Union men out of state office and appointing scores of returned Confederate soldiers and "the worst kind of Rebels," including some who had signed the ordinance of secession in 1861. An Illinois colonel on duty in Mississippi apprised Senator Lyman Trumbull that national loyalty could not be said to exist there: the convention that wrote emancipation into the new state constitution was, he said, as pro-slave as the one that passed the secession ordinance. In a letter to Sumner, Wade revealed his nagging fear that Johnson's generosity toward the Southern states would hamstring the Republican Party, leaving it at the mercy of Southern Democrats and "their copper head allies in the north."[28]

Early on, Radicals began to press Johnson on black suffrage. Sumner tried hinting to him about it early in the summer, to no avail, and by August Sumner assured Wade that the president's provisional governors and white men's governments could never pass muster with Congress. In the middle of August Johnson urged his governor in Mississippi to set an example for returning states by granting a very limited franchise to those who, besides owning taxable property, could read the Constitution and sign their names. That, he supposed, would disarm proponents of the black vote without the risk of lending serious political power to that constituency. Johnson might have shown a Radical streak in his antagonism toward the Southern aristocracy, which he blamed for secession, but he held little of the egalitarian sentiment shared by many of the Radicals in Congress. He was, instead, steeped in the attitudes of Tennessee, where racial prejudice flourished at least as intensely as it did in less loyal areas of the South. He insisted, besides, that regulating the franchise was a state prerogative.[29]

After touring the South in May, Chief Justice Chase had told Johnson that freedmen valued the right to vote only a little less than they did liberty itself. Chase urged Stanton to read his letters to the president, predicting that if universal suffrage were pursued "firmly but kindly" at that moment of Southern subjugation it would probably meet with little opposition. Stanton, who had been so ardent for black suffrage in a cabinet meeting of early May, sensed the president's reluctance on that point, and by August Chase found Stanton unwilling to even try persuading him otherwise. Unlike Lincoln, whose easygoing nature had allowed Stanton to push him on different points without the danger of more than a mild rebuff, Johnson had an obstinate streak and could be testy. At first Stanton's belligerent example had drawn the new president into remarks that promised a harsh and punitive peace. That success inevitably encouraged Stanton to suppose he could dominate Johnson, but he found the Tennessean far less receptive to pressure from below than his predecessor had been. Like the Radicals who pointed out the political vulnerability of disenfranchised former slaves, Chase began to suspect by September of 1865 that only Congress could "save the country" from a new incarnation of the old slave power.[30]

With Johnson still enjoying broad support, and especially while congressional Radicals refrained from criticism, Stanton felt powerless to confront him and reverted to an air of submissive compliance. Dana had resigned as assistant secretary, taking a job as editor of a Chicago newspaper, so Stanton immersed himself in the diminished affairs of his department, where he still exerted complete control. The sudden loss of executive influence and wartime power may have lent a rare touch of sincerity to Stanton's periodic private intimation—voiced again that summer—about leaving the War Department. However, that presented the problem of what he would do next, and without executive favor he stood little chance of securing a significant federal appointment or a return to the remunerative special-attorney contracts he had enjoyed under Buchanan and Lincoln.[31]

As the controversy over how to restore the Southern states built to a crescendo, Stanton and Ellen left sweltering Washington for a month's vacation, but because of Stanton's dwindling financial resources they traveled at government expense, calling it a tour of inspection. Surgeon General Barnes went along as private physician, while Mrs. Barnes joined them as a companion for Ellen. They took a telegrapher to communicate with Stanton's former telegraph chief, Thomas Eckert, who had filled Dana's place as assistant secretary. Accepting invitations to stay with private parties, Stanton lounged ten days or more on the Jersey shore, making his way from Sandy Hook up the Hudson to the spectacular views at West Point, where his nephew had just returned to his studies. After a few days they sailed back down the Hudson, around Long Island, and into Narragansett Bay, stopping with a wealthy family at Newport, Rhode Island.[32] A local reporter noted the stately manner in which Stanton and his entourage traveled, while soldiers' widows struggled to feed their children. Stanton still owned a reputation for autocratic oppression: when the horrified Newport editor belatedly saw his reporter's insinuation about the secretary, he defended the luxurious accommodations as the trappings of a cabinet officer on official tour, sending the retraction to Stanton inside an obsequious letter.[33]

Disturbed, perhaps, by the newspaper observation, Stanton took Ellen from Newport to Boston by train, at his own expense. The old abolitionist William Lloyd Garrison heard of his arrival and wrote to thank him for his invitation to the Fort Sumter flag-raising, in April. Stanton replied with abject admiration, claiming to have held Garrison in awe since "earliest youth," but the two appear to have missed each other. After five days at the home of Samuel Hooper the Stantons started back for New York City, lodging a few days at Senator Edwin Morgan's mansion at Fifth Avenue and Thirty-seventh Street, where Morgan held a huge party in his honor, filled with soldiers and celebrities. The list of public and private luminaries spilled over two columns on the front page of the *New York Times*, right alongside the daily grist from the military commission that would hang Henry Wirz. Stanton left New York on the morning of September 23, returning to Washington just as Radical anxiety over Johnson's brand of Reconstruction came to a head. The *New York Herald* was then advising the constitutional convention in South Carolina to accept the president's condition of emancipation before the state had to face even more stringent demands. "The President desires reconciliation, peace and renovation," the *Herald* warned. "The extremists aspire after continued separation, disorder and ruin."[34]

While Stanton had been enjoying New Jersey's seashore, Montgomery Blair was denouncing him as one of those extremists in a speech at Rockville, Maryland. Even more fervently than the president and Welles, Blair resented the Radical aim of disenfranchising most white Southern voters while offering suffrage to the freedmen: that seemed profoundly hypocritical to men of his mold, considering that most Northern states had yet to extend the vote to their own black residents. From Blair's conservative perspective, Southern Unionists like the Confederate vice president, Alexander Stephens—who had fulminated publicly against secession before his native state of Georgia departed the Union—had been left helpless by the dilatory policy of the Buchanan administration, and had been forced to swim with the tide of secession. Buchanan's coterie at that critical period had included Stanton and Holt, Blair noted, and he described them acting with far less determined nationalism than they later claimed. Now, Blair asserted, Stanton and Holt were to serve as the executioners for reluctant former Confederates like Stephens. Reminding his audience that Stanton had privately sympathized with the complaints of Southern secessionists during the crisis of 1861, Blair asked whether Stephens or Stanton was the real traitor. Humphrey Leavitt, the federal district judge in Cincinnati, offered to counter

Blair's accusation with his own recollections of Stanton's vociferously pro-Union comments, late in 1860, but Stanton never took advantage of the offer—which might have done nothing more than bring others forward to testify to his duplicity.[35]

That Stanton continued to express different opinions before different factions became clear soon after Congress met, in December, when Radicals launched their attack on Johnson's Reconstruction policies. The president had still considered Stanton his loyal ally that summer, chastising Blair for his attack on the secretary of war at Rockville. From their discussions in cabinet, Gideon Welles supposed that Stanton had suspended his early support for freedmen's voting rights in the face of Johnson's view that such a decision was constitutionally reserved to the states. Stanton did make some show of neutrality between the warring factions, but probably with less than sincere purpose, as illustrated, perhaps, by his introduction of Johnson's provisional Alabama governor, Lewis Parsons, to Senator Sumner. Well familiar with Sumner's views on universal suffrage, Stanton may have hoped for the negative reaction that Sumner registered so swiftly: Parsons could exert only a "pernicious" influence, Sumner said, after hearing Parsons say that "rather than allow negroes to vote he would emigrate."[36]

One week into the congressional session, Sumner told Welles that Stanton had complimented a fiercely Radical speech of Sumner's from the previous September. Sumner convincingly replicated the war secretary's fondness for hyperbolic flattery and absolute concurrence, maintaining that "he approved every sentiment, every opinion and word of it"—apparently including the demand for enfranchising the former slaves. When Welles repeated Sumner's story to Treasury Secretary Hugh McCulloch, a week or so later, McCulloch replied that if Sumner were telling the truth Stanton "was a double-dealer—wore two faces," and if he did not agree with the president he should resign. Sumner was telling the truth, it seemed, and McCulloch was hardly the first person to accuse Stanton of talking out of both sides of his mouth. As the Radical cause gained political strength, Stanton's support for it grew more confident and conspicuous.[37]

The contest between Johnson and the Radicals—with Thad Stevens as their champion—began in the opening moments of the session. As Stevens, Sumner, and other Radicals had feared, Johnson's Reconstruction policy brought an array of defiant Southern congressmen-elect to Washington, including the former Confederate vice president, Stephens. Before the first gavel fell, caucusing Republicans decided to establish a joint committee of fifteen members from the House and Senate to oversee the readmission of states. Then, by prearrangement, when the clerk of the House of Representatives called the roster of members on the opening day, he failed to name any of those elected from the former Confederate states. When the most undeniably loyal of those excluded representatives tried to object, he was told that he was not a member of the body and could not be heard. Because each chamber of Congress held final authority over members' qualifications for office, the excluded representatives could only retire, leaving both houses with heavy Republican majorities. That assured passage of the resolution creating the Joint Committee of Fifteen. Stanton, a friendly correspondent of the Speaker of the House, may have known it would happen.[38]

In his first message to Congress, Johnson outlined his conservative view of the relations between the federal and state governments, contending as he and Lincoln had from the start that the secession ordinances were "null and void," and that the states themselves had never ceased to exist. Subjecting them to indefinite military rule would divide the country into conquerors and conquered, he said, and burden the treasury unnecessarily, besides discouraging the immigration that the end of slavery could be expected to inspire. Once the states had ratified the Thirteenth Amendment, he continued, the House and Senate should seat their elected representatives and senators, but in the matter of deciding suffrage the Constitution prevented him from interfering in that state prerogative. The national debt had soared to nearly $3 billion, but Johnson pointed to the immigrants teeming the country's shores as evidence of a prosperous future, and he invited the members of Congress to join him in achieving "a perfect restoration of fraternal affection," rather than nourishing wartime antagonism.[39]

Welles thought the message might change people's minds. He was mistaken, but his optimism was reinforced by the return of General Grant from a tour of the South, ten days before Christmas. Still warmed by the reconciliation he had fostered at Appomattox, Grant contradicted descriptions of rebellious resurgence, reporting that Southern people showed more loyalty than he had expected, and appeared well prepared to resume their places in the Union. He noted that freed slaves seemed to feel entitled to the lands of their former masters, which disinclined them to labor, and he pointed out that the potential for collisions between the white population and black troops dictated that the occupation forces should be white. To Grant, a rapid reunion was perfectly feasible, and Welles urged him to put his observations on paper. For all the commanding general's confidence, Stanton remained secretly and increasingly hostile to the idea, perhaps taking his cue from the impressive coalition of Radical and moderate Republicans Stevens and Sumner were beginning to muster against the president.[40]

Hours after Grant reported his observations, Stanton left by rail for Steubenville and Gambier, where he spent his fifty-first birthday with his mother and Pamphila. He had to cover the last few miles from Mount Vernon by sleigh over a frozen landscape, which could not have failed to provoke reflection on his college days and what the intervening years had wrought. He hurried back to Washington to spend Christmas with his family—the one place on earth where he may have felt safe removing the mask he seemed to wear each day—and his nephew Christopher came down from West Point for the holiday. Not until the last cabinet meeting of the year did Stanton reappear at the White House, theatrically disparaging Senator Sumner for the benefit of his increasingly suspicious cabinet colleagues.[41]

Johnson submitted Grant's report on Southern conditions to Congress, but at Sumner's insistence he accompanied it with the far-less-rosy impressions of Carl Schurz. Johnson had sent the Radical Schurz on a tour of inspection in the Deep South, assuming he would also find conditions there promising, but Schurz had investigated from a different perspective. He went at the urging of Senator Sumner and Stanton, who seemed to be working together to provide the new president with the Radical viewpoint. Stanton told Schurz it was "absolutely necessary" for him to go, since his findings would be "of the most vital interest in the discussions of the next Congress." Johnson would not be able to simply put Schurz's report "in his pocket," Stanton promised, and Sumner's demand for that report fulfilled Stanton's promise.[42]

As Schurz candidly admitted to his wife, in the midst of his tour, "I have found all my preconceived notions verified fully." In the five states he visited, he reported that government agents or soldiers could not travel safely alone, and Union men lived in perpetual danger. Freedmen had been restored to a semblance of servitude through oppressive legislation and a judicial system harshly weighted against them. New vagrancy laws provided fines and near-certain imprisonment for men who lacked a means of support, and in the immediate postwar era that consisted of an active contract for labor with a planter or other employer, usually for a year at a time. The threat of prison, which meant forced labor, discouraged freedmen from negotiating for better wages: in some states that right was specifically proscribed by expanding the description of vagrancy to include those who refused to work for "the usual and common wages," which often fell below the level of subsistence. Because employers lacked much incentive to preserve the health of their laborers, many newly liberated blacks found the cost of freedom high. Southern whites considered such laws crucial to the restoration of their economy and to the control of so large a population of displaced workers. Even officers in the occupation force sometimes felt that only compulsion would teach the former slaves the responsibility of supporting themselves, but to outside observers those methods reflected the resurrection of human bondage.[43]

Schurz assumed Johnson objected to his report because it contradicted the image he wished to project, but the president had reason to suspect Schurz's own impartiality by the time he returned to Washington. If Grant's report suffered from wishful thinking, Schurz's inspection had been conducted with an agenda. Johnson had declined to reinstate Schurz as a major general for the tour, and Schurz balked at going because of financial concerns, so Senator Sumner offered to find fellow Radicals to subsidize his travels: he finally arranged for Schurz to write about his observations for the *Boston Advertiser*, which would pay for the critical view Sumner expected him to take. Schurz agreed, but he cautioned Sumner to keep his association with the newspaper secret. "You can easily divine the reason," he wrote early in August. A month later he had been identified as the *Advertiser*'s correspondent, and had to explain why he had been releasing his conclusions to an opposition paper rather than submitting them confidentially to the president, whose emissary he was supposed to be. Schurz pleaded economic need, but he also defended himself with the excuse that he had informed the secretary of war about the journalistic arrangement before he left. That Stanton would approve so clear a Radical ploy ought to have given Johnson some pause, and he may well have noted it, but he said nothing at the time. Perhaps Schurz's report more closely reflected reality than Grant's, but Johnson doubted as much after Schurz's preexisting bias became clear, and in that respect Sumner's (and Stanton's) scheme further alienated Johnson from Radical opinion. Schurz's views seemed all the more suspect when General Sheridan submitted a far more favorable opinion: from New Orleans, where Schurz had stopped, Sheridan let the president know that he had "the most abiding faith" in the success of the conciliatory policy Johnson was pursuing.[44]

The day those dueling reports reached the Capitol, Thad Stevens delivered a long speech arguing that the Confederate states had most certainly gone out of the Union, because they had been accorded belligerent rights during the war. They were no longer states, he insisted: they could only rejoin the Union with congressional permission, and the president could have no hand in it. The state governments Johnson had established would have to give way to martial law. He even advocated distributing confiscated lands among the freedmen—a logical enough economic rationale, because the labor of the owners' slaves had improved or paid for most of that land, but in December of 1865 that idea appealed only to a minority in Congress, and it never took firm root.[45]

Early in the new year, Sumner confided to Gideon Welles that most of Johnson's cabinet concurred in the Radical aims, moving Welles to reply that he knew nothing of the kind. By Sumner's reckoning, not only did Stanton hold a different view than he pretended, but Interior Secretary James Harlan, Attorney General James Speed, and to an extent Postmaster General William Dennison also disagreed with the president's course. Three of the four sided with him "entirely," Sumner claimed (apparently qualifying

Dennison's position), while only Seward, Welles, and Hugh McCulloch, of the Treasury, supported the president. Welles said he doubted the senator's assessment, but Sumner replied that one of the cabinet dissidents had advised Sumner to compose a bill that would override presidential policy and put Congress in charge of Reconstruction. Sumner did not name Stanton as the adviser, but it seems more than probable, for eight months later Stanton did make such a suggestion to an extreme Radical in the House.[46]

The first legislative battles between Johnson and Congress proved Sumner's point about dissention in the cabinet, and demonstrated that Johnson's stubbornness only stiffened the resistance against him. The president complained that the congressional initiatives emanated from Republican caucuses that excluded Northern Democrats and all representatives from the eleven Southern states. That was true, but Lincoln would have let it pass in the interests of compromise, and might have allied himself with moderate Republicans to bolster and expand his support within the party, but Johnson obdurately stood his ground, yielding no point, and in the process made enemies of some of his strongest potential collaborators.[47]

Charles Dana became one of those enemies. Hoping to capitalize on his service under Stanton, he appealed to Johnson for appointment as the collector of New York City—one of the most profitable government posts the president or his treasury secretary could bestow, and one that seemed to invite graft. Dana listed Stanton as his foremost supporter, but Johnson's friends were already warning him of Stanton's secret antagonism, and that luscious morsel of executive patronage went to someone else. When Dana learned that he had been passed over, he opened a searing editorial campaign against Johnson's policies. He would prove similarly treacherous to Johnson's successor, Grant, after that old friend refused Dana the same collectorship.[48]

Johnson also lost the support of Lyman Trumbull, a onetime Radical who had softened his views during the war. Trumbull tried to correct the repressive laws of the reconstituted Southern legislatures by extending the authority of the Freedmen's Bureau and proposing a civil rights bill. His constituents recognized that his bills would have hamstrung the Democratic Party, yet the Freedmen's Bureau bill would have allowed executive control over the agency, whereas the Radicals wished to wrest that power from the president and exercise it themselves. Disturbed by the revolutionary congressional intrigues that he associated with the bill, and by its provision for a semblance of martial law that seemed designed to favor freedmen, Johnson decided to veto it. None of his cabinet officers objected when he informed them, but Welles thought Stanton, Harlan, and Speed regretted it. Stanton remarked that the bill might have been improved with a couple of changes, but he seemed to assent to the veto. Friendly newspapers reported that Johnson's cabinet unanimously rejected the bill, and Horace White of the *Chicago Tribune* chastised Stanton for that assumed support. Stanton's private replies to such criticism, flavored as usual with exaggeration, may account for Welles hearing, later, that Stanton had told his Radical friends he was entirely opposed to the veto. Harlan, who had joined the cabinet believing that Johnson held firm Republican ideas about Reconstruction, wrote Trumbull to assure him that the department heads had not all agreed; he nonetheless warned that correcting the misunderstanding might do more harm than good, because open warfare between the president and Congress could only hurt the party. Unaccustomed to so intransigent and confrontational a chief executive, Congress failed by two votes to mount the two-thirds majority necessary to override the veto.[49]

On Washington's birthday in 1866, Radicals requested an adjournment of Congress so the Capitol could be given over to a eulogy for Henry Winter Davis. Davis had not been reelected to the House in 1864, largely because of his effort to undermine Lincoln's reelection and Reconstruction plans, and Secretary Welles thought it highly inappropriate for the national legislature to accord such an honor to a private citizen who had served only one term in Congress. He correctly gauged the affair as a Radical display, and he might have added something about Stanton's political alliances had he known that Stanton attended the ceremony, sitting with Chief Justice Chase and William Lloyd Garrison—just as he had traveled all the way to Baltimore the previous winter to appear at Davis's funeral.[50]

Four days after Johnson vetoed the Freedmen's Bureau bill, he met with Orville Hickman Browning and old Tom Ewing of Ohio, who had served twice in the Senate and held cabinet posts under Harrison and Taylor. Broaching the subject of cabinet unity, Browning reflected that it would soon be necessary to make a change in the War Department: he suggested that Ewing's son, Tom Jr. (who had defended Dr. Mudd and Ned Spangler in the conspiracy trial), would make a satisfactory replacement for Stanton. Johnson conceded that Stanton's departure "must come." That same day, Welles mentioned to the president Stanton's favoritism to John Forney's Radical newspaper, the *Washington Chronicle*, while he bought no department advertising through the administration-friendly *National Intelligencer*. Johnson evidently spoke to Stanton about dispensing department funds to hostile critics, but he had to issue specific orders on particular newspapers before Stanton would desist. Welles had also noticed the detectives and other War Department "creatures" with whom Stanton surrounded the president, ostensibly for his personal protection but really— Welles firmly believed—to collect White House information for Stanton's Radical friends.[51]

The cabinet discussion over Senator Trumbull's civil rights bill better illustrated the looming division in the cabinet. Seward favored only the portion that made citizens of the freedmen, while the provision for federal enforcement of equal-rights clauses struck him as unconstitutional because it infringed on state sovereignty. Welles felt much the same. Dennison and Harlan both thought Johnson should endorse it—especially after Stanton argued for a favorable reading of its text, defending it as palatable under his interpretation. Speed was not present, and McCulloch said he had not given the bill close consideration, but even he hoped it could be signed to avoid further trouble with Congress. In the end Johnson vetoed that bill, as well, but this time both chambers overrode the president's veto for the first time. Welles noted that "all of Stanton's pets" in Congress either voted against the veto or paired off with absent members, so they would not have to vote.[52]

In all the grappling over Reconstruction issues, Stanton and the president still managed to act in concert on military matters and foreign affairs. While the rejected civil rights bill went back to Congress, Stanton handled tensions on the Mexican border in a fashion the president at least seemed to approve. Late in March General Grant asked Stanton for permission to sell five thousand rifles, with fifty rounds apiece, to a Mexican commission merchant in New York for shipment to the liberal government of Mexico in its struggle against the French imperialists. Anticipating that Stanton might refuse, Grant asked him to forward the idea to Johnson. Stanton replied that he thought the proposal imprudent, but promised to show it to the president. He waited an entire month to do so, perhaps presenting it in a pejorative light, and Johnson refused. Phil Sheridan, who held command in that theater, made the same request of Grant's chief of staff a couple of months later, and Grant passed that up the chain of command with his endorsement, only to see it refused again as a potential act of war.[53]

The president and his secretary of war enjoyed no such agreement when the focus turned back to the South. The abrupt end of slavery, along with the presence of large numbers of U.S. Colored Troops among the occupying forces, bred serious racial tensions that erupted in violence at Memphis, Tennessee, on April 30. A fracas between a group of black men and some white policemen that day led to a more dangerous confrontation the next afternoon, as police tried to arrest some intoxicated black soldiers, and the police began shooting indiscriminately. Then a posse of white men rode into town and attacked the freedmen's neighborhood without provocation, initiating three days of murder and arson. Conservatives like Johnson regarded such mayhem as the predictable result of military occupation, especially by black soldiers, while the Radicals saw it as evidence that a military presence was crucial to the safety of Southern freedmen.[54]

While the Memphis riot raged, Johnson confronted the proposed Fourteenth Amendment, which reiterated Trumbull's civil rights legislation and went even further. Besides establishing citizenship for all native-born Americans, the amendment provided for congressional representation based on the extent of the franchise, imposed office-holding restrictions for former rebels, and sanctified the nation's war debt while repudiating once and for all the Confederate debt. The first draft of the Senate resolution appeared on April 30, and the next day Johnson gathered his department heads, asking whether they supported the amendment or his conservative, conciliatory policies. Stanton jumped in ahead of everyone, out of the traditional order that dictated Seward should speak first. He said he was glad Johnson brought it up, claiming he had supported the president from the beginning, although differing initially on giving the vote to freedmen. He waxed loud and emphatic for some time, but he never said whether he favored the amendment. When Welles called him on that, Stanton would only say he did not approve of the amendment in its present form, but thought it might be reconciled with Johnson's thinking. Later that day someone leaked this exchange to the *National Intelligencer*, with Stanton's expression of opposition to the amendment somewhat amplified. Welles chuckled at Stanton's likely discomfort at facing his Radical friends, whom he had probably told an entirely different story.[55]

With the biennial elections only months away, supporters of the president had organized into political clubs. Prompted by Stanton's own statements, Radicals like Sumner were boasting that the president's inner circle was "nearly equally divided" over the subject of Reconstruction, so the National Union Club of Washington set out to press for more definitive statements from the cabinet officers. Hundreds of people gathered outside the White House on the evening of May 23, seeking Johnson's attention with the blaring of a band. After he addressed them, they glided over to Lafayette Square, where they drew brief, supportive remarks from a reluctant Welles (who disliked such spectacles) before moving on to each of the other ministers' homes. Seward was away. Harlan and Speed, who were beginning to distance themselves from Johnson, declined to speak. Dennison called for party unity, and McCulloch supported the president's program.[56]

When the serenade reached Stanton's house, he read a long, handwritten speech from his doorstep by the light of candles held by men at either elbow, while the crowd spilled across K Street into Franklin Park. In as many words as possible he said as little as possible, quoting heavily from Johnson's December message to Congress. Admitting that he had originally advocated universal suffrage, he excused himself for abandoning that cause on the same constitutional grounds Johnson had argued, besides which he noted that Johnson's reconstruction proclamations had restricted the organizing power in each state to those who were "loyal" to the United States. "Who are loyal people is a question that ought not to be difficult of decision," he contended, leaving adherents of the political extremes to interpret his ambiguous remark as each preferred. He conceded that he had advised the president to approve the Freedmen's Bureau bill, observing with some justification that it reflected "an honest desire to conform" to Johnson's views, but he deftly avoided making any comment on the civil rights bill, which he had tried to defend in council. Of the Fourteenth Amendment, he would say only that he objected to a four-year voting ban proposed for former Confederate soldiers.[57]

That long and largely evasive response left the illusion of a fairly loyal and generally conservative secretary. Johnson men who heard it doubtless went home satisfied, if they believed it, and Stanton's partisans maintained that he had absolved himself of any suspicion of treachery. The next night Surgeon General Barnes—the friend, personal physician, and professional beneficiary of Mr. Stanton—assured ex-Senator Browning, a Johnson supporter, that Stanton had made "an explicit declaration of approval of the President's policy." Barnes insisted that Stanton "was not a radical and never would be—that he had no sympathy with the course of Stevens and Sumner, and would not cooperate with them even if turned out of the cabinet." The man Barnes described bore no resemblance to the one Sumner and other Radicals trusted and eventually revered, and apparently Stanton was striving again to misrepresent himself to one faction or the other—if not to both.[58]

Stanton had good reason to cling tenaciously to his office that spring. He had exhausted his savings, and probably saw little promise in resuming a profession increasingly dominated by younger, better-educated men. The most lucrative cases of his career had emanated from a cultivated relationship with the Buchanan administration, and he had deftly transferred that connection to Buchanan's successor, but leaving Johnson's cabinet at that juncture would deprive him of executive influence. Not only would he have to build a practice of his own privately, from scratch, but he might have to hire an attorney himself: two men, including the wealthy banker William Smithson, had already filed actions against him for false imprisonment, asking heavy damages. Both had been arrested before Stanton took office, but he had been responsible for their prolonged detention. Thus far Stanton had filed his own answer to a suit by Joseph Maddox, and he seemed ready to act as his own attorney if it came to trial, but so long as he remained in the cabinet he enjoyed the option of hiring additional counsel at War Department expense. While Maddox dropped his civil action a few weeks after Stanton's cautious reply to the National Union Club, plenty of other potential litigants could have mounted cases against him. Only ironclad statutory immunity would have given him complete security, and the procedural and technical objections he raised in the Maddox case telegraphed his uncertainty on that score.[59]

By the beginning of summer, as the election season increased the political pressure to reveal allegiances, Johnson's cabinet began to disintegrate. James Doolittle, the very conservative senator from Wisconsin, sent each cabinet member an invitation to come to Philadelphia for the Union Party convention, which Johnson hoped would inaugurate a new coalition, named after the one he and Lincoln had run under in 1864. He expected it to consist of Democrats, conservative Republicans, and at least some moderates. Speed and Dennison had spurned this initiative, and Dennison submitted his resignation first. Speed began to miss cabinet meetings, and in the middle of July he, too, resigned. Johnson waited patiently for Harlan to follow, not wishing to dismiss him, but finally he had to make it clear that the Interior secretary's resignation would be agreeable. Harlan complied, asking for a month's stay, and Johnson acceded. To replace Speed as attorney general Johnson named an able Ohio lawyer, Henry Stanbery, who had worked with Stanton and had faced him in the Ohio Supreme Court—and beaten him. Former Wisconsin governor Alexander W. Randall, the president of Washington's National Union Club, became postmaster general in place of Dennison. In Harlan's stead, Johnson appointed Browning, who was also involved in the National Union movement. All three new members could be depended on for political loyalty.[60]

That left Stanton. Gideon Welles assumed that Stanton still embraced the Radical faction, but that he was pretending to abandon each of their policies as Johnson took a stance against them. Characterizing Stanton as "selfish, insincere, a dissembler, and treacherous," Welles suspected that he would not leave the cabinet—or, if he did, he would turn downright malevolent. Sam Barlow thought it crucial to remove him, reminding Montgomery Blair that Stanton was "faithless & treacherous in the highest degree." Johnson had decided in the spring that he would push no one from the cabinet involuntarily until after the fall elections, so Stanton had little to fear at the moment. With no real hope of influencing the president's decisions, Stanton remained in office to preserve his salary, his perquisites, and whatever power his status as least-favored secretary would yield him. Welles may have correctly analyzed Stanton's political purposes when he suspected him of spying on the administration for his Radical friends and of hoping to embarrass and confound Johnson by manipulating affairs within his own department.[61] The Republicans he would please by discomfiting the president held the keys to Stanton's future in government, which he seemed by then to realize was the only future he had.

Stanton composed a perfectly insulting letter to Senator Doolittle, refusing to even address him by name, and he repudiated the aims of the party, dismissing it as an alliance of rebels and Copperheads. "So far as the terms of the call and the purposes and objects of the convention are designed to oppose the Constitutional authority of Congress," Stanton concluded, "I condemn them." Had he mailed that letter he would have had to accompany it with his resignation, and Welles might then have complimented him for a frank admission of differences, but Edwin Stanton did not have such candor in him. He directed a clerk to copy the letter in a more legible hand, and then he filed both copies in his papers, as though planting evidence of his intentions to show his Radical friends, or to preserve for posterity. The next day he entered the cabinet room, still in the guise of the faithful counselor to a president whose enemies he actively served.[62]

17

THE TROJAN HORSE

On Sunday morning, July 29, 1866, a War Department messenger came to the door of 320 K Street with an urgent message from Brigadier General Absalom Baird. Phil Sheridan had gone out to Texas to consider the situation on the Mexican border, leaving Baird in command at New Orleans, where the Radical faction intended to reconvene the 1864 constitutional convention—hoping to expand the suffrage to freedmen and, some thought, to disenfranchise all former Confederates. Louisiana's attorney general and lieutenant governor deemed the meeting illegal, and a local judge evidently agreed, so the mayor of New Orleans planned to arrest the members as they gathered at Mechanics Hall. Baird, who was merely the commander of the Freedmen's Bureau in that department, anticipated trouble and warned Stanton by telegraph, pleading for instructions.[1]

Through either negligence or design—and far more likely the latter, since he was not prone to negligence—Stanton gave no instructions, or any answer at all. He failed even to show the dispatch to the president, later making an excuse for that strange lapse. This was not the first time he had seemed to manipulate his communications to army commanders with an eye to embarrassing the president, and if that was his hope he met with unusual success. Johnson heard directly from the lieutenant governor and the state attorney general, who wondered whether federal troops would interfere in the arrest of delegates, and Johnson, who had not seen Baird's nervous telegram, told them he expected the military not to interfere with the civil courts, but to sustain them. The convention did gather, but without the army standing by, and dozens of black demonstrators who marched in support of the convention became embroiled in a gunfight with the police, who chased them into the convention hall with pistols blazing. The police and a phalanx of armed civilians slaughtered a couple of dozen men and wounded scores more, some of whom later died. Baird imposed martial law to bring the violence to an end.[2]

The New Orleans riot marked a watershed in Johnson's administration. The president's obstinacy had alienated him from a solid majority in Congress, but Stanton did his best to widen that breach, informing Senator

Sumner that Johnson was the "author" of the New Orleans eruption. The Memphis riot had caused General Grant to doubt the president's conciliatory policy, and the bloodshed in New Orleans confirmed his suspicion that the conservative element in the South was taking advantage of Northern magnanimity. General Sheridan, who had dismissed Carl Schurz's cautions late in 1865, still cast a suspicious eye on Louisiana Radicals, but he regarded the mayhem of July 30 as little more than organized murder by the police, and he felt the need of a stronger military hand. Johnson had retained a large measure of popular support thus far, but the riot cost him much of the moderate public. Reflecting that shift, George Templeton Strong thought Johnson at fault for the blood spilled in Louisiana, and confessed: "I begin to fear that Sumner and Stevens may be right about him." The National Union Party convention that met in Philadelphia a couple of weeks later did the president no good. By the time it met, Strong had concluded that Johnson's new party consisted of "Rebels and Copperheads mostly." To the extent that Stanton's suppression of the Baird telegram allowed the riot to erupt, he could congratulate himself on striking a blow against the president through what might be characterized as political passive aggression.[3]

Secretary Welles parlayed a cabinet discussion about the Philadelphia convention into a revelation of Stanton's disloyalty. It happened a week before the new party adherents were to gather, and the discussion still focused on the New Orleans police and the passivity of General Baird—whose frantic dispatch Johnson had still not seen, or heard of. Stanton remarked that the War Department had been asked for bunting to decorate the convention hall. The war office usually supplied patriotic displays, but with more sarcasm than sincerity Stanton replied that he had none to give, suggesting that the organizing committee might appeal to the navy. Welles answered that he always displayed his bunting, challenging Stanton to "Show your flag."

"You mean the convention?" Stanton asked. Refraining from the acerbic tenor of his drafted reply to Senator Doolittle's invitation, he at least went so far as to say "I am against it." To that rare admission of open opposition Welles replied that he was sorry to hear Stanton's opinion but glad to know it, and undoubtedly so was the president. Welles thought the illuminating exchange troubled Seward, who remained loyal to both Johnson and Stanton. Having finally drawn out Stanton's secret, Welles felt convinced of what he had long suspected—that the war secretary allied himself with the Radicals to protect himself politically. Everything in Stanton's background and character supports the navy secretary's interpretation, however much Welles's observations were flavored by personal dislike: that dislike, after all, seemed to have been founded as much on Stanton's frequent deceit and intrigue as on his surly, condescending manner. Welles observed that

Stanton "seems to have personal apprehensions" about "the real Unionists" coming to power, supposing that he would rather see the government "overthrown" first.[4]

In the wake of the ineffective Philadelphia convention, Johnson embarked for Chicago, nominally to dedicate a memorial for Senator Stephen A. Douglas. Turning that appearance into a Homeric speaking tour, Johnson persuaded a file of celebrities to accompany him, including Seward, Welles, Grant, Admiral Farragut, and half a dozen other well-known army and navy officers. Welles suggested inviting the secretary of war, partly to dissuade the Radicals from orchestrating any violent political demonstrations, but Stanton begged off with the excuse that Ellen was ill; Welles thought he exaggerated her condition, but eight weeks later Stanton said he was afraid she was lapsing into consumption, and her condition remained "very infirm" at the end of the year.[5]

Just before the entourage departed, Browning and McCulloch tried to dissuade Johnson from making any speeches, knowing how hecklers provoked him to intemperate rhetoric, but he came to life on the stump, appearing to relish applause and confrontation. He spoke nearly every time the train stopped, occasionally falling into the trap his confidants feared. He and his companions made a broad circuit up the East Coast to Albany, westward along the shores of the Great Lakes, and from Chicago down to St. Louis, returning by a zigzag route along the Ohio River. Passing through Harrisburg and Baltimore, they reached Washington on September 15, after nearly three weeks. Johnson referred fondly to the journey as his "swing around the circle," but critics used that very phrase to lampoon it. So successfully did his friends and opponents goad him to excessive bombast, and so tenaciously did the memory of his bibulous vice presidential inauguration linger that it was widely believed among Republicans that Johnson was drunk, or crazy. Several witnesses reported that General Grant did get drunk at one point, yet Grant viewed Johnson's speeches as "a National disgrace": thenceforward Grant began to drift away from the president personally and politically— although, characteristically, he kept those differences to himself.[6]

During the president's tour of the North, Stanton took a ride to the Washington Arsenal with the new attorney general, Henry Stanbery. When Stanbery entered the cabinet, he thought Stanton and Johnson were "in perfect harmony," perhaps because of the sycophantic manner Stanton adopted to mask any disagreement, and he observed that the president seemed to confide more in Stanton than in Seward.

"Well," Stanbery remembered Stanton replying, "I believe he does."[7]

Stanton may not have revealed the depth of his antagonism to Johnson, but he made a special effort to describe it for Radical congressmen. In a letter to Representative James Ashley, the Radical's Radical, he suggested that Grant compromised his own reputation by his close association with Johnson. Not for the first time in his public life, Stanton characterized himself as the one true friend of the government, hinting that with its ready majority Congress could shackle the president and Seward before they had a chance to "wreck the country." Turning treacherously on the political benefactor who had brought him into the cabinet, and the friend who so often invited him to dinner and whist parties while Ellen recuperated in Pittsburgh or New York, Stanton warned Ashley that Seward and Johnson had already assured "a reign of chaos and bloodshed in the South." Complaining that he was wracked by asthma and headaches, Stanton implied that he could not battle Johnson and the rest of the cabinet alone, and he implored Ashley to come to Washington in advance of the session, probably so they could plan strategy.[8]

Seward fell grievously ill on Johnson's speaking tour. Cholera had come back to the Ohio River Valley that summer, despite strenuous efforts by various boards of health, and Seward came down with symptoms of it as the president's party steamed upriver from Louisville. He took leave of his colleagues to start for home in a special rail car, apparently dying, and he seemed no better at Harrisburg, where his children met him. When the train pulled into the Washington depot on the afternoon of September 15 Stanton—who had so venomously disparaged Seward to Congressman Ashley, only the day before—came aboard the car to greet them, all sweetness and light; he had brought an ambulance and stretcher to carry Seward home. That evening Stanton returned to the depot with the rest of the cabinet, to greet the president as a conquering hero.[9]

To everyone's surprise, Seward recovered well enough to resume work by the second cabinet meeting after Johnson's return. On that occasion, Stanton presented a request from Judge Advocate General Holt for a court of inquiry to acquit him of any malfeasance in prosecuting the accused conspirators in the assassination. The previous spring Holt had been called before a congressional committee to account for his reliance on perjurers like Charles Dunham, alias Conover. The Radicals who dominated the committee deemed Holt's excuses perfectly satisfactory, but their lone Democratic colleague, Andrew Rogers, presented a minority report illuminating inconsistencies and improbabilities in Holt's testimony, and implying that Holt had actively participated in suborning perjury. General Dix had apprised Stanton of Conover's bad character and his propensity for falsehood and fraud in June of 1865, but Rogers observed that Holt had still employed Conover through the rest of that year to procure witnesses to Jefferson Davis's complicity in the assassination. The *New York Herald* brought suspicion to a boil by publishing letters purportedly written by two of Conover's contracted perjurers and one by Holt himself, all dated in

April of 1866, that suggested a conspiracy to present false testimony and implicated the judge advocate general. Rather than resort to a libel suit, Holt addressed those incriminating insinuations through John Forney's Radical organ, the *Washington Chronicle*, and he filed an official, novella-length report—ostensibly to explain the untrustworthiness of the witnesses Conover had produced, but more obviously to counteract the supposition that Holt had been in on the scheme. Then he appealed to his crony Stanton for official exoneration by a court, to lend a semblance of authority to another rescue of his reputation.[10]

Stanton, who would have selected the members of any court of inquiry, pressed Holt's case before the cabinet and the president on the grounds that such a devoted patriot deserved a hearing. Welles, who had recently heard of "some queer legislation to secure a military life office for Holt," contended that the judge advocate general was a civil officer, and so would have to bear political criticism without recourse to a military court. Stanton argued that he was a brigadier general, although he never wore a uniform. The rest of the cabinet agreed with Welles, but afterward Holt asked several members to "indorse" him if they would not grant him a court: they declined doing so because it would have entailed extensive investigation of their own. Browning suspected it might be one of Stanton's tricks, intended to embarrass the administration again and aid Radicals on the eve of the election, and Stanton may well have seen such an opportunity, but Holt appeared intent merely on rehabilitating his tarnished reputation. His anxiety probably increased in November, when the federal court for the District of Columbia arraigned Conover on a charge of perjury, for which he was ultimately convicted and sentenced to ten years in prison. At last Stanton gave Holt the only official exoneration he was to receive from the executive branch, in a letter offering "my own conviction that all charges and imputations against your official conduct and character are in my judgment entirely groundless." Still not satisfied, Holt produced the first of his self-exculpatory pamphlets, casting himself as the innocent and infinitely honorable victim of traitors in league with Jefferson Davis.[11]

Seward joined the rest of the cabinet in opposing Stanton over Holt's court of inquiry, and perhaps to make amends he invited Stanton to dinner at his home that evening, with a couple of knighted British guests. Stanton sat beside Seward's frail but devoted daughter Fanny, who was tottering in the last stages of tuberculosis, and the girl touched a soft spot in him that few ever found. He and Eddie came to play whist with her another evening, and a few days later, in a rare example of obvious compassion, Stanton asked her to go for an afternoon drive with him, if her health permitted. Probably it did not, for she died twelve days afterward.[12]

September of 1866 brought confirmation that the Northern public had turned as sternly against Johnson as Congress had. Hints had emerged from the March elections in New Hampshire, where the Radical candidate for governor won that conservative state by seven percentage points, and Connecticut's April elections generally went to Johnson's enemies, although his champion in the gubernatorial race won by a razor-thin majority. Ambrose Burnside, now a Radical candidate for governor of Rhode Island with the Republican Union Party, carried his state by a substantial majority. Johnson dismissed those spring losses as predictable, but on September 4 little Vermont, which had gone heavily for Lincoln in 1864 and for Republican regulars in 1865, added several thousand more to the Republican majority. A week later Maine elected a Republican governor by a landslide, and gave a substantial majority to the anti-Johnson candidate for Congress. Johnson newspapers still found excuses for the losses, but the tide showed no sign of ebbing.[13]

As early as September of 1865, Andrew Johnson's friends in New York began to notice that Radicals were using federal patronage against them, and Johnson chose to rectify that in time for the 1866 elections. Since spring he had wielded the executive ax indiscriminately against federal officeholders who seemed hesitant about supporting his policies, or who owed their positions to unfriendly congressmen. That strategy sometimes backfired, as it did when former vice president Hannibal Hamlin resigned as collector at the Boston Custom House after publishing a letter critical of Johnson—and then started campaigning against him. The October and November elections in the Mid-Atlantic and the Midwest proved perfectly disastrous to the president, leaving both houses of Congress with two-thirds Republican majorities. Johnson's refusal to compromise had, moreover, pushed virtually all of those Republicans toward the Radical camp.[14]

The mounting power of the Radicals only emboldened Stanton, who began more obviously administering his department to Johnson's disadvantage. The president had already considered luring him out of office by appointing him minister to Spain, hoping to install General Sherman as a friendlier secretary of war, but Sherman wanted nothing to do with a political position and Stanton had no wish to go to Spain. Stanton told Senator Fessenden it would actually please him to be removed from office, although he also listed numerous reasons why Republicans ought to fight for his retention.[15]

Stanton began to find Grant an ally against Johnson, as discussion over the Maryland election illustrated. Tension between the governor and Baltimore's police commissioners had grown so sharp that violence again seemed likely in that riot-prone city, and the president suggested sending troops to Fort McHenry, where they would be handy in an emergency.

Grant, whose own drift toward the Radicals had attracted attention in the cabinet, initially doubted the chances of trouble and resisted Johnson's request, but even he considered a riot "very probable" four days before the election. Stanton, who had so readily posted soldiers at Maryland polling places during the war to encourage Republican victories, opposed that precautionary measure with unusual vigor, especially for someone who had been so critical of the New Orleans riot. Grant expressed a hope never to deploy troops during an election in a state that was "in full relations with the General Government" (although he did precisely that in Tennessee, a few months later), but the president instructed him to give any aid the Maryland governor should request. Recruits bound for Texas landed at Fort McHenry until the election passed.[16]

Those recruits represented reinforcements Grant had promised to send Phil Sheridan after the New Orleans riot. The administration of military rule in the occupied states had grown complicated, in the wake of a Supreme Court decision and a pair of presidential proclamations. First, in the spring the court had decided against the government in the case of Lambden P. Milligan, one of the defendants condemned in Indianapolis in 1864: a majority declared the military prosecution of civilians unconstitutional where the civil courts were in operation. About the same time, the president proclaimed the rebellion ended everywhere except in Texas, and in August he declared it over altogether, which nominally closed the war—and ended the war powers on which the authority for military arrests and trials had been predicated. In response to reports of violence against Freedmen's Bureau officials, Union men, and freedmen, General Grant tried to reconcile military justice with the Milligan decision by a general order for commanding officers to arrest malefactors wherever civil authorities would not or could not bring them to trial. That nevertheless conflicted with the high court's as-yet-unpublished insistence that military courts were justified only in a theater of war, where civil justice was interrupted. After Johnson's second proclamation, department commanders wondered whether they could still ignore writs of habeas corpus, and how they could administer their bailiwicks without such extraordinary powers in the face of a hostile population. Grant equivocated on the viability of his general order, but doubted that the congressional guarantees of civil rights could be enforced without something similar, and the same problem would face any further federal legislation designed to protect freedmen and federal loyalists in the South.[17]

Despite *ex parte Milligan*, Stanton also strove to retain control over prosecutions, which military tribunals had long afforded him. Not until the middle of December did the Supreme Court release its full decision, in which Lincoln's close friend David Davis severely chastised the Lincoln administration. A few days before that, Stanton was still urging the trial of Major General George Pickett for hanging Confederate deserters captured in Union service in 1864. Joseph Holt wanted to arrest Pickett and try him before a military commission, but worried that the Milligan case prevented it. Subordinating legal logic to emotional argument, Stanton insisted that "the magnitude of the offense alleged against Pickett is such that there should be no room to contest the jurisdiction of the tribunal." In December and January he and Holt appointed courts of inquiry composed of junior officers, but neither brought Pickett to trial, and even General Grant recommended against trying a soldier he had paroled at Appomattox. While Stanton ultimately hesitated to approve executions ordered by military courts in the wake of the Milligan decision, he admitted to a congressional committee that he considered the ruling mistaken, and that Milligan had been "properly convicted." He also deemed the murder of soldiers to lie within the jurisdiction of military tribunals, although *ex parte Milligan* clearly dictated otherwise.[18]

So divergent had the aims of the president and Congress become that the new session had not even convened before some Republicans started hinting at using their overwhelming majority to remove Johnson altogether. The voice of Ben Butler rose loudest among the early advocates of impeachment, enumerating a litany of crimes exaggerated and imagined. So rash had the rhetoric become immediately after the election that some in the cabinet feared revolution. Even without the majorities of three and four to one that would soon fill the House and Senate, Congress went to work on its own agenda, appointing committees to investigate different aspects of presidential Reconstruction. Given the Republican majorities and the political polarization, committees were necessarily all chaired and dominated by men hostile to the president.[19]

A special joint committee went to New Orleans in December to look into the riot there. Chairman Thomas Eliot of Massachusetts maintained a private correspondence with Stanton, sending an envoy to warn him that the lone Democrat on the committee would present a dissenting report. When questions arose about Stanton's failure to answer General Baird's plaintive telegram of July 28, Eliot gave Stanton nearly two weeks' notice to prepare a response, which Stanton took through several drafts before he submitted it. Eliot also forewarned him about unfriendly testimony on the subject, evidently so Stanton could frame his response accordingly. So close did the secretary of war seem to the opposition, and so consistently had he proven faithless, that even his steadfast friend Seward began to feel, as 1866 drew to a close, that Stanton could not be trusted with confidential information.[20]

In addition to its investigations, the latest session of Congress initiated a flurry of legislation designed to undo and commandeer Johnson's

Reconstruction efforts, and to curtail his constitutional powers. First came the Tenure of Office Act, originally introduced to strip him of the patronage nineteenth-century presidents normally enjoyed through their appointment authority. The impetus had been Johnson's wholesale removal of Republican officeholders who failed to support his policies, and congressmen intended to require any discharge of appointees to first have the consent of the Senate, which had approved those same nominees in the first place. Representative Thomas Williams, a colleague of Stanton's from the Pittsburgh bar, presented the bill on the third day of the new session. Williams's draft would have applied the restriction to cabinet officers, but an amendment was soon inserted exempting the heads of departments and their first assistants.[21]

The House passed the amended bill and sent it to the Senate. Wisconsin Senator Timothy Howe, whose friends had lost heavily when Johnson cleaned house, tried to remove the exemption for department heads, and mentioned the secretary of war in particular: Stanton's impending removal had been rumored, Howe warned, and Congress should not allow it to happen. His plea failed, but weeks later the House did eliminate the exception on another reconsideration. When the Senate took up the change, Democrats who had opposed the bill in the first place denounced it vigorously, none of them more fervently than Republican John Sherman, who deplored the possibility of forcing a president to retain a cabinet officer he could not work with, or trust. Sherman could not understand how "any gentleman" would hold onto an office against the wishes of his chief, objecting that the revised bill would require a president to keep such a person against his will. Personal and political confidence were necessary to the performance of executive functions, Sherman insisted, adding that he would not support the continuance of any cabinet officer who had lost that confidence. Thomas Hendricks of Indiana argued that the man who most deserved removal would be the only one to remain in office under the amended bill. Wisconsin's Doolittle reminded the chamber that "the late lamented Mr. Lincoln" had found it crucial to replace some of his cabinet, and he pointed out a technical flaw in the bill: if Stanton were the man it aimed to protect, it failed to do so because it only guaranteed the tenure of officers appointed by the sitting president, while Stanton had been appointed under a previous administration.[22]

Meanwhile, Congress had concurrently developed its own Reconstruction legislation that created the conquered provinces Radicals preferred. Dismantling all the state governments of the old Confederacy save that of Tennessee, the House had already passed what would become known as the First Reconstruction Act, dividing the region into five military districts under generals who would command with virtual omnipotence. The prominence of military rule under the congressional plan required sympathetic oversight in the War Department, and that consideration likely drove the relatively conservative Senate to support the amendment to the Tenure of Office Act. Outvoted on that point, Senator Sherman assented to the bill itself, but not without a Parthian shot. He acknowledged Doolittle's observation that the secretaries of war, navy, and state seemed not to fall under the protection of the bill, but added that even if the bill did apply to them he would consent to their removal at any time if one of them was "so wanting in manhood, in honor, as to hold his place after the politest intimation by the President of the United States that his services were no longer needed."[23]

While the Tenure of Office bill made its way to approval, the House again sallied forth against presidential power by inserting administrative changes into the army appropriations bill that even some Republicans thought irrelevant to a financial bill. Like the Tenure of Office Act, one of the insertions stipulated that the general in chief could not be removed from command without prior approval of the Senate: that would have forced Lincoln to keep McClellan, but the bill was designed with General Grant in mind. His headquarters were also fixed in Washington—in apparent reaction to a suspicion of presidential chicanery. Just before the November elections, Johnson had tried to order Grant to Mexico, while he brought General Sherman to Washington, where it was supposed that he would install Sherman in Stanton's place and send Stanton abroad to a diplomatic post. The conservative Sherman met Johnson's political standards, while his prestige would have aided Senate confirmation, but Sherman precluded any such arrangement when he refused to accept any post superior to Grant's.[24]

The appropriations bill also eliminated the president's constitutional authority as commander in chief—and thus the principle of civilian control over the military—by requiring all orders issued to subordinate commanders by the president or secretary of war to go through the general in chief. The idea was Stanton's, as he revealed to Grant on January 23. He may have included it to prevent Johnson from deploying the army against Congress: such a coup could be averted by forcing him to act through Grant, whom Radicals had begun to see as an ally. If Johnson could not replace Grant, he would have no means of enforcing the orders he issued through him, and he could not pass them down to other officers if Grant refused to obey. In essence the proposal left the general in chief independent of everyone, and so intently did Republicans train their antagonism on Johnson that they overwhelmingly waived the constitutional protection against military dictatorship. A generation later, Massachusetts Radical George Boutwell claimed that Stanton had dictated that amendment to him, verbatim.[25]

In cabinet discussion about the new legislation, Stanton voiced the most vehement opposition to the Tenure of Office Act, contending in a line of reasoning the president found especially able that it violated the Constitution. At one point Stanton mimicked Senator Sherman, remarking that no one who was fit for a cabinet post would remain in office if he were not wanted. Welles supposed that Stanton made the most of an opportunity to express concurrence with the rest of the cabinet, just as Browning had found him peculiarly agreeable over a minor issue the previous year, but Stanton's enthusiasm evaporated when Johnson asked him to put his argument on paper for use in the formal veto message. Lamely pleading a lack of time and rheumatism in his writing arm, he asked to be excused from preparing the message, probably to avoid having Radicals associate his name with opposition to their bill. Attorney General Stanbery declared that he could not possibly do it with his workload, and others also shied from the task, but Seward finally offered to compose it if Stanton would help him.[26]

As though in answer to Stanton's appeal for help, James Ashley voted in favor of the House amendment that included cabinet officers in the Tenure of Office Act, but he went a step further. Barely a month into the congressional session he accused Johnson of high crimes and misdemeanors, introducing a resolution for a committee to conduct an investigation. His list of crimes, some of them ludicrous, consisted mainly of legitimate executive functions to which Ashley added the adverb "corruptly": "corruptly" using the appointing power, for instance, or "corruptly" using the pardoning or veto powers. A veto had just come in that morning on a bill to award suffrage to black residents of the District of Columbia, and Congress summarily overrode the veto. Johnson's defiance inflamed the House (even though Grant and everyone in the cabinet but Stanton had also opposed the bill), and Ashley's impeachment resolution passed in a few minutes.[27]

In the next day's cabinet meeting, Johnson asked each department head to elaborate on his opinion of congressional Reconstruction plans— which, now that Tennessee had been restored to full statehood, would effectively dismantle the other ten states of the former Confederacy. Seeking a solid front against the House attack, Johnson achieved at least nominal unity in his official household. One by one his ministers acknowledged their allegiance to presidential policy by expressing doubt that a state could be reduced to a territory, even by Congress. Stanton concurred, or said he did, insisting that he had always approved of Johnson's reorganization of the state governments. Claiming that he had discussed the president's methods with no member of Congress but Senator Sumner, a full year before, he said he disagreed with Sumner then and had never since "conversed" with him. That was not true, for Sumner had assured others that Stanton agreed with him "entirely" a year before, and Stanton had been belittling Johnson's policy to Sumner and other Radicals at least as recently as the previous autumn.[28]

That very day, Congress passed another resolution calling on the president for any information he had relating to failures to enforce the Civil Rights Act in the South. Stanton suggested directing it to the attorney general, with copies forwarded to each department head. Welles responded immediately, and supposed that others had, as well. More than five weeks passed before Stanton submitted an undocumented list of alleged crimes against freedmen and soldiers through 1866 and early 1867; he had solicited it from the chief of the Freedmen's Bureau, and presented it in cabinet, asking to have it inserted as his part of the answer to the resolution. Several of those present doubted the relevance of Stanton's list, which Welles dismissed as "negro quarrels." The understanding seemed general that Stanton had dredged up as many potential violations as he could find, to throw doubt on executive enforcement and force the president to submit those allegations as proof. For once the secretary of war gave himself away, virtually daring his colleagues to suppress the information and warning that some members of Congress already had copies of his list. That inadvertent admission made it obvious that he had provided those copies himself—if he had not proposed the congressional inquiry in the first place. It was equally clear that he had meant from the start to embarrass Johnson, or to put him in the position of seeming to lie to Congress, perhaps as yet another excuse for impeachment. If Stanton's words had not betrayed him, his nervous facial expressions and body language would have. His only remaining friend in the cabinet, Seward, felt so embarrassed for him that he dropped out of the discussion and started reading a book.[29]

"He has no sincerity of character," Browning wrote of Stanton that evening, "but is hypocritical and malicious." When they compared notes on the incident the next day, Browning and Welles concluded that Stanton was involved in "villainy, if not absolute treachery" with the Radical leaders in Congress. Welles then took the matter up with the president, hypothesizing that Stanton's trumped-up report was part of a Radical scheme to justify a congressional plan for Reconstruction that relied on martial law. It also seemed increasingly apparent, Welles added, that Grant was falling into step with Stanton.[30]

Stanton's faithlessness to the president's Southern policy seemed corroborated by the eerie similarity of the Radical plan for Reconstruction to the one he had brought to Lincoln's last cabinet meeting: that blueprint had lumped Virginia and North Carolina into one military district under martial law, commanded by a single general, with the apparent aims of superseding the state governments and ignoring the original state boundaries. He had proposed as well that all loyal males of any color be allowed to vote, while the "disloyal" should be excluded from the franchise. The Reconstruction bill then afloat in Congress matched Stanton's original plan almost exactly, with at least two states combined in each new military district (except Virginia) and a general in firm military control; the bill also distributed voting privileges along the lines Stanton had suggested. Looking back on those similarities, Gideon Welles suspected that Stanton had provided his own rejected statehood scheme for Radical use against the president.[31]

Four days before his revealing blunder in council, Stanton had begun testifying before the House committee that was collecting information for impeachment—a body that Welles dismissed as a mere fishing expedition. Stanton would come before it again several times through the spring, and on one occasion he offered the committee Radicals the comfort of his opinion that Congress owned complete authority over "the whole subject of reconstruction." That statement conflicted with his January assurance to the president and cabinet that he had "cordially approved of every step which had been taken to reorganize the governments of the States which had rebelled." His contradictory testimony would soon be published as part of the propaganda campaign against the president, but with his Radical friends in the ascendance he seemed to worry less about betraying such mendacity—especially after those Radicals had specifically brought his office under the protection of their tenure bill.[32]

By March of 1867 Andrew Johnson began to comprehend that Congress had reduced his administration to impotence, if not to irrelevance. The Senate routinely rejected his nominees, and Congress regularly passed legislation without concern for either executive objection or constitutional compatibility. So hamstrung was the president that most of his cabinet finally consented to have him sign the army appropriations bill with nothing more pugnacious than an innocuous protest: even Browning, who dubbed it the "Military despotism bill" and had prepared a veto message, finally acceded to that virtual surrender. As they sat in the president's room at the Capitol, Johnson asked Stanton whether he approved of the protest, but Stanton smugly refused to answer. "I approve you taking whatever course you may think best," he replied. With that, control of the army effectively passed from the president to Stanton and Grant, and Stanton's collusion with the Radical majority meant that Congress could exercise an influence over the military that it was denied by the Constitution. Grant's staff detected just then that he, too, was creeping into the Radical camp. Stanton immediately began working with congressional Radicals to encourage editorial support for the plan in the South, using the old trick of government advertising to reward friendly journalists and punish the critical.[33]

With some suggestions from James Buchanan's former attorney general, Jeremiah Black, Johnson had already vetoed the First Reconstruction Act, characterizing it as nothing less than the imposition of military dictatorship for the purpose of coercing the people of the Southern states into accepting principles and measures they opposed. He had sent it to the Capitol, along with the veto of the Tenure of Office Act, on March 2, but Congress easily overrode both of them before the day ended. It was two days later that the president and cabinet discussed the army appropriations bill at the Capitol, when Stanton so curtly refused to answer Johnson's question. Johnson, Welles, and Buchanan had noted how obsequious Stanton could be, but suddenly that changed: safe inside the forum of those Radical allies who had just granted him their official protection, he evidently felt secure enough to speak flippantly to the president.[34]

The Thirty-ninth Congress adjourned at noon on March 4, and the resolution for impeachment died with it. Congress would normally have met next in early December, but by prior arrangement the members reassembled almost immediately to convene the Fortieth Congress, with its overwhelming Republican majorities. This ploy assured their uninterrupted domination of the president.[35]

Judge Black's early hesitation about Buchanan's constitutional options in the secession crisis remained an infuriating memory among militant Unionists, and many still blamed Black for Buchanan's failure to crush the rebellion in its infancy. The opprobrium then associated with Black's name may have accounted for the clandestine manner in which he contributed to the veto message. Secretary Welles was certain he recognized Black sitting in the president's office, scribbling at what Welles even then supposed was the veto message, although he never lifted his head from the paper. Stanton or one of his spies must have seen him there as well, for General Grant cited Black as the suspected author of the message within two days after it was delivered, and Stanton would have been Grant's principal conduit for White House information. Within a few more days Black's participation was known to the Radicals on the impeachment committee, probably through the same source, and they quickly subpoenaed him to testify, forcing him to admit his role in the veto for no apparent reason beyond embarrassing Johnson by the association.[36]

That veto, and the stubbornness that Johnson had so often demonstrated, left some doubt whether he would enforce the new Reconstruction Act. He might have stymied implementation of the law by judicious appointments to head the five military districts of the South—for moderate last-minute amendments to the bill had allowed Johnson, rather than Grant, to appoint the commanding generals. Stanton surely feared executive resistance, but even the president seemed momentarily stunned at how badly he had been beaten: he virtually abdicated the appointments to Grant, with whom he conferred for several hours on March 9. Welles frowned on Johnson's choice of adviser, suspecting that Grant had absorbed the Radical line through

Stanton and Holt. There may have been some substance to that suspicion, for when Johnson revealed his selections to the cabinet a few days later Stanton turned fairly giddy, joking uncharacteristically and showing uncontrollable jubilation. Stanton's steadfast old friend, Dan Sickles, and Grant's protégé, Phil Sheridan, were named to head two of the districts.[37]

Sheridan, who remained in his old department of Louisiana and Texas, celebrated his new authority by removing the Louisiana attorney general, the New Orleans mayor, and the judge who had opposed reassembly of the constitutional convention, all of whom Sheridan appeared to blame for the New Orleans riot. Within the next couple of months he removed the board of levee commissioners and finally the governor, as well, and his actions drew applause from Grant and Stanton, who were by then allied against the president and cabinet. Focusing their attention on Sheridan's more Radical appointments, conservatives perceived a dictatorial trend in the general that they had anticipated from the military "satraps" (as Welles characterized them), and that only confirmed their repugnance for the congressional version of Reconstruction.[38]

Frank Blair, a former Union general and member of Congress, believed Grant had started lusting after the presidency, with which his name had begun to be connected, and Blair supposed that the role of dictator might suit him, too. Blair saw Stanton as the "evil genius" behind the general's ambitions, ready to play Bismarck to Grant's Emperor Wilhelm, and he supposed that the uniform tactics of the five Reconstruction generals, including the high-handed Sheridan, reflected the instructions Stanton had issued to all of them. After the election defeat of the previous year, Blair had urged his brother, Montgomery, to persuade the president to abandon both Seward and Stanton, as a signal to conservative supporters that he had learned his lesson, but now disposing of either might be interpreted as a violation of the Tenure of Office Act. With Congress still in nominal session, producing only an occasional quorum, Johnson could not even appoint interim replacements; the Senate seemed to meet solely for the purpose of approving hostile legislation and rejecting even his most minor nominations. The only concession came when Johnson submitted a treaty with Russia, ceding Alaska to the United States for $7 million in gold. All but two senators approved the agreement, which had also won unanimous support in the cabinet, although Stanton appeared to lend it backing merely for the sake of his relations with Seward, who had negotiated the deal. In conversation with the president after Seward departed, Stanton ranted about spending so much for "a country of ice and rock," and lamented the additional cost of defending so vast a territory. It would have been better to leave it in the hands of a friendly power, he argued, although he had entered no objections when it would have mattered.[39]

Seward remained as loyal to Johnson as Stanton was not, and he may have accounted for the president's patience with Stanton. Seward was still a friend to the war secretary (he praised him as "the divine Stanton"), and Stanton portrayed himself as a friend to Seward. Seward was the most politically resourceful member of the cabinet, and Johnson held him in high esteem, having spent five years in the Senate with him when Seward was the rising star of that body. Welles overheard Seward tell Johnson of an understanding between him and Stanton that when one of them left the cabinet, so would the other. Johnson may have taken that seriously, tolerating Stanton for the sake of keeping Seward.[40]

Conservative Republicans who were turning gradually into Democrats— Montgomery Blair among them—took heart at the spring elections. New Hampshiremen went to the polls in March, just as civil government gave way to military rule in the South, and Republican candidates for governor and Congress still won all their contests, but they did so with smaller majorities than they had the year before. Democrats carried half the counties in the state, and added a fair percentage to their representation in the legislature. Three weeks later, just as the news of Sheridan's initial interference with civil government reached the North, Connecticut voters deposed their Republican governor and three of their four Republican congressmen. A reversal like that hinted that public patience with the Radicals had reached its limits, but even if that reactionary trend accelerated it could not dilute the Radical majority in Congress before Johnson's term ended.[41]

In decisions like the Milligan case, the Supreme Court had shown its own conservative side, and those who opposed the Radical agenda saw the court as the president's potential ally against the overweening ambition and unprecedented power of the latest Congress. The governors of Mississippi and Georgia tried to enlist the justices in the battle for constitutional supremacy, filing injunctions to stop implementation of the Reconstruction Acts—a second Reconstruction bill already having been passed, vetoed, and overridden less than three weeks after Congress reconvened. Mississippi governor William Sharkey filed his petition against the president himself, "to prevent irreparable mischief." Despite Johnson's criticism of the law for creating a "military despotism," his appointment of military commanders suggested that he would enforce it, and Sharkey condemned the law as a violation of several compacts between the federal government and the states, including the Ordinance of 1787. "These acts annihilate a State," Sharkey complained; "they destroy the State Constitution of Mississippi of 1817, accepted by Congress, as well as the amended Constitution of 1865, accepted by the people."[42]

The Supreme Court scheduled a hearing for eleven o'clock on Friday morning, April 5. Attorney General Stanbery wanted instructions, so the president called a cabinet meeting for nine o'clock, at which most members recommended that Stanbery appear and fight the petition: as sympathetic as they all might be to it, the principle of executive immunity to civil suit seemed worth preserving. Predictably, only Stanton argued against an appearance, suggesting illogically that they wait and see how the plaintiff's attorney fared. Stanbery made the objection, and the court dismissed *Mississippi v. Johnson* on the grounds of executive immunity Johnson had posed, so the Georgia governor modified his petition to make Stanton the defendant, as the head of the department that would rule his state under the new law. Many of the rulings on war powers and Reconstruction had come down with a bare majority, and in the absence of one justice the court deadlocked four to four on the question of accepting *Georgia v. Stanton.* That tie vote amounted to a refusal, killing any hope that the ten states could fend off military rule.[43]

Andrew Johnson earned no credit from Radicals for defending their legislation. Antagonism between the Capitol and White House only intensified as the president and Stanbery consistently applied permissive interpretations to laws Congress had designed for intrusive federal control. Stanton fought the president and the rest of the cabinet at every step. More than once during the spring, Stanton's defense of the Reconstruction Acts waxed so warm, and he displayed such intimate familiarity with the legislation, that the ever-suspicious Welles concluded he had written the original bills himself. "He defended it with all the earnestness and tenacity of an author," Welles observed once, "and took such ground as would suit the strongest Radicals."[44]

While the injunctions occupied the attorney general, another legal issue arose when the commanding general at Fort Monroe asked for orders in the case of Jefferson Davis. After two years of confinement, the erstwhile Confederate president had still not had a hearing, although an indictment for treason had been brought at Norfolk, Virginia. In May his attorney filed a writ of habeas corpus with the federal district court in Richmond, and the U.S. Attorney there asked for an order to release Davis from military custody so he could come to court. Stanton, just back from a visit with his mother in Ohio, handed the request to the president at the cabinet session of May 7, and Johnson read it, asking what recommendation Stanton might have. For the past two years Francis Lieber's legion of clerks had been scouring the rebel archives in the vain hope of finding correspondence that might link Davis or his government to the Lincoln assassination, which Stanton and Holt had insisted from the outset was the work of Davis and his "Canadian cabinet." Johnson, who had issued a proclamation to that effect on the authority of Stanton and Holt, might reasonably have expected Stanton to have developed a plan, but the secretary dodged an admission that no evidence could be found, saying again that he had no recommenda-tion. Still eager to try Davis for treason, Johnson directed Stanton to issue the order. Despite Stanton's avoidance of responsibility, he took undeserved credit before the Judiciary Committee for advising compliance with the writ, and he optimistically introduced the commanding officer at Richmond to the government's special prosecutor, William Evarts.[45]

The assassination, and Stanton's part in the aftermath, kept resurfac-ing that spring and summer of 1867. In the opening days of the Forti-eth Congress, James Ashley, who had uttered the first formal appeal for impeachment, alluded ominously to suspicions that Johnson was involved in the murder of Lincoln, and in a bitter exchange with John Bingham on the floor of the House a couple of weeks later, Ben Butler carried that insinuation a step further. In its impeachment investigation the Judiciary Committee had learned of the existence of the diary taken from the body of John Wilkes Booth, and Butler accused Bingham of having deliberately withheld it from evidence in the trial of the conspirators. Noting that the first eighteen pages of the diary were missing, Butler suggested that they would have proven Booth's original plan of kidnapping the president, which might have saved Mary Surratt from the gallows. He implied that someone in the government had cut those pages out, adding that the missing segment might also have indicated "who it was that could profit from assassination who could not profit by capture and abduction of the President." Combined with Ashley's scornful reference to Andrew Johnson as a "man who came into the Presidency through the door of assassination," Butler's remarks implied that the conspiracy extended to Johnson and those associates who had conducted the investigation and prosecution.[46]

Within a week after Butler's last barb, the Judiciary Committee called Stanton to the stand in an effort to track the whereabouts of the diary from the moment it left Booth's pocket. His testimony conflicted with that of the men who brought him Booth's effects, and that inconsistency evidently raised some eyebrows. Lafayette Baker had said, weeks before, that he ex-amined the diary at Stanton's home the evening he and Conger announced Booth's death, finding it more complete than its current condition, and both he and Conger testified that they left the diary with Stanton. When Stanton appeared before the committee, he maintained that he gave the book either to Baker or to Thomas Eckert for delivery to Holt. According to the oth-ers, Eckert had not even been present, but Stanton said Eckert had either arrived with them or "was sent for."[47]

That suggested Stanton had kept the diary long enough to remove incrim-inating content, and his contradictory testimony helped fuel speculation that he might have been involved in the assassination. Revelations from the committee's investigation came much slower to the president than to

Stanton, and more than a month passed before Johnson learned of the discrepancy in Stanton's story, but on May 9 Johnson directed him to produce a certified copy of the contents of Booth's diary, along with everything he knew about its capture and possession by the War Department. With great caution, Stanton composed numerous drafts of his reply, and he also passed the request on to the judge advocate general for comment. Holt leaped to Stanton's defense with more loyalty than logic, boldly assuring the president that it was "absolutely certain" the diary had not been tampered with—a patently worthless assurance, because Holt was the last person to come into possession of the book and could not even remember who delivered it to him.[48]

Not until the end of May was the contradiction reconciled, and even then it was not resolved to the satisfaction of the more skeptical. Eckert, who had resigned, returned to Washington and told the committee that he reached Stanton's home after Baker and Conger. Stanton gave him the diary, he said, and he locked it in his office safe until turning it over to Holt some time later. He failed to specify whether Baker and Conger were still at Stanton's home when he arrived: they had denied seeing him, but he was not asked whether they had already left, although any lag between their departure and Eckert's arrival would have given Stanton time to remove pages from the book. The impeachment committee inquired no further into that yawning gap in the testimony, perhaps because the only suspicion it raised about the mutilated diary implicated their friend Stanton, rather than Johnson or someone who might have acted in his behalf.[49]

Nor was that the last public reminder of the assassination. Mary Surratt's son John, who had long been sought as an early accomplice of Booth's, had fled the country and gone finally to Europe, where he was discovered in Vatican City as a soldier in the Papal Guard late in 1866. He was brought back across the Atlantic in a gunboat and jailed. In the wake of the Milligan decision, he, unlike his mother, was brought before a civil judge and jury in the District of Columbia courthouse early in June.[50]

That trial was just starting when the president and cabinet entered another long, contentious debate over Henry Stanbery's evolving interpretation of the Reconstruction Acts. The dispute consumed most of a workweek, beginning with an introduction on Monday, June 17, and only concluding the following Thursday. Stanbery's opinion, published finally in an eighteen-page pamphlet, characterized the commanders of the military districts as the guardians of the provisional governments, rather than substitutes for them, while Stanton insisted that the commanders of the departments in the South amounted to military governors with "omnipotent" authority. Welles, who had often enough regretted the need for military intrusion into civil government during the war, objected to it all the more in peace, and at one juncture he agreed with Stanton that the intent of the Reconstruction Acts was to "strike down" popular government in favor of military rule: the difference between them, Welles implied, was that Stanton applauded the new law while he deplored it. Stanbery's numerous legal points occasionally met unanimous approval from the cabinet, but in most cases Stanton offered the only dissenting opinion. In an unusual move for him, he kept a record of each day's developments, and of all the votes cast, but Welles also documented their sessions, after cringing at an account he found in the newspapers on Friday morning.[51]

On that same Friday, Stanton sent a telegram to Norman Judd, a newly elected Illinois congressman and a close friend of Lyman Trumbull. Stanton requested Judd to come to Washington "immediately," for reasons that became evident when Congress reconvened on July 3. During that first day's session Stanton's friend Thomas Eliot entered a resolution for a third, supplementary Reconstruction bill to counteract Stanbery's mild interpretations, and a few moments later Judd rose with another resolution to require of Stanton "copies of all instructions, orders, and correspondence" related to enforcement of the earlier acts. So many of the minority Democrats had not bothered to attend that both resolutions passed without debate or objection. Stanton, who had undoubtedly proposed Judd's resolution and may have written Eliot's as well, promptly supplied the requested materials.[52]

Within a couple of weeks that third Reconstruction Act came to Johnson's desk. It helped clarify congressional intent behind the previous acts in full accordance with the spirit of military rule that Stanton had espoused in council—condoning Sheridan's removal of public officials up to and including the governor of a state, and authorizing other district commanders to do the same, subject only to the approval of General Grant. Rather than give political privileges to black residents and disenfranchise many white voters, some Southern state officials were hesitating to establish the constitutional conventions, opting instead to remain under military control. One aging South Carolinian, though cherishing the old "Union of Equal Sovereigns," preferred living forever under the rule of General Sickles to holding a constitutional convention that would create a "Negroe Legislature." The supplementary act mandated those conventions, setting deadlines barely two months away. This third act all but emasculated the president insofar as the ten ex-rebel states were concerned, giving utmost authority to the commanding general. Johnson sent a futile veto message, but Congress passed it again over that veto the same day, and then adjourned the following morning.[53]

The adjournment left Stanton alone in his house, where he had been hosting Congressman Samuel Hooper. With too little money left to afford a private summer resort, Stanton had again sent Ellen and the children to their cottage at the Soldiers' Home during the intense humidity of July and August: in their absence the congressman had supplied Stanton with companionship and a handy line of communications with the Radicals on Capitol Hill, but after Congress left town Hooper returned to Boston.[54]

A young woman came to the White House on Saturday, July 27, introducing herself as the wife of Sandford Conover—or Charles Dunham, who had sat in the district jail for months, waiting to go to the Albany penitentiary to begin his ten-year sentence for perjury. She carried Conover's request for a presidential pardon, which was supported by recommendations from Joseph Holt and Albert Gallatin Riddle. Riddle, like Stanton's good friend Edwards Pierrepont, had been hired by the government—which was to say by the War Department—for the prosecution of John Surratt, since Holt and the Bureau of Military Justice remained intently interested in the case. Both Holt and Riddle urged the president to grant the pardon because they insisted that, while waiting at the jail, Conover had contributed materially to the case against Surratt.[55]

That was a lie. Conover had offered nothing useful to the prosecution, as Riddle admitted a few days later, notwithstanding his earlier statement to the contrary. Only a year before, Holt had defended his own damaged reputation by denouncing Conover as a wily, untrustworthy character, but the judge advocate general still seemed willing to rely on such a rascal for the third time. To the detriment of Holt's credibility, and Riddle's, Mrs. Conover's packet contained another missive that suggested a far more sinister motive for the recommendations of clemency than any pretense of aid in Surratt's trial. Inadvertently mixed with the petition and supporting documents was a note to Holt and Riddle from James Ashley, the ultra-Radical impeachment advocate from Ohio. Ashley had arranged the delay in Conover's transfer, and he solicited Holt and Riddle to help with Conover's pardon—not for anything concerning the Surratt trial, but to prove his reckless insinuation that Johnson had participated in the plot to kill Lincoln: all that effort on behalf of Conover, including the recommendations falsified by Riddle and Holt, emanated from the hope that Conover would use his peculiar talents toward that end. Ashley later admitted most of this when examined by the Judiciary Committee.[56]

Two nights after the woman visited the White House, her husband was suddenly plucked from his cell and shuffled off to Albany, but not before he directed his wife (if she really was his wife) to take another packet of letters to the president. The packet included Conover's own account of efforts by Ashley and others to have him supply witnesses who would produce false testimony and evidence showing that Johnson had taken an active role in the plot to kill Lincoln. Several letters written by Ashley to Conover appeared to confirm it, as did a memorandum of the script Conover's witnesses should follow, written in what certainly appeared to be the hand-writing of a clerk for the Judiciary Committee that had charge of the impeachment investigation.[57]

It seemed particularly suspicious that, after his transfer had been deferred for nearly six months, Conover should be packed off to Albany so soon after his wife showed up at the White House. Welles strongly suspected spies within Johnson's inner circle: any of the War Department detectives who loitered about the president's house might have recognized Mrs. Conover and mentioned it to Stanton, who was fairly intimate with Riddle and remained so close to Holt that he seemed a prime suspect. Stanton may well have been privy to the campaign to employ Conover against the president, but neither he nor any of his usual informants likely caused the prisoner's abrupt delivery to the penitentiary: Conover's motion to suspend his sentence had been denied in district court the day before his wife appealed to the president, and she had come there as a last resort, supposing that Ashley, Holt, and the rest had forsaken him.[58]

Both Seward and Stanbery missed the Tuesday cabinet meeting of July 30, and the president waited until Stanton had left before briefing Welles, Browning, McCulloch, and Randall on the incriminating materials. Welles and McCulloch urged Johnson to have the entire correspondence published immediately, and both Browning and the president seemed to agree. Randall thought publication should wait until they could determine who the false witnesses were, and obtain letters they had supposedly received from the Judiciary Committee clerk, instructing them how to testify. Randall proposed going to Albany himself that very night with Mrs. Conover, to secure a lawyer for her husband and get the papers, and his sudden enthusiasm persuaded the others to wait.[59]

Not until Stanton left the next cabinet meeting, on Friday, did Randall report that Mrs. Conover had declined to accompany him to Albany or hand over anything further until her husband had been pardoned. Welles expected to see the letters all published forthwith, but the president held off sending everything to the newspapers for another week, perhaps because other developments distracted him.[60]

Johnson had finally concluded that Stanton had to leave the cabinet. On August 1 he dictated a single sentence asking the secretary for his resignation, but he withheld that, too, until he could persuade Grant to accept the office. So great was the general's prestige that it seemed unlikely the Senate would stand in the way of his elevation to the War Department—and, while Grant had come to adopt the Radical viewpoint in most aspects of Reconstruction, he could at least be expected to fill the office with a more honest opposition than Stanton had shown. He demonstrated as much when, in interviews with the president, he admitted his differences over policy, and argued in favor of retaining Stanton. Grant said he would obey orders, but he observed that those who wanted Stanton removed were largely the same men who had opposed the war, and he implied that dismissing the secretary would only further associate the administration with that disloyal element. Most important of all, he felt, was his impression that Congress had passed the Tenure of Office Act primarily for Stanton's benefit: even if the law could be circumvented, public sentiment would weigh against the president.[61]

Grant's reluctance frustrated Welles, who thought Stanton would resign on demand: after the truculent comments Stanton had made against the Tenure of Office Act, Welles doubted that even he would have the gall to remain, once asked to retire. Welles recognized that Stanton would cling to his post as long as he dared "from personal considerations," by which he may have meant the salary, the power, or both, but he did not expect he would have the audacity to defy a direct request to leave.[62]

It would take one more provocation to prod the president to action. On the evening of August 4 he saw the *Star*'s account of that day's proceedings in the Surratt trial, in which prosecutor Edwards Pierrepont had mentioned the defendant's mother: her part in the conspiracy was believed to have been so prominent, Pierrepont said, brandishing Holt's summary of that earlier case, that the president had rejected the court's plea for mercy. "I hold in my hand the original papers signed by the President," Pierrepont was quoted as saying, "after it had been suggested and recommended that Mrs. Surratt's sentence be commuted." The *Star* reporter described Pierrepont throwing the sheaf of papers on the table in front of the defense lawyers, inviting them to look at it.[63]

The next morning Johnson sent for the documents Pierrepont had mentioned, declaring to his secretary, Colonel William Moore, that he had never before seen any petition for clemency. Neither had Holt mentioned one, Johnson insisted, and he immediately suspected skullduggery. Holt and Stanton seemed such close allies in their opposition to the administration that the president instructed Moore to deliver the letter seeking Stanton's resignation. Just before noon the next day Stanton's reply came back to the White House, declining to resign until Congress reconvened: he obviously intended to hide behind the Tenure of Office Act that he had so scorned as unconstitutional only five months previously. Welles in particular recalled Stanton damning the bill up and down, and insisting that he would not stay a moment if his departure were desired. Those assertions stuck with the navy secretary all the more vividly because, as Stanton raged self-righteously about the moral obligations of a cabinet officer, Welles had been thinking how unfaithful Stanton had been to President Buchanan.[64]

The cabinet members met again that morning, without Stanton. The lawyers among them hesitated to advise his outright dismissal, although his appointment by Lincoln seemed to preclude any protection under the tenure law, which covered officeholders for only thirty days beyond the term of the appointing president. They considered the law so unconstitutional in any case that it demanded a challenge, but with Congress still discussing impeachment that seemed a rash course. They did agree that temporary suspension was still permissible under the new law during the adjournment of Congress, and Johnson decided to take that avenue, but again he waited a few days. In the meantime he released all the correspondence from Conover and Ashley to the press, as though to curry public sympathy for himself with a sample of Radical villainy. Johnson invited Grant in for another interview on August 11, and Grant agreed to accept the post rather than let it go to someone less familiar with the army, or less friendly to it. The next day Johnson sent Stanton the order to turn his books and papers over to Grant, as secretary ad interim. Stanton blustered a bit against any executive authority to suspend him, but he seemed unconvinced by his own argument. On the excuse that Grant's acceptance posed a "superior force" he could not resist, he meekly turned his back on the department he had not so much administered as dominated for five and a half years.[65]

18

END OF THE TETHER

Even as he declined the president's request to resign, Stanton must have known Johnson would take further steps to push him out of office. Horatio Woodman had invited the Stantons up to Boston, and from there Congressman Samuel Hooper wished to take them to his cottage at Cotuit, on the south shore of Cape Cod. Stanton sent his defiant answer to the president, but then informed Woodman that he and Ellen hoped to see him soon. Vermont's wartime governor, J. Gregory Smith, had long before made a similar offer from his home at St. Albans, and Stanton intimated that he might soon be able to come there, as well. On August 12, 1867, when he conceded at least temporary defeat in his battle to remain in office, he sent a note to Ellen, who had been pressing him to leave the cabinet anyway. Allowing her to think his removal would be permanent, he said it would let them pursue the northern vacation she had been hoping for. Taking final advantage of his cachet as secretary, he called for a special railroad car to carry them to New York, and they arrived at Hooper's home in Boston on the morning of August 16.[1]

Publicity over her husband's situation would have been disturbing enough to Ellen, but alongside the inevitable personal agitation of the conflict she may have been concerned with the depletion of family funds. In 1863 the California reporter Noah Brooks had noticed that they lived well beyond the salary of a cabinet officer, but the luxuries had begun to fade with the shrinking of their cash reserves: the expensive hot-weather sojourns at spas had given way to summers at the Soldiers' Home, and Stanton had disguised their latest getaway as an inspection junket. Like many women of her era, Ellen may not have known much about their finances, but she probably hoped that her husband's return to the legal profession would quickly restore them to prosperity. Stanton labored under no such assumption. The friends he had represented in private cases were now largely his enemies, alienated by his political metamorphosis, while his new friends had never known him as an attorney. The Supreme Court, where he had earned generous fees and had been so well regarded by the majority before the war, now included more men who would view him with suspicion, despite his long association with the chief justice. If Stanton was confident he could resume a lucrative practice, his suspension from office gave him a perfect opportunity to do so, but despite economic need he made no effort in that direction. Stanton had good reason to doubt his prospects in private practice, and such doubts inevitably contributed to his reluctance to leave the cabinet. He seemed only to be waiting for the U.S. Senate to decide whether to approve his suspension, in compliance with the Tenure of Office Act.[2]

Bravely did he feign satisfaction with the change. Just over a week after turning the office over to Grant, while he and Ellen enjoyed the breezes off Nantucket Sound, he assured Eddie (who was still at work in the department) how glad he was to be out of it. From all quarters came invitations to visit, but while he said nothing about offers of employment he insisted that he would follow "professional designs," to the exclusion of public affairs. Yet no correspondence suggests that he had any business prospects, or even the hope of any, and their vacation dragged on well into the autumn.[3]

From Cotuit, Hooper put Stanton and another friend aboard a revenue cutter and sailed southwest a few miles to Naushon Island for an overnight stay. The following weekend they sailed the thirty miles to Nantucket, traversing the island to Siasconset and sleeping in Nantucket village, where Hooper introduced Stanton to some of his own cousins through his grandmother, Abigail Macy; the family included George Macy, whom Stanton had brevetted all the way to major general.[4] Leaving Cape Cod on the afternoon of September 3, the Stantons reached Boston that night, lodged with Woodman, and boarded a train for St. Albans the next day. Ellen, whose pulmonary difficulties had persisted from the previous summer, revived rapidly in the sea air of the cape, and Stanton's asthma abated in St. Albans. They spent a week with Governor and Mrs. Smith, inevitably hearing much about the Confederate raid on the local banks, not quite three years before, in which the governor's wife had stood guard at her front door with her husband's unloaded revolver.[5]

At St. Albans, Stanton learned of a nearby mineral spring that boasted remarkable curative powers, including some alleged success with cancer. It had been some time since he had corresponded with Senator Henry Wilson, his old ally from the Military Affairs Committee, and in a solicitous letter he mailed a brochure from the owners of that spring to Wilson, whose wife was suffering from cancer. Worry about Ellen's health, and the memory of Mary's inexorable decline, may have triggered a moment of pity for the soon-to-be-widowed Wilson, who had always been one of Stanton's champions in the Senate.[6]

The tedium of inactivity and uncertainty about his future began to wear on Stanton's nerves, and Ellen chastised Eddie for sending depressing letters filled with news about the department. Early in the long vacation she had tried to keep newspapers away from her husband, and she went so far as to censor his mail, opening at least one letter and destroying it when it failed to convey a "cheerful" tone. "Your father is in very bad spirits," she cautioned Eddie; "the least thing upsets him." The situation in Washington brought additional worry for Stanton, who may have originally supposed that Grant was merely holding the War Department open for him until the Senate came to his rescue: Francis Lieber, after all, had satisfied himself that Grant was "'fixed' on our side," and, unbeknownst to Stanton, Grant mistrusted Johnson enough that he dared not leave Washington. Yet, soon after Grant accepted the War Office, Johnson had removed Sheridan from command at New Orleans, and struck at an old Stanton ally by relieving Dan Sickles from duty in Charleston, all without any visible protest from Grant. The fall elections began to reverse the previous year's Radical victories, boding ill for Stanton in the long term, and Gideon Welles thought Stanton's suspension hurt the Republicans because it prevented him from devoting so many War Department resources to electioneering. Stanton's agitation would have only been aggravated by his own financial worries: he had left the War Department with no ready cash, evidently borrowing money to fund his travel and support his family until the Senate reinstated him—if it did.[7]

On the way home from Vermont the Stantons stopped in New York City and Hoboken, New Jersey, with other friends; they returned to Washington a week into October. With the congressional session impending, Stanton wrote to another senator, John Sherman. In reply, Sherman invited him to his home in Mansfield, Ohio, barely thirty miles from Gambier, where Stanton's mother and sister were then living. Leaving Ellen and the younger children in Washington, Stanton took Eddie with him, and after stopping in Mansfield they moved on to Gambier for a few nostalgic days where they had both attended college, and where Eddie's mother had grown up.[8]

During Stanton's absence from Washington the president had grown fearful that Grant's sympathies inclined too sharply toward Congress, and toward Stanton, and he toyed again with the idea of replacing his ad interim secretary with General Sherman, whose conservative nature better suited him. Sherman declined once more to supplant his old friend, whom he deemed not nearly so close to the Radicals as many in and out of the administration seemed to think. Sherman's father-in-law, old Tom Ewing, wondered whether Sherman miscalculated on that point; considering Grant as a moderate candidate for president, he inquired whether Grant had been "Stantonized, and delivered over to the extreme Radicals." Ewing's son, Tom Jr., suspected that Grant wanted to remain secretary of war, where he might run the army as he saw fit, and Sherman agreed, although he credited Grant's asserted disinclination to run for president. The underlying tensions in the department failed to reach Stanton through Eddie, increasing his anxiety over his chances of reinstatement. At the same time, the president seemed to fear that the Senate would restore Stanton to office, and he questioned Grant about his course if that happened: would the general submit? Grant replied that the matter would have to be resolved judicially, which Johnson optimistically interpreted to mean that he would not surrender the office directly to Stanton and might put the issue to a legal test.[9]

The confrontation with the Senate began early in the session. On December 3 the president delivered his annual message, beginning with an argument against the Radical denial of statehood in the former rebel states, but most of the members had no interest in hearing it. Johnson outlined his irreconcilable political differences with Stanton, adding such details as the secretary's failure to warn him of General Baird's alarming dispatch before the New Orleans riot, or to give Baird any instructions. He accused Stanton of first supporting presidential Reconstruction and then using his office to undermine it, as well as providing the template for the competing congressional plan. For an ironic conclusion, the president described the vehement objection Stanton himself had raised to the Tenure of Office Act. Fervent Radicals in the House made a second pitch for impeachment a few days later, based on Stanton's suspension and the removal of Sheridan and Sickles, but the resolution failed. The Senate merely awaited Johnson's request to approve Stanton's suspension, and he submitted it on December 12, thereby complying with the Tenure of Office Act and compromising any hope of challenging its constitutionality.[10]

Stanton was not in town to respond, and the Senate postponed action through the holidays. His nephew David Stanton, Darwin's only son, died at Steubenville during the first days of the congressional session, and when the telegram arrived Stanton made the trek back to Steubenville alone. The young man, only about a year older than Eddie, was laid to rest in the family lot on December 10, and Stanton appears not to have arrived in time. So hard did the loss of her only son strike Nancy Hooker Stanton that Stanton lingered in Steubenville a week after the funeral, taking the train and the stage out to Gambier to pass his fifty-third birthday with his mother and Pamphila. Snow fell during much of the visit, and he had to travel part of the way by sleigh again, returning to Steubenville on December 20.[11]

He reached Washington in plenty of time for Christmas, finding Ellen anxious over their unsettled situation and uncertain future. Wheezing from what he supposed was furnace smoke at 320 K Street, Stanton composed a lengthy retort to Johnson's Senate message that was perhaps not even necessary to assure his restoration to office. After Christmas the president had deposed two more of the five commanding generals in the South—John Pope, who administered Florida, Georgia, and Alabama, and E. O. C. Ord, who had overseen Arkansas and Mississippi. Pope, like Sheridan and Sickles, had irked Johnson with the arbitrary removal of state officials. Johnson regretted losing the conscientious and discreet Ord, but the general had sought reassignment for months, so he could take his consumptive wife to a drier climate. In September Grant had hesitated to send Ord elsewhere, lest it be mistaken for another punitive removal, but in December he relented and recommended Ord's transfer. Radicals nevertheless greeted both changes as more blows to congressional Reconstruction by a defiant president.[12]

Johnson remained confident, as he had since the autumn elections. He instructed his secretary to draft an undated letter removing Stanton from office, should the Senate reinstate him. He even seemed hopeful that Grant might yield the post—still assuming that he would leave it under Johnson's control, and that a more compatible interim appointee could be found. In his impatience to complete the Reconstruction process and relieve the army of that obnoxious duty, Grant was incurring presidential annoyance by subverting some of Johnson's aims in the Southern military districts.[13]

Predictably, the question of Stanton's removal went to Senator Wilson's Military Affairs Committee, which disapproved it and then leaked its decision to the press. On Saturday, January 11, 1868, the full Senate discussed Stanton's fate in executive session. Senator Doolittle, who had been the only dissenting member of the committee, sought to arouse animosity against Stanton by resurrecting his part in the interruption of prisoner exchanges during the war, which had had such devastating effects on the health of Union soldiers. Stanton heard of Doolittle's attack right away, and on Sunday he dug out General Hitchcock's report on prisoners of war, garnishing it with his own bloody-shirt brief contending that the mistreatment of Union prisoners was a diabolical plot of the rebels designed "to secure the overthrow of the United States government." Henry Wirz had gone to the gallows, after all, to absolve Union authorities, including Stanton, by burning that image of deliberate Confederate cruelty into the American memory. Presenting this rebuttal to Senator Fessenden, Stanton asked him to use it to counter the "false and malicious" allegations among his fellow senators.[14]

General Grant dropped in on the president that Saturday, telling him that he had read the text of the Tenure of Office Act more closely. The law would subject him to a $10,000 fine and a five-year sentence, he said, if the Senate restored Stanton to duty and he failed to surrender the office. Knowing that he would be the likely Republican presidential nominee in a few months, Grant had no wish to commit even a technical violation, but he told Johnson that he especially feared such harsh penalties. Johnson remonstrated with him at length, arguing that the law was unconstitutional, and he seemed deaf to Grant's protests. They wrangled for an hour or more, with Grant perhaps satisfied that he had warned the president of his intentions and Johnson apparently convinced that he had brought Grant back to a point of uncertainty from which he could be persuaded to hold out against Stanton and test the law. Johnson dismissed him finally with the remark that they would talk again on Monday.[15]

Johnson wanted someone in the War Department willing to hold the position and challenge the law, but he would have accepted some moderate who might win Senate approval. Grant suggested Governor Jacob Cox of Ohio, a former Union general whose Canadian birth precluded any presidential ambitions. General Sherman was in the capital, visiting with his brother the senator (who lived next door to the Stanton home), and at Grant's request he saw the president to suggest Cox. No successor would have suited, however, and on Monday evening the Senate voted nearly six to one to reject Stanton's suspension. The debate included a rousing defense by Fessenden of Stanton's handling of the prisoner exchanges: the senator used Stanton's brief, which diverted attention from the secretary's opposition to exchanges by castigating the Confederates for deliberate maltreatment. Stanton promised Fessenden "gratitude ever and forever."[16]

Grant and the president did not meet formally on Monday, although they saw each other at a levee that evening. Early Tuesday morning Grant locked the doors to the secretary's office in the War Department and gave the keys to the adjutant general. Returning to his office at army headquarters, across the street, he sent a staff officer to the White House with a letter announcing that the Senate disapproval of Stanton's suspension ended his tenure as secretary ad interim. Johnson, who may or may not have read that letter yet, called Grant to the regular cabinet meeting that day, where the general informed him of his action. A tense interview followed, with the president asserting that Grant had promised to either retain the office until the courts decided the issue or resign beforehand, so a more determined nominee could be appointed. Johnson took umbrage that Grant had said nothing at the Monday levee. Grant, evidently unsettled by Johnson's seething indignation, explained that his intentions had changed when he learned of the penalties prescribed by the tenure law, but Welles and Browning heard him concede that he had agreed to see the president on Monday to give his final answer. The rest of those present later corroborated that recollection. Perhaps Grant had hoped Sherman would persuade Johnson to appoint Cox on Monday, as an alternative, or he may simply have forgotten the appointment. At least twice the general mumbled about the press of business on Sunday and Monday, as if excusing an oversight, and he admitted that the president may have been under the impression that they were to meet, but he denied ever afterward having agreed to the Monday meeting. The two surviving descriptions of his January 14 appearance, both recorded by Johnson partisans, portray an uncharacteristically stammering and apologetic general in chief backing out of the room. The scene seemed to permanently tarnish his image for those who witnessed it.[17]

Georges Clemenceau, a young French doctor visiting the United States, admired Johnson's determination and tenacity in his unequal contest with Congress, and in this episode he thought Grant came out looking much the worst of all the actors. In a letter to *Le Temps* at the time of Stanton's reinstatement, Clemenceau noted that the Democrats "turned all the vials of their wrath" on Grant because of his broken promise. "But who knows whether the General really made such a promise?" he concluded.[18]

While Johnson belabored Grant, a brash Stanton bustled back into the War Department. The next day's papers depicted him in unusually fine spirits and chatting casually—which, one editor noted wryly, was often said of men about to be hanged. Henry Raymond of the *New York Times* no longer held the president in very high esteem: he blamed Johnson for defying the law before it had been tested (although until it was defied there could have been no test). Raymond nevertheless chastised Stanton for lacking the grace to withdraw from a position of confidence when asked, and he considered the secretary's conduct still more questionable than Johnson's. Stanton's continuation in office could yield neither honors nor an opportunity for usefulness, thought Raymond, wondering what motive he might have. Word circulated that Stanton immediately drew his pay for the previous five months, suggesting he did it for the money, but Chief Clerk John Potts denied it.[19]

Other rumors, likely spawned by Stanton himself, predicted that he would resign as soon as the Senate restored the office to him, but he gave no indication of doing so. He told his sister that "Republican Members of Congress" insisted that he stay on, while Ellen very much wished him to quit. Although he reportedly conferred at length with Ben Wade in the vice president's chamber at the Senate on Wednesday, he was back in his office in time for General Sherman to drop in on him from an army board meeting. Sherman, who had accompanied Grant to see the president that morning, intended to suggest that Stanton resign, but Stanton never gave him the chance. Supposing that Sherman had been called to Washington to replace him, Stanton used the visit to express what great respect and admiration he felt for him ("all very loving," noted a cynically amused Sherman). The proud general had not yet forgotten Stanton's humiliating public tirade, and he demonstrated as much when he responded with an offer not to "recall the past," saying only that he did not want to see the army entangled in Stanton's feud with the president.[20]

The contest between Johnson and Stanton involved nothing less than complete control of the army. Johnson told Grant not to obey Stanton's orders unless he knew they really came from the White House, for Stanton often signed orders "by direction of the president" when the president never even knew of their existence: he had often done the same under Lincoln. Grant, who might otherwise have sympathized with Johnson's plight, bristled after the *National Intelligencer* began publishing Johnson's insinuations that Grant had schemed with Stanton to return him to office, and the general insisted on having it in writing if he was to ignore the secretary. Johnson put it on paper, but when Grant took it to Stanton the secretary replied that he had no instructions from the president limiting his authority to issue orders in his name "as has heretofore been his practice under the law." Coyly cooperating with Stanton, Grant sent that message back to the president, with notice that he would regard all such orders from Stanton as though the president had issued them until that authority was formally rescinded. Johnson refused to recognize Stanton officially by issuing such an order, but he noted the irony of Grant obeying indirect orders through Stanton while refusing to obey a direct one from the president.[21]

When paperwork came from the War Department, Johnson would endorse it and pass it on to Grant, rather than return it to Stanton: he said he would reduce the secretary's office to a "mere clerkship," but that plan collapsed when he failed to bar his other department heads from recognizing Stanton as the secretary. If Stanton could sign warrants on the Treasury, he still retained significant power.[22]

Someone who must have been informed by Stanton alerted House members to the exchanges between Johnson and Grant over Stanton's authority. Hoping the letters might reveal a technical violation of the tenure law, a young Radical congressman introduced a resolution calling for the correspondence. Grant volunteered copies of his replies for Stanton to submit, but to the disappointment of Johnson's enemies it fell short of an impeachable offense for the president to insist on having control over orders issued in his name. Still, so long as Congress sustained him, Stanton could use the army as he pleased, ignoring the wishes of the president and even violating his direct orders.[23]

Unconvinced by friends who assured him Grant was innocent of any conniving, Johnson sputtered periodically about what he characterized as Grant's faithless collusion with Stanton, and those accusations kept creeping into print. Had Johnson not offended Grant with such remarks, they might still have allied against the renegade secretary, for Grant had not turned completely Radical. He shared Sherman's apprehensions about potential entanglements for the army, and the Radical-driven supplemental Reconstruction Act of the previous summer had embroiled the army in Southern politics. Grant also resented Radical retaliation against General Winfield Hancock, whose administration of Sheridan's former military district dissatisfied them: they were then trying to reduce the number of major generals in the army, to force Hancock's discharge. Furthermore, Ord had become the defendant in a Supreme Court suit designed to test the legality of military rule on which congressional Reconstruction depended; in an attempt to avoid an unfavorable decision Republicans prevented Johnson from replacing a deceased justice by reducing the size of the court—much as they had tried to restructure the executive branch to exploit the political loyalties of the incumbents. Grant was apparently also annoyed with Stanton for reoccupying his office hastily enough to make the general look complicit. But for the mistrust the president had aroused in the general in chief, Grant might have been more open to helping him find a way around the dog in the manger at the War Department.[24]

Well might Henry Raymond wonder what Stanton intended to do with the office he had regained. His pecuniary situation made the income important, and he always valued the prestige of high office, but these were no longer the incentives that drove him to entrench himself in an inimical administration. The primary appeal of the War Department, after the break with Johnson became open and irrevocable, was the opportunity it gave him to thwart and provoke Johnson—and the power that opportunity could represent. Stanton's suspension in August had initiated a blizzard of complimentary mail such as he had not seen since he accepted the post in 1862, and none of those more recent letters could have represented the strategic flattery of prospective favor-seekers, as so many of the earlier ones had. His return in January launched a similar flood of congratulation, by note and by handshake, on Capitol Hill, and these accolades reflected a perverse appreciation for the mortification Stanton could cause the unpopular president. However dark the talents and powers that won him the attention of the dominant Radicals, their support served as his best assurance of future indulgence: his disinclination or inability to resurrect his legal practice during five idle months dictated that his future comfort and security lay in some form of government office that his admirers in Congress might accommodate. If he could survive the final 400 days of Johnson's term, or if the hostile majority in Congress found an excuse for impeachment beforehand, a more congenial and grateful chief executive might exercise the power of federal appointments.

In desperation Johnson cast about again for someone to replace Stanton whom the Senate might approve. As always, he thought first of General Sherman, who refused one last time on personal and political grounds. When Sherman returned to his department headquarters in St. Louis, Johnson tried to bring him back East on a permanent basis, probably for future courting as war secretary, by sending his name to Congress for promotion to brevet general and assigning him to command a huge new Military Division of the Atlantic, with headquarters in Washington. Sherman, who wanted nothing to do with the politics of Washington, begged him to desist from so unwelcome a favor, and to his great relief Johnson finally let it drop.[25]

Stanton's first days back at his desk must have passed in heightened tension, as both he and the president wondered what the other would do. After a few weeks, with Johnson seemingly reconciled to the unavoidable, Stanton began to relax. Keeping possession of the war office precluded travel, which his finances would not allow anyway, and during his suspension the Stanton home had ceased to ring with the laughter of dinner guests, but three weeks after his return he received an invitation he could not refuse. Charles Sumner apprised him on Sunday afternoon, February 2, that Charles Dickens, who was touring the United States, would be at Sumner's Washington lodgings that evening, and if Stanton wished to come over they would be alone. Dickens was Stanton's favorite author, whom he often quoted in letters, and the three of them sat together long into the night, smoking cigars while the admiring reader impressed the celebrity by his familiarity with the Dickens canon. If Stanton applied his customary veneer of flattery Dickens may have been reminded of his character Uriah Heep, but any impression Stanton made on the author seems to have gone unrecorded.[26]

That late night notwithstanding, Stanton appeared at his desk as usual the next morning. To prolong his incumbency he followed the path of least resistance, attending to routine inquiries while relying on his mere presence to serve as an annoyance to the president. With his return, department correspondence resumed the tone of businesslike insensitivity that he always modeled, at least in dealing with those without influence. One of the early letters passing through his office came from semiliterate Eliza Crewson, back in Steubenville, whose husband had served throughout the war and then joined one of the veteran volunteer regiments raised by General Hancock in 1865. He had been discharged again in the spring of 1866, sick, and died about a year later. With seven children to feed, his struggling widow sought the balance of his bounty from his second enlistment, and Stanton assigned a staff officer to investigate the claim. The officer found that William Crewson's final muster roll made no reference to any bounty, yet at that stage of the war he must have enlisted for one. Sharing the same home town with the secretary of war did not even avail Mrs. Crewson advice for further relief, and two more decades passed before anyone so much as suggested that she apply for a pension. The most common correspondence that winter involved Southerners trying to recover confiscated property, which usually elicited a similar lack of sympathy, even for elderly veterans of earlier American wars with no record of disloyalty to the Union.[27]

By mid-February Stanton had resumed regular communications with the other cabinet departments. To Hugh McCulloch, at the Treasury, he forwarded a report on the evils of department employees selling liquor to laborers on the Union Pacific Railroad. To Attorney General Henry Stanbery he conveyed titles obtained by the Quartermaster Bureau for land to accommodate national cemeteries. The establishment of new national cemeteries consumed several quires of War Department stationery in February.[28]

Stanton's own actions came back to haunt him when, on February 20, the firm of Carlisle & McPherson obtained an order from the Court of Claims for Stanton to provide information about a large supply of cotton owned by neutral parties that Sherman's army had captured at Savannah. This represented some of the cotton Stanton had found there in January of 1865, from which he had ordered the owners' identifications removed, and that action prevented the government from documenting any fraudulent claims.[29]

However little actual damage Stanton might do to Johnson politically from within the War Department, the knowledge that he occupied that nearby building drove the temperamental president to exasperation and finally provoked the very act that Johnson's enemies had long awaited. No longer able to bear the congressional insult of an enemy imposed on his official family, Johnson began to ponder removing Stanton outright and replacing him with someone palatable enough to win Senate approval. The lopsided rejection of Stanton's suspension ought to have persuaded the president that it could no longer be done, but the taunting proximity of his tormentor seemed to rob him of reason, and in his monomania he thought of installing the chief clerk, Potts, as interim secretary until he found someone permanent. Potts confided that he was indebted to Stanton for giving his son an army commission, and he would find it very uncomfortable to supplant him, so Johnson turned next to Lorenzo Thomas, the adjutant general.[30]

Thomas, whom Stanton had sent away during the war to recruit Southern slaves into Union service, had never resumed his original assignment. In his place stood his assistant, Colonel Edward Townsend, who enjoyed a much more intimate relationship with Stanton. The president interviewed Thomas, and early on Friday morning, February 21, Johnson instructed his private secretary, Colonel Moore, to prepare one order for Stanton's removal, one for Thomas's appointment as secretary of war ad interim, and a message for the Senate announcing the change. Thomas personally delivered the news to Stanton, and Stanton dropped onto one of the divans to read the dismissal order, asking if he could have some time to collect his private property. Thomas agreed, and when Stanton asked for a copy of the order Thomas returned to his office to have Townsend make one. Certifying it as a true copy with his own signature as secretary ad interim, Thomas gave it to Stanton, who asked for time to decide whether to obey the order.[31]

Several sealed messages from the White House reached the Senate an hour after lunch, with the announcement of Stanton's removal among them, but Stanton had already sent word of his plight to House Speaker Schuyler Colfax and Ben Wade, now president pro tem of the Senate. When a messenger handed Stanton's note to Colfax he interrupted the afternoon's proceedings to read it, while Wade promptly ejected all reporters and visitors sometime after two o'clock, taking the Senate into executive session. General Grant's patron, Elihu Washburne, instantly moved that the House refer the issue to the Committee on Reconstruction. Congressmen and senators bombarded Stanton with messages to stand at his post, including a single-word note in Senator Sumner's inscrutable scrawl admonishing him to "Stick!"[32] Four Radical senators left the discussion to join the embattled secretary at the War Department. Late that evening the Senate doors opened to emit a resolution declaring that the president had no legal right to remove his secretary of war, as if to reveal a predetermination that Johnson had broken the law and encourage the House of Representatives to initiate impeachment proceedings. The House needed no such encouragement, for John Covode had long since risen, as the sky darkened over Washington City, to enter the third impeachment resolution in fourteen months. Tammany Hall Democrat Fernando Wood objected, but Colfax overruled him, whereupon the congressmen voted and headed home for the night.[33]

That evening General Thomas escorted his daughters to a masquerade ball, where he imbibed a little too freely. By 9:00 P.M. gossip trickled back to the War Department that Thomas was boasting he would take possession of the building the next morning, by force if necessary, and Stanton scratched off a message to three senators—Fessenden of Maine, Jacob Howard of Michigan, and George Edmunds of Vermont—alerting them to the threat. "If the Senate does not declare their opinion of the law," he asked them, "how am I to hold possession?" At that hour the Senate had not yet adjourned, and his message probably precipitated the last-minute resolution proclaiming the removal illegal. Stanton had ordered the War Department closed in observance of Washington's birthday, the next day, but the lights there burned late into the night. He remained in his office with his congressional visitors until after midnight, when most of them left him to bed down on one of the divans, with a single officer to keep him company.[34]

Holiday or not, the War Department doors opened the next morning for visitors with any official clout, some of whom witnessed a comic opera between the contending secretaries. Stanton had filed a complaint with his Radical friend David Cartter, the chief justice of the District of Columbia

Supreme Court, charging General Thomas with violating the Tenure of Office Act, and Cartter issued a warrant for Thomas's arrest. The general had not fully recovered from the previous evening's festivities, and had not eaten breakfast when the U.S. marshal took him from his home on H Street for arraignment before Cartter, who let him post bail at 10:30 A.M. From there Thomas took the F Street horsecar to Fourteenth Street, where he stopped to see the attorney general. After reporting his misadventure to the president, Thomas proceeded to the War Department at noon with his stomach still grumbling, finding his rival huddled with a semicircle of congressmen. The old general straightened his tall, suffering frame and told Stanton he had come to take possession of the office as interim secretary. Stanton replied that he was secretary, and ordered Thomas to his own office. The general refused, insisting that he would act as secretary, and Stanton reiterated his order to leave the room. Again Thomas declined, repeating that he would act as secretary. Stanton barked back that he might stand there as long as he wished, but he would not be secretary of war. Thomas left the room then for Colonel Edmund Schriver's office, and Stanton followed him in to try a friendlier tack. Thomas complained that his arrest had deprived him of any food or drink that morning, and Stanton sidled sympathetically up to him, putting one arm around his neck and running the fingers of his other hand through Thomas's white mane, calling on Schriver at the same time to provide a little stimulant from a bottle he kept there. Stanton poured some into two tumblers, studied them against the light for equal measure, and the two of them drank together. A messenger brought a full bottle, and they shared another glass. Thus ended the only physical attempt to wrest the office from Stanton.[35]

While that farce entertained Stanton's visitors, the House of Representatives also ignored the holiday. Old Thad Stevens introduced the correspondence between Johnson and Stanton as the Committee on Reconstruction interpreted it, along with Covode's motion for impeachment. Republicans ruled the day, defeating Democratic motions to read Washington's Farewell Address and adjourn. A Democrat from Indiana objected when Speaker Colfax announced a wire from Governor Richard Oglesby of Illinois, the Radical who had presided over the prosecution of Surgeon General Hammond. Colfax drew howls of laughter when he replied that he would rule on whether the telegram was in order after he had read it. Remarking on the "treason" of Andrew Johnson, Oglesby urged Congress to do its duty. Stanton's special prosecutor of yore, John Bingham, bade his colleagues consider the Senate's eager hint of the night before, when it had formally declared Stanton's removal illegal.[36]

The result was never in doubt, but individual members felt constrained to impress their constituents with their indignation. With further speeches limited to half an hour they went to dinner, reconvening at seven o'clock and going late into the night. Debate resumed Monday morning, apparently with the record distorted to pretend it was still Saturday, but at noon a Pennsylvania Democrat proposed abandoning that charade to "begin" Monday's session. That deterred Republicans from nominally impeaching the president on Washington's birthday, and the decision came in the afternoon, with 125 Republicans supporting Covode's resolution and 47 Democrats opposed. At the end of the counting Speaker Colfax added his vote to impeach, raising the total to 126.[37]

Six inches of fresh snow blanketed Washington the next morning, and it was still falling. Everyone had already read the news in the Monday edition of the *Washington Evening Star*, but the House had appointed Thad Stevens and Bingham as a committee to make formal delivery of the impeachment resolution to the upper chamber, and the sergeant at arms announced them at the Senate door just after one o'clock. Leaning on Bingham's arm, the lame, pale, and clearly failing Stevens hobbled down the aisle to within earshot of Ben Wade's chair. Their entrance had interrupted a Kentucky senator, who objected to being silenced, but Wade (who would assume the presidency if Johnson were removed) gave Stevens the floor. In the name of the House of Representatives "and all of the people of the United States," Stevens made his announcement. "We do impeach Andrew Johnson, President of the United States, of high crimes and misdemeanors in office, and we further inform the Senate that the House of Representatives will in due time exhibit articles against him."[38]

While this drama unfolded, Stanton continued to live in his office, having food and clothing brought to him. Five years afterward, a local woman remembered seeing him take half an hour of exercise each day on the walkway in front of the department, pacing back and forth. Thirty-five years later, an old soldier who served as sergeant of a guard detail at the War Department told of being sent by Stanton to 320 K Street for blankets and pillows, to ease the nights on the divan, but, according to the sergeant, Ellen refused to provide him with anything from the house and demanded that her husband give up and come home. She stopped by once, early in his long confinement, and her impatience drove him to some utterance of irritation or self-pity that sent her home angry; after a few more days she wrote him a conciliatory note, and he apologized.[39]

Congressmen crowded Stanton's office, wishing him well and encouraging continued resistance. When he wanted to consult with senators on strategy, he sent a carriage to bring them to his office, not daring to leave it empty for an hour. Like Grant, whose soured relations with Johnson had made him all the more willing to cooperate with the impeachment managers, he rifled department files for evidence damaging to the president's case. He busied himself with routine paperwork, signing discharges, court-martial recommendations, and requisitions on the Treasury Department, a sheaf of which he dispatched to Secretary McCulloch, to test whether he would still honor them. Perhaps because a refusal would only handicap the army, McCulloch accepted the bills, implicitly recognizing Stanton as the rightful secretary. He forwarded one letter to General Thomas as adjutant general, but Thomas appears to have returned it. A petition for habeas corpus by General Thomas, who was still technically under arrest, offered the president his last hope of challenging the constitutionality of the Tenure of Office Act in time to avert impeachment, but Stanton was still a wily enough lawyer to ask Judge Cartter to dismiss his complaint. Thomas retaliated with a civil suit for damage to his reputation, "interference with business," and legal expenses, asking a phenomenal sum that only brought him editorial ridicule.[40]

The House appointed a committee of seven Republicans to oversee the impeachment, with Bingham and Stevens among them, and more than a week later Bingham submitted their handiwork to the consideration of the full House. The managers broke a single incident into as many technical violations as possible, the better to obtain a conviction on something. Eight different articles charged Johnson with one violation of the tenure law. He had committed "a high misdemeanor" for removing Stanton without the advice and consent of the Senate; he had committed another for appointing Thomas when there was no vacancy, and a third for doing so while the Senate was in session, available for consultation. For "conspiring" with Thomas to hinder Stanton in his duties, Johnson was charged with both a "high crime" and a "high misdemeanor," in two separate articles. That alleged conspiracy furthermore subjected him to two more counts for the same action, both as crime and as misdemeanor, under an 1861 law passed to punish disloyal intrigue. The eighth article accused him and Thomas of conspiring to "control the disbursements of the moneys appropriated for the military service and for the Department of War."[41]

The next article fell under the provision of the army appropriations bill that prohibited Johnson from issuing orders to the army without going through Grant. It stemmed from a conversation between Johnson and William Emory, commander of the forces in Washington, on February 22, when the sudden activation of troops sparked some worry over a military coup against the administration. The president commented sarcastically to Emory on the prohibition, and the impeachment committee tried to twist that offhand remark into an effort to persuade the general to violate that congressional stricture. Ben Butler wrote a long and laughable tenth article complaining of Johnson's political speeches before and during his "swing around the circle," charging him with a high misdemeanor for bringing the presidency into disrepute and trying to "excite the odium and resentment of all good people" by expressing his political sentiments "in a loud voice" to large public assemblages.[42]

Those ten articles, ranging from the picayune to the absurd, would attract the votes of many senators, but conviction required a two-thirds majority. A majority would probably support some or all of the technical criminal violations in the first eight articles, as well as the violation implied by the ninth. Butler's political accusation promised to be popular, too, but even so Radical a Senate might not produce the two-thirds vote required to convict on any one of those counts. An eleventh omnibus article vastly improved the odds for conviction by combining the technical criminal accusations with subjective political allegations as silly as Butler's and presenting them all in a single charge, designed to appeal equally to the legally fastidious and the politically vengeful.[43]

The Senate sergeant at arms called at the White House on the evening of March 7 to deliver the summons to the president. Chief Justice Chase opened the pretrial phase of the process in the Senate chamber less than a week later, hearing the articles read and granting delays requested by the president's attorneys—among whom Henry Stanbery stood foremost, having resigned as attorney general to avoid complaints that Johnson was defending himself at government expense. Visitors filled the galleries to watch the unprecedented event. Ellen Stanton's mother had come down from Pittsburgh, perhaps to keep Ellen company while Stanton slept at the department, and women looking for celebrities at the Senate noticed her there.[44]

The actual trial opened at the end of March, and few of those involved did more than pretend to engage in open-minded consideration of evidence. Politics drove the contest from the start, with party faithful hard at work lobbying senators to cast their votes for or against conviction. With only a dozen Democrats among the fifty-four senators, the outcome seemed preordained, but soon enough doubts arose about a few of the Republicans. John Sherman, for instance, had notoriously argued during deliberation on the Tenure of Office Act that it should not have applied to the cabinet posts, and that he would not hesitate to approve the removal of a stubborn secretary: a vote for conviction would suggest partisan hypocrisy.[45]

The vote of Senator Fessenden, Stanton's ally for most of the past six years, also came into doubt early. As late as March 27 he had defended Stanton on the Senate floor from criticism by Kentucky's Garrett Davis, and the secretary used Fessenden as his conduit to more moderate senators. For the apparent benefit of his Senate colleagues, Stanton told Fessenden that he wished to leave public life "forever," partly to avoid such "malignant assaults" as Davis's: that gratuitous remark seemed to imply that he only clung to office out of self-sacrifice to the party and its principles—and, perhaps, that he would not complicate matters with the presidential candidacy that some were suggesting for him.[46] Fessenden may have passed that hint along, but he was no friend or admirer of Ben Wade, and impeachment would thrust Wade into the presidency. Besides, Fessenden had distanced himself from the Radical caucus. Stanton may not have been unaware of Fessenden's potential wavering when he reciprocated the senator's kindness with a favor of his own. With a small flood of claims for confiscated property pouring through the war office that spring, Stanton formed a three-man commission to review and rule on those claims, and it was Fessenden's son whom Stanton chose first for the sinecure, offering him a chance, as well, to name at least one friend to the same commission. This small reward for young General Fessenden, written just as the impeachment trial opened, may have been intended to remind Senator Fessenden of the even-greater favors Stanton had previously bestowed on two of his soldier-sons.[47]

From New York, Edwards Pierrepont forwarded what he considered reliable information that "Ruffians," rather than soldiers, would come take possession of the war office. Speaker Colfax informed the *New York Tribune* editor when he heard that scores of strangers had come to Washington with carpetbags that seemed to be bulging with revolvers. To the consternation of his wife, Stanton remained in his office day and night through March, declining even to respond to a subpoena from the commissioner of Chancery on the grounds that "Duties prevent him from leaving the War Department." Eight weeks into the siege he finally dared slip away to his house, and could not resist spending one night in his own bed, asking his son to send his cough medicine home and stand guard at the office in his place: at the first sign of trouble, Eddie was to send back the enclosed army ambulance that had probably carried Stanton home, to avoid having anyone see him outside his office.[48]

That first visit home coincided with Ben Butler's appearance at the department. Unable to find Stanton, Butler finally left a note explaining that he and George Boutwell, another of the impeachment managers, thought it would be helpful to publicize a list of all the federal officials Johnson would be able to remove if the tenure law were not sustained. He added that the salaries of those men would be good to have, as well, to illustrate how much patronage the president would gain and how much Republicans would lose as a result of acquittal. All of that would put a little more pressure on senators to support conviction, and Butler admitted that the only reason he and Boutwell did not do it themselves was because they lacked the "clerical force." Henry Stanbery dared not defend the president while collecting his government salary as attorney general, but Stanton had no qualms about diverting government resources to assure conviction, and War Department scriveners came up with that voluminous list three days later, after Butler sent another impatient note.[49]

Friends tried to lure Stanton away from his self-imposed imprisonment with offers of other, more pleasant appointments. In trying to solve the impeachment dilemma, lest it end in acquittal, some schemers thought that a cabinet shuffle might satisfy both the president and Congress, and one proposed slate of ministers included Frederick P. Stanton, an attorney who had practiced before the Supreme Court and had served in Congress and as governor of Kansas Territory. That man was only three days younger than the presumptive secretary of war, and the similarities in name may have ignited a confused tale that reached the War Department, suggesting that Stanton was to be moved to the Treasury Department. That post traditionally carried greater stature and would have kept Stanton in the cabinet while also preventing him from meddling in army affairs, but Stanton discouraged such a tactic himself. Again affecting fatigue with public service, he implied that he wished to retire from government as soon as an acceptable successor could be found. In the remaining twenty months of his life he did nothing to corroborate that claim, and much to discredit it: in all probability, he simply recognized that his greatest value to Radical Republicans still lay in acting as a burr under Johnson's saddle, and as a fulcrum for prying him out of the White House.[50]

Edwards Pierrepont broached the subject of a choice foreign mission with Ellen, suggesting that negotiations would soon be initiated between the United States and England, probably over claims for damages incurred by the British-built Confederate cruiser *Alabama*. That work would require a good lawyer, Pierrepont intimated, or perhaps even a minister, for Charles Francis Adams had finally given up the London portfolio. "Now I write to know whether *you* will take the place," Pierrepont asked Ellen, as though she were the one to make the decision. "I think you would like it, and the change of climate & all would put the secretary in good health. Now tell me what you think of it. I know it can be done."[51]

Stanton's old friend from Steubenville, John Oliver, tried to cheer him with a little flattery. Oliver would be a delegate to the Republican convention in Chicago, scheduled for the third week of May, and apparently he had planned to support his fellow Ohioan Ben Wade for vice president, but if impeachment made Wade president it seemed unlikely that he would accept a nomination as vice president. Oliver wanted to know if Stanton would allow his name to go forward for that office.[52]

Any reply to Oliver does not survive, but Stanton never relished elective office, and the powerless position of vice president might have appealed to him least of all. It was the relative certainty of appointment that he sought, especially while he enjoyed so friendly a Senate, and if Ben Wade became president Stanton could probably have any position he wanted. His professed disinclination for further service in the cabinet may have reflected a touch of sincerity, for merely transferring to another department within the Johnson administration would have only prolonged the uncertain personal prospects that so agitated Ellen. Johnson would leave office in less than a year in any case, and the fall elections might return a less Radical Congress if Stanton allowed the fury of the impeachment battle to subside by submitting to such a compromise. A blunder like that would also cost him friends among the dominant faction of the Republican Party, and that would have posed the ultimate disaster to Stanton, who had probably already begun to calculate his chances for a less ephemeral and more prestigious gift from an appreciative president and Senate. The death of James Wayne had left one vacancy on the Supreme Court that Congress had postponed filling by reducing the number of justices, but the seat would reopen with a timely reversal of that reduction, as soon as a sound Republican entered the White House. Stanton's well-cultivated friend, seventy-four-year-old associate justice Robert Grier, had suffered a stroke, and he may have confided his thoughts about retirement, while Justice Samuel Nelson was nearing the end of his eighth decade. As a lawyer whose courtroom reputation had not entirely faded from memory, with a significant claim to party gratitude, Stanton had good reason to anticipate a lifetime post at the pinnacle of his profession—if the Radical majority continued in power long enough, and if it remained convinced of his doctrinal purity.[53]

Eventually Stanton concluded that Johnson had no intention of wresting the office from him by force, and he started spending more evenings at home. Mrs. Hutchison returned to Pittsburgh, and Ellen even hosted a few parties. Precarious health sent her to bed now and then, but whenever she regained her strength she spent an occasional day at the Capitol, bathing in the society that had gravitated to the impeachment carnival. Even at the height of uncertainty, an element of routine returned to life on K Street.[54]

As though to calm fears that he might use an acquittal to wreak conservative vengeance on the Republican Party (as that list of vulnerable officeholders was meant to suggest), Johnson sent up a nomination for Major General John Schofield as secretary of war. Schofield seemed moderate enough to be acceptable to the Radicals. The gesture may have had an effect, and by the end of April no fewer than four Republican senators were expected to vote for the president's acquittal. All of them—Fessenden, Sherman, Lyman Trumbull of Illinois, and James Grimes of Iowa—were friends of Stanton's, and he flew into a rage at what he considered their defection. Through a Regular Army colonel with business at the War Department, the president learned that Stanton "cursed and swore terrifically" at the news. Stanton also took steps to make examples of the turncoats.[55]

Fessenden was the first to show his hand. The senator had smoothed Stanton's Senate confirmation in 1862, and had always cleared a path for department funding through the Senate Finance Committee. They had served in the cabinet together for the better part of a year, and Fessenden had recently defended Stanton, more than once, from accusations of misconduct and misfeasance. Stanton had addressed him as "My Dear Friend" in conveying his thanks and promising lifelong gratitude, but none of that mattered any longer. Stanton knew how traitors should be dealt with—which helped explain his dread of Democratic dominance in Congress. The editor of the *New York Tribune*, John Russell Young, was visiting Washington, and Stanton called him in to propose a fit punishment: pillory Fessenden in the press, and invite his constituents to express their contempt for him. The *Tribune* man obliged, laying into the senator with a vengeance. He thanked Stanton for suggesting the article and sent him a clipping of it, noting that it was "intended to prepare the minds of our party for the sentence we must pronounce upon any senator who proves recreant to his country in this hour of its agony." That diatribe falsely implied corruption, combining rumors of millions of dollars in bribe money with the insinuation that Fessenden was trying to sway fellow senators toward acquittal.[56]

The president relied on gossip from the War Department to gauge the morale and plans of his tormentors, while the impeachment managers benefited from White House documents filched by one of the sweepers. Johnson reveled in a report that Stanton had ordered his Steubenville home readied for occupancy within two weeks, and the impeachers read a letter from one of Johnson's lawyers who predicted that "defeat stares us in the face." Both sides lobbied ferociously, with promises of patronage and perhaps, as Ben Butler later insinuated, outright cash payment. The foregone conclusion of conviction evaporated, and those who expressed perfect confidence in it suddenly reversed themselves. Stanton himself saw "very little doubt" of anything but conviction in early April, and a week later Pierrepont assured him that everyone in New York still expected a guilty verdict, while acquittal would "astound all." At the beginning of May the situation began to change, and Pierrepont warned that one of the president's attorneys, William Evarts, had assured him that Johnson would be acquitted. Uncertainty heightened as the vote came closer. "The hour of judgment is nigh at hand," Stanton himself wrote on May 10, speculating that "the great criminal" would be convicted, but—just in case—he composed his formal surrender of the War Department the next day. "The Conviction of the President Considered Certain," read the main headline of the *New York Times* on May 14, but the following morning the same paper announced "The President's Acquittal Considered Certain."[57]

Ben Wade postponed the vote for several days when Radical Jacob Howard turned seriously ill. When Senator Grimes suffered a stroke Wade tried to persuade him to "pair" with him and Howard—that is, to agree not to vote, in return for the same consideration from a senator on the other side of the question. Grimes declined, and promised that he would be present when the time came, as did the others.[58]

Some wanted to postpone the vote longer still, because five of the Southern states had completed the requirements for congressional Reconstruction. With their new constituencies of black voters, those states had elected ten Radical senators who would all vote for conviction, thereby nullifying the seven Republicans who seemed prepared to buck party discipline. The House hurried through the five-states bill on May 15, probably hoping for the votes of what the *New York World* called the "Carpet Bagger" senators, but the Senate would have to approve the bill and send it to the president, who could hold it for ten more days, and so long a postponement of the vote would too obviously reveal the motivation. Even Thad Stevens doubted the new senators could be seated in time to affect the verdict.[59]

The showdown finally came at noon on Saturday, May 16. Grimes and Howard both showed up, feeble but firm in their opposing opinions. It seemed logical to some that they should begin with the last article—the omnibus article that offered the most promise of a conviction, rather than plod through the earlier articles and risk losing momentum with a series of decisions to acquit. There had been some changing of sides over the past few days, and no one seemed sure how the verdict would fall. Senator Sherman, so long thought sure to support the president, had lit upon a tortured technicality that allowed him to overlook his public criticism of the tenure law. That left the defense one man shy of the seven Republicans it needed. "It has been the work of the week to get the seventh man," observed the *New York Times*, but at last he was found. Edmund Ross, a new senator from Kansas, had consistently indicated he would vote for conviction, but when the roll call came to his name he responded with "not guilty." With the six others who were already known, that single vote revealed the outcome before the last senator was even called. Johnson survived by a vote of nineteen to acquit and thirty-five to convict: Ross had prevented a precise two-thirds majority. That amounted to "virtual acquittal" on all charges, crowed the *New York Herald*. Messengers flew from the chamber with the news.[60]

Stanton had already composed the letter to the president, informing him that he relinquished control of the War Department "and left all the books, archives, and papers in possession of General Townsend." He dated it, but did not send it yet. The other ten impeachment articles remained to be voted on, and the most optimistic Radicals hoped for a conviction on something, but the Senate had adjourned for ten days, to allow for the Republican convention in Chicago. As expected, the party nominated Grant for president. One of Grant's staff officers later alleged that Stanton himself brought word to Grant of the nomination, running across the street from the War Department and hurrying up the stairs, out of breath, "lest some one should precede him."[61]

The senators began drifting back into town over the next weekend, meeting again on May 26 to consider the rest of the charges, but after two more articles failed by the same count of 19-35 the managers gave up the fight. When Stanton heard of it that afternoon, he drew the letter to Johnson from his desk drawer and, in a final token of defiance, signed it as secretary of war. General Townsend later claimed that Stanton asked Eddie to take it to the White House, but Eddie came to him first, giving him the instructions to take charge of the department paperwork: Townsend said he was on the way to the White House and took the letter for him, saving Eddie the humiliation of delivering his own father's admission of defeat. It reached the president at 3:25 P.M.[62]

It was over. Stanton walked down a flight of stairs and through the front door to Seventeenth Street. There is no evidence that he ever entered the War Department again. Unless General Townsend exaggerated for dramatic effect, the building had not closed for business that day when the oblong, faded sign that had hung for so many years over Stanton's office door broke loose and fell flat on the floor, face down.[63]

19

THE STEALTHY APPLICANT

After professing such impatience to return to private practice, Stanton remained unusually idle the rest of that spring and summer. A childhood friend invited him to come stay in Nebraska for a season, but as much as Stanton thought it might help his lungs he held off answering, hoping to make a conspicuous contribution to Grant's election campaign. He must have spent part of the summer tutoring Eddie in the law, for his son had also left the War Department and by autumn had begun his own practice.[1]

Between January and May Stanton had earned another $3,000 in salary, but living expenses had consumed some of that, besides the debt that likely remained from his five-month suspension. Threats of legal judgments lingered, too, in the form of the outstanding litigation by Smithson and a new action filed just before he gave up the war office: two northern Virginia farmers, charging that Stanton had arbitrarily ordered an army officer to force them from their land a month after Lee's surrender, sought $50,000 as compensation for the crops and livestock the eviction had cost them. In anticipation of such claims, Stanton had taken steps to protect at least some of his assets, transferring them in trust to Ellen. The onetime bitter foe of the Farmers and Mechanics Bank now owned some valuable stock in the Mechanics National Bank, which he assigned to Ellen's brother to administer for her benefit.[2]

Three weeks after Stanton left the War Department, Senator Edwin Morgan asked him to come to New York and speak for Morgan's reelection. John Russell Young of the *Tribune* noticed Stanton's own name mentioned for the Senate seat of a Pennsylvania Democrat, and offered to help him win it if he was inclined, but elective office still held no charm for the former secretary. His friend Pierrepont expected no political activity until after the Democratic convention, which met in New York over the Fourth of July weekend. Stanton won dishonorable mention in a sideshow to that long, contentious gathering: Democratic veterans of the army and navy held a convention of their own while the party wrangled over nominees, with William B. Franklin presiding, and the many resolutions they passed included one thanking President Johnson for removing Stanton from office.

They charged that Stanton had "disgraced and dishonored" his position "by his many acts of cruelty (both to Union and Confederate soldiers) and by his official acts of tyranny." All soldiers, they suggested, should greet Stanton with "the same feelings of outraged dignity and patriotism that he was received with on that ever memorable occasion in the city of Washington from the great and gracious soldier, General W. T. Sherman."[3]

The soldiers' and sailors' convention in New York made no effort to hide its conservative flavor, preferring a soldier as the Democratic presidential candidate to compete with Grant and condemning "the appointment of negroes to govern white men." With terse sarcasm the veterans "thanked" the Radicals who constituted the majority of Congress for adding $33 a year to the pay of the common soldier, at the same time they increased their own salaries by $2,000 apiece, but the veterans' loudest tribute to class distinctions came in their support for the new proposal to pay off wartime government bonds with paper currency, rather than gold.[4]

The bond issue constituted an echo of the class struggle that had murmured through the war as an undercurrent to recruiting and the draft. When bankers hesitated to lend money to the government early in the conflict, Secretary Chase had resorted to the printing of paper money and a widespread offer of war bonds. The most common bonds were the "five-twenty" issue, carrying 6 percent interest and redeemable anywhere from five to twenty years after purchase. The earliest of them matured early in 1867, and by the terms of their original sale the interest was to be paid in gold coin, as an additional incentive; whether the principal was also to be paid in gold remained questionable, although those who had bought them insisted that the mature bond should be entirely redeemable in gold. The Legal Tender Act that had created those bonds also initiated the paper notes that indicated (in the green ink on the reverse that gave them the nickname "greenbacks") that those bills were legal tender for all debts. Based on that, populist Democrats maintained that the easily depreciated paper currency should be just as acceptable as the more valuable and stable gold in paying off the bond principle as well as the interest. Presidential contender George Pendleton supported the paper-money payments, but Republicans and well-heeled Democrats countered that the greenback claim of legal tender applied only to private debts. Those bills merely stood for "a promise to pay an actual dollar at a future day," wrote Mr. Raymond of the *New York Times*, while the bondholders had been promised the actual dollar.[5]

Few citizens of modest resources had bought any bonds, and they naturally favored greenback payments. So did the veterans at the soldiers' and sailors' convention, who declared that "if greenbacks were good enough to pay soldiers, merchants, mechanics, newsboys and bootblacks with, they are good enough for the pampered bondholder. . . ." Stanton, the hard-money advocate of the 1840s, had indeed seemed happy to compensate his soldiers in depreciated paper during the fighting, but he sided with the bankers and bondholders in this postwar dispute. Like many better-paid government officials, he evidently held some of those bonds himself, and they were just beginning to mature; some of them may have supported his family through the idle months of 1868. He scorned the reluctance to pay in gold as a stain on the national honor, exaggerating it as an outright repudiation of the public war debt.[6]

An Ohio delegation petitioned Stanton to "take the stump" for the Republican ticket, and in the waning weeks of the presidential campaign he did, playing the paper-money question for all it was worth. Robert Schenck, who had served during the war as a general and congressman, still held Clement Vallandigham's former seat in the House, and he asked Stanton to come speak for him. Stanton evidently kept the extent of his plans from Ellen, but he told Schenck he meant to take part in the campaign in Ohio, and late in September he headed west on the dual mission of supporting Republicans and visiting his family—but primarily to politic. The train trip aggravated his asthma, and with archaic superstition he blamed it on having crossed the mountains during the autumnal equinox, but prolonged exposure to the choking billows pouring out of the locomotive's smokestack probably explained that latest paroxysm.[7]

During his sojourn in his native town he stayed in his big house at Third and Logan. A visit to Union Cemetery may have filled him with melancholy, for some years later the cemetery superintendent recalled Stanton asking for the plat of his family's lot, on which he marked the spot beside Mary where he wished to be buried. The weather did nothing to improve his health or his lugubrious mood: a cold, dreary rain fell for days, continuing through Friday, September 25, when he was supposed to address his first outdoor crowd of the campaign. At the last minute the local Republican committee rented Kilgore Hall, on Market Street, accommodating a fair number of those who had wanted to catch a glimpse of Steubenville's notorious native son. The local photographer came by to ask him to stand for a portrait, and in the developed image he appeared to enjoy his usual health, his complaints to the contrary notwithstanding. Some of his old friends among the Democrats may have dropped in out of nostalgia, although they surely expected him to wave the bloody shirt, and he did not disappoint them."[8]

He took the stage at two o'clock that afternoon. "The graves of 300,000 patriot soldiers slain in battle by the Rebels are still green," he reminded his listeners early in his delivery. "The tears of widows, orphans, and bereaved parents still flow, and the maimed and wounded soldiers around us are living memorials of the cruelty of the Rebels in their war against the United

States Government." He blended the image of the Democratic Party with that of the Confederacy in gargantuan sentences of confusing complexity. He lavished praise on Grant, beginning with the West Point education that Stanton had so mistrusted in others: he explained Grant's resignation after the Mexican War by his aversion to being a "drone" in peacetime, thereby avoiding the issue of alcoholism, which had helped compel Grant's departure from the antebellum army. He detailed Grant's every victory during the war, and then asked, "what reason has any man to vote against Gen. Grant?"

Launching instinctively into the emotionally distracting ministerial singsong that had served him so well before juries, Stanton sought to drive a deep wedge between the nation's sections. "If any man among you would hide from the boy the musket and knapsack that his father carried at Donelson, at Vicksburg, upon Lookout Mountain, throughout the Wilderness before Richmond, at Five Forks, at Appomattox Court House, and shouldering proudly marched with 200,000 of his fellow-soldiers through the streets of Washington and around the Capitol and Executive Mansion that he defended with his life for years in the long march, the wearisome siege, and the storm of battle, let such [a] man vote against Grant. Is there any man among you that would compel the armies of the Potomac, of the James, of the Ohio, of the Cumberland, of the Tennessee and of the Gulf to be again gathered at the tap of the drum and surrendered as prisoners of war to Lee and Johnson [sic], Beauregard and Forrest, and Preston, let him vote against Gen. Grant."[9]

"But what," he then asked, lurching into the realm of finance, "is this public debt manifested by the bonds, and the notes of the United States, and about which the bowels of the financiers of the New-York convention are so severely moved?" With turbid logic he smeared the furor over bond payments as "a provisionary step to smooth the path of the restoration of the slaveholders." Ignoring the ambiguity of the statute on the payment of bond principal, he clung to the specification that the interest should be paid in gold, characterizing anything less as repudiation. On uttering that word he thought to remind his audience that Jefferson Davis had supported repudiation of Mississippi debts thirty years before—and by that double leap of logic he linked the Democrats who favored greenback payments to the nation's arch-traitor. They wished to destroy the national credit, he shouted, for the bond debt represented "a thousand brilliant achievements on land and sea that would render illustrious any nation upon earth, and that will be renowned upon the pages of history to the end of all time." After an hour or more, stopping frequently enough to cough that one newspaperman supposed he had a bad cold, Stanton concluded that the election of Grant and a Republican Congress would be "a crowning blessing on you and your posterity forever."[10]

The Steubenville daily filled half a page with his speech in dense type, leaving no room for the local speaker who followed him. The next day Stanton wrote to Ellen, telling her the event was well received and assuring her that he would give no more speeches even though he was receiving "scores" of urgent requests to speak every day. "My political labors are over," he promised, but that was not the case and he knew it: he had arranged a skeleton speaking tour over a week before, and had added to it since. He had promised to appear in John Bingham's district in Harrison County on October 2, and he had long since told Schenck he would come help him around Dayton, including a speech for an ambitious rally at Carlisle Station of October 3, which was already advertised before he made his promise to Ellen. From there he would go to Mount Vernon, stopping afterward in Gambier for a day to see his mother and Pamphila before doubling back to Cambridge and continuing on to Cleveland for a massive Republican gathering on October 8. The crowd at Cleveland reportedly exceeded that city's population, and Stanton spoke alongside Governor Rutherford B. Hayes after watching a torchlight procession two miles long. Stanton had begun tiring out by then, but the chances for Grant seemed good, and that encouraged him to further effort. The Democratic Party had embraced Horatio Seymour as its candidate, and Seymour had chosen Frank Blair as his running mate: their victory would quash any hope Stanton cherished for a satisfactory appointment, and the battle he waged might decide his own future.[11]

He returned to the hustings two weeks later, at Pittsburgh, and on the way back to Washington he stopped at Philadelphia for the grand finale of the campaign. The Union League of Philadelphia had asked him to speak for Grant at the Academy of Music, and he arrived on the last day of October, three days before the election. The doors opened at six o'clock, and from that moment the crowd effectively blocked the street outside. Reporters described the hall "packed from pit to dome," but, for all the enthusiastic coverage by politically sympathetic newspapers, his delivery fell short of expectations. His lungs suffered from five weeks of near-constant travel on dusty, smoky railroads, with long discourses in a projected voice and the inevitable succession of smoke-filled rooms—his own ubiquitous cigar contributing to the choking haze. Two decades later a Pennsylvania party leader recalled that Stanton had grown feeble by the time he reached his room at the Continental Hotel that morning, and the increasingly difficult struggle for breath appeared to have dulled his focus: names and events escaped his memory as he addressed the audience, and other speakers behind him on the stage had to prompt him when he groped for words. Afterward the Union League swept him away for a reception on the front steps of its headquarters house on Broad Street, where he could nurse the embarrassment of his disappointing performance under a spectacular display of fireworks.[12]

He reached home on Monday, November 2, in what he called "great exhaustion," and found Ellen in the same precarious health of recent years. The next day Seymour polled nearly half a million votes more than Lincoln had won four years before, but the expansion of Republican votes in seven Southern states—and the restriction of Democratic votes—gave Grant the victory, albeit at barely half the margin of the Republican triumph in 1864. The election did not end the campaigning. New state legislatures would choose about two dozen new senators over the next few months, and the Southern states could be relied on to supply Radicals for that institution, but the unrestricted Northern electorate could not. Interested parties carried on senatorial-level campaigning by private letter, and Stanton contributed his share. His old friend Ben Wade lost to a Democratic challenger in Ohio, but Zachariah Chandler survived a similar attempt in Michigan.[13]

Four months would pass before Grant could begin dispensing patronage. Stanton again found himself in enough need of money that he picked up some legal work, perhaps partly to offer some practice for Eddie, who was taking clients as a government claims agent. *Thompson, et al v. Edwards, et al*, a suit for the ownership of vast, mineral-rich tracts in the Kanawha Valley of West Virginia, may have come Stanton's way because of his lingering reputation in the Wheeling bridge case, for the dispute was waged in the federal appeals court in Wheeling. Stanton evidently accepted a retainer on the case in late November or early December of 1868, but he had spent it by the first of the year, when he admitted to Peter Watson that he was "straitened for money" and asked if Watson could lend him any. Watson himself could not, but he mentioned Stanton's plight to a wealthy associate, who immediately sent Stanton a draft for $5,000 without asking for security. Stanton gratefully replied with a promissory note on a one-year term, although he must have wondered then how he would repay it in time.[14]

The West Virginia case took both the father and son to Wheeling in mid-January. Stanton felt reasonably hale when they departed, but again the trip over the mountains left him wheezing and weak, and again he blamed it on the atmosphere or altitude of the trip, rather than on creeping over mountain passes in a plume of engine smoke. By the time they reached Wheeling on January 15 the prolonged fits of coughing had resumed. Four days later he made an argument against a motion by the plaintiffs, following a local attorney his clients had hired for hometown advantage, and in his usual exaggerated literary style he judged that this courtroom performance had exceeded anything in his former career. "I never made an argument with more ease and effect and success," he assured Watson, and ultimately his clients did prevail, at least on the motion he argued.[15]

In the early discussion of Grant's cabinet, Stanton was reportedly "the most prominently suggested." By the end of January, Stanton knew that

Grant had chosen all his ministers, but if he did not know their names he did know that his own was not among them. As though to refute suspicions of disappointment that he had not been asked to serve in the administration of a fourth consecutive president, he discounted a purported scheme to include him in Grant's cabinet with the assertion that he would rather burn his arm off at the socket than accept another such position. He averred that "no earthly influence" could induce him to accept any government post "at home or abroad."[16]

In fact, he betrayed singular disappointment. He had probably referred to himself when he said he expected Grant to be "considerate" in forming his cabinet, but the only morsel the new president offered him came in the form of an appointment as ambassador to Mexico, and in the hierarchy of governmental aristocracy that fell far below even the attorney generalship he had held at the beginning of the decade. Had he really not wanted a federal post he might have replied that his commitments prevented him from accepting the position, which would have implied that he was unavailable for public service, at least at that particular time. He could also have declined on the excuse of health, which would have been credible enough, especially if the duty required him to endure the oxygen-thin air of lofty Mexico City, but that, too, might have discouraged further offers. Instead, he showed outright petulance, hinting broadly to Grant's new secretary of state that the Mexican mission "would not be agreeable to me." No other offers came, and while he continued to protest that he wanted no government office he grumbled so persistently about Grant ignoring him that his friends understood otherwise.[17]

In the spring and early summer of 1869 Stanton's asthma had begun to worsen enough to alarm him. By July his extremities were swelling, sometimes to the point that he found it difficult to write, which hinted that the laboring of his lungs had started straining his heart. Perhaps in desperation, he began corresponding with a doctor of dubious pedigree by the name of John Bayne. Surgeon General Barnes, who still acted as Stanton's personal physician, apparently mistrusted this practitioner, and when Bayne stopped by Stanton kept it from the surgeon, although he eventually persuaded Barnes to let the new man examine him. Bayne's treatment leaned toward increasing his patient's intake of fruits and vegetables, and that prescription may have accounted for the sudden urgency to buy a stockpile of berries in the week after one of his visits. Ellen must not have been well herself, for even in her husband's questionable condition she left him in broiling Washington, caring for the children, while she visited with her mother.[18]

In addition to his physical decline, Stanton sank into prolonged dejection after Grant's snub, and the interminable prosecution of his onetime prisoner William Smithson could only have deepened that gloom. Stanton's friends on the bench at the District of Columbia Supreme Court seemed to be dragging the case out for his benefit, and one motion that Smithson had filed over a year previously only came to the docket at the end of June, demanding that Stanton turn over books and documents pertinent to the case that had been in his possession as secretary of war. The obliging judge denied the motion on two conflicting grounds: first, that it was premature, because the case had not come to trial, and then that it was too late, because Stanton was no longer secretary of war. This accommodating decision notwithstanding, the case continued on the docket, posing a perpetual liability.[19]

Samuel Hooper recognized Stanton's persistent brooding weeks later, confiding to Senator Sumner his regret that Stanton "takes things so much at heart," but he conceded that there was reason enough for it. Stanton's friend Pierrepont kept in close touch with the administration, to the point of socializing with the Grants, and late in June he tried to encourage Stanton by recounting a recent conversation with the president and Mrs. Grant. In a long chat, Grant had spoken of Stanton with special regard, and Mrs. Grant had chastised her husband for failing to appoint the former secretary to a position of the "highest honor." It was an "emphatic" discussion, Pierrepont assured him, "and has some specific meaning." The letter may have initiated a burst of confidence, judging by Stanton's response to a prospective client a few days later. This man had sought his services to pursue claims against the French government, and Stanton had delayed responding for six weeks, ostensibly hoping his health would improve enough to take the case, but he failed to respond even after he recovered. When the man inquired again, early in July, Stanton admitted that he felt better, but he turned the case down anyway, as though he had better prospects.[20]

The "specific meaning" of Pierrepont's talk with the Grants did not become apparent that summer, however, and the disintegration of that hope coincided with a respiratory relapse that plunged Stanton into a depression from which he never really recovered. A generous and forgiving William Sherman heard about his weakened state and invited him to come out to the Rocky Mountains by train, coach, and army wagon, with an escort and comfortable quarters all along the way. Stanton admitted that he had always wanted to see those mountains, but he lacked the money for so long a journey. Instead, he and Ellen decided to pass the worst of the summer heat in New England, but before leaving home Stanton took the precaution of drawing up a will. He asked Adjutant General Edward Townsend to serve as an executor—and, as Townsend recalled later, Stanton mentioned again that he wished to be buried in Steubenville, where his father, brother, and first wife already lay.[21]

On August 4 Stanton, Ellen, and the younger children started north. Eddie remained behind in Washington, working, and they stopped in

Baltimore to board the girls for the rest of the summer. After a few days in Philadelphia they made their way to New Hampshire, where newspaper gossip predicted they would gravitate to Conway: tourism there was picking up steam, with two stagecoaches a day spinning into the White Mountains from the seacoast, but the isolation there made it expensive. "The most economical tourist should carry ten dollars in his pocket for every day he intends to stay," warned a Concord weekly, so Stanton took Ellen and Lewis to Wolfeboro, on Lake Winnipesaukee. The president made a trip through the middle of the Granite State a few days later, but he seemed not to know that Stanton was close by.[22]

After leaving New Hampshire, Grant went to Utica, New York, on a long-promised visit to Senator Roscoe Conkling, and while there he asked Conkling if he knew where Stanton was. Conkling dispatched a flurry of telegrams over the course of two days, asking everyone he could think of, and finally someone misinformed him that the old war minister was summering at the Wachusett House in Princeton, Massachusetts. Conkling addressed a note to him there, asking him to bring Ellen to Utica and telling him, as Pierrepont had, that the president had expressed strong friendship for him, and wished to write to him. Conkling's letter spent many weeks in search of its peripatetic addressee, beginning with the Wachusett House, where the manager certainly recognized the name and probably forwarded it to Washington. By the time the postmaster there sent it along to New Hampshire the vagabond family had departed for Cape Cod, for another long stay with Hooper at his Cotuit cottage. The hotelkeeper in Wolfeboro returned it to the home address Stanton had entered in the ledger.[23]

Conkling and Pierrepont must have exaggerated how friendly Grant felt toward Stanton: he probably valued him as an icon of the Radical wing, which Grant sought to appease without bending too far in that direction himself. John Russell Young, the *Tribune* editor, recorded Grant claiming a decade later that he and the war secretary had become increasingly friendly the more they worked together, but that conflicts with Grant's own description of their relations and with those of the president's more intimate acquaintances, who believed his regard for Stanton to be waning.[24]

When Stanton reached Cotuit, Hooper found him in sorry shape. He remained feeble until the last few days of his vacation there, when the sea air finally revived him a little, but he and Ellen left the cape on September 28, returning home directly. The letter from Conkling was waiting at 320 K Street when they arrived, and it must have ignited particular excitement. With Grant coming into office, Congress had reauthorized a ninth Supreme Court justice, and that had created an immediate vacancy, but for all the suggestive talk of presidential esteem Stanton heard nothing from the White House. Eagerness might be unseemly in a candidate for so exalted a post, not to mention inconsistent with Stanton's oft-repeated disdain for public office, but with no official connection to the president he could not allude to the subject incidentally, in casual conversation. In his hunger for the position he resorted to the clumsy approach of an unannounced social call, driving over to the White House in the carriage with Ellen. They sent their cards in for Mrs. Grant, but she was not at home, and they drove away without descending from the carriage.[25]

The Grants must have learned of the aborted call, but it elicited no message of regret or invitation. Stanton's only hope lay in some lobbying from a seemingly disinterested proxy of sufficient influence, and Stanton put his faith in Methodist Episcopal bishop Matthew Simpson of Philadelphia. In a confidential letter asking Simpson to see the president for him, he carefully tread a fine line between desperate need and adequate capacity, contending that his health was too fragile for the rigors of the bar, but perfectly suitable for the demands of the bench. The country owed him the appointment, he implied, grandiosely asserting that he had left "the best professional practice in the United States" to serve his country, for a salary so small that he had exhausted his personal fortune. The president also owed him the place, he argued, because no one had supported Grant during the war as much as Edwin Stanton. "His name & fortune he owed at a critical moment to me," he added, perhaps implying (as he had to McClellan) that he had interceded with Lincoln on Grant's behalf. As one last inducement for his appointment, Stanton told the bishop that the president could depend on no one else to support his administration more loyally from the high court, as though offering favorable opinions in return for life tenure. In conclusion, Stanton jeopardized his claim of sufficiently sound health by admitting that the appointment might make the difference for him between life and death.[26]

Simpson did as requested, but the president—however friendly he may have professed to be toward Stanton—did not intend to appoint him. Instead he settled on his own attorney general, Ebenezer Rockwood Hoar, partly to relieve himself of the political faux pas of having chosen too many cabinet members from Massachusetts. He also appears to have decided against Stanton because of his poor health, as described by an informant within the administration whom Stanton characterized as a grafter and a personal enemy. Stanton thanked the bishop and begged him not to reveal the attempt to anyone. As for Grant, Stanton bitterly remarked that he would "be influenced by his judgment as to his own interest."[27]

Pierrepont thought his own name might be entertained as a replacement for Hoar as attorney general, and Grant gave him serious consideration. Pierrepont consoled Stanton with an offer to take Eddie in as an assistant attorney general, or permanent special prosecutor, but it never came to pass. The Senate remained too Radical, while Hoar had grown too moderate, and eventually he failed of confirmation.[28]

Even as he assured Bishop Simpson that his health had stabilized, Stanton cast about for another doctor who might reverse the course of his decline. He wrote to a recovered asthmatic on the staff of the *New York Times* who recommended a specialist in chronic diseases, but with limited resources Stanton stuck with his fruit-and-vegetable therapist and Dr. Barnes, who still apparently treated him without charge. Since September, at least, Stanton had remained healthy during the daytime: the coughing spasms began with darkness (and perhaps with the need to light the furnace), keeping him from sleep until well after midnight. Even with that torment, he considered his health "very much improved" after Dr. Bayne had seen him again, although he had begun inhaling pure oxygen to counteract the asphyxiating effects of his asthma.[29]

By Thanksgiving he confessed to Watson that he was "entirely out of money," asking him to help sell off his undeveloped lands along the Monongahela River and in eastern Ohio. He evidently did not expect to pay off his imminent note to Watson's partner, hoping only to provide himself with $5,000 more for another year's living expenses. Had he but lived as frugally through the war as he had in 1869, his savings and his salary would still have left him comfortable.[30]

Driven by the wolf at the door, Stanton gathered his last reserves of strength and prepared a long argument in the patent case of *Whitney v. Mowry*. In mid-December Justice Noah Swayne, whose son had benefited more than once from Stanton's favoritism, reputedly allowed the weakened former secretary to present his argument "in chambers," and on the fourth day those chambers consisted of Stanton's library, in his own home, because he was too ill to leave the house. After that, he returned to his bed in the front room on the second floor and never ventured outdoors again.[31]

The Senate had not yet tabled Grant's appointment of Rockwell Hoar when Justice Grier, Stanton's longtime friend, decided to take advantage of a new law allowing retirement pay for aging members of the Supreme Court. In the early part of December Grier notified President Grant that he wished to retire as of February 1, and he probably alerted Stanton, whom he had thought worthy to be chief justice. Stanton in turn appears to have notified Matthew Carpenter, the junior senator from Wisconsin. Carpenter remained grateful to Stanton for employing him as a special counsel in several Reconstruction cases, in addition to recommending him to Ben Wade for further employment, and the young senator undertook to aid his former benefactor. Two days before Grier formally announced his retirement, Carpenter entered a bill to raise the pay of associate justices from $6,000 to $8,000 a year; then, as soon as the president officially responded to Grier,

Carpenter circulated a petition in the upper chamber asking Grant to appoint Stanton to the vacancy. Within twenty minutes he had collected 38 signatures; John Bingham did the same in the House, and in short order he had 118 names. On Saturday morning Carpenter and Zachariah Chandler took the Senate petition to the president, and on the way Carpenter stopped by Stanton's home to show it to him. That unusual display of Republican solidarity overcame every objection Grant had entertained, which seemed to demonstrate that he was guided by political prudence rather than personal admiration. The next day—Sunday, December 19, which was Stanton's fifty-fifth birthday—Grant and Vice President Colfax appeared at 320 K Street to apprise the former war secretary personally that he would take Grier's place. "So far as Mr. Stanton is concerned," the *New York Times* correspondent naively reported, "the tender was unsolicited, as I believe he had not permitted any one to understand that he was a candidate for the position."[32]

On December 21, Stanton scrawled his acceptance from his sickbed, alluding to an intimate relationship he claimed to share with Grant, and pledging to serve with "diligence, impartiality, and integrity"—notwithstanding his earlier intimation of favorable court judgments. The appointment specified an effective date of February 1, at which time Grier was to leave, but the Senate confirmed the nomination immediately.[33]

Two nights later, as Washington lay blanketed in fresh snow, Stanton felt so weak that Ellen sent for the surgeon general. Her husband complained of pain in the back of his head, neck, and upper spine, as though from meningitis, but once the sun set he began his nightly struggle for breath. Barnes found his pulse sluggish, and later in the evening the constriction of his lungs gravitated to the heart, finally bringing such crushing pressure that Stanton and Barnes both grew anxious. Toward midnight the pressure on his chest subsided enough that Barnes prepared to leave, while Ellen and the children started for bed. Before the doctor left the house the pain grew worse and Stanton gasped so strenuously for air that someone ran for the pastor of the Church of the Epiphany, and soon after he arrived Stanton lost consciousness. Ellen and the children returned to the bedside and they, Barnes, the minister, and the governess remained there until sometime between three and four o'clock in the morning on Christmas Eve, when Barnes checked for a pulse, found none, and put a hand on Stanton's chest. He felt nothing, and pronounced his most famous patient dead.[34]

Obituaries appeared as early as that same evening. Nearly every newspaper, including the *Steubenville Daily Herald*, misdated his birth in 1815. The president ordered the White House and government buildings adorned with crepe, but Ellen resisted suggestions of a state funeral. Dressed in broadcloth and tucked into a black coffin lined with white satin, the body lay in the second-floor bedroom until late on Monday morning, December 27, when ten soldiers from the 5th U.S. Artillery carried it down to the parlor. Grant, Colfax, the cabinet, senators, army officers galore, and a host of other dignitaries poured into the house while a cold rain set the atmosphere. Inside, Charles Sumner towered over everyone. Stanton's mother sat there, with Pamphila and Nancy, all of them having spent Christmas Day riding from Gambier and Steubenville in a special railroad car. The Supreme Court attended in a body, including Robert Grier, whom Stanton was intended to succeed. Also present was Hiram Revels, a black man waiting to take his seat as a senator from Mississippi, along with two black army doctors—perhaps the first of their color to enter the Stanton home as anything but servants. Three ministers spoke, including one of Stanton's Kenyon professors. After the eulogy the artillerymen lifted the coffin into a hearse drawn by four grey horses, and that somber vehicle led a mile-long procession of hacks and carriages to Oak Hill Cemetery, through streets cleared by police and lined with the umbrellas of spectators. The family crowded around the open grave while the president and the rest stood ten yards away, hatless, as the drizzle intensified to a heavy shower. Against the wish that Stanton had repeatedly expressed to spend eternity beside Mary, three hundred miles away, the soldiers lowered his casket into the earth by the infant James. Twenty minutes later only the sexton remained, shoveling mud into the grave.[35]

That evening Congressman Hooper called the mourners to his lodging to start a fund for the family, for Stanton had made his poverty well-known among his more powerful acquaintances. Horrified at the prospect of publicly accepting charity, a few weeks before his death he had declined a Pittsburgh friend's offer to raise a subscription for him: when the Pittsburgh Union League met to honor Stanton on the day of his funeral, former congressman James K. Moorhead read Stanton's letter refusing such ostentatious alms. Emphasizing his sacrifice of a prosperous practice and bodily vigor for an arduous public duty he had not sought, Stanton—who was then eagerly borrowing money he knew he could not repay, and resenting the president who denied him adequate reward—pretended he was satisfied to have exhausted his wealth and health in patriotic service. "In all the dark years of discouragement, disaster, persecution and calumny," he had written, "my heart was strengthened and my courage upheld by the reflection that such troubles could only be for a brief period compared with the great hereafter. I am, therefore, cheerfully resigned to my own lot for the short term of service that remains, not envying the apparent prosperity of those who have prospered by the fortunes of war, and I trust that strength will be given for my 'soul to march on,' however rugged and weary the march."[36]

The self-pitying tone of that letter leaves the distinct impression that he hoped it would persuade his would-be benefactors to raise the money anyway, and the circulation of his refusal among potential donors certainly helped to inspire the generosity Samuel Hooper sought. Grant offered the first thousand dollars, followed by some of his cabinet officers and senators, and some contributed much more. Stanton's will specified that Ellen should receive two-thirds of his estate and his mother one-third, but each was to shoulder a commensurate share of his debts, and by then they had sold off nearly everything but the two houses and their personal effects. The sale of the Steubenville house and his law library might have covered the debts, leaving only the proceeds of the house on K Street, and the fund proved essential. Eddie received nothing—not even the library—and he, too, had already borrowed money that he could not now repay.[37]

Three weeks after Stanton's funeral, John Bingham introduced a bill in the House of Representatives proposing to give Stanton's family one year's salary of an associate justice of the Supreme Court. After it went through the Committee on Appropriations the language was amended to pay the money to Ellen specifically, to use for herself and her children, as though to exclude Eddie and the Ohio relatives. At the Ides of March the Republican majority in the Senate passed the bill in haste at the request of Henry Wilson. By then the gesture might have seemed superfluous, as Hooper's private subscription fund had already exceeded $100,000. That covered the debts Stanton had incurred and provided enough to educate Ellie, Lewis, and Bessie, with plenty left over to sustain the family comfortably for years.[38]

Such extensive support proved unnecessary. Ellen endured another cold all through the rest of the winter, keeping to the house through at least January. After the house was sold she moved to Philadelphia, but less than four years after Stanton died she followed him to the lot at Oak Hill, probably succumbing to the consumption her husband had so long feared; she had just turned forty-three.[39] Stanton's mother had died less than two weeks before.[40] His son by Mary Lamson, Eddie, perished a few days past his thirty-fifth birthday, in 1877, and likely from tuberculosis as well; Ohio relatives brought Eddie's body back to Steubenville, and buried it in the spot beside his mother where his father had hoped to lie.[41] The "darling" Bessie, as Stanton called her, evidently died within a decade of her father. Eleanor and Lewis lived to adulthood, but only Lewis survived to old age, and his father's name is perpetuated through him.[42]

Stanton's eulogists inadvertently emphasized his least admirable traits in the course of their adulation. Widespread references to "the organizer of victory" would have amused those who had witnessed Stanton's panic at any threat to Washington, as well as those who remembered his disastrous closing of the recruiting stations or his divisive vendettas. Most seemed to accept the assertion that Stanton had worked himself to death, but few who ever knew his alternately obsequious and bullying nature could have swallowed the gratuitous accolade of one obituary that painted Stanton as the champion of the downtrodden. "The highest in rank generally received the least consideration," claimed that panegyric, "but to the weak and defenseless he was as gentle as a woman."[43]

Senator Wilson sought to pay another tribute to Lincoln's secretary of war with an article in the February issue of the *Atlantic Monthly*, describing him as no less a martyr to the Union than "Sedgwick, Wadsworth, and Lincoln." Stanton had saved the nation from the pusillanimous Buchanan administration, Wilson claimed, repeating the heroic story Stanton so often told of himself in private. That version necessarily portrayed Buchanan and Jeremiah Black as weak-kneed dupes of the slave power, and Isaac Toucey as a traitor to the Navy Department he administered; for the first time, Wilson revealed that Stanton's malicious whispering had inspired a hostile House resolution against Toucey. Borrowing from the self-made Stanton myth, Wilson sketched an ardent patriot of determined unionism and devoted antislavery sentiments who supplied backbone for President Lincoln. Like similar tales that emerged from the more laudatory obituaries, Wilson's article produced amused disgust among those who had known Stanton better—men who had long suspected him of duplicity but who only began then to understand how deeply that trait penetrated his character. Jeremiah Black responded to Wilson in *The Galaxy*, treating the senator's revelations with exquisitely subtle sarcasm as he accused the would-be eulogist of having slandered the deceased hero as a two-faced hypocrite. For years afterward Black, Gideon Welles, Jacob Thompson, and the viciously antagonistic Montgomery Blair compared the Wilson legend with the Stanton they had known, seasoning the inescapably unflattering results of those conflicting images with the flavor of their pity, contempt, and downright hatred.[44]

In the end, one of Stanton's own friends may have pronounced the final judgment on the worst aspect of his character, coming closer to the mark than he realized. It happened late in the spring of 1872, after the disintegrating Radical faction had begun to bare its teeth to Grant. Matthew Carpenter was sitting in the Senate when Charles Sumner rose, pompous as ever, to deal Grant a vicarious blow from Stanton's own lips. Sumner said he had just returned for the first session of the Forty-first Congress in December of 1869 when he made his last visit to the ailing ex-secretary, whom he found reclining on a divan at 320 K Street and waiting for his final "furlough." Stanton abruptly told him he had something to say, and Sumner sat down to hear it.

"I know General Grant better than any other person in the country can know him," Sumner remembered Stanton saying. "It was my duty to study him, and I did so day and night, when I saw him and when I did not see him, and now I tell you what I know, *he cannot govern this country.*" Sumner said he remonstrated with Stanton, reminding him that the criticism came too late, and that he should have voiced his apprehension before the nomination, rather than campaigning so diligently for Grant. According to Sumner, Stanton replied that he was not consulted about the nomination, and that he was too concerned with his official duties and his fight with Johnson. Sumner also claimed that Stanton said he never mentioned Grant's name on the campaign trail, instead speaking for the success of the Republican Party and Republican candidates.[45]

A few days later Senator Zachariah Chandler recalled a different Stanton, telling his colleagues that he and Ben Wade knew the old war secretary well, and always believed that he considered Grant highly capable. He said he made a visit to the Stanton home one week before black crepe decorated the windows, and Stanton praised Grant both as a soldier and as an administrator. Chandler added that Stanton had told Wade, in front of witnesses, that Grant had shown himself a great warrior and was also certain to prove himself "a great civilian."[46]

As Chandler demonstrated by reading from Stanton's published speeches during the 1868 campaign, Stanton had often endorsed Grant by name. That all seemed to discredit Sumner, who had earned a reputation for strident opinions and a willingness to support them with any unfounded rumor, but he was not known for overt prevarication. Senator Carpenter corroborated Chandler's memory of Stanton's views, and by implication assailed Sumner's, by offering his own recollections of the war minister. Stanton had used his association with Senator Wade to have Carpenter assigned as a special counsel in a Supreme Court challenge to the Reconstruction laws, and while Stanton was "imprisoned" in the War Department Carpenter had occupied a room there, where Stanton frequently came to smoke. In the scores of times Grant's name came up, Carpenter said he remembered none in which Stanton did not speak of the general in anything but terms of great respect and confidence. Carpenter described bringing Stanton the news that Grant had appointed him to the Supreme Court, at which the dying man expressed abundant regard for Grant and appreciation for his "characteristic" kindness.

Then Carpenter addressed the anecdote Sumner had told on May 31. "If Mr. Stanton made that declaration to the Senator from Massachusetts under the circumstances detailed by him," he said, "if there is a word of substantial truth in that whole paragraph, if it is not an infamous fabrication from first to last, then Mr. Stanton was the most double-faced and dishonest man that ever lived."[47] Both Sumner and Carpenter may have been telling the truth, and in their quest to claim Edwin Stanton's posthumous imprimatur they illustrated the character flaw that had ultimately consumed him.

APPENDIX : THE CINCINNATI SNUB

The image of Edwin Stanton snubbing Abraham Lincoln on the steps of the Burnet House in September of 1855 has long served as the foremost example of Stanton's surly, condescending manner, and Lincoln's forgiveness for that slight is often cited as evidence of his generous nature. However accurate those respective characterizations may be, the story itself probably originated in the imagination of George Harding. There may have been an uncomfortable encounter at the hotel, but if so it was not at Stanton's instigation: Peter Watson and perhaps Harding, the senior members of John H. Manny's legal team, had decided to drop Lincoln from the reaper case long before, as was illustrated by their failure to send him any of the promised documentation, or to answer any of his communications.

The tale has also been widely embellished by others. According to Charles Benjamin, a War Department clerk under Stanton, Harding added an incompatible epilogue to the story. In Benjamin's account, Harding characterized himself as a peacemaker between Stanton and Lincoln, both in Cincinnati and in Washington, more than six years later. In Benjamin's version, Harding said he remained friendly with Lincoln after the trial, and that he even suggested or recommended Stanton for the War Office, but that also seems unlikely. The antebellum disdain for Lincoln that Harding described to his novice associate in 1876 would preclude sufficient intimacy for him to offer advice on prospective cabinet officers, and Lincoln's correspondence does not sustain the cordiality that Harding alleged. Their putative friendship seemed necessary if Harding was to plausibly assert that when Stanton first visited Lincoln at the White House, he came along to reintroduce them and help them smooth over any hard feelings. This smacks of still more invention (by Harding or Benjamin), because Lincoln would already have encountered Stanton a few days before his inauguration as president, when President Buchanan introduced him to the members of a cabinet that included then-Attorney General Edwin Stanton. Furthermore, a couple of weeks after Stanton's appointment as secretary of war, Harding lamented to a colleague that he had not associated with Stanton for some time, which reduced any potential for influence. If any more evidence were needed to discredit this mythical addendum, Stanton himself mentioned in an 1862 letter that Lincoln already knew him personally when he appointed him secretary of war, although Stanton had not spoken a word to him between March 4, 1861, and the day Lincoln handed him his commission.[1]

Harding's apparent attempt to inflate his association with Lincoln casts a shadow over his entire story. The same is true of a little memoir by Ralph Emerson, whose father-in-law, Wait Talcott, was involved on Manny's side of the McCormick suit. In a heavily padded presentation booklet published on the centennial of Lincoln's birth, Emerson asserted that he was, "for a time, intimate with Abraham Lincoln," and that on a private stroll with him Lincoln offered the advice that led Emerson to choose his life's course. Emerson also claimed that he suggested hiring Lincoln in the first place, but that is not true: it was Congressman Elihu B. Washburne who proposed Lincoln's services to Watson, in Washington. Emerson described a rapt Lincoln hanging on every word of Stanton's argument at the Cincinnati trial, and then confiding to Emerson his humble admiration for such persuasive eloquence and legal brilliance. He added a scene of Stanton exploding in fury at the mere suggestion of compromise in what would have been a private conference of Manny's legal team, proclaiming that he knew "but one way to compromise with an enemy, and that is with a sword in your hand, and to smite, and keep smiting!" Emerson suggested that this bellicose display must have impressed Lincoln with Stanton's qualifications for managing the War Department, but the unmistakable rebuff Lincoln had received from the legal team leaves little room to suppose that he would have been invited to such a session. Although Emerson had been retailing his familiarity with Lincoln for years, most of his booklet can probably be discounted as imaginary.[2]

Long afterward, a Cincinnati lawyer named William Dickson claimed that Lincoln lodged at his home during the reaper trial. According to Dickson, Lincoln said Stanton had volunteered to give way to him in the courtroom, and Lincoln insisted that Stanton argue the case because McLean was unfriendly to him, but Lincoln could not have known McLean at all. Furthermore, Dickson appears not to have ever met Lincoln until 1859, which fatally undermines his credibility. Joseph Gillespie's 1866 recollection, if true, may reflect Lincoln's generous memory of the episode. An old acquaintance of Lincoln's, Gillespie wrote that Lincoln told him his "young associate" in the case showed so much more familiarity with the mechanical details of the reapers that Lincoln stood aside for him—but Harding, rather than Stanton, would have been the "young associate."[3]

Donn Piatt, an Ohio attorney and Washington newspaper editor, published a dubious anthology of elaborate tales about the close personal relationships he claimed to enjoy with five legendary figures, including Lincoln and Stanton. Piatt's portrait of Stanton entailed a particularly unconvincing glimpse of Stanton's stern public visage melting into tears when he thought he was alone, and includes what was purportedly Stanton's own narration of his Cincinnati encounter with Lincoln, punctuated with indignation. After describing Lincoln's stained provincial attire, Stanton supposedly boasted that he threatened to withdraw from the case if "that giraffe" were allowed to participate. Like Harding, Piatt used Lincoln's later appointment of Stanton to illustrate the selflessness and magnanimity of the Great Emancipator, whom he described as having overheard the insult.[4]

Certainly the legend of Lincoln's rude treatment at the hands of Manny's lawyers made the rounds, at least after Lincoln and Stanton were dead. Piatt could have learned of the incident from Charles Benjamin, the War Department clerk, or from someone else Harding had regaled with the story. He may also have taken it from Lincoln's law partner, William H. Herndon, who wrote a similar account of the Cincinnati snub. In Herndon's story, Stanton and Manny stood on one side of a closed door, and the shabbily dressed Lincoln on the other side, while Stanton ranted audibly at his client for bringing along "that damned long-armed ape." Herndon had Gillespie's letter about Lincoln's comment in January of 1866, but he implied that he had heard numerous contradictory versions of the episode, some of which brought an indignant Lincoln storming home immediately, while others had him sitting out the trial. Herndon insisted that he never asked Lincoln what had happened, so he could testify to nothing of his own knowledge, except that Lincoln came back to Springfield "sad and sour and gloomy."[5] In all probability, that was not the fault of his future secretary of war.

NOTES

ABBREVIATIONS

AAS	American Antiquarian Society
ADAH	Alabama Department of Archives and History
ALP	Abraham Lincoln Papers, Library of Congress
ALPLM	Abraham Lincoln Presidential Library and Museum
BPL	Boston Public Library
CCHS	Chautauqua County Historical Society
CG	U.S. Congress, *Congressional Globe*
CHC	Chicago History Center (formerly Chicago Historical Society)
CHS	Connecticut Historical Society
CL	Clements Library, University of Michigan
CWL	Basler, Roy P., ed. *The Collected Works of Abraham Lincoln*
DC	Dartmouth College
Doyle	Joseph B. Doyle, *In Memoriam: Edwin McMasters Stanton, His Life and Work*
Drozdowski	Eugene C. Drozdowski, "Edwin M. Stanton, Lincoln's Secretary of War: Toward Victory." Ph.D. diss., Duke University
ED	Enumeration District (of the U.S. Census)
ELS	Edwin Lamson Stanton
EMS	Edwin M. Stanton
Flower	Frank Abial Flower, *Edwin McMasters Stanton: The Autocrat of Rebellion, Emancipation, and Reconstruction*
GBM	George B. McClellan
Gorham	George C. Gorham, *Life and Public Services of Edwin M. Stanton*
Graves	Frederick J. Graves, "The Early Life and Career of Edwin M. Stanton." Ph.D. diss., University of Kentucky
GTS	Gideon Townsend Stanton, "Edwin M. Stanton: A Personal Portrait"
HCC	Harrison County Courthouse
HHC	Heinz History Center (formerly Western Pennsylvania Historical Society)
HL	Huntington Library
HML	Hagley Museum and Library
HSP	Historical Society of Pennsylvania
Hyman	Benjamin P. Thomas and Harold M. Hyman, *Stanton: The Life and Times of Lincoln's Secretary of War* (unless another Hyman title is specified)
IHS	Indiana Historical Society
ISL	Indiana State Library

JCC	Jefferson County Chapter of the Ohio Genealogical Society
KSHS	Kansas State Historical Society
LC	Library of Congress
LFFC	Lincoln Financial Foundation Collection, Allen County Public Library
LOV	Library of Virginia
LSU	Louisiana State University
MEHS	Maine Historical Society
MHS	Massachusetts Historical Society
MNHS	Minnesota Historical Society
MOHS	Missouri Historical Society
NA	National Archives
NHHS	New Hampshire Historical Society
NYHS	New-York Historical Society
NYPL	New York Public Library
OHS	Ohio Historical Society
OR	*War of the Rebellion: A Compilation of the Official Records of the Union and Confederate Armies* (all citations from Series 1 unless otherwise noted)
OR Atlas	*Atlas to Accompany the Official Records of the Union and Confederate Armies*
ORN	*Official Records of the Union and Confederate Navies in the War of the Rebellion* (all citations from Series 1 unless otherwise noted)
Pratt	Fletcher Pratt, *Stanton: Lincoln's Secretary of War*
PVA&M	Prairie View A&M University
RBHPL	Rutherford B. Hayes Presidential Library
RG	Record Group (National Archives)
RJCCW	*Report of the Joint Committee on the Conduct of the War* (37th Congress)
RJCCW2	*Report of the Joint Committee on the Conduct of the War, at the Second Session, Thirty-eighth Congress*
SCL	South Caroliniana Library, University of South Carolina
SHSI-DM	State Historical Society of Iowa, Des Moines
SHSI-IC	State Historical Society of Iowa, Iowa City
SP	Edwin M. Stanton Papers, Library of Congress
UCB	University of California, Berkeley
UIA	University of Iowa
UME	University of Maine
UMI	University of Michigan
USAMHI	U.S. Army Military History Institute
USG	John Y. Simon, ed., *The Papers of Ulysses S. Grant*
UVA	University of Virginia
UVM	University of Vermont
VFM	Vertical File Manuscripts (Ohio Historical Society)
VHS	Virginia Historical Society

WHS   Wisconsin Historical Society
Wolcott   Pamphila S. Wolcott, "Edwin M. Stanton: A Biographical Sketch by
            His Sister," OHS
WRHS   Western Reserve Historical Society

CHAPTER 1

1. This story relies on Thomas S. Forbes to J. M. Grinnan, January 12, 1931, LC, in which Forbes relates his father's version of meeting Mrs. Wale: the details are consistent with Eighth Census of the U.S. (M653), Reel 1341, Culpeper County, Va., 907, and Ninth Census of the U.S. (M593), Reel 1641, Culpeper County, 671, RG 29, NA. Clark B. Hall, the premier historian of 1860s Culpeper County, pinpointed the location of the dwellings for me and photographed the still-extant Zimmerman's Tavern.

2. Norman's pay record and declaration of June 7, 1832, in widow's pension claim 26580, and Joseph Yeadon's affidavit of August 20, 1832, veteran's pension certificate 8040, both in Revolutionary War Pension Applications (M804), RG 15, NA.

3. Norman, "History," Culpeper County Library; certification of Bible entry, June 16, 1854, in Fannie Norman's widow's pension claim 26580, Revolutionary War Pension Applications (M804), RG 15, NA.

4. Copy of Henry Stanton's will, May 25, 1751, and map of Benjamin Stanton's property, Friends Historical Collection, Guilford College; Minutes of the Core Sound, Westland, and Short Creek Monthly Meetings in Hinshaw, *Encyclopedia of Quaker Genealogy*, 1:276, and 4:60–61, 279; Brian Hellen to Benjamin Stanton Jr., February 22, 1815, William M. Stanton Papers (HM37001), HL. Howells, *Recollections*, 14, 21–30, describes the Quaker community at Mount Pleasant in some detail.

5. Stanton, *A Book Called Our Ancestors*, 39–40; David Stanton to "Dear Brother," April 29, 1821, William M. Stanton Papers (HM37005), HL; Howells, *Recollections*, 33. Benjamin Stanton inherited one slave and acquired another by 1790 (Clark, *State Records*, 26:362), but was ostensibly prevented by state law from freeing them.

6. Wilson, "Jeremiah S. Black," 469–70. An 1864 letter from William Lloyd Garrison to Henry Wilson made it clear that Wilson had conveyed Stanton's tale of David Stanton giving Lundy money for his abolition newspaper, and Garrison approvingly replied of Stanton that the abolitionist spirit "runs in the blood" (Merrill, *Garrison Letters*, 5:191).

7. Jefferson County Marriage Books, 2:38, JCC. According to her daughter (Wolcott, 160) and her gravestone in Steubenville's Union Cemetery, Lucy Norman Stanton was born November 17, 1793. The pagination of the vanished Wolcott manuscript used by Hyman and Graves evidently differed from that of the OHS microfilm copy.

8. Minutes of Short Creek Monthly Meeting, in Hinshaw, *Encyclopedia of Quaker Genealogy*, 4:279. Unless John Murray Forbes (or his minister son) misrepresented his notes on his conversation with Martha Wale (Thomas S. Forbes to J. M. Grinnan, January 12, 1931, LC), the rumor of Lucy Stanton's premature pregnancy flourished in Culpeper County before Edwin Stanton acquired the enemies who might have invented it maliciously, but Forbes himself may well have been hostile to Stanton. There is no other evidence that Lucy became pregnant before marriage, although it

would hardly have been unusual for a bride to be with child in 1814 Ohio: Stanton himself documented a spate of illegitimate births among Methodists there in 1842 (EMS to Benjamin Tappan Sr., April 22, 1842, Tappan Papers, OHS). In *The Market Revolution*, 258–59, Sellers notes that a bridal pregnancy rate of 23.7 percent between 1800 and 1840 was actually a substantial decrease from eighteenth-century frequency; he attributes the decline to a focus on market production and an obsession with material success.

9. Barrett, *Correspondence*, 2:115–17; *Hartford Convention Resolutions of 1815*, 4–22.

10. Wolcott, 18; Howells, *Recollections*, 37. Most of the businesses Howells listed were mentioned in various issues of the *Steubenville Western Herald* between 1816 and 1818.

11. Thomas S. Forbes to J. M. Grinnan, January 12, 1931, LC; Wolcott, 18–21; David Stanton medical license, Reel 14, SP. Wolcott's memoir includes some complete and excerpted transcripts of original letters. Erasmus Darwin Stanton later reversed his first and middle names.

12. Deed of March 1, 1818, Book F, 517, Jefferson County Courthouse. Lucy Stanton's small inheritance from her wealthy father suggests an earlier beneficence, such as this home.

13. Wolcott, 20–22; Flower, 22–23; Gorham, 1:7–10, and quoting Frances Wilson to EMS, ca. 1865, 7–8; Howells, *Recollections*, 42, 97–98. Stanton's early schooling is only recounted in conflicting memoirs.

14. Post-1873 memorandum in Schuckers Papers, LC; James Buchanan to Harriet Lane, January 16, "1861" [1862], Buchanan-Johnston Papers, LC; William G. Moore Diary, July 5, 1867, Johnson Papers, LC; John P. Hatch to "Dear Father," April 1, 1863, LC; James H. Wilson to Adam Badeau, August 5, 1865, LC; Charles C. Morey to "Dear Parents," July 8, 1864, USAMHI; Zealous B. Tower to William P. Fessenden, May 31, 1865, CL.

15. *Steubenville Western Herald*, February 20, March 27, and April 24, 1819, March 11 and June 24, 1820. Marc Egnal observed that the generally wealthier, commercially oriented Whig Party of 1840s Ohio was concentrated along the National (i.e. Cumberland) Road, which missed Jefferson County (*Clash of Extremes*, 46–52).

16. *Steubenville Western Herald*, March 10 and July 7, 1821.

17. Deed of March 1, 1818, Book F, 517, Jefferson County Courthouse; David Stanton to "Dear Brother," April 29, 1821, William M. Stanton Papers (HM37005), HL; Norman, "History," Culpeper County Library; interment records of Union Cemetery, Steubenville.

18. Letter of Jane Catherine Duerson (Lucy Norman Stanton's half-sister), date unknown, quoted in Flower, 27; EMS to "My dear Mother," December 16, 1868, in Wolcott, 175; *New England Farrier and Family Physician*, 65, 72, 102–3.

19. Wolcott, 21; Norman, "History," Culpeper County Library; interment records of Union Cemetery, Steubenville. Oella's headstone in Oak Dale Cemetery, Urbana, Ohio, records that she was born on May 3, 1822. Pamphila's stone in Steubenville's Union Cemetery mistakenly dates her birth in 1829—more than a year after her father's death.

20. Wolcott, 24; *Steubenville Republican Ledger*, January 2, 1828. This cemetery is located on an early plat of Steubenville in Heald, *Bezaleel Wells*, 26. Dr. John Andrews, a colleague of David Stanton's, identified the cause of his death as "apoplexy" (*Ohio State Journal*, May 24, 1866).

21. Land Grant assignment from Joseph McFarland, SP; *Steubenville Republican Ledger*, April 9, 1828; Common Pleas Journal F, 52, 283, 359, 360, JCC; *Western Herald and Steubenville Gazette*, July 31, 1833; letter of Jane Catherine Duerson, date unknown, quoted in Flower, 23.

22. Wolcott, 28; *Steubenville Western Herald*, March 11, 1820; *Western Herald and Steubenville Gazette*, November 22, 1828, and March 28, 1829.

23. *Ohio State Journal*, August 11, 1832; *American Union*, August 7, 1841.

24. John P. Lloyd to EMS, April 10, 1865, SP; EMS to Daniel Collier, September 14, 1833, Kenyon; Wolcott, 39–40; statements of J. F. Oliver, Margaret Clemson, James Gallagher, and John Harper, quoted in Flower, 23–24.

25. According to Flower (23), Stanton's apprenticeship compensation was $50 for the first year, $100 for the second, and $150 for the third; on Stanton's college financing see his account with Collier, February 21, 1840, GTS, LSU.

26. Parker, "Edwin M. Stanton at Kenyon," 235–43; excised account book page, SP.

27. *Catalogue of Kenyon College*, 11; Chase circular to Kenyon faculty, July 14, 1831, and "The Professors of Kenyon College" to Chase, July 21, 1831, both at Kenyon; *Journal of the Proceedings of the Fourteenth Annual Convention*, cited in Parker, "Edwin M. Stanton at Kenyon," 236. More than half a century later Reverend Heman Dyer told a suspiciously didactic story in which Stanton stole Bishop Chase's horse for an evening excursion. This would have had to happen during Stanton's first four months at Kenyon (Dyer, *Records of an Active Life*, 69–73), but it seems unlikely that Stanton would have jeopardized his coveted educational opportunity. Dyer acted as something of a personal publicist for Stanton during the Civil War, and apparently resumed that role after Stanton's death, crafting anecdotes to highlight his former student's virtues. After the story of the stolen horse appeared in Dyer's memoir, another Kenyon alumnus insinuated himself into it (Flower, 28; Parker, "Edwin M. Stanton at Kenyon," 236).

28. Parker, "Edwin M. Stanton at Kenyon," 245 (quoting the Kenyon calendar for 1832); excised account book page, SP; EMS to Daniel L. Collier, August 18, 1831, Kenyon.

29. *National Journal*, April 7, 1832; U.S. House, *Memorial of the Ladies of Steubenville*.

30. Philomathesian Society Treasurer's Book, 22, and Minute Books, July 13, 20, and 27 and August 3, 1832, Kenyon.

31. Philomathesian Society Minute Books, June 25 and July 6, 1832, Kenyon; Sherlock A. Bronson to Pamphila Wolcott, June 25, 1886, quoted in Gorham, 1:16.

32. Gorham (1:11) presents the nullification crisis as the impetus for Stanton siding with Jackson, as though to postulate that he was motivated by a devotion to the Union, but there is no evidence that he yet identified with the Jackson faction. Ohio had, however, gone strong for Jackson in both 1828 and 1832: his candidacy has

been credited with more than doubling voter participation between 1824 and 1828 (McCormick, "New Perspectives on Jacksonian Politics," 110–11).

33. "Our Admiration of Military Character Unmerited," SP.

34. EMS to Alexander J. Beatty, July 21, 1832, Kenyon.

35. Ibid.

36. *New York Evening Post*, July 3 and 23, 1832, quoted in Rosenberg, *The Cholera Years*, 28, 32–34; *Ohio State Journal*, June 30 and August 11, 1832; EMS to Alexander Beatty, July 21, 1832, Kenyon.

37. EMS to Daniel L. Collier, August 18, 1832, and EMS to Andrew T. McClintock, October 10, 1832, Kenyon.

38. *Western Herald and Steubenville Gazette*, January 10, 1829; Common Pleas Journal G, 283, JCC.

39. *Ohio State Journal*, June 2, 1832; EMS to Daniel L. Collier, September 14, 1833, and EMS to McClintock, October 10, 1832, Kenyon.

40. Wolcott, 42–43; Benjamin, "Recollections," 760; EMS to McClintock, October 26, 1832, LSU.

41. *Ohio State Journal*, September 8, 1832, July 6, 1833.

42. EMS to McClintock, November 2, 1832, and EMS to Daniel L. Collier, September 14, 1833, both at Kenyon.

43. EMS to McClintock, November 2, 1832, Kenyon. In "Edwin M. Stanton at Kenyon" Parker deleted the paragraph about Stanton's pants, along with other crude passages in Stanton's letters, after discussion about their impropriety with Stanton's grandson Gideon Townsend Stanton, who supplied transcripts of the letters. See their correspondence of April 18, July 5, 30, 1950, Kenyon.

44. EMS to McClintock, January 30, [1834], Kenyon; Wolcott, 40–44, 112–13; Nevins and Thomas, *Strong Diary*, 1:203; Parker, "Edwin M. Stanton at Kenyon," 238. In a letter to Marie Bates in the late 1840s, Stanton described meeting Mary at a lecture in Columbus, and he mentioned a miniature portrait of her that has never surfaced (Wolcott, 118, 119).

45. EMS to Daniel L. Collier, September 14, 1833, Kenyon; Common Pleas Journal G, 283, JCC; *Western Herald and Steubenville Gazette*, July 31, 1833; Wolcott, 38.

46. *Ohio State Journal*, June 15, July 20, 27, and August 3, 17, 24, and September 7, 1833.

47. Flower, 30.

48. Wolcott, 29, 36; Flower, 30. Flower's Columbus informant was Arthur H. Smythe, whose father was a contemporary of Stanton, but not necessarily an acquaintance [Eighth Census of the U.S. (M653), Reel 964, Ward 2, Columbus, 165, and Thirteenth Census of the U.S. (T624), Reel 1180, Franklin County, ED 102, Sheet 6, RG 29, NA]. Stanton's sister gave family letters to George Gorham for his biography (Pamphila Wolcott to Belmont Perry, August 11, 1888, Eldridge Collection, HL), but her letter to Joseph A. Howells (March 28, 1897, RBHPL) suggests that Gorham did not use her memoir, and he never alluded to Ann Howard or the cholera epidemic. Pamphila's childhood memory may have prompted Flower's cursory inquiry into the alleged episode.

49. EMS to Daniel L. Collier, September 14, 1833, Kenyon.

50. Ibid.; EMS to McClintock and Joseph Mitchell, September 27, 1833, Kenyon.

51. EMS to McClintock and Mitchell, September 27, 1833, Kenyon; *Ohio State Journal*, September 14, 21, and 28, 1833.

52. EMS to McClintock and Mitchell, September 27, 1833, Kenyon; *Ohio State Journal*, September 28, 1833.

53. EMS to McClintock, January 30, [1834], Kenyon; *Republican Ledger*, January 30, 1828.

54. EMS to McClintock, January 30, [1834], Kenyon; Wolcott, 39.

55. EMS to McClintock, January 30, [1834], Kenyon; EMS to McClintock, June 5, 1834, CHC.

CHAPTER 2

1. EMS to McClintock, January 30, 1834, Kenyon, and June 5, 1834, CHC; McClintock to Edwin L. Stanton, December 25, 1869, SP. The lewd passages of the January 30 letter, which were expurgated from Wyman's published version in all the Kenyon letters, evidently included the inquiry whether the face of one professor's wife was still "sicklied o'er with the pale cast of—cunt?"

2. Wolcott, 103–11, quoted several letters between Mary and EMS; Graves, 32, quoted one of Mary's letters from Edward S. Corwin's unpublished (and apparently unfinished) biography.

3. *Washington Globe*, December 13, 1832, March 4, August 25, 1834, June 10, 1835; Wainwright, *Fisher Diary*, 2. The Bank War is recounted through the lenses of different generations in Schlesinger, *The Age of Jackson*, 74–87, and Sellers, *The Market Revolution*, 321–26.

4. John Miner to EMS, November 18, 1835, and John S. Patterson to Benjamin Tappan Sr., January 15, 1836, Tappan Papers, LC; Wolcott, 53, 81; Seventh Census of the U.S. (M432), Reel 693, Harrison County, 374, RG 29, NA. The flour case was *Joshua Woods v. Beverly McGee*: see *Condensed Reports*, 466. Larson, *The Market Revolution*, 178–79, equated Jackson's bank fight to modern deregulation campaigns.

5. William Boyce to EMS, June 8, 1836, SP; Common Pleas Journal C, 454–59, HCC; *New York Evening Post*, April 1, 1836. Graves, 33, cites an 1836–39 Appearance Docket and Common Pleas Records that are no longer extant at the Harrison County Courthouse.

6. Wolcott, 53–55; *Ohio State Journal*, May 24, 1866; Benjamin Tappan Jr. to EMS, February 26, 1837, Tappan Papers, LC. Despite his sister's claim that Darwin attended Harvard (Wolcott, 53), the University of Pennsylvania granted his degree in 1838.

7. Wolcott, 54, 105; Benjamin Tappan Sr. to Tappan Jr., December 28, 1836, and Benjamin Tappan Jr. to EMS, February 26, 1837, Tappan Papers, LC; *Ohio State Journal*, January 3, 1837; EMS to Salmon P. Chase, December 2, 1847, HSP.

8. Benjamin Tappan Sr. to Tappan Jr., December 28, 1836, and March 8, 1837, Tappan Papers, LC; Wolcott, 54–59; Culpeper County Will Book O, 356–59, 404–8, LOV.

9. *Washington Globe*, April 24, 25, 1837; Wainwright, *Fisher Diary*, 27, 29–32; Nevins and Thomas, *Strong Diary*, 1:62–65. Modern proponents of centralized banking tend to blame the inflation on Jackson's transfer of federal funds from the Bank of the United States to "pet" banks, which they say fueled speculation. They also credit the Specie Circular for creating the panic. See Kaplan, *The Bank of the United States*, 160; Matson, *The Economy of Early America*, 55; Howe, *What Hath God Wrought*, 503.

10. Benjamin Tappan Sr. to EMS, January 9, 1840, quoted in Gorham, 1:25.

11. Adams Jewett to Benjamin Tappan Sr., May 20, 30, 1837, Tappan Sr. to Tappan Jr., June 16, 1837, and Tappan Jr. to Tappan Sr., March 18, 1837, Tappan Papers, LC; *American Union*, June 12, 1838.

12. EMS to Benjamin Tappan Sr., July 24, 1837, Tappan Papers, OHS; *American Union*, May 31, 1837; Wolcott, 60–62. The association with Dewey lasted until at least 1839 (*The Organ*, April 18, 1839).

13. Common Pleas Journal D, 1–2, 74–75, 114, 130, 132, 138–39, 160, 162, 165–68, 171–75, 195–97, 203–6, 209, 212, 251–54, 281, 289, HCC; Wolcott, 85–86. Jean H. Baker claimed in *Affairs of Party*, 111–14, that the Democratic Party had no name until the 1840s; she apparently meant that the name was applied to "a series of tribelike local units" instead of to a large national organization with an organized platform.

14. EMS to Salmon P. Chase, December 2, 1847, HSP; numerous entries in Common Pleas Journals C, D, and E, HCC.

15. *American Union*, June 12, 26, 1838; M. Birchard to Benjamin Tappan Sr., December 24, 25, 1838, Tappan Papers, LC; *The Organ*, December 27, 1838; EMS to Tappan Sr., January 14, "1839" [1840], SP.

16. Commencement program and Minutes of the Trustees, April 6, 1838, University of Pennsylvania Archives; Wolcott, 71–73; *American Union*, September 13, 1837, July 9, 1839; Common Pleas Journal I, 222, JCC; Wolcott, 73. Nancy Hooker Stanton's gravestone in Union Cemetery records that she was born on October 23, 1823.

17. Common Pleas Journal I, 222, 382, JCC; Wolcott, 120; statement of account with Daniel L. Collier by EMS, with release dated February 21, 1840, GTS, LSU.

18. EMS to Benjamin Tappan Sr., January 14, "1839" [1840], Tappan Papers, OHS; "Buckeye" letter, SP.

19. EMS to Benjamin Tappan Sr., January 14, "1839" [1840], Tappan Papers, OHS; Resolution of January 8, 1840, Corrington Searles to "Gentlemen," December 27, 1839, and Reuben Wood to David Tod et al., January 7, 1840, SP.

20. EMS to Benjamin Tappan Sr., January 7, 1840, Tappan Papers, OHS, and same to same, January 22, 1840, SP.

21. Wolcott, 71; Deed Book I, 586–87, HCC; Deed Book V, 191, Jefferson County Courthouse.

22. EMS to William L. Hatch, January 27, 1840, EMS to "Gentlemen," February 1, 1840, and Robert Maxwell and A. G. Dimmock to EMS, June 4, 1840, SP.

23. *New York Evening Post*, March 10, 1840; *Washington Globe*, April 13, 1840.

24. *Sangamo Journal*, May 15, 1840, quoted in *CWL*, 1:209–10; French, *Journals*, 102; Nevins and Thomas, *Strong Diary*, 1:137; Niven, *Chase Papers*, 2:70–71.

Outdated as Schlesinger's *Age of Jackson* may be, it offers an amusing sketch of the 1840 campaign (290–99).

25. *Log Cabin Farmer*, July 23, 30, August 13, 27, 1840.

26. Ibid., July 23, 1840; John H. Forester to EMS, July 21, 1840, LC; "Bill to Regulate Banking," in the handwriting of EMS, SP. This manuscript editorial is labeled "[1844?]," but it refers to a bill incorporating banks in the District of Columbia that was debated in the early summer of 1840 (*CG*, 26th Cong., 1st sess., 504). Sellers, *The Market Revolution*, 358, identifies the banning of paper currency in lower denominations as a favorite Democratic ploy for forcing specie into circulation.

27. *Log Cabin Farmer*, July 23, August 27, and September 3, 1840; Wainwright, *Fisher Diary*, 102; French, *Journals*, 104. Howe, *What Hath God Wrought*, 505, credits the lingering effects of the Panic of 1837 to a second panic in 1839, caused by a glut of cotton in England that sent prices plummeting. Others had previously recognized the Panic of 1839 as a specific, separate depression: Watson, *Liberty and Power*, 206, deemed it far more devastating than the Panic of 1837.

28. EMS to Tappan, February 12, 1841, and James Means and EMS to Tappan, February 22, 1841, Tappan Papers, LC; EMS to Tappan, February 6 and March 7, 1841, SP.

29. EMS to Benjamin Tappan Sr., February 6, 1841, May 31, 1842, SP; same to same, June 27, 1841, Tappan Papers, OHS. Years later Stanton prosecuted Stokely, unsuccessfully, over a disputed inheritance (*Ohio Reports* 5:195–98).

30. Common Pleas Journal I, 102, 335, and J, 127, JCC; Deed Book V, 367, Jefferson County Courthouse; Deed of Trust, May 1, 1843, Tappan Papers, OHS. Gaddis had settled in the region in the 1790s (Carter, *Territorial Papers*, 3:54–57).

31. Common Pleas Journal E, 153, 205, 209, 213, 215, 230, HCC; Harrison County Common Pleas Record, 1839–1841, 508–12 (no longer extant), cited in Graves, 35. On Stanton's aggressiveness see, for instance, EMS to Benjamin Tappan Sr., July 24, 1837, May 31, 1842, OHS.

32. *American Union*, July 31, August 28, 1841; Christopher P. Wolcott to Tappan, August 27, 1841, and Tappan to Wolcott, September 4, 1841, Tappan Papers, LC; William Stanton Buchanan, quoted in Flower, 38; *Union Cemetery*, 1. Buchanan named Samuel Wilson, a coppersmith, as the workman who brazed up the remains: Seventh Census of the U.S. (M432), Reel 699, 144, RG 29, NA.

33. Wolcott, 74. Probably on the authority of Stanton family members, Flower (38) dates the birth of ELS as August 11, 1842, but no documentation survives.

34. See, for example, Jefferson County Common Pleas Journals 12 through 16, JCC. After Volume J, Jefferson County started numbering its common pleas journals, beginning with 11.

35. Seventh Census of the U.S. (M432), Reel 699, 936, RG 29, NA; Common Pleas Journal 12, 130, 304–5, 587, JCC.

36. *Moore v. Gano and Thoms*, *Ohio Reports*, 12:300–304; *U.S. Reports* 54: 218.

37. EMS to Benjamin Tappan Sr., March 7, 1841 and May 31, 1842, SP; Seventh Census of the U.S. (M432), Reel 699, 1064, RG 29, NA; Sixth Census of the U.S. (M704), Reel 405, Jefferson County, 66, RG 29, NA; Common Pleas Journal J, 107, 191, 261, 394, 422, 428, JCC.

38. EMS to Tappan, April 22, 1842, Tappan Papers, OHS.

39. EMS to Tappan, April 2, 1842, Tappan Papers, OHS.

40. *American Union*, January 1, 1842; EMS to [Bela Latham?], February 26, 1842, LSU; EMS to Tappan, February 6, 1841 and April 20, 1842, SP; Tappan to EMS, May 5, 1842, Tappan Papers, OHS; Seventh Census of the U.S. (M432), Reel 699, Jefferson County, 114, RG 29, NA.

41. *American Union*, September 4, November 6, 1841, January 15, 1842; EMS to Benjamin Tappan Sr., May 31, 1842, SP.

42. *American Union*, April 16, May 21, 1842; EMS to Benjamin Tappan Sr., May 31, 1842, SP, and same to same, July 17, 1842, Tappan Papers, OHS. Tyler's defection is detailed in Holt, *Rise and Fall of the Whig Party*, 127–50.

43. *Ohio State Journal*, December 7, 1842; EMS to Benjamin Tappan Sr., July 17, 1842, OHS.

44. Tappan to EMS, March 3, 1840, quoted in Gorham, 1:26; *Ohio State Journal*, December 7, 1842.

45. EMS to "My Dear Sister," December 25, 1842, quoted in Wolcott, 75–77; EMS to Tappan, December 27, 1842, SP.

46. EMS to Tappan, February 8, 1843, SP; EMS to Ebenezer Lane, February 10, 1843, Lee Kohns Collection, NYPL.

47. *American Union*, May 27, June 24, July 8, August 19, October 21, November 18, 1843; *Ohio State Journal*, September 2, 1843.

48. Wolcott, 109; EMS to Wilkins, October 12, "1843" [1842] and September 25, 1843, HHC. Tuberculosis carried such a stigma by the late nineteenth century that families began to disguise it, and Pamphila Wolcott attributed Mary's decline to "bilious fever."

49. Wolcott, 99, 108–9; Deed Book X, 428–30, Jefferson County Courthouse; Theobald Umbstaetter to Benjamin Tappan Sr., December 22, 1843, LC.

50. EMS to Tappan, January 8, "1843" [1844], SP; William Medill to Tappan, January 12, 1844, LC, and to William Allen, January 11, 1844, LC; W. Blacksom to Tappan, January 18, 1844, LC. Sharp, *The Jacksonians versus the Banks*, 136, apparently underestimated the size of the "hard-money clique" when he said it involved only 10 percent of the Democratic Party.

51. Wolcott, 99–100; *Ohio State Journal*, March 19, 1844. Steubenville's business district was already crowding its cemeteries by 1844, when Stanton bought a family plot in the graveyard of the Presbyterian Church, at the corner of Fourth and South streets. Little Lucy's coffin went into this grave with her mother's, only to be moved again a decade later: Deed Book X, 460, Jefferson County Courthouse; *Union Cemetery*, 1.

52. EMS to Lewis Tappan, March 20, 1844, Lewis Tappan Papers, LC.

CHAPTER 3

1. *Ohio State Journal*, March 14, 23, 28, 1844; *Washington Globe*, April 27, 1844; EMS to Tappan, April 28, 1844, SP.

2. *Washington Globe*, May 30, 1844; Nevins and Thomas, *Strong Diary*, 1:235. This episode is similarly described in, for instance, Schelesinger, *The Age of Jackson*,

435–37; Sellers, *The Market Revolution*, 414–17; Howe, *What Hath God Wrought*, 682–84.

3. William Buchanan and Alfred Taylor, quoted in Flower, 39–40; EMS to Salmon P. Chase, December 2, 1847, HSP; *American Union*, July 11, August 15, September 5, 19, 1844.

4. French, *Journals*, 157–58, 608; EMS to Benjamin Tappan Sr., January 27, 1845, SP.

5. *American Union*, September 5 and 19, 1844; *CG*, 28th Cong., 1st sess., 620, 658.

6. *Ohio State Journal*, October 12, 15, 17, 1844.

7. EMS to Tappan, December 5, 1844, OHS, and December 26, 1844, SP.

8. *American Union*, July 25, August 1, 8, 1844, May 14, 1846; Common Pleas Journal 12, 530, JCC; EMS to Tappan, March 26, 1845, SP; Common Pleas Journal 12, 570, JCC.

9. *American Union*, March 25, 1845; EMS to William Allen, February 20, 1846, Allen Papers, LC; EMS to Jacob Brinkerhoff, January 19, 1845, SP.

10. EMS to Tappan, January 30, 1842, January 27, 1845, SP; *American Union*, November 4, 11, 18, 1843; Benjamin Tappan Jr. to Tappan Sr., March 2, 1845, LC.

11. EMS to Tappan, January 27, 1845, SP.

12. *CG*, 28th Cong., 2nd sess., 149–52.

13. Ibid., 152–53.

14. *Baltimore Sun*, December 19, 1845.

15. *National Intelligencer*, December 9, 1845; Darwin Stanton to Pamphila Stanton, December 11, 1845, quoted in Wolcott, 90–91; Benjamin B. French Journal, December 17, 1845, LC; *Daily Union*, December 17, 1845; *Baltimore Sun*, December 18, 1845.

16. *Baltimore Sun*, December 18, 1845; *Washington Evening Star*, April 7, 1859.

17. *Baltimore Sun*, December 20, 1845.

18. Ibid., December 22, 23, 1845.

19. Ibid., December 23, 1845.

20. Ibid., December 23, 24, 25, 1845; *Ohio Statesman*, December 29, 1845, and *American Union*, January 1, 1846 (both quoted in Graves, 50).

21. *Ohio Statesman*, January 8, 10, 1846; *CG*, 28th Cong., 2nd sess., 131–32, 29th Cong., 1st sess., 197–98; EMS to Brinkerhoff, January "19," 1845 (postmarked January 18), SP; EMS to Allen, February 20, 1846, Allen Papers, LC.

22. *American Union*, May 14, 21, and 28, 1846.

23. *American Union*, May 28, June 11, 1846; Muster-in and Muster-out Rolls of Company B, 2nd Ohio Volunteers, Caleb J. McNulty service file, Reel 25, Index to Compiled Service Records of Volunteer Soldiers Who Served During the Mexican War (M616), RG 94, NA; EMS to Allen, July 13, 1846, January 16, 1847, Allen Papers, LC.

24. *American Union*, September 24, 1846. Flower, whose biography appeared while Nancy Stanton was still alive, first revealed the suicide (45). Hyman, 40–41, citing Alexander Reid's privately owned memoir, describes Darwin cutting his throat: Reid, however, only came to Steubenville years afterward, and probably

repeated the story as he heard it, although that may demonstrate that the community believed Darwin had killed himself.

25. Flower, 45, cited separate statements from Taylor and Brown.

26. Common Pleas Journal 12:213, 475, JCC; EMS to Lewis Tappan, November 23, 1846, Lewis Tappan Papers, LC; Seventh Census of the U.S. (M432), Reel 699, 114, RG 29, NA; headstone inscriptions, Stanton lot, Union Cemetery; Nancy Hooker Stanton never remarried, and died on May 29, 1913.

27. *Keene Sentinel*, August 9, 1817; Niven, *Chase Papers*, 1:xix, xxiii, 117; Chase to John P. Hale, June 30, 1846, Hale Papers, NHHS; EMS to Chase, ca. August, 1846, January 5, 1847, HSP.

28. EMS to Chase, November 30, 1846, HSP. Citing 1870 correspondence with Jeremiah Black, Chase biographer John Niven concluded that Chase blamed Stanton's reluctance to join the antislavery cause on his attachment to the Democratic Party, but in an 1870 letter to Henry Wilson, Chase seemed to attribute it to Stanton's exaggeration (*Salmon P. Chase: A Biography*, 104; Chase to Black, July 4, 1870, Black Papers, LC; Chase to Wilson, May 25, 1870, Chase Papers, LC). Neither Niven nor Frederick Blue (*Salmon P. Chase*) made much of Stanton's antebellum relationship with Chase, but before the war he evidently put too much stock in Stanton's professions of ideological sympathy.

29. EMS to Chase, November 30, 1846, January 5, March 11, May 1, 1847, HSP; letterbook registers for January through April, 1847, Reel 27, Chase Papers, LC.

30. EMS to Chase, November 30, 1846, January 5, March 11, 1847; Gorham, 9; Flower, 23; EMS to Marie Bates, July 22, 1848, VFM 1243, OHS; Wolcott, 105, 115–19, 131–41.

31. *American Union*, March 25, June 17, July 8, 1847; George W. McCook to "My dear Mother," July 22, 1847, and EMS to Margaret Dick Beattie, undated, McCook Papers, LC; Loomis, *Steubenville Directory*, 43; EMS to Chase, July 30, 1847, HSP; Niven, *Chase Papers*, 2:155.

32. Seventh Census of the U.S. (M432), Reel 745, Ward 4, Pittsburgh, 247, RG 29, NA; Harris, *General Business Directory* for 1847, 137, lists "Shaler & Simpson."

33. EMS to John Sanders, November 17, 1847, SP; Deed Book Z, 456–57, 476, Jefferson County Courthouse; Doyle, 29–30. Ohio Route 7, called Dean Martin Boulevard in Steubenville after another native son, now jogs diagonally across what was Stanton's Patch in front of Steubenville High School; it then turns north again and runs directly over the site of Stanton's house at the corner of Logan Street.

34. *Daily Morning Post*, October 29, 30, 1847.

35. Harris, *General Business Directory*, iii–iv; John Harper to "Dear Albert," May 14, 1862, HHC; "City of Pittsburgh," *Gleason's Pictorial Drawing-Room Companion*, April 30, 1853, 280.

36. Harris, *General Business Directory*, 10; EMS to John Sanders, November 17, 1847, SP.

37. *Wheeling Bridge Case*, 4. Stanton's premature preparation for action in this case (EMS to John Sanders, November 17, 1847, SP) appears to have gone undetected.

38. Wolcott, 144–45; *New York Sun*, March 14, 1892; John Harper to "My dear Son," October 16, 1856, HHC; EMS to Chase, December 2, 15, 1847, February 16,

1848, HSP; Chase to EMS, January 9, 1848, SP. On Wolcott's fervent idealism, see his letter to "My Dear Wife," December 30, 1851, EG Box 66, Eldridge Collection, HL.

39. Chase to Tappan, March 30, 1848; Niven, *Chase Papers*, 2:167–78; letterbooks, May 14 and 24, 1848, Reel 27, Chase Papers, LC; Wolcott, 146; Edson B. Olds to EMS, March 11, 1848, and Clement L. Vallandigham to EMS, June 26, 1848, SP.

40. Wilson, "Jeremiah S. Black and Edwin M. Stanton," 469–70, relates Stanton's story of Lundy; on September 18, 1865, Stanton wrote William Lloyd Garrison that the renowned abolitionist had been "an object of my respect and admiration" since "earliest youth" (Garrison Letters, BPL).

41. *Pittsburgh Daily Gazette*, July 6, August 1, 3, 1848, January 16–18, 1849; *Daily Morning Post*, January 17, 18, 1849; *Daily Commercial Journal*, August 1, 1848.

42. *Daily Commercial Journal*, August 4, 1848; *Pittsburgh Daily Gazette*, August 3, 5, 16, September 14, 1848; *The Factory Riots*, 1–2.

43. *Pittsburgh Daily Gazette*, December 2, 1848, January 16, 1849. Patton and Stanton maintained a personal correspondence, part of which is published in Flower, 56–57.

44. *Pittsburgh Daily Gazette*, January 16–18, 1849; *Daily Morning Post*, January 17, 18, 1849; *Daily Dispatch*, January 16, 18, 1849.

45. *Pittsburgh Daily Gazette*, January 19, 20, 22, 1849; *Daily Morning Post*, January 19, 1849; *Daily Dispatch*, January 19, 20, 1849; *The Factory Riots*, 8–15.

46. Wolcott, 124–25; EMS to Chase, January 5, 1847, HSP; Williams, *Diary and Letters of Rutherford Birchard Hayes*, 5:149. Most lawyers serve a diverse clientele, but newspaper coverage suggests that Stanton's proportion of wealthy or corporate clients increased significantly and abruptly, at least partly because of the clients he chose to accept. That trend also helps to demonstrate his tendency to align himself with majorities: in *Clash of Extremes*, 52–55, Egnal identified Jefferson County, Ohio, at that period as solidly Democratic, and Allegheny County, Pennsylvania, as firmly Whig. The shift may also have reflected Stanton's own success: as Sellers pointed out in *The Market Revolution*, 47, "only the best-heeled clients could afford the superior representation provided by the most successful lawyers."

47. Harris, *General Business Directory*, 137; Thurston, *Directory*, 44, 141. Stanton was an avid fan of Dickens, whose character Mr. Omer remarks in *David Copperfield*, "I smoke, myself, for the asthma," According to a War Department clerk, so did Stanton (Benjamin, "Recollections," 760).

48. Wolcott, 115–19, 123–24; EMS to Chase, December 2, 1847, HSP; Yulee to EMS, February 23, 1848, SP; Common Pleas Journals 14:105, 118, 153, 177, 179, 183, 225, 238, 15:9, 102, 154, 162; *Ohio Reports*, 1:206–21; EMS to Maria K. Bates, July 22, 1848, VFM, OHS; EMS to John Sanders, June 13, 1849, SP.

49. *Pittsburgh Daily Gazette*, April 12, 13, 1849; *Daily Morning Post*, April 18, 1849.

50. *Pittsburgh Daily Gazette*, August 11, 1849; *U.S. Reports* 50:647.

51. *U.S. Reports* 54:520–22; [Wheeling] *Daily Gazette*, August 20, 1849; *Pittsburgh Daily Gazette*, September 4, 1849; EMS to John Sanders, "1848" [September 1, 1849], and "Thursday" [September 6, 1849], SP.

52. [Wheeling] *Daily Gazette*, October 22, November 17, 1849; *Pittsburgh Daily Gazette*, November 5, 1849.

53. *U.S. Reports* 50:652–54; *Wheeling Bridge Case*, 6, 11, 19, 26.

54. *U.S. Reports* 50:655–56; *Wheeling Bridge Case*, 17–18. The inflated story of the *Hibernia* first appeared in Flower, 55, and is repeated in Hyman, 62.

55. Wolcott, 128, 131; EMS to Walker, November 20, 1849, Miscellaneous Manuscripts (HM27125), HL; James Baker to Charles Ellet, December 9, 1849, Hatcher Library, UMI; EMS to Benjamin Patton, December 11, 1849, quoted in Flower, 56–57; Chase to EMS, December 14, 1849, May 27, 1850, SP; *Daily Commercial Journal*, February 18, 1850.

56. *National Intelligencer*, February 26, 1850; *Pittsburgh Daily Gazette*, March 1, 1850; *U.S. Reports* 50:659, 54 (13 Howard):522–29.

57. *U.S. Reports* 50:658–59, 54 (13 Howard):530–37.

58. *Pittsburgh Daily Gazette*, December 14, 1850; December 22, 1851, February 5, 1852; *Morning Chronicle*, February 7, 1851; *Daily Commercial Journal*, December 14, 1850, February 20, 1851, February 9, 10, May 29, 1852; Harding, *Argument for the Complainant*, 3–12; *U.S. Reports* 54:622–27.

59. *Daily Commercial Journal*, July 13, 1852; *U.S. Reports* 59:422–28, 436–37; *Morning Chronicle*, March 23, 1855; H. Hepburn to A. V. Parsons, August 11, 1849, SP.

CHAPTER 4

1. *CG*, 31st Cong., 1st sess., 412. The courtroom is described in EMS to Ellen Hutchison, [December 4, 1854] (HM27100), HL.

2. Chase to EMS, March 15, May 27, 1850, SP.

3. EMS to Chase, June 28, 1850, HSP; Chase to EMS, July 16, 1850, SP.

4. EMS to Chase, June 28, 1850, HSP; EMS to John Sanders, June 28, 1850, SP. On June 25, three days before Stanton wrote these letters, compromise opponent Charles Sumner predicted it would pass both the Senate and House (Palmer, *Sumner Letters*, 1:298).

5. Chase to Sarah Bella Chase, July 12, 1850, Chase Papers, LC. Senator William Gwin hailed from Mississippi. Remini's *At the Edge of the Precipice* has supplanted Hamilton's *Prologue to Conflict* on the Compromise of 1850, but Michael Holt gave it more comprehensive attention than either in *Rise and Fall of the Whig Party*.

6. Niven, *Chase Papers*, 2:310–11; *Daily Commercial Journal*, November 25, 1850; *National Intelligencer*, November 10, 1853; Nevins and Thomas, *Strong Diary*, 2:24–25.

7. *True American*, February 8, 1855; EMS to Benjamin Tappan Sr., August 4, 1851, Tappan Papers, LC; EMS to Chase, September 7, 1851, HSP; *Daily Commercial Journal*, March 14, 1851.

8. *Daily Morning Post*, January 29, 1851; *Daily Commercial Journal*, February 7, 8, 1851; *Morning Chronicle*, February 7, 1851; EMS to Reuben H. Walworth, January 30, February 26, April 11, July 7, 1851, SP.

9. EMS to Chase, June 28, 1850, September 7, 1851, HSP.

10. *Daily Commercial Journal*, February 8, 1851.

11. *U.S. Reports* 60:126–28. Nordhoff, *Communistic Societies*, 63–95, provides some background on Rapp and New Harmony. In that era each Supreme Court justice was also assigned to individual duty in federal circuit courts.

12. *U.S. Reports* 60:126–30; Dockets of the Supreme Court (M216), Reel 2, 3418, RG 267, NA.

13. EMS to Reuben H. Walworth, February 26, 1851, SP; EMS to Benjamin Tappan Sr., February 9, 26, 1852, Tappan Papers, OHS.

14. *Florida Contested Election*, 3–7, 36.

15. Benjamin Tappan Sr. to "Dear Brother," May 17, 1853, OHS.

16. Common Pleas Journal 16:344–49, 387, JCC; Benjamin Tappan Sr. to "Dear Brother," August 10, 1853, November 13, 1853, and to "Brother Lewis," August 22, 1853, OHS; L. Hastings to Benjamin Tappan Jr., July 11, 1853, and Lewis Tappan to Benjamin Tappan Sr., August 11, 1853, Benjamin Tappan Papers, LC. While he was in Steubenville, Stanton helped defend his old political foe, Colonel James Collier, from a charge of misappropriating public funds; he freed the old man from jail on a writ of habeas corpus.

17. Benjamin Tappan Sr. to "Dear Brother," November 13, 1853, OHS. Had the judge lived another decade, he might have heard abundant confirmation that his elder son had become a sot. Eight years after his first wife left him, Dr. Tappan would go to war as the surgeon of the 8th Ohio Infantry, but the professional soldier who took over his brigade early in 1862 explained long after the war that Tappan's "habits of intemperance were such" that he asked him to resign. When Tappan declined to do so, the general sent him home on a furlough "with the understanding that he would never return." In old age the erstwhile surgeon applied for a pension for a trumped-up injury he claimed to have endured in the line of duty, but it was rejected: one of his colleagues told a pension examiner that it was known around camp that Dr. Tappan "was on a spree and probably fell off his horse while drunk and broke his arm." See reports of H. P. Maxwell, March 17, 1887, D. M. Hamlin, May 7, 1887, and Benjamin Tappan Jr. to Nancy Tappan, October 27, 1861, all in Benjamin Tappan pension application 470166, RG 15, NA.

18. Common Pleas Journal 16:379–80; Benjamin Tappan Sr. to "Dear Brother," November 13, 1853, December 28, 1853, August 21, 1854, OHS; Tappan Sr. to Tappan Jr., May 10, 1854, LC.

19. Wolcott, 131; Benjamin Tappan Sr. to "Dear Brother," November 13, 1853, OHS; Jinnett Rowan to Benjamin Tappan Jr., August 11, 1859, LC.

20. *Daily Morning Post*, November 18, 19, 1853.

21. EMS to Reuben H. Walworth, December 6, 1851, SP.

22. *Pennsylvania Reports* 20–25, numerous cases, and particularly 22:22–25, 52–54, 54–68, 102–15, 320–24.

23. *Pittsburgh Daily Gazette*, December 12, 1853; *Daily Morning Post*, January 20, 1854.

24. *Daily Morning Post*, January 12, 13, 20, 24, 1854; *Pittsburgh Daily Gazette*, January 23, 1854; *Pennsylvania Reports* 26:287–326, 27:339–89.

25. *Pennsylvania Reports* 20:18–22; *Pittsburgh Daily Gazette*, May 9, 12, 1854; *Ohio Reports* 5:568–79.

26. *Weekly Picayune*, January 8, 1849; *New York Tribune*, May 17, 1849; Salmon P. Chase to John F. Morse, August 6, 1849, and to John C. Vaughan, August 7, 1849; Cincinnati Historical Society; EMS to Reuben H. Walworth, July 29, August 27, 1850, SP; EMS to McLean, September 26, 1854, McLean Papers, LC; *U.S. Reports* 54:624–25.

27. EMS to William F. Johnston, July 18, 1855, quoted in "List of Articles," 266; Seventh Census of the U.S. (M432), Reel 806, Ward 4, Pittsburgh, 249, and Reel 699, 114, RG 29, NA; Harris, *General Business Directory*, 77; Thurston, *Directory*, 66, 141.

28. EMS to Ellen Hutchison, [summer, 1854], letter fragment, GTS, LSU; Edwin M. Van Deusen to Ellen Stanton, January 4, "1869" [1870], SP; EMS to Ellen, "Thursday night, October 10" [12], and October 28, 1854 (HM27097, HM27098), HL.

29. EMS to William Stanton, October 26, 1854 (HM37012), HL.

30. EMS to Ellen Hutchison, December 3, 11, 12, 13, "15" [16], and "Monday evening" [December 4], 1854, (HM27099 through HM27104), HL.

31. EMS acknowledged Ellen's demand in an undated letter from about April, 1856 (HM27118, HL).

32. EMS to Ellen, "Monday evening" [December 4], December "15" [16], December 27, 30, 1854, February 13, 1855 (HM27100, HM27104 through HM 27107), HL.

33. *True American*, February 8, 1855. The idea of Senator Stanton holding Wade's seat until at least 1863 invites provocative if pointless speculation on what might have been.

34. *Daily Dispatch*, January 24, 1855; *Pittsburgh Daily Gazette*, January 24, 26, 1855; *Daily Morning Journal*, January 26, 1855.

35. *U.S. Reports* 59:385–94.

36. The adage is credited to James T. Brady, with whom Stanton later worked (*New York Times*, October 22, 1898), although Brady may merely have repeated it.

37. *CWL* 2:314–15, 325. The amount of the retainer is found in a list of Manny's expenses cited in Harry E. Pratt, *Personal Finances of Abraham Lincoln*, 55.

38. Robert H. Parkinson to Albert J. Beveridge, May 28, 1923, quoted in Beveridge, *Abraham Lincoln*, 1:576–78; A. E. H. Johnson statement, Flower Collection, WHS.

39. Beveridge, *Abraham Lincoln*, 1:579–83. Harding also claimed that President Lincoln generously offered to appoint him commissioner of patents; his name does appear beside the Board of Patent Appeals on a list of appointments Lincoln was considering in 1861, but not for the post of commissioner (*CWL*, 4:295).

40. The reliability of the Cincinnati incident is further analyzed in the Appendix.

41. *Cincinnati Commercial*, September 22, 24, 25, 1855.

42. Ibid., September 26, 27, 28, 1855; EMS to Ellen, September 25, 26, 1855 (HM27111, HM27112), HL.

43. *Cincinnati Commercial*, September 29, 1855.

44. Ibid., October 1, 3, 1855.

45. *Pittsburgh Daily Gazette*, January 17, 1856; Dockets of the Supreme Court (M216), Reel 2, 3613, RG 267, NA; *U.S. Reports* 60:96–107, and 61:402–3. Manny died two weeks after the ruling.

46. Flower, "McCormick v. Manny," 1–7, WHS.

47. Ibid., 9–12.

48. Ibid., 16–17; A. E. H. Johnson statement and Flower to Salem G. Pattison, April 29, 1903, Flower Collection, WHS.

49. *Washington Star*, March 21, 1903; *Washington Post*, March 21, 1903; *U.S. Reports* 61:408–12. Hinchliff, "Lincoln and the 'Reaper Case,'" 364–65, treats Wood's story as a hoax "bought and paid for" by Flower, whom he accused of falsifying other evidence in his Stanton biography.

50. *OR*, Series 2, 5:251–52, 354, 368, 400–403, 413, 488–91.

51. *Steubenville Daily Herald*, May 12, 1855; *Union Cemetery*, 1–2; EMS to "Dear Madam," July, 1849, quoted in Wolcott, 114–15; EMS to Ellen Hutchison, January 4, February 13, 1856 (HM 27113 and 27114), HL.

52. EMS to Ellen Hutchison, February 13, 1856 (HM 27114), HL; Dockets of the Supreme Court (M216), Reel 2, 3395, and Minutes of the Supreme Court (M215), Reel 5, 8271, RG 267, NA.

53. *Morning Chronicle*, March 14, 23, 1856; Dockets of the Supreme Court (M216), Reel 2, 3395, RG 267, NA. About this time Stanton was pursuing one action against an indigent Steubenville neighbor on behalf of a corporation (EMS to William R. Prince & Co., February 25, 1856, Montague Collection, NYPL). It bears repeating that the resources of an attorney's clients are bound to vary, but Stanton's had once been mainly poor and had become primarily wealthy, no doubt partly as a result of his effectiveness but perhaps also because of diminishing sympathy for the class with which he once identified.

54. EMS to Ellen, two undated letters and March 10, 14, 1856 (HM 27116 through 27119), HL. The nature of the offense can only be inferred from Stanton's defensive letters; his side of their correspondence reveals only the shadows of their relationship, and most of her surviving letters have apparently passed into the hands of unknown descendants.

55. Burlingame and Ettlinger, *Hay Diary*, 37; "An Iowa Woman in Washington," 85–86. Days before his wedding, for instance, Stanton wrote a gratuitously flattering letter to Supreme Court Justice McLean: EMS to McLean, June 21, 1856, McLean Papers, LC.

56. *Pittsburgh Daily Gazette*, June 27, 1856; *True American*, July 2, 1856; James A. Hutchison to "Dear Little Daughter," June 27, 1856, and EMS to Ellen, February 25, 1858, GTS, LSU; Wolcott, 128. Hyman, 70, mistakenly locates the wedding at the Hutchison home, naming another minister.

CHAPTER 5

1. *CG*, 33rd Cong., 1st sess., 221–22, 275–82; Niven, *Chase Papers*, 2:382, 389.

2. U.S. House, *Howard Report*, 829–1187.

3. *CG*, 34th Cong., 1st sess., Appendix, 529–47; U.S. House, *Alleged Assault upon Senator Sumner*; *New York Tribune*, May 23, 1856; *Richmond Enquirer*, June 6, 1856.

4. Palmer, *Sumner Letters*, 1:460–68; *Advertiser*, November 4, 1856. Donald (*Sumner*, 271–73) discounts the accusations of malingering by "later historians of

pronounced antiabolitionist sympathies," yet admits that Sumner's prolonged inca-
pacitation lacked medical explanation and that Republicans "skillfully exploited" it
for party advantage and Sumner's reelection. Hoffer, *The Caning of Charles Sumner*,
73–77, believes Sumner suffered severe injuries, but the doctor who first treated him
did not (*CG*, 34th Cong., 1st sess., 1359–60). Sumner apparently developed an infection from the wounds, and probably suffered a concussion. Barnes, *Medical and
Surgical History of the Rebellion* (7:20–23) lists numerous soldiers who suffered
severe saber wounds to the head, even with cranial fractures, and returned to duty
within weeks or months, but some also died.

5. *Daily Constitutionalist*, September 20, 1856; Samuel J. Reader Diary, July 29–
August 9, 1856, KSHS. In "The Crime Against Sumner," William Gienapp credited
the assault with initiating a tremendous surge in the ranks of the new Republican
Party, a theme he revisited in *The Origins of the Republican Party*.

6. John Harper to "My dear Son," October 16, 1856, HHC; Wolcott, 128; Dockets
of the Supreme Court (M216), Reel 2, 3418, and Minutes of the Supreme Court
(M215), Reel 5, 8478, 8501–11, RG 267, NA; EMS to Alfred Taylor, February 16,
1857, SP.

7. EMS to William Stanton, January 26, 1858 (HM37106), HL; Wainwright,
Fisher Diary, 245; Weld, *A Vacation Tour*, 284, quoted in Brown, "Residence Patterns of Negroes," 78; Adams, *Education*, 44–45.

8. Wolcott, 128–29; *New York Times*, March 23, May 4, June 9, 1857; John P.
Hale to Mason W. Tappan, March 21, 1857, and to Theodore Parker, April 3, 1857,
NHHS.

9. Deed Book J.A.S. 130:45–46, District of Columbia Archives. Harrold, *Gamaliel Bailey*, 191–92, describes Bailey scrambling for loans and liquidating property
in 1856–58.

10. EMS to Alfred Taylor, February 16, March 5, 1857, SP; Lomax, *Diary*, 67;
French, *Journals*, 279–80; *New York Times*, March 6, 1857.

11. Moore, *Works*, 10:114; EMS to Black, March 12, 16, 30, 31, May 14, 1857,
Black Papers, LC; Black to EMS, undated [but March, 1857], SP; EMS to James
Buchanan, April 2, 1858, BPL.

12. *New York Times*, March 7, 1857; Moore, *Works of Buchanan*, 10:106–8; Minutes of the Supreme Court (M215), 8421–30, 8764. For a minute examination of the
case and its consequences see Fehrenbacher, *Dred Scott*.

13. Minutes of the Supreme Court (M215), 8765; *U.S. Reports* 59:436–37.

14. Dockets of the Supreme Court (M216), 3653, 3669; EMS to William L. Hirsch,
November 28, 1857, Lee Kohns Collection, NYPL; EMS to Alfred Taylor, April 5,
1857, SP; EMS to Jeremiah Black, March 31, April 13, 1857, Black Papers, LC.

15. EMS to Alfred Taylor, May 26, 1857, SP; Ellen to EMS, June 10, July 1, 1857,
GTS, LSU. Graves, 201, cites Stanton's grandson, Gideon T. Stanton, for the information that Eleanor was born April 9, but her gravestone records her birth date as
May 9; in the April 13 letter to Black cited above, Stanton relayed Ellen's request that
Black's wife and daughter stop by for the day and stay for dinner, and Ellen would
not likely have made that invitation if she had just delivered four days before, especially since she came down with childbed fever immediately after the birth.

16. EMS to Alfred Taylor, February 16, 1857, SP; EMS to Jeremiah Black, August 25, 1857, Black Papers, LC.

17. EMS to Ellen, September 18, 1857, GTS, LSU.

18. *Cincinnati Enquirer*, August 28, 1857; *Cleveland Plain Dealer*, September 2, 1857; Nevins and Thomas, *Strong Diary*, 2:352–62; *New York Times*, October 14, 1857; *Richmond Enquirer*, October 16, 1857; *Richmond Whig*, November 27, December 18, 25, 1857; *Lynchburg Virginian*, November 23, 1857, February 5, 8, March 17, 18, April 7, June 14, 1858.

19. R. H. Gillett to Black, March 25, 1857, Letters Received, 1818–1870, 4:96, Entry 10, RG 60, NA; Auguste Jouan to Black, May 18, 1857, Black Papers, LC.

20. *U.S. Reports* 61:418–27.

21. EMS to Black, October 26, 1857, Black Papers, LC; EMS to John C. Knox, January 26, 1858, LSU; Black to EMS, November 20, 1857, and John B. S. Dunstry to EMS, January 18, "1857" [1858], January 26, 1858, all in Box 4, Correspondence on Land Claims, Entry 27, RG 60, NA. Hyman, 75, cites a letter from Lewis Hutchison to Mary Hutchison, October 7, 1857, for the Stantons' October trip; the whereabouts of that letter is not now known, but on May 1, 1859, Stanton wrote that he had last visited Pittsburgh eighteen months previously (EMS to Black, Black Papers, LC).

22. *CG*, 35th Cong., 1st sess., 5–8, 14–19; *National Intelligencer*, December 12, 1857.

23. Nevins and Thomas, *Strong Diary*, 2:376; EMS to Douglas, December 11, 1857, University of Chicago.

24. *New York Times*, February 17, 1858; EMS to Black, February 17, 1858, Black Papers, LC; U.S. House, *Expenditures on Account of Private Land Claims*, 3.

25. EMS to Black, July 1, 1859, Box 6, Correspondence on Land Claims, Entry 27, RG 60, NA; EMS to Ellen, March 15, 1858, GTS, LSU; U.S. House, *Expenditures on Account of Private Land Claims*, 2, 10; EMS to Black, February 19, 1858, Black Papers, LC; *Defence of Lieutenant H. N. Harrison*, 3–21; *Registry of the Commissioned and Warrant Officers of the Navy*, 20.

26. EMS to Ellenore Adams Hutchison, February 20, 1858, HHC; EMS to Ellen, February "29" [20], 21, 1858, GTS, LSU. The February 20 letter to Ellen from New York is misdated February 29 in Gideon T. Stanton's transcription of his grandfather's letters.

27. EMS to Ellen, February 21–25, 1857, GTS, LSU; EMS to Watson, March 2, 1858, quoted in Flower, 68.

28. EMS to Ellen, February 25–27, 1858, GTS, LSU.

29. Ibid., February 28, 1858; *ORN*, 25:756.

30. EMS to Ellen, March 3–4, 1858, GTS, LSU

31. EMS to Watson, March 10, 1858, quoted in Flower, 68–69; EMS to Ellen, March 5–7, 12, 16, 1858, GTS, LSU; U.S. House, *Expenditures on Account of Private Land Claims*, 10.

32. EMS to Ellen, March 8–12, 1858, GTS, LSU.

33. Ibid., March 13–19, 21, 1858; EMS to Peter Watson, March 19, 1858, quoted in Flower, 69.

34. EMS to Ellen, March 21, 1858, GTS, LSU.

35. Black to EMS, April 27, 1858, quoted and reprinted in facsimile in Gorham, 1:55–56. Like Stanton's diary and other manuscripts that Gorham used in his 1899 biography, the original of this letter seems to have disappeared.

36. EMS to Ellen, April 11, 1858, GTS, LSU. At the December term of 1857 alone, the Supreme Court handled thirty-six appeals of decisions in land cases from the District Court of Northern California: Dockets of the Supreme Court (M216), Reel 2, 3715–3876, RG 267, NA.

37. EMS to Ellen, April 4, 11, 1858, GTS, LSU; EMS to Black, April 16, 1858, Harrison to Black, June 4, 1858, and Buchanan to Black, June 20, 1858, all in the Black Papers, LC; EMS to James Buchanan, July 19, August 4, 1858, HSP.

38. EMS to Black, April 16, 1858, Black Papers, LC; U.S. House, *Expenditures on Account of Private Land Claims*, 1–3; 32; EMS to Ellen, April 18, 21, 26, 1858, GTS, LSU; EMS diary, April 27, 1858, quoted in Gorham, 1:63; EMS to Pablo de la Guerra, June 3, 15, 1858, FAC667 (938), HL; EMS to Peter Watson, May 2, 1858, quoted in Flower, 70–71; EMS to James Buchanan, July 19, 1858, HSP.

39. James F. Shunk to Black, November 14, 1860, LC. Bancroft, *History of California*, 6:533, conceded that bribery was often used "to oil the machinery of government and overcome the Mexican tendency to delay." Both Smith (*The Enemy Within*, 82) and Summers (*The Plundering Generation*, 70, 71, 159–61) comment on the corruption for which California was then infamous.

40. EMS to Ellen, April 26, 1858, GTS, LSU; *"New Almaden,"* 468; Williams, *Cases Argued*, 362; Black to EMS, July 19, August 4, 1858, Box 6, Correspondence on Land Claims, Entry 27, RG 60, NA. For the association of Stanton and especially Black with Eldredge and the Quicksilver Mining Company, see William Bond to Black, November 25, December 16, 1861, and Eldredge to Black, April 6, 1862, Black Papers, LC.

41. EMS to Ellen, April 26, 1858, GTS, LSU; Robert C. Wright to Faxon, October, 1855, Western Americana Collection, Yale; EMS to Faxon, June 20, 1859, Gratz Papers, HSP.

42. E. W. Burr to Black, November 19, 1857, Box 1, F. H. Banks to Jacob Thompson and Black, March 18, 1858, and Montgomery Blair to Black, April 2, 1858, both in Box 2, and all three in Correspondence on Land Claims, Entry 27, RG 60, NA; U.S. House, *Expenditures on Account of Private Land Claims*, 3–4, 30–32; 38–39. Gorham (1:53) credited Stanton with drafting those congressional bills, but in fact Stanton advised Black that the prosecution of fraud probably could not be "maintained." Black to EMS, August 4, 1858, Letters Received, 5:12, Entry 10, RG 60, NA.

43. EMS diary, April 27, 1858, quoted in Gorham, 1:63; J. S. Black to Jacob Thompson, March 19, 1859, Box 4, and R. C. Hopkins to Black [presumably], "October, 1859," Box 9, Correspondence on Land Claims, Entry 27, RG 60, NA; Eighth Census of the U.S. (M653), Reel 67, 498, RG 29, NA.

44. *Daily Alta California*, July 15, August 7, 1858.

45. Ibid., August 1, 6, 21, September 21, 25, October 8, 15, 1858; U.S. House, *Expenditures on Account of Private Land Claims*, 33. In some cases, and perhaps many, squatting Forty-Niners used the Board of Land Commissioners to swindle Mexican

settlers who had occupied their property well before the war with the United States. One sympathetic Yankee exposed that land-grabbing in a San Francisco newspaper, and many suspected that the federal government pursued a similar strategy, hoping to seize the most valuable property in the national interests. See *Daily Alta California*, March 19, July 4, 1858, and Bancroft, *History of California*, 6:535–36.

46. Oella Stanton Wright to Ellen, June 24, 1860, HM27123, HL; EMS to Black, August 1, 1858, Black Papers, LC; EMS to Ellen, May 7, August 17, [September 5], 1858, GTS, LSU; EMS to Watson, May 2 and September 3, 1858, quoted in Flower, 70–71.

47. EMS to Peter Watson, August 4, 1858, CHC; Black to EMS, August 18, 1858, Letters Received, 5:24, Entry 10, RG 60, NA; U.S. House, *Expenditures on Account of Private Land Claims*, 33; EMS to Ellen, September 19, 1858, GTS, LSU.

48. *New York World*, August 17, 1863; Black to EMS, July 19, August 4, 1858, Letters Received, 5:1, 11–12, Entry 10, RG 60, NA.

49. *Daily Alta California*, July 15, August 19, 20, September 1, October 31, November 7, 1858; U.S. House, *Expenditures on Account of Private Land Claims*, 7.

50. "*New Almaden*," 338; Halleck to Ethan Allen Hitchcock, March 31, 1862, LC.

51. EMS to Edmund Randolph, February 22, 1861, Letters Received, 6:572–73, Entry 10, RG 60, NA; Minutes of the Supreme Court (M215), Reel 3, 4913, RG 267, NA.

52. *Daily Alta California*, February 2, 1859; *Daily Evening Bulletin*, May 1, 1858, and February 4, 1859, quoted in Graves, 238. Bancroft repeated a San Francisco judge's allegation that the attorney general who tried to undermine this Supreme Court challenge held an interest in the Santillian grant, apparently through the Philadelphia Land Company, which bought the claim. See Bancroft, *History of California*, 7:243–44; *New York World*, August 17, 1863; E. W. Burr to Black, November 19, 1857, Box 1, Correspondence on Land Claims, Entry 27, RG 60, NA; *U.S. Reports* 64:341–53. Black's biographer deemed Bancroft biased (Brigance, *Black*).

53. *Daily Alta California*, July 14, 1863; *Daily Evening Bulletin*, July 23, 1863, quoted in Ascher, "Lincoln's Administration and the New Almaden Scandal," 47. Hyman, 79, cited "rumors" that Stanton "had been counsel for a company which held dubious title to lands he was now examining," and "had profited from this connection." Hyman seemed to confirm those rumors by admitting that Stanton had "severed this affiliation before leaving the East." He did not name the client or cite a source for any of his assertions, and he may have been referring to the Santillian claim, Stanton's connection to James Eldredge and the Quicksilver Mining Company, or yet another conflict of interest. Ascher's 1936 article somewhat clarifies the confusing details of the New Almaden case and follows the questionable involvement of Stanton and Black. Smith, *The Enemy Within*, 3–4, described the growing intensity of public apprehension over government corruption, especially during the Buchanan and Lincoln administrations; Summers, *The Plundering Generation*, 239–60, devoted an entire chapter to "The Buchaneers," but conceded, 297, that corruption in the Grant administration equaled that in Buchanan's.

54. Montgomery Blair, who served in Lincoln's cabinet with Stanton, believed at least as early as 1861 that Stanton had taken a bribe (Beale, *Welles Diary*, 1:56–57; Blair

to Gideon Welles, February 25, 1873, Welles Papers, CHS). Summers, *The Plundering Generation*, 91–92, 94–95, explains how the attitude of that era blurred the line between outright bribery and overly generous compensation for goods or services rendered.

55. EMS to Ellen, November 4, 1858, GTS, LSU; *Daily Alta California*, November 7, 9, 10, 1858; *Philadelphia Press*, August 20, 1883. To prove that the mine belonged to the U.S. government, the Castillero mineral claim had to be discredited, because a mineral claim did not require ownership of the land. If the Berreyesa and Larios land grants could not be proven fraudulent as well, they had to be eliminated by a boundary challenge. The mineral deposits appeared to lie beneath the Berreyesa grant, favoring Barron, Forbes & Co., but the Supreme Court finally decreed that the mine lay within the Larios grant, controlled by the Fossat-Quicksilver interests. Judge Black's role involved great personal profit and apparent silence about (and thus tolerance of) Eldredge's boasted bribery.

56. EMS to Ellen, November 4, 1858, GTS, LSU.

57. Ibid., ca. November 20, 1858, January 14, 1859; EMS to Lewis Hutchison, January 5, 1859, HHC; *American Union*, February 9, 1859. Lewis Hutchison Stanton was born January 12, 1860 (Ernest Lee Jahncke Jr. membership application no. 74014, National Society of the Sons of the American Revolution).

58. In commenting on the rampant corruption in (and over) California, Summers, *The Plundering Generation*, 161, noted that—before Stanton traveled there—it appeared to inspire the first law prohibiting bribery and forbidding department officers from aiding or representing those pursuing claims against the United States. Smith. *The Enemy Within*, 82, remarked that "California society seemed, to many Northerners, to be 'wanting in terms of order and public virtue,' especially among its financial elite."

CHAPTER 6

1. *New-Yorker*, July 7, 1838; *National Intelligencer*, March 28, 1857; *New York Times*, March 2, 1859; *Harper's Weekly*, March 12, 1859; J. B. Gray to James Buchanan, July 13, 1859, and J. S. Black to Louis Janin, September 19, 1859, both in Box 2, Correspondence on Land Claims, Entry 27, RG 60, NA.

2. *Washington Evening Star*, February 28, March 2, 1859; *New York Times*, March 2, 3, 1859; *Harper's Weekly*, March 12, 1859. Jackson Square was then occasionally called Lafayette Square, as it is now exclusively known.

3. *Frank Leslie's*, March 12, 1859; *Harper's Weekly*, March 19, April 9, 1859.

4. *Washington Evening Star*, February 28, 1859; *Harper's Weekly*, March 19, 1859; *New York Times*, March 2, 1859; Nevins and Thomas, *Strong Diary*, 2:438; French, *Journals*, 308–9.

5. *Harper's Weekly*, March 12, 1859; EMS to Matthew [?] G. Upton, March 1, 1859 (HM19272), HL; Supreme Court Minutes, March 4, 1859 (M215), RG 267, NA. Brandt, *The Congressman Who Got Away with Murder*, 154, speculated that Buchanan himself might have asked Stanton to serve.

6. *New York Times*, April 8, 1859; *Harper's Weekly*, April 16, 1859; *New York Tribune*, April 5, 1859; *Washington Evening Star*, March 16, 1859.

7. *New York Herald*, March 1, 1859; *Harper's Weekly*, March 12, 26, 1859; *Washington Evening Star*, March 2, 1859; *New York Tribune*, April 4, 1859.

8. Nevins and Thomas, *Strong Diary*, 2:440–41; *Washington Evening Star*, March 2, 1859; Aldrich Diary, April 9, 26, 1859, AAS.

9. *Washington Evening Star*, March 21, 24, 25, 1859.

10. Ibid., March 16, 1859.

11. *New York Times*, April 4, 1859.

12. *Washington Evening Star*, April 5, 6, 7, 1859; *New York Tribune*, April 7, 1859; *New York Times*, April 7, 1859.

13. *New York Tribune*, April 7, 1859; *New York Times*, April 7, 1859.

14. *Washington Evening Star*, April 5, 1859; *New York Times*, April 8, 1859.

15. *Washington Evening Star*, April 7, 8, 1859; *New York Tribune*, April 8, 1859; *New York Times*, April 8, 1859.

16. DeFontaine, *Trial*, 23–24; *New York Times*, April 9, 1859; *Baltimore Patriot*, April 27, 1859.

17. *Washington Evening Star*, April 9, 11, 1859; *Harper's Weekly*, April 23, 1859; *New York Times*, April 12, 1859; *New York Tribune*, April 5, 8, 15, 1859. Stanton is usually credited with making this "temporary insanity" defense—ostensibly for the first time in an American courtroom. Yet Brady and Graham appear to have decided to use it in the Sickles case, and the same defense had been made in that very courtroom a year before (*Washington Evening Star*, April 14, 15, 1859; *New York Tribune*, April 5, 15, 16, 1859).

18. *New York Times*, April 13, 15, 1859; *Harper's Weekly*, April 23, 1859.

19. DeFontaine, *Trial*, 44–46; *Washington Evening Star*, April 13, 1859; *New York Times*, April 13, 1859; *Harper's Weekly*, April 23, 1859.

20. *Washington Evening Star*, April 14, 1859; *New York Times*, April 15, 1859; *New York Tribune*, April 15, 1859; *Harper's Weekly*, April 23, 1859.

21. *New York Times*, April 15, 1859; *New York Tribune*, April 15, 1859; *Washington Evening Star*, April 7, 14, 15, 1859; *Harper's Weekly*, April 16, 1859.

22. *New York Tribune*, April 15, 1859; *Harper's Weekly*, April 16, 1859.

23. DeFontaine, *Trial*, 66–70; *Washington Evening Star*, April 18, 19, 1859; *New York Times*, April 15, 1859.

24. *Washington Evening Star*, April 21, 1859; DeFontaine, *Trial*, 81–85. Ould also tried to call the manager of Barnum's Hotel in Baltimore, who had brought the hotel register for January 16 bearing the signatures of Daniel E. Sickles and a "Mrs. Sickles" who was not Teresa, but Judge Crawford refused to allow his testimony (*Harper's Weekly*, May 14, 1859, with a *Baltimore Exchange* citation of uncertain date; DeFontaine, *Trial*, 85–86).

25. French, *Journal*, 312; Wainwright, *Fisher Diary*, 323; Nevins and Thomas, *Strong Diary*, 2:448.

26. *Washington Evening Star*, April 23, 25, 1859; *New York Tribune*, April 25, 1859; DeFontaine, *Trial*, 89–90.

27. DeFontaine, *Trial*, 91–93; *Washington Evening Star*, April 23, 25, 26, 1859; *New York Tribune*, April 25, 1859.

28. DeFontaine, *Trial*, 95–100; *New York Times*, April 26, 1859. Stanton's digression from the temporary insanity plea further discredits the notion that he suggested this strategy.

29. DeFontaine, *Trial*, 103–6; *New York Times*, April 26, 1859; *New York Tribune*, April 28, 1859.

30. *Washington Evening Star*, April 26, 1859; *New York Times*, April 27, 1859; *Harper's Weekly*, May 7, 1859; Aldrich Diary, April 26, 1859, AAS; Baltimore *Patriot*, April 27, 1859, quoted in Swanberg, *Sickles the Incredible*, 66.

31. EMS to Ogden Hoffman, April 27, 1859 (HM19008), HL; EMS to Black, May 1, 1859, Black Papers, LC.

32. EMS to William Stanton, May 18, 26, 1859 (HM37022, HM37023), HL; EMS to Eben Faxon, June 20, 1859, Gratz Collection, HSP; *Pennsylvania Reports* 32:345; EMS to John F. James, June 29, 1859, Stuart Collection, LC; Reports on *U.S. v. Hiram Grime, U.S. v. Ellen E. White*, and *U.S. v. Heirs of José R. Berreyesa*, all dated July 6, 1859, Box 6, Correspondence on Land Claims, Entry 27, RG 60, NA.

33. EMS to Eben Faxon, June 20, 1859, Gratz Collection, HSP; EMS to Black, July 1, 1859, Box 6, and Black's approval of Stanton's fee, September 3, 1859, Box 5, Correspondence on Land Claims, Entry 27, RG 60, NA; "J.A.S.," 169:183–84, 185:136–37, District of Columbia Archives.

34. EMS to Lewis Hutchison, October 27, 1859, Lee Kohns Collection, NYPL; EMS to "My Dear Son," October 31, 1859, GTS, LSU; EMS to Dr. William Addison, October 27, 1859. HHC.

35. Oella Stanton Wright to Ellen Stanton, June 24, 1860 (HM27123), HL; Plat of Square No. 248, L&B 859–1852, RG 23, NA; Eighth Census of the U.S. (M653), Reel 103, 26, RG 29, NA. This description is based on heavily retouched photos in Gorham, 1:188, and Flower, 24. Lot numbers on the deed and plat do not match, so the exact location is uncertain, but the house sat toward the middle of the current 1300 block of K Street NW, on the north side, where a complex called One Franklin Square now stands.

36. Reynolds, *John Brown*, presents the raid and its leader in a somewhat glorified light.

37. Wolcott, 146; Supreme Court Minutes, January 23–April 24, 1860 (M215), RG 267, NA; EMS to Dr. William Addison, October 27, 1859, HHC.

38. EMS to Mason & "Estess" [spelling uncertain], May 2, 1860, LSU.

39. EMS to Lewis Hutchison, November 30, 1859, HHC; *U.S. Reports* 64:117–32, 435–38.

40. EMS to William Wilkins, January 25, 1860, HHC; Oella Stanton Wright to Ellen Stanton, June 24, 1860 (HM 27123), HL.

41. Supreme Court Minutes, January 23–April 24, 1860 (M215), RG 267, NA.

42. *CG*, 36th Cong., 1st sess., 995, 997–98; EMS to Ellen, May 9, 1860, GTS, LSU; EMS to Lewis Hutchison, April 13, 1860, HHC.

43. Moore, *Works of Buchanan*, 10:104, 433; Buchanan to EMS, June 10, 1860, SP.

44. U.S. House, *Covode Report*, 1, 291–304.

45. EMS to Samuel Medary, June 4, 1860, Brown University; Wolcott, 147; EMS to Charles Shaler, July 2, 1860, quoted in Flower, 80; Black, "Mr. Black to Mr. Wilson," 263; "To the Public," Reel 26, Black Papers, LC; John F. Oliver, quoted in Gorham, 1:79; *Springfield Republican*, January 18, 1862; *New York Sun*, February 28, 1892.

46. "To the Public," Reel 26, Black Papers, LC.

47. Buchanan to Harriet Lane, January 16, "1861" [1862], Buchanan-Johnston Papers, LC.

48. Phillips to EMS, July 27, 1860, SP; EMS to Phillips, February 21, 1861, and Phillips, "A Summary of the Principle Events of My Life," 44, Phillips Papers, LC; Beale, *Welles Diary*, 1:355. Stanton helped free Phillips's wife from arrest early in the war.

49. James E. Harvey to Black, October 2, 1870, LC; *New York Herald*, February 4, 1865; Montgomery Blair to Robert Tyler, ca. 1865, "Original Letters," 123.

50. Wolcott, 129–30; EMS to James A. Hutchison, September 7, 1860, HHC; EMS to "My Dear Son," October 31, 1859, GTS, LSU; ELS to Eben Sturges, May 21, 1870, Kenyon.

51. EMS to William Stanton, September 29, 1860 (HM37027), HL; Buchanan to EMS, October 11, 1860, SP; Moore, *Works of Buchanan*, 11:2; Nevins and Thomas, *Strong Diary*, 3:45.

52. Jacob Thompson to Jeremiah Black, October 10, 1870, LC; John C. Ropes notes on his 1869 interview with Stanton, Woodman Papers, MHS.

53. Buchanan to Harriet Lane, November 4, 1860, Buchanan-Johnston Papers, LC; Wilson, "Jeremiah S. Black and Edwin M. Stanton," 468–69; John C. Ropes's notes on his 1869 interview with Stanton, Woodman Papers, MHS; Jacob Thompson to Jeremiah Black, October 10, 1870, LC. Some of Stanton's flattering self-portrayals are described in more detail in Chapter 7.

54. Moore, *Works of Buchanan*, 11:20–23.

55. "To the Public" memo, Black Papers, LC.

56. *Constitution*, December 1, 1860; William G. Reed to Black, December 1, 1860, G. W. Woodward to Black, December 10, 1860, and Caleb Cushing to Black, December 11, 1860, LC; Moore, *Works of Buchanan*, 11:12–23, 62, 75; *New York Times*, December 5, 10, 1859; *New York Evening Post*, December 10, 1860.

57. John C. Ropes notes on his 1869 interview with Stanton, Woodman Papers, MHS; Wilson, "Jeremiah S. Black and Edwin M. Stanton," 468–69.

58. *New York Times*, December 8, 11, 1860; Moore, *Works of Buchanan*, 11:57–63.

59. Black, "Mr. Black to Mr. Wilson," 260–61; James Buchanan to Harriet Lane, January 16, "1861" [1862], Buchanan-Johnston Papers, LC; Humphrey H. Leavitt to EMS, October 3, 1865, SP; John C. Ropes notes on his 1869 interview with Stanton, Woodman Papers, MHS.

CHAPTER 7

1. Black, "Mr. Black to Mr. Wilson," 261; Shunk to Black, November 10, 14, 23, 1860, Black Papers, LC; Black to Shunk, December 12, 1860, 6:504–7, Letters Received, Entry 10, RG 60, NA.

2. *CG*, 36th Cong., 2nd sess., 159; EMS to Jacob Thompson and P. L. Solomon (three letters), December 24, 1860, 6:509–11, Letters Received, Entry 10, RG 60, NA.

3. *New York Times*, December 24, 25, 1860, February 13, 1861; Moore, *Works of Buchanan*, 11:252. Summers, *The Plundering Generation*, 242–46, did not doubt

Floyd's corruption, although there remains some question about whether he profited personally.

4. *Washington Evening Star*, December 27, 1860; *OR*, 1:89–90; Hunt, "Narrative and Letter of William Henry Trescot," 543–45.

5. Wolcott, 148–49; Burlingame, *With Lincoln in the White House*, 69–70; Moore, *Rebellion Record*, 1:Documents, 10.

6. Wolcott, 149; Nicolay and Hay, *Abraham Lincoln*, 3:73–74; Burlingame, *With Lincoln in the White House*, 69–70.

7. *New York Times*, December 31, 1860; Wolcott, 149; Burlingame, *With Lincoln in the White House*, 70.

8. *The Observer*, February 9, 1862; *New York Herald*, March 4, 1862; Carpenter, *The Inner Life of Abraham Lincoln*, 54–55; Beale, *Welles Diary*, 2:273–74.

9. Jeremiah Black to Augustus Schell, August 6, 1863, James Buchanan to Black, September 25, 1863, and Jacob Thompson to Black, June 7, October 10, 1870, all in Black Papers, LC; Moore, *Works of Buchanan*, 11:84–91, 263, 269; "To the Public" memo, Reel 26, Black Papers, LC. Stanton drafted a reply to Schell, calling the "allegation" (which he had originated) "substantially true." He addressed some points ambiguously, avoiding any assertion that anyone had threatened to resign, but he never sent even that equivocal confirmation (EMS to Schell, October 8, 1863, SP).

10. Moore, *Rebellion Record*, 1:Documents, 10; *OR*, 1:252; Phillips, "Correspondence," 532; Joseph Holt to "My dear Maggie," September 26, 1857, Holt Papers, LC.

11. *OR*, 1:109–10.

12. "Memorandum to the President," undated [but December 30, 1860], Black Papers, LC.

13. Black to Joseph Holt, marked "1861? Feb.?" by a curator, [but clearly December 30, 1860], Holt Papers, LC; *Weekly Press*, September 10, 1883, quoted in Auchampaugh, *James Buchanan and His Cabinet*, 161–63; James F. Shunk to Black, November 23, 1860, and George W. Woodward to Black, December 10, 1860, Black papers, LC. By now Black had borrowed money from President Buchanan's nephew, among others (James Buchanan Jr. to Black, November 13, 1860, Black Papers, LC).

14. *Press*, August 11, 1881, September 10, 1883, quoted in Auchampaugh, *Buchanan and His Cabinet*, 161–63; "Memorandum for the President," Buchanan Papers, HSP and Black Papers, LC; EMS to William Robinson, December 30, 1860, quoted in Flower, 90–91; Black to EMS, September 3, 1864, Black Papers, LC.

15. Holt to James Buchanan Henry, May 26, 1884, in Moore, *Works of Buchanan*, 11:86; *Press*, September 17, 1883, quoted in Auchampaugh, *Buchanan and His Cabinet*, 164.

16. *New York Times*, December 31, 1860; Phillips, "Correspondence," 530; Moore, *Works of Buchanan*, 11:86–87.

17. *OR*, 1:115–18, 120–25; *Press*, August 4, 1881, quoted in Auchampaugh, *Buchanan and His Cabinet*, 165.

18. Holt's purported description of a quailing Buchanan, posthumously published in Gorham, 1:158–59, is altogether inconsistent with the respectful and even complimentary account Holt gave in Moore, *Works of Buchanan*, 11:84–91.

19. *New York Times*, December 31, 1860; Wilson, "Jeremiah S. Black and Edwin M. Stanton," 464–65; Bernitt, "Two Manuscripts of Gideon Welles," 589; Thurlow Weed to Abraham Lincoln, January 10, 1861, and Seward to Lincoln, December 29, 1860, ALP.

20. *McCormick Extension Case*, 347, cited in Graves, 309.

21. Brigance, *Jeremiah Sullivan Black*, 74; James Buchanan to Harriet Lane, January 16, "1861" [1862], Buchanan-Johnston Papers, LC. In the year before he became attorney general Stanton had appeared in at least forty cases before the Supreme Court, and he had represented the U.S. government in all but four of those cases (Supreme Court Minutes, December 26, 1859 through December 26, 1860 [M215], RG 267, NA).

22. *OR*, 1:114, 119, 128–32.

23. Ibid., 9–10, 120; *ORN*, 4:220–21.

24. *Atlas and Argus*, January 11, 1861; *New York Times*, January 12, 1861; H. P. Laird to Jeremiah Black, January 16, 1861, Black Papers, LC; Nevins and Thomas, *Strong Diary*, 3:88–89; Wainwright, *Fisher Diary*, 377.

25. *New York Herald*, February 4, 1865. Brown's assertion, quoted by the *Herald* from a Confederate paper, comports with several other recollections of pro-Southern remarks Stanton made during the secession crisis that were recorded during and after the war.

26. *New York Times*, January 9–12, 1861; *OR*, 1:252; *National Intelligencer*, March 2, 1861; *Philadelphia Inquirer*, March 6, 1861; Phillips, "Correspondence," 532.

27. Wilson, "Edwin M. Stanton and Jeremiah S. Black," 467–68; Dawes, "Washington the Winter before the War," 163; Beale, *Welles Diary*, 1:355.

28. EMS to James A. Hutchison, January 15, 1861, HHC; EMS to Chase, January 23, 1861, HSP; Charles Francis Adams to John Andrew, January 4, 1861, MHS; R. C. Weightman to Samuel Cooper, February 6, 1861, Frank B. Schaeffer to Weightman, February 9, 1861, Weightman to Cooper, February 14, 1861, and Charles P. Stone to Lorenzo Thomas, February 26, 1861, all in Letters Received (M619), RG 94, NA. The prevalence of disloyalty among District of Columbia residents was wildly exaggerated. In a study of military service by district residents, Whyte, "Divided Loyalties," 111, 121, found that only about 400 served the Confederacy in some capacity, while 16,872 joined the Union army (including U.S. Colored Troops).

29. Black, "Senator Wilson and Edwin M. Stanton," 822–23, and "Mr. Black to Mr. Wilson," 262; Sumner to John Andrew, January 26, 28, 1861, MHS; John H. Clifford and Stephen H. Phillips to Andrew, January 30, 1861, NYHS; Phillips to Horace Gray, January 31, 1861, Gray Papers, LC.

30. Black to Buchanan, January 22, 1861, Black Papers, LC; Benjamin to S. L. M. Barlow, December 9, 1860, HL; *Richmond Examiner*, December 25, 1860; Buchanan to Horatio King, April 21, 1866, King Papers, LC; *OR*, 51(1):312, 314. Black's cautionary advice of January 22 is still consistent with his later admission that "no tangible evidence" of a plot to seize Washington was ever found (Black, "Mr. Black to Mr. Wilson," 268), although he had apparently forgotten his own apprehension about the possibility at the time.

31. *Steubenville Weekly Herald*, January 23, 1861; EMS to John Oliver, January 20, 1861, quoted in Gorham, 180.

32. EMS to McCook, February 4, 1861, McCook Family Papers, LC.

33. Seward to EMS, February 16 [1861], SP.

34. *Washington Evening Star*, February 23, 1861; *National Intelligencer*, February 26, 1861; *Illinois State Register*, February 27, 1861; Black, "Senator Wilson and Edwin M. Stanton," 813.

35. Assorted correspondence, Letters Received, 6:553–76, 7:1–32, Entry 10, RG 60, NA; Shunk to EMS, January 17, 1861, Box 6, Correspondence on Land Claims, Entry 27, RG 60, NA; EMS to Della Torre, March 4, 1861, SP. The original of Della Torre's letter, at Brown University, was miscataloged in 2011 as being addressed to "P. D. Lowe."

36. Heintzelman Diary, March 4, 1861, LC; French, *Journals*, 348; *CWL* 4:262–71.

37. French, *Journals*, 348–49; EMS to Della Torre, March 4, 1861, SP; Moore, *Works of Buchanan*, 11:156. John Dix identified Ould's home as their meeting place the night of March 4 in a March 14 letter to Buchanan (Moore, *Works of Buchanan*, 11:168–69).

38. Anderson to Samuel Cooper, February 28, 1861, and Holt to Lincoln, with Scott's endorsement, March 5, 1861, ALP. Over the next dozen years Holt would spend much time preparing personal defenses against explicit and implicit accusations of malfeasance, confidently declaring himself fully vindicated in each instance; his March 5 letter to Lincoln foreshadows that defensive pattern.

39. EMS to Buchanan, March 10, 1861, HSP; EMS to Lincoln, March 6, 1861, ALP; Beale, *Bates Diary*, 176–77.

40. *New York Times*, September 7, 1865; Moore, *Works of Buchanan*, 11:178.

41. Beale, *Welles Diary*, 1:56–57; Meneely, "Three Manuscripts of Gideon Welles," 492; Montgomery Blair to Gideon Welles, February 25, 1873, Welles Papers, CHS. Welles, whose diary and correspondence with Blair reveals the charge of bribe-taking, later turned intensely hostile to Stanton, and Blair came to despise him as well, but the accusation was apparently not the fruit of those animosities: it arose in a cabinet meeting in the spring of 1861, before Welles knew Stanton, and before Blair grew to hate him.

42. EMS to Dix, March 16, 19, 1861, Dix Papers, Columbia; EMS to Buchanan, March 12, 14, 16 (two letters), April 3, 10, 11, 12, 1861, Buchanan Papers, HSP.

43. Caleb Smith to R. W. Thompson, April 16, 1861, LFFC; Beale, *Diary of Edward Bates*, 178–80; Stephen Hurlbut to Lincoln, March 27, 1861, and Gustavus Fox to Lincoln, March 28, 1861, ALP. Thurlow Weed had commented to Lincoln on the *Star of the West* incident "arousing the whole North" (January 10, 1861, ALP), and Lincoln himself could not have missed that effect.

44. Montgomery Meigs Diary, April 2, 3, 1861, LC; *ORN*, 4:248–49.

45. Horatio Taft Diary, April 5–10, 1861, LC; Burlingame, *With Lincoln in the White House*, 33; EMS to Dix, April 8, 1861, Dix Papers, Columbia.

46. Horatio Taft Diary, April 13, 1861, LC; *OR*, 1:245; *ORN*, 4:249–50.

47. *OR*, Series 3, 1:67–70, 76, 79–83, 114. Six governors refused; two replied equivocally.

48. EMS to Dix, March 16, 19, April 8, 1861, Dix Papers, Columbia; EMS to James Hutchison, April 15, 1861, HHC.

49. Horatio Taft Diary, April 16–25, 1861, LC; *Philadelphia Inquirer*, April 19, 1861; *OR*, 2:7–21; David Creamer Diary, June–July, 1861, Maryland Historical Society.

50. Moore, *Works of Buchanan*, 11:190–91; Horatio Taft Diary, January 9, April 8, 9, 21–23, 1861, LC; EMS to Edwin L. Stanton, May 1, 1861, quoted in Hyman, 122; EMS to Dix, April 23, 1861, quoted in Gorham, 1:213; French, *Journals*, 351–52.

51. Moore, *Works of Buchanan*, 11:190–91, 193–94; Duncan, *Shaw Letters*, 75–76, 79–82; *OR*, Series 3, 1:165; T. Y. Johnson to EMS, April 28, 1861, SP.

52. Moore, *Works of Buchanan*, 11:190–91; Jeremiah Black to EMS, August 12, 1861, SP.

53. EMS to Horatio King, March 15, 1861, King Papers, LC; EMS to Buchanan, June 8, 12, 20, 1861, HSP; EMS to Cameron, May 29, 1861, Lincoln Memorial University; EMS to Chase, June 9, 1861, HSP.

54. Moore, *Works of Buchanan*, 11:199–200; Supreme Court Minutes, December 16, 1861 (M215), RG 267, NA; *New York Times*, July 18, August 27–29, 1861; Moore, *Rebellion Record*, 2: Diary, 29, 50, and Documents, 297–303; Holt to Abraham Lincoln, October 29, 1861, ALP; P. H. Watson to Holt, March 14, 1862, Box 4, Holt Papers, HL.

55. Order in Stanton's hand dated October 11, 1861, SP; Winfield Scott to EMS, October 15, 1861, SP; EMS to Joseph Holt, January 29, 1861, Holt Papers, HL.

56. Memo dated November 21, 1861, signed by Simon Cameron but in the hand of EMS, SP; EMS to Jeremiah Black, February 19, 1858, Black Papers, LC.

57. EMS to Dix, June 11, 1861, quoted in both Gorham, 1:217–18 and Flower, 110–11; EMS to Buchanan, July 26, 1861, HSP.

58. Moore, *Works of Buchanan*, 11:190–91; EMS to Buchanan, July 26, 1861, HSP; EMS to Dix, June 11, 1861, quoted in Gorham, 1:218; EMS to John Oliver, June 29, 1861, SP.

59. *National Intelligencer*, September 10, 1861; *Messenger*, September 10, 1861; *Pioneer and Democrat*, September 25, 1861. This incident is described in both Imholte, *The First Volunteers*, 60–69, and Moe, *The Last Full Measure*, 68–72.

60. ELS to Eben Sturges, August 19, 1861, Edwin L. Stanton file, Kenyon.

61. *OR*, Series 2, 2:237; Eugenia Phillips Journal, Phillips Family Papers, September 10, 12, 16, 1861, LC.

62. *OR*, 2:763, 766, 5:639; Burlingame and Ettlinger, *Hay Diary*, 28–29; Zachariah Chandler to "My dear Wife," October 27, 1861, LC; Sears, *McClellan Papers*, 113–18.

63. EMS to "My dear Sister," March 24, 1862, VFM, OHS. The Stanton monument on Oak Hill Cemetery records this child's birthdate as October 17, 1861.

64. Beale, *Bates Diary*, 201–2, 215–17; Sears, *McClellan Papers*, 135; Barlow to GBM, November 18, 1861, to EMS, November 18, 21, 1861, and to August Belmont, January 17, 1862, Letterbook 7, Barlow Papers, HL; memo dated November 21, 1861, SP.

65. William Bond to Jeremiah Black, November 25, 1861, Black Papers, LC; Supreme Court Minutes, December 23, 24, 1861 (M215), RG 267, NA.

66. Moore, *Works of Buchanan*, 11:227; Buchanan to King, September 18, 1861, quoted in King, *Turning on the Light*, 96.

CHAPTER 8

1. EMS to Wolcott, July 25, 1861, and Wolcott to EMS, August 13, 16, 1861, quoted in Wolcott, 151–52; *New York Times*, August 17, 1861; William P. Fessenden to Cameron, August 28, 1861, Cameron to Fessenden August 29, 1861, and R. M. Blatchford to Cameron, September 6, 1861, all in Cameron Papers, LC.

2. Beale, *Bates Diary*, 203; Wilson, "Jeremiah S. Black and Edward M. Stanton," 470; Welles to Montgomery Blair, September 24, 1870, Welles Papers, LC; Welles memo on the nomination of EMS (WE528), HL.

3. Blair to Andrew, January 7, 1861, MHS.

4. Beale, *Bates Diary*, 226; *CWL*, 5:96–97; Alexander K. McClure to Gideon Welles, September 22, 1870, and Welles to Montgomery Blair, September 24, 1870, both in Welles Papers, LC; Niven, *Chase Papers*, 5:336–38; memo on Chase's letter to Jeremiah Black, July 4, 1870, Schuckers Papers, LC; Blair to Welles, November 24, 1870, CHS; Cameron to Frank Flower, March 6, 1887, Cameron Papers, LC.

5. Niven, *Chase Papers*, 1:325–26. Niven, *Salmon P. Chase*, 284–85, and Stahr, *Seward*, 324–25, recount similar versions of this episode.

6. *New York Times*, July 16, 1865; Cameron to F. P. Blair, February 8, 1862, Princeton; Beale, *Bates Diary*, 226; *CWL*, 5:97; Pease and Randall, *Browning Diary*, 1:524.

7. Malcolm Ives to James Gordon Bennett, January 15, 1862, Bennett Papers, LC. This would have been George Harding's only chance to reintroduce Lincoln and Stanton (Charles Benjamin to Horace White, June 1, 1914, ALPLM); on the credibility of Harding's story see Chapter 4 and the Appendix.

8. Grier to EMS, January 13, 1862, SP; Sam Ward to Seward, January 14, 1862, UR.

9. Chase to Fessenden, January "15" [14], 1862, with Fessenden's endorsement, SP; Niven, *Chase Papers*, 1:326; EMS to Black, undated [but January 14 or 15, 1862], misfiled under 1858, Black Papers, LC; Horatio Taft's Diary, January 13–15, 1862, LC.

10. Wolcott, 154. Cabinet officers drew salaries of $8,000 in 1862: Hyman, 137, credits Stanton with private income of over $50,000 a year before joining the cabinet, but the *Philadelphia Inquirer* (December 25, 1869) put the figure more reasonably at $20,000, reflected mostly by California cases that were then petering out.

11. Sears, *McClellan Papers*, 154; McClellan, *Own Story*, 154.

12. Niven, *Chase Papers*, 1:324–26; McClellan, *Own Story*, 155–57; Meigs, "Conduct of the Civil War," 292–93. The January 13 conference is described mainly in memoirs.

13. Malcolm Ives to James Gordon Bennett, January 15, 1862, Bennett Papers, LC; S. L. M. Barlow to GBM, January 25, 1862, Letterbook 7, Barlow Papers, HL.

14. *CG*, 37th Cong., 2nd sess., part 1, 344, and *Senate Executive Journal*, 78; *New York Herald*, January 16, 1862; George Carlisle to Chandler, January 18, 1862, Chandler Papers, LC.

15. "An Iowa Woman in Washington," 65, 67; Nevins, *Wainwright Journals*, 10.

16. Buchanan to "My dear Harriet," November 4, 1860, and January 16, "1861" [1862], Buchanan-Johnston Papers, LC; Buchanan to Horatio King, January 28, 1862, King Papers, LC.

17. Memorandum on the January 19, 1862, meeting with Butler, SP.

18. Simon Cameron to Lorenzo Thomas, January 20, 1862, *Letters Sent by the Secretary of War* (M6), RG 107, NA; Sears, *McClellan Papers*, 154; Sparks, *Patrick Diary*, 32; *Philadelphia Inquirer* and *New York Herald*, January 21, 1862; *RJCCW*, 1:75–76.

19. *RJCCW*, 1:68; Hyman, 139, describes Wade and Chandler joining Stanton for breakfast at Cameron's house on January 16, citing Cameron's endorsement on a letter of February 2, 1862, in the "Lamon Collection, LC." An October, 2010 search of the Lamon Papers (actually at the Huntington) did not produce that letter, nor is it in the Cameron Papers.

20. EMS to Wade, January 27, 1862, SP; Niven, *Chase* Papers, 3:267; RJCCW, 1:78; *OR*, 5:341.

21. *CG*, 37th Cong., 2nd sess., 130; Stone to Sumner, December 23, 1861, Sumner Papers, Harvard; *RJCCW*, 2:295–306, 319–20, 335–37, 343, 365–67, 370, 384, 387–92, 395, 402.

22. *RJCCW*, 1:79, 2:18, 426–33; Stone to GBM, December 29, 30, 1861, Reel 120, Telegrams, Unbound (M504), RG 107, NA.

23. Allan Pinkerton to GBM, February 6, 1862, McClellan Papers, LC; *RJCCW*, 2:18, 504, 509–10; *OR*, 5:341; *CWL*, 7:285; *CG*, 37th Cong., 2nd sess., 1662–66 and Appendix, 414. Sears, *Controversies and Commanders*, 29–50, exonerates Stone and offers a deservedly scathing assessment of Stanton's role in the general's persecution.

24. *OR*, Series 2, 2:226, 236, 528–29; *New York Herald*, February 11, 1862; *Philadelphia Inquirer*, February 12, 1862.

25. *OR*, Series 2, 2:221–23, 225–38, 249, 250–52, 264–68. Neely, *The Fate of Liberty*, 62, credited Seward with arresting 864 Americans nationwide over the course of ten months; by the late summer of 1862, Stanton was arresting at least 643 in a single month.

26. *OR*, Series 3, 1:964; *CG*, 37th Cong., 2nd sess., 1734; Nevins and Thomas, *Strong Diary*, 3:181, 204, 418, 476.

27. *OR*, Series 3, 2:956; EMS to Frederick Law Olmsted, January 18, 1862, Letters Sent (M6), RG 107, NA; Nevins and Thomas, *Strong Diary*, 3:187, 218, 313–14.

28. EMS to Dana, January 24, February 1, 19, 23, 1862, Dana Papers, LC; EMS to Dana February 7, 1862, Abraham Lincoln Papers, Yale; Dana to Sumner, February 21, 1862, Sumner Papers, Harvard.

29. *New York Times*, October 28, 1861; *CWL*, 5:21–22; commission report, quoted in Wilson, *The Business of Civil War*, 158.

30. Wade to Dana, February 3, 1862, and EMS to Dana, February 1, 1862, Dana Papers, LC; Frémont to EMS, February 10, 1862, SP; Malcolm Ives to James Gordon Bennett, January 27, 1862, Bennett Papers, LC. After six weeks Wade's committee finally said that enough evidence could not be gathered for a comprehensive report, and focused instead on exaggerating Frémont's accomplishments (*RJCCW*, 3:3–279).

31. *OR*, 8:482, 525, 529–30, 551, 829–31; Hunter to EMS, January 29, 1862, SP; Lincoln to EMS, January 31, 1862, McGarrah Collection, LC.

32. Henry Halleck to Elizabeth Halleck, January 15, 1862, CL; *OR*, 8:832–33; McClellan, *Own Story*, 137; Halleck to Ethan Allen Hitchcock, March 31, 1862, Hitchcock Papers, LC.

33. *CG*, 37th Cong., 2nd sess., 386, 444; EMS to Hannibal Hamlin, January 27, 1862, SP; Henry D. Bacon to S. L. M. Barlow, January 16, 1862 (BW Box 39), Barlow Papers, HL. Scott and Tucker were probably the two Cameron "cronies" at whom Buchanan had cringed.

34. Johnson, "Reminiscences," 88–89; Benjamin, "Recollections"; Benjamin to Horace White, June 1, 1914, White Papers, ALPLM.

35. *CG*, 37th Cong., 2nd sess., 50, 89, 240, 334; John W. Forney to EMS, February 1, 1862, with Peter Watson's endorsement, SP; EMS to John L. Graham, June 9, 1862 (GM404), HL; Stewart Van Vliet to S. L. M. Barlow, February 10, 1862 (BW Box 44), Barlow Papers, HL; Samuel Wilkeson to Simon Cameron, February 12, 1862, Cameron Papers, LC; *OR*, Series 3, 1:884; Beale, *Bates Diary*, 231; *Washington Star*, February 18, 1862. For the location of Stanton's office see Benjamin, "Recollections," 760.

36. *CWL*, 5:111, 135.

37. *OR*, 7:546, Series 3, 1:807–8; EMS to Lincoln, January 24, 1862, SP; Scott to EMS, February 1, 12, 1862, SP. Hatch was the brother of Lincoln's close friend Ozias Hatch: Lincoln saved him by appointing a friendly commission that approved his expenditures (*CWL*, 4:461, 5:116, 177); Colonel Hatch was also conspicuous in the overloading of the doomed steamer *Sultana* in 1865: see Marvel, *Tarnished Victory*, 339–40, 419n6.

38. GBM to EMS, "Sunday," SP; Beale, *Bates Diary*, 232. McClellan's note is addressed to "My dear Stanton," so the Sunday in question was probably January 26, 1862: such friendly salutations disappeared from McClellan's letters to Stanton soon thereafter.

39. *OR*, 7:124–25, 159–60, 327–28, 571–72, 617–20, 626–28; *CWL*, 5:135. Simpson, *Ulysses S. Grant*, 110–18, offers a good synopsis of this campaign, which is more thoroughly examined in Cooling, *Forts Henry and Donelson*.

40. *New York Times*, February 12, 1861; Horatio Taft Diary, February 12, 17, 1862, LC; K. Pritchett to Simon Cameron, February 17, 1862, Cameron Papers, LC.

41. Burlingame, *With Lincoln in the White House*, 69–70.

42. *Washington Evening Star*, February 21, 1862; EMS to Dana, February 23, 1862, Dana Papers, LC; S. L. M. Barlow to EMS, February 22 and "29," 1862, Letterbook 7, HL.

43. Deming to Barlow, February 22, 1862 (BW Box 41), Barlow Papers, HL.

44. *RJCCW*, 1:84–85; R. F. Paine to J. W. Irving, February 15, 1862, and Joseph Geiger to Wade, February 20, 1862, both in the Wade Papers, LC.

45. *RJCCW*, 1:84–85; 2:426).

46. Burlingame, *With Lincoln in the White House*, 71; Pease and Randall, *Browning Diary*, 1:530–31; EMS to Oella Stanton Wright, March 24, 1862, Stanton Papers, OHS; EMS to James A. Hutchison, April 30, 1862, HHC.

47. EMS to Scott, February 21, 1862 (two letters), SP; GBM to Scott, February 20, 1862, Reel 12, Telegrams, Bound (M473), RG 107, NA.

48. Beale, *Bates Diary*, 236–37; draft of order, February 25, 1862, SP; *OR*, Series 3, 1:899.

49. Scott to EMS, February 6, 1862, SP. Pound, "The Military Telegraph in the Civil War," and Scheips, "Albert James Myer," first presented the problems caused by Stanton's control of the telegraph service; Burton, in "'No Turning Back,'" 284–91, recognized Stanton's goal of censoring the press and distorting news in favor of the government.

50. *USG*, 16:412 (on changes in the role of the adjutant general).

51. *OR*, 5:41–45.

52. *CWL*, 5:118–25. These plans are detailed in Sears, *To the Gates of Richmond*. 5–16.

53. *OR*, 5:39–40; 7:930–31.

54. Sears, *McClellan Papers*, 191–92; *OR*, 5:727–28.

55. Burlingame, *With Lincoln in the White House*, 72–73; Horace White to Joseph Medill, March 3, 1862 (RY220), Ray Papers, HL.

56. Sumner to John A. Andrew, March 2, 1862, Andrew Papers, MHS; *OR*, 5:48–49, 731; Eby, *Strother Diaries*, 12; Quaife, *Williams Letters*, 62; John Codman Ropes notes on Stanton interview, Woodman Papers, MHS. McClellan cited Stanton's disingenuous remark more than a year later, in an official report that Stanton authorized.

57. *OR*, 7:423–25, 436–37, 8:191–93. Halleck, who oversaw all those victories, chastised McClellan for not appointing an overall commander in the West (*OR*, 8:602).

58. Scott to Stanton, February 17, March 3, 4, 1862, and Johnson's appointment and commission, March 3, 1862, SP.

59. Heintzelman Diary, March 8, 1862, LC; "S. P. H." to Lincoln, March 8, 1862, ALP; Burlingame and Ettlinger, *Hay Diary*, 35; President's General War Order No. 2, SP; CWL, 5:150–51. In 1992 Stephen Sears realized that the "S.P.H." of the March 8 letter was Samuel P. Heintzelman, and obviously not Salmon P. Chase (*To the Gates of Richmond*, 396n3), under whose name it is nevertheless still misfiled.

60. *RJCCW*, 1:85–86, 88; *CWL*, 5:149–50; Horatio Taft Diary, March 8, 1862, LC.

61. Burlingame, *With Lincoln in the White House*, 75; *OR*, 5:739–41.

62. Peter Cooper to EMS, April 24, 1862, SP; Pease and Randall, *Browning Diary*, 1:532–33; Burlingame, *With Lincoln in the White House*, 74; Burlingame and Ettlinger, *Hay Diary*, 35; Beale, *Welles Diary*, 1:61–63; Sears, *McClellan Papers*, 199; Dahlgren to Ulric Dahlgren, March 11, 1862, Dahlgren Papers, LC.

63. Burlingame, *With Lincoln in the White House*, 74–75; Sears, *McClellan Papers*, 199.

64. Pease and Randall, *Browning Diary*, 1:533; Beale, *Welles Diary*, 1:66; EMS to John Wool, March 12, 1862, SP; Proceedings of the War Board, March 13, 1862, SP.

65. Pease and Randall, *Browning Diary*, 1:533; Nevins and Thomas, *Strong Diary*, 3:211; Ethan Allen Hitchcock to Henry Hitchcock, March 10, 1862, MOHS.

66. OR, 7:594; Edward Bates to Halleck, January 31, 1862, LFFC; Ethan Allen Hitchcock to Mrs. Horace Mann, March 15, 1862, and to EMS, March 11, 1862 (first letter of that date), Hitchcock Papers, LC.

67. Beale, *Bates Diary*, 239; copies of President's War Order No. 3, SP; Burlingame and Ettlinger, *Hay Diary*, 36.

68. Hitchcock to EMS, March 11, 1862 (second letter of that date), Hitchcock Papers, LC; *OR*, 5:54.

69. Sears, *McClellan Papers*, 206–7; S. L. M. Barlow to August Belmont, March 18, 1862, Letterbook 7, Barlow Papers, HL.

70. Proceedings of the War Board, March 13, 1862, SP; *OR*, 5:1099. In the spring of 1862 Robert E. Lee became Jefferson Davis's general in chief in fact, if not in name. Weigley, *Quartermaster General*, 216, noted that the constitutional role of the secretary of war effectively obviated the position of general in chief over the U.S. Army.

71. *OR*, 5:55–56; EMS to GBM, March 13, 1862, 5:20 P.M., Hitchcock Papers, LC; Sears, *McClellan Papers*, 207.

72. This incident is recorded only in memoirs. David Homer Bates had it in February, 1862 (*Lincoln in the Telegraph Office*, 137), but Johnson, "Reminiscences," 73–74, made it "soon after" Stanton became secretary of war; McClellan, *Own Story*, 217–18, dated it during his brief absence from Washington "for a couple of days in March," and mentions his removal as general in chief as though the two events happened separately. Yet he does not appear to have left Washington at any other time in early March.

73. Barlow to H. D. Bacon, March 15, 1862, Letterbook 7, Barlow Papers, HL.

74. Hitchcock Diary, March 15, 1862, Gilcrease Institute; Hitchcock to Henry Hitchcock, March 15, 17, 1862, Hitchcock Collection, MOHS; Hitchcock to Mrs. Horace Mann, March 15, 1862, and Hitchcock's memo, March 17, 1862, Hitchcock Papers, LC.

75. Samuel Ward to Samuel Barlow, March 16, 1862 (BW Box 44), Barlow Papers, HL; Hitchcock Diary, March 17, 1862, Gilcrease Institute; John Barnard to McClellan, March 19, 1862, McClellan Papers, LC; GBM to EMS, March 18, 1862, Reel 98, Telegrams, Bound (M473), RG 107, NA; *RJCCW*, 1:91. Julian, *Recollections*, 210–11, corroborates the March 24 meeting with Stanton, whom he described projecting (or affecting) an air of utter discouragement over McClellan's continuation in command.

76. Pease and Randall, *Browning Diary*, 1:537–39.

77. Ibid.; Jacob Rister to Benjamin Wade, March 30, 1862, Wade Papers, LC. Various versions of the KGC rumor were making the rounds: William T. Sherman's wife, Ellen, conveyed it to Senator John Sherman on March 24, when she thought McClellan was trying to shelve her husband (Sherman Family Papers, LC).

CHAPTER 9

1. Beale, *Bates Diary*, 239; Proceedings of the War Board, March 13, 1862, SP; EMS to Charles Dana, January 24, 1862, Dana Papers, LC; Joseph Medill to EMS, January 21, 1862, SP; EMS to William Fessenden, February 3, 1862, Reports to Congress (M220), RG 107, NA; Edwards Pierrepont to William Seward, February 9, 1862, UR; Samuel Barlow to Sam Ward, March 26, 1862, Letterbook 7, Barlow Papers, HL.

2. *CG*, 37th Cong., 2nd sess., 615–17, 695; Niven, *Chase Papers*, 3:141–42; Chase to EMS, March 28, 1862, SP. The cost of the war led to the modern U.S. use of "billion," which debuted in Webster's *American Dictionary of the English Language* in 1864.

3. John Dahlgren to Ulric Dahlgren, March 11, 1862, Dahlgren Papers, LC; *Harper's Weekly*, March 1, 1862; *New York Times*, March 12, 14–20, 23–26, 29–31, 1862; James H. Roberts to EMS, April 14, 1862, Miscellaneous Collections: U.S. Army, NYPL; *Cleveland Plain Dealer*, March 18–21, 24, 1862; Mohr and Winslow, *The Cormany Diaries*, 188; Engs and Brooks, *Evans Letters*, 9; Mushkat, *Voris Letters*, 39–41.

4. French, *Journals*, 392; Nevins and Thomas, *Strong Diary*, 3:215; Laas, *Elizabeth Lee Letters*, 111, 116.

5. Stanton to Irenius Prime, March 26, 1862, Gratz Collection, HSP; Wilson, "Edwin M. Stanton," 239; *OR*, Series 3, 2:2–3, 16, 29; Burlingame, *Dispatches from Lincoln's White House*, 70; George Redlon to "Dear Father," April 13, 1862, MEHS.

6. McClellan, *Own Story*, 258; *RJCCW*, 1:91; Julian, *Political Recollections*, 210. Rafuse, *McClellan's War*, 242, concluded that the suspension of recruiting did effectively prevent Lincoln from reinforcing McClellan.

7. Horace Greeley to Margaret Allen, June 17, 1861, LC; Norton and Howe, *Norton Letters*, 1:237–38; Palmer, *Sumner Letters*, 2:183–84; J. H. Jordan to Lyman Trumbull, February 20, 1862, and A. B. Campbell to Trumbull, March 6, 1862, Trumbull Papers, LC. Radicals reversed this accusation, alleging that conservative Union generals sought to avoid conclusive victory so a negotiated peace might salvage slavery.

8. *OR*, 10(1):108, 395–96, 406, 463–64, 567; *Cleveland Plain Dealer*, April 9, 1862; *Waterloo Courier*, April 16, 1862; *Northern Advocate*, May 13, 1862; Andrew Davis to Sarah Davis, April 17, 1862, UIA; John St. John to "Dear Father," April 14, 1862, LC. McDonough, in *Shiloh*, 219–25, focused on the battle as a watershed defeat for the Confederacy, but McPherson, *Battle Cry of Freedom*, 413–14, emphasized how abruptly it reversed Northern optimism about imminent victory.

9. Hitchcock to "Dear Cox" [April, 1862], and Halleck to Hitchcock, April 18, 1862, Hitchcock Papers, LC.

10. *OR*, 7:660, 661, 664, 671, 678, 682–83, 10(1):98–99, 10(2):77, 79, 126, 128–29, 138.

11. *OR*, 9:370, 380, 10(2): 57–62, 64–68, 71–74, 76–80, 86–92, 94–100, 102–3, 105–8.

12. *OR*, 11(1):9, 13; Sears, *McClellan Papers*, 225–27.

13. Sears, *McClellan Papers*, 227–29.

14. *OR*, 5:58, 62, 12(3):32–34; Frémont to EMS, March 30, 1862, SP; EMS to "Mr. President," March 30, 1862, SP; memo, March 30, 1862, and Hitchcock to Winfield Scott, May 28, 1862, Hitchcock Papers, LC; Hitchcock to Henry Hitchcock, May 30, 1862, MOHS. Stanton acted very deferentially toward Frémont and his Radical supporters: when one of Frémont's influential friends asked to have a favorite appointed to Frémont's staff, Stanton replied that Frémont need only ask and it would be done "at once." See Proceedings of the War Board, March 21, 1862, SP; EMS to Parke Godwin, April 11, 1862, Bryant-Godwin Papers, NYPL.

15. *OR*, 5:63, 11(3):59–62; War Board minutes, March 27, 1862, SP; *RJCCW*, 1:304. Sears did the troop calculation in *To the Gates of Richmond*, 34; Rafuse, in *McClellan's War*, 206, was less critical of McClellan's dispositions, and more so of Hitchcock and Thomas. Winfield Scott, who had no reason to favor McClellan, considered the Shenandoah force close enough to defend Washington (Scott memorandum, June 24, 1862, ALP).

16. *RJCCW*, 1:92, 251–53; *OR*, 11(1):10, 11(3):73.

17. *OR*, 11(1):321, 11(3):71–72; Arthur McClellan Diary, April 5, 1862, McClellan Papers, LC. In *George B. McClellan* (430n9), Sears times the order for the siege train before 1:00 P.M. on April 5, noting that McClellan's telegram to Lincoln, headed at 7:30 P.M., implied that news of McDowell's retention had just been received.

18. Sears, *McClellan Papers*, 228–31; *OR*, 11(3):67–68.

19. Sears, *McClellan Papers*, 231; *New York Herald*, April 22, 27, 1862; *New York World*, May 3, 1862; *Detroit Free Press*, July 16, 1862.

20. *OR*, 6:714, 716–17, 10(2):138–39, Series 4, 1:1095.

21. Russell to EMS, April 2, 1862, SP; Proceedings of the War Board, March 27, 1862, SP; *Washington Evening Star*, March 31, 1862; Russell, *Diary*, 338–40; James Wadsworth to EMS, April 2, 1862, and C. C. Fulton to EMS, April 9, 1862, SP.

22. *OR*, Series 2, 2:221–23, Series 3, 1:899; Beale, *Welles Diary*, 1:67. The use of the past tense reveals that Welles revised this diary entry after the fact.

23. *CG*, 37th Cong., 2nd sess., 1735.

24. EMS to James Wadsworth, March 17, 1862, SP; *New York Times*, April 12, 1862. On Forney's admitted determination to offer the Lincoln administration no criticism whatever, see Forney to Lincoln, May 12, 1863, ALP.

25. Simon Cameron to "Proprietors," December 11, 1861, Raymond Papers, NYPL; *New York Times*, April 17, 1862; John Tucker to EMS, April 20, 1862, SP; *OR*, 25(2):239–41. The favored *New York Times* even published the intended route and destination of Sherman's March to the Sea, angering General Grant and jeopardizing Sherman's success, but Stanton merely blamed it on Sherman's volubility, and on loose lips among his staff: *OR*, 39(3):740.

26. *New York Times*, April 15, 1862. Mindich analyzes Stanton's bulletins in *Just the Facts*, 64–94, as does Burton in "'No Turning Back,'" 281–91.

27. Hitchcock to EMS, April 19, 1862, SP.

28. *OR*, 11(1):18, 11(3):13–33; Sears, *McClellan Papers*, 253–56.

29. *OR*, 11(3):138, 145: EMS to "Dear Sir" [Salmon P. Chase], May 5, 1862, HSP; Hitchcock Diary, May 8, 1862, Gilcrease Institute; Beale, *Bates Diary*, 255; Niven, *Chase Papers*, 1:336–37, 3:185–87. In "A Trip with Lincoln, Chase and Stanton," 813, Viele misremembered the date of their departure. Chase later revealed that the trip was Stanton's idea (Niven, *Chase Papers*, 3:267).

30. Niven, *Chase Papers*, 3:189–90, 267; *OR*, 11(3):146–47.

31. Niven, *Chase Papers*, 1:339, 3:190; EMS to Ellen, May 8, 1862, SP; *OR*, 11(3):153; *ORN*, 7:330–35.

32. Niven, *Chase Papers*, 1:340–42, 3:193–95, 267–68; *OR*, 11(3):157; EMS to Peter Watson, May 10, 1862, Miscellaneous Personal Files, NYPL.

33. *OR*, 11(3):157, 160, 163–64; Niven, *Chase Papers*, 1:340–44, 3:193–97.

34. *OR*, 11(3):153–55; Sears, *McClellan Papers*, 257–58; Sprague to EMS, May 3, 1862, SP.

35. *OR*, 11(3):153–55. McClellan's relationship with Lincoln started deteriorating as soon as Stanton entered the War Department and began interposing himself between them.

36. Hitchcock Diary, May 12, 1862, Gilcrease Institute; Hitchcock to EMS May 13, 1862, Hitchcock Papers, LC; Hitchcock to Henry Hitchcock, April 25, 1862, MOHS. Hitchcock expanded on the incident in his memoir (Croffut, *Fifty Years in Camp and Field*, 442–43).

37. *New York Times*, May 16, 1862.

38. David Davis to Joseph Holt, April 28, 1862, Holt Papers, LC.

39. See, for instance, Wilson, "Jeremiah S. Black and Edwin M. Stanton," 469–70, EMS to William Lloyd Garrison, September 18, 1865, BPL, and Merrill, *Garrison Letters*, 5:190–91, 210, for Stanton trying to paint himself as a lifelong abolitionist to those who were.

40. Joshua Speed to Joseph Holt, December 8, 1861, Holt Papers, LC.

41. Heman Dyer to EMS, May 16, 1862, SP.

42. EMS to Oella Wright, March 24, 1862, Stanton Papers, OHS; EMS to Dyer, May 18, 1862, SP. This letter appears out of chronological sequence in *OR*, 19(2):725–28.

43. EMS to Dyer, May 18, 1862, Dyer to EMS, May 24, 1862, SP; Palmer, *Sumner Letters*, 103, 112, 114–15; Samuel Hooper to Horatio Woodman, June 5, 1862, Woodman Papers, MHS; Horatio Woodman to EMS, June 22, 1862, SP.

44. Dahlgren, *Memoir*, 368; *OR*, Series 2, 3:244; Palmer, *Sumner Letters*, 2:113; Thompson and Wainwright, *Fox Correspondence*, 2:297. Dahlgren's "memoir" actually consists of his diaries and correspondence, edited by his daughter.

45. *CG*, 37th Cong., 2nd sess., 2041; Sears, *McClellan Papers*, 254, 260, 262–63, 264; GBM to EMS, May 10, 1862, SP; *OR*, 11(3):166–67, 169–70, 174–75, 181–82.

46. *OR*, 11(1):26–28, 11(3):173.

47. *OR*, 11(3):176–77; GBM to Ellen McClellan, May 18, 1862, McClellan Papers, LC; Sears, *McClellan Papers*, 270–72.

48. Quaife, *Williams Letters*, 73–87; Eby, *Strother Diaries*, 38–45; Duncan, *Shaw Letters*, 203–5; Jordan, *Gould Journals*, 131–36.

49. Pease and Randall, *Browning Diary*, 1:546–47; Dahlgren, *Memoir*, 368–70; Niven, *Chase Papers*, 1:345; Sparks, *Patrick Diary*, 82; *OR*, 12(3):216–17, 51(1):75. Telegrams dated from the War Department the night of May 23, signed with Stanton's name, were sent when Stanton would have been asleep on the steamer in mid-Potomac.

50. Pease and Randall, *Browning Diary*, 1:547; *OR*, 12(3):219–21.

51. *OR*, Series 3, 2:44–47, 61–65, 68–72; *Cleveland Plain Dealer*, May 27, 1862; Laas, *Elizabeth Lee Letters*, 152; Henry L. Dawes to Ella Dawes, May 29, 1862, Dawes Papers, LC.

52. "Horace Binney" to EMS, May 27, 1862, EMS to Binney, June 2, Binney to EMS, June 4, and Peter Watson to Binney, June 11, 1862, all in SP; Niven, *Chase Papers*, 3:205–6.

53. Proceedings of the War Board, March 13, 1862, SP; *OR*, Series 3, 2:183–85.

54. Niven, *Chase Papers*, 1:346; Pease and Randall, *Browning Diary*, 1:547; Palmer, *Sumner Letters*, 2:114–15; *OR*, 11(1):31–32.

55. *OR*, Series 3, 2:69–70, Series 1, 12(3):235–60; Blair, *Geary Letters*, 46.

56. *OR*, 11(3):189–93, 199; Sears, *Haydon Journal*, 245.

57. *OR*, 11(3):201.

58. Heintzelman Diary, May 31–June 1, 1862, LC; Philip Kearny to Cortlandt Parker, "Just after Fair Oaks," Kearny Papers, LC; Sears, *McClellan Papers*, 285, 287–88; *OR*, 11(3):208–9.

59. *OR*, 11(3):206–7, 211; *CWL*, 5:255.

60. Heintzelman Diary, June 3, 1862, LC; *CWL*, 5:255; *OR*, 11(3):569.

61. EMS to GBM, June 7, 8, 1862, and GBM to EMS, June 7, 1862, all SP; *OR*, 11(1):204–5; unsigned, undated note in Stanton's hand, on Executive Mansion stationery, declining to forward the correspondence about the White House property (filed between June 30 and July 1, 1862), SP; Sears, *McClellan Papers*, 304; Samuel Barlow to Benjamin Stark, June 28, 1862, Letterbook 7, Barlow Papers, HL.

62. William A. Hammond to EMS, June 16, 1862, and C. P. Wolcott to GBM, June 16, 1862, SP; Wolcott, 155–56.

63. Flower, 367; Hyman, 165–66; Johnson, "Reminiscences," 92; Register of Enlistments in the United States Army (M233), RG 94, NA; Lincoln's instruction of May 13, 1862, with Stanton's endorsement of May 14, reproduced in Hyman, 167; Ben Wade to William Stanton, March 9, 1863, and February 5, 1864 (HM37033 and 37034), HL; *CWL*, 6:185; Register of Cadet Appointments, 1819–1867 (M2037), RG 94, NA.

64. *OR*, 11(3):216–17, 219, 223, 225, 11(1):46–47.

65. *OR*, 11(1):47; *Boston Evening Transcript*, June 2, 1862; Horatio Woodman to EMS, June 22, 1862, SP; Sparks, *Patrick Diary*, 103; *Cleveland Plain Dealer*, July 11, 1862; Sears, *McClellan Papers*, 297, 305; Joseph C. G. Kennedy to McClellan, June 12, 1862, Reel 25, McClellan Papers, LC (quoted in Rafuse, *McClellan's War*, 219).

66. *OR*, 11(1):48–49, 268–69, 11(3):237, 240.

67. *OR*, 11(1):49, 51.

68. *OR*, 11(3):259; Niven, *Chase Papers*, 3:221; Scott memorandum, June 24, 1862, ALP.

CHAPTER 10

1. Pease and Randall, *Browning Diary*, 1:552; *OR*, 10(1):669, 17(2):17–18, 20.

2. *OR*, 51(1):79; Sparks, *Patrick Diary*, 97; Joseph Willard Diary, June 18, 19, 1862, LC.

3. *OR*, 12(3):435.

4. Sutherland made these points in "Abraham Lincoln, John Pope, and the Origins of Total War," 569–70, 574, persuasively arguing that Lincoln chose Pope for compatibility, contrary to the stubborn tradition that Lincoln selected him under Radical pressure—for which see, for instance, Blue, *Salmon P. Chase*, 177.

5. *RJCCW*, 1:276–78.

6. *OR*, 11(1):49, 51, 12(3):438; Eby, *Strother Diaries*, 64–66. Frémont's complaint to Charles Sumner that Stanton was his "insidious enemy" may have been founded

on this rebuke, although Stanton said he later offered Frémont another command. See Frémont to Sumner, December 14, 1863, Sumner Papers, Harvard; Palmer, *Sumner Letters*, 2:174.

7. Heintzelman Diary, June 26–July 3, 1862, LC; GBM to Lincoln, July 7, 1862, Reel 50, Telegrams, Bound (M473), RG 107, NA; GBM to EMS, July 3, 1862, McClellan File, Harvard.

8. Sears, *McClellan Papers*, 322–23.

9. Pease and Randall, *Browning Diary*, 1:559.

10. *RJCCW*, 1:339–40; *Letter of the Secretary of War*, 131–32; *McClellan's Own Story*, 10–11; Bates, *Lincoln in the Telegraph Office*, 109–11; Johnson, "Reminiscences," 81–82.

11. Bates, *Lincoln in the Telegraph Office*, 112; *OR*, 12(1):218–22; Sanford to EMS, April 9, 1862, SP.

12. *OR*, 11(3):274–75, 16(2):69–70, 74–76; Watson to EMS, June 29, 1862, and EMS to David Hunter, July 3, 1862, SP.

13. *CG*, 37th Cong., 2nd sess., 3220; *New York Herald*, July 4, 7, 1862, *New York Times*, July 10, 1862.

14. EMS to Olmsted, January 18, 1862, *Letters Sent by the Secretary of War* (M6), RG 107, NA; Olmsted, *Papers*, 4:399–400, 402, 413–14.

15. EMS to GBM, July 5, 1862 (two letters), McClellan Papers, LC; Sears, *McClellan Papers*, 346–47; George T. Balch to Harriet Balch, July 16, 1862, UCB.

16. Chandler to "My dear Wife," July 6, 1862, LC.

17. *OR*, 11(3):314; Beale, *Welles Diary*, 1:105, 108; Laas, *Elizabeth Lee Letters*, 166. See Schutz and Trenerry, *Abandoned by Lincoln*, 100, and Sutherland, "Abraham Lincoln, John Pope, and the Origins of Total War," 574, on Pope's influence on Halleck's appointment and his motivation for recommending him.

18. Sears, *McClellan Papers*, 354–55, 368; Barlow to GBM, July 18, 1862, and to Henry Bacon, July 19, 1862, Letterbook 7, Barlow Papers, HL; George T. Balch to Harriet Balch, July 16, 1862, UCB; Barlow to GBM, August 9, 1862, McClellan Papers, LC.

19. Nevins and Thomas, *Strong Diary*, 3:236.

20. *OR*, Series 3, 2:179–88, 199–200; *CWL*, 5:298, 301, 304.

21. Recruiting estimates extrapolated from unit records in Dyer, *Compendium*, 1002–1681.

22. Alfred Pleasonton to Joseph Holt, July 14, 1862, Holt Papers, LC; French, *Journals*, 401; Laas, *Elizabeth Lee Letters*, 160, 185, 186n4; John R. P. Martin to "Dear father," July 17, 1862 (HM32131), HL; *Detroit Free Press*, July 16, 1862.

23. *OR*, Series 3, 2:198, 280–82; *CG*, 37th Cong., 2 sess., 3178, 3227, 3320–23, 3338–40, 3351, 3394, 3397–98, 3404.

24. Beale, *Welles Diary*, 1:70; EMS to Lincoln, June 29, 1862, ALP; Peter Watson to EMS, June 29, 1862, SP; Wolcott, 157b; George T. Balch to Harriet Balch, July 13, 1862, UCB; Burlingame, *With Lincoln in the White House*, 85.

25. *OR*, 17(2):90; Records of Lot 675, Oak Hill Cemetery; Beale, *Welles Diary*, 1:70–71.

26. Robert Dale Owen to EMS, July 23, 1862, LC; Nevins and Thomas, *Strong Diary*, 3:160; Cutting to EMS, February 20, 1867, SP.

27. Memo dated July 22, 1862, SP; Niven, *Chase Papers*, 1:350–51;Wolcott, 157b–158a; Lewis Campbell to Andrew Johnson, November 20, 1865, Johnson Papers, LC; Cutting to EMS, February 20, 1867, SP; *OR*, Series 3, 2:274–76.

28. Pease and Randall, *Browning Diary*, 1:562; statement of volunteers, July 29, 1862, SP.

29. Sears, *McClellan Papers*, 344–45, 346–47.

30. Niven, *Chase Papers*, 1:352; *CWL*, 5:338; Pease and Randall, *Browning Diary*, 1:562.

31. *OR*, Series 2, 3:515, 4:20–21, 36, 266–68.

32. Sam Ward to Seward, July 23, 1862, Seward Papers, UR; Wolcott, 157b.

33. *New York Times*, July 23, 1862; *RJCCW*, 1:637–39; Daniel Larned to "Dear Helen," July 21, 1862, and to "My Dear Sister," July "21" [26], 1862, Larned Papers, LC.

34. *OR*, 11(3):337–38; Heintzelman Diary, July 26, 1862, LC.

35. Pease and Randall, *Browning Diary*, 1:563; Sears, *McClellan Papers*, 372.

36. Sears, *McClellan Papers*, 376–77; *RJCCW*, 1:650; *OR*, 11(1):75–81, 11(3):342, 344, 345–46.

37. *OR*, 12(3):473–74; Sparks, *Patrick Diary*, 108; Jacob Cox, who was truthful enough himself, wrote that Pope told him of Stanton's part in composing the address (*Military Reminiscences*, 1:222). Schutz and Trenerry, *Abandoned by Lincoln*, 103, hypothesized that Stanton "was using Pope's address as a trial balloon to test public reaction." Pope's latest biographer (Cozzens, *General John Pope*, 83–86) seemed to credit Pope as author.

38. *OR*, 12(3):513, 573; Orlando Poe to "My dear," August 25, 1862, Poe Papers, LC.

39. Daniel Larned to "My Dear Sister," August 3, 1862, Larned Papers, LC; *OR*, 12(3):528–29; Sears, *McClellan Papers*, 397, 399–400.

40. *OR*, Series 3, 2:292–92; Niven, *Chase Papers*, 1:360; Halleck to EMS, August 3, 1862, SP.

41. *CWL*, 5:358–59; *New York Times*, August 7, 1862.

42. *New York Herald*, August 8, 1862; Barlow to GBM, July 18, 1862, Letterbook 7, Barlow Papers, HL.

43. *OR*, Series 3, 2:321; *Baltimore Sun*, December 23, 1845. In a communication he seems never to have sent, Stanton later claimed that Lincoln directed him to issue the order (undated replies to questionnaire, filed under August 8, 1862, SP). Neely (*The Fate of Liberty*, 232–35) identified nearly 14,000 military arrests, but discounted the impact on civil liberty, contending that many were neither political nor arbitrary, and he dated the worst of them in the late summer of 1862. Hyman and Wiecek, in *Equal Justice*, 233, estimated 18,000 arrests. Stanton was directly responsible for that season of heightened tyranny, and he persistently tried to expand the reach of his authority over the civilian population. Early in 1863 Senator Garrett Davis detected Stanton's influence in a bill to give military courts jurisdiction over fraud in military claims, complaining that Stanton was "prone to bring every person and every act within military law and military courts." *CG*, 37th Cong., 3rd sess., 957.

44. *OR*, Series 3, 2:370; Niven, *Chase Papers*, 1:362.

45. Case 413, Reel 14, Turner-Baker Case Files (M797), RG 94, NA; *Daily Gate City*, August 15, 18, 27, 1862; *Dubuque Daily Times*, August 17, 1862; *OR*, Series 2, 5:117–18; Mahony to Charles Mason, October 4, 1862, SHSI-DM.

46. *Daily Morning Chronicle*, September 1, 22, and October 9, 1862; Cases No. 200 and 201, Case Files of Investigations (M797), RG 94, NA; *The Crisis*, August 20, 1862; *Chicago Tribune*, August 18, 1862.

47. Case Nos. 14, 153, 202, Case Files of Investigations (M797), RG 94, NA; Wainwright, *Fisher Diary*, 433–34; Israel Washburn Jr. to EMS, August 18, 1862, Letters Received, Main Series (M221), RG 107, NA. So numerous did the arrests become that the Turner-Baker Case Files (M797) fill 137 reels of microfilm, and all were not filmed.

48. *OR*, Series 3, 587–88. Hyman, 375, justified Stanton's crackdown with the observation that "most of the civilians who were arrested for disloyalty and tried before military commissions on that charge were found to be guilty." It was, however, precisely in order to produce convictions that Stanton ordered defendants tried by military commissions rather than in civilian courts. In a 1973 book on the war's constitutional effects (*A More Perfect Union*, 65–80), Hyman acknowledged that even some of the most loyal Northern citizens were uncomfortable with the arbitrary arrests, but he dismissed this as an immature reaction emanating from "the belief that America was an Eden whose people need never suffer repressive devices familiar abroad." He seemed to argue that to preserve civil liberties, it was necessary to violate them, and he repeated this argument in muted form in 1982 (Hyman and Wiecek, *Equal Justice*, 232–38). Mark Neely, in *Lincoln and the Triumph of the Nation*, 90, 109, concluded that the United States avoided "one man rule" in the 1860s, but the era did see the first steps in that direction. Daniel Farber observed in *Lincoln's Constitution*, 4, that "most of Lincoln's actions (contrary to common belief) were generally in line with our current view of executive authority," perhaps overlooking how much Lincoln's (and Stanton's) unfortunate precedents have molded that current view.

49. EMS to Ambrose Burnside, May 20, 1862, Stanton Collection, ALPLM; Edward Atkinson to "Ned," June 10, 1862, MHS; EMS to George F. Shepley, June 10, 1862, and Shepley to EMS, November 6, 1862, SP; John S. Phelps to EMS, July 7, 1862, and (unsigned) October 20, 1862, SP; EMS to Andrew J. Hamilton, November 14, 1862, SP; Abraham Lincoln to Andrew J. Hamilton, September 19, 1863, SP.

50. *OR*, Series 3, 2:439–41, 518, 522–23.

51. *CG*, 37th Cong., 2nd sess., 1083, 1188, 1624, 1662–64, 1678–79, 1732–42, 1913.

52. Stone to Benjamin Lossing, November 5, 1866, Schoff Collection, CL.

53. Charles G. Greene et al. to Abraham Lincoln, March, 1862, ALP; *CWL*, 7:285–86; McClure, *Abraham Lincoln and Men of War-Times*, 186. Lincoln scholars often ignore General Stone's ordeal (see, for instance, Miller, *Lee's Virtues*; Gienapp, *Abraham Lincoln and Civil War America*; Perret, *Lincoln's War*; and Davis, *Lincoln's Men*). In *Lincoln*, 319, Donald only mentioned "a growing suspicion" that Stone was disloyal. Brevity may sometimes account for the absence: McPherson did not address Stone in *Tried by War* but did in *Battle Cry of Freedom*, 363–64. In *The Presidency of Abraham Lincoln*, 104–5, Paludan implied that Lincoln may

have found credibility in Stanton's justification for what even Paludan recognized as Stanton's persecution of Stone. The sufferance of that injustice blemishes Lincoln's record of fairness to the fighting men, posing special difficulty in an increasingly laudatory interpretive atmosphere.

54. *OR*, 13, 658–59. Stanton refused to postpone the draft during the Sioux uprising in Minnesota, and Lincoln had to reverse him (*CWL*, 5:396–99).

55. *OR*, 6:263–64; *New York Times*, April 9, 1862.

56. *CWL*, 5:219, 222–23; Edward Atkinson to "Ned," June 10, 1862, MHS; Niven, *Chase Papers*, 1:349, 351; *OR*, Series 3, 2:292, 346.

57. *OR*, Series 3, 2:294–95, 417, 431, 582.

58. Butler, *Correspondence*, 2:192; Niven, *Chase Papers*, 3:234–37; *OR*, Series 3, 2:436–38.

59. *CG*, 37th Cong., 2nd sess., 3125.

60. *OR*, 14:374–76, 377; Hunter to EMS, August 15, 1862, SP.

61. *CWL*, 5:388–89; Niven, *Chase Papers*, 1:351–52.

62. *OR*, 12(3):613–14, 676, 684–85, 720–21, 741, 796–97; Sears, *McClellan Papers*, 406; Heintzelman Diary, August 28–September 1, 1862, LC.

63. *OR*, 12(3):706, 739–41.

64. Niven, *Chase Papers*, 366–67; Beale, *Welles Diary*, 1:93–95. Welles (*Diary*, 1:100), noted that the original, strident draft of the petition was in Stanton's hand, but a photoduplication of the revised version in Flower (180–81) appears to be in Watson's.

65. Beale, *Welles Diary*, 1:93–99, 101; Burlingame and Ettlinger, *Hay Diary*, 37.

66. Burlingame and Ettlinger, *Hay Diary*, 37; Halleck to Elizabeth Halleck, September 5, 1862, CL; Beale, *Welles Diary*, 1:95–98.

67. GBM to Halleck, August 31, 1862 (three telegrams), Reel 65, Telegrams, Unbound (M504), RG 107, NA; Burlingame and Ettlinger, *Hay Diary*, 37; *OR*, 11(1):102–3, 12(3):775–76; *Letter of the Secretary of War*, 182–83; Sears, *McClellan Papers*, 428; Niven, *Chase Papers*, 1:367.

68. Sears, *McClellan Papers*, 428; *Letter of the Secretary of War*, 183–84; *OR*, 12(3):807.

69. Beale, *Welles Diary*, 1:104–5; Niven, *Chase Papers*, 1:368–69.

70. Bates's draft of the petition, ALP; Beale, *Welles Diary*, 1:94; Niven, *Chase Papers*, 1:369. From Bates's notes on this draft, Sears debunked the long-standing belief that Lincoln never actually saw the petition (*The Civil War: The Second Year*, 428–29).

71. Horatio Woodman to Francis Lieber, January 9, 1870 (LI4643), Lieber Papers, HL.

72. *OR*, 19(2):169, 175, 182, 188; *RJCCW*, 1:453, 650; Brinkerhoff Miner to Nathaniel Banks, September 4, 1862, quoted in Fishel, *Secret War for the Union*, 211; Sparks, *Patrick Diary*, 139; Sears, *McClellan Papers*, 435. I am indebted to Stephen Sears for engaging in the patient correspondence that deduced the timing of these offers of command.

73. Niven, *Chase Papers*, 369. 370; Beale, *Welles Diary*, 1:109–10; *OR*, 12(2):12–18, 12(3):811.

74. Sears, *McClellan Papers*, 436–37.

CHAPTER 11

1. *OR*, Series 3, 2:280–81; C. P. Wolcott to Holt, July 9, 18, 1862, Holt Papers, LC.

2. EMS to Holt, January 25, March 4, 1862, Box 5, Holt Papers, HL; Holt to EMS, February 27, 1862, SP.

3. Bartman, "The Contribution of Joseph Holt," 12–14, quoted in Leonard, *Lincoln's Forgotten Ally*, 66–67. On the new judge advocate general's sudden support for Lincoln's proclamation, see Holt to Bellamy Storer, September 24, 1862, Cincinnati Historical Society (Storer's correspondent is mistakenly identified as "George F." Holt). Leonard, *Lincoln's Forgotten Ally*, skips over the six months that saw Holt's political conversion.

4. Dozens of Amelie's letters from March of 1859 to December of 1860 are filed with his letters to Margaret in Box 99 of the Holt Papers, LC. The translations are mine: the ambiguity that made French useful in diplomacy also recommends it for illicit liaisons: for instance "mon cher ami" (which more likely meant "my precious lover" in these intimate letters) could have been interpreted as "my dear friend," had Margaret found them.

5. Julia Beckham to "My dearest sister," September 6, 1857, William Merrick to "My dear sister," September 10, 1857, "Nanny" to "My dear Maggie," September 11, 1857, and to "My dear Sister," September 25, 1857, and Holt to "My dear Maggie," September 26, 1857, all in Holt Papers, LC; P. H. Watson to Holt March 12, 14, 1862, Holt Papers, HL; *CWL*, 5:21–22; commission appointment dated March 13, 1862, SP; *OR*, Series 3, 2:509. In September of 1864, Holt was still pleading limited pecuniary resources (Rebecca Cox to Holt, September 29, 1864, LC), but after nine more years in government employ his fortunes rebounded from the outright financial embarrassment of 1857 to a level of prosperity that might have piqued the suspicion of an auditor: the 1870 census credits him with a personal fortune of $145,000 (M593, Reel 125, 152, RG 29, NA).

6. H. M. Bowman to Samuel Kirkwood, undated, and B. McCarty to "Dear Sir," August 27, 1862, Disloyal Sentiments File, Adjutant General's Correspondence, SHSI-DM; John A. Logan to Abraham Lincoln, August 30, 1862, Case 142, EMS to Holt, September 9, 1862, with Holt's endorsement, Case 200, Case Files of Investigations (M797), RG 94, NA; *OR*, Series 3, 2:525–26. Batchelder was ordered released on $10,000 bond in late September, but apparently was held until the second half of October: see L. C. Turner to Jacob Ela, October 15, 1862, Case 200, Case Files of Investigations (M797), RG 94, NA.

7. *OR*, 12(3):811.

8. GBM to Halleck, September 9, 14, 1862, and to Lincoln, September 13, 1862, Reel 50, Telegrams, Bound (M473), RG 107, NA. The best book on the Maryland campaign is still Sears, *Landscape Turned Red*.

9. Samuel Butterworth to Samuel Barlow, September 23, 1862, and T. J. Barnett to Barlow, same date, Box 40, Barlow Papers, HL.

10. Chandler to EMS, September 10, 1862, SP; EMS to Chandler, September 18, 1862, Chandler Papers, LC; EMS to George Harrington, September 14, 1862, MOHS; Olmsted, *Papers*, 4:418–20, 449–51.

11. *OR*, Series 3, 2:584–85.

12. Ibid., 587–88. Congress approved his actions March 3, 1863 (*OR*, Series 3, 3:95–97).

13. Beale, *Welles Diary*, 1:150; undated interrogatories, filed under August 8, 1862, SP.

14. *OR*, Series 3, 2:569, 663; *Chicago Times*, October 26, 1862. Stanton later rescinded the authority, but (as Paludan observed in *"A People's Contest,"* 248) the damage was done.

15. *The Crisis*, August 20, 1862; *Chicago Tribune*, August 18, 1862; *Prairie du Chien Courier*, December 18, 25, 1862; *CWL*, 5:413; James Speed to Joseph Holt, November 8, 1862, Holt Papers, LC; *OR*, 16(2):519; Thomas Ewing and H. H. Hunter to EMS, October 12, 1863, Letters Received (M221), RG 107, NA; John L. Mayer et al. to EMS, October 28, 1862, Reel 31, Letters Received, Irregular Series (M492), RG 107, NA; Case 1397, Case Files of Investigations (M797), RG 94, NA; Solomon Hamrick to A. D. Hamrick, undated (late summer or early fall, 1862), IHS; David Dudley Field to Abraham Lincoln, November 8, 1862, ALP. Public indignation over the arbitrary arrests may have been permanently desensitized: retrospective studies like Hyman's *A More Perfect Union*, Neely's *The Fate of Liberty*, and Farber's *Lincoln's Constitution* seem more impressed with the ameliorating effects of Lincoln's benevolent executive influence than with the repressive precedent of the crackdown itself.

16. *OR*, 17(2):300, 332, 849–53; Niven, *Chase Papers*, 1:416, 417; Beale, *Welles Diary*, 1:167, 386–87; *CWL*, 5:468–69.

17. *OR*, 17(2):345, 348–49, 401, 412–15, 420, 425, 528–30; Beale, *Welles Diary*, 1:217.

18. McClernand to Lincoln, January 7, 1863, ALP; *CWL*, 6:70–71; Ewing to Sherman, February 8, 1863, and to Ellen Sherman, February 13, 1863, Ewing Family Papers, LC. Grant's poor opinion of McClernand is noted by Simpson, *Ulysses S. Grant*, 140, 167.

19. *OR*, 16(2):555, 650, 651, 652, 662; George Landrum to "Dear Amanda," October 12, 1862, WRHS; Alexander Varian to "Dear Father," October 15, 1862, WRHS; Andrew Davis to "My dear Wife," October 16, 1862, UIA; *New York Times*, October 31, 1862. Just as he had tried to substantiate court-martial charges against McClellan, Stanton created a military commission to find charges that might be brought against Buell: Engle, *Don Carlos Buell*, 323–36, documented it as another court packed with Stanton cronies and Buell antagonists, who failed through no lack of effort. See also *OR*, 16(1):6–20.

20. *OR*, 19(2):484–85; Henry Halleck to Elizabeth Halleck, October 7, 1862, CL; Sparks, *Patrick Diary*, 168; Sears, *Haydon Journal*, 283; Halleck to EMS, October 28, 1862, with transcription of an endorsement presumably by EMS, SP.

21. Williams, *Garfield Letters*, 153–54, 160–61. Halleck thought Lincoln and Stanton were afraid to remove McClellan (to Elizabeth Halleck, August 9, 1862, CL).

22. Beale, *Welles Diary*, 1:182; EMS to Horace Greeley, October 4, 1862, Indiana University (on suspicions of a coup); *OR*, 21:82; *Chicago Tribune*, September 6, 1875 (page misdated September 5); Herman Haupt to "Dear Sis," November 9, 1862, Haupt Papers, LC; Sparks, *Patrick Diary*, 172; Sears, *McClellan Papers*, 519–20.

23. *OR*, 19(2):545, 569; Sparks, *Patrick Diary*, 175.

24. Nevins, *Wainwright Journals*, 134; *OR*, 12(2):821; Williams, *Garfield Letters*, 306–15; Beale, *Welles Diary*, 2:171; Niven, *Chase Papers*, 1:422.

25. *OR*, 12(2):821, 824; Sears, *McClellan Papers*, 532. Enough other disinterested generals were awaiting orders then to suggest careful bias in the selection of Porter's judges.

26. *OR*, 12(2):824.

27. *New York Times*, November 13, 1862.

28. *OR*, 21:101–4, 105; *CWL*, 5:509–10, 511, 514–15; Sparks, *Patrick Diary*, 182–83.

29. *OR*, 20(2):40–45; Hooker to EMS, November 13, 1862, Dearborn Collection, Harvard, and November 19, December 4, 1862, SP.

30. Meade, *Life and Letters*, 1:337–38; Acken, *Inside the Army of the Potomac*, 176–93. Rable, *Fredericksburg!*, 289, found that Union soldiers considered their casualties much higher than the official count of 12,653, while some morale-conscious newspaper editors reported them much lower.

31. Nevins and Thomas, *Strong Diary*, 3:281; Beale, *Welles Diary*, 1:193, 206; Heman Dyer to EMS, November 11, 1862, SP; "Extracts from the Journal of Henry J. Raymond," 424.

32. Fessenden memorandum, Bowdoin; Pease and Randall, *Browning Diary*, 1:596–97.

33. Pease and Randall, *Browning Diary*, 1:598, 601; Fessenden memorandum, Bowdoin; Nevins and Thomas, *Strong Diary*, 3:281; Blair to Lincoln, December 18, 1862, ALP.

34. Fessenden memorandum, Bowdoin; Beale *Welles Diary*, 1:196–98; Beale, *Bates Diary*, 269–70. Fessenden's account appears to have been composed soon after these events.

35. Beale, *Welles Diary*, 1:200. Citing Frederick Seward's memoir (*Seward at Washington*, 2:147), Stahr, *Seward*, 358, and Goodwin, *Team of Rivals*, 492–93, depict Stanton urging Seward not to resign, but what Welles overheard did not seem to show vigorous support.

36. Fessenden memorandum, Bowdoin.

37. Fessenden to Samuel Fessenden, December 20, 1862, and to Elizabeth Warriner, December 21, 1862, Bowdoin.

38. Beale, *Welles Diary*, 1:201–2.

39. Ibid., 203; Charles Gibson to Hamilton Gamble, January 6, 1863, MOHS; Nevins and Thomas, *Strong Diary*, 1:284.

40. Beale, *Welles Diary*, 1:60, 200–202. See, for instance, David Hunter's belief that Stanton "wears two faces" and was "not sincere," in Niven, *Chase Papers*, 1:422.

41. Beale, *Bates Diary*, 483; Pease and Randall, *Browning Diary*, 2:109, 130; Niven, *Chase Papers*, 5:335.

42. Johnson, "Reminiscences," 72, 82–83, 89–90, 92–94, 97; [Benjamin], "Recollections," 760–61, 763, 765; Benjamin to Horace White, June 1, 1914, White Papers, ALPLM. Piatt, *Memories*, tells several tales that invite doubt; Ward Hill Lamon's recollection of Lincoln tearfully rejecting Stanton's resignation originated

with Stanton himself, and Johnson may have taken it from either of them (Lamon, *Recollections*, 239; EMS to Ashley, September 14, 1866, quoted in Flower, 310–12). See Benjamin's biographical sketch for an article in *Century* (reprinted in *Battles and Leaders*, 3:239).

43. Julian, *Political Recollections*, 211–12.

44. Bates, *Lincoln in the Telegraph Office*, 390–91; Julian, *Political Recollections*, 211.

45. Burlingame, *Lincoln Observed*, 47, 97–98; Brooks, *Washington in Lincoln's Time*, 37.

46. Julian, *Recollections*, 211. McPherson, *Tried by War*, 68–69, and Davis, *Lincoln's Men*, 125, seem not to consider this weakness of the president's. In *Partners in Command*, Glatthaar (231) adopted Hyman's interpretation, remarking that "Edwin M. Stanton never bullied Lincoln into anything." That may not be accurate.

47. *CWL*, 7:285–86.

48. Joshua Speed to Joseph Holt, December 8, 1861, Holt Papers, LC.

49. Beale, *Bates Diary*, 271; Beale, *Welles Diary*, 1:206–9; opinion of EMS, December 26, 1862, SP. Lincoln called this partition of Virginia "secession in favor of the constitution" (*CWL*, 6:26–28), and Brian Dirck supportively characterized that reasoning as a search for "elasticity" in the Constitution, meanwhile criticizing the rigidity of strict constructionists (*Lincoln and the Constitution*, 72–73).

50. Daniel Larned to "My Dear Uncle," January 1, 1863, Larned Papers, LC; Beale, *Welles Diary*, 1:211; *OR*, 21(941–42, 944–45, 1001; Burnside to Lincoln, January 1, 5, 1863, letterbook labeled "Copies of Private & Important Dispatches & Letters," Rhode Island Historical Society. See, for instance, Weld, *War Diary*, 153, and Nevins, *Wainwright Journals*, 156, for conservative officers' poor opinions of Stanton and Halleck.

51. *OR*, 12(1):36–270, 12(2, supplement):1041–49.

52. Porter to Barlow, December 29, 1862 (BW Box 41), Barlow Papers, HL; *OR*, 12(2, supplement), 1035–37.

53. *OR*, 12(2, supplement), 918–19, 923, 925, 937–38, 953–54, 1054–57, 1073–74.

54. Ibid., 1050–52, 1075–1112; *New York Times*, January 12, 1863; Beale, *Welles Diary*, 1:221, 225.

55. *OR*, 12(2, supplement), 1052, 1112–33, 1134; *CWL*, 2:53–54, 78–79; *New York Herald*, January 16, 1863.

56. *CG*, 37th Cong., 2nd sess., *Senate Executive Journal*, 33, 59, 86–87, 89–90; *OR*, 14:391–92; Hitchcock to Holt, January 10, 1863, Holt Papers, HL. In Stephen Sears's essay on the Porter trial in *Controversies and Commanders*, 53–73, he finds a trace of justice in the outcome despite recognizing the bias of the court. Otto Eisenschiml's *Celebrated Case of Fitz John Porter* lacks annotation and objectivity, often straining mightily to polish Porter's image, while Elizabeth Leonard's rendition of the case in *Lincoln's Forgotten Ally* (166–73) leans just as far in the opposite direction to praise Holt.

57. *Proceedings of a General Court Martial*; Beale, *Welles Diary*, 1:229; *Review by the Judge Advocate General*; Nevins, *Wainwright Journals*, 182; Nevins and Thomas, *Strong Diary*, 2:37, 3:291.

58. *RJCCW*, 1:721; Beale, *Welles Diary*, 1:229–30; Pease and Randall, *Browning Diary*, 1:619. A postwar article of doubtful reliability suggests that Stanton thought of resigning over Hooker's appointment (*Battles and Leaders*, 3:240).

59. Wilson, *The Business of Civil War*, 227–29, calculated an inflation rate of 75 percent between 1861 and 1864. Abundant evidence for depression, discouragement, and dissatisfaction at this juncture can be found in soldiers' correspondence, such as this sampling: Jacob Haas to "My Dear Bro.," December 18, 1862, USAMHI; Milton Bassett to "Dear Julia," December 31, 1862, CHS; Edward Hall to "My dear Susan and Eddie," January 1, 1863, NHHS; Solomon Dodge to "Dear Sister Eliza," January 17, 1863, NHHS; James Gillette to "Dear Mother," January 29, 1863, LC; Franklin Sawyer to Samuel Sexton, February 20, 1863, OHS; William Stow to "Dear Father & Mother," February 23, 1863, UVM. See also *RJCCW2*, 1:3, and soldier letters to conservative newspapers like *The Crisis*, December 31, 1862; *Detroit Free Press*, January 1, 1863; *Prairie du Chien* Courier, January 22, 1863; New *Hampshire Patriot*, February 4, 1863; *Portland Advertiser*, March 6, 1863. On inflation and soldiers' pay see, for example, Joseph Medill to Lyman Trumbull, January 28, 1863, LC; Niven, *Chase Papers*, 3:357–59, 366–68; *CG*, 37th Cong., 3rd sess., 199–200, 381; Francis Boland to John Brislin, December 2, 1862, USAMHI; Lewis Cleveland to "Dear Louise," December 2, 1862, USAMHI; William Thompson to Jane Thompson, December 22, 1862, February 2, 1863, SHSI-DM; William Presley to "Dear Father," December 23, 1862, USAMHI; Adoniram Withrow to Libertatia Withrow, January 3, 1863, SHSI-IC; Levi Shell to "Dear Brother," January 5, 1863, WHS; Solomon Hamrick to "Brother Charley," January 16, 1863, IHS; Elijah Cavins to "Dear Ann," January 18, 1863, IHS; Daniel W. Perkins to George Wheeler, January 23, 1863, DC.

60. *RJCCW2*, 1:3, 73, 112; *OR*, 17(1):515–16, 17(2):590–91, 23(2):65, 24(1):68.

61. Charles Turner to "Dear Parents," March 31, 1863, WRHS; Cyrus H. Stockwell to "Dear Parents," March 14, 1863, WRHS; Levi Shell to "Dear Brother," February 7, 1863, WHS; Jim Giauque to "Folks at Home," January 23, 1863, UIA; Beale, *Welles Diary*, 1:232; *CWL*, 6:132–33; Pease and Randall, *Browning Diary*, 1:618; Frank Sterns to "Dear Parents," postmarked February 24, 1863, CL; Joel Glover to "Dear Wife," March 20, 1863, UVM; Richard Irwin to "Dear Mother & Sister," March 21, 1863, UVM.

62. Report of December 1, 1862, 19, Annual Reports of the Secretary of War (M997), RG 107, NA; *CG*, 37th Cong., 3rd sess., 558, 715–16, Appendix, 30; Beale, *Welles Diary*, 1:396–97. Stanton's vigorous support for the draft illustrated his sudden distance from the party to which he had belonged all his adult life: Baker, *Affairs of Party*, 156, noted that Democrats objected wholeheartedly to the Conscription Act, on many principles.

63. *CG*, 37th Cong., 3rd sess., 706, 708–9; *Chicago Tribune*, July 4, 1862; Pease and Randall, *Browning Diary*, 1:618–19.

64. *CG*, 37th Cong., 3rd sess., 728–39, 816, 976, 978, 981–84, 990–91, 995, 1002, 1202, 1213–16, 1218–19, 1224, 1226–27, 1229, 1235, 1404–5, 1454.

65. *CG*, 37th Cong., 3rd sess., 1229–35; *OR*, Series 3, 4:421. EMS to E. D. Morgan, July 17, 1863, quoted in Gorham, 2:107–8.

66. Sumner to Charles Scribner, December 27, 1862, Myers Collection, NYPL; *OR*, Series 3, 3:100–102; Lorenzo Thomas to Simon Cameron, March 18, 1863, Cameron Papers, LC; Townsend, *Anecdotes*, 79.

67. Frémont to EMS, March 31, 1863, SP; Palmer, *Sumner Letters*, 2:174; Charles Dana to James Pike, August 18, 1863, UME; *OR*, Series 3, 3:103, 215–16, 1111–13.

CHAPTER 12

1. Beale, *Welles Diary*, 1:387; Hitchcock to "Dear Cox," undated but April, 1862, LC; charges preferred by Captain Kountz, January 26, 1862, and February 8, 1862 (filed under February 12), SP. Grant had arrested both Kountz and one of his witnesses, Reuben Hatch, for suspected fraud, although neither was convicted.

2. EMS to McClernand, January 23, 24, 1863, McClernand to Grant, January 30, February 1, 1863, Grant to J. C. Kelton, February 1, 1863, all in SP; Kountz to McClernand, February 25, 1863, quoted in *USG*, 7:275; McClernand to Lincoln, March 15, 1863, Murat Halstead to Salmon P. Chase, April 1, 1863, and Chase to Lincoln, April 4, 1863, ALP.

3. EMS to Dana, June 16, 1862, Dana Papers, LC; Dana to EMS, December 19, 1862, SP; *OR*, 17(2):575–76; Dana to James Pike, March 13, 1863, UME; Dana to EMS, January 21, 1863, quoted in Dana, *Recollections*, 18–19; OR, Series 3, 3:63; EMS to Dana, March 11, 1863, SP. The friends Stanton appointed to salaried commissions included Robert Dale Owen, Edwards Pierrepont, Holt, Dana, three neighbors from Steubenville and nearby (James A. Hardie to Adjutant General, November 5, 1863, Letters Sent by the Secretary of War to the President [M421], RG 107, NA), and a professor from Kenyon (Edwin L. Stanton to Eben Sturges, April 21, 1863, Kenyon). He also promised employment to friends of friends: see, for instance, EMS to Thomas McCrary, June 24, 1863, Bingham Papers, OHS. Again, this was a common practice at the time, and was less frowned upon than today, but Stanton pretended to shun such personal patronage.

4. *OR*, Series 3, 3:75; James Wilson to Adam Badeau, March 22, 1867, Wilson Papers, LC; Simpson and Berlin, *Sherman Correspondence*, 450.

5. Wilson Diary, June 7, 1863, Delaware Historical Society; Nevins and Thomas, *Strong Diary*, 3:352; Dana to Elihu Washburne, August 29, 1863, Washburne Papers, LC. James H. Wilson learned early in 1862 that "Grant drinks all the time" (Hayes, *Du Pont Letters*, 2:22); as a member of Grant's staff he noted that the general was "intoxicated" on June 7, and Dana witnessed that incident. Simpson, *Grant*, 206–8, observes that the June bender was later exaggerated, including by a much-less-friendly Dana, who described Grant as "stupidly drunk" (*New York Sun*, April 28, 1891). Dana biographer Janet Steele concluded that Dana attached himself to Grant in order to tie his fortunes to the general's, which he expected to rise; her description of Dana's "fascination with rich and powerful men" sounds much like Stanton (*The Sun Shines for All*, 53–54, 71).

6. Dana to EMS, April 27, 29, 30, May 4, 5, 1863, and EMS to Dana, May 6, 1863, SP; *OR*, 24(1):30–31. On Stanton's spontaneous, stubborn prejudices see E. A. Hitchcock to Henry Hitchcock, April 25, 1862, MOHS, and Wolcott, 67.

7. EMS to Wolcott, September 30, 1862, and Watson to Wolcott, January 21, 1863, quoted in Wolcott, 158b-59; *OR*, Series 3, 3:1199.

8. *CG*, 37th Cong., 3rd sess., 451, 691, 38th Cong., 1st sess., 210, 233; *OR*, 24(1):93.

9. Benjamin, "Recollections," 761; Hardie to E. E. Bedee, May 5, 1865, Hardie Papers, LC.

10. *Delaware Gazette*, November 7, 11, 25, 1862; *Delaware Journal*, November 11, 1862; *Delaware Republican*, November 13, 1862; William Cannon to EMS, January 29, 1863, SP.

11. *Portland Daily Press*, March 3, 1863; *Daily Morning* Chronicle, March 13, 16, 26, 1863; *Carroll County Register*, June 11, 1863; E. H. Rollins to Abraham Lincoln, July 14, 1863, and Nehemiah Ordway to Lincoln July 23, 24, 1863, ALP; Ordway to Stanton, December 22, 1869, SP.

12. Sylvester Hadley Diary, February 28, March 5, 10, May 25, 26, 1863, NHHS; *Daily Morning Chronicle*, April 13, 1863. Harriman only won a brevet as brigadier in 1865.

13. George Towle to Charles Brewster, April 3, 1863, NHHS; *Cleveland Plain Dealer*, April 8, 1863; *New York Times*, April 26, 1863; *Crisis*, April 29, 1863.

14. EMS to Buckingham, March 21, 1863, Letterbooks, SP; William Church to Alexander Long, April 12, 1863, Cincinnati Historical Society; "Cousin Henry" to Timothy Loomis, April 5, 1863, CHS; Sears, *Fiske Letters*, 66; *Crisis*, April 8, 15, 1863; *New York Times*, April 8, 1863; Buckingham to EMS, April 8, 1863, SP. The same trick was repeated in Connecticut in 1864 (Robert Hale Kellogg to "Dear Father," March 25, 1864, CHS).

15. Nevins, *Wainwright Journals*, 179; Jordan, *Gould Journals*, 264; Heintzelman Diary, April 6–8, 1863, LC.

16. Wolcott, 130a, 158a; *CWL*, 6:165.

17. Wolcott, 130a; ELS to Eben Sturges, May 28, 1863, Kenyon; *CWL*, 6:171, 185; Register of Cadet Applicants (M2037), Vol. 35, p. 104, RG 94, NA.

18. *RJCCW2*, 1:116; Sparks, *Patrick Diary*, 234; *Correspondence of John Sedgwick*, 2:90–91; Andrew Young to "My Dear Susan," April 21, 1863, DC; Racine, *Mattocks Journal*, 6; *OR*, 25(1):351–52, 25(2):302; Chesson, *Dyer Journal*, 73.

19. Sparks, *Patrick Diary*, 236–43; Meade, *Life and Letters*, 1:370–71; Nevins, *Wainwright Journals*, 190–97; Dowdey and Manarin, *Lee Papers*, 444–57; *Correspondence of John Sedgwick*, 2:110–26; Quaife, *Williams Letters*, 179–202; George Marden to unidentified recipient, May 4, 8, 1863, DC; John Judd Diary, May 1–3, 1863, KSHS; William West Diary, April 28–May 5, 1863, MHS; Henry Comey to "My Dear Father," May 5, 1863, and to "Dear Sister Mary," May 8, 1863, AAS; Weld, *War Diary*, 183–93.

20. Beale, *Bates Diary*, 289–90; Laas, *Elizabeth Lee Letters*, 266–68; Beale, *Welles Diary*, 1:293–94; Nevins and Thomas, *Strong Diary*, 3:318–19; Hammond, *Diary of a Union Lady*, 237–38. Sears, *Chancellorsville*, 440–43, noted that Lee had more men killed than Hooker did.

21. *OR*, Series 2, 5:555, 566, 567.

22. Ibid., 717; Beale, *Welles Diary*, 1:306.

23. *OR*, Series 2, 573–84; Lincoln to EMS, May 13, 1863, SP. In *Lincoln's Constitution*, 174, Daniel Farber conceded that "the very infrequency and arbitrariness" of First Amendment violations like this "strongly suggest that these actions were not truly necessary," adding that Lincoln must have felt so himself, despite his reliance on the claim of necessity. Brian McGinty, *The Body of John Merryman*, 140, points out that Leavitt based his refusal to interfere on a lack of authority over a military commission, but in James McPherson's interpretation, *Tried by War*, 175, Leavitt "endorsed Lincoln's understanding of his constitutional powers as commander in chief."

24. Palmer, *Sumner Letters*, 2:184; Watson to Holt, May 13, 1863, Holt Papers, LC; *CWL*, 6:303; *OR*, Series 2, 5:765–66. Jonathan White observed Holt's evasion of the law in *Abraham Lincoln and Treason*, 84, while Mark Neely, *The Fate of Liberty*, 174, detected deliberate untruthfulness in Lincoln's published statement that military arrests were preventive only, and had not resulted in punishment "in a single case."

25. Beale, *Welles Diary*, 2:205–7.

26. Lieber to Halleck, November 13, 1862, SCL; Halleck to Lieber, April 23, 1863, Lieber Papers, HL; *OR*, Series 3, 2:951 and 3:148–64. For Lieber's theories on liberty and despotism, including a somewhat equivocal view of the evils of centralization, see Gilman, *Miscellaneous Writings*, especially 2:226, 371–73. On Lieber's code in particular, see Witt, *Lincoln's Code*; Grimsley, *Hard Hand of War*, 149–51; Sutherland, *A Savage Conflict*, 126–28, and *American Civil War Guerrillas*, 50–54.

27. Wainwright, *Fisher Diary*, 433–35; Harvey Bloom essay, October, 1862, Yale; George Landrum to "Dear Amanda," February 6, 1863, WRHS; *War Letters*, 6, 13; Pease and Randall, *Browning Diary*, 1:632–33; George Weston to Lyman Trumbull, June 11, 1863, Trumbull Papers, LC; *OR*, Series 2, 5:717. Neely noted that "most Democrats and a few influential Republicans criticized most of the arrests made north of the border states." More significantly, Neely also observed that once the war ended, "some people could see that there really had been little need" for most of those arrests (*The Fate of Liberty*, 127).

28. Blair to Lincoln, May 17, 1863, ALP.

29. Chandler to his wife, May 20, 1863, LC; Whiting to Woodman, May 10, 1863, MHS.

30. *OR*, 21:142, 25(1):173–85; Barnes, *Medical and Surgical History*, 1:177.

31. *OR*, 24(1):4–5, 9, 18–24, 49; Charles Dana to EMS, May 3, 5, 6, 24, 1863, SP; William Christie to "Dear Brother," June 6, 1863, Thomas Christie to "My Dear Sister," June 7, 1863, both MNHS; Halleck to Grant, Burnside, and John Schofield, all June 2, 1863, SP.

32. Thomas Barnett Diary, June 10–20, 1863, Earlham; *Oxford Democrat*, July 31, 1863; *OR*, Series 3, 3:330–32, 3338–41, 351–52, 357, 372–73, 395–97; *The Crisis*, July 1, 1863; *North Missouri Courier*, July 2, 1863; Orlando Willcox to Ambrose Burnside, June 17, 1863, Burnside Papers, RG 94, NA; Charles Branich to "Dear Brother in law and Sister," June 9, 1863, MNHS; *Chicago Tribune*, June 26, 27, 1863; *Louisville Daily Democrat*, June 13, 16, 18, 1863; *Daily Constitutional Union*,

June 11, 1863; Joseph Wetherill to Samuel Yohe, June 11, 1863, Letters Received, RG 110, NA.

33. *OR*, Series 3, 3:371, 391–92.

34. Hitchcock Diary, May 24, 1863, Gilcrease Institute; Heintzelman Diary, May 20, 24–26, 1863, LC.

35. Hitchcock Diary, May 24, 1863, Gilcrease Institute.

36. *OR*, 27(1):34–35; Sparks, *Patrick Diary*, 258–61; Matthew Marvin Diary, June 17, 18, 1863, MNHS; William West Diary, June 15, 1863, MHS; Levi Perry to "Dear Sister," June 18, 1863, MEHS; Clinton Morrill to "Dear Carrie," June 23, 1863, Ingersoll Collection, MEHS.

37. Nevins, *Wainwright Journals*, 229; William Henry to Mary Jane Henry, July 1, 1863, VTHS; William Stow to "Dear Friends one & all," July 6, 1863, UVM; John Proudfit to "Dear Sister," June 1, 1863, University of Kansas; Boyd Hamilton to "My dear Mother," June 30, 1863, LC; *CWL*, 6:311–12; *New York Herald*, June 18, 1863.

38. *OR*, 27(1):55, 59–60; Beale, *Welles Diary*, 1:348. Stanton later cast the Harper's Ferry flap as a misunderstanding, arguing that had Hooker asked for the garrison he could have had it. Instead, Stanton said, Hooker ordered it to join him without asking permission. Ignoring Hooker's authority over those forces, Stanton said he and Halleck together countermanded the order, precipitating Hooker's request to be relieved (John C. Ropes memo of February 8, 1870, Woodman Papers, MHS). Charles Benjamin claimed that Stanton, Halleck, and Lincoln conspired to induce Hooker to resign, to avoid losing the support of his political friends or embarrassing Chase (*Battles and Leaders*, 3:239–43). Stephen Sears called this article "largely fictional" (*Controversies and Commanders*, 165n32), and Benjamin is indeed a very dubious source: he did not enter the War Department until late in 1864, based the story on hearsay if he did not invent it altogether, and only wrote it after all the other participants were dead.

39. Meade, *Life and Letters*, 2:11–12.

40. Charles Cummings to "My Dear Wife," July 6, 1863, Roswell Farnham to "Dear Mary," June 29, 1863, and Olney Seaver to "Dear Father," July 3, 1863, all VTHS.

41. James Brown to "Dear Friends," June 18, 1863, Leonard Valentine to "Dear Father and Mother," June 3, 1863, and Mark Waterman to "Dear Wife and Children," June 10, 1863, all at MEHS.

42. Heintzelman Diary, June 28, 29, 1863, LC; Horatio Taft Diary, June 29, 1863, LC; EMS to Daniel E. Somes, June 28, 1863, quoted in Stone, *History of the Twenty-seventh Maine*, 34–35; *OR*, 27(3):441, 637; *General Orders*, 138, quoted in Pullen, *A Shower of Stars*, 73.

43. Browne, *Complete Works*, 431. This was probably not among the Ward stories that Lincoln read to his cabinet.

44. Meade, *Life and Letters*, 2:132–34; Nevins, *Wainwright Journals*, 232–62; Sparks, *Patrick Diary*, 266–72.

45. Beale, *Welles Diary*, 1:369–70.

46. Sparks, *Patrick Diary*, 271; Dana to James Pike, July 29, 1863, UME; *OR*, 27(1):92–94; *CWL*, 6:327–29.

47. EMS to A. K. McClure, July 22, 1863, Letterbooks, SP; Eby, *Strother Diaries*, 193–94.

48. *OR*, 27(2):886–87; EMS telegram to Ellen Stanton, July 7, 1863, SP.

49. Greeley to "Dear Sir," June 12, 1863, SP, *New York Times*, July 14, 1863.

50. *New York Times*, July 14–18, 1863; *New York Tribune*, July 15, 1863; *Boston Journal*, July 15–17, 1863; Helen McCalla Diary, July 17, 1863, LC; Nevins and Thomas, *Strong Diary*, 3:335–40; Seymour to Abraham Lincoln, August 3, 1863, Lincoln Papers, LC.

51. *Louisville Daily Democrat*, August 4–7, 1863; *Cleveland Plain Dealer*, August 7, 1863.

52. *U.S. Reports* 67:360–72; Beale, *Bates Diary*, 282. Stanton had initiated the government's challenge to the Castillero and Berreyesa claims in 1858 (*Daily Alta California*, July 15, August 19, 20, September 1, 1858).

53. *CWL*, 6:205–6; Swett to William W. Orme, May 23, 1863, quoted in Ascher, "New Almaden Scandal," 49–50; *Daily Alta California*, July 11, 1863. In "An Uncertain Influence," 234, Robert Chandler attributed the decision to "a confused Supreme Court." Usher is described betraying Indian tribes to railroad interests in Bain, *Empire Express*, 108, 131–32, 168, 186. See James Eldredge to Jeremiah Black, April 6, 1862, Black Papers, LC, for a thinly disguised discussion of bribery in pursuit of the Fossat claim.

54. *Daily Alta California*, July 11, 1863; OR, 50(2):514–19, 522; CWL, 6:322.

55. *Daily Alta California*, July 14, 1863; *Sacramento Union*, May 27, 1863. Summers, *The Plundering Generation*, 161, asserts that Congress first prohibited lawyers from serving both the government and its litigants in 1853, but Quicksilver was not a claimant against the government, so Stanton might have legally represented the syndicate in 1858 while foiling one of its competitors as a special prosecutor. Comments like those in the *Daily Alta California* show that such conflicting alliances were still not regarded as innocent.

56. *New York World*, August 7, 17, 1863; *CWL*, 6:333–34; Beale, *Bates Diary*, 340, 354; *U.S. Reports* 69:649.

57. Beale, *Welles Diary*, 1:397–98; Blair to Gideon Welles, February 25, 1873, CHS.

58. Beale, *Welles Diary*, 1:397, 407. Chase soon overcame any annoyance; a few weeks later he was complimenting Stanton in his diary (Niven, *Chase Papers*, 4:133–34).

59. Williams and Atwater, *Catalogue of the Kenyon Chapter*, 41; Wolcott, 161.

60. Johnson, "Reminiscences," 92; Charles Benjamin to Horace White, June 1, 1914, White Papers, ALPLM.

61. Ben Wade to William Stanton, March 9, 1863, February 5, 1864, HM37033 and HM37034, and William Stanton to "Dear Daughter," October 12, 1907, HM37046, HL.

62. S. W. Jans to Henry Jackson, July 29, 1863, WHS; *OR*, 23(2):592–98, 30(3):32–33; Niven, *Chase Papers*, 4:103.

63. EMS to Ellen, August 25, 1863, GTS, LSU; *Sacramento Union*, May 27, 1863; *CWL*. 6:436; *OR*, 30(3):486–87; Lincoln's order, September 4, 1863, Letters Sent to the President (M127), RG 107. Stanton's absence is revealed in his letterbooks, SP.

64. David Nichol to "Dear Sister," September 18, 1863, USAMHI; Isaac Gardner to "Dear Parents," August 23, 1863, USAMHI; *Correspondence of John Sedgwick*, 2:145–54; Styple, *De Trobriand Letters*, 132; William Hamilton to "My dear Mother," September 4, 1863, LC; Nevins, *Wainwright Journals*, 277–78; Meade, *Life and Letters*, 2:145; *New York Tribune*, August 31, 1863; *OR*, 29(2):261–62.

65. *Correspondence of John Sedgwick*, 2:155; Nevins, *Wainwright Journals*, 282; Niven, *Chase Papers*, 1:449.

66. Halleck to Meade, September 22, 1863, and Meade to Halleck, same date, SP; Meade, *Life and Letters*, 2:150; *OR*, 29(2):227, 261–62; Nevins, *Wainwright Journals*, 282.

67. Sears, *McClellan Papers*, 581–82; Charles Morey to "Dear Parents," July 8, 1864, USAMHI; *OR*, 43(2):517, 46(3):1039.

68. Meade, *Life and Letters*, 2:150; *OR*, 29(2):207–8; Charles Dana to EMS, numerous telegrams, September 19–22, 1863, SP.

69. Burlingame and Ettlinger, *Hay Diary*, 85–86; Dana to EMS, 1:40 P.M. and 5:00 P.M., September 23, 1863, SP.

70. Burlingame and Ettlinger, *Hay Diary*, 86; Niven, *Chase Papers*, 1:450.

71. Niven, *Chase Papers*, 1:450–52.

72. Ibid., 452–54. In one of his two journals Chase mistook the meeting for September 24.

73. *OR*, 29(1):146–95; Niven, *Chase Papers*, 1:454.

74. *OR*, 29(1):158, 172–80, 190–92; Rufus Mead to "Dear Folks at Home," September 25, 29, and October 4, 1863, LC; James Miller to "Dear Mother," October 11, 1863, CL; L. M. Cole to EMS, October 6, 1863, SP.

75. Supposing that Stanton had moved 30,000 men, Phillip Paludan noted in *"A People's Contest,"* 298–99, that he had "pulled off the most remarkable feats of transport and organization in the entire war." It was still impressive with only 18,000 troops.

76. Samuel Allen to "My Dear Father," October 12, 1863, CCHS; Davis, *Butler Family Letters*, 48; Margaret Jones Diary, September 28, 1862, Earlham.

77. Beale, *Welles Diary*, 1:471; Edwin May et al. to Oliver P. Morton, [September 28, 1863], SP; Morton to EMS, October 1, 1863, SP; EMS to R. P. Spaulding, September 10, 1863, to O. B. Matteson, October 16, 1863, to William Pitt Fessenden, August 3, 1863, and to Hannibal Hamlin, August 20, 1863, Letterbooks, SP; Alfred Denny to John Sherman, October 15, 1863, John Sherman Papers, LC; *Oxford Democrat*, September 18, 1863.

CHAPTER 13

1. Beale, *Welles Diary*, 1:446–47; *USG*, 9:273; Nathaniel Banks to Mary Banks, September 5, 1863, LC; C. C. Washburn to Elihu Washburne, September 5, 1863, LC.

2. *USG*, 9:281, 283, 296–98; Grant, *Personal Memoirs*, 2:17–19; Burlingame and Ettlinger, *Hay Diary*, 94.

3. *USG*, 9:296–98, 302–3, 308; *OR*, 30(4):434, 31(1):684; Montgomery Meigs to "My dear Father," October 22, 1863, LC; John Hay to Charles Halpine, October 24, 1863, LC.

4. *OR*, Series 2, 5:128, 394, 397, 795–97, 6:380–81.

5. Nathaniel Banks to "My Dearest Mary," January 15, 1863, LC; *OR*, Series 2, 5:940–41.

6. *OR*, Series 2, 3:244, 254.

7. Ibid., 3:301–2, 310, 322, 341, 376, 588, 4:174, 266–68, 278, 821, and Series 1, 11(2):37, 973–84.

8. *OR*, Series 2, 4:267–68, 6:78–79.

9. Ibid., 6:163–64, 381. White was still a prisoner ten months later. Ibid., 7:679–80.

10. William Cabot Russell to "Dear Ellen," September 7, 1863, and John Murray Forbes to "my dear Shaw," September 6, 1863, both in Russell Papers, NYPL; Lamon manuscript (LN2454), HL; *OR*, Series 2, 7:62–63, 606–7. Hyman, 374, cited a copy of an undated memo in the estate of Benjamin Thomas, ostensibly prepared for Grant by Stanton, in which Stanton proposed the manpower argument for ending exchanges. In *Andersonvilles of the North*, 37–38, 86–94, James Gillispie noted that Union authorities had to consider the numbers and condition of the prisoners to be exchanged, lest Confederates profit by an exchange, but the mathematical arguments posed by Grant and Stanton, and Lincoln's confession to the New Yorkers, show that concern over black prisoners was not the only reason for suspending exchanges, and may not even have been the paramount reason.

11. *OR*, Series 2, 6:457–58, 468, 485–86; Hitchcock to Mrs. Horace Mann, November 25, 1863, Ethan Allen Hitchcock Papers, LC.

12. *OR*, Series 2, 7:101, 113–14, 150–51, 183–84, Series 3, 3:1130; *Harper's Weekly* and *Leslie's Illustrated Newspaper*, June 18, 1864; EMS to Wade, May 4, 1864, cited in Trefousse, *Benjamin Franklin Wade*, 215. Barnes, *Medical and Surgical History*, 3:49–65, 103–264, recounts the case histories of hundreds of men who died in Union hospitals from chronic diarrhea or dysentery, most of whom showed extreme emaciation despite close care and adequate food. Horigan, *Elmira* (87), rejects Hyman's lenient interpretation of Stanton's proposal, but it should be pointed out that the reduced diet Stanton approved was still more than the Confederate army issued to its own soldiers and prisoners (*OR*, Series 2, 7:521–22).

13. *OR*, Series 2, 6:439, 497–98, 558; Testimony of Uriah B. Harrold, Isaac Turner Case No.11496, Congressional Jurisdiction Case Files, RG 123, NA.

14. *OR*, 31(1):273–78, 31(2):31–36; William Draper to "My dear Wife," December 1, 1863, LC; Daniel Larned to "Dear Sister" and to "Dear Henry," November 14, 1863, Larned Papers, LC; Willard Templeton memorandum, November 26, 1863, New Hampshire State Library; George Hodges to "Dear Wife," November 18, 1863, WRHS; W. C. Patton Diary, November 24, 25, 1863, IHS; William Swayze to "Dear Mother," December 3, 1863, HIS; Henry Robinson to wife, [December, 1863], IHS; Charles Caley to "My Dear Wife," November 27, 1863, Notre Dame; J. Dexter Cotton to "My dear wife," November 26, 1863, LC; Alexander Varian to "Dear Father," November 27, 1863, WRHS; Albion Tourgee to "Darling Wife," November 29, 1863, CCHS; Myron Wood to "Dear Father," February 12, 1864, MHS; John Whitten Diary, November 25, 1863, SHSI-DM.

15. *RJCCW2*, 2:343–47; Meade, *Life and Letters*, 2:156–59; Sparks, *Patrick Diary*, 313–19; Joseph C. Rutherford to "My dear wife," December 13, 1863, UVM; Sidney Burbank Diary, November 30, 1863, LC; Nevins, *Wainwright Journals*, 308.

16. Wolcott, 160; Burlingame and Ettlinger, *Hay Diary*, 111–12. The limits of the trip are again defined by the gap in Stanton's letterbook (SP) between November 24 and 30.

17. Beale, *Bates Diary*, 318; Beale, *Welles Diary*, 1:480; Horatio Taft Diary, December 3, 1863, LC; *CWL*, 7:53–56.

18. *OR*, Series 3, 3:231–35, 711–12; Niven, *Chase Papers*, 4:133–35; Banks to Lincoln, December 30, 1863, ALP; *CWL*, 7:123–25, 243. Banks's objection to black suffrage is missing from the version of this letter published in *CWL*. Foner, *The Fiery Trial*, 282, alleges that Stanton made the revision "with Lincoln's approval," perhaps on Chase's comment that "Mr. Stanton & the President" were responsible for the instructions, but those orders do not include the usual note that they are "by order of the president."

19. Burlingame and Ettlinger, *Hay Diary*, 120; William Orton to Chase, December 5, 1863, HSP; EMS to Harriet Beecher Stowe, December 7, 1863, Letterbooks, SP; Henry Ward Beecher to EMS, December 14, 1863, Letters Received (M221), RG 107, NA; *Independent*, October 15, November 5, 1863; EMS to Salmon P. Chase, December 30, 1863, HSP; Arden Smith to Andrew Johnson, February 27, 1866, Johnson Papers, LC; Williams, *Garfield Letters*, 301.

20. U.S. House, *Hurtt Court Martial*, 5–6; *Cincinnati Daily Commercial*, April 23, 1863; *The Crisis*, May 6, July 29, 1863; Burnett to EMS, December 10, 14, 1863, Letters Sent by the Secretary of War Relating to Military Affairs (M6), RG 107, NA. Wilson, *The Business of Civil War* (186–88, 273n75), found fraud rife in supply departments during the second half of the war, and dozens of government contractors were court-martialed, including two friends of the Speed brothers whom Lincoln pardoned.

21. Barnes, *Medical and Surgical History*, 12:930–31, 933–35; *CG*, 37th Cong., 2nd sess., 3062, 37th Cong. 3rd sess., 194, 523, 719–21; Nevins and Thomas, *Strong Diary*, 3:227, 234, 248–49, 257, 306.

22. Barnes, *Medical and Surgical History*, 4:717–22.

23. EMS to Hammond, May 26, 1863, Letters Sent (M-421), RG 107, NA; Nevins and Thomas, *Strong Diary*, 3: 353; [Hammond], *Statement*, 24–25, 29.

24. Nevins and Thomas, *Strong Diary*, 3:358–59. 393, 418; E. D. Townsend to Hammond, December 2, 1863, Letterbooks, SP; [Hammond], *Statement*, 26–28; *CWL*, 7:93.

25. Special Order 24, Court Martial of Surgeon General William A. Hammond, MM1430, 173–196, Court Martial Case Files, RG 153, NA; [Hammond], *Statement*, 68–69; *OR*, 33:617. A witness later testified to a congressional committee that General Slough was "a warm personal friend of Secretary Stanton" (*Impeachment Investigation*, 665). On Stanton's unsuccessful attempt to find Starkweather an assignment, see *OR*, 43(2):725.

26. Chase to Bingham, November 4, 1859, Bingham Papers, OHS; *CWL*, 6:363; [Hammond], *Statement*, 68–69.

27. U.S. House, *Hurtt Court Martial*, 5–354; Court Martial of Surgeon General William A. Hammond, MM1430, 173–196, Court Martial Case Files, RG 153, NA; Niven, *Chase Papers*, 4:21; Nevins and Thomas, *Strong Diary*, 3:418–19; *Reply of the Judge Advocate*, 2–3.

28. Nevins and Thomas, *Strong Diary*, 3:418; [Hammond], *Statement*, 33, 35–36, 38, 41–43, 48, 51–52, 55, 57–58; *Reply of the Judge Advocate*, 20–21

29. [Hammond], *Statement*, 32–33; 54, 65–66, 73; *New York Times*, August 22, 1864.

30. [Hammond], *Statement*, 72; Court Martial of Surgeon General William A. Hammond, MM1430, Court Martial Case Files, RG 153, NA (pages 1963 through 2124 are missing).

31. *New York Times*, August 22, 1864; *Reply of the Judge Advocate*, 24; [Hammond], *Statement*, 71–73.

32. *New York Times*, August 24, 1864.

33. EMS to Benjamin Loan, February 22, 1864 (on department advertising with supportive newspapers), SP; EMS to Joshua Speed, February 18, 1864, Letterbooks, SP; Speed to Holt, September 8, 12, 1864, H. W. Allen to Holt, September 11, 1864, and Rosecrans to Holt, September 14, 1864, all in Holt Papers, LC. Gideon Welles resisted similar pressure to extort campaign funds from Navy Yard employees, considering it unethical and obnoxious (Beale, *Welles Diary*, 2:123, 137). Wilson, *The Business of Civil War*, 170–73, recounted the ordeal of a career army quartermaster who was acquitted by a court martial of skimming money this way, but was still arbitrarily dismissed by Stanton.

34. On pressure from the War Department, just before the election, one quartermaster arranged several million dollars' worth of contracts for overcoats with a Philadelphia company that had never made clothing, and a Nashville quartermaster openly solicited Republican campaign contributions from contractors, implying that those who did not donate might be cut off: Herman Biggs to Montgomery Meigs, November 5, 1864, Meigs Papers, LC; John Crane to William Browning, October 26, 1864, Johnson Papers, LC, cited in Wilson, *The Business of Civil War*, 178. Wilson (178) also found correspondence indicating that another Philadelphia contractor paid several thousand dollars in "election expenses." Smith, *The Enemy Within*, 3–4, noted that illicit campaign-funding schemes like the one pursued by Stanton and Holt netted far less than they do in modern times, but that at the time the public seemed to view them as even more deplorable.

35. Barnes, *Medical and Surgical History*, 4:720–22. Adams, *Doctors in Blue* (41), considered Hammond's conviction a victory for hidebound traditionalists.

36. Richard Henry Dana to "My Dear Lathrop," May 4, 1864, MHS; John Harper to EMS, December 25, 1863, May 4, 1865, with Special Order No. 5, January 5, 1864, and EMS to Harper and to Godfrey Weitzel, May 31, 1865, HHC; EMS to "Dear Madam," December 1, 1863, Worthington Family Papers, OHS; EMS to Robert C. Grier, November 30, 1863, April 20, 1864, to Thomas S. Jewett, December 2, 1863, to Harriet Beecher Stowe, December 7, 1863, and to George Julian, December 16, 1863, Letterbooks, SP; John Catron to EMS, January 26, [1864], Lamon Papers, HL; Charles Sumner to Horace Gray, December 30, 1863, LC.; Lincoln to EMS,

July 12, 1862, with endorsement, Lincoln Collection, NYPL; EMS to Parke Godwin, April 22, 1863, Bryant-Godwin Papers, NYPL; Palmer and Ochoa, *Selected Papers of Thaddeus Stevens*, 1:420–21. Stevens considered the letter "too mendicant" and asked Stanton to return it.

37. See, for example, E. R. S. Canby to William Blanchard, December 26, 1863, to Lucy Harris, January 6, 1864, to Hewitt & Edminston, January 23, 1864, to Nancy Baldwin, January 25, 1864, to James H. Campbell, February 3, 1864, to Mary Hagerty, February 5, 1864, to Reverend W. Fass, February 5, 1864, to George Babcock, February 29, 1864, and to Eliza Elder, March 7, 1864; James Hardie to V. B. Horton, December 5, 1863, and to L. A. Baker, January 2, 1864, all in Letters Sent (M6), RG 107, NA; John P. Hatch to "Dear Father," April 1, 1863, LC; Lincoln to EMS, and EMS to Lincoln, both March 1, 1864, SP; draft of a pledge for cadets, January 14, 1864, approved by EMS, Orders and Endorsements Sent (M444), RG 107, NA.

38. *CG*, 37th Cong., 2nd sess., 386, 444, 37th Cong. 3rd sess., 451, 691, and 38th Cong., 1st sess., 210, 233; James Wilson to "Dear Ad," March 22, 1867, Wilson Papers, LC; Wolcott, 159, 160; Charles Benjamin to Horace White, June 1, 1914, White Papers, ALPLM; ELS to Eben Sturges, May 16, 1864, Kenyon. Dana's official service as assistant secretary began January 28, 1864 (*OR*, Series 3, 4:1035) after Congress reauthorized another assistant, but he had been calling himself the assistant secretary for months by then (Dana to James Pike, July 29 and August 18, 1863, UME). Despite his intimacy with Dana, Stanton remained cordial with the influential Horace Greeley, whom Dana had left with hard feelings (EMS to Greeley, February 10, 1864, NYPL).

39. *CG*, 37th Cong., 2nd sess., 334; inspection report of R. S. Alexander, February 3, 1865, Register of Reports, 1864, Entry 2, RG 159, NA; George Ramsay to EMS, December 3, 1863, Reel 29, Letters Received (M494), RG 107, NA.

40. *OR*, Series 3, 3:1199; EMS to George Opdyke, September 19, 1863, Letterbooks, SP. For Opdyke's interest in the Gibbs carbine, see Edwards, *Civil War Guns*, 123–24. Wilson, *The Business of Civil War*, 180–81, relates Thurlow Weed's accusation of wartime profiteering against Opdyke, who sued unsuccessfully for libel.

41. Ramsay to EMS, October 17, December 3, 1863, Letters Received (M494), RG 107, NA; *Proceedings of a Court of Inquiry*, 1:189, 192, 500–502; *OR*, Series 3, 4:1035.

42. EMS to Meigs, September 24, 1863, SP; *New York Herald*, September 15, 1863; Hay to "Miles" [i.e., Halpine], October 24, 1863, Hay Papers, LC.

43. W. A. Nichols to Myer, September 22, 1863, quoted in Scheips, "Albert James Myer," 567–68; Anson Stager to Edwin Stanton, October 27, 1863, quoted in Plum, *The Military Telegraph*, 2:100–101; *OR*, Series 3, 3:948–61, 968–72; Circular of September 18, 1863, quoted in Brown, *The Signal Corps*, 180–81.

44. EMS to Joseph Taylor, February 5, 1864, Letterbooks, SP; *OR*, Series 3, 3:892, 4:59, 67–68; EMS to Fessenden, February 11, 1864, and joint resolution, Letterbooks, SP.

45. J. H. Ela to John P. Hale, February 3, 1864, NHHS; *OR*, Series 3, 4:93, 99–102; *Dover Enquirer*, February 18, 1864.

46. Child, *Letters*, 203; Chandler to Gilmore, December 14, 1863, Gilmore Papers, NHHS; Augustus Paddock to "Dear Father," February 25, 1864, UVM; Leander Harris to "Dear Emmy," January 6, February 7, 1864, UNH; *OR*, Series 3, 4:101; Chandler to "My Dear Sir" [Frank E. Howe], February 17, 1864, Chandler Papers, NHHS; *New Hampshire Patriot*, March 2, 1864.

47. Robert Hale Kellogg to "Dear Father," March 25, 1864, CHS; *OR*, Series 3, 4:160, 181, 232; Beale, *Welles Diary*, 1:541–42; *Daily Chronicle*, April 7, 12, 1864.

48. *OR*, 24(3):547, 32(3):18; Burlingame, *With Lincoln in the White House*, 129–30; *New York Tribune*, September 2, 1863; *CG*, 38th Cong., 1st sess., 434, 586–94, 842, 874, 936.

49. Burlingame, *With Lincoln in the White House*, 121, 130–31; Hunter to Charles Halpine, October 16, December 18, 1863 (HP129), HL; Halleck to Lieber, January 11, March 7, 1864 (LI1690, LI1694), HL.

50. Hunter to Charles Halpine, March 10, 1864 (HP129), HL; *RJCCW2*, 1:388; *OR*, 33:717–18; Meade, *Life and Letters*, 2:169, 182–83; Daniel Spofford to "Dear Mother," March 30, 1864, MHS; Washington Roebling to "Dear Em," April 10, 1864, Rutgers.

51. *RJCCW2*, 1:ix, xix, 295–329; Meade, *Life and Letters*, 2:160.

52. Meade, *Life and Letters*, 2:169–70; *RJCCW2*, 1:329–47.

53. Meade, *Life and Letters*, 2:176–78, 183–84, 186–87; *RJCCW2*, 1:xx–xxi, 347–51, 359–76, 417–75; *OR*, 27(1):127–37.

54. *OR*, 34(2):756; Heitman, *Register*, 1:92.

55. *The Crisis*, February 3, March 9, April 6, 27, 1863; *Illinois State Journal*, April 4, 1864; *OR*, Series 3, 4:148–53, 155; Heintzelman Diary, March 4, 5, 29, April 28, 1864, LC; James Hardie to Heintzelman, April 20, 1864, Letterbooks, SP; Wright to Joseph Holt, October 17, 1864, Holt Papers, LC.

56. *OR*, Series 2, 7: 658, 660, 8:523–25; The careers of Bickley and Wright are detailed in Klement, *Dark Lanterns*, 7–33, 64–90: recent attempts at revising Klement's depiction of the secret societies' impotence (Weber, *Copperheads*, and van der Linden, *The Dark Intrigue*) seem unduly credulous of the government case, which was largely a propaganda ploy.

57. Wright to Holt, October 17, 1864, and to Theodore Romeyn, November 27, 1864, Holt Papers, LC; William S. Buchanan to EMS, November 30, 1863, with endorsement, and EMS to Buchanan, December 8, 1863, Letters Received (M221), RG 107, NA; T. J. Barnett to Barlow, May 23, 1863, March 20, 1864 (BW Boxes 43 and 49), and Barlow to Blair, May 28, 1864, Letterbook 7, Barlow Papers, HL.

58. James E. Love to "Molly," December 14, 1863, MOHS; *OR*, Series 2, 6:659, 691.

59. Butler, *Correspondence*, 3:373–74; *CWL*, 7:202–3; *OR*, 33:118, 140, 519–22, 541.

60. *OR*, 33:172–73; Meade, *Life and Letters*, 2:166–68. A photograph of Fairfield as the headquarters of Kilpatrick's quartermaster appears in Miller's *Photographic History*, 4:51; the scene is mislabeled Brandy Station, but Clark B. Hall identified the actual site when researching the army's Stevensburg encampment ("Season of Change," 50).

61. *OR*, 33:183–88, 194–96; Washington Roebling to John Roebling, March 1, "1863" [1864], Rutgers; Charles Greenleaf to "Dear Father & Mother," February 26, 1864, CHS; George Lyon to "Dear Friend," March 6, 1864, VTHS; John Sheahan to "My Dear Father and Mother," and to "My Dear Father," both March 5, 1864, MEHS; William Wells to "Dear Friend Anna," March 25, 1864, UVM; William Hills Diary, March 1, 1864, LC.

62. *OR*, 33:178–80; Henry Higginbotham to Thomas Higginbotham, March 15, 1864, Schary Collection, NYPL.

63. *OR*, Series 2, 7:62–63.

64. William Hoffman's report of May 2, 1864, Register of Reports, 1864, Entry 2, RG 159, NA; Consolidated Morning Reports, May 1–4, 1864, Entry 111, RG 249, NA.

65. *OR*, Series 3, 4:237–44; Maggie Wade to "My Dear Aunt," May 13, 1864, Wade Papers, LC; E. A. Miller to "My dear Clason," May 15, 1864, and Catherine Fisk to "Dear Cousin," May 16, 1864, Schwab Letters, Cincinnati Historical Society; Davis, *Butler Letters*, 78, 81.

66. Ohio Provost Marshal's Papers, 52, 262, OHS; *OR*, Series 3, 4:131, 473, 966, 1225.

CHAPTER 14

1. *OR*, 37(1):10, 41; Longacre, *Wightman Letters*, 173; George Julian to "My dear Parents & Sister," May 11, 1864, UNH; Andrew Linscott to "Dear Parents," May 19, 1864, MHS; George Cobham Diary, May 6, 1864, CCHS.

2. Andrew Linscott to "Dear Parents," May 19, 1864, MHS; Samuel Pingree to "Cousin Hunton," June 10, 1864, VTHS; Charles Richardson Diary, May 5, 1864, LC; John Bailey Journal, May 6–15, 1864, NHHS; Charles Cummings to "My Dear Wife," May 15, 1864, VTHS. From May 5 to June 1 Grant's forces reported 40,051 casualties, and on June 4 Charles Dana forwarded Stanton an estimate of up to 7,500 lost in the action of June 2–4 (*OR*, 36[1]:89, 133, 149, 164); McClellan lost about 25,370 in his Peninsula campaign (Sears, *To the Gates of Richmond*, 355), and 15,220 in the Maryland campaign.

3. Leander Harris to Emily Harris, May 11, 17, 1864, UNH; George Julian to "My dear Parents & Sister," May 11, 18, 1864, UNH; Mushkat, *Voris Letters*, 166–69; Longacre, *Wightman Letters*, 175–81; William Willoughby to "My Dear Wife," May [13 or 14], 15, 22, 1864, AAS; Charles Paine to "Dear Father," May 17, 1864, MHS.

4. *OR*, 38(1):63–64; Quaife, *Williams Letters*, 306; George Hodges to "Dear Wife," May 20, 1864, WRHS; J. B. Dawley to "Dear Brother," June 1, 1864, Yale; Francis Crowninshield Journal, May 15, 16, 1864, Peabody Essex Museum; Charles Senior to "Dear Father," May 17, 1864, UVA.

5. French, *Journals*, 450; Nevins and Thomas, *Strong Diary*, 3:447; Beale, *Welles Diary*, 2:33, 35.

6. Beale, *Welles Diary*, 2:35; *OR*, Series 3, 4:387–89; *CWL*, 7:347–48. Stahr, *Seward* (395–96), seemed to question Welles's description of Seward driving the newspaper shutdown.

7. Beale, *Welles Diary*, 1:321–22; *OR*, Series 2, 5:723–24.

8. *OR*, Series 3, 4:388–89.

9. Ibid., 389–94; Barlow to McClellan, May 18, 1864, Letterbook 9, Barlow Papers, HL.

10. *OR*, Series 3, 4:390; *CWL*, 7:512–13.

11. *CG*, 38th Cong., 1st sess., 258.

12. Ibid., 3448–49.

13. Henry Winter Davis to Wade, undated (June, 1864), Wade Papers, LC; *CG*, 38th Cong., 1st sess., 2108, 3407, 3457–61, 3518, 3491. The creation of West Virginia had, inconsistently, included the retention of Carlile (who was from Wheeling) as a "Virginia" senator.

14. Burlingame and Ettlinger, *Hay Diary*, 217–18; *CWL*, 7:433–34.

15. *CG*, 38th Cong., 1st sess., 259; EMS to Davis, January 26, 1864, Letterbooks, SP; Davis to Samuel F. Du Pont, April 8, 1864, Box 43, Du Pont Papers, HML.

16. *OR*, 29(2):290, 394–95, 547; Davis to Samuel F. Du Pont, November 4, 1863, January 9, 1864, Box 43, Du Pont Papers, HML.

17. Chase to Lincoln, February 22, 1864, Lincoln to Chase February 23, 29, 1864, and Jesse Dubois to Lincoln, February 25, 1864, all ALP; Chase to Albert Gallatin Riddle, March 11, 1864, WRHS; *CWL*, 7:412–14, 419.

18. Hyman, 91, credits EMS with income of at least $40,000 in 1859, but $20,000 of the amount he collected reflected the final payment for his 1858 work in California, and he also received a considerable amount for expenses incurred on that mission: U.S. House, *Expenditures on Account of Private Land Claims*, 3, 7, 10, 11, 13–15, 28, 50.

19. The Stantons kept four servants and a carriage, and Ellen held weekly receptions: Eighth U.S. Census (M653), Reel 103, 375, RG 29, NA; "An Iowa Woman," 66–67. Bates, (*Lincoln in the Telegraph Office*, 397–98), placed the Stantons at the Soldiers' Home in the summer of 1864. Late in life Lewis Stanton, who was born in 1860, remembered staying at the Soldiers' Home "in the summer from 1861 to 1867" (letter excerpt, January 4, 1930, transcript at PVA&M). He was clearly mistaken about 1861, and they rented a house west of Georgetown in 1862; in 1863 Ellen summered at Bedford Springs.

20. *CWL*, 7:417; William McVey Diary, July 8, 9, 1864, OHS; William Henry to "My Darling Wife," July 12, 1864, VTHS; D. B. Harmon to Eron N. Thomas, July 22, 1864, Civil War Collection, AAS.

21. David Homer Bates Diary, July 10, 1864, LC; Benjamin French to Pamela French, July 17, 1864, NHHS; Horatio Taft Diary, July 9–11, 1864, LC.

22. EMS to Lincoln, July 9, 10, 1864, ALP; *Sacramento Union*, August 10, 1864; Beale, *Welles Diary*, 2:71–74, 78; Burlingame and Ettlinger, *Hay Diary*, 221–22; Beale, *Bates Diary*, 384; David Homer Bates Diary, July 11, 1864, LC; Richard Auchmuty to Samuel Wylie Crawford, July 25, 1864, CL; Sarah Low to "Dear Mother," July 11, 1864, NHHS; Lyman Holford Diary, July 11, 1864, LC; *OR*, 37(2):188, 191, 195, 220.

23. Niven, *Chase Papers*, 1:480; Wolcott, 161; *OR*, 37(1):265; 37(2):204, 265; Brun, "Fleming Letters," 34–35.

24. *OR*, 37(1):349; Beale, *Welles Diary*, 2:72; Burlingame and Ettlinger, *Hay Diary*, 221; Lyman Holford Diary, July 11, 1864, LC; John Peirce to "My Dear Wife," July 15, 1864, Peabody Essex Museum.

25. Lorenzo Miles Diary, July 11, 1864, VTHS; Edward Roberts Diary, July 12, 1864, CHS; Chandler Watts Diary, July 11, 12, 1864, Cheney-Watts Collection, VTHS; William West Diary, July 12, 1864, MHS; William Adams Diary, July 12, 1864, MEHS; Beale, *Welles Diary*, 2:74–75; George Stevens to "Darling Hattie," July 12, 1864, CL; *OR*, 37(2):195, 259; Wolcott, 161–62; Pease and Randall, *Browning Diary*, 1:676.

26. *OR*, 37(2):262–63; Beale, *Welles Diary*, 2:76–77; Sylvester Bishop to "Dear Mother," July 29, 1864, IHS; Niven, *Chase Papers*, 1:479. Early himself reckoned his infantry at no more than ten thousand men (*OR*, 37[1]:348).

27. *CG*, 37th Cong., 3rd sess., 691, 1054–55, 1151; Palmer, *Sumner Letters*, 2:184; *OR*, Series 3, 368–70, 460–61; Beale, *Welles Diary*, 2:84–85.

28. *New York Tribune*, August 5, 1864.

29. Davis to Wade, undated (filed between August 2 and 3, 1864), Wade Papers, LC; Niven, *Chase Papers*, 4:420–22; James Ashley to Chase, August 5, 1864, LC; Orson S. Murray to Benjamin Wade, September 6, 1864, LC; Palmer, *Sumner Letters*, 2:249, 251; Raymond to Fessenden, August 11, 1864, Goodyear Collection, Yale; Raymond to Lincoln and Weed to Seward, both August 22, 1864, ALP.

30. *CWL*, 7:514; Burlingame and Ettlinger, *Hay Diary*, 247–48.

31. *CWL*, 7:517–18; Burlingame, *With Lincoln in the White House*, 152. Nicolay's personal memorandum on this meeting of "the stronger half of the cabinet," ostensibly "made at the time," appears in Nicolay and Hay, *Abraham Lincoln*, 9:221, but is not included in the published collection of his various writings.

32. Beale, *Welles Diary*, 2:102; Niven, *Chase Papers*, 1:602.

33. Black to EMS, August 24, September 3, 1864, and EMS to Black, August 31, 1864, Black Papers, LC; Thompson to John Mason and John Slidell, August "28," 1864, quoted in Hines, "The Northwestern Conspiracy," 508–9; *OR*, Series 4, 3:636–38. The date of Thompson's letter was probably misread by the typesetter and was likely August 23: had he written on August 28, Black's visit "three days" before would have fallen on August 25, but Black was back in Washington by August 24, reporting to Stanton on the meeting.

34. Greeley to "My Friend," August 30, 1864, Palmer Collection, WRHS; Weed to Seward, September 10, 1864, ALP; Palmer, *Sumner Letters*, 2:251–52.

35. *CWL*, 7:461; William Cassidy to Samuel Barlow, September 5, 1864 (BW Box 50), Barlow Papers, HL; George Codman to "Little Sissie," September 11, 1864, DC; James Rickard to "Dear Brother," September 12, 1864, AAS; "John" to "Forrest," September 14, 1864, William Hunter Papers, OHS; George Stearns to "Dear Mother," September 18, 1864, NHHS. Waugh, *Reelecting Lincoln*, 285–86, dates the adoption of the peace plank.

36. *OR*, 23(2):193–94, Series 2, 5:363–67; Jonathan Joseph to "Dear Sister," April 10, 1863, ISL; James Moses to Jacob Ammen, April 24, 1863, OHS; Wayne Morris to "My Beloved Companion," May 27, 1863, BL. By the 1863 elections in the West, Gettysburg and Vicksburg had been offset by Chickamauga, and Carrington's propaganda may have played a greater role in the spectacular Republican resurgence than has been supposed.

37. Sanderson to Rosecrans, May 31, 1864, with numerous lettered attachments, and H. W. Reid to Rosecrans, March 8, 1864, Sanderson Papers, OHS. An extended report dated June 12, 1864 (but containing material of later date) is in *OR*, Series 2, 7:228–366.

38. *CWL*, 7:379, 386–88; Burlingame and Ettlinger, *Hay Diary*, 204–7.

39. *Daily Journal*, June 30, 1864; *Missouri Democrat*, July 28, 1864.

40. *OR*, Series 3, 4:488. Leonard (*Lincoln's Forgotten Ally*, 176) remarked that it would be "simply impossible" to examine in detail the "tens of thousands of cases" that came under Holt's authority, which raises the question of how Holt did so, especially when pet cases and political errands occupied so much of his time.

41. Holt to EMS, July 29, 1864, SP; *OR*, 39(2):208, 212–15, Series 3, 4:577–79.

42. Sanderson to Rosecrans, August 20, 1864, with attachments, OHS; Stanton to Holt, August 31, 1864, SP; Carrington to Richard Thompson, September 4, 1864, ISL; *Report of the Judge Advocate General* [this is the pamphlet form of Holt's report, published in *OR*, Series 2, 7:930–53]; *Detroit Free Press*, October 20, 1864; *OR*, Series 3, 4:702–3, 711–12, 714, 716–17; EMS to Edwin Morgan, September 4, 1864, SP.

43. See, for instance, *ORN*, Series 2, 3:1234–39; *OR*, 43(2):930–36. Weber, *Copperheads*, 148–49, 243n35, appears not to consider how extensively military authorities exaggerated the threat of the secret societies for Republican propaganda purposes.

44. Pittman, *Trials for Treason*, 9, 80–81; *Chicago Times*, October 22, 1864; *OR*, Series 3, 4:716–17. On Hovey and the depredations of his division see Thomas Hughes to "My Dear Wife," December 21, 1862, CL; John Barney to "All at Home," January 2, 1863, WHS; Thomas Sterns to "Dear Wife," January 1, 1863, UIA; Woodworth, *Musick of the Mocking Birds*, 13; John S. Phelps to EMS (report, unsigned), October 20, 1862, SP.

45. Pittman, *Trials for Treason*, 17–72; *Daily Journal*, October 8, 1864; *Chicago Times*, October 22, 1864.

46. Burlingame and Ettlinger, *Hay Diary*, 239–41; Dana, *Recollections*, 261–62; Oliver P. Morton to EMS, October 12, 1864, and Union State Central Committee (of Pennsylvania) to EMS, November 10, 1864, SP. Dana misremembered the incident as happening the night of the presidential election, at which time Stanton was confined to his bed.

47. Hoar to Evarts, February, 1864, May 26, October 30, November 16, 1864, CL; Pease and Randall, *Browning Diary*, 1:688; Chase to EMS, October 13, 1864, SP.

48. EMS to Chase, October 13, 1864, HSP; Grier to EMS, October 13, 1864, reproduced in Gorham, 2:470–71; Pease and Randall, *Browning Diary*, 1:687–88. Stanton and three bureau chiefs visited City Point, Bermuda Hundred, and the Petersburg trenches on October 16 and 17 (Sparks, *Patrick Diary*, 430–31; EMS to Lincoln, October 16, "1863" [1864], filed under the mistaken date, SP).

49. William Evarts to Richard Henry Dana, November 16, 1864, and Dana to Thornton Lothrop, November 21, 1864, Dana Family Papers, MHS; Pease and Randall, *Browning Diary*, 1:688; Sparks, *Patrick Diary*, 442, 445.

50. Hoar to Evarts, November 16, 1864, CL; Beale, *Bates Diary*, 427; Edwards Pierrepont to Lincoln, November 24, 1864, ALP; Beale, *Welles Diary*, 2:181–82,

183, 192; Dana to James Pike, December 12, 1864, UME. The story of the Kilkenny cats describes them fighting each other until nothing remained of either but the tail.

51. Pittman, *Trials for Treason*, 73–157. *Ex parte Milligan* declared military commissions like the one at Indianapolis unconstitutional in 1866.

52. Nevins and Thomas, *Strong Diary*, 3:489.

53. *OR*, Series 3, 4:709–10, 712–13.

54. *CWL*, 8:18–20; Alexander Black to Jane Black, September 25, 1864, Hagaman Collection, MOHS; *Prairie Du Chien Courier*, November 3, 1864; Weed to Lincoln, November 6, 1864 (second letter of that date), ALP.

55. William Cannon to EMS, October 27, 1864 (three letters), SP; *Delaware Journal*, November 8, 1864; *OR*, 42(3):471; voter authorization of William Bennit, CL; Thurlow Weed to Lincoln, November 6, 1864 (both letters of that date), ALP; *OR*, 42(3):470; Burlingame and Ettlinger, *Hay Diary*, 243.

56. *OR*, 42(3):470, 480–81, 489, 491; Nevins and Thomas, *Strong Diary*, 3:509, 510.

57. Burlingame and Ettlinger, *Hay Diary*, 242–46; *Sacramento Union*, December 10, 1864; Beale, *Welles Diary*, 2:178–79; Burlingame and Ettlinger, *Hay Diary*, 246; Dana to James Pike, December 12, 1864, UME.

58. Brooks, *Washington*, 36; Report of R. S. Alexander, February 3, 1865, Register of Reports, 1864, Entry 2, RG 159, NA. The War Department building was demolished and replaced in the 1870s (Ames, *Ten Years in Washington*, 465).

59. Beale, *Welles Diary*, 2:179.

60. Ibid., 2:187; Edward Bates to "My Dear Son," December 25, 1864, VHS; "Your loving M." to "My beloved Cousin," December 18, [1864; misfiled as 1862], Holt Papers, LC. Holt, who had been unemployed and financially embarrassed in 1857, retired from the judge advocate general's office in 1875 with a sizable fortune.

61. *New York Times*, September 7, 1864; Gideon Welles to Montgomery Blair, November 18, 1872, Blair Family Papers, LC.

62. Both Farber (*Lincoln's Constitution*, 174) and Neely (*The Fate of Liberty*, 127) acknowledged one way or another that the repressive arrests of Northern citizens were not necessary. Farber specifically criticized First Amendment violations, which represented the brunt of Stanton's 1862 crackdown and periodically discouraged free speech thereafter. Neely more tentatively acknowledged that after the war "some people could see" that there had been little need of vast arbitrary arrests in the loyal states. Because Lincoln justified such constitutional violations on his "doctrine of necessity," those arrests remained unconstitutional: they did not further the war effort, and may have impeded it, while posing a dangerous precedent.

CHAPTER 15

1. John Murray Forbes to John Andrew, February 11, 1865, MHS; Lamon memorandum, LN2427, HL (incorporated in Lamon's *Recollections*, 239). This John Murray Forbes was no immediate relation to the Virginian of the same name who appears in the opening paragraph of this book.

2. EMS to Ashley, September 14, 1866, quoted in Flower, 310–12.

3. Sherman to EMS, December 13, 1864, SP, and to Lincoln, December 22, 1864, ALP.

4. Sumner, *Comstock Diary*, 298–99, 301; Beale, *Welles Diary*, 2:215.

5. Beale, *Welles Diary*, 2:219; French, *Journals*, 462; Montgomery Meigs Diary, January 2, 1865 (small pocket diary), LC. Furgurson, *Freedom Rising*, 147, mistakenly described French as an "admirer" of Mary Lincoln, whom French came to particularly dislike.

6. *OR*, 47(2):5–6. Townsend, *Anecdotes*, 114, claimed the cotton was only an excuse.

7. Montgomery Meigs Diary, January 5, 1865 (large pocket diary), LC; Beale, *Welles Diary*, 2:219–20; Burlingame and Ettlinger, *Hay Diary*, 92.

8. Meigs Diary, January 5–10, 1865 (large pocket diary), LC; *War Letters*, 442.

9. *OR*, 44:809, 47(2):35–37; Sherman, *Memoirs*, 2:243; Carlisle & McPherson to EMS, February 20, 1868, Letters Received (M221), RG 107, NA. Smith, *The Enemy Within*, 168–70, believed Sherman strove to smear Stanton with the taint of the corrupt cotton trade out of "intense animosity" over Stanton's published reprimand for Sherman's generous surrender terms to Joe Johnston's army, but Sherman only accused Stanton of administrative error: his anger at Stanton had cooled by the time he wrote his memoirs, as shown by his friendly letter to EMS of July 29, 1869 (GTS, LSU).

10. Simpson and Berlin, *Sherman* Letters, 762, 794–95; Niven, *Chase Papers*, 5:3–4; *OR*, 44:836–37, 846, 847, 47(2):18, 21, 37–41; Sherman, *Memoirs*, 2:244–45.

11. *OR*, 47(2):37–41.

12. Niven, *Chase Papers*, 1:602–3; 5:335. For a good example of the uncharacteristically pious tone Stanton affected in correspondence with the clergy, see EMS to Reverend Irenius Prime, March 6, 1862, Gratz Collection, HSP.

13. *OR*, 47(2):87; EMS to Garrison, February 12, 1865, BPL; EMS to Sumner, February 12, 1865, Fields Papers (FI5270), HL.

14. *War Letters*, 442; *CWL*, 8:238; *OR*, 46(2):155–57; Sumner, *Comstock Diary*, 305–6.

15. *OR*, 46(1):399, 46(2):178, Series 2, 8:89, 122–23; *Harper's Weekly*, December 10, 1864, January 14, 1865.

16. *OR*, Series 2, 7:606–7, 8:174; Lamon manuscript (LN2454), HL; Beale, *Welles Diary*, 2:168–71.

17. *OR*, Series 2, 8:170; *Sumter Republican*, February 4, 1865; George Shearer Diary, January 19–28, February 4, 1864, SHSI-IC; Amos Ames Diary, January 19–26, February 4, March 6, 7, 18, 1865, SHSI-DM; John Whitten Diary, January 17–25, February 2–8, March 6, 7, 18, 1865, SHSI-DM; J. G. Thomas to Robert Ould, July 31, 1868, Carrington Papers, Duke.

18. *CWL*, 8:253–54. The Constitution requires no executive endorsement on an amendment.

19. *OR*, 47(1):1018–20, 47(2):508; Samuel Duncan to "My Dear Bro.," February 25, 1865, DC; James Congleton Diary, March 4, 1865, LC.

20. Beale, *Welles Diary*, 2:251–52; Pease and Randall, *Browning Diary*, 2:9; Zachariah Chandler to "My dear wife," March 6, 1865, Chandler Papers, LC.

21. Burlingame, *With Lincoln in the White House*, 175; diaries of David Bates and Jeremiah Lockwood, March 4, 1865, LC; *CWL*, 8:332–33.

22. John P. Hale, Daniel Clark, and E. H. Rollins to EMS, March 1, 1865, Letters Received (M221), RG 107, NA; *CWL*, 8:359–60; *OR*, Series 3, 4:1203, 1252; Agassiz to EMS, January 20, 1865, SP. Agassiz asked for "one or two handsome fellows & the heads of two or three more."

23. *USG*, 14:158; John Darrah Wilkins to "My dear Child," March 17, 1865, CL; Theodore Lyman to Mrs. Lyman, March 16, 17, 1865, MHS.

24. Wilson to Adam Badeau, August 5, 1865, Wilson Papers, LC.

25. *USG*, 14:158; *OR*, 46(3):50, 86–87.

26. Bushrod Johnson Diary, March 25, 1865, RG 109, NA; William Boston to "Dear Aunt," March 25, 1865, BL; Warren Goodale to "Dear Children," March 25, 1865, MHS; Oscar Robinson to "Dear Mother," March 25, 1865, DC; Ransom Sargent to "My ever dear Maria," March 26, 1865, DC. The common understanding that Lee intended to break out of Petersburg on March 25 is, I think, mistaken. That would have left the Confederate government trapped in Richmond, because Lee had made no plans with President Davis to evacuate the capital. As he explained in a letter on March 26, Lee hoped only to shrink Grant's lines enough to allow a "select body" of his army to join Johnston when Sherman approached, weeks later (Freeman, *Lee's Dispatches*, 342–43). More than a decade later, Jefferson Davis remembered that they at least hoped to stop Grant's perpetual flanking movements long enough to postpone the eventual evacuation until the roads dried (Davis, *Rise and Fall*, 2:648). The 20th-century recollection of John B. Gordon, the general who made the attack, implied that the plan involved the immediate escape of Lee's entire army, but that is manifestly exaggerated (Gordon, *Reminiscences*, 403).

27. Sherman, *Memoirs*, 2:324–31; Gerry, *Through Five Administrations*, 43; J. R. Hamilton to "Dear Swinton," March 28, 1865, VHS; Bushrod Johnson Diary, March 28–31, 1865, RG 109, NA; Holcomb Harvey Diary, March 29–31, 1865, Duke; Francis Sherman Diary, March 31, April 1, 1865, UVA; Andrew Linscott to "Dear Parents," April 18, 1865, MHS; Daniel Himes Diary, April 2, 3, 1865, USAMHI; Alexander Rose Diary, March 31–April 2, 1865, USAMHI; Caleb Beal to "Dear Parents," April 3, 1865, MHS.

28. Edward Roberts Diary, April 3, 1865, CHS; John Bailey Journal, April 3, 1865, NHHS; Jones, *Diary*, 532; Henry Marshall to "Dear Folks at Home," April 5, 1865, CL; *CWL*, 8:386–87, 389; *OR*, 46(3):575, 612.

29. *CWL*, 8:388–92; John Macomber Diary, April 8, 1865, MNHS. Lincoln stayed at the front until April 8; his boat left Fort Monroe before dawn on April 9 (*OR*, 47[3]:139).

30. *OR*, 46(3):677–68, 696–97, 711, 724; *CWL*, 8:405–6. Rable, *God's Almost Chosen Peoples* (323), notes that Episcopal, Presbyterian, and Catholic churches regularly included prayers for the president and civil officials.

31. Beale, *Welles Diary*, 2:279; *CWL*, 8:406–7; Palmer, *Sumner Letters*, 2:284.

32. Palmer, *Sumner Letters*, 2:283.

33. The only Virginia units surviving after April 9 consisted of an artillery battery and a consolidated infantry battalion with Johnston, in North Carolina: *OR*, 47(1):1063, 1065.

34. Beale, *Welles Diary*, 2:281–83; Welles, "Lincoln and Johnson," 526–27. Benedict, in *A Compromise of Principle* (99), interpreted Stanton's plan as a reaction to Lincoln allowing the Virginia legislature to reconvene, in fear that he would do the same across the South.

35. *OR*, 47(3):59, 109; *War Letters*, 469; *New York Times*, April 18, 1865.

36. Pease and Randall, *Browning Diary*, 2:20; ELS to "Dear Aunt," April 28, 1865, quoted in Wolcott, 164–65; diary of an unidentified War Department clerk, "Lincoln Photostat Collection," LC, cited in Hyman, 396 (evidently no longer extant); Beale, *Welles Diary*, 2:283–85; *Washington Evening Star*, April 18, 1865; Fanny Seward's account and rewritten diary entry, April 14, 1865, Reel 198, Seward Papers, UR.

37. Beale, *Welles Diary*, 2:286–88; *OR*, 46(3):780–81

38. See, for instance, Warren Goodale to "Dear Children," April 15, 1865, MHS; J. Warren Keifer to his wife, April 15, 1865, LC; J. F. Lovering Diary, April 16, 1865, Indiana University; Louise Titcomb to Rebecca Usher, April 20, 1865, MEHS; Elizabeth Livermore Diary, April 15, 1865, NHHS; Francis Thomas Diary, April 15, 1865, Earlham; Nevins and Thomas, *Strong Diary*, 3:582.

39. *New York Herald*, April 15, 1865; *New York Tribune*, April 17, 1865; *New York Sun*, April 16, 1905; Beale, *Welles Diary*, 2:287–88, 290; *New York Times*, April 15, 21, 1865. Lincoln's role as Stanton's political guardian discredits the attempts to implicate Stanton in the assassination, which rest on the assumption that he sincerely supported Radical policies, rather than embracing them as a matter of personal political strategy. Stanton's reflexive duplicity and his zeal in convicting and executing the conspirators made him an inviting target for the dark insinuations forwarded by Eisenschiml in 1937 (*Why Was Lincoln Murdered?*) and resurrected by O'Reilly in 2011 (*Killing Lincoln*), but a deeper understanding of Stanton's nature reveals the absurdity of such fantasies.

40. *OR*, 46(3):744–45, 756–57.

41. Beale, *Welles Diary*, 2:289–90; *New York Herald*, April 15, 1865; *New York Tribune*, April 17, 1865; *Philadelphia Inquirer*, April 17, 1865; Nicolay and Hay, "A History of Abraham Lincoln," 436. In 1893, army surgeon Charles Taft echoed Nicolay and Hay when he claimed that Stanton said "He now belongs to the ages" ("Lincoln's Last Hours," 634, 635). Forty years after the assassination Corporal James Tanner, the Veteran Reserve Corps stenographer, remembered Stanton saying "He belongs to the ages now" (*New York Sun*, April 16, 1905). A decade later still, former provost marshal James O'Beirne asserted that he alone stood near enough to Stanton to hear him say "now he belongs to history" (*New York Evening World*, April 21, 1915).

42. Niven, *Chase Papers*, 1:529–30; Memo dated April "15" [16], 1865, Chase Papers, Cincinnati Historical Society; Beale, *Welles Diary*, 2:289–90; *OR*, 46(3):781–82. Castel, *The Presidency of Andrew Johnson*, 24, judged Stanton "the most important man in Johnson's administration during its early weeks," and in the absence of Seward, that was certainly true: his domination of the cabinet council suggests an effort to take control.

43. Beale, *Welles Diary*, 2:290–91.

44. *RJCCW2*, 1:xxxvi; *War Letters*, 472; Julian, *Political Recollections*, 257.

45. Beale, *Welles Diary*, 2:291; Welles, "Lincoln and Johnson," 528. On Weed and Ewing see *The Observer*, February 9, 1862, and *Cincinnati Commercial*, November 4, 1864.

46. *OR*, 46(3):806–8, 821, 845–47; Edward S. Burbank receipt for Samuel Arnold, April 18, 1865, Union Provost Marshal's File of Papers (M345), RG 109, NA; EMS to James L. McPhail, April 18, 1865, SP; *Trial of John H. Surratt*, 327, 486–87.

47. War Department order dated April 20, 1865, SP; order dated April 21, 1865, Letterbooks, SP; *Cincinnati Daily Commercial*, March 11–April 13, 1865. Stanton's order assigning Holt is marked "Confidential," and is not signed in Stanton's hand.

48. *OR*, 47(3):263.

49. Beale, *Welles Diary*, 2:294–97; *OR*, 47(3):263, 285–86. Davis and the remnants of his government had already fled beyond Sherman's reach before the truce began.

50. Chandler to "My dear Wife," April 23, 1865, LC.

51. Welles to Andrew Johnson, July 27, 1869, Johnson Papers, LC. Stanton was ultimately prosecuted at least three times: see his answer to the complaint of J. H. Maddox, December 5, 1865, Cushing Papers, LC; *Smithson v. Stanton*, Case 2724, Equity Docket, Entry 33, RG 21, NA; *New York Herald*, May 19, 1868.

52. *OR*, 47(3):286, 311–12; John Sherman to EMS, April 27, 1865, SP; Sherman to John Rawlins, April 29, 1865, SP; Brooks and Berlin, *Sherman Letters*, 892–93, 897.

53. Kennedy, *History of the Ohio Society*, 596; Burnett to Christopher C. Augur, April 26 (four letters), April 28, 1865 (two letters), and Burnett to S. J. Bowen, April 28, 1865 all on Reel 1, Investigation and Trial Papers (M599), RG 153, NA.

54. *New York Herald*, April 25, 1865; Von Steinacker statement, Reel 2, Investigation and Trial Papers (M599), RG 153, NA. Von Steinacker was released from Fort Delaware and allowed to rejoin the U.S. Army without punishment, despite having deserted to the enemy. See Register of U.S. Army Enlistments, April 15, 1861 (as Von Winkelstein) and May 19, 1865 (as Von Steinacker); Muster Rolls of Company K, 2nd Virginia, May, 1863 through April, 1864, Henry Von Steinacker file, Compiled Service Records of Confederate Soldiers from the State of Virginia (M324), Reel 381, RG 109, NA.

55. *OR*, Series 2, 8:523–25; EMS to Holt, May 2, 1865, Reel 16, Investigation and Trial Papers (M599), RG 153, NA; Beale, *Welles Diary*, 2:296, 299–300, 303.

56. Kauffman, *American Brutus*, 273–75, debunks the myth that Booth broke his leg jumping to the stage after he shot Lincoln.

57. *Impeachment Investigation*, 280–81, 285–86, 324, 333, 408, 451–52.

58. Beale, *Welles Diary*, 2:303; Pitman, *The Assassination*, 17; Beale, *Bates Diary*, 483.

59. Turner, *Beware the People Weeping* (144) doubted Holt was "a mere puppet of Stanton's," but the two at least shared a collaborative understanding of purpose.

60. Beale, *Welles Diary*, 2:301, 303.

61. Nevins and Thomas, *Strong Diary*, 3:595–96; *OR*, 46(3):1141–42, 1149; *Boston Evening Transcript*, June 20, 1865. The Greeley lawsuit seems never to have taken root.

62. Sumner, *Comstock Diary*, 317; Pitman, *The Assassination*, 409. General August Kautz recoiled at the hooding and chaining of the defendants, too (Journal, May 9, 1865, LC); both he and Comstock implied that Mrs. Surratt was also subjected to that humiliating torment, and contemporary newspaper engravings offer further evidence that she was.

63. Sumner, *Comstock Diary*, 317–18; Horatio Taft Diary, May 22, "1864" [1865], LC; Abiah Clough to "Dear Little Son," June 4, 1865, DC.

64. Hunt, *Brevet Brigadier Generals*, 116, 189, 621; Pitman, *The Assassination*, 64.

65. Winfield Hancock to John Hartranft, and C. H. Morgan to Christopher Augur, both May 10, 1865, Letters Received, RG 153, NA; Pitman, *The Assassination*, 21, 24–37, 39–43; Dix to EMS, June 24, 1865, SP. Leonard, *Lincoln's Forgotten Ally*, 49, 247, 249–50, describes Holt as "brilliant," although she accepted his contention that Conover duped him completely, but in *Lincoln's Avengers*, 151–52, she cited Holt's "gullibility." Charitable reasoning might portray Holt as so intent on proving his (and Stanton's) preconceived theory that he eagerly accepted any testimony or evidence, however disreputable; even that excuse suffers in light of Holt's subsequent recommendation for Conover's pardon—apparently offered in the equally single-minded pursuit of false testimony against Andrew Johnson. In "The Man Who Shifted the Blame," William Tidwell imagines that Conover was planted by rebel agents in an implausibly complicated scheme to discredit the claim of Confederate involvement.

66. J. W. Shaffer to Ben Butler, May 14, 1865, Butler Papers, LC.

67. John Bailey Journal, May 23, 1865, NHHS; Horatio Taft Diary, May 24, 1865, LC; John Peirce to "My Dear Wife," May 24, 1865, PEM; J. F. Lovering Diary, May 23, 1865, Indiana University; Willis Porter to "My dear Wife," May 25, 1865, MEHS.

68. Nathaniel Parmeter Diary, May 24, 1865, OHS; John McIntosh to "Dear Sister," May 26, 1865, WRHS; James Stillwell to "My dear wife and Children" May 24, 1865, OHS.

69. Samuel Hooper to Charles Sumner, May 22, 1865, Sumner Papers, Harvard; Horatio Taft Diary, May 24, 1865, LC; Henry Hitchcock to "My darling," May 26, 1865, LC; *New York Times*, May 25, 1865.

70. Davis and Schurz to Andrew Johnson, both May 13, 1865, Johnson Papers, LC; *OR*, 47(3):576, Series 3, 5:25, 42–44; Pease and Randall, *Browning Diary*, 2:30.

CHAPTER 16

1. EMS to Christopher C. Augur, May 17(two letters), 22, 1865, SP letterbooks; Holt to EMS, June 16, 1865, Reel 1, Investigation and Trial Papers (M599), RG 153, NA.

2. *Trial of the Conspirators*, 11–14, 53–54, 99–104; Weichmann to Holt, October 10, November 12, 23, 28, December 18, 1865, and to Ekin, November 21, 1865, all in Holt Papers, LC; Pitman, *The Assassination*, 122, 127.

3. Holt to John Forney, October 2, 1865, Letters Sent, 679–80, Entry 1, RG 153, NA.

4. Pitman, *The Assassination*, 97, 107, 117, 247–50. In Steers, *The Trial*, li, Betty Ownsbey notes that Spangler signed his first name "Edman."

5. Turner, *Beware the People Weeping*, 203, came to this same conclusion.

6. Kautz, "Reminiscences," 111, LC. Leonard, in *Lincoln's Forgotten Ally*, 216, doubted Kautz's description of the judge advocates' chagrin over the lesser sentences, arguing that what Kautz "claimed to recall" was colored by subsequent events: presumably she alluded to the controversy over whether Holt later withheld the clemency petition from President Johnson, but Kautz's memoir supported Holt's version of that episode.

7. Frederick Aiken and William Doster, quoted in Moore, *The Case of Mrs. Surratt*, 23; EMS to Hancock, June 19, 1865, SP. This physiological explanation for the petition seems never before to have been considered.

8. *New York Times*, July 4, 6, 1865; *Vindication of Hon. Joseph Holt*, 3–6, 12. This is essentially the hypothesis of George Fort Milton, a Johnson admirer who found the original documents arranged this way in 1929, with the petition reinserted after being torn from the packet (*Age of Hate*, 207–8). The modern microfilm version reflects Milton's description, and somewhat substantiates his theory of this transaction: see Reel 14, Investigation and Trial Papers (M599), RG 153, NA. Trefousse hypothesized, in *Andrew Johnson*, 223, that Johnson was so ill he may not have even realized what he had seen.

9. *Vindication*, 6; Grant to Johnson, February 3, 1868, Johnson Papers, LC; "Zaydee" to Holt, November 1, 1866, and numerous unsigned, mutilated letters in a feminine hand, mostly dated "1866" by a curator, Holt Papers, LC. This was not Holt's last dalliance with married women, one of whom was evidently a friend's wife: see, for instance, unidentified correspondent to Holt, August 24, 1876, Margaret Crosby to Holt, July 20, 1869, February 11, 1870. Holt seems to have ended some of these relationships abruptly, on apparent pretexts: see Mary (last name illegible) to Holt (undated, filed between October 8 and 9, 1864), and Margaret Crosby to Holt, December 27, 1887, Holt Papers, LC.

10. *New York Times*, July 6, 1865; Holt's report, Reel 14, Investigation and Trial Papers (M599), RG 153, NA. Turner, *Beware the People Weeping*, 177, concluded (as I do) that the evidence points to Holt actively withholding the petition.

11. *New York Times*, July 7, 1865; Pease and Randall, *Browning Diary*, 2:155.

12. Speed to Holt, March 30, 1873, Holt Papers, LC; *New York Times*, July 4, 6, 1865; *Washington Chronicle*, November 11, 1873, quoted in Trefousse, *Andrew Johnson*, 366.

13. Holt, *Vindication of Hon. Joseph Holt*, 6–7; Holt to Bingham, February 18, 1873, Bingham Papers, OHS. Gideon Welles thought Bingham's claim "incorrect," since he remembered no cabinet meeting during that period and recorded none in his diary (Welles to Andrew Johnson, November 5, 1873, Johnson Papers, LC).

14. Holt, *Vindication of Hon. Joseph Holt*, 7–13; Speed to Holt, March 30, 1873, and R. D. Mussey to Holt, August 19, 1873, Holt Papers, LC.

15. Holt, *Vindication of Hon. Joseph Holt*, 7; T. H. Duval to Holt, September 22, 1873, Box 4, Holt Papers, HL. Holt's similar 1866 pamphlet, *Vindication of Judge Advocate General Holt*, demonized all his accusers as lying, vindictive Confederate sympathizers. Both pamphlets leave the distinct impression of Holt protesting too much.

16. E. D. Townsend to Anna Surratt, July 20, 1865, SP letterbooks; Nevins and Thomas, *Strong Diary*, 4:15–17; U. S. House, *Trial of Henry Wirz*, 2.

17. *OR*, 46(3):584, 659, 944, 1132, 1152, 1158; Younger, *Kean Diary*, 206–7.

18. EMS to Woodman, May 18, 1865, Woodman Papers, MHS; W. W. Winthrop to EMS, June 15, 1865, Letters Sent, 357, Entry 1, RG 153, NA; *OR*, Series 3, 5:95.

19. Charles C. Pomeroy to Allen C. Fuller, October 10, 1864, and Fuller to Elihu B. Washburne, October 12, 1864, Washburne Papers, LC; *OR*, Series 2, 8:537–38. The parents of a Vermont cavalryman who died at Andersonville erected a tombstone noting that he died September 11, 1864, "wholly neglected by President Lincoln" (Joseph P. Brainerd tombstone, Greenwood Cemetery, St. Albans, Vt.).

20. *OR*, Series 2, 8:555, 558–60.

21. Wallce to "My dear Wife," August 21, 1865, and to "My dear Sue," September 1, 1865, Wallace Collection, IHS.

22. U.S. House, *Trial of Henry Wirz*, 61–66, 181, 355–62, 371–72, 414–15, 427, 695–700; Younger, *Kean Diary*, 228–30; Benjamin Dykes to EMS, February 1, 1866, Consolidated Correspondence File, Entry 225, RG 92, NA. Stories of monstrous cruelty permeate the *Trial of Henry Wirz*, but most do not jibe with original prison diaries, and it is noteworthy that those historians who have given the most credence to the worst horror stories made no effort to compare trial testimony with those original, unedited accounts of daily life at Andersonville. The prisoners carrying the petition reentered Union lines at Hilton Head, but were not given an audience with the president (*New York Times*, August 30, 1864).

23. Thomas Eckert to EMS, August 26, 1865, SP; *New York Times*, September 3, 1865.

24. U.S. House, *Trial of Henry Wirz*, 80–81; *Macon Daily Telegraph*, September 28, 1865; Sue Wallace to "My dear Brother," September 30, 1865, Wallace Collection, IHS. For two contrasting interpretations of the case against Wirz, see Marvel, *Andersonville: The Last Depot*, 243–47, and Leonard, *Lincoln's Avengers*, 154–61.

25. U.S. House, *Trial of Henry Wirz*, 803–8; *OR*, Series 2, 8:794.

26. *OR*, Series 3, 5:13–15, 37–39, Series 2, 8:578–80.

27. Stevens to Johnson, May 16, 1865, Johnson Papers, LC; Stevens to Sumner, May 10, June 3, June 14, 1865, Sumner Papers, Harvard; Sumner to Stevens, June 19, July 12, 1865, Palmer, *Sumner Letters*, 2:313–15, 324–25.

28. John Covode to Wade, July 11, 1865, Wade to Sumner, July 29, 1865, and Sumner to Wade, August 5, 1865, Wade Papers, LC; Charles E. Lippincott to Trumbull, August 29, 1865, Trumbull Papers, LC.

29. William Kelley to Johnson, May 12, 1865, and Sumner to Johnson, June 30, 1865, Johnson Papers, LC; Johnson to William Sharkey, August 15, 1865, quoted in Fleming, *Documentary History of Reconstruction*, 1:177. Simpson, *The Reconstruction Presidents*, 79, observed that Johnson's advice to Sharkey reflected a similar proposal Lincoln had made to Louisiana governor Michael Hahn on March 13, 1864, as that state considered a new constitution, but Simpson noted that Johnson wanted to use the idea to confound his Republican critics; Lincoln's advice to Hahn, by contrast, had been meant "to keep the jewel of liberty within the family of freedom." Trefousse, *Andrew Johnson*, 224, faulted Johnson for not pressuring Sharkey

to encourage compliance, but neither did Lincoln use coercion with Hahn, calling that limited suffrage "only a suggestion" (*CWL*, 7:243).

30. Chase to Johnson, May 17, 1865, Johnson Papers, LC; Chase to Sumner, August 20, 1865, Chase Papers, LC; Chase to EMS, May 20, 1865, SP; Chase to William Sprague, September 6, 1865, Chase Papers, LC. Trefousse, *Andrew Johnson*, 232, believed that Johnson might have imposed almost any conditions on the conquered states in the spring of 1865, and encouraged resistance by his lenience; that is probably true, but Lincoln's own actions and statements suggest that he would have begun with at least as conciliatory an attitude.

31. EMS to James Bates, August 14, 1865, SP.

32. *OR*, Series 3, 5:581; John Potts to EMS, August 24, 1865, Eckert to EMS, August 26–September 12, 1865, Barnes to EMS, September 2, 1865, ELS to Ellen Stanton, September 4, 1865, and EMS to Mrs. Isaac Bell, September 12, 1865, all in SP; Bergeron, *Papers of Andrew Johnson*, 9:58.

33. *Daily News*, September 14, 15, 1865; George T. Hammond to EMS, September 15, 1865, SP.

34. *Daily News*, September 15, 1865; Garrison to EMS, September 15, 1865, SP; EMS to Garrison, September 18, 1865, Garrison Letters, BPL; EMS to Eckert, September 15, 1865, EMS to E. D. Morgan, September 19, 1865, and Eckert to EMS, September 20, 1865, all in SP; *New York Times*, September 23, 1865. Hyman, 457–58, claims that during this Boston sojourn Senator Sumner transformed a skeptical Stanton into a supporter of black voting, but more than four months previously Stanton had advocated that very measure in cabinet council (Beale, *Welles Diary*, 2:303).

35. Eckert to EMS, September 5, 1865, SP; *Speeches of Hon. Montgomery Blair*, 14–16; Leavitt to EMS, October 3, 1865, SP. Citing two congressmen as sources, Blair referred to Stanton's reported encouragement of secessionist Albert G. Brown, as he left the U.S. Senate for his home in Mississippi. Brown told that story in the Confederate Senate (*New York Herald*, February 4, 1865), and others remembered Stanton making disloyal statements in 1861, which was consistent with his habit of preserving his political options by playing both sides of the fence: see, for instance, James Harvey to Jeremiah Black, October 2, 1870, Black Papers, LC; Phillips, "Summary," 44, LC.

36. Thomas Eckert to EMS, September 5, 1865, SP; EMS to Sumner, November "6," 1865, Sumner Papers, Harvard; Sumner to EMS, November "5," 1865, SP. Either Stanton's telegram or Sumner's letter is obviously misdated, and probably Sumner's letter.

37. Beale, *Welles Diary*, 2:394, 398.

38. Ibid., 2:387; *CG*, 39th Cong., 1st sess., 4, 6, 30; EMS to Schuyler Colfax, October 15, 1866, Colfax Papers, IHS.

39. *A Compilation of the Messages and Papers of the Presidents*, 5:3551–3569.

40. Beale, *Welles Diary*, 2:392, 396–97; *USG*, 15:434–37.

41. EMS to Thomas Eckert, December 16, 17, 1865, SP; Wolcott, 167–68; EMS to Mrs. Hutchison, December 25, 1865, GTS, LSU; Beale, *Welles Diary*, 401, 405–6.

42. Bancoft, *Speeches, Correspondence, and Political Papers of Carl Schurz*, 1:264–65.

43. Ibid., 1:268; U.S. Senate, *Message of the President . . . Accompanied by a Report of Carl Schurz*, 8–16; *The Condition of the South*, 1–24; *Acts of the General Assembly*, 91–93; James Geiser to Charles Dibble, August 18, 1865, and to J. H. Jewett, August 31, September 8, 1865, Reports Received, Department of Virginia, Entry 7005, RG 393, NA. For varying court treatment of freedmen see, for example, Records Relating to Court Cases, Records of the Assistant Commissioner for the State of Virginia (M1048), RG 105, NA, and Narrative Reports of Criminal Cases, Records of the Field Officers for the State of Louisiana (M1905), RG 105, NA. Similar records survive for most of the occupied states.

44. Schafer, *Intimate Letters of Carl Schurz*, 354; Bancroft, *Speeches, Correspondence, and Political Papers of Carl Schurz*, 1:264–68, 270–71; Sheridan to Johnson, November 26, 1865, Johnson Papers, LC. Perman, *Reunion without Compromise*, felt that optional, conciliatory Reconstruction was impossible with the antebellum elite still in control, and that only federal imposition of the Radical program could have succeeded. Rable, *But There Was No Peace*, 189–90, argued that a longer, more coercive Reconstruction policy would have demanded greater military force than the country would have tolerated.

45. *CG*, 39th Cong., 1st sess., 72–75. Stevens may have used the excuse of belligerent rights at the suggestion of Sumner, to whom Chief Justice Chase had pointed out that legal inconsistency the previous summer (Chase to Sumner, August 20, 1865, Harvard).

46. Beale, *Welles Diary*, 2:414–17; EMS to James Ashley, September 14, 1866, quoted in Flower, 311–12.

47. In *With Charity for All*, 74, Harris rightly doubted that Lincoln, "despite his wartime reluctance to dictate to loyal Southern governments, would have permitted events to take the calamitous course that followed under Johnson."

48. Bergeron, *Papers of Andrew Johnson*, 9:608, 612; *Chicago Republican*, March 15, April 5, 1866, quoted in Steele, *The Sun Shines for All*, 69. See Steele, 90–93, Wilson, *Life of Charles A. Dana*, 406–7, and *New York Sun*, April 17, 1869, for Dana's wish that President Grant would appoint him collector, and his subsequent tirades against Grant.

49. D. L. Phillips to Trumbull, January 7, 1866, W. H. Underwood to Trumbull, January 15, 1866, and Harlan to Trumbull, February 26, 1866, Trumbull Papers, LC; White to EMS, March 15, 1866, SP; Beale, *Welles Diary*, 2:434–35, 439; Harlan to Elihu Washburne, June 12, 1865, Washburne Papers, LC; Timothy Howe to "My dear Grace," February 21, 1866, WHS.

50. William Lloyd Garrison to Wendell P. Garrison, February 22, 1866, BPL; Niven, *Chase Papers*, 1:602–3.

51. Pease and Randall, *Browning Diary*, 2:63; Beale, *Welles Diary*, 2:403–4, 439; EMS to Johnson, March 10, 1866, Johnson Papers, LC.

52. Beale, *Welles Diary*, 2:463–64, 479.

53. Grant to EMS, March 25, 28, July 18, 1866, EMS to Grant, March 26, 1866; unsigned note, "July 17, 1866," SP. In an unlikely memoir, *Civil War Echoes*, 225–28,

Hamilton Howard has a tipsy Stanton boasting that Sheridan would drive the French into the sea.

54. F. W. Gilbreth to O. O. Howard, May 22, 1866, and Benjamin P. Runkle to Clinton Fisk, May 23, 1866, both in Reports of Outrages, Reel 34, Records of the Assistant Commissioner for the State of Tennessee (M999), RG 105, NA; U.S. House, *Memphis Riots and Massacres*, 2–3, 367–69.

55. Beale, *Welles Diary*, 2:495–98; Pease and Randall, *Browning Diary*, 2:74–75.

56. Palmer, *Sumner Letters*, 2:365–66; Beale, *Welles Diary*, 2:512–13.

57. Beale, *Welles Diary*, 2:513. The speech is published in Gorham, 2:302–10.

58. Pease and Randall, *Browning Diary*, 2:77.

59. Stanton's answer of December 5, 1865, in *Maddox v. Stanton*, J. H. Maddox to Caleb Cushing, June 15, 1866, and EMS to Cushing, June 13, 1866, all in Cushing Papers, LC; Mackey, *Reports*, 6–8; *OR*, Series 2, 2:904, 1354–55.

60. Beale, *Welles Diary*, 2:536, 551–52, 554, 555; *Ohio Reports*, 5:195–98; Pease and Randall, *Browning Diary*, 2:85–86; platform of the National Union Club, Reel 11, SP.

61. Beale, *Welles Diary*, 2:403, 552, 554–55, 557; Barlow to Blair, July 16, 1866, Letterbook 13, Barlow Papers, HL; Francis Lieber to Henry Halleck, May 23, 1866 (LI1742), Lieber Papers, HL. When Welles edited his diary entry a few years later, he inserted the qualification "I believe" before "treacherous." Benedict, *A Compromise of Principle*, 194n32, illustrated the interpretive influence of Hyman's friendly portrait: remarking on the earlier view that Stanton's tenacity in the cabinet eventually reflected hypocrisy and treachery, Benedict wrote that Stanton's "most recent biographers [i.e., Hyman and his deceased coauthor, Thomas] have argued cogently that in fact he made a significant sacrifice to stay where he was." Citing Hyman again, Benedict also noted that "leading military men, and Republicans felt duty required him to remain," and that was true, but it was personal considerations rather than duty that led him to stay.

62. Two copies of unsigned letter of July 16, 1866, SP; Beale, *Welles Diary*, 2:554–55.

CHAPTER 17

1. *Impeachment Investigation*, 398; U.S. House, *New Orleans Riots*, 28, 37, 238, 451, 458; Albert Voorhies and Andrew Herron to Johnson, received July 28, 1866, SP.

2. U.S. House, *New Orleans Riots*, 12–15, 27, 49, 534–35, 547; Andrew Herron to Johnson, July 31, 1866, SP; Sheridan to Johnson, August 6, 1866, and William Moore Diary, undated (between October 23 and November 6, 1866), Johnson Papers, LC. Hyman, 496, also thought Stanton deliberately left Baird without instructions. Even Eric Foner, no conservative apologist, conceded it was "irregular" to reconvene the convention after two years, and concluded that blame for the resulting violence was "widely shared" among government officials—including Stanton, for his failure to respond to Baird (*Reconstruction*, 263).

3. Palmer, *Sumner Letters*, 2:380; *New York Times*, May 24, 1866; Sheridan to Johnson, November 26, 1865, Johnson Papers, LC; *USG*, 16:288–89; Nevins and

Thomas, *Strong Diary*, 4:96–97. Rable, *But There Was No Peace*, 58, identified the New Orleans riot as the spark that ignited the violent resistance that finally defeated the Radical agenda.

4. Beale, *Welles Diary*, 2:572–73. If support for rapid Reconstruction showed nationalism, as Jean Baker argued in *Affairs of Party*, 319, resistance to it implied the opposite. In recent decades, Reconstruction studies have focused on the egalitarian and humanitarian motives of the Radicals, but through 1866 they must also have feared domination by a coalition of Northern and Southern conservatives when Reconstruction ended.

5. Beale, *Welles Diary*, 2:587–89; EMS to Peter Watson, October 19, 1866, published in Flower, 313–14; EMS to George G. Meade, December 14, 1866 (HM23337), HL.

6. Pease and Randall, *Browning Diary*, 2:91, 93; Beale, *Welles Diary*, 2:588–96; Williams, *Hayes Diary and Letters*, 3:33; Vickery, *Godfrey Journals*, 238; *USG*, 16:308. Welles noted in postdated addenda to his diary (2:591, 593) that between Buffalo and Cleveland Grant became "somewhat inebriated" and had to be hustled aboard a boat for Detroit with Surgeon General Barnes, who was in the same condition. Representative James Ashley and Postmaster General Alexander Randall independently confirmed that Grant was drunk at Cleveland and had to be hidden away, but Ashley implied that Johnson was intoxicated, too. See Stanton's reply to Ashley's accusation, quoted in Flower, 310, and Browning on Randall's statement, Pease and Randall, *Browning Diary*, 2:115.

7. William Moore Diary, March 16, 1868, Johnson Papers, LC.

8. EMS to Ashley, September 14, 1866, quoted in Flower, 312; EMS to Ellen, October 2, December 4, 1866, GTS, LSU.

9. *Cincinnati Gazette*, August 9, 1866; Beale, *Welles Diary*, 2:594–95; Fanny Seward Diary, September 14, 15, 1866, Reel 198, Seward Papers, UR; Pease and Randall, *Browning Diary*, 2:93; *New York Tribune*, September 17, 1866.

10. Beale, *Welles Diary*, 2:601; U.S. House, *Assassination of Lincoln*, 1, 28–29, 30–41; Dix to EMS, June 24, 1865, Letters Sent, Department of the East, 9:282–84, Entry 1394, Part I, RG 393, NA; *New York Herald*, August 12, 24, 1866; *Washington Chronicle*, September 3, 1866; *OR*, Series 2, 8:931–45; Holt to EMS, September 11, 1866, Letters Received (M494), RG 107, NA. In "Subornation of Perjury in the Lincoln Conspiracy Trial?" Joseph George Jr. persuasively documented his assertion that Holt actively sought to use perjured testimony and manufactured evidence to connect Jefferson Davis to the assassination.

11. Beale, *Welles Diary*, 2:601, 604, 616; Pease and Randall, *Browning Diary*, 2:95, 96; *Daily Whig and Courier*, February 13, 1867; *Davenport Daily Gazette*, July 31, 1867; EMS to Holt, November 14, 1866, Letters Sent (M421), RG 107, NA; Holt, *Vindication of Judge Advocate General Holt*. Conover was arraigned on November 2, 1866, and was sentenced to ten years on February 11, 1867, but his appeal for presidential pardon (endorsed by Holt) was ultimately granted: Criminal Docket, Vol. 4, Case 4525, Entry 4, RG 21, NA; Criminal Case Files, Case 4525, Entry 77, RG 21, NA.

12. Fanny Seward Diary, September 25, October 1, 1866, Reel 198, and EMS to Fanny Seward, October 17, 1866, Reel 97, Seward Papers, UR.

13. *Free Press*, March 24, 1866; Pease and Randall, *Browning* Diary, 2:68; *Oxford Democrat*, September 7, 14, 1866; *New York Herald*, September 12, 1866.

14. Samuel Barlow to Montgomery Blair, September 11, 1865, and Blair to Johnson, September 12, 1865, Johnson Papers, LC; Joseph Geiger to James Doolittle, June 25, 1866, WHS; Pease and Randall, *Browning Diary*, 2:77–79; Timothy Howe to "My dear Grace," June 2, 1866, WHS; *Oxford Democrat*, September 7, 1866 (with Hamlin's letter); *New York Times*, November 8, 1866; Beale, *Welles Diary*, 2:616–17.

15. EMS to William Fessenden, October 25, 1866 (HM4642), HL.

16. *USG*, 16:350–55; Pease and Randall, *Browning Diary*, 2:105–6; William Moore Diary, November 6, 1866, and "July, 1867," Johnson Papers, LC.

17. *USG*, 16:228, 297, 389–92; *A Compilation of the Messages and Papers of the Presidents*, 5:3627–30, 3632–36.

18. *New York Tribune*, December 18, 1866; EMS to Andrew Johnson, December 10, 1866, Letters Sent (M421), RG 107, NA; *USG*, 17:220–21; Stanton's testimony before the Select Committee on the Murder of United States Soldiers, January 30, 1867, SP; EMS to Henry Stanbery, January 25, 1867, Letters Sent (M421), RG 107, NA. I am obliged to Pickett scholar Richard Selcer for details about the efforts of Stanton and Holt to arraign Pickett before military courts of inquiry even after *ex parte Milligan*.

19. *Cincinnati Commercial*, October 8, 1866; *Chicago Tribune*, November 28, 1866; Pease and Randall, *Browning Diary*, 2:109–10; U.S. House, *New Orleans Riots*, 1; James H. Wilson to EMS, February 9, 1867, SP.

20. U.S. House, *New Orleans Riots*, 547; D. L. Eaton to EMS, January 9, 1867, Eliot to EMS, January 19, 30, 1867, and EMS to Eliot, January 31, 1867 (numerous drafts), all in SP; Pease and Randall, *Browning Diary*, 2:109. In the spring of 1866 Montgomery Blair thought Stanton protected Seward from the Radicals (Blair to Andrew Johnson, April 11, 1866, Johnson Papers, LC), but if there was any truth to that in the spring there was not by the end of summer, as Stanton's September 14 letter to Ashley reveals (Flower, 310–12).

21. *CG*, 39th Cong., 2nd sess., 17, 22, 73.

22. Ibid., 547–48, 550, 969–70, 1046, 1515, 1516. Stanton's appeals to Radicals like James Ashley probably inspired the amendment protecting cabinet officers from removal, and its introduction by one of Stanton's own acquaintances adds to the suspicion that the secretary had a hand in it.

23. Ibid., 1205–15, 1518.

24. Ibid., 1351–56, 1404; *USG*, 16:338–40; W. P. Fessenden to EMS, October 20, 1866, SP.

25. *CG*, 39th Cong., 2nd sess., 1404, 1851–55; Sumner, *Comstock Diary*, 341; Boutwell, *Reminiscences*, 2:107–9. Hyman, 493, claimed that Stanton feared Johnson might use the army "for the purpose of unseating the Republican congressional majority," adding that "Grant and [General John] Pope shared these fears." For documentation, however, Hyman cited only two letters that have no evident relation to this subject. Then, using that unsupported passage as his own authority, David Stewart (*Impeached*, 70) wrote: "Stanton told congressional allies that he and Grant

feared an armed takeover by the president." No evidence for such a claim has yet been furnished, and nothing indicates that Johnson even considered such mischief.

26. Beale, *Welles Diary*, 3:50–51. 158; Pease and Randall, *Browning Diary*, 2:108, 132.

27. *CG*, 39th Cong., 2nd sess., 320–21; Beale, *Welles Diary*, 3:5, 8. In *Andrew Johnson*, 282–83, Trefousse argued that the House still remained relatively moderate, noting that it referred the "perfectly fanatical" Ashley's resolution to the Judiciary Committee, consisting of four moderate Republicans, three Radicals, and one Democrat.

28. Beale, *Welles Diary*, 2:414–17, 3:9–13; Palmer, *Sumner Letters*, 2:359, 365–66, 380; EMS to James Ashley, September 14, 1866, quoted in Flower, 310–12.

29. Beale, *Welles Diary*, 3:42–44; Pease and Randall, *Browning Diary*, 2:130; William Moore Diary, August 12, 1867, Johnson Papers, LC; List of Outrages, Reel 11, SP.

30. Pease and Randall, *Browning Diary*, 2:130; Beale, *Welles Diary*, 3:45–46.

31. Welles to Andrew Johnson, July 27, 1869, Johnson Papers, LC; *Impeachment Investigation*, 401–2. Flower, 327, noted that the Radical Reconstruction plan essentially replicated the one "Stanton conceived, prepared, and handed to Lincoln."

32. *Impeachment Investigation*, 406; Beale, *Welles Diary*, 3:11, 90.

33. Pease and Randall, *Browning Diary*, 2:134–35; Beale, *Welles Diary*, 3:58–59; William Moore Diary, March 4, 1867, Johnson Papers, LC; Sumner, *Comstock Diary*, 344; James Dunning to EMS, March 5, 1867, and EMS to Edward McPherson, March 7, 1867, McPherson Papers, LC.

34. *A Compilation of the Messages and Papers of the Presidents*, 5:3696–3709 (especially 3698); *Impeachment Investigation*, 271; William Moore Diary, "July" [April] 5, 1867, Johnson Papers, LC; Beale, *Welles Diary*, 3:134. Johnson's observation about Stanton's erstwhile obsequious manner is in the Moore diary, but is missing from the published version of the April 5 entry (Sioussat, "Notes," 107).

35. Beale, *Welles Diary*, 3:58–59; *CG*, 40th Cong., 1st sess., 1–2.

36. Beale, *Welles Diary*, 3:51–52; *USG*, 17:76; *Impeachment Investigation*, 271–73.

37. Pease and Randall, *Browning Diary*, 2:135; Beale, *Welles Diary*, 3:62, 64–65; *USG*, 17:80–81.

38. *USG*, 17:93, 96–97, 185; Beale, *Welles Diary*, 3:93, 104–5.

39. Frank Blair to "Dear Father," August 2, 1867, and to "Dear Judge," December 6, 1866, Princeton; Beale, *Welles Diary*, 3:66, 68, 83–84, 85; William Moore Diary, May 2, 1867, Johnson Papers, LC.

40. Welles to Montgomery Blair, November 18, 1872, Blair Family Papers, LC.

41. *New Hampshire Patriot*, March 13, 20, 1867; Thomas Hendricks to Johnson, March 23, 1867, Johnson Papers, LC; Beale, *Welles Diary*, 3:77–78; Nevins and Thomas, *Strong Diary*, 4:128–29. Welles considered all the defeated Republicans Radicals.

42. *New York Times*, April 6, 13, 1867.

43. Pease and Randall, *Browning Diary*, 2:142; Beale, *Welles Diary*, 80–81; William Moore Diary, "July" [April] 5, 1867, Johnson Papers, LC; *New York Times*, April 27, May 4, 7, 15, 18, 1867.

44. Pease and Randall, *Browning Diary*, 2:145; Beale, *Welles Diary*, 3:93–94, 96, 98.

45. L. H. Chandler to EMS, May 4, 1867, with endorsement of EMS and Johnson, SP; Thomas Shankland to Joseph Holt, April 30, 1867, Holt Papers, LC (on the Ohio trip); William Moore Diary, May 7, 1867, Johnson Papers, LC; *Impeachment Investigation*, 396; EMS to John Schofield, May 11, 1867, Barney Collection (HB Box 27), HL. Evarts was still not ready for trial, so Davis went free on bail (*New York Times*, May 14, 1867).

46. *CG*, 40th Cong., 1st sess., 18–19, 262–63, 362–64.

47. *Impeachment Investigation*, 32–33, 280–81, 323–25, 332–33.

48. Johnson to EMS, May 9, 1867, endorsed by EMS and Holt, and several complete and partial drafts of EMS to Johnson, May 14, 1867, SP; *Impeachment Investigation*, 28.

49. *Impeachment Investigation*, 673. Stanton may have had a chance to mutilate the diary, but he had no reason to do so. Booth probably used the missing pages for messages during his flight: Kauffman, *American Brutus*, 329, quotes one of those messages.

50. *New York Herald*, January 4, 1867; Beale, *Welles Diary*, 3:31; *Washington Evening Star*, June 10, 17, 1867.

51. Beale, *Welles Diary*, 3:105, 109–14, 117; *Opinion of Attorney General Stanbery*; Stanton memoranda of June 18–20, 1867, SP.

52. EMS to Judd, June 21, 1867, SP; Beale, *Welles Diary*, 3:128; *CG*, 40th Cong., 1st sess., 463, 468, 480.

53. Beale, *Welles* Diary, 3:132–33, 137; Alfred Huger to Benjamin Perry, July 4, 1867, ADAH; *A Compilation of the Messages and Papers of the Presidents*, 5:3734–3743; *CG*, 40th Cong., 1st sess., 767.

54. Hooper to Horatio Woodman, July 28, 1867, Woodman Papers, MHS.

55. Criminal Docket, Vol. 4, Case 4525, Entry 4, RG 21, NA; Beale, *Welles Diary*, 3:143–44; Pease and Randall, *Browning Diary*, 2:152–53; Holt to Johnson, July 23, 1867, with Riddle's affidavit, Holt Papers, LC; Riddle to EMS, June 21, 1867 (HM25600), HL.

56. Pease and Randall, *Browning Diary*, 2:152–53, 156; Beale, *Welles Diary*, 3:143–44, 170–71; *Impeachment Investigation*, 1202–3.

57. Beale, *Welles Diary*, 3:144–45; Pease and Randall, *Browning Diary*, 2:152–53; *Washington Evening Star*, August 10, 1867; *Impeachment Investigation*, 1194–1208 (with the incriminating letters).

58. Beale, *Welles Diary*, 3:145; Criminal Docket, Vol. 4, Case 4525, Entry 4, RG 21, NA.

59. Beale, *Welles Diary*, 3:143–46; Pease and Randall, *Browning Diary*, 2:152–53.

60. Pease and Randall, *Browning Diary*, 2:153; Beale, *Welles Diary*, 3:149, 157.

61. Johnson to EMS, August 5, 1867, Letters Received (M421), RG 107, NA; William Moore Diary, August 1, 11, 1867, Johnson Papers, LC; *USG*, 17:250–52.

62. Beale, *Welles Diary*, 3:155–56.

63. *Washington Evening Star*, August 4, 1867.

64. William Moore Diary, August 5, 6, 1867; Johnson Papers, LC; Beale, *Welles Diary*, 3:158; Pease and Randall, *Browning Diary*, 2:155.

65. Beale, *Welles Diary*, 158–60, 167–69; Pease and Randall, *Browning Diary*, 2:154; Johnson to EMS, August 12, 1867, SP; William Moore Diary, August 11, 12, 1867, and EMS to Johnson, August 12, 1867, Johnson Papers, LC; *Washington Evening Star*, August 10, 1867. Within days newspapers carried purported affidavits from Conover's cronies, claiming that Conover sought to destroy the credibility of Holt and the Bureau of Military Justice in a convoluted scheme to damage the case against Jefferson Davis (*New York Times*, August 15, 1867). When Johnson asked to see Conover's pardon petition and the affidavits, Holt replied that no such papers were ever received by his bureau, and none were found anywhere else in the War Department (*USG*, 17:285–86).

CHAPTER 18

1. EMS to Woodman, August 6, 1867, Woodman Papers, MHS; Smith to EMS, August 10, 1867, SP; EMS to Ellen, August 12, 1867, GTS, LSU; Palmer, *Sumner Letters*, 2:401.

2. Edwards Pierrepont told one of General Grant's staff that Ellen Stanton wanted her husband out of the cabinet (Badeau, *Grant in Peace*, 139–40), as is implied in Pierrepont's letter to her dated April 15, 1868, SP; Stanton confirmed that she wanted him to quit (EMS to Pamphila, January 18, 1868, quoted in Wolcott, 170).

3. EMS to ELS, August 22, 1867, GTS, LSU.

4. Samuel Hooper to Woodman, August 23, 29, 1867, Woodman Papers, MHS; Hooper to Charles Sumner, September 2, 1867, Sumner Papers, Harvard; EMS to "My Dear Friend," August 28, 1867, Clifford Papers, MHS.

5. EMS to ELS, September 4, 1867, Pratt Collection, Columbia; EMS to Ann E. Smith, August 31, 1868, and Smith to Frank Flower, date not stated, both quoted in Flower, 324–25; Ann E. Smith to J. Gregory Smith, October 20, 1864, St. Albans Historical Society.

6. EMS to Wilson, September 11, 1867, Wilson Papers, LC.

7. Ellen to ELS, September 29, 1867, quoted in Gorham, 2:410; Palmer, *Sumner Letters*, 2:401; Lieber to Henry Halleck, August 30, 1867, HL; *USG*, 17:279, 297–98, 18:8; Wolcott, 170; Nevins and Thomas, *Strong Diary*, 4:150, 163. Flower, 324, quoted Stanton's letter asking for a $3,000 loan from Congressman James K. Moorhead and claimed it was granted; no further documentation of that loan appears to survive.

8. Sherman to EMS, October 16, 1867; Wolcott, 168–69; EMS to John W. Draper, November 20, 1867, quoted in Gorham, 2:411–12.

9. Thomas Ewing Jr. to Thomas Ewing Sr., September 17, October 12, 19, 1867, Ewing Sr. to Ewing Jr., October 15, 1867, and William T. Sherman to Ewing Jr., October 18, 1867, Ewing Family Papers, LC; *USG*, 18:116–21.

10. *A Compilation of the Messages and Papers of the Presidents*, 5:3756–79, 3781–92; *USG*, 18:56–58; *CG*, 40th Cong., 2nd sess., 64–68.

11. Wolcott, 170, including EMS to Pamphila Wolcott, December 20, 1867; Union Cemetery interment records; EMS to James Hutchison, December 16, 1867, HHC. In contrast to his sympathetic reaction to that nephew's death, Stanton seems not to have taken any notice at all when Oella's refractory son, Benjamin, was killed in

a fight with Apaches in Arizona, on March 22, 1866 (Heitman, *Historical Register*, 1:944).

12. Beale, *Welles Diary*, 3:246, 249, 251; EMS to Lucy Stanton, January 8, 1868, CHC; *USG*, 17:321–23, 354–55. Hyman's quotes about Ellen's anxiety (561) evidently came from Stanton's letter to her of December 19, 1867, which—like all the letters he wrote on that trip—was privately owned when Hyman saw it, and has since dropped from sight.

13. William Moore Diary, January 7, 1868, Johnson Papers, LC; *USG*, 17:354.

14. Beale, *Welles Diary*, 3:255–56; EMS to Fessenden, January 13, 1868 (HM23176), HL. The brief, which Stanton pressed Fessenden to present, is quoted in Gorham, 2:427.

15. *USG*, 18:116–18. By early 1868, Grant was the front-runner: see John Binney to William Pitt Fessenden, December 30, 1867, February 5, 1868, Fessenden Papers, LC, and J. R. Doolittle to Manton Marble, January 2, 6, 1868, Marble Papers, LC.

16. Grant to Johnson, January 28, 1868, Johnson Papers, LC; W. T. Sherman to Johnson, January 18, 1868 (addressed from 322 K Street), Johnson Papers, LC; E. D. Morgan and George Edmunds to EMS, both January 13, 1868, SP; *New York Times*, January 14, 1868; EMS to Fessenden, January 14, 1868, Fessenden Papers, Bowdoin.

17. *USG*, 18:102–3, 118; Pease and Randall, *Browning Diary*, 2:174, 179–80; Beale, *Welles Diary*, 3:259–61, 269–72; William Moore Diary, January 14, 1868, Johnson Papers, LC.

18. Clemenceau, *American Reconstruction*, 102–3, 144.

19. *New York Times*, January 15, 16, 1868; *New York World*, January 15, 1868.

20. EMS to Pamphila Wolcott, January 18, 1868, quoted in Wolcott, 170; *New York Herald*, January 16, 1868; Sherman to Grant, January 27, 1868, Sherman Papers, LC; Howe, *Home Letters*, 365–66.

21. *National Intelligencer*, January 15, 1868; Grant to Johnson, January 24, 1868, EG Box 22, Eldridge Collection, HL; Grant to Johnson, January 30, 1868, Letters Sent by the Headquarters of the Army (M857), RG 108, NA; Johnson to Grant, February 10, 1868, Johnson Papers, LC.

22. *New York Times*, January 17, 1868.

23. *CG*, 40th Cong., 2nd sess., 936, 977; Grant to Johnson, February 3, 1868, Letters Sent (M857), RG 108, NA.

24. William Hillyer to Andrew Johnson, January 14, 1868, Johnson Papers, LC; J. B. Stillson to Samuel Barlow, January 27, February 12, 1868 (Box 68), Barlow Papers, HL; *New York World*, January 14, 27, 1868; Howe, *Home Letters*, 365, 367; William Moore Diary, February 3, 1868, Johnson Papers, LC.

25. Sherman to Thomas Ewing Sr., January 25, February 14, 1868, Ewing Family Papers, LC; Sherman to Johnson, February 14, 20, 1868, and William Moore Diary, February 3, 19, 1868, Johnson Papers, LC.

26. Sumner to EMS February 2, 1868 (misfiled in correspondence of December, 1867), SP; Palmer, *Sumner Letters*, 2:416; *Letters of Charles Dickens*, 3:245–49.

27. Eliza Crewson to "Mr. Marden," January 27, 1868, and L. H. Pelouze to Mrs. Crewson, February 3, 1868, Letters Received (M221), RG 107, NA; pension

application, certificate 373695, Reel 103, General Index to Civil War Pension Applications (T288), RG 15, NA; see also W. K. Browne to U. S. Grant, with E. D. Townsend's endorsement of January 20, 1868, and much other correspondence between then and May, 1868, Letters Received (M221), RG 107, NA.

28. EMS to McCulloch, February 18, 1868, and to Stanbery, February 19, 1868, Letters Sent (M421), RG 107, NA.

29. Carlisle & McPherson to EMS, February 20, 1868, Letters Received (M221), RG 107, NA; Sherman, *Memoirs*, 2:243.

30. William Moore Diary, February 17–19, 1868, Johnson Papers, LC; *CG*, 40th Cong., 2nd sess., supplement, 142.

31. William Moore Diary, February 21, 1868, Johnson Papers, LC.

32. Ibid.; EMS to Colfax, Wade, George Boutwell, Jacob Howard, Henry Wilson, Charles Sumner, and Richard Yates, and John M. Thayer to EMS, all February 21, 1868; SP; *New York World*, February 22, 1868.

33. *New York Times*, February 22, 1868; *New York World*, February 23, 1868; *CG*, 40th Cong., 2nd sess., 1316, 1326–27, 1329–30.

34. *CG*, 40th Cong., 2nd sess., supplement, 71, 75; William Moore Diary, February 22, 1868, Johnson Papers, LC; EMS to Fessenden, Howard, and Edmunds, February 21, 1868, SP; *New York Times*, February 22, 1868. In 1897 Senator John M. Thayer claimed he stayed with Stanton that night ("A Night with Stanton," 441–42), but on the following day the *Times* identified Stanton's companion as Colonel Edmund Schriver of the general staff.

35. William Moore Diary, February 22, 1868, Johnson Papers, LC; *New York Times*, February 23, 24, 1868; *CG*, 40th Cong., 2nd sess., supplement, 140–41.

36. *CG*, 40th Cong., 2nd sess., 1330–1346; *New York Times*, February 23, 1868.

37. *CG*, 40th Cong., 2nd sess., 1346–69, 1382–1400.

38. French, *Journals*, 558–59; *Washington Evening Star*, February 24, 1868; *CG*, 40th Cong., 2nd sess., 1405; *New York Times*, February 26, 1868.

39. Ames, *Ten Years in Washington*, 465–66; *Commercial Advertiser*, May 24, 1903; EMS to Ellen, late February or early March, 1868, GTS, LSU.

40. *New York World*, February 24, 1868; *New York Times*, February 26–28, 1868; EMS to Jacob Howard, February 25, 1868, SP; *USG*, 18:190, 242–43, 549, 556, 557; M. B. Lamar to EMS, April 8, 1868, SP; undated draft of a letter to Cartter on War Department stationery, presumably from EMS, alleging that Stanton had only arrested Thomas to test the Tenure of Office Act, which impeachment would do anyway, SP.

41. *CG*, 40th Cong., 2nd sess., 1647–49; Bingham to "My dear Lucy & Emma," April 11, 1868, Bingham Papers, OHS. Benedict, *Preserving the Constitution*, 239n57, contended that Johnson's compliance with the Tenure of Office Act in suspending Stanton, and Stanton's resumption of the office when the Senate demurred, "seemed to have settled the question of whether Stanton was covered by the act." That was the same argument made by the Republicans who led impeachment, but the question was never decided judicially.

42. *CG*, 40th Cong., 2nd sess., 1647–49; *New York World*, February 24, 1868; Beale, *Welles Diary*, 3:288–89.

43. *CG*, 40th Cong., 2nd sess., 1648–49, supplement, 78–90. Stewart, *Impeached*, 157, subjects the articles to legal and logical analysis.

44. William Moore Diary, March 7, 10, 11, 13, 1868, Johnson Papers, LC; Beale, *Welles Diary*, 3:312; Briggs, *The Olivia Letters*, 48–50.

45. *National Intelligencer*, March 31, 1868; Beale, *Welles Diary*, 3:326. Dewitt's *The Impeachment and Trial of Andrew Johnson* derided the constitutional excesses and inconsistencies of congressional Radicals with biting irony, betraying conservative sympathy for Johnson's Reconstruction policy. Evolving views on race and equality have since subjected Johnson's presidency to increasingly pejorative revision, for example in Michael Les Benedict's 1973 book of the same name, in Trefousse's *Impeachment of a President*, and in Stewart's *Impeached: The Trial of President Andrew Johnson*. While acknowledging the partisan logic and constitutional implications of the Radical argument for impeachment, Stewart virtually endorsed using impeachment to force political conformity from a coequal branch of government.

46. EMS to Fessenden, March 28, 1868, Bowdoin.

47. Various letters from the Court of Claims, February and March, 1868, Letters Received (M221), RG 107, NA; EMS to Francis Fessenden, April 1, 1868, SP. Stanton breveted James and Francis Fessenden as major generals—retiring Francis as a full brigadier, although his highest rank had been colonel, and offering him a lieutenant colonelcy in the Regular Army: EMS to William P. Fessenden, November 5, 1864, to James D. Fessenden, August 8, 1864, December 2, 1865, and to Francis Fessenden, August 7, 1866, Bowdoin.

48. Pierrepont to Stanton, undated, SP; Colfax to John Russell Young, March 11, 1868, Young Papers, LC; EMS motion to the District of Columbia Supreme Court, March 23, 1868, SP; EMS to "Dear Eddie," April 17, 1868, SP.

49. Butler to EMS, April 17, 20, 1868, and EMS to Butler, April 20, 1868, SP.

50. William Moore Diary, March 17, 1868, Johnson Papers, LC; EMS to Simon Cameron, April 14, 1868, SP.

51. Pierrepont to Ellen Stanton, April 15, 1868, SP.

52. Oliver to EMS, April 8, 1868, SP.

53. Niven, *Chase Papers*, 5:120.

54. EMS to Ellenore Adams Hutchison, May 1, 1868, HHC.

55. William Moore Diary, April 21, 23, 25, 1868, Johnson Papers, LC.

56. John Russell Young to EMS, May 6, 1868, SP; *New York Tribune*, May 6, 1868; *New York Times*, May 6, 1868.

57. William Moore Diary, April 25, 1868, January 6, 1870, Johnson Papers, LC; EMS to James Hutchison, April 6, 1868, HHC; Pierrepont to EMS, April 13, May 3, 1868; SP; *Chicago Tribune*, quoted in *New York Herald*, May 14, 1868; EMS to John Russell Young, May 10, 1868, Young Papers, LC; EMS to Andrew Johnson, May 11, 1868, SP; *New York Times*, May 14, 15, 1868. Butler later launched a House investigation into Johnson's defense fund, insinuating that direct bribes had been paid, but he produced no convincing evidence (U.S. House, *Raising of Money to Be Used in Impeachment*, 3–34).

58. *New York Times*, May 13, 14, 1868; *New York Herald*, May 14, 1868.

59. *National Intelligencer*, May 15, 16, 1868; *New York Times*, May 15, 1868; *New York World*, May 16, 1868.

60. *Washington Evening Star*, May 16, 1868; *New York Times*, May 17, 1868; *New York Herald*, May 19, 1868. No bribery was ever proven, but Johnson did not withhold traditional political rewards for those who acquitted him, and Ross received abundant patronage favors over the next couple of months: see Bergeron, Graf, et al., *Andrew Johnson Papers*, 14:177–78, 215–16, 295, 346.

61. EMS to Johnson, "May 11, 1868" [redated May 26, 1868], SP; Badeau, *Grant in Peace*, 144. Badeau's recollection appears to be deliberately unflattering, but Stanton's control of the telegraph would have given him the earliest word of the nomination, and his later efforts to curry favor with Grant lend this vignette some credibility.

62. *New York Herald*, May 27, 1868; *New York World*, May 27, 1868; *Washington Evening Star*, May 26, 27, 1868; Townsend, *Anecdotes*, 132; William Moore Diary, May 26, 1868, Johnson Papers, LC.

63. This adornment comes from Townsend's *Anecdotes*, 135.

CHAPTER 19

1. EMS to Louis A. Walker, November 16, 1868, quoted in Wolcott 174; EMS to Lucy Stanton, December 16, 1868, quoted in Wolcott, 175.

2. *New York Herald*, May 19, 1868; EMS to James Hutchison, April 6, 1868, HHC.

3. Morgan to EMS, June 16, 1868, Young to EMS, June 17, 1868, and Pierrepont to EMS, June 24, 1868, all in SP; EMS to Young, June 24, 1868, Young Papers, LC; *New York Times*, July 5, 7, 1868. The text of the resolution is reproduced in Flower, 394.

4. *New York Times*, July 7, 1868.

5. *CG*, 37th Cong., 2nd sess., 787–804; *New York Times*, July 6, 7, 1868.

6. *New York Times*, July 7, 1868; "George W. Julian's Journal," 325. Hyman, 615, remarks without documentation that at this stage "Ellen began to dispose of her government bonds, their only wartime investment."

7. William Jordan to EMS, August 14, 1868, Schenck to EMS, August 24, 1868, EMS to Schenck, August 27, 1868, and EMS to Isaac Bell, September 29, 1868, all in SP.

8. Ninth Census of the U.S. (M593), Reel 1233, Ward 4, Steubenville, 16, RG 29, NA; John McCracken, quoted in Flower, 410; *New York Tribune, Steubenville Daily Herald*, and *Cincinnati Gazette*, all September 26, 1868. This Stanton portrait is in Doyle, 294.

9. *New York Tribune, Steubenville Daily Herald, Cincinnati Gazette*, September 26, 1868.

10. *New York Tribune* and *Cincinnati Daily Gazette*, September 28, 1868; *New York Times*, September 27, 1868; *Steubenville Daily Herald*, September 26, 1868.

11. *Steubenville Daily Herald*, September 26, 1868; EMS to Ellen, September 27, 1868, quoted in Hyman, 618; Wolcott, 171; EMS to John Russell Young, September 19, 1868, Young Papers, LC; *Ohio State Journal*, September 26, 1868; *Cincinnati Daily Gazette*, October 5, 1868; EMS to Zachariah Chandler, October 1, 1868,

Chandler Papers, LC; *Washington Evening Star*, October 8, 1868; *Cleveland Leader*, October 9, 1868, *Philadelphia Inquirer*, October 9, 1868; *Cincinnati Daily Gazette*, October 27, 1868.

12. EMS to Peter Watson, November 8, 1868, quoted in Flower, 399; *Philadelphia Inquirer*, October 31, November 2, 1868; McClure, *Lincoln and Men of War-Times*, 187. The *New York Times* of October 30, 1868, mistook the Pittsburgh speech as another appearance in Steubenville, but Stanton did not return there after September.

13. EMS to Peter Watson, November 8, 1868, quoted in Flower, 399; EMS to Noah Brooks, December 22, 1868, Chandler Papers, LC.

14. EMS to Watson, January 3, 29, 1869, quoted in Flower, 400–401; ELS to John Schofield, September 26, 1868, Register of Letters Received (M22), RG 107, NA; Watson to EMS, January 15, 1869, and EMS to L. Witt, January 29, 1869, SP.

15. *Wheeling Intelligencer*, January 16, 20, September 4, 1869; EMS to Watson, January 29, 1869, quoted in Flower, 401; W. H. Edwards to EMS, September 7, 1869, SP.

16. *Cleveland Leader*, November 12, 1868; EMS to Watson, January 29, 1869, quoted in Flower, 401; EMS to L. Witt, January 29, 1869, SP.

17. Samuel Hooper to Charles Sumner, November 17, 1868, June 13, 1869, Sumner Papers, Harvard; EMS to Hamilton Fish, April 15, 1869, Fish Papers, LC.

18. EMS to Ellen, July 2, 3, 1869, HHC; EMS to Bayne, May 17, June 26, 1869, SP.

19. Mackey, *Reports*, 6–8.

20. Hooper to Sumner, September 17, 1869, Sumner Papers, Harvard; Pierrepont to EMS, June 23, 1869, SP; EMS to Watson, June 11, 1869, quoted in Flower, 403; David Paul Brown to EMS, July 6, 1869, with Stanton's endorsement, SP.

21. Sherman to EMS, July 28, 1869, GTS, LSU; EMS to Lucy Stanton, June, 1869, quoted in Wolcott, 176; *New York Times*, January 30, 1870; Townsend, quoted in Flower, 410.

22. *Washington Evening Star*, August 4, 13, 1869; EMS to Peter Watson, November 25, 1869, quoted in Flower, 403–4; EMS to Lucy Stanton, September 18, 1869, quoted in Wolcott, 177; *Great Falls Journal*, August 14, 21, 1869; *New Hampshire Gazette*, August 14, 28, 1869; *Republican Statesman*, August 6, 27, 1869.

23. Conkling to EMS, September 6, 1869, SP.

24. Young, *Around the World with General Grant*, 333–34; Grant, *Personal Memoirs*, 2:104–5, 536–37; Sherman, *Memoirs*, 2:422. Hyman, 574, cites John Schofield's manuscript memoir in Box 49 of the Hamlin Garland Papers at the University of Southern California as further evidence of Grant's growing dislike of Stanton.

25. Hooper to Charles Sumner, September 22, 27, 28, 1869, Sumner Papers, Harvard; EMS to Conkling, November 4, 1869, Conkling Papers, LC; *Washington Evening Star*, November 15, 1869.

26. EMS to Simpson, October 26, 1869, LFFC.

27. Hamilton Fish Diary, November 3, 1869, quoted in Nevins, *Hamilton Fish*, 1:304; EMS to Simpson, November 3, 1869, LFFC; Edwards Pierrepont to Hamilton Fish, November 18, 1869, Fish Papers, LC; *Washington Evening Star*, December 15, 1869.

28. Pierrepont to EMS, November 21, 1869, SP; Nevins and Thomas, *Strong Diary*, 4:243; Beale, *Welles Diary*, 3:550–51.

29. Hooper to Charles Sumner, September 22, 1869, Sumner Papers, Harvard; George Jones to EMS, November 2, 1869, and EMS to John Bayne, November 27, 1869, SP.

30. EMS to Watson, November 25, 1869, quoted in Flower, 403–4. By the end of 1869 Stanton had evidently let most of his servants go, but despite the family's financial straits at least a governess was still employed at the house until the evening he died; by the following June, even she had left the household (Ninth Census of the U.S. [M593], Reel 123, Ward 2, Washington, D.C., 119).

31. Edwin L. Stanton, quoted in Gorham, 2:470–71; *New York Times* and *New York World*, December 25, 1869. Despite Eddie's quoted letter and newspaper stories describing the in-chambers argument, the Supreme Court docket and minutes for December 9, 10, 13, and 14 indicate that Justice Swayne was sitting with the full court on other cases at that time, while court news from the *Washington Evening Star* makes no mention of either *Whitney v. Mowry* or Stanton himself between December 9 and 16. Like Senator Fessenden's son, Colonel Wager Swayne was promoted to brigadier and major general, although he never commanded more than a regiment. After the war Stanton also offered him an appointment to the same government commission with General Fessenden (EMS to Francis Fessenden, April 1, 1868, SP).

32. *Washington Evening Star*, December 23, 1869; *USG*, 19:52, 67; Carpenter to EMS, April 24, 1868, SP; petitions dated December 16, 18, 1869, SP; *CG*, 42nd Cong., 2nd sess., Appendix, 560; ELS to Lucy Stanton, December 21, 1869, quoted in Wolcott, 178; *New York Times*, December 20, 1869.

33. EMS to Grant, December 21, 1869, LSU; *Washington Evening Star*, December 20, 1869.

34. *New York Times*, December 25, 1869, April 20, 1879; *New York World*, December 25, 1869.

35. *Washington Evening Star*, December 24, 27, 1869; *Steubenville Daily Herald*, December 31, 1869; *New York Times*, December 28, 1869.

36. *New York Times*, December 31, 1869.

37. Hooper to Horatio Woodman, December 25, 1869, January 31, 1870, Woodman Papers, MHS; *CG*, 42nd Cong., 2nd sess., 4283; *New York Times*, January 30, 1870; ELS to Eben Sturges, January 5, 1870, ELS File, Kenyon.

38. *CG*, 41st Cong., 2nd sess., 519, 1799–1800, 1923, 1946, 1986; Samuel Hooper to Horatio Woodman, January 31, 1870, Woodman Papers, MHS; *USG*, 20:80.

39. Samuel Hooper to Horatio Woodman, January 16, 1870, Woodman Papers, MHS; *Philadelphia Inquirer*, November 19, 1873.

40. Stanton's mother was buried November 8, 1873 (Union Cemetery interment records).

41. *Washington Evening Star*, August 31, 1877. Edwin L. Stanton married in November of 1874 and fathered two children before he died: his widow lived until 1914; his son, First Sergeant Edwin M. Stanton, was killed in the Meuse-Argonne offensive on October 14, 1918, apparently unmarried, and the line of Edwin L. Stanton ended when his spinster daughter Sophy Carr Stanton died in 1942 (headstone and cenotaph inscriptions, cemetery of St. James the Less Episcopal Church, Philadelphia).

42. EMS to Ellen, July 2, 3, 1869, HHC; *Ohio Press*, November 21, 1879 (article about Eleanor and Eddie, suggesting that Bessie was already dead). Eleanor Stanton Bush died September 26, 1910, and is buried in the Oak Hill lot; Lewis moved to New Orleans, where he died in 1938 (headstone, Metairie Cemetery); his father's name survives in the person of Lewis's great-grandson, Captain Edwin M. Stanton (U.S. Coast Guard, retired).

43. *Wheeling Intelligencer*, December 25, 1869.

44. Wilson, "Edwin M. Stanton" and "Jeremiah S. Black and Edwin M. Stanton"; Black, "Senator Wilson and Edwin M. Stanton" and "Mr. Black to Mr. Wilson." Letters concerning inconsistencies in the Radical impression of Stanton include J. Ashton to Black, January 3, 1870, Jacob Thompson to Black, June 7, October 10, 1870, Salmon P. Chase to Black, July 4, 1870, James E. Harvey to Black, October 2, 1870, all in Black Papers, LC; Gideon Welles to Montgomery Blair, January 17, 25, June [27], November 22, 1870, January 21, 1871, November 18, 1872, July 10, October 16, 1873, Blair Papers, LC; E. R. Hoar to Zachariah Chandler, January 20, 1870, Chandler Papers, LC; Salmon P. Chase to Wilson, May 25, 1870, Chase Papers, LC; Welles to Blair, September 24, 1870, Welles Papers, LC; Blair to Welles, June 18, November 24, 1870, February 25, 1873, Welles Papers, CHS.

45. *CG*, 42nd Cong., 2nd sess., 4112–13.

46. Ibid., 4282–83.

47. Ibid., Appendix, 559–60; Carpenter to EMS, April 24, 1868, SP.

APPENDIX

1. *CG*, 42nd Cong., 2nd sess., Appendix, 583; Charles Benjamin to Horace White, June 1, 1914, ALPLM; *Illinois State Register*, February 27, 1861; Harding to Alexander Dallas Bache, January 27, 1862 (RH1441), HL; EMS to Heman Dyer, May 18, 1862, SP. Harding's only extant letter to Lincoln is a routine 1863 recommendation for an applicant to West Point.

2. *Mr. & Mrs. Ralph Emerson's Personal Recollections of Abraham Lincoln*, 5, 7, 9; Beveridge, *Abraham Lincoln*, 1:580–82; Washburne to Lincoln, January 17, 1855, Lincoln Papers, LC. William Lee Miller, *Lincoln's Virtues*, 410–18, 490–91, accorded Harding more credence than close scrutiny warrants, but he did doubt the truth of Emerson's account.

3. Wilson and Davis, *Herndon's Informants*, 186, 655; *CWL*, 3:491.

4. Piatt, *Memories*, 54–57.

5. Hertz, *The Hidden Lincoln*, 153–54.

BIBLIOGRAPHY

MANUSCRIPTS

Alabama Department of Archives and History, Montgomery
   Benjamin F. Perry Papers
Allen County Public Library, Fort Wayne, Ind.
   Lincoln Financial Foundation Collection: Cabinet Member Letters
American Antiquarian Society, Worcester, Mass.
   Lee Pardon Aldrich Diary
   Civil War Collection
   Comey Family Papers
   James Helme Rickard Letters
   William A. Willoughby Papers
Boston Public Library, Boston, Mass.
   William Lloyd Garrison Letters
   Edwin M. Stanton Letters
Bowdoin College, Brunswick, Maine
   Fessenden Family Papers
Brown University, Providence, R.I.
   Edwin M. Stanton Letters
Chautauqua County Historical Society, Westfield, N.Y.
   Samuel T. Allen Letters
   George A. Cobham Jr. Diary
   Albion W. Tourgee Letters
Chicago History Center, Chicago, Ill.
   Edwin M. Stanton Letters
Cincinnati Historical Society, Cincinnati, Ohio
   Salmon P. Chase Papers
   Alexander Long Papers
   Miller Family Collection
   Mathias Schwab Letters
   Bellamy Storer Letters
Columbia University, New York, N.Y.
   John Adams Dix Papers
   Fletcher Pratt Collection
Connecticut Historical Society, Hartford
   Milton H. Bassett Papers
   Charles Greenleaf Letters
   Robert Hale Kellogg Papers
   Timothy Loomis Letters

Edward S. Roberts Diary

Gideon Welles Papers

Culpeper County Library, Culpeper, Va.

Norman, Nellie Virginia. "History of the Culpeper County Normans"

Dartmouth College, Hanover, N.H.

Joseph Messer Clough Letters

George Benton Codman Letters

Samuel Duncan Letters (in Duncan Family Papers)

George Marden Letters

Oscar D. Robinson Papers

Ransom F. Sargent Papers

George Wheeler and D. W. Perkins Letters

Andrew Hale Young Correspondence

Delaware Historical Society, Wilmington

James Harrison Wilson Collection

District of Columbia Archives, Washington

Deed Books

Duke University, Durham, N.C.

Isaac H. Carrington Papers

Drozdowski, Eugene C. "Edwin M. Stanton, Lincoln's Secretary of War: Toward Victory." Ph.D. diss., 1964.

Holcomb P. Harvey Diary (in William Clifton Harvey Papers)

Earlham College, Richmond, Ind.

Thomas W. Barnett Diary

Margaret Jones Diary

Francis W. Thomas Papers

Gilcrease Museum, Tulsa, Okla.

Ethan Allen Hitchcock Diaries

Guilford College, Greensboro, N.C.

Friends Historical Collection: Stanton Family Papers

Hagley Museum and Library, Wilmington, Del.

Winterthur Manuscripts: Samuel F. du Pont Papers

Harrison County Courthouse, Cadiz, Ohio

Common Pleas Journals

Deed Books

Harvard University, Cambridge, Mass.

Frederick M. Dearborn Collection

George B. McClellan Autograph File

Charles Sumner Papers

Rutherford B. Hayes Presidential Library, Fremont, Ohio

Pamphila Wolcott Letter

Heinz History Center, Pittsburgh, Pa.

Harper Family Papers

Wilkins Family Papers (including Edwin M. Stanton Correspondence)

Historical Society of Pennsylvania, Philadelphia
    James Buchanan Papers
    Salmon P. Chase Papers
    Simon Gratz Collection
Huntington Library, San Marino, Calif.
    Alexander Dallas Bache Papers
    Hiram Barney Collection
    Thomas H. Dudley Papers
    James T. Eldridge Civil War Collection
    James Thomas Fields Papers
    John Lorimer Graham Papers
    Charles G. Halpine Papers
    Joseph Holt Papers
    Ward Hill Lamon Papers
    Francis Lieber Papers
    Miscellaneous Manuscripts
    Charles H. Ray Papers
    William M. Stanton Papers
Indiana Historical Society, Indianapolis
    Sylvester C. Bishop Letters
    Elijah H. C. Cavins Papers
    Schuyler Colfax Papers
    Solomon S. Hamrick Letters
    W. C. Patton Diaries
    Henry A. Robinson Letters
    William A. Swayze Letters
    Lew Wallace Collection
Indiana State Library, Indianapolis
    Jonathan Joseph Letters
    Richard W. Thompson Collection
Indiana University, Bloomington
    Horace Greeley Letter
    J. F. Lovering Diary
Jefferson County Chapter of the Ohio Genealogical Society, Wintersville, Ohio
    Jefferson County Common Pleas Journals
    Jefferson County Marriage Books
Jefferson County Courthouse, Steubenville, Ohio
    Deed Books
Kansas State Historical Society, Topeka
    Judd Family Diaries
    Samuel J. Reader Papers
Kansas University, Lawrence
    John Kerr Proudfit Letters
Kenyon College, Gambier, Ohio
    Edwin L. Stanton Manuscript File

Edwin M. Stanton Manuscript File
Philomathesian Society Records
Library of Congress, Washington, D.C.
William Allen Papers
Nathaniel Banks Papers
David Homer Bates Diary
Jeremiah S. Black Papers
Buchanan-Johnston Papers
Burbank-Van Voorhis Family Papers
Simon Cameron Papers
Zachariah Chandler Papers
Salmon P. Chase Papers
James A. Congleton Diary
Roscoe Conkling Papers
J. Dexter Cotton Papers
Caleb Cushing Papers
William Franklin Draper Papers
Thomas Ewing Family Papers
William Pitt Fessenden Papers
Hamilton Fish Papers
Thomas S. Forbes Letter
Benjamin Brown French Family Papers
James J. Gillette Papers
Horace Gray Papers
Horace Greeley Papers
Hamilton Family Papers
John P. Hatch Papers
Lewis M. Haupt Family Papers
John Hay Papers
Samuel P. Heintzelman Diary
Ethan Allen Hitchcock Papers
Lyman Holford Diary
Joseph Holt Papers
Andrew Johnson Papers
August V. Kautz Papers
Philip Kearny Papers
J. Warren Keifer Papers
Horatio King Papers
Daniel Read Larned Papers
Abraham Lincoln Papers
Jeremiah T. Lockwood Papers
George B. McClellan Papers
Gates W. McGarrah Collection
Edward McPherson Papers
Manton Marble Papers

Rufus Mead Papers
Montgomery Meigs Papers
Robert Dale Owen Letter
Philip Phillips Family Papers
Charles H. Richardson Diary
Bela T. St. John Papers
Jacob Schuckers Papers
John Sherman Papers
William T. Sherman Papers
Edwin M. Stanton Papers
George Hay Stuart Collection
Horatio Nelson Taft Diary
Benjamin Tappan Papers
Lewis Tappan Papers
Lyman Trumbull Papers
Benjamin Wade Papers
Elihu B. Washburne Papers
Gideon Welles Papers
Willard Family Papers
James H. Wilson Papers
Library of Virginia, Richmond
Culpeper County Will Books
Lincoln Memorial University, Harrogate, Tenn.
Papers of Lincoln's Cabinet Members
Abraham Lincoln Presidential Library and Museum,
        Springfield, Ill.
Henry Halleck Letters
Edwin M. Stanton Collection
Horace White Letters
Louisiana State University, Baton Rouge
Edwin M. Stanton Papers
Stanton, Gideon Townsend. "Edwin M. Stanton: A Personal Portrait."
Maine Historical Society, Portland
William Bryant Adams Papers
James Brown Papers
H. C. Ingersoll Collection
Perry Family Correspondence
Willis M. Porter Papers
George M. Redlon Letters
John Parris Sheahan Correspondence
Rebecca Usher Collection
Leonard Valentine Correspondence
Mark P. Waterman Letters
Maryland Historical Society, Baltimore
David Creamer Diary

Massachusetts Historical Society, Boston
    John A. Andrew Papers
    Edward Atkinson Papers
    Caleb Hadley Beal Papers
    John Henry Clifford Papers
    Dana Family Papers
    Warren Goodale Letters
    Andrew R. Linscott Papers
    Theodore Lyman Papers
    Charles J. Paine Letters
    Daniel H. Spofford Letters
    William H. West Diaries
    Myron Rice Wood Papers
    Horatio Woodman Papers
Minnesota Historical Society, St. Paul
    Charles J. Branich (Karl Josef Breunig) Papers
    Christie Family Papers
    John H. Macomber Papers
    Matthew Marvin Papers
Missouri Historical Society, St. Louis
    Hamilton Gamble Collection
    Abraham Hagaman Collection
    George R. Harrington Papers
    Henry and Ethan Allen Hitchcock Collection
    James E. Love Papers
National Archives, Washington, D.C.
    Records of the Veterans Administration, Record Group 15
        General Index to Civil War Pension Records (T288)
        Revolutionary War Pension and Bounty Land Warrant Applications (M804)
    Records of the Supreme Court of the District of Columbia, Record Group 21
        Criminal Docket, Entry 4
        Criminal Case Files, Entry 77
    Records of the Coast and Geodetic Survey, Record Group 23
        Land and Building Surveys, Washington, D.C.
    Records of the Bureau of the Census, Record Group 29
        Sixth Census of the United States (M704)
        Seventh Census of the United States (M432)
        Eighth Census of the United States (M653)
        Ninth Census of the United States (M593)
        Thirteenth Census of the United States (T624)
    Records of the Department of Justice, Record Group 60
        Letters Received, 1818–1870, Entry 10
        Correspondence on Land Claims, 1855–1870, Entry 27
    Records of the Quartermaster General, Record Group 92
        Consolidated Correspondence File, Entry 225

Records of the Adjutant General, Record Group 94
    Case Files of Investigations by Levi C. Turner and Lafayette C. Baker (M797)
    Generals' Papers and Generals' Reports and Books
        Ambrose E. Burnside Papers
    Index to Compiled Service Records of Volunteer Soldiers Who Served
        During the Mexican War (M616)
    Individual Service Records
    Letters Received (M619)
    Register of Cadet Appointments, 1819–1867 (M2037)
    Register of Enlistments in the United States Army, 1798–1914 (M233)
Records of the Bureau of Refugees, Freedmen, and Abandoned Lands, Record
        Group 105
    Records of the Assistant Commissioner for the State of Tennessee (M999)
    Records of the Assistant Commissioner for the State of Virginia (M1048)
    Records of the Field Officers for the State of Louisiana (M1905)
Records of the Office of the Secretary of War, Record Group 107
    Annual Reports of the War Department, 1822–1907 (M997)
    Letters Received by the Secretary of War, Main Series (M221)
    Letters Received by the Secretary of War, Irregular Series (M492)
    Letters Received by the Secretary of War from the President, Executive
        Departments, and War Department Bureaus, 1862–70 (M494)
    Letters Sent by the Secretary of War Relating to Military Affairs (M6)
    Letters Sent by the Secretary of War to the President (M421)
    Letters Sent to the President (M127)
    Orders and Endorsements Sent by the Secretary of War (M444)
    Registers of Letters Received by the Office of the Secretary of War, Main
        Series, 1800–1870 (M22)
    Reports to Congress from the Secretary of War (M220)
    Telegrams Collected by the Office of the Secretary of War, Bound, 1861–1882
        (M473)
    Telegrams Collected by the Office of the Secretary of War, Unbound,
        1860–1870 (M504)
Records of the Headquarters of the Army, Record Group 108
    Letters Sent by the Headquarters of the Army, Main Series, 1828–1903
        (M857)
War Department Collection of Confederate Records, Record Group 109
    Combined Service Records of Confederate Soldiers from the State of
        Virginia (M324)
    Bushrod Rust Johnson Diary
    Union Provost Marshal's File of Papers Relating to Individual Citizens
        (M345)
Records of the Provost Marshal General's Bureau, Record Group 110
    Letters Received, Eleventh District of Pennsylvania
Records of the United States Court of Claims, Record Group 123
    Congressional Jurisdiction Case Files, 1884–1943

        Isaac Turner Case File, Claim No. 11496
    Records of the Judge Advocate General, Record Group 153
       Court-Martial Case Files
          Court-Martial of Surgeon General William A. Hammond, MM1430
          Court-Martial of Henry Wirz, MM2975
          Investigation and Trial Papers Relating to Suspects in the Lincoln
             Assassination (M599)
          Letters Received, 1854–1894, Entry 6
          Letters Sent ("Record Books"), 1842–1889, Entry 1
    Records of the Office of the Inspector General, Record Group 159
       Register of Reports, 1864, Entry 2
    Records of the Commissary General of Prisoners, Record Group 249
       Consolidated Morning Reports of Prisoners at Andersonville, Entry 111
    Records of the Supreme Court of the United States, Record Group 267
       Dockets of the Supreme Court (M216)
       Minutes of the Supreme Court (M215)
    Records of U.S. Army Continental Commands, Record Group 393
       Part I, Geographical Divisions and Departments and Military Districts
          Department of the East
             Letters Sent, January 1863–December 1872, Entry 1394
          Department of Virginia
             Reports Received, Entry 7005
National Society of the Sons of the American Revolution, Louisville, Ky.
    Membership Applications
New Hampshire Historical Society, Concord
    John Batchelder Bailey Journal
    Charles Gilman Brewster Letters from George Francis Towle
    William E. Chandler Papers
    Solomon Dodge Letters
    Benjamin B. and Henry F. French Correspondence
    Joseph A. Gilmore Papers
    Sylvester Erwin Hadley Diary
    John P. Hale Papers
    Edward F. Hall Letters
    Elizabeth Livermore Diary
    Sarah Low Papers
    George Stearns Papers
New Hampshire State Library, Concord
    Willard J. Templeton Letters
New-York Historical Society, New York
    John H. Clifford Letter
New York Public Library
    Bryant-Godwin Papers
    Horace Greeley Papers
    Lee Kohns Collection
    Abraham Lincoln Collection

Miscellaneous Collections: U.S. Army
Miscellaneous Personal Files
Montague Collection of Historical Autographs
Theodorus Bailey Myers Collection
Henry J. Raymond Papers
Cabot Jackson Russell Papers
Dore Schary Collection
Ohio Historical Society, Columbus
Jacob Ammen Papers
John A. Bingham Papers
William F. Hunter Papers
William McVey Papers
Nathaniel L. Parmeter Diary
Samuel Sexton Papers
Edwin M. Stanton Papers
James R. Stillwell Papers
Benjamin Tappan Papers
Vertical File Manuscripts
Wolcott, Pamphila S. "Edwin M. Stanton: A Biographical Sketch by His Sister."
Worthington Family Papers
Peabody Essex Museum, Salem, Mass.
Francis Crowninshield Papers
John Peirce Letters
Prairie View A&M University, Prairie View, Tex.
Harold M. Hyman Papers
Princeton University, Princeton, N.J.
Blair-Lee Family Papers
Rhode Island Historical Society, Providence
Ambrose E. Burnside Papers
Rutgers University, New Brunswick, N.J.
Roebling Family Papers
St. Albans Historical Society, St. Albans, Vt.
Smith Family Papers
State Historical Society of Iowa, Des Moines
Adjutant General's Correspondence: Disloyal Sentiments File
Amos W. Ames Diary
Charles Mason Papers
William and Jane Thompson Letters
John Whitten Diary
State Historical Society of Iowa, Iowa City
George Marion Shearer Diary
Adoniram Judson Withrow Letters
U.S. Army Military History Institute, Carlisle Barracks, Pa.
John Brislin Letters
Lewis Frederick Cleveland Letters
Isaac Gardner Letters

Jacob W. Haas Papers
Daniel Himes Diary
Charles C. Morey Papers
David Nichol Papers
William Presley Letters
Alexander Rose Diary
University of California, Berkeley
George T. Balch Letters
University of Chicago, Chicago, Ill.
Stephen A. Douglas Papers
University of Iowa, Iowa City
Andrew F. Davis Papers
Giauque Family Papers
Papers of the Sterns Family
University of Kentucky, Lexington
Graves, Frederick J. "The Early Life and Career of Edwin M. Stanton." Ph.D.
diss., 1955.
University of Maine, Orono
James S. Pike Papers
University of Michigan, Ann Arbor
Bentley Library
William Boston Papers
Charles Ellet Papers
Wayne E. Morris Papers
Clements Library
William Bennit Voter Proxy
Samuel Wylie Crawford Letters
Henry Wager Halleck Letters
Ebenezer Rockwood Hoar Letters
Thomas Hughes Letters
Henry Grimes Marshall Letters
James T. Miller Letters
Frank Sterns Letter
George T. Stevens Letters
Zealous B. Tower Letter
John Darrah Wilkins Letters
Hatcher Library
Transportation History Collection
Charles Ellet Papers
University of New Hampshire, Durham
Leander Harris Letters
George Naylor Julian Papers
University of Notre Dame, Notre Dame, Ind.
Caley Family Correspondence
University of Pennsylvania, Philadelphia

Trustee Minutes
Commencement Programs
University of Rochester, Rochester, N.Y.
William H. Seward Papers
University of South Carolina, Columbia
South Caroliniana Library
Francis Lieber Papers
University of Southern California, Los Angeles
Hamlin Garland Papers
University of Vermont, Burlington
Joel Glover Letters
Richard Irwin Letters
Augustus Paddock Papers
Joseph C. Rutherford Papers
William Stow Letters
William Wells Papers
University of Virginia, Charlottesville
Charles B. Senior Letters
Francis T. Sherman Diary
Vermont Historical Society, Barre
Cheney-Watts Collection
Charles Cummings Papers
Roswell Farnham Correspondence
William Wirt Henry Papers
George S. Lyon Letters
Lorenzo Miles Diary
Pingree-Hunton-Stickney Family Papers (Lyndon State College Collection)
Seaver Family Letters
Virginia Historical Society, Richmond
Edward Bates Papers
J. R. Hamilton Letter
Western Reserve Historical Society, Cleveland, Ohio
George W. Hodges Letters
George W. Landrum Letters
John A. McIntosh Letters
William P. Palmer Collection
Albert Gallatin Riddle Papers
Cyrus H. Stockwell Papers
Charles Albert Turner Papers
Alexander Varian Letters
Wisconsin Historical Society, Madison
John J. Barney Papers
James R. Doolittle Papers
Frank Abial Flower Collection
Timothy O. Howe Papers

Henry W. Jackson Letters
Levi Shell Letters
Yale University, New Haven, Conn.
Beinecke Library
Abraham Lincoln Papers
Western Americana Collection
Sterling Library
J. B. Dawley Correspondence
A. Conger Goodyear Collection

PUBLISHED SOURCES

Acken, J. Gregory, ed. *Inside the Army of the Potomac: The Civil War Experience of Captain Francis Adams Donaldson*. Mechanicsburg, Pa.: Stackpole Books, 1998.

Acts of the General Assembly of the State of Virginia Passed in 1865–66. Richmond, Va.: Allegre and Goode, 1866.

Adams, George Worthington. *Doctors in Blue*. New York: Henry Schuman, 1952.

Adams, Henry. *The Education of Henry Adams*. Boston: Houghton Mifflin, 1918. Reprinted with an introduction by D. W. Brogan. Boston: Houghton Mifflin, 1961.

Ames, Mary Clemmer. *Ten Years in Washington: Life and Scenes in the National Capital, as a Woman Sees Them*. Hartford, Conn.: A. D. Worthington, 1873.

Ascher, Leonard. "Lincoln's Administration and the New Almaden Scandal." *Pacific Historical Review* 5, no. 1 (March, 1936): 38–51.

Auchampaugh, Philip G. *James Buchanan and His Cabinet on the Eve of Secession*. Lancaster, Pa.: privately printed, 1926.

Badeau, Adam. *Grant in Peace, from Appomattox to Mount McGregor: A Personal Memoir*. Hartford, Conn.: S. S. Scranton & Co., 1887.

Bain, David Haward. *Empire Express: Building the First Transcontinental Railroad*. New York: Viking, 1999.

Baker, Jean H. *Affairs of Party: The Political Culture of Northern Democrats in the Mid-Nineteenth Century*. New York: Fordham University Press, 1998.

Bancroft, Frederic, ed. *Speeches, Correspondence, and Political Papers of Carl Schurz*. 6 vols. New York: G. P. Putnam's Sons, 1913.

Bancroft, Hubert Howe. *History of California*. 7 vols. San Francisco: The History Company, 1884–90.

Barnes, Joseph K. *The Medical and Surgical History of the War of the Rebellion (1861–65)*. 15 vols. 1870. Reprinted, Wilmington, N.C.: Broadfoot Publishing, 1990.

Barrett, John Spencer, ed. *Correspondence of Andrew Jackson*. 7 vols. Washington, D.C.: Carnegie Institute of Washington, 1926–35.

Basler, Roy P., ed. *The Collected Works of Abraham Lincoln*. 8 vols. New Brunswick, N.J.: Rutgers University Press, 1953.

Batchelor, Charles W. *Incidents in My Life*. Pittsburgh, Pa.: J. Eichbaum, 1887.

Bates, David Homer. *Lincoln in the Telegraph Office: Recollections of the United States Military Telegraph Corps during the Civil War*. New York: The Century Co., 1907.

Battles and Leaders of the Civil War. 4 vols. New York: The Century Co., 1884–88.

Beale, Howard K., ed. *The Diary of Edward Bates.* Washington: Government Printing Office, 1933.

——, ed. *The Diary of Gideon Welles, Secretary of the Navy Under Lincoln and Johnson.* 3 vols. New York, W. W. Norton, 1960.

Benedict, Michael Les. *A Compromise of Principle: Congressional Republicans and Reconstruction, 1863–1869.* New York: W. W. Norton, 1974.

——. *The Impeachment and Trial of Andrew Johnson.* New York: W. W. Norton, 1973.

——. *Preserving the Constitution: Essays on Politics and the Constitution in the Reconstruction Era.* New York: Fordham University Press, 2006.

[Benjamin, Charles F.] "Recollections of Secretary Stanton." *Century Magazine* 33, no. 5 (March, 1887): 758–68.

Bergeron, Paul H., Leroy P. Graf, et al., eds. *The Papers of Andrew Johnson.* 16 vols. Knoxville: University of Tennessee Press, 1967–2000.

Bernitt, Muriel, ed. "Two Manuscripts of Gideon Welles." *New England Quarterly* 11, no. 3 (September, 1938): 576–605.

Beveridge, Albert J. *Abraham Lincoln, 1809–1858.* 2 vols. Boston: Houghton Mifflin, 1928.

Black, Jeremiah S. "Mr. Black to Mr. Wilson." *The Galaxy* 11, no. 2 (February, 1871): 257–76.

——. "Senator Wilson and Edwin M. Stanton." *The Galaxy* 9, no. 6 (June, 1870): 817–31.

Blair, William Alan, ed. *A Politician Goes to War: The Civil War Letters of John White Geary.* University Park, Pa.: The Pennsylvania State University Press, 1995.

Blue, Frederick J. *Salmon P. Chase: A Life in Politics.* Kent, Ohio: Kent State University Press, 1987.

Boutwell, George S. *Reminiscences of Sixty Years in Public Affairs.* 2 vols. New York: McClure, Phillips & Company, 1902.

Brandt, Nat. *The Congressman Who Got Away with Murder.* Syracuse, N.Y.: Syracuse University Press, 1991.

Brigance, William N. *Jeremiah Sullivan Black: A Defender of the Constitution and the Ten Commandments.* 1934. Reprinted, New York: Da Capo Press, 1971.

Briggs, Emily Edson. *The Olivia Letters, Being Some History of Washington City for Forty Years as Told by the Letters of a Newspaper Correspondent.* New York: Neale Publishing Co., 1906.

Brooks, Noah. *Washington in Lincoln's Time.* New York: The Century Co., 1895. Reprinted with an introduction by Herbert Mitgang. Athens, Ga.: University of Georgia Press, 1989.

Brown, J. Willard. *The Signal Corps, U.S.A., in the War of the Rebellion.* Boston: U.S. Veteran Signal Corps Association, 1896.

Brown, Letitia W. "Residence Patterns of Negroes in the District of Columbia, 1800–1869." *Records of the Columbia Historical Society* 47 (1969–70), 66–79.

Browne, Charles Farrar. *The Complete Works of Artemus Ward.* New York: G. W. Dillingham Co., 1898.

Brun, Christian. "A Palace Guard View of Lincoln (The Civil War Letters of John H. Fleming)." *Soundings* 3, no. 1 (May, 1971): 18–39.

Bullard, F. Lauriston, ed. *The Diary of a Public Man.* New Brunswick, N.J.: Rutgers University Press, 1946

Burlingame, Michael, ed. *Dispatches from Lincoln's White House: The Anonymous Civil War Journalism of Presidential Secretary William O. Stoddard.* Lincoln: University of Nebraska Press, 2002.

———, ed. *Lincoln Observed: Civil War Dispatches of Noah Brooks.* Baltimore, Md.: The Johns Hopkins University Press, 1998.

———, ed. *With Lincoln in the White House: Letters, Memoranda, and Other Writings of John G. Nicolay, 1860–65.* Carbondale: Southern Illinois University Press, 2000.

Burlingame, Michael, and John R. Turner Ettlinger, eds. *Inside Lincoln's White House: The Complete Civil War Diary of John Hay.* Carbondale: Southern Illinois University Press, 1997.

Burton, Crompton. "'No Turning Back': The Official Bulletins of Secretary of War Edwin M. Stanton." In *Words at War: The Civil War and American Journalism,* edited by David B. Sachsman, S. Kittrell Rushing, and Roy Morris Jr. West Lafayette, Ind.: Purdue University Press, 2008.

Butler, Benjamin F. *Private and Official Correspondence of Ben Butler.* 5 vols. Norwood, Mass.: privately printed, 1917.

Carpenter, Francis B. *The Inner Life of Abraham Lincoln: Six Months at the White House.* New York: Hurd and Houghton, 1867. Reprinted with an introduction by Mark E. Neely Jr. Lincoln: University of Nebraska Press, 1995.

Carter, Clarence Edwin, ed. *The Territorial Papers of the United States.* Vol. 3. Washington, D.C.: Government Printing Office, 1934.

Castel, Albert E. *The Presidency of Andrew Johnson.* Lawrence: The Regents Press of Kansas, 1979.

Catalogue of Kenyon College and of the Theological Seminary of the Diocese of Ohio, 1825 to 1872. Gambier, Ohio: Edmonds and Hunt, 1873.

Chandler, Robert J. "An Uncertain Influence: The Role of the Federal Government in California, 1846–1880." *California Historical Quarterly* 81, no. 3/4 (2003): 224–71.

Chesson, Michael B., ed. *J. Franklin Dyer: The Journal of a Civil War Surgeon.* Lincoln: University of Nebraska Press, 2003.

Child, William. *Letters from a Civil War Surgeon: Dr. William Child of the Fifth New Hampshire Volunteers.* Edited by Merrill C. Sawyer, Betty Sawyer, and Timothy C. Sawyer. Solon, Maine: Polar Bear & Company, 2001.

"City of Pittsburgh." In *Gleason's Pictorial Drawing-Room Companion.* Harrisburg, Pa.: F. Gleason. April 30, 1853, 280.

Clark, Walter, William L. Saunders, and Stephen B. Weeks, eds. *The State Records of North Carolina.* 16 vols., nos. 11–26. Winston and Goldsboro: State of North Carolina, 1895–1907.

Clemenceau, Georges. *American Reconstruction, 1865–1870, and the Impeachment of President Johnson.* New York: The Dial Press, 1928.

A Compilation of the Messages and Papers of the Presidents. 11 vols. Washington, D.C.: Bureau of National Literature, 1913.

Condensed Reports of Decisions in the Supreme Court of Ohio, Containing All the Cases in the Sixth and Seventh Volumes of Hammond's Reports. Columbus, Ohio: Isaac N. Whiting, 1840.

The Condition of the South: Extracts from the Report of Major-General Carl Schurz, on the States of South Carolina, Georgia, Alabama, Mississippi, and Louisiana. Washington, D.C.: n.p., 1866.

Cooling, Benjamin F. *Forts Henry and Donelson: Key to the Confederate Heartland.* Knoxville: University of Tennessee Press, 1988.

Correspondence of John Sedgwick, Major-General. 2 vols. New York: C. and E. B. Stoeckel, 1902–03.

Cox, Jacob D. *Military Reminiscences of the Civil War.* 2 vols. New York: Scribner's, 1900.

Cozzens, Peter. *General John Pope: A Life for the Nation.* Urbana: University of Illinois Press, 2000.

Croffut, W. A., ed. *Fifty Years in Camp and Field: Diary of Major-General Ethan Allen Hitchcock, U.S.A.* New York: Putnam's Sons, 1909.

Dahlgren, Madeleine Vinton. *Memoir of John A. Dahlgren, Rear-Admiral United States Navy.* Boston: James R. Osgood & Co., 1882.

Dana, Charles A. *Recollections of the Civil War.* New York: D. Appleton and Co., 1898. Reprinted with an introduction by Charles E. Rankin. Lincoln: University of Nebraska Press, 1996.

Davis, Barbara Butler, ed. *Affectionately Yours: The Civil War Home-Front Letters of the Ovid Butler Family.* Indianapolis: Indiana Historical Society, 2004.

Davis, Jefferson. *The Rise and Fall of the Confederate Government.* 2 vols. New York: D. Appleton and Co., 1881. Reprinted, with a foreword by Bell I. Wiley, New York: Thomas Yoseloff, 1958.

Davis, William C. *Lincoln's Men: How President Lincoln Became Father to an Army and a Nation.* New York: The Free Press, 1999.

Dawes, Henry L. "Washington the Winter before the War." *Atlantic Monthly* 72, no. 430 (August, 1893): 160–67.

Defence of Lieutenant H. N. Harrison before the Court of Inquiry No. 2, Convened at Washington City. Washington, D.C.: Buell & Blanchard, 1858.

DeFontaine, Felix G. *Trial of the Hon. Daniel E. Sickles: for Shooting Philip Barton Key, Esq., U.S. District Attorney, of Washington, D.C., February 27th, 1859.* New York: R. M. De Witt, 1859.

Dewitt, David Miller. *The Impeachment and Trial of Andrew Johnson, Seventeenth President of the United States.* New York: Macmillan Company, 1903.

Dirck, Brian R. *Lincoln and the Constitution.* Carbondale: Southern Illinois University Press, 2012.

Donald, David Herbert. *Charles Sumner and the Coming of the Civil War.* 1960. Reprinted, Napierville, Ill.: Sourcebooks, 2009.

Dowdey, Clifford, and Louis H. Manarin, eds. *The Wartime Papers of R. E. Lee.* New York: Virginia Civil War Commission, 1961.

Doyle, Joseph B. *In Memoriam: Edwin McMasters Stanton, His Life and Work*. Steubenville, Ohio: Herald Printing Company, 1911.

Duncan, Russell, ed. *Blue-Eyed Child of Fortune: The Civil War Letters of Colonel Robert Gould Shaw*. Athens, Ga.: The University of Georgia Press, 1992.

Dyer, Heman. *Records of an Active Life*. New York: Thomas Whittaker, 1886.

Eby, Cecil B. Jr., ed. *A Virginia Yankee in the Civil War: The Diaries of David Hunter Strother*. Chapel Hill: University of North Carolina Press, 1961.

Edwards, William B. *Civil War Guns: The Complete Story of Federal and Confederate Small Arms*. Harrisburg, Pa.: Stackpole, 1962.

Egnal, Marc. *Clash of Extremes: The Economic Origins of the Civil War*. New York: Hill and Wang, 2009.

Eisenschiml, Otto. *The Celebrated Case of Fitz John Porter: An American Dreyfus Affair*. Indianapolis, Ind.: Bobbs-Merrill Co, 1950.

———. *Why Was Lincoln Murdered?* Boston: Little, Brown & Co., 1937.

Engle, Stephen D. *Don Carlos Buell: Most Promising of All*. Chapel Hill: University of North Carolina Press, 1999.

Engs, Robert F., and Corey M. Brooks, eds. *Their Patriotic Duty: The Civil War Letters of the Evans Family of Brown County, Ohio*. New York: Fordham University Press, 2007.

"Extracts from the Journal of Henry J. Raymond." *Scribner's Monthly* 19, no. 3 (January, 1880): 419–24.

The Factory Riots in Allegheny City: Judge Patton's Charge. Pittsburgh, Pa.: Blackstone et al., 1849.

Farber, Daniel. *Lincoln's Constitution*. Chicago: University of Chicago Press, 2003.

Fehrenbacher, Don E. *The Dred Scott Case: Its Significance in American Law and Politics*. New York: Oxford University Press, 1978.

Fessenden, Francis. *The Life and Public Services of William Pitt Fessenden*. 2 vols. Boston: Houghton Mifflin, 1907.

Fishel, Edwin C. *The Secret War for the Union: The Untold Story of Military Intelligence in the Civil War*. Boston: Houghton Mifflin, 1996.

Fleming, Walter. *Documentary History of Reconstruction: Political, Military, Social, Religious, Educational & Industrial, 1863 to the Present Time*. 2 vols. Cleveland, Ohio: Arthur H. Clark Co., 1906.

Florida Contested Election of U.S. Senator. Argument before the Select Committee of the U.S. Senate, Thursday, June 10th, 1852, by Edwin M. Stanton, of Counsel for the Complainant. Washington, D.C.: Gideon & Co., 1852.

Flower, Frank Abial. *Edwin McMasters Stanton: The Autocrat of Rebellion, Emancipation, and Reconstruction*. Akron, Ohio: Saalfield Publishing Co., 1905.

Foner, Eric. *The Fiery Trial: Abraham Lincoln and American Slavery*. New York: W. W. Norton, 2010.

———. *Reconstruction: America's Unfinished Revolution, 1863–1877*. New York: Harper & Row, 1988.

Frank, Seymour J. "The Conspiracy to Implicate Confederate Leaders in Lincoln's Assassination." *Mississippi Valley Historical Review* 40, no. 4 (March, 1954): 629–36.

Freeman, Douglas Southall, ed. *Lee's Dispatches: Unpublished Letters of General Robert E. Lee, C.S.A., to Jefferson Davis and the War Department of the Confederate States of America, 1862–65.* New York: Putnam, 1957. Reprinted with a foreword by Grady McWhiney. Baton Rouge: Louisiana State University Press, 1994.

French, Benjamin Brown. *Witness to the Young Republic: A Yankee's Journals, 1828–1870.* Edited by Donald B. Cole and John J. McDonough. Hanover, N.H.: University Press of New England, 1989.

Furgurson, Ernest B. *Freedom Rising: Washington in the Civil War.* New York: Alfred A. Knopf, 2004.

Geary, James W. *We Need Men: The Union Draft in the Civil War.* DeKalb, Ill.: Northern Illinois University Press, 1991.

General Orders Affecting the Volunteer Force. Washington, D.C.: Adjutant General's Office, 1863.

George, Joseph, Jr. "Subornation of Perjury in the Lincoln Conspiracy Trial? Joseph Holt, Robert Purdy, and the Lon Letter." *Civil War History* 38, no. 3 (September, 1992): 232–41.

"George W. Julian's Journal—The Assassination of Abraham Lincoln." *Indiana Magazine of History* 11, no. 4 (December, 1915): 324–37.

Gerry, Margarita Spalding, ed. *Through Five Administrations: Reminiscences of Colonel William H. Crook, Body-Guard to President Lincoln.* New York: Harper & Brothers, 1910.

Gienapp, William E. "The Crime Against Sumner: The Caning of Charles Sumner and the Rise of the Republican Party." *Civil War History* 25, no. 3 (September, 1979): 218–45.

———. *The Origins of the Republican Party, 1852–1856.* New York: Oxford University Press, 1987.

Gillispie, James M. *Andersonvilles of the North: Myths and Realities of Northern Treatment of Civil War Confederate Prisoners.* Denton: University of North Texas, 2008.

Gilman, Daniel C., ed. *The Miscellaneous Writings of Francis Lieber.* 2 vols. Philadelphia: J. B. Lippincott, 1881.

Glatthaar, Joseph T. *Partners in Command: The Relationship Between Leaders in the Civil War.* New York: The Free Press, 1994.

Goodwin, Doris Kearns. *Team of Rivals: The Political Genius of Abraham Lincoln.* New York: Simon & Schuster, 2005.

Gordon, John B. *Reminiscences of the Civil War.* New York: Charles Scribner's Sons, 1903.

Gorham, George C. *Life and Public Services of Edwin M. Stanton.* 2 vols. Boston: Houghton Mifflin, 1899.

Grant, Ulysses S. *Personal Memoirs of U. S. Grant.* 2 vols. New York: Charles L. Webster & Co., 1886.

Grimsley, Mark. *The Hard Hand of War: Union Military Policy Toward Southern Civilians, 1861–1865.* Cambridge: Cambridge University Press, 1995.

Gunderson, Robert Gray. *Old Gentlemen's Convention: The Washington Peace Conference of 1861.* Madison: University of Wisconsin Press, 1961.

Hall, Clark B. "Season of Change." *Blue & Gray Magazine* 8, no. 4 (April, 1991): 8–20, 48–62.

Hamilton, Holman. *Prologue to Conflict: The Crisis and Compromise of 1850.* New York: W. W. Norton, 1964.

Hammond, Harold Earl, ed. *Diary of a Union Lady, 1861–1865.* New York: Funk & Wagnalls, 1962. Reprinted with an introduction by Jean V. Berlin. Lincoln: University of Nebraska Press, 2000.

[Hammond, William A.] *A Statement of the Causes Which Led to the Dismissal of Surgeon General William A. Hammond from the Army.* Washington, D.C.: n.p., 1864.

Harding, George. *Argument for the Complainant, in the Case of the State of Pennsylvania v. The Wheeling and Belmont Bridge Company.* Washington, D.C.: n.p., 1851.

Harris, Isaac. *Harris's General Business Directory of the Cities of Pittsburgh & Allegheny, With the Environs.* Pittsburgh, Pa.: A. A. Andres, 1847.

Harris, William C. *With Charity for All: Lincoln and the Restoration of the Union.* Lexington: University Press of Kentucky, 1997.

Harrold, Stanley. *Gamaliel Bailey and Antislavery Union.* Kent, Ohio: Kent State University Press, 1986.

Hartford Convention Resolutions of 1815. Toledo, Ohio: Great Neck Publishing, 2009.

Hayes, John D., ed. *Samuel Francis Du Pont: A Selection from His Civil War Letters.* 3 vols. Ithaca, N.Y.: Cornell University Press, 1969.

Heald, Edward Thornton. *Bezaleel Wells, Founder of Canton and Steubenville, Ohio.* Canton, Ohio: Stark County Historical Society, 1948.

Heitman, Francis B. *Historical Register and Dictionary of the United States Army, from its Organization, September 29, 1789, to March 2, 1903.* 2 vols. Washington, D.C.: Government Printing Office, 1903.

Hennessy, John J. *Return to Bull Run: The Campaign and Battle of Second Manassas.* New York: Simon & Schuster, 1993.

Hertz, Emanuel. *The Hidden Lincoln: From the Letters and Papers of William H. Herndon.* New York: The Viking Press, 1938.

Hinchliff, Emerson. "Lincoln and the 'Reaper Case.'" *Journal of the Illinois Historical Society* 33, no. 3 (September, 1940): 361–65.

Hines, Thomas H. "The Northwestern Conspiracy." *The Southern Bivouac: A Monthly Literary and Historical Magazine,* New Series 2, vol. 2, no. 8 (January, 1887): 500–510.

Hinshaw, William Wade. *Encyclopedia of American Quaker Genealogy.* 5 vols. Ann Arbor, Mich.: Edwards Brothers, 1936–46.

Hoffer, Williamjames Hull. *The Caning of Charles Sumner: Honor, Idealism, and the Origins of the Civil War.* Baltimore, Md.: Johns Hopkins University Press, 2010.

Holt, Joseph. *Vindication of Hon. Joseph Holt, Judge Advocate General of the United States Army.* Washington, D.C.: Chronicle Publishing Co., 1873.

——. *Vindication of Judge Advocate General Holt, from the Foul Slanders of Traitors, Confessed Perjurers and Suborners, Acting in the Interest of Jefferson Davis*. Washington, D.C.: Chronicle Publishing Co., 1866.

Holt, Michael F. *The Rise and Fall of the American Whig Party*. New York: Oxford University Press, 1999.

Horigan, Michael. *Elmira: Death Camp of the North*. Mechanicsburg, Pa.: Stackpole Books, 2002.

Howard, Hamilton G. *Civil War Echoes: Character Sketches and State Secrets, by a United States Senator's Son and Secretary, Hamilton Gay Howard*. Washington, D.C.: Howard Publishing Company, 1907.

Howe, Daniel Walker. *What Hath God Wrought: The Transformation of America, 1815–1848*. New York: Oxford University Press, 2007.

Howe, M. A. DeWolfe, ed. *Home Letters of General Sherman*. New York: Scribner's Sons, 1909.

Howells, William Cooper. *Recollections of Life in Ohio from 1813 to 1840*. 1895. Reprinted, Gainesville, Fla.: Scholars' Facsimiles & Reprints, 1963.

Hunt, Gaillard. "Narrative and Letter of William Henry Trescot, Concerning the Negotiations between South Carolina and President Buchanan in December, 1860." *American Historical Review* 13, no. 3 (April, 1908): 528–56.

Hunt, Roger D. *Brevet Brigadier Generals in Blue*. Gaithersburg, Md.: Olde Soldier Books, 1990.

Hyman, Harold M. *A More Perfect Union: The Impact of the Civil War and Reconstruction on the Constitution*. New York: Alfred A. Knopf, 1973.

Hyman, Harold M., and William M. Wiecek. *Equal Justice under Law: Constitutional Justice, 1835–1875*. New York: Harper & Row, 1982.

Imholte, John Quinn. *The First Volunteers: History of the First Minnesota Volunteer Regiment, 1861–1865*. Minneapolis, Minn.: Ross & Haines, 1963.

Impeachment Investigation: Testimony Taken Before the Judiciary Committee of the House of Representatives in the Investigation of the Charges Against Andrew Johnson. Washington, D.C.: Government Printing Office, 1867.

"An Iowa Woman in Washington, D.C., 1861–1865." *Iowa Journal of History* 52, no. 1 (January 1954): 61–90.

Johnson, Albert E. H. "Reminiscences of the Hon. Edwin M. Stanton, Secretary of War." *Records of the Columbia Historical Society* 13 (1910): 69–97.

Jones, John B. *A Rebel War Clerk's Diary at the Confederate States Capital*. 2 vols. Philadelphia: Lippincott, 1866. Reprinted (2 vols. in 1), edited and annotated by Earl Schenck Miers. New York: Sagamore Press, 1958.

Jordan, William B. Jr., ed. *The Civil War Journals of John Mead Gould*. Baltimore, Md.: Butternut and Blue, 1997.

Journal of the Proceedings of the Fourteenth Annual Convention of the Protestant Episcopal Church in the Diocese of Ohio. Gambier, Ohio: Diocese of Ohio, 1831.

Julian, George W. *Political Recollections, 1840 to 1872*. Chicago, Ill.: Jansen, McClurg & Co., 1884.

Kaplan, Edward S. *The Bank of the United States and the American Economy*. Westport, Conn.: Greenwood Press, 1999.

Kauffman, Michael W. *American Brutus: John Wilkes Booth and the Lincoln Conspiracies*. New York: Random House, 2004.

Keneally, Thomas. *American Scoundrel: The Life of the Notorious Civil War General Dan Sickles*. New York: Nan A. Talese, 2002. Reprinted, New York: Anchor Books, 2003.

Kennedy, James H., ed. *History of the Ohio Society of New York, 1885–1905*. New York: Grafton Press, 1906.

King, Horatio. *Turning on the Light: A Dispassionate Survey of President Buchanan's Administration, from 1860 to Its Close*. Philadelphia, Pa.: J. B. Lippincott, 1895.

Klement, Frank L. *Dark Lanterns: Secret Political Societies, Conspiracies, and Treason Trials in the Civil War*. Baton Rouge: Louisiana State University Press, 1984.

Laas, Virginia Jeans, ed. *Wartime Washington: The Civil War Letters of Elizabeth Blair Lee*. Urbana: University of Illinois Press, 1991.

Lamon, Ward Hill. *Recollections of Abraham Lincoln, 1847–1865*. Edited by Dorothy Lamon Teillard. Washington, D.C.: privately published, 1911.

Larson, John Lauritz. *The Market Revolution in America: Liberty, Ambition, and the Eclipse of the Common Good*. Cambridge: Cambridge University Press, 2010.

Leonard, Elizabeth D. *Lincoln's Avengers: Justice, Revenge, and Reunion after the Civil War*. New York: W. W. Norton, 2004.

———. *Lincoln's Forgotten Ally: Judge Advocate General Joseph Holt of Kentucky*. Chapel Hill: University of North Carolina Press, 2011.

Letter of the Secretary of War, Transmitting Report of the Organization of the Army of the Potomac, and of Its Campaigns in Virginia and Maryland, under the Command of Maj. Gen. George W. McClellan, from July 26, 1861, to November 7, 1862. Washington, D.C.: Government Printing Office, 1864.

The Letters of Charles Dickens, Edited by His Sister-in-Law and His Eldest Daughter. 3 vols. London: Chapman and Hall, 1879–80.

Letters of William Carey Jones in Review of Attorney General Black's Report to the President of the United States, on the Subject of Land Titles in California. San Francisco: Commercial Steam Book and Job Printing Establishment, 1860.

"List of Articles Presented to the Historical Society of Western Pennsylvania." *Western Pennsylvania Historical Society* 12, no. 4 (October, 1929): 265–66.

Lomax, Elizabeth Lindsay. *Leaves from an Old Washington Diary, 1854–1863*. Edited by Lindsay Lomax Wood. Mount Vernon, N.Y.: E. P. Dutton & Co., 1943.

Longacre, Edward G., ed. *From Antietam to Fort Fisher: The Civil War Letters of Edward King Wightman, 1862–1865*. Madison, N.J.: Fairleigh Dickinson University Press, 1985.

Loomis, H. J. *Steubenville Business and Local Directory*. Steubenville, Ohio: Daily Herald Book and Job Office, 1850.

McClellan, George B. *McClellan's Own Story*. New York: Charles L. Webster & Co., 1887.

McClure, Alexander K. *Abraham Lincoln and Men of War-Times*. 1892. Reprinted, Lincoln: University of Nebraska Press, 1996.

McCormick Extension Case: Patent of 1847. Washington, D.C.: n.p., 1861.

McCormick, Richard P. "New Perspectives on Jacksonian Politics." In *Political Ideology and Voting Behavior in the Age of Jackson,* edited by Joel H. Silbey, 106–17. Englewood Cliffs, N.J.: Prentice-Hall, 1973.

McDonough, James Lee. *Shiloh: In Hell Before Night.* Knoxville: University of Tennessee Press, 1977.

McGinty, Brian. *The Body of John Merryman: Abraham Lincoln and the Suspension of Habeas Corpus.* Cambridge, Mass.: Harvard University Press, 2011.

Mackey, Franklin H. *Reports of Cases Argued and Adjudged in the Supreme Court of the District of Columbia in the General Term of February 1869 to February 1872, Inclusive.* Washington, D.C.: The Law Reporter Co., 1891.

McPherson, Edward. *A Political History of the United States of America during the Period of Reconstruction.* Washington, D.C.: Solomons & Chapman, 1875.

McPherson, James M. *Battle Cry of Freedom: The Civil War Era.* New York: Oxford University Press, 1988.

———. *Tried by War: Abraham Lincoln as Commander in Chief.* New York: Penguin Press, 2008.

Marvel, William. *Andersonville: The Last Depot.* Chapel Hill: University of North Carolina Press, 1994.

———. *Tarnished Victory: Finishing Lincoln's War.* Boston: Houghton Mifflin Harcourt, 2011.

Matson, Cathy, ed. *The Economy of Early America: Historical Perspectives and New Directions.* University Park: Pennsylvania State University Press, 2006.

Meade, George. *The Life and Letters of George Gordon Meade, Major-General United States Army.* 2 vols. New York: Charles Scribner's Sons, 1913.

Meigs, Montgomery C. "General M. C. Meigs on the Conduct of the Civil War." *American Historical Review* 26, no. 2 (January, 1921): 285–303.

Meneely, A. Howard. "Three Manuscripts of Gideon Welles." *American Historical Review* 31, no. 3 (April, 1926): 484–94.

Merrill, Walter M., ed. *The Letters of William Lloyd Garrison.* 6 vols. Cambridge, Mass.: Harvard University Press, 1971–81.

Miller, Francis Trevelyan, ed. *The Photographic History of the Civil War: Thousands of Scenes Photographed, 1861–1865.* 10 vols. New York: Review of Reviews Co., 1911.

Miller, William Lee. *Lincoln's Virtues: An Ethical Biography.* New York: Alfred A. Knopf, 2002.

Milton, George Fort. *The Age of Hate: Andrew Johnson and the Radicals.* New York: Coward-McCann, 1930.

Mindich, David T. Z. *Just the Facts: How "Objectivity" Came to Define American Journalism.* New York: New York University Press, 1998.

Mr. & Mrs. Ralph Emerson's Personal Recollections of Abraham Lincoln. Rockford, Ill.: Wilson Brothers, 1909.

Moe, Richard. *The Last Full Measure: The Life and Death of the First Minnesota Volunteers.* New York: Henry Holt & Co., 1993.

Mohr, James C., and Richard E. Winslow III, eds., *The Cormany Diaries: A Northern Family in the Civil War*. Pittsburgh, Pa.: University of Pittsburgh Press, 1982.

Moore, Frank, ed. *The Rebellion Record, a Diary of Events with Documents, Narratives, Illustrative Incidents, Poetry, etc.* 12 vols. 1861–69. Reprinted, New York: Arno Press, 1977.

Moore, Guy W. *The Case of Mrs. Surratt: Her Controversial Trial and Execution for Conspiracy in the Lincoln Assassination*. Norman: University of Oklahoma Press, 1954.

Moore, J. B., ed. *Works of James Buchanan*. 12 vols. Philadelphia: Lippincott, 1911.

Mushkat, Jerome, ed. *A Citizen-Soldier's Civil War: The Letters of Brevet Major General Alvin C. Voris*. DeKalb: Northern Illinois University Press, 2002.

Neely, Mark E. Jr. *The Fate of Liberty: Abraham Lincoln and Civil Liberties*. New York: Oxford University Press, 1991.

——. *Lincoln and the Triumph of the Nation: Constitutional Conflict in the American Civil War*. Chapel Hill: University of North Carolina Press, 2011.

Nevins, Allan, ed. *A Diary of Battle: The Personal Journals of Colonel Charles S. Wainwright, 1861-1865*. New York: Harcourt, Brace, & World, 1962.

——, ed. *Hamilton Fish: The Inner History of the Grant Administration*. 2 vols. New York: Frederick Ungar Publishing, 1936.

Nevins, Allan, and Milton Halsey Thomas, eds. *The Diary of George Templeton Strong*. 4 vols. New York: Macmillan Company, 1952.

"New Almaden." Transcript of the Record. San Francisco: n.p., 1859.

New England Farrier and Family Physician. Exeter, N.H.: Josiah Richardson, 1828.

Nicolay, John G., and John Hay. *Abraham Lincoln: A History*. 10 vols. New York: Century Company, 1890.

Nicolay, John G., and John Hay. "A History of Abraham Lincoln." *Century Magazine* 39, no. 3 (January, 1890): 428–43.

Niven, John, ed. *The Salmon P. Chase Papers*, 5 vols. Kent, Ohio: Kent State University Press, 1993–98.

——. *Salmon P. Chase: A Biography*. New York: Oxford University Press, 1995.

Noe, Kenneth W. *Perryville: This Grand Havoc of Battle*. Lexington: University Press of Kentucky, 2001.

Nordhoff, Charles. *The Communistic Societies of the United States, from Personal Visit and Observation . . .* New York: Harper & Brothers, 1875.

Norton, Sara, and M. A. DeWolfe Howe, eds. *Letters of Charles Eliot Norton*. 2 vols. Boston: Houghton Mifflin, 1913.

Official Records of the Union and Confederate Navies in the War of the Rebellion. 31 vols. Washington, D.C.: Government Printing Office, 1894–1927.

Ohio Reports: Reports of Cases Argued and Determined in the Supreme Court of Ohio. Vols. 1–12. Cleveland, Cincinnati, and Columbus, Ohio: Various publishers, 1853–1873.

Olmsted, Frederick Law. *The Papers of Frederick Law Olmsted*. 7 vols. Baltimore: Johns Hopkins University Press, 1977–2007.

Opinion of Attorney General Stanbery, under the Reconstruction Laws.
Washington, D.C.: Government Printing Office, 1867.

O'Reilly, Bill, and Martin Dugard. *Killing Lincoln: The Shocking Assassination that Changed America Forever*. New York: Henry Holt & Co., 2011.

O'Reilly, Francis Augustin. *The Fredericksburg Campaign: Winter War on the Rappahannock*. Baton Rouge: Louisiana State University Press, 2003.

"Original Letters." *William and Mary Quarterly* 20, no. 2 (October, 1911): 114–23.

Palmer, Beverly Wilson, ed. *The Selected Letters of Charles Sumner*. 2 vols. Boston: Northeastern University Press, 1990.

Palmer, Beverly Wilson, and Holly Byers Ochoa, eds. *The Selected Papers of Thaddeus Stevens*. 2 vols. Pittsburgh, Pa.: University of Pittsburgh Press, 1997–98.

Paludan, Phillip Shaw. *"A People's Contest": The Union and the Civil War, 1861–1865*. New York: Harper & Row, 1988.

———. *The Presidency of Abraham Lincoln*. Lawrence: University Press of Kansas, 1994.

Parker, Wyman W. "Edwin M. Stanton at Kenyon." *Ohio State Archaeological and Historical Quarterly* 60, no. 3 (July, 1951): 233–60.

Pease, Theodore Calvin, and James G. Randall, eds. *The Diary of Orville Hickman Browning*. 2 vols. Springfield, Ill.: Illinois State Historical Library, 1925, 1933.

Pennsylvania Reports: Comprising Cases Adjudged in the Supreme Court of Pennsylvania. Vols. 20–32. Philadelphia: Various publishers, 1854–60.

Perman, Michael. *Reunion without Compromise, The South and Reconstruction: 1865–1868*. Cambridge: Cambridge University Press, 1973.

Perret, Geoffrey. *Lincoln's War: The Untold Story of America's Greatest President as Commander in Chief*. New York: Random House, 2004.

Phillips, Ulrich B., ed. "The Correspondence of Robert Toombs, Alexander H. Stephens, and Howell Cobb." *Annual Report of the American Historical Association for the Year 1911*. Vol. 2. Washington, D.C.: Government Printing Office, 53–743.

Piatt, Donn. *Memories of the Men Who Saved the Union*. New York: Belford, Clarke & Co., 1887.

Pitman, Benn, ed. *The Assassination of President Lincoln and the Trial of the Conspirators*. New York: Moore, Wilstach & Baldwin, 1865.

———. *The Trials for Treason at Indianapolis, Disclosing the Plans for Establishing a North-Western Confederacy*. New York: Moore, Wilstach & Baldwin, 1865.

Plum, William R. *The Military Telegraph during the Civil War in the United States*. 2 vols. Chicago: Jansen, McClurg & Co., 1882.

Pound, Roscoe. "The Military Telegraph in the Civil War." *Proceedings of the Massachusetts Historical Society*. Series 3, vol. 66. (October, 1936–May, 1941): 185–203.

Pratt, Fletcher. *Stanton: Lincoln's Secretary of War*. New York: W. W. Norton, 1953.

Pratt, Harry E. *The Personal Finances of Abraham Lincoln*. Springfield, Ill.: Abraham Lincoln Association, 1943.

Proceedings of a Court of Inquiry Convened at Washington, D.C., November 9, 1868 by Special Order No. 217 War Department, to Examine into the Accusations Against Brig. And Bvt. Major General A. B. Dyer, Chief of Ordnance. 2 parts. Washington, D.C.: Government Printing Office, 1869.

Proceedings of a General Court Martial for the Trial of Maj. Gen. Fitz John Porter, U.S. Vols. Washington, D.C.: n.p., 1862.

Pullen, John J. A Shower of Stars: The Medal of Honor and the 27th Maine. Philadelphia: J. B. Lippincott, 1966.

Quaife, Milo M., ed. From the Cannon's Mouth: The Civil War Letters of General Alpheus S. Williams. Detroit, Mich.: Wayne State University Press, 1959.

Rable, George C. But There Was No Peace: The Role of Violence in the Politics of Reconstruction. Athens: University of Georgia Press, 1984.

———. Fredericksburg! Fredericksburg! Chapel Hill: University of North Carolina Press, 2002.

———. God's Almost Chosen Peoples: A Religious History of the American Civil War. Chapel Hill: University of North Carolina Press, 2010.

Racine, Philip N., ed. Unspoiled Heart: The Journal of Charles Mattocks of the 17th Maine. Knoxville: University of Tennessee Press, 1994.

Rafuse, Ethan S. McClellan's War: The Failure of Moderation in the Struggle for the Union. Bloomington and Indianapolis: Indiana University Press, 2005.

Register of the Commissioned and Warrant Officers of the Navy of the United States, Including Officers of the Marine Corps, for the Year 1842. Washington, D.C.: Alexander & Barnard, 1842.

Remini, Robert V. At the Edge of the Precipice: Henry Clay and the Compromise That Saved the Union. New York: Basic Books, 2010.

Reply of the Judge Advocate, John A. Bingham, to the Defence of the Accused, Before a General Court-Martial for the Trial of Brig. Gen. William A. Hammond. Washington, D.C.: Government Printing Office, 1864.

Report of the Joint Committee on the Conduct of the War. 3 vols. Washington, D.C.: Government Printing Office, 1863.

Report of the Joint Committee on the Conduct of the War, at the Second Session Thirty-eighth Congress. 3 vols. Washington, D.C.: Government Printing Office, 1865.

Report of the Judge Advocate General on the "Order of American Knights" or "Sons of Liberty," a Western Conspiracy in Aid of the Southern Rebellion. Washington, D.C.: n.p., 1864.

Review of the Judge Advocate General of the Proceedings, Findings, and Sentence of a General Court Martial Held in the City of Washington for the Trial of Major General Fitz John Porter of the United States Volunteers. Washington, D.C.: Daily Chronicle Press, 1863.

Reynolds, David S. John Brown, Abolitionist. New York: Alfred A. Knopf, 2005.

Rosenberg, Charles E. The Cholera Years: The United States in 1832, 1849, and 1866. Chicago, Ill.: University of Chicago Press, 1962.

Russell, William H. My Diary North and South. London: Bradbury and Evans, 1863. Reprinted, edited with a preface and introduction by Eugene H. Berwanger. New York: McGraw-Hill, 1988.

Schafer, Joseph, ed. *Intimate Letters of Carl Schurz, 1841–1869.* Madison: State Historical Society of Wisconsin, 1928.

Scheips, Paul J. "Albert James Myer, Founder of the Army Signal Corps: A Biographical Study." Ph.D. diss., American University, 1966.

Schutz, Wallace J., and Walter N. Trenerry. *Abandoned by Lincoln: A Military Biography of John Pope.* Urbana: University of Illinois Press, 1990.

Sears, Stephen W. *Chancellorsville.* Boston: Houghton Mifflin, 1996.

———, ed. *The Civil War Papers of George B. McClellan.* New York: Ticknor & Fields, 1989.

———, ed. *The Civil War: The Second Year Told by Those Who Lived It.* New York: Library of America, 2012.

———. *Controversies and Commanders: Dispatches from the Army of the Potomac.* Boston: Houghton Mifflin, 1999.

———, ed. *For Country, Cause & Leader: The Civil War Journal of Charles B. Haydon.* New York: Ticknor & Fields, 1993.

———. *Landscape Turned Red: The Battle of Antietam.* New York: Ticknor & Fields, 1983.

———, ed. *Mr. Dunn Browne's Experiences in the Army: The Civil War Letters of Samuel W. Fiske.* New York: Fordham University Press, 1998.

———. *To the Gates of Richmond: The Peninsula Campaign.* New York: Ticknor & Fields, 1992.

Seward, Frederick W. *Seward at Washington, as Senator and Secretary of State: A Memoir of His Life, With Selections from His Letters, 1861–1872.* 2 vols. New York: Derby and Miller, 1891.

Sharp, James Roger. *The Jacksonians versus the Banks: Politics in the States after the Panic of 1837.* New York: Columbia University Press, 1970.

Sherman, William T. *Memoirs of Gen. W. T. Sherman.* 4th ed., 2 vols. in 1. New York: Charles L. Webster, 1891.

Simon, John Y., ed. *The Papers of Ulysses S. Grant.* 30 vols. Carbondale: Southern Illinois University Press, 1967–2008.

Simpson, Brooks D. *Ulysses S. Grant: Triumph over Adversity, 1822–1865.* Boston: Houghton Mifflin, 2000.

———. *The Reconstruction Presidents.* Lawrence: University Press of Kansas, 1998.

Simpson, Brooks D., and Jean V. Berlin, eds. *Sherman's Civil War: Selected Correspondence of William T. Sherman, 1860–1865.* Chapel Hill: University of North Carolina Press, 1999.

Sioussat, St. George L. "Notes of Colonel W. G. Moore, Private Secretary to President Johnson, 1866–1868." *American Historical Review* 19, no. 1 (October 1913): 98–132.

Smith, Michael Thomas. *The Enemy Within: Fears of Corruption in the Civil War North.* Charlottesville: University of Virginia Press, 2011.

Sparks, David S., ed. *Inside Lincoln's Army: The Diary of Marsena Rudolph Patrick, Provost Marshal General, Army of the Potomac.* New York: Thomas Yoseloff, 1964.

Speeches of Hon. Montgomery Blair. Washington, D.C.: H. Polkinhorn & Sons, 1865.

Stahr, Walter. *Seward: Lincoln's Indispensable Man*. New York: Simon & Schuster, 2012.

Stanton, William Henry. *A Book Called Our Ancestors the Stantons*. Philadelphia: Privately printed, 1922.

Steele, Janet E. *The Sun Shines for All: Journalism and Ideology in the Life of Charles A. Dana*. Syracuse, N.Y.: Syracuse University Press, 1993.

Steers, Edward Jr. *The Trial: The Assassination of President Lincoln and the Trial of the Conspirators*. Lexington: University Press of Kentucky, 2003.

Stewart, David O. *Impeached: The Trial of President Andrew Johnson and the Fight for Lincoln's Legacy*. New York: Simon & Schuster, 2009.

Stone, James M. *The History of the Twenty-seventh Regiment Maine Volunteer Infantry*. Portland, Maine: Thurston Print, 1895.

Styple, William B., ed. *Our Noble Blood: The Civil War Letters of Regis de Trobriand*. Kearny, N.J.: Belle Grove Publishing, 1997.

Summers, Mark W. *The Plundering Generation: Corruption and the Crisis of the Union, 1849–1861*. New York: Oxford University Press, 1987.

Sutherland, Daniel E. "Abraham Lincoln, John Pope, and the Origins of Total War." *Journal of Military History* 56 (October, 1992): 567–86.

———. *American Civil War Guerrillas: Changing the Rules of Warfare*. Santa Barbara, Calif.: Praeger, 2013.

———. *A Savage Conflict: The Decisive Role of Guerrillas in the American Civil War*. Chapel Hill: University of North Carolina Press, 2009.

Swanberg, W. A. *Sickles the Incredible*. New York: Charles Scribner's Sons, 1956.

Taft, Charles Sabin. "Abraham Lincoln's Last Hours." *Century Magazine* 45, no. 4 (February, 1893): 634–36.

Testimony Taken by the Joint Select Committee to Enquire into the Condition of Affairs in the Late Insurrectionary States. 13 vols. Washington: Government Printing Office, 1872.

Thayer. John M. "A Night with Stanton in the War Office." *McClure's Magazine* 8, no. 6 (April, 1897): 438–42.

Thomas, Benjamin P., and Harold M. Hyman. *Stanton: The Life and Times of Lincoln's Secretary of War*. New York: Alfred A. Knopf, 1962.

Thompson, Richard Means, and Richard Wainwright, eds. *Confidential Correspondence of Gustavus Vasa Fox, Assistant Secretary of the Navy, 1861–1865*. 2 vols. New York: Naval Historical Society, 1918–19.

Thurston, George H. *Directory for 1856–'57 of Pittsburgh and Allegheny Cities*. Pittsburgh, Pa.: W. S. Haven, 1856.

Tidwell, William A. "The Man Who Shifted the Blame." *Civil War Times Illustrated* 40, no. 3 (June, 2001): 50–59.

Townsend, E. D. *Anecdotes of the Civil War in the United States*. New York: D. Appleton Co., 1884.

Trefousse, Hans L. *Andrew Johnson: A Biography*. New York: W. W. Norton, 1989.

———. *Benjamin Franklin Wade: Radical Representative from Ohio*. New York: Twayne Publishers, 1963.

————. *Impeachment of a President: Andrew Johnson, the Blacks, and Reconstruction.* Knoxville: University of Tennessee Press, 1975.

Trial of John H. Surratt in the Criminal Court for the District of Columbia. Washington, D.C.: Government Printing Office, 1867.

Trial of the Conspirators for the Assassination of Abraham Lincoln, &c. Argument of John A. Bingham, Special Judge Advocate. Washington, D.C.: Government Printing Office, 1865.

Turner, Thomas Reed. *Beware the People Weeping: Public Opinion and the Assassination of Abraham Lincoln.* Baton Rouge: Louisiana State University Press, 1982.

Union Cemetery, Steubenville, Ohio. Steubenville: Public Library of Steubenville, 2004.

U.S. Congress. *Congressional Globe.* 26th-42nd Congresses.

U.S. House. *Alleged Assault upon Senator Sumner: Report of the Select Committee.* 34th Cong., 1st sess., 1856. H. Report 182.

U.S. House. *Assassination of Lincoln.* 39th Cong., 1st sess. 1866. H. Report 104.

U.S. House. *Covode Report: Select Committee on Alleged Corruptions in Government.* 36th Cong., 1st sess., 1860. H. Report 648.

U.S. House. *Expenditures on Account of Private Land Claims in California.* 36th Cong., 1st sess., 1860. Ex. Doc. 84.

U.S. House. *Howard Report: the Special Committee Appointed to Investigate the Troubles in the Territory of Kansas.* 34th Cong., 1st sess., 1856. H. Report 200.

U.S. House. *Hurtt Court Martial.* 43rd Cong., 1st sess., 1874. Ex. Doc. 255.

U.S. House. *Memorial of the Ladies of Steubenville, Ohio.* 21st Cong., 1st sess., 1830. H. Report 209.

U.S. House. *Memphis Riots and Massacres.* 39th Cong., 1st sess., 1866. H. Report 101.

U.S. House. *New Orleans Riots.* 39th Cong., 2nd sess., 1867. H. Report 16.

U.S. House. *Raising of Money to Be Used in Impeachment.* 40th Cong., 2nd sess., 1868. H. Report 75.

U.S. House. *Trial of Henry Wirz.* 40th Cong., 2nd sess., 1867. Ex. Doc. 23.

U.S. Reports: Reports of Cases Argued and Adjudged in the Supreme Court of the United States. Vols. 50–69. Boston and Washington, D.C.: Various publishers, 1851–1903.

U.S. Senate. *Message of the President, Communication in Compliance with a Resolution of the Senate of the 12th Instant, Information in Relation to the States of the Union Lately in Rebellion, Accompanied by a Report of Carl Schurz, on the States of South Carolina, Georgia, Alabama, Mississippi, and Louisiana; also a Report of Lieutenant General Grant on the Same Subject.* Ex. Doc. 2, 39th Cong., 1st sess., 1865.

van der Linden, Frank. *The Dark Intrigue: The True Story of a Civil War Conspiracy.* Golden, Colo.: Fulcrum Publishing, 2007.

Vickery, James B., ed. *The Journals of John Edwards Godfrey, Bangor, Maine, 1863-1869.* Rockland, Maine: Courier-Gazette, 1979.

Viele, Egbert L. "A Trip with Lincoln, Chase and Stanton." *Scribner's Monthly* 16, no. 6 (October, 1878): 813–22.

Wainwright, Nicholas B., ed. *A Philadelphia Perspective: The Diary of Sidney George Fisher, Covering the Years 1834–1871.* Philadelphia: Historical Society of Pennsylvania, 1967.

War Letters, 1862–1865, of John Chipman Gray and John Codman Ropes. Cambridge: Massachusetts Historical Society, 1927.

War of the Rebellion: A Compilation of the Official Records of the Union and Confederate Armies, 128 vols. Washington, D.C.: Government Printing Office, 1880–1901.

Watson, Harry L. *Liberty and Power: The Politics of Jacksonian America.* New York: Hill and Wang, 1990.

Waugh, John C. *Reelecting Lincoln: The Battle for the 1864 Presidency.* 1997. Reprinted, New York: Da Capo Press, 2001.

Weber, Jennifer L. *Copperheads: The Rise and Fall of Lincoln's Opponents in the North.* New York: Oxford University Press, 2006.

Weigley, Russell F. *Quartermaster General of the Union Army: A Biography of M. C. Meigs.* New York: Columbia University Press, 1959.

Weld, Stephen M. *War Diary and Letters of Stephen Minot Weld, 1861–1865.* 2nd ed. Boston: Massachusetts Historical Society, 1979.

Welles, Gideon. "Lincoln and Johnson." *The Galaxy* 14, no. 4 (April, 1872): 521–32.

The Wheeling Bridge Case: Mr. Stanton's Argument. In the Supreme Court of the United States: Chancery No. 2, December term, 1849.

White, Jonathan W. *Abraham Lincoln and Treason in the Civil War: The Trials of John Merryman.* Baton Rouge: Louisiana State University Press, 2011.

Whyte, James H. "Divided Loyalties in Washington during the Civil War." *Records of the Columbia Historical Society* 44 (1960–62): 103–22.

Williams, Charles Richard, ed. *Diary and Letters of Rutherford Birchard Hayes, Nineteenth President of the United States,* 5 vols. Columbus: Ohio State Archaeological and Historical Society, 1914–26.

Williams, Frederick D., ed. *The Wild Life of the Army: Civil War Letters of James A. Garfield.* East Lansing: Michigan State University Press, 1964.

Williams, Lewis Caleb, and George Parkin Atwater, eds. *Catalogue of the Kenyon Chapter, Phi Beta Kappa.* New York: John C. Rankin Co., 1899.

Williams, Stephen K., ed. *Cases Argued and Decided in the Supreme Court of the United States: 1, 2 Black; 1, 2 Wallace.* Rochester, N.Y.: Lawyers Cooperative Publishing Co., 1884.

Wilson, Douglas L., and Rodney O. Davis, eds. *Herndon's Informants: Letters, Interviews, and Statements about Abraham Lincoln.* Urbanna: University of Illinois Press, 1998.

Wilson, Henry. "Edwin M. Stanton." *Atlantic Monthly* 25, no. 148 (February, 1870): 234–45.

———. "Jeremiah S. Black and Edwin M. Stanton." *Atlantic Monthly* 26, no. 156 (October, 1870): 463–75.

Wilson, James H. *The Life of Charles A. Dana.* New York: Harper and Brothers, 1907.

Wilson, Mark R. *The Business of Civil War: Military Mobilization and the State, 1861–1865.* Baltimore: Johns Hopkins University Press, 2006.

Witt, John Fabian. *Lincoln's Code: The Laws of War in American History*. New York: Free Press, 2012.

Woodworth, Steven E., ed. *The Musick of the Mocking Birds, the Roar of the Cannon: The Civil War Diary and Letters of William Winters*. Lincoln: University of Nebraska Press, 1998.

Young, John Russell. *Around the World with General Grant*. New York: American News Co., 1879. Reprinted; abridged, edited, and with an introduction by Michael Fellman. Baltimore: Johns Hopkins University Press, 2002.

Younger, Edward, ed. *Inside the Confederate Government: The Diary of Robert Garlick Hill Kean*. Baton Rouge: Louisiana University Press, 1973.

NEWSPAPERS

Advertiser, Boston, Mass.
American Union, Steubenville, Ohio
Atlas and Argus, Albany, N.Y.
Baltimore (Md.) Exchange
Baltimore (Md.) Sun
Boston (Mass.) Evening Transcript
Carroll County Register, Ossipee, N.H.
Chicago Times
Chicago Tribune
Cincinnati (Ohio) Commercial
Cincinnati (Ohio) Daily Commercial
Cincinnati (Ohio) Daily Gazette
Cincinnati (Ohio) Enquirer
Cleveland (Ohio) Leader
Cleveland (Ohio) Plain Dealer
Commercial Advertiser, New York City
Constitution, Washington, D.C.
The Crisis, Columbus, Ohio
Daily Alta California, San Francisco
Daily Commercial Journal, Pittsburgh, Pa.
Daily Constitutional Union, Washington, D.C.
Daily Constitutionalist, Augusta, Ga.
Daily Evening Bulletin, San Francisco, Calif.
Daily Gate City, Keokuk, Iowa
Daily Gazette, Wheeling, [W.]Va.
Daily Journal, Indianapolis, Ind.
Daily Morning Chronicle, Portsmouth, N.H.
Daily Morning Post, Pittsburgh, Pa.
Daily News, Newport, R.I.

Daily Union, Washington, D.C.
Daily Whig and Courier, Bangor, Maine
Davenport (Iowa) Daily Gazette
Delaware Gazette, Wilmington
Delaware Journal, Wilmington
Delaware Republican, Wilmington
Detroit (Mich.) Free Press
Dover (N.H.) Enquirer
Dubuque (Iowa) Daily Times
Frank Leslie's Illustrated Newspaper, New York
Free Press, Lebanon, N.H.
Great Falls (N.H.) Journal
Harper's Weekly, New York
Illinois State Journal, Springfield
The Independent, New York
Keene (N.H.) Sentinel
Log Cabin Farmer, Steubenville, Ohio
Louisville (Ky.) Daily Democrat
Lynchburg Virginian
Macon (Ga.) Daily Telegraph
Messenger, Stillwater, Minn.
Missouri Democrat, St. Louis
Morning Chronicle, Pittsburgh, Pa.
National Intelligencer, Washington, D.C.
National Journal, Washington, D.C.
New Hampshire Gazette, Portsmouth
New Hampshire Patriot, Concord
New York Evening Post
New York Sun
New York Tribune
New York World
New-Yorker

North Missouri Courier, Hannibal
Northern Advocate, Claremont, N.H.
The Observer, London, England
Ohio State Journal, Columbus
Ohio Statesman, Columbus
The Organ, Cadiz, Ohio
Oxford Democrat, Paris, Maine
Philadelphia (Pa.) Inquirer
Philadelphia (Pa.) Press
Pioneer and Democrat, St. Paul, Minn.
Pittsburgh (Pa.) Daily Gazette
Portland (Me.) Daily Press
Prairie du Chien (Wis.) Courier
The Press, Philadelphia, Pa.
Republican Statesman, Concord, N.H.
Richmond (Va.) Enquirer
Richmond (Va.) Examiner

Richmond (Va.) Whig
Republican Ledger, Steubenville, Ohio
Sacramento (Calif.) Union
Steubenville (Ohio) Daily Herald
Steubenville (Ohio) Western Herald
Sumter Republican, Americus, Ga.
True American, Steubenville, Ohio
Washington Chronicle
Washington Evening Star
Washington Globe
Washington Post
Waterloo (Iowa) Courier
Weekly Picayune, New Orleans, La.
Weekly Press, Philadelphia, Pa.
Western Herald and Steubenville (Ohio)
  Gazette
Wheeling (W.Va.) Intelligencer

MISCELLANEOUS

Greenwood Cemetery, St. Albans, Vt.: Headstone Inscriptions
Metairie Cemetery, New Orleans, La.: Headstone Inscriptions
Oak Dale Cemetery, Urbana, Ohio: Headstone Inscriptions
Oak Hill Cemetery, Washington, D.C.: Lot Records and Headstone Inscriptions
St. James the Less Episcopal Church, Philadelphia: Headstone and Cenotaph
    Inscriptions
Union Cemetery, Steubenville, Ohio: Interment Records and Headstone
    Inscriptions

ACKNOWLEDGMENTS

Research for this book indebted me to scores of people, whom I will attempt to acknowledge in the order I approached them about the project. The list begins with Sandy Day, local historian at the Schiappa branch of the Public Library of Steubenville and Jefferson County, Ohio, who provided long-distance assistance and also gave my inquiries close attention every time I made the trip to Stanton's birthplace. From there my benefactors included John E. Haas, at the Ohio Historical Society in Columbus; Ethan Henderson and Darko Gligorovski, at Kenyon College in Gambier, Ohio; Nan Card, of the Rutherford B. Hayes Presidential Library in Fremont, Ohio; Janet Bloom, of the Clements Library and Kate Hutchens, of the Special Collections Library at the University of Michigan in Ann Arbor; Cindy VanHorn, Lincoln librarian at the Allen County Public Library in Fort Wayne, Indiana; Isabel Planton, at Indiana University's Lilly Library in Bloomington; Peter Lido, of Special Collections at the University of Chicago; Lee Grady, Eric Willey, and Spencer Brayton, of the Wisconsin Historical Society in Madison; Daniel Lewis, Olga Tsapina, Juan Gomez, and Manuel Flores, at the Huntington Library in San Marino, California; David Kessler, of the Bancroft Library of the University of California at Berkeley; Ollie Mayberry, at the John B. Coleman Library of Prairie View A&M University in Prairie View, Texas; Dara Flinn, of the Fondren Library at Rice University in Houston; Renee Harvey, of the Gilcrease Museum in Tulsa, Oklahoma; Dennis Northcott, at the Missouri Historical Society in St. Louis; Judy Bolton, of Special Collections at Louisiana State University in Baton Rouge; Norwood Kerr, at the Alabama Department of Archives and History in Montgomery; Michelle Ganz, at the Lincoln Memorial University Archives in Harrogate, Tennessee; David R. Grinnell, chief archivist at the Senator John Heinz History Center in Pittsburgh; David Haugaard, director of research at the Historical Society of Pennsylvania in Philadelphia; Nancy R. Miller, at the University of Pennsylvania Archives in Philadelphia; Ed Richi, at the Delaware Historical Society in Wilmington; Lucas R. Clawson, at the Hagley Museum's Eleutherian Mills Historical Library in Wilmington; Gabriel Swift and AnnaLee Pauls, of Special Collections at Princeton University; Tal Nadan, at the New York Public Library; Eric Wakin and Tara Craig, at the Butler Library of Columbia University in New York; Tammy Kiter, of the New-York Historical Society in New York; Adrienne Sharpe, of the Beinecke Library at Yale in New Haven, Connecticut; Holly Snyder and Kathleen Brooks, in the John Hay Library at Brown University in Providence, Rhode Island; Peter Drummey's friendly staff at the Massachusetts Historical Society in Boston; Susan Halpert, at Harvard's Houghton Library in Cambridge; Sarah Hartwell, at Dartmouth's Rauner Library in Hanover, New Hampshire; Bill Copeley and Peter Wallner, at the New Hampshire Historical Society in Concord; Joyce Rumery and Brenda Steeves, of the Raymond H. Fogler Library at the University of Maine in Orono; Sally Moir, at the Calais Public Library in Calais, Maine; Ella S. Pozell, superintendent of Oak Hill Cemetery in Washington, D.C.; Clarence Davis and Bill Branch, at the District of Columbia Archives; Graham Duncan, in the Manuscripts Department of the South Caroliniana Library in Columbia; and—last but certainly not least—the eternally patient and helpful staff in the manuscript reading room at the Library of Congress, including Jeff Flannery, Bruce Kirby, Patrick Kerwin, Joseph Jackson, and Jennifer Brathovde.

I owe a particular debt to Harold Hyman, who guided me to some of his dispersed papers, and whose 1962 biography of Stanton provided a foundation on which to build. The half-century gap between our treatments necessarily created much disagreement, primarily because of new information, differing perspectives, and the difficulty he faced in taking up the project of a coauthor who could answer none of his inevitable questions. While I tend to be critical of Mr. Hyman's book, I can hardly deny that the research he and Benjamin Thomas did from scratch made my work much easier.

Stanton's great-great-grandson, Frank Mevers (who is also a personal friend and colleague), tipped me off to a small trove of family papers that he had personally delivered to Louisiana State University. Historians Mark Grimsley and Daniel Sutherland cordially answered questions within their areas of study, or directed me to where they could be answered. Clark B. Hall's phenomenal knowledge about the Stevensburg vicinity in Virginia yielded information about Edwin Stanton's grandfather and the family farm, as well as a photograph of the surviving Zimmerman Tavern, where in 1862 a traveler first heard the local legend surrounding Stanton's birth. My nephew Matthew Hoppock, Esq., introduced me to some handy sources for case law, and Jeff Wieand explained some of the ethical issues and attitudes in the legal profession.

To Stephen Sears I am grateful, as always, not only for his opinions on various characters and topics but also for his willingness to debate minor details that sometimes lead to subtle interpretive revisions. Brooks Simpson of Arizona State University gave me the benefit of his views on different aspects of Ulysses Grant's career and character. George Rable, Will Greene, and Jeff Wieand all did me the great favor of reading a cruelly long original manuscript, and offering their observations on myriad matters of history, logic, and style. George offered priceless advice on emphasis and delivery, and on relevant secondary sources, and he did yeoman service as a copyeditor to boot. Will also extensively criticized my angles of analysis and attack, besides saving me from innumerable overt and implied factual errors through his incomparable knowledge of the military end of the Civil War and Southern geography. Jeff likewise made valuable suggestions about where I could alternately let up on my subject or lay into him. Since I did not always take their advice, none of them can be held accountable for surviving flaws, but an honest opinion is the greatest gift a friend can give, regardless of how the recipient uses it.

To an author, the major benefit of a university press is the peer review process, which can be frustrating and even infuriating, but almost always yields a better result. Pete Carmichael's review of this manuscript for the Civil War America series was the first of the official readings, and so was also the most productive of them, but even the much less friendly review that followed his proved surprisingly useful;

the final reader left hints of a particular expertise on the subject of Lincoln's official family. Expert copyediting by Scott Rohrer and the eternally sensitive editorial advice of Ron Maner provided the other noteworthy advantages of choosing the University of North Carolina Press.

Ellen Schwindt is always my first reader. Her scrawled questions, circled passages, and advisory arrows provide constant reminders that the cleverest literary style is not always the clearest, and she tries valiantly to contribute balance to my opinionated prose. In the realm of biography, as in everyday life, she also serves as my sounding board for the subject of human nature, which she seems to understand with far more sympathy and patience than I. Perhaps that is why she puts up with me.

INDEX

opposes black troops, 148; opposes partition of Virginia, 269; on panic over Early's raid, 339; on "reckless extravagance" of the army, 173; resigns, 355; seeks chief justiceship, 350; Trent Affair, 146–47

Bates, Marie, 55, 77

Bayne, John, 457, 461

Beall, John Yates, 374–75

Beatty, Alexander, 11, 12–13, 16

Beauregard, Pierre G. T., 199–200, 202, 332

Beecher, Henry Ward, 312, 335, 371

Bell, John, 116

Belmont, August, 354

Benjamin, Charles: credibility of, 266–67; on EMS, 159; on hiring of Edwin L. Stanton, 298; on the Lincoln snub, 467, 469

Benjamin, Judah P., 135

Bennett, James Gordon, 4–5

Bermuda Hundred, 332

Berryesa, José, 87, 97, 295

Bestor, Chauncey, 43

Bickley, George, 326, 528 (n. 56)

Biddle, Charles, 213

Bingham, John A.: antebellum Whig orator, 28; as congressman, 275, 422; EMS campaigns for, 455; and EMS's nomination to Supreme Court, 462; impeachment, 441, 443; salary for Ellen Stanton, 464; special prosecutor, 315, 316, 372, 381, 382; Surratt clemency recommendation, 382–83, 385–86

Binney, Horace, 198

Black, Jeremiah S.: attorney general, 84; Buchanan biography, 143; on EMS, 116–17, 123, 126, 136, 465; and EMS mission to California, 87, 88, 89, 92–93, 94–95, 96, 98–99; and Johnson, 417; New Almaden suit, 98–99, 114, 147, 295–96; peace mission, 344; recommends EMS for attorney general, 121; secession

crisis, 120–21, 125, 127–28, 130, 132, 134–35; and Sickles, 102; as special counsel, 137

Black, Samuel, 53

Black troops: recruiting of, 225–28, 275–76, 306; treatment of, as prisoners, 305, 309, 329, 362

Blair, Francis P., Jr., 160, 357, 419, 455

Blair, Francis P., Sr., 263–64, 287, 357

Blair, Montgomery: cabinet crisis, 264, 265; criticizes Cameron, 149; defends McClernand, 256; Dred Scott case, 77; on EMS, 139, 149, 197, 296, 357, 393, 465; hatred of EMS, 266; loyalty to Lincoln, 343; opposes evacuating Fort Sumter, 140; opposes partition of Virginia, 269; prospective chief justice, 351; resignation, 353, 355; urges removal of EMS and Seward, 419

Blenker, Louis, 183, 197

Bogus proclamation, 333–35

Bonds, 452–53, 454

Booth, John Wilkes: assassination of Lincoln, 368; capture, 375; diary, 422–23, 547 (n. 49); flight, 372; letter from Arnold, 371; and Mudd, 382

Border ruffians, 80, 82

Boutwell, George S., 445

Bowman, Alexander H., 300, 301

Brady, James T., 103, 109

Bragg, Braxton: Chattanooga, 298, 303, 310; Chickamauga, 301; Kentucky invasion, 257; Stone's River, 288

Breckinridge, John C.: preserves Confederate records, 387; as presidential candidate, 116, 119; as vice president, 83, 137

Bribery of government officials, 94

Brinkerhoff, Jacob, 45, 118

Brooks, Noah, 267–68, 429

Brooks, Preston, 81

Brough, John, 305, 342

Brown, Albert G., 133, 541 (n. 35)
Brown, Benjamin Gratz, 336
Brown, John, 80–81, 112, 113
Brown, Nancy, 108
Brown, William, 46
Browne, Charles Farrar, 292
Browning, Orville Hickman: on army appropriations bill, 417; assured of EMS's conservatism, 402; cabinet crisis, 263, 264, 265; Conover revelations, 426; dispute between Grant and Johnson, 434; and Early's raid, 340; on EMS, 172, 176–77, 266, 409, 415, 416; Interior secretary, 403; intermediary for Mrs. Sherman, 380; Lincoln confidant, 171, 205, 215; lobbies for EMS as chief justice, 350; suggests EMS's removal, 399; Surratt clemency recommendation, 384, 385; touts McClellan's popularity, 273; urges Johnson not to speak, 407
Buchanan, James: candidate for the presidency, 65, 82; confers with EMS, 118–19; Covode committee investigates, 114–16; disloyalty of EMS to, 344; and Dred Scott case, 84–85; EMS on, 63, 125, 126, 130–31, 136; on EMS, 117, 132, 147, 152, 418; and Holt, 252; Lecompton Constitution, 88; and Lincoln, 136, 137, 467; National Hotel disease, 83, 84; pursues California claims, 87, 89–90, 93; secession crisis, 121, 124, 125–26, 127–28, 130, 134, 136; and Sickles, 102, 106; supports Breckinridge, 119
Buchanan, William, 31
Buckingham, Catharinus P., 259
Buckingham, William A., 281, 282
Buckner, Simon B., 163, 216
Buell, Don C., 160, 181, 257–58, 288
Buford, John, 259
Buford, Napoleon B., 176, 259
Bull Run, First Battle of, 145; Second Battle of, 229
Bureau of Colored Troops, 276

Bureau of Military Justice, 355, 375, 389
Burnett, Henry L.: Hurtt trial, 313; Indianapolis trials, 349, 351; trial of Lincoln conspirators, 372, 374, 375, 382
Burnside, Ambrose E.: Antietam, 253; commands Department of the Ohio, 284, 285, 289, 333–34; in east Tennessee, 298, 299, 303, 310; friendship with McClellan, 217; governor of Rhode Island, 410; leads Army of the Potomac, 258–59, 261, 262–63, 269–70, 272–73, 282; in North Carolina, 163, 203; refuses army command, 217–18, 233; sends troops to Pope, 218; under Grant, 331
Bush, Charles, 222
Butler, Andrew P., 81
Butler, Benjamin F.: at Bermuda Hundred, 331, 332; and Booth's diary, 422; challenge to Lincoln nomination, 345; commands at New Orleans, 225, 226–27, 228, 306; considered for secretary of war, 350–51; conversion to Radicalism, 153; impeachment manager, 412, 443–44, 445–46, 448, 551 (n. 57), 552 (n. 60); monitors New York elections, 354; Richmond raids, 328, 329
Butterworth, Samuel F.: background, 101; on John Tucker, 158; and Key murder, 101–2, 105, 106; legislation favoring, 114; and New Almaden, 101, 295, 296

Cadiz Antislavery Society, 21
Calhoun, John C., 36
Cameron, Simon: competence, 166, 355; dissatisfaction with, 148; expelled from cabinet, 149; hires EMS, 145;
Campbell, John A., 366
Campbell, John W., 17

Carlile, John S., 274

Carlisle, James M.: in McNulty trial, 43, 44; in Sickles trial, 105, 107, 108–9

Carlisle & McPherson, 439

Carpenter, Matthew H., 461–62, 465–66

Carrington, Henry B., 345–46, 347, 348, 351

Cartter, David K., 440–41, 443

Casey, Silas, 200, 259, 272

Cass, Lewis: advice to EMS, 172; presidential contender, 35–36, 51, 65; secretary of state, 120–21; senator, 81

Castillero, Andrés, 87, 97, 98, 294, 295

Chancellorsville, Battle of, 283, 287

Chandler, William E., 321–22

Chandler, Zachariah: backs Hooker, 287–88; complains of McClellan reinstatement, 254; demands removal of Meade, 324; EMS disparages McClellan to, 211; on EMS opinion of Grant, 466; notes outcry against himself, Wade, and EMS, 210; reelected, 456

Chase, Philander, 8, 9, 47

Chase, Salmon P.: admitted to practice before Supreme Court, 58; and Bingham, 315; and Butler, 226–27, 228; in cabinet crisis, 263, 264, 265; and cabinet petition, 230, 231; calculates cost of war, 178; and Cameron's removal, 149–50; chastises Sherman, 359; as chief justice, 350, 351, 444; and corruption in Treasury permits, 358; at Davis eulogy, 399; and Early's raid, 341; in emancipation debate, 215; employees drafted, 297; on EMS's real devotion to antislavery cause, 360; hosts Garfield, 258, 260; invites EMS into antislavery crusade, 47–48, 51, 60–61, 62, 63; and McClellan tribute, 300; midnight conference, 302; Norfolk

expedition, 189–91; on partition of Virginia, 269; presidential ambitions, 337; reelected senator, 134; on reinstatement of McClellan, 232, 233; resigns, 337; solicits government loans, 148; on suffrage for freedmen, 312, 391–92; takes Treasury post, 143; on three-month regiments, 198

Chickamauga, Battle of, 301, 303–4

Chilton, Samuel, 103

Cholera, 12, 15–16, 68

Clay, Henry, 39, 56, 60, 61, 135

Clemenceau, Georges, 435

Clendennin, David, 377

Cobb, Howell, 121, 127

Colfax, Schuyler: at EMS's funeral, 463; and impeachment, 440, 441, 442, 445; in nomination of EMS, 462

Collier, Daniel L.: administrator of B. Wells & Co., 32–33; EMS scorns, 34; as EMS's guardian, 8, 12, 13, 14, 18, 25; EMS tries cases with, 41; legal mentor to EMS, 17, 18; legal opponent of EMS, 21

Collier, James, 12, 29, 485 (n. 16)

Compromise of 1850, 60, 61, 135

Commutation clause, 275

Comstock, Cyrus B., 377, 378

Conger, Everton J., 375, 422–23

Conkling, Roscoe, 459

Connecticut elections, 281–82

Conover, Mrs. Sandford, 425, 426

Conover, Sandford: bad character discovered, 408; negotiations for pardon, 425–26; and perjury, 378, 381, 386

Conscription Act, 274–75

Cooke, Jay, 313

Cooper, George, 315

Corcoran, William W., 144

Corinth campaign, 186

Corruption in supply departments, 525 (n. 20), 526 (nn. 33, 34)

Couch, Darius N., 291

Hayes, Rutherford B., 455
Heep, Uriah, 438
Heintzelman, Samuel P., 169, 290
Hendricks, Thomas A., 413
Herndon, William H., 469
Herold, David, 372, 382
Hibernia, 57
Hill, Ambrose P., 253
Hill, Daniel H., 216
Hitchcock, Ethan Allen: EMS calls
  to Washington, 172–73, 175–76;
  on EMS, 191; on Grant, 181, 277;
  and Halleck, 158; and mutilated
  telegram, 208, 209; on Porter court
  martial, 259, 272; and prisoners,
  309; resignations, 191–92; and rules
  of war, 286; as War Department
  advisor, 183, 184, 188
Hoar, Ebenezer R., 350, 351, 460–61
Holt, Joseph: advocates hanging
  prisoners of war, 216; appointed
  judge advocate general, 250, 252;
  background, 250–51; Blair on,
  393; blames Anderson for plight
  of Fort Sumter, 138; and Booth's
  diary, 422–23; in Buchanan cabinet,
  125, 126–27, 130, 133; considered
  for office under Lincoln, 150, 351,
  355; conversion to Radicalism, 251,
  260–61, 511 (n. 3); as corroboration
  for EMS, 268; credibility, 539
  (n. 15); disdain for civil liberties,
  253; extramarital affairs, 251–52,
  384, 513 (n. 4), 539 (n. 9); finances
  of, 513 (n. 5); fondness for control,
  355; holds prisoners incommuni-
  cado, 326; ignores Habeas Corpus
  Act, 285–86; investigates assassination, 372, 374, 375; investigates
  Frémont, 157; life tenure in office,
  409; and military trial of Lincoln
  conspirators, 376, 378, 381–82;
  obsession with self-vindication,
  385–86, 408, 409, 498 (n. 38), 539
  (n. 15); offends Buchanan, 147, 153;

and Pickett, 412; and plausible deniability, 329; potential for retribution
  against, 373; and propaganda, 271,
  272, 317, 347–48, 351, 353, 381–82,
  389; and prosecution of EMS foes,
  253, 260, 270–72, 314–15, 316, 317;
  quartermaster extortions, 317, 526
  (n. 33); rewards government witnesses, 381; in secession crisis, 128,
  130; speaking tour, 144; suborning
  perjury, 378, 408–9, 425, 426, 538
  (n. 65), 544 (n. 10), 548 (n. 65);
  Surratt clemency recommendation,
  382–86, 539 (n. 8)
Holt, Margaret, 251
Hooker, Joseph: Chancellorsville, 283,
  287, 289; considered for command,
  232; EMS and, 183, 261–62, 283,
  290; favored by Radicals, 287–88,
  324, 325; and Halleck, 283, 290; at
  Lookout Mountain, 310; relieved
  from command, 290, 521 (n. 38);
  and troop transfer, 302, 303, 304,
  305; undermines and replaces
  Burnside, 272, 273
Hooper, Samuel: EMS arranges son's
  release, 307; EMS visits, 393, 429,
  430, 459; and newspaper defense
  of EMS, 194; raises fund for EMS's
  family, 463, 464; visits army with
  EMS, 364; visits EMS, 424–25
Houston, Sam, 64
Hovey, Alvin P., 349
Howard, Ann, 15, 476 (n. 48)
Howard, Hannah, 14
Howard, Horton, 14, 15, 16
Howard, Jacob M., 440, 448–49
Howard, James, 335
Howard, William A., 133
Howe, Albion P., 315, 324, 377, 378
Howe, Timothy O., 413
Hoxie, H. M., 221
Hundred-days regiments, 329–30
Hunter, David: as courts-martial
  president, 259, 270, 272, 377; in

Kansas, 158; and McClellan, 230; raising black troops, 225–26, 227, 228; seeks command, 323–24; in Shenandoah Valley, 338

Hurtt, Francis, 313, 315

Hutchison, James, 141

Hutchison, Lewis, 68–69, 111, 112, 115

Ives, Malcolm, 152, 155, 158

Jackson, Andrew, 9, 10, 17, 20, 22–23

Jackson, Thomas J. ("Stonewall"): and Chancellorsville, 283, 284; at Harper's Ferry, 308; at Second Bull Run, 229; in Shenandoah Valley, 168, 183, 195–96, 202

Johnson, Albert E. H.: chief clerk, 159, 201; and EMS favoritism, 266; on hiring of Edwin L. Stanton, 298; and mutilated telegram, 208–9; and reaper case fraud, 75–76

Johnson, Andrew: approves trial sentences, 352, 383; cabinet resignations, 403; and civil rights bill, 400; on Committee on the Conduct of the War, 153, 164; and Conover revelations, 426–27; considers Sherman for War Department, 414, 431, 435, 437–38; and Davis, 421–22; dispute with Grant, 384, 433–35; drinking, 363, 544 (n. 6); on EMS, 418; and fears of army takeover, 545 (n. 25); flagging public support, 406, 410; and Fourteenth Amendment, 401; impeachment, 415, 441–49, 552 (n. 60); inauguration scene, 363; loses control of the army, 435–36, 443; as military governor, 169, 223, 306; and military trial of conspirators, 376; New Orleans riot, 405–6; and presidential Reconstruction, 390–91, 394–95, 398, 541 (n. 30); proclaims end of rebellion, 411; removal of EMS, 427–28, 432, 439; removal of Sheridan and Sickles,

431; stubbornness of, 398; submits Grant and Schurz reports, 395–96; on suffrage for freedmen, 540 (n. 29); Surratt clemency recommendation, 383–85, 427, 539 (n. 8); and "swing around the circle," 407, 408; sworn in as president, 370

Johnson, Reverdy: in bridge case, 70; in Dred Scott case, 77; and Mrs. Phillips, 146; in Porter court martial, 260; in reaper case, 74, 89; at Sickles trial, 103

Johnston, Albert S., 199

Johnston, Joseph E.: in Atlanta campaign, 331, 332, 333; in Carolinas campaign, 365; surrender convention with Sherman, 372; surrender of, 368, 372, 373–74; in Vicksburg campaign, 289; in Virginia, 167, 171, 172, 174, 201

Johnston, William, 67

Joint Committee on the Conduct of the War: cooperates with EMS against McClellan, 164–65, 170, 184; EMS meets with, 153–54, 176; meets with Johnson, 371; meets with Pope, 206; and the mutilated telegram, 208; and prisoners, 309; publishes reports, 282; and reduction of corps, 324; targets Stone, 154–55

Jouan, Auguste, 87, 95

Judd, Norman B., 424

Julian, George W., 180, 268, 371

Kansas-Nebraska Act, 80

Kansas troubles, 80–81, 82

Kautz, August V., 377, 382, 538 (n. 62), 539 (n. 6)

Kennedy, R. T., 52, 53

Kenyon College: Edwin L. Stanton attends, 111, 112, 116, 118, 145, 282, 297, 298; EMS acquaintances from, 193, 250, 259, 335, 463, 475 (n. 27), 518 (n. 3); EMS attends, 8–12, 16

Key, Francis Scott, 101

Key, Philip Barton: affair with Teresa Sickles, 101, 103, 107, 108, 109; confrontation with Sickles, 103; murder of, 102, 105, 109

Keyes, Erasmus D., 170

Kilpatrick, H. Judson, 327–28, 329

King, Alfred, 67

King, Horatio, 127, 147

King, Rufus, 259, 270, 272, 377

Knights of the Golden Circle, 177, 326, 346, 375

Kountz, William, 277, 518 (n. 1)

Lamon, Ward Hill, 308–9, 357, 515 (n. 42)

Lamson, Nathan, 37

Lamson, William K., 9, 14

Lane, James H., 158, 226

"Lapsley, Aglai," 251–52

Larios, Justo, 87, 97, 98, 295

Lawrence, Kan., 80

Leavitt, Humphrey, 41, 121–22, 285, 393–94, 520 (n. 23)

Lecompton Constitution, 88, 115, 116, 287

Lee, Elizabeth Blair, 179

Lee, John, 117

Lee, Robert E.: assumes command, 196, 201; detaches Early, 338; Fredericksburg, 262; and John Brown's raid, 112; in Maryland, 253; and Meade, 310, 311, 328; at Petersburg, 344, 365, 535 (n. 26); on prisoner exchange, 307, 327; surrender of, 367, 373; Wilderness campaign, 331, 332, 333

Legal Tender Act, 178

Liberty Party, 47

Lieber, Francis, 286, 323, 387, 421, 431

Limantour, José, 87, 93, 94–96, 97

Lincoln, Abraham: appoints Meade, 290–91; assassination of, 368–70; on black soldiers, 276; blamed for prisoners' suffering, 388, 540 (n. 19); and Burnside, 217, 233, 261,

269–70; cabinet crisis, 264–65; cabinet letter, 342–43; calls for troops, 141, 212, 213, 216, 320; and Cameron, 148–49, 149–50; as candidate, 116; chastises EMS for anti-Semitism, 361; and civil liberties, 254–55, 285–86, 334; conciliatory policy, 367, 374, 541 (n. 30); considers emancipation, 214–15, 228; discounts OAK threat, 346; and doctrine of necessity, 287, 520 (n. 27), 533 (n. 62); election night, 349; EMS criticizes, 148; and EMS as secretary of war, 159, 160, 219, 267–69, 302, 356, 357, 515 (n. 42); and Fort Sumter, 138, 140; and Frémont, 157; at Gettysburg, 311; and Grant, 277, 323, 365; and Greeley, 228; and Halleck, 158, 211; and Hammond, 316; hears EMS stories, 126, 163; inaugurations, 137–38, 363; and McClellan, 146, 168–69, 170, 177, 184, 185, 191, 198, 203, 215, 217, 231–33, 253–54, 258, 300; and mutilated telegram, 208–9; and New Almaden, 295; and peace mission, 343, 344; and Pope, 205–6; as president-elect, 136; readiness to compromise, 398; and reaper trial, 72–73, 467–69; and reelection of, 343–44, 353–54; and Scott, 146, 204; and son Willie, 165, 166; and Stone, 268, 511 (n. 53); as strategist, 167, 183, 197, 198; stumps for Harrison, 28; and suffrage for freedmen, 312, 540 (n. 29); and *Virginia*, 171, 189–91; visits army, 282, 364–65, 366, 368

Lincoln, Mary Todd, 358, 365, 369

Lincoln, Robert Todd, 298, 369

Lincoln, Thomas ("Tad"), 369

Lincoln, William W., 165, 166

Lloyd, John, 7

Logan, John A., 252

Longstreet, James, 310, 331, 332

Perryville, Battle of, 257

Petersburg, Siege of, 332, 344, 350, 365–66

Peterson, William, 368

Phillips, Eugenia, 145–46

Phillips, Philip, 103, 117, 145–46

Phillips, Wendell, 192, 194

Philomathesian Society, 9–10

Piatt, Donn, 468–69

Pickett, George E., 412, 545 (n. 18)

Pickett's Charge, 344

Pierce, Franklin, 69, 70, 82, 116

Pierrepont, Edwards: on Grant's intentions, 458; and Greeley action, 376; on impeachment, 448; offers to hire Edwin L. Stanton, 460; and Surratt trial, 427; warns of "Ruffians," 445

Pinkerton, Allan, 203

Pittsburgh & Steubenville R.R., 111

Pittsburgh mill riot, 52–53

Polk, James K., 39, 40, 45

Pomeroy, Samuel C., 152

Pony Express, 123

Pope, John: administrative capacity, 355; brought east, 205–6; commands Army of Virginia, 218, 225, 229; as district commander, 432–33; and Halleck, 211; introductory order, 510 (n. 37); and Porter, 270; report, 233

Porter, Fitz John: court martial of, 270–72, 316, 317, 348, 377; at Gaines's Mill, 207; at Hanover Court House, 199; McClellan favors, 191; relieved of duty, 259–60

Porter, Horace, 377, 378

Potts, John, 435, 439

Powell, Lewis, 368, 382

Preston, William, 13, 14, 22

Prime, William, 208, 209

Prisoners of war: exchange, 216, 306–9, 329, 362, 524 (n. 10); health of, 309, 310, 361–62; rations, 524 (n. 12); treatment of, 388–89, 540 (n. 22)

Propaganda. *See under* Stanton, Edwin M.; Holt, Joseph

Quicksilver Mining Co.: attempts to seize New Almaden mine, 87, 94, 99, 101, 295–97; Black represents, 99, 295–96; EMS as attorney for, 87–88, 94, 99, 100, 296–97

Ramsay, George, 320

Randall, Alexander W., 403, 426

Rapp, George, 63, 64

Ratliffe, Daniel, 103, 105

Raymond, Henry J.: on bond payments, 452; and Lincoln's reelection, 342, 353; and peace mission, 343, 344; questions EMS's motives, 435, 437; relationship with Seward, 131

Reconstruction: Civil Rights Act, 416; Committee of Fifteen, 395; First Reconstruction Act, 413, 417, 418; Fourteenth Amendment, 401, 402; Freedmen's Bureau Bill, 398–99; Second Reconstruction Act, 420; Southern representatives refused seats, 394–95; Supplementary Reconstruction Act, 424

Reams's Station, Battle of, 344

Recruiting, 179–80, 212

Reeder, Andrew H., 314

Revels, Hiram R., 463

Richardson, William A., 274

Ricketts, James B., 259, 272

Riddle, Albert G., 425, 426

Riggs & Co., 144

Ripley, James, 319–20

Roanoke Island, Battle of, 163

Rocky Face Ridge, Battle of, 332

Rogers, Andrew J., 408

Rosecrans, William S.: captures Chattanooga, 298, 299; at Chickamauga, 301; and contractor extortions, 317; and OAK myth, 346, 347; replaces Buell, 257, 261; at Stone's River, 288

Ross, Edmund G., 449, 552 (n. 60)
Russell, William, 186–87

Sanders, John, 61
Sanderson, John P., 346, 347, 348
Sanford, Edward S., 166, 208, 209
Sanitary Commission, 156, 210, 254, 313
Santa Clara Mining Company, 94, 97
Savannah, Ga.: EMS visits, 357–60
Schell, Augustus, 126
Schenck, Robert C., 337, 452, 455
Schriver, Edmund, 441, 550 (n. 34)
Schurz, Carl, 300, 379, 396–97, 406
Scott, John, 53
Scott, Thomas A.: as assistant secretary, 158, 159–60, 166, 169, 201; and Nashville railroad, 306; and troop transfer, 302
Scott, Winfield: advises Lincoln, 204, 205, 206; and First Bull Run; and Fort Sumter, 132, 136, 138; and McClellan, 146; and Stone, 134
Secession crisis, 120–21, 123–28, 130–36, 138–40
Seddon, James A., 310
Sedgwick, John, 299, 300, 465
Seven Days Battles, 207, 209, 307
Seward, Fanny, 409
Seward, Frederick, 201–2, 214, 368
Seward, William H.: and Alaska, 419; attack on, 368, 369; and bogus proclamation, 333; in cabinet crisis, 263, 264; and civil rights bill, 400; and clemency petition, 385; and draft, 275; and emancipation, 214–15, 254; and EMS, 125, 126, 131, 136, 139, 141, 173, 355, 406, 409, 420; health, 366, 408; hires son, 201–2; and Lincoln, 136, 342, 343, 345; loyalty to Johnson, 398, 420; midnight conference, 302; on partition of Virginia, 269; and peace mission, 343; and political arrests, 155–56; relationship with Raymond, 131;

and Sumter crisis, 140–41; "swing around the circle," 407, 408
Seymour, Horatio, 294, 353, 455
Seymour, Thomas, 281
Shaler, Charles: partnership with EMS, 49, 50, 54, 55, 82; riot case, 53
Shannon, Wilson, 34, 35, 37
Sharkey, William, 420
Shenandoah Valley campaign, 195–96, 352
Sheridan, Philip H.: in Appomattox campaign, 365; and arms for Mexican revolutionaries, 400; and New Orleans riot, 405, 406; removed from command, 431, 433; removes Louisiana officials, 419; in Shenandoah Valley, 352; on success of conciliatory Reconstruction, 397
Sherman, Ellen, 380, 504 (n. 77)
Sherman, John: and cabinet crisis, 263; EMS visits, 431; and impeachment, 444, 447, 449; and Tenure of Office Act, 413, 414, 415
Sherman, William T.: Atlanta campaign of, 331, 332, 333, 341–42; Carolina campaign, 363, 365, 372; and Chickasaw Bluffs, 256; conference with Lincoln and Grant, 365; and Cox nomination, 434, 435; Johnson considers for secretary of war, 410, 414, 431, 437; and McClernand, 277; offers EMS western vacation, 458; resentment toward EMS, 374, 378, 379–80, 534 (n. 9); Savannah visit of EMS, 357–58, 359–60, 534 (n. 9); snubs Halleck, 378; surrender convention with Johnston, 372–74
Shields, James, 199
Shiloh, Battle of, 181
Show trials, 349, 351
Shunk, James, 123, 137
Sickles, Daniel E.: attorneys of, 103; as district commander, 419; and Key murder, 101–2; philandering of, 493

(n. 24); removed from command, 431, 433; testifies against Meade, 324; trial of, 104–10

Sickles, Teresa: affair with Key, 101, 103, 107, 108, 109; confession, 101, 103, 106

Sigel, Franz, 331

Signal Corps, 320

Simpson, Matthew, 460

Slough, John P., 315, 525 (n. 25)

Smith, Ann, 430

Smith, Caleb B., 143, 148, 231, 269

Smith, J. Gregory, 429, 430

Smith, William F., 191

Smithson, William, 402, 451, 457–58

Soldiers' Home, 338, 429, 530 (n. 19)

Sonora, 91–92

Sons of Liberty, 347, 348

South Carolina commissioners, 127–28, 130

South Mountain, Battle of, 253

Spangler, Edman, 382, 399

Specie Circular, 22–23

Speed, James: approves military tribunal, 376; diverges from Johnson, 363, 397, 398, 401; resigns, 403; sees onset of military despotism, 255; on Sherman's surrender convention, 373; on Surratt clemency recommendation, 384–85

Speed, Joshua F.: on Lincoln newspaper, 317; on Lincoln's gullibility, 193, 268–69

Sprague, William, 189, 190

Stanbery, Henry: as attorney general, 403, 420–21; defends Johnson, 444, 445; and EMS, 32, 407, 439; interprets Reconstruction Acts, 421, 423, 424; and Tenure of Office Act, 415

Stanton, Abigail Macy (grandmother), 2, 4, 430

Stanton, Bessie (daughter), 312, 464

Stanton, Darwin E. (brother): birth, 4; death of, 46–47, 481 (n. 24); education, 17, 21, 25, 477 (n. 6);

impractical nature, 33, 40; marriage, 25; political pursuits, 33, 34, 40

Stanton, David (father): antislavery sentiments, 2, 473 (n. 6); death of, 6; early life, 2–3; education, 3–4; political leaning, 5, 17

Stanton, David (nephew), 33, 83, 432

Stanton, Edwin L. (son): birth, 31, 479 (n. 33); at Buchanan's inauguration, 83; California mission, 89, 90, 93, 94, 99–100; death of, 464; guards EMS's office, 445; inheritance, 464; at Kenyon, 111, 112, 118, 145; letters to EMS, 430–31, 432; marriage and children, 554 (n. 41); and Oella's funeral, 282; seeks army commission, 145; and the Sewards, 409; studies law, 451; visits grandmother, 86, 311, 319, 431; at War Department, 279, 297–98, 430

Stanton, Edwin M.: administrative ability, 355–56; ambition for Supreme Court, 350, 351, 357, 459–60; apparent anti-Semitism, 359, 361; appointment as secretary of war arranged, 149–51; apprenticeship, 7–8; association with Judge Tappan, 23, 30, 41, 42; attempts to control, confound, undermine, or remove McClellan, 164, 165, 166, 168, 169, 170, 173–74, 175–76, 177, 180, 183, 184, 185, 191, 198, 206, 230–31, 232, 254, 258, 288, 348; attempts to ingratiate McClellan, 146, 176, 202–3, 211–12, 213–14; avoids antislavery struggle, 21, 47–48, 60–61, 62, 63; 51, 52; avoids elective office, 34–35, 70–71, 446; Baird telegram, 405, 406, 412, 543 (n. 2); Barlow on EMS, 403; birth, 3, 473 (n. 8); and Black, 87, 88, 89, 92–93, 94–95, 96, 98–99, 121, 123, 126, 128, 134, 137, 344; Black on EMS, 116–17, 123, 126, 136,

465; and bogus proclamation, 333–35; and Booth's diary, 422–23, 547 (n. 49); as Breckinridge Democrat, 116, 147, 150; bribery allegations, 139, 149, 296–97; Browning on EMS, 416; and Buchanan, 118–19, 121–22, 123, 125, 126, 130–31, 136, 139–40, 142, 143, 145, 163, 344; and Burnside, 217, 262, 263; and cabinet crisis, 263–64, 265–66; California claims, 89–100, 111, 136–37, 254; closes recruiting offices, 179–80, 198, 212, 356; and Confederate records, 386–87; conflicts of interest, 94, 97, 98, 111, 296, 522 (n. 55); consolidation of power, 155–56, 166, 186–87, 187–88, 199, 356; contest with Thomas, 439–41, 443; and cotton controversy, 359, 439, 534 (n. 9); courtroom demeanor, 43–44, 44–45, 55, 105, 107, 109, 110; courtship of Mary Lamson, 14, 16–17, 18, 19, 21, 22; courtship of Ellen Hutchison, 69, 70–71, 78–79, 80, 81; and Dana, 156–57, 157–58, 160, 164, 277–79, 319, 349, 351, 354, 366–67; death and funeral of, 462–63; as Democratic committeeman and delegate, 25, 26, 33, 37, 45, 49; devotion to family, 31, 66, 113–14; devotion to first wife's memory, 48, 55, 66, 77, 78, 96, 118, 453, 458, 463; disdain for those without influence, 52, 91, 319, 360–61, 438; disloyalty to Fessenden, 444, 448; disloyalty to Seward, 408, 545 (n. 20); and the draft, 213, 216, 219, 274–75, 352–53, 517 (n. 62); duplicity, 394, 541 (n. 35); and Early's raid, 338–39, 340, 341; education, 4, 7, 8–12, 19, 20–21; efforts to remove EMS from office, 399, 427, 446; and emancipation, 214; employment, 12–13, 14, 15, 16; expands War Department, 159, 278–79, 280, 297–98, 341; and *Ex*

parte Milligan, 411–12; expensive living habits, 296, 299; expresses contradictory opinions to opposing factions, 45, 118, 135–36, 139, 176, 465–66; family tragedies, 6, 31, 37–38, 46–47, 213–14; favoritism and nepotism of, 145, 201–2, 266, 298, 320, 461, 518 (n. 3); finances, 69, 78, 85, 99, 111, 337–38, 424–25, 453, 456, 461, 500 (n. 10), 530 (n. 18), 548 (n. 7), 554 (n. 30); focuses on Virginia theater, 182; and Frémont, 157–58, 174, 180, 182, 183, 192, 206, 276, 505 (n. 14), 508 (n. 6); Gaddis murder case, 30, 31; and Garfield, 260, 312–13; government employment, 115, 143, 144, 145, 497 (n. 21); and Grant, 305–6, 323, 418–19, 428, 450, 453–55, 456–57, 458, 459–60, 462, 463; gravitates toward wealthy and privileged, 54, 77–78, 79, 99, 312, 319, 483 (n. 46), 487 (n. 53); and Halleck, 97–98, 158, 174, 182, 209, 229, 254; health, 6, 11, 13, 16, 57–58, 61, 79, 86, 90, 91, 93, 354, 358, 384, 408, 430, 453, 457, 458, 459, 460, 461, 462, 483 (n. 47); homes of, 24, 27, 37, 49–50, 111, 112; and Hooker, 261–62, 283, 291, 521 (n. 38); and impeachment, 440, 442, 445–46; indifference to civil liberties, 220, 221–22, 223, 252–53, 255, 285, 286, 326, 382, 510 (n. 43), 511 (n. 48); ingratiating letters to the powerful and influential, 45, 68, 88–89, 361, 430, 431; intrigue between Buchanan and Lincoln administrations, 126, 131–32, 135; intrigue between Lincoln and Radicals, 336–37, 343–44; and Jefferson Davis, 388, 390, 421; Lincoln and EMS, 72–73, 136, 139–40, 148, 149, 152, 194, 267–69, 343–44, 347, 348, 349–50, 357, 366–67, 467–69, 515 (n. 42); and Lincoln assassination,